ENTREPRENEURSHIP & SMALL BUSINESS MANAGEMENT

Steve Mariotti • Caroline Glackin

Prentice Hall
Boston Columbus Indianapolis New York San Francisco Upper Saddle River
Amsterdam Cape Town Dubai London Madrid Milan Munich Paris Montreal Toronto
Delhi Mexico City Sao Paulo Sydney Hong Kong Seoul Singapore Taipei Tokyo

Editorial Director: Vernon Anthony
Executive Acquisitions Editor: Gary Bauer
Development Editor: Linda Cupp
Editorial Assistant: Tanika Henderson
Director of Marketing: David Gessel
Senior Marketing Manager: Stacy Martinez
Marketing Assistant: Les Roberts
Senior Managing Editor: JoEllen Gohr
Project Manager: Christina Taylor
Senior Operations Specialist: Pat Tonneman
Senior Art Director: Diane Ernsberger
Manager Cover Visual Research & Permissions: Karen Sanatar
Cover Art: Getty One
Full-Service Project Management: Donna Lee Lurker, PreMediaGlobal
Composition: PreMediaGlobal

Credits and acknowledgments borrowed from other sources and reproduced, with permission, in this textbook appear on appropriate page within text.

Photo Credits: Page 1: Jupiter Images—Thinkstock Images Royalty Free, Page 2: Getty Images Editorial, Page 8: Alamy Images, Page 14: Shutterstock, Page 17: Alamy Images, Page 19: Getty Images Inc., Page 31: Alamy Images, Page 36: Alamy Images, Page 38: Alamy Images Royalty Free, Page 40: Alamy Images, Page 41: Getty Images Thinkstock, Alamy Images, Page 51: Alamy Images, Page 55: Thinkstock Royalty Free, Page 58: Getty Images Thinkstock, Page 59: Alamy Images, Page 62: Horseneck Wines, Page 63: Honeecakes Bakery, Page 69: Alamy Images Royalty Free, Page 74: Alamy Images, Page 76: iStockphoto.com, Page 77: Alamy Images, Page 78: Shutterstock, Page 89: Bigfoot Networks Inc., Page 90: Getty Images/Digital Vision, Page 105: Getty Images Thinkstock, Page 106: Getty Images Editorial, Page 108: Getty Images Editorial, Page 132: Dorling Kindersley Media Library, Page 134: Thinkstock Royalty Free, Page 135: Alamy Images, Page 136: CORBIS–NY, Page 142: Photo Researchers, Inc., Page 144: Alamy Images Royalty Free, Page 149: Getty Images/Time Life Pictures, Page 156: American Electrical, Inc., Page 157: Getty Images Inc., Page 159: Getty Images Editorial, Page 164: Alamy Images Royalty Free, Page 165: Alamy Images Royalty Free, Page 168: AP Wide World Photos, Page 169: CORBIS–NY, Page 170: Evesoar, Inc., Page 173: Corbis, Page 182: Getty Images Editorial, Page 184: Getty Images Inc. –Image Bank, Page 186: Thinkstock Royalty Free, Page 187: Alamy Images, Page 195: Getty Images Inc. —Hulton Archive Photos, Page 208: iStockphoto.com, Page 209: Alamy Images, Page 216: Alamy Images, Page 221: Alamy Images, Page 226: Dreamstime LLC–Royalty Free, Page 229: Alamy Images, Page 248: iStock, Page 249: Alamy Images, Page 252: Alamy Images, Page 256: Daniel Uribe, Page 261: Getty Images–Thinkstock, Alamy Images, Page 277: Thinkstock Royalty Free, Page 278: Shutterstock, Page 280: Getty Images–Thinkstock, Page 281: Alamy Images Royalty Free, Page 289: Getty Images/Digital Vision, Page 290: Steve Smolinsky and Kay Keenan, Page 292: T. Scott Gross, Page 293: Stock Connection, Page 312: Getty Images, Inc. –Jupiter Images, Page 313: Alamy Images Royalty Free, Page 314: Getty Images–Thinkstock, Page 317: Getty Images–Thinkstock, Page 320: Alamy Images, Page 324: Bob Kaufman, Page 326: Getty Images–Hulton Archive Photos, Page 333: Thinkstock Royalty Free, Page 336: Getty Images–Thinkstock, Page 337: Alamy Images Royalty Free, Page 340: Omni-Photo Communications, Inc., Page 345: Getty Images Inc.–PhotoDisc, Page 349: Alamy Images, Page 352: Getty Images Editorial, Page 361: Small Business World, Page 363: Getty Images, Inc.–Photodisc/Royalty Free, Page 372: SuperStock Royalty Free, Page 373: Getty Images–Photodisc/Royalty Free, Page 378: AP Wide World Photos, Page 382: SuperStock/Art Life Images, Page 390: SuperStock Royalty Free, Page 392: Getty Images–Thinkstock, Page 397: Alamy Images, Page 400: SuperStock, Page 401: Alamy Images, Page 403: Alamy Images Royalty Free, Page 406: AP Wide World Photos, Page 407: Getty Images Editorial, Page 419: Creative Eye/MIRA.com, Page 425: PhotoEdit, Page 432: Corbis RF, Page 433: CORBIS–NY, Page 435: SuperStock Royalty Free, Page 437: Thinkstock Royalty Free, Page 450: Old Dartmouth Historical Society, Page 452: Stock Connection, Page 454: Shutterstock, Page 464: Shutterstock, Page 465: Corbis, Page 472: Getty Images, Page 475: Shutterstock, Getty Images Editorial, Page 481: Corbis NY, Page 490: Alamy Images Royalty Free, Page 491: Alamy Images, Page 493: José Echeverri, Page 494: Shutterstock, Page 496: Alamy Images Royalty Free, Page 497: Alamy Images, Page 504: Alamy Images, Page 505: Alamy Images Royalty Free, Page 509: ONLC Training Centers, Page 511: SuperStock Royalty Free, Page 514: Shutterstock, Page 515: Library of Congress, Page 518: Thinkstock, Page 522: Thinkstock Royalty Free, Page 525: Getty Images Editorial, Page 540: Alamy, Page 542: Alamy Images Royalty Free, Page 551: Thinkstock Royalty Free, Page 554: iStockphoto.com, Page 557: AP Wide World Photos, Page 561: Getty Images–Thinkstock, Page 564: Getty Images Editorial, Page 572: Thinkstock Royalty Free, Page 573: Getty Images Editorial, Page 575: Creative Eye/MIRA.com, Page 578: Getty Images Thinkstock, Page 581: Alamy Images, Page 586: AP Wide World Photos, Page 587: AP Wide World Photos.

Library of Congress Cataloging-in-Publication Data

Mariotti, Steve, 1953–
Entrepreneurship & small business management / Steve Mariotti and Caroline Glackin. — 1st ed.
p. cm.
ISBN-13: 978-0-13-503031-8
ISBN-10: 0-13-503031-5
1. Small business—Management. 2. Entrepreneurship. I. Glackin, Caroline. II. Title.
HD62.7.M3768 2012
658.02'2—dc22

2010047714

10 9 8 7 6 5 4 3 2

Prentice Hall
is an imprint of

www.pearsonhighered.com

ISBN 10: 0-13-503031-5
ISBN 13: 978-0-13-503031-8

Special thanks to Shelby Cullom Davis.
Also thanks to Kathryn Davis, Shelby M.C. Davis,
Kimberly La Manna, Abby Moffat, and
Diana Davis Spencer.

—Steve Mariotti

To my children, Elise and Spencer, whose support and love
are essential parts of this book.
To my parents, Howard and Maria Wiedenman,
who truly understood the importance
of education. My love and gratitude.

—Caroline Glackin

Brief Contents

Contents

Helping Students Own Their Future

Entrepreneurship and Small Business Management (ESBM) is the newest textbook in a line of entrepreneurship textbooks written by Steve Mariotti, founder of the Network for Teaching Entrepreneurship (NFTE). This is the second written with professor and entrepreneur Caroline Glackin, and it promotes entrepreneurship as a career option from middle school though college. It is built upon the success of *Entrepreneurship: Starting and Operating a Small Business,* Second Edition, with greatly expanded coverage of the details of managing and growing a small business.

Business students, as well as those from other disciplines, can benefit from *ESBM*. For business students, it recasts their prior learning from a typical corporate context and focuses it on small and entrepreneurial enterprises. For students in such fields as hospitality, the arts, engineering, and fashion merchandising, the text introduces key business concepts and provides examples from a broad range of careers. Cases from hospitality, technology, retail, manufacturing, distribution, real estate, finance, and not-for-profit organizations bring a wealth of learning opportunities. Most importantly, *ESBM* is a balanced mix of the academic and applied components of entrepreneurship education. Students are introduced to the theories, methods, and requisite knowledge and skills required of entrepreneurs and are immediately given practical examples and discussion opportunities. Using the Application Exercises and Exploring Online features at the end of each chapter, they are encouraged to take this new knowledge and apply it in their own lives, so that the course materials are reinforced and internalized.

Combining Street Smarts and Academic Smarts

Entrepreneurship and Small Business Management is an extension of the academic programs developed by Steve Mariotti under the auspices of NFTE. Since 1987, NFTE has reached over 180,000 students and professionals, and certified more than 3,500 instructors to impart its innovative entrepreneurship curriculum. NFTE is widely viewed as a world leader in promoting entrepreneurial literacy and has a proven track record of helping young people start a great variety of successful ventures.

This textbook unites Steve Mariotti's experience as an entrepreneur with relevant academic theory and practice, supported by a rich variety of examples and stories that include experiences from NFTE program graduates who have started their own businesses. Caroline Glackin brings years of experience in the university classroom, as a lender to small and microbusinesses, and as an entrepreneur and former small business owner. Together, these two authors have produced a text that is practical, useful, and academically solid.

Organization

Entrepreneurship and Small Business Management is organized to follow the life cycle of an entrepreneurial venture from concept through implementation into harvesting or replication. It is a comprehensive text written in light of the reality that college students often take only one course in entrepreneurship, which is covered in a multitude of ways. For instructors who will teach the course as a "business plan," *ESBM* offers step-by-step content to build a plan over a semester or a quarter. For those who focus on the management of small and entrepreneurial ventures, there is an abundance of high-quality material on the critical topics of management, marketing, and operations for such ventures. For those charged with teaching a comprehensive introductory course, all of the components are provided.

Never underestimate the power of a simple idea executed with a lot of energy and persistence. This book will enable college students to execute their ideas, grow their businesses, and tap into a greater power—the ability to use their ideas and energies to then achieve social and political goals that will empower their communities.

—Russell Simmons,
Chairman & CEO, Rush Communications

Chapter Learning System

Chapter **5**

CREATING BUSINESS FROM OPPORTUNITY

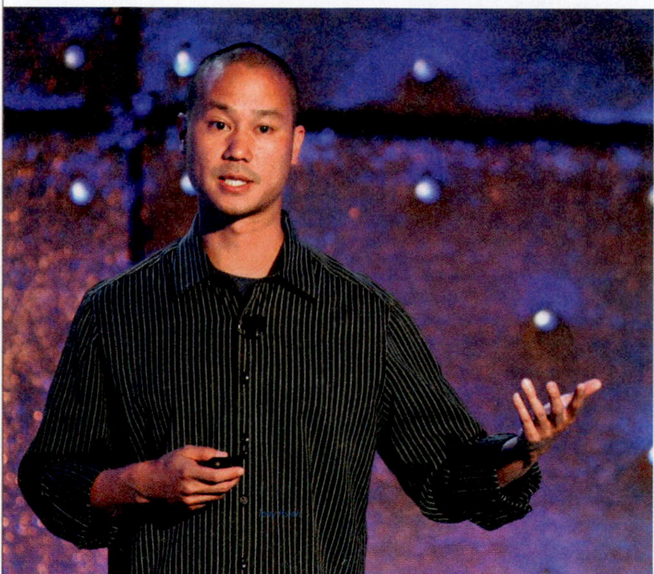

"Problems are only opportunities in work clothes."

—Henry J. Kaiser, American industrialist

Entrepreneurs find and exploit opportunities that others don't recognize or cannot access the resources to exploit. When Zappos.com founder Nick Swinmurn became frustrated by looking for shoes in a mall and online, he saw an opportunity to create an online megastore with a multitude of sizes, styles, and colors. Swinmurn was three years out of college when he launched Shoesite.com with $150,000 in 1999. Within one month, he relaunched as Zappos.com. In 2000, Tony Hsieh of Venture Frog Incubators saw the opportunity in Zappos, investing $1.1 million and joining Swinmurn. The company thrives on providing the best selection and service with a focus on the wow factor. Zappos.com carries more than 1100 brands, stocks more than three million shoes, employs more than 1300 people, and has annual revenues in excess of $1 billion.[1]

Performance Objectives

1. Define your business.
2. Articulate your core beliefs, mission, and vision.
3. Analyze your competitive advantage.
4. Perform viability testing using the Economics of One Unit.

Apple and the Personal Computer

In 1943, IBM's founder Thomas Watson said, "I think there is a world market for about five computers." A **market** is a group of people or organizations that may be interested in buying a given product or service, has the resources to purchase it, and is permitted by law and regulation to do so. When Watson made his statement, computers were forbiddingly large and expensive machines that only the government, universities, and a few giant corporations could afford. That was the market for computers at the time.

market a group of people or organizations that may be interested in buying a given product or service, has the resources to purchase it, and is permitted by law and regulation to do so.

By the 1970s, however, a few people were talking about creating personal computers. These enthusiasts were outside of mainstream thinking. One such visionary was Stephen Wozniak, who had landed his first job at Hewlett-Packard, then as now, a major company. He was also attending meetings of the Homebrew Club, a Palo Alto-based group of electronics hobbyists. Wozniak was determined to build a small, personal computer to show the club members using existing technology. He believed that there was a much larger market for hobbyist computers than IBM and Hewlett-Packard thought. Tandy, Hewlett-Packard, and IBM all had personal computers on the market but not of the sort Wozniak envisioned.

Wozniak offered Hewlett-Packard a chance to codevelop his small computer. The company was not focused on desktop computing, and the technology did not fit within its computer or calculator strategies, so they turned him down. Wozniak's friend Steve Jobs also was interested in the technology and set out to sell some hobbyist computers. Jobs sold 100 circuit boards to a local start-up computer shop, and Wozniak, Jobs, and three others soldered together components in the garage of Jobs' home in Cupertino, California.

[1]Zappos.com, Inc., http://www.zappos.com (accessed February 12, 2010).

37

Chapter Openers Set the Stage

Each chapter starts with an inspirational quote, an introduction, and then Performance Objectives that provide a "road map" so readers know where they are headed. The reader connects with a story of a real business in the opening vignette that sets the stage for upcoming material.

Step into the Shoes

Putting Spring into a Third-Generation Business

Brothers Tom and David Walker grew up at Oregon Mattress Company in Newburg. Their grandfather founded the company in 1932, and their father operated it into the 1990s. Tom and David worked with their father for a number of years to expand the business and enhance its overall viability. They moved from producing under the Lady Americana label to Restonic, a well-respected national brand, and Sleep E-Z, their own brand.

Late in 2009, Oregon Mattress opened two retail stores featuring mattresses produced in its Portland-area factory. The BedCo Mattress Superstores are located in Lake Oswego and Beaverton.[3] The Walkers saw an opportunity to increase their share of the local market through direct retail sales of locally produced mattresses, including hard-to-find custom sizes and shapes, and their signature round beds. Now, as the fourth generation of Walkers joins Oregon Mattress Company, the firm is bouncing back in a weak economy.

Source: Courtesy of Oregon Mattress Company.

"Step into the Shoes" of the Experts

Step into the Shoes appears in each chapter and gives insight into the business practices of entrepreneurs and an opportunity to discuss the brief example.

BizFacts

BizFacts impart useful information regarding entrepreneurship statistics, company practices, or certain business applications.

BizFacts

- There are 27.2 million businesses in the United States; approximately 99.9 percent of them are small companies with fewer than 500 employees.
- Small businesses in America have employed about half the country's private (non-government) workforce, hired 40 percent of high-tech workers, and created 60 to 80 percent of net new jobs annually over the last decade.
- Home-based businesses make up 52 percent and franchises compose 2 percent of small firms.
- Small businesses represent 99.7 percent of all companies with employees.
- Small firms constituted 97.3 percent of all identified exporters and produced 28.9 percent of the country's known export value in Fiscal Year (FY) 2006.

Source: Accessed from http://www.sba.gov on March 16, 2009.

Entrepreneurial Wisdom

Entrepreneurial Wisdom contains insights or advice that will help students in the preparation of a business plan or management of an enterprise.

Entrepreneurial Wisdom…

A useful way to evaluate a business idea is to look at its Strengths, Weaknesses, Opportunities, and Threats (**SWOT**). This is called **SWOT Analysis**.

- *Strengths*—All the capabilities and positive points that the entrepreneur has, from experience to contacts. These are internal to the organization.
- *Weaknesses*—All of the negatives that the entrepreneur faces, such as lack of capital or training, or failure to set up a workable accounting system. These are internal to the organization.
- *Opportunities*—Any positive external event or circumstance (including lucky breaks) that can help the entrepreneur get ahead of the competition.
- *Threats*—Any external factor, event, or circumstance that can harm the business, such as competitors, legal issues, or declining economies.

Global Impact

Global Impact, featured in each chapter, provides examples of entrepreneurial ventures around the world, or information that can be applied in international trade.

Global Impact…

Free Trade

For much of recorded history, international trade was difficult and hazardous. To sell products in another country often required long and dangerous journeys overland or by ship. Many countries were closed to outside trade. Governments also used their power to give their own businesspeople a competitive advantage over those from other countries by imposing trade barriers, such as imposing taxes (tariffs) on foreign goods that made them very expensive. Governments could also enforce restrictions on how many imports or exports could cross their borders.

Today, trade barriers have fallen in most parts of the world. The North American Free Trade Agreement (NAFTA) of 1994 ended trade barriers between the United States, Mexico, and Canada. This turned the entire continent into a free-trade zone. The General Agreement on Tariffs and Trade (GATT) cut or eliminated tariffs between 117 countries. Where entrepreneurs are free to trade voluntarily to as large a market as possible, their ability to find someone to buy their goods or services increases as well as their ability to meet consumer needs.

Meanwhile, the Internet has made it much easier for businesses to sell to customers all over the world. Shipping, too, has become much faster and less expensive.

End-of-Chapter Learning Portfolio

End-of-chapter materials help students develop a working understanding of key concepts and develop critical-thinking skills.

All chapters include the following:

- **Key Terms** list.
- **Critical Thinking Exercises** that require readers to ponder important issues and support a thoughtful response.
- **Key Concept Questions** that review core topics.
- **Application Exercises** that give readers a structured opportunity to reinforce chapter topics through experience.
- **Exploring Your Community** and **Exploring Online** assignments that invite readers to go into their respective local business communities or search online material for information.
- **Cases for Analysis** include one short case and one long case, with analytical questions. Cases cover a variety of issues and draw on real business scenarios. Examples of businesses that may be familiar to students include Craigslist, Krispy Kreme, Honest Tea Company, and Russell Simmons (Rush Communications). Other organizations that may be less familiar include Dogfish Head, Harold Imports, Luggage Concierge, MIDA Trade Ventures, Conversation on Networking, and Enablemart. These cases reflect a diverse set of entrepreneurs, industries, and geographic locations.

Entrepreneurship Portfolio

Critical Thinking Exercises

1. What would be the best thing about owning your own business? What would be the worst?
2. Identify three nonfinancial benefits of entrepreneurship that be important to you. Write a paragraph about each.
3. If you were to start a business, what would be your opportu cost? In other words, what is the next-best use of your time? much money could you make working at a job instead? The to this question will give you a rough idea of how to value y when you start a business and have to figure out how much yourself.
4. Describe an idea that you have for a business. Explain how it satisfy a consumer need.
5. Explain how a business opportunity differs from a business i
6. Give an example of a change that has occurred or is about to in your area/neighborhood. Discuss any business opportuniti change might create.
7. List five business opportunities in your area/neighborhood an need(s) each would satisfy. Note whether the opportunity you is internal, external, or a mix.

Key Concepts Questions

1. Define small business.
2. Explain how profit works as a signal to the entrepreneur.
3. Do you agree that it will probably take about three months for your business to start earning a profit? Why or why not? If not, how long do you expect it to take and why?
4. Describe three things you have learned about capitalism.
5. Visit the U.S. Small Business Administration for brochures and other materials. Find an office in your area or go to *http://ww.sba.gov.*

Application Exercises

Have a conversation with a friend or relative. Ask this person to tell you about which things he or she finds frustrating in the area/neighborhood. Write down these complaints.

Step 1: Generate at least three business opportunities from this conversation.

Step 2: Use the checklists below to evaluate your three business ideas as opportunities.

Step 3: Choose the best of the business opportunities and write a SWOT analysis for it.

Step 4: Create a benefit/cost analysis for starting this business. Use the analysis to explain why you would or would not actually start it.

Business Idea 3	Critical Evaluation	
Would it be attractive to potential customers?	Yes ______	No ______
Would it work in your business environment?	Yes ______	No ______
Is there a window of opportunity?	Yes ______	No ______
Do you have the skills and resources to create this business?	Yes ______	No ______
If you do not have the skills and resources to create this business, do you know someone who does and might want to create the business with you?	Yes ______	No ______

Exploring Your Community

Interview an entrepreneur in your community. Entrepreneurs are busy people, but most are willing to spend time talking with someone who is interested in what they are doing. Meeting over a meal might be the most efficient use of the entrepreneur's time. Before the interview, brainstorm 10 questions in the following four categories. If you can, tape the interview with the entrepreneur's permission. After the interview, be sure to write a thank-you note.

MyBizSkillsKit for Entrepreneurship

Included with the purchase of a new textbook is access to *MyBizSkillsKit for Entrepreneurship*, a resource site containing video cases, business-simulation cases, planning worksheets and templates, links to helpful Internet resources, test-prep quizzes, and access to Business Plan Pro online.

MyBizSkillsKit Components:

① BizBuilder Business Plan Worksheets and Templates Online

Go to www.prenhall.com/mariotti to download business plan and presentation templates that will help students write a plan and present it.

- ***BizBuilder Business Plan Worksheets*** provide step-by-step instructions on building a business plan.
- ***BizBuilder Business Plan Template*** provides a professional-looking format for a business plan that ties in with assignments in the text.
- ***BizBuilder Business Plan Presentation Template*** guides the student through the process of creating a PowerPoint presentation for a business plan.

Students can build their business plans using the BizBuilder worksheets. Appendix 4 provides students with instructions on how to use the worksheets that mirror the planning process in the book, and contains more questions in some areas than are found in commercially available planning software. Once they have created a plan using the worksheets, students can generate a professional-looking document using the BizBuilder Business Plan Template or Business Plan Pro software.

② Business Plan Pro Software Online

Business Plan Pro is the most widely used professional business planning software in the nation. Students can download the Business Plan Pro program to a personal computer from within MyBizSkillsKit. Once a student has created a business plan using the BizBuilder worksheet, it will be easy to cut and paste that information into Business Plan Pro. BPP includes a number of very useful features:

- Sample business plans students can study and compare with their own, using the Sample Plan Browser to search the library.
- Easy Plan Wizard guides students through writing a plan.
- Spreadsheet tables with columns, rows, and formulas to automatically calculate totals.
- Pie and bar charts can be automatically created from spreadsheets.
- Financial statements can be customized.
- Professional-looking printout of the business plan.
- Appendix 8 provides students with an overview of how to get started using Business Plan Pro.

③ Entrepreneurship Videos in MyBizSkillsKit

Included in MyBizSkillsKit are ten video case studies, produced by the Small Business School that accompany the written cases in the textbook.

Bridgecreek Development

Meet Frank Jao, an immigrant from Vietnam and founder of Bridgecreek Development, who grew a successful land development company in California from virtually nothing. Frank Jao teaches that it is key to envision a new future, invest not spend, combine tangible services and products with good feelings, and learn to speak the language of bankers. This is a story about adapting to a new environment, the power of capital, and the power of ideas.

Nicole Miller

Go to the heart of the fashion industry and behind the scenes of Nicole Miller, a fashion house on Seventh Avenue, to meet the founders, Nicole Miller and Bud Konheim. Starting in 1986, Nicole built her success upon the idea that women want well-made fashionable dresses. Today, their company earns $300 million in annual revenue.

Texas Jet

Texas Jet is a gas station for airplanes. Fortunately, owner Reed Pigman doesn't use today's gas station as a model for his business. He knows the tastes and expectations of owners of private airplanes and uses the Ritz Carlton Hotel customer-service model as his guide. By copying the strategies of top service providers, Reed sells more fuel than his competitors while charging the highest prices.

eHarmony

Dr. Neil Clark Warren, the founder of the online matchmaking service eHarmony, spent 35 years as a marriage counselor, frustrated because he couldn't help married couples fix their relationships. He discovered that many couples were not well matched for marriage. His solution was to use the power of the Web to reach a market of 93 million single Americans and help them find other people with similar interests. This is the story of how Neil started and grew a business that is being used by 20 million paying customers today.

Ken Done Studios

This is the story of an accidental business. The founder calls it an accident because he never intended to sell anything but his paintings. When a T-shirt he designed as a marketing gimmick turned out to be a hit, he decided he should listen to the marketplace and do more than paint. Ken Done is now Australia's most recognized modern artist and employs more than 100 people. Ken Done teaches that owners must do what works, and then repeat it to achieve profits through scale.

Cactus & Tropicals

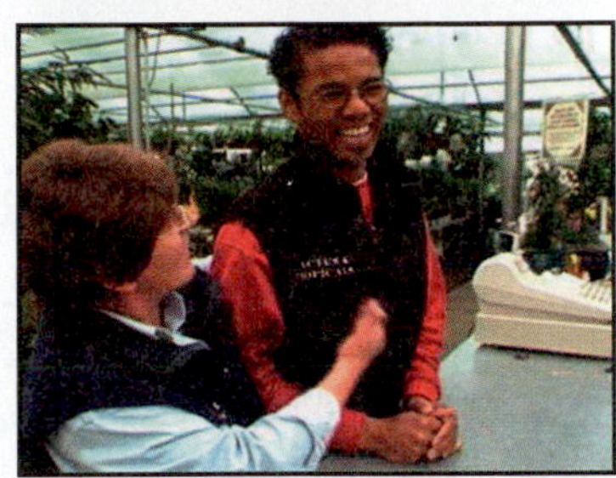

Cactus & Tropicals is an indoor and outdoor landscaping company based in Salt Lake City, Utah. Founder Lorraine Miller's goal at Cactus & Tropicals is to deliver to customers more than they paid for through highly motivated, self-guided employees. Lorraine teaches that you have to be the teacher, leader, and mentor, not "the boss"—boss is a four-letter word that is not allowed at Cactus & Tropicals.

FASTSIGNS

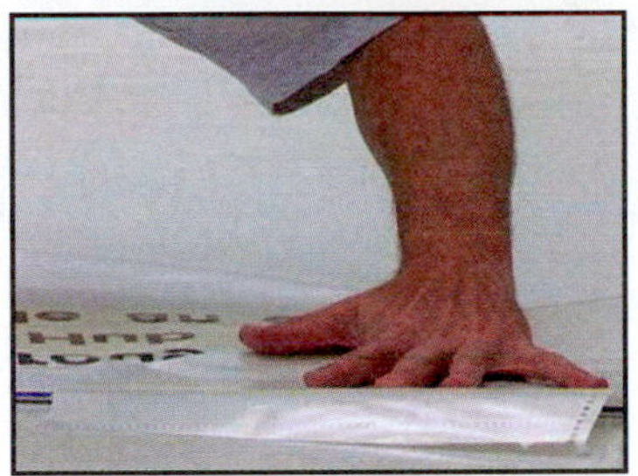

This business began on the back of a paper napkin. FASTSIGNS founder, Gary Salomon, saw how a computer could make high-quality signs in hours instead of days. He jumped at the opportunity to build a business offering this service internationally. Today, FASTSIGNS is America's leading sign company with more than 550 locations worldwide.

On Target Supplies and Logistics

Albert Black founded On Target Supplies and Logistics in 1982 as a janitorial supply business. He perfected his delivery systems and changed his mission so that today the company is known for its supply-chain management. Albert explains that his leadership strategy requires him to preach, teach, coach, and counsel so that everyone on the payroll is working to achieve his or her potential.

Mo's Chowder

Mo's Restaurants are famous for serving hot clam chowder since 1951. There are three locations on the Oregon coast, and a chowder-base factory. When Mo opened for business the town of Newport had a lively fishing industry with hundreds of fisherman. Back then, Mo's was a fisherman's hangout. Now it is a key component of local tourism in Newport. The evolution of Mo's demonstrates both the principle of adapting to a changing market and the personal business acumen of its present owner.

Avocent

Avocent is a manufacturing company that makes a box to remotely control PCs and servers—from 25 feet to 25,000 miles. This story illustrates what can happen when a founder starts a business to solve a very big problem for customers who have the money to pay for solutions.

Small Business School is the television series made for PBS and Voice of America. On the Web, at http://smallBusinessSchool.org, students will discover the largest video library about small business in the world.

④ Additional Resources in MyBizSkillsKit:

- **Test-Prep Quizzes** for each chapter, including true/false, multiple choice, and short essay.
- **PowerPoint Chapter Review of Key Topics**
- **Links to Web-based Video Assignments at the Small Business School**
- **Web Links to Additional Resources**
- **Pearson's MySearchLab: Research, Grammar, and Writing Tips** is a great source of research tips, access to the EBSCO document database, writing assessment and instruction, and access to the Longman Online Handbook for writers.

Value Package

Entrepreneurship and Small Business Management can be value packaged with MyBizSkillsKit for Entrepreneurship. Contact your local Pearson representative or visit www.pearsonhighered.com for more information.

Instructor Resources

All instructor resources can be downloaded from the Prentice Hall Instructor's Resources Website: **www.pearsonhighered.com**.

- TestGen, a computerized Test Generator
- PowerPoint Lecture Presentation Package
- The Instructor's Manual includes:
  - Answers to all end-of-chapter material, including teaching notes for short and long case studies.
  - Additional instructional material on how to teach students to write a business plan, to supplement end-of-unit business plan sections.
  - Course outlines for 8-week term (short course), 12-week term (3 hours/week), and 15-week term (3 hours/week).
  - Additional resources (print and Web sites) for each chapter.
  - Test Item File.

CourseConnect Entrepreneurship Online Course: Convenience, Simplicity, Success

courseconnect™

Looking for robust online course content to reinforce and enhance student learning? Course Connect courses contain customizable modules of content mapped to major learning outcomes. Each learning object contains interactive tutorials, rich media, discussion questions, MP3 downloadable lectures, assessments, and interactive activities that address different learning styles. CourseConnect courses can be delivered in any commercial platform, such as WebCT, BlackBoard, Angel, Moodle, or eCollege. For more information, call 800-635-1579.

About the Authors

STEVE MARIOTTI, founder of the Network for Teaching Entrepreneurship (NFTE), is an expert in education for at-risk youth. He has been helping young people develop marketable skills by learning about entrepreneurship for more than 25 years.

Mariotti received an M.B.A. from the University of Michigan and has studied at Harvard University, Stanford University, and Brooklyn College. His professional career began as a Treasury Analyst for Ford Motor Co. He then founded Mason Import/Export Services in New York, eventually acting as sales representative and purchasing agent for 32 overseas firms. In 1982, Mariotti made a significant career change and became a Special Education/Business Teacher in the New York City school system, choosing to teach in inner-city neighborhoods in Brooklyn and the South Bronx. It was at Jane Addams Vocational High School in the Bronx that he developed the insight and inspiration to bring entrepreneurial education to low-income youth. This led to the founding of NFTE in 1987.

Steve Mariotti and NFTE have received numerous awards, including the 2004 Ernst & Young National Entrepreneur of the Year Award; the Golden Lamp Award from the Association of Educational Publishers (2002); and the National Federation of Independent Businesses—Best Business Teacher, 1988, as well as major media exposure in *The New York Times* and other prominent publications, and profiles on ABC News and CNN. Mariotti has coauthored some two dozen books and manuals that have sold over half a million copies.

CAROLINE GLACKIN, PhD, is a "pracademic" who has successfully worked as a microenterprise and small business owner and manager, as an executive director of a community-development financial institution, and as an academic in areas of community-development finance, entrepreneurship, and management. She has been assisting entrepreneurs in achieving their dreams for over 25 years.

Glackin earned a doctorate from the University of Delaware, where her research emphasis was on microfinance. She received an M.B.A. from The Wharton School at the University of Pennsylvania and a B.A. from Bryn Mawr College. Her professional career began with the DuPont Company, American Bell, Bell Atlantic, and American Management Systems. She has consulted for businesses and not-for-profit agencies in turnaround and high-growth situations. After exiting a family business, she became the executive director of a Community-Development Financial Institution serving businesses and not-for-profits.

Dr. Glackin has succeeded in leading change in the practical fields of her research and has received numerous honors and awards. Thse include the first Gloeckner Business Plan Award at The Wharton School, the Minority Business Advocate of the Year for Delaware from the U.S. Small Business Administration, and the She Knows Where She's Going Award from Girls Inc. Dr. Glackin co-chaired the Delaware Governor's Task Force for Financial Independence and has participated in the Cornell University Emerging Markets Think Tank Series.

Acknowledgments

First, sincere thanks to the team of reviewers who provided insightful feedback during the development of this book:

Harvey Lon Addams, *Weber State University, Ogden, UT*
John R. Callister, *Cornell University, Ithaca, NY*
Joyce Ezrow, *Anne Arundel Community College, Arnold, MD*
Rita Friberg, *Pueblo Community College, Pueblo, CO*
Vada Grantham, *Des Moines Area Community College, Ankeny, IA*
Linda Ross, *Rowan University, Glassboro, NJ*
William Searle, *Asnuntuck Community College, Enfield, CT*
Dennis R. Williams, *Pennsylvania College of Technology, Penn State, Williamsport, PA*

And thank you to all the consultants and reviewers who assisted in the development of *Entrepreneurship*, Second Edition:

Elaine Allen, *CPA, Vice Chair, Not-for-Profit Sector, Mitchell & Titus, LLP*
Larry Bennett, *President, Benland Innovations, LLC*
Sunne Brandmeyer, *Retired Lecturer/Advisor, Center for Economic Education, University of South Florida, Tampa, FL*
Stanlee Brimberg, *Teacher, Bank Street School for Children, New York, NY*
Howard W. Buffett, Jr.
John D. Christesen, *SUNY Westchester Community College, Valhalla, NY*
Steve Colyer, *Miami Dade College, Miami, FL*
Laura Portolese-Dias, *Shoreline Community College, Seattle, WA*
Alex Dontoh, *New York University, New York, NY*
Alan J. Dlugash, *CPA, Partner, Marks Paneth & Shron LLP*
Thomas Emrick, *Ed.D.*
George Gannage, Jr., *West Georgia Technical College, Carrollton, GA*
Thomas Goodrow, *Springfield Technical Community College, Springfield, MA*
Janet P. Graham, *Coastal Carolina University, Conway, SC*
John Harris, *Eastern High School, Bristol, CT*
Deborah Hoffman, *CPA, Director of Finance, Math for America*
Donald Hoy, *Benedictine College, Atchison, KS*
Samira Hussein, *Johnson County Community College, Overland Park, KS*
Eileen M. Kearney, *Montgomery County Community College, Blue Bell, PA*
Sanford Krieger, Esq., *General Counsel & Managing Director, AEA Investors LP*
Jawanza Kunjufu, D.B.A. *President, African-American Images*
Corey Kupfer, Esq., *Partner, Hamburger Law Firm, LLC*
Emily H. Martin, *Faulkner State College, Bay Minette, AL*
Alaire Mitchell, *Former Assistant Director of Curriculum Research, New York City Board of Education*
Timothy R. Mittan, *Southeast Community College, Lincoln, NE*
Eric Mulkowsky, *Engagement Manager, McKinsey and Company, Inc.*
Raffiq Nathoo, *Senior Managing Director, The Blackstone Group, LLP*
Ray E. Newton, III, *Senior Managing Director, Evercore Partners Inc.*

Arnold Ng, *Pepperdine University, Rancho Palos Verdes, CA*
William H. Painter, *Retired Professor of Law, George Washington University*
Peter Patch, *Patch and Associates*
Alan Patricof, *Founder, Apax Partners and Greycroft Partners*
Carolyn J. Christensen Perricone, *CPA, SUNY, Westchester Community College, Valhalla, NY*
Robert Plain, *Guilford Technical Community College, Jamestown, NC*
Christopher P. Puto, *University of St. Thomas, Minneapolis, MN*
Richard Relyea, *President, NY Private Equity Network (NYPEN)*
Ira Sacks, Esq., *Partner, Law Offices of Ira S. Sacks LLP*
William Sahlman, *Harvard Business School, Cambridge, MA*
Arnold Scheibel, MD, *Professor of Neurobiology, University of California at Los Angeles*
LaVerne Tilley, *Gwinnett Technical College, Lawrenceville, GA*
Marsha Wender Timmerman, *LaSalle University, Philadelphia, PA*
Liza Vertinsky, *Emory University, Atlanta, GA*
Peter B. Walker, *Managing Director, McKinsey and Company, Inc.*
Walter Lara, *Florida Community College, Jacksonville, FL*
Larry Weaver, *Navarro College, Corsicana, TX*
Donald A. Wells, *University of Arizona, Tucson, AZ*

I would like to thank my coauthor, Caroline Glackin, without whose talent and expertise this text would not have been possible, and Tony Towle, who from NFTE's inception has helped me organize my thoughts and experiences. I must single out the help of two outstanding educators: John Harris and Peter Patch. I would also like to acknowledge the significant contributions of NFTE executives Amy Rosen, Michael J. Caslin, III, J. David Nelson, Julie Silard Kantor, Leslie Pechman Koch, Jane Walsh, Neelam Patel, Daniel Rabuzzi, Victor Salama, Del Daniels, Jonathan Weininger, Deirdre Lee, Rupa Mohan, Christine Poorman, Joel Warren, and Essye Klempner.

Special thanks as well to Gary Bauer and the team at Prentice Hall, for their professionalism and for their editorial assistance.

Thanks also to Tom Goodrow of the Springfield Enterprise Center and the National Association of Community College Entrepreneurship (NACCE), and to John Christesen of SUNY Westchester Community College.

Thanks also to Howard Stevenson, the late Jeffry Timmons, William Bygrave, Bob Pritzker, and NFTE Board Member Stephen Spinelli for imparting their wisdom, and to Richard Fink of Koch Industries, Carl Schramm of the Ewing Marion Kauffman Foundation, and Mike Hennessy and John Hughes of the Coleman Foundation. Special thanks to Eddy Bayardelle and Melanie Mortimer of Merrill Lynch Global Philanthropy, and Kim Davis of the JPMorganChase Foundation.

In addition, I would like to recognize the efforts and contributions of members of NFTE's National Board of Directors, and I would like to acknowledge the inspired guidance provided by our National Executive Committee. I am deeply grateful as well to the many philanthropists who have supported our work, including the Scaife Family Foundation, the Newark Boys' and Girls' Clubs, the William Zimmerman Foundation, the Goldman Sachs Foundation, The Shelby Cullom Davis Foundation, the Microsoft Corporation, The Nasdaq Educational Foundation, and Ronald McDonald House Children's Charities.

Further, I would like to acknowledge Steve Alcock, Harsh and Aruna Bhargava, Lena Bondue, Dawn Bowlus, Shelly Chenoweth, Janet McKinstry Cort, Erik Dauwen, Clara Del Villar, Christine Chambers Gilfillan, Andrew Hahn, Kathleen Kirkwood, Michael Simmons, Sheena Lindahl, Cynthia Miree, Henry To, Carol Tully, Dilia Wood, and Elizabeth Wright, as well as Peter Cowie, Joseph Dominic, Paul DeF. Hicks, Jr., Ann Mahoney, David Roodberg, Phyllis Ross Schless, and Remi Vermeir, who have provided countless insights into providing entrepreneurial opportunities to young people.

In addition, I would like to thank my brother, Jack, the best CPA I know, and my father, John, for financing much of NFTE's early work, and for their continuing love and guidance. Thanks are due to all the other teachers, students, experts, and friends who were kind enough to look over this book and help us improve it. Finally, I want to thank my mother, Nancy, a wonderful special education instructor who showed me that one great teacher can affect eternity.

Steve Mariotti

To my coauthor Steve Mariotti, who brought hope, opportunity, and change out of adversity to create the Network for Teaching Entrepreneurship and started this journey—many thanks. Also thanks to Tony Towle, who has provided numerous insights to make this text sing. Hattie Bryant and Lois Ann Freier brought a number of the stories to life. As Steve noted, the team at Prentice Hall has been wonderful to work with again. Faculty reviewers and faculty members who have contacted me directly regarding earlier materials are always a valued source of insights.

Most importantly, I appreciate the terrific entrepreneurs who shared their stories with me, including the good, the bad, and the downright ugly! Their interest in sharing their experiences with students and willingness to carve out time to tell their tales demonstrates the kind of energy and enthusiasm we associate with successful entrepreneurs. They have made this endeavor interesting and engaging.

On a more personal note, I would like to thank my "families" at Delaware State University and Shepherd University for their support and tolerance as I worked on *Entrepreneurship and Small Business Management*. Special thanks to Bridget Anakwe, Kimble Byrd, Gabrielle Capitanio, Cynthia deLeon, Heidi Golding, Terri Hasson, Young-Sik Kwak, Ron Nordheimer, Anne Rhoads, Linda Ross, Milos Velickovic, and Carol Ann Weisenfeld, and the folks at Over Coffee Café. Finally, to Elise and Spencer for being the best cheering section a mother could ever have—thanks and love to you both.

Caroline Glackin

UNIT 1

ENTREPRENEURIAL PATHWAYS

Chapter 1

ENTREPRENEURS RECOGNIZE OPPORTUNITIES

Tom Szaky from TerraCycle Inc.

> **"Everyone lives by selling something."**
>
> —Robert Louis Stevenson, Scottish author

Tom Szaky was a 19-year-old college student in need of inspiration for a business plan competition, when he happened to visit friends who were using red worms to compost waste that they then used as plant fertilizer. The idea captured his imagination, and he created a business plan for an environmentally friendly company that would convert trash into fertilizer. Although he finished in fifth place in the competition, Szaky moved ahead to make the company a viable venture.[1]

TerraCycle, Inc. has expanded its product lines to encompass a wide range of recycling and upcycling, including branded products for Target and Kraft Foods. The company is the producer of the world's first product made from and packed in waste. Szaky sells to some of the world's largest retailers, including Wal-Mart, Target, and Home Depot and has programs that involve entire communities in recycling products. Sales exceed $20 million per year, and the company has collected literally billions of pieces of waste. TerraCycle plant food was named the most eco-friendly product in Home Depot, twice. Tom Szaky and TerraCycle have turned trash into treasure.

Performance Objectives

1. Explain what entrepreneurs do.
2. Describe how free-enterprise economies work and how entrepreneurs fit into them.
3. Find and evaluate opportunities to start your own business.
4. Explain how profit works as a signal to the entrepreneur.

Entrepreneurship Defined

Have you ever eaten a Mrs. Fields cookie? Used an Apple computer? Listened to a hip-hop CD? The entrepreneurs that founded these companies brought these products into your world.

What Is an Entrepreneur?

Most Americans earn money by working in *business*. They are engaged in the buying and selling of products or services in order to make money.

product something tangible that exists in nature or is made by human beings.

service intangible work that provides time, skills, or expertise in exchange for money.

- A **product** is something that exists in nature or is made by human beings. It is *tangible*, meaning that it can be physically touched.
- A **service** is labor or expertise (rather than a tangible commodity) exchanged for money. It is *intangible*. You cannot actually touch it.

Someone who earns a living by working for someone else's business is an employee of that business. There are many kinds of employees. At Ford Motor Company, for instance, some employees build the cars, some sell the cars, and some manage the company. But employees all have one thing in common—they do not own the business; they work for others who do. They know how much money they can earn, and that amount is limited to salary plus bonuses and any stock options they may receive.

entrepreneur a person who organizes and manages a business, assuming the risk for the sake of potential return.

Some people start their own businesses and work for themselves. They are called **entrepreneurs**. Entrepreneurs are often both owners and employees. For an entrepreneur, the sky is the limit as far as earnings are concerned. Unlike an employee, an entrepreneur owns the profit that his

[1]TerraCycle, Inc., www.terracycle.net (accessed February 4, 2010).

or her business earns and may choose whether to reinvest it in the business or take it as payment.

Performance Objective 1
Explain what entrepreneurs do.

An entrepreneur is someone who recognizes an opportunity to start a business that other people may not have noticed and jumps on it. As economist Jeffry A. Timmons writes in the preface of *New Venture Creation: Entrepreneurship for the 21st Century*, "A skillful entrepreneur can shape and create an opportunity where others see little or nothing—or see it too early or too late."

The French word *entrepreneur* began to take on its present-day meaning in the seventeenth century. It was used to describe someone who undertook any project that entailed risk—military, legal, political, as well as economic. Eventually it came to mean someone who started a new business—often a new kind of business or a new (and improved) way of doing business. French economist Jean-Baptiste Say wrote at the turn of the nineteenth century: "The entrepreneur shifts economic resources [like wood or coal] out of an area of lower and into an area of higher productivity and greater yield." By doing this, Say argued, entrepreneurs added value to scarce resources. Coal is a resource because it is used as fuel. Wood is a resource because it can be used to build a house or a table or to make paper (as well as used for fuel). Economists consider *scarce* all resources that are worth money.

Debbi Fields took resources—eggs, butter, flour, sugar, and chocolate chips—and turned them into cookies. People liked what she did with those resources so much that they were willing to pay her more for the cookies than it cost her to buy the resources to make them. She added value to the resources she purchased by what she did with them and created a multimillion-dollar business in the process.

Entrepreneurs may have different reasons to start and continue their businesses, but they share the common focus of creating sustained value for themselves. Entrepreneurs seek opportunities that they envision as generators of incremental income, or wealth. Whether the business is intended to meet short-term household cash needs or to grow into a publicly traded company, viability is critical. Each activity of the firm should be driven by this need.

The Economic Questions[2]

Since the beginnings of human society, people have had to answer the same basic questions:

- What should be produced?
- When will it be produced?
- How will it be produced?
- Who will produce it?
- Who gets to have what is produced?

Families and individuals, as well as businesspeople, charitable organizations, corporations, and governments all have had to answer these questions. The system created by making these decisions is called an *economy*. The study of how different groups answer the questions is called *economics*.

free-enterprise system
economic system in which businesses are privately owned and operate relatively free of government interference.

An economy is a country's financial structure. It is the system that produces and distributes wealth in a country. The United States economy is a **free-enterprise system** because anyone is free to start a business.

[2]Source of definitions: United States Small Business Administration (SBA): *http://www.sba.gov*. Accessed August 3, 2010.

You do not have to get permission from the government to start a business, although you will be expected to obey laws and regulations.

The free-market system is also called **capitalism** and is characterized by the following attributes:

- Individuals and companies may compete for their own economic gains,
- private property ownership and wealth are permissible, and
- free-market forces determine prices.

Cash or goods invested to generate income and wealth is called **capital**, and in a free-enterprise system anyone who can raise the necessary capital may start a business.

Performance Objective 2

Describe how free-enterprise economies work and how entrepreneurs fit into them.

capitalism the free-market system; characterized by individuals and companies competing for economic gains, private property ownership and wealth, and free-market forces determine prices.

capital money or property owned or used in business.

Voluntary Exchange

The free-enterprise system is also sometimes referred to as a free-trade system because it is based on **voluntary exchange**. Voluntary exchange is a transaction between two parties who agree to trade money for a product or service. Each is eager to take advantage of what the trade offers. The parties agree to the exchange because each will benefit.

voluntary exchange a transaction between two parties who agree to trade money for a product or service.

Let's say you have a contracting business, and your busy neighbors hire you to renovate their kitchen. You need money and are willing to use your skills and time to earn it. They want their kitchen renovated and are willing to give up money to get it done. You each have something the other wants, so you are willing to trade. Trading only takes place when both parties believe they will benefit. Robbery, in contrast, is an *involuntary* trade.

Benefits and Challenges of Free Enterprise

The public benefits from living in a free-enterprise system because it discourages entrepreneurs who waste resources by driving them out of business. It encourages entrepreneurs who use resources efficiently to satisfy consumer needs by rewarding them with profit.

Global Impact...

Free Trade

For much of recorded history, international trade was difficult and hazardous. To sell products in another country often required long and dangerous journeys overland or by ship. Many countries were closed to outside trade. Governments also used their power to give their own businesspeople a competitive advantage over those from other countries by establishing trade barriers, such as imposing taxes (tariffs) on foreign goods that made them very expensive. Governments could also enforce restrictions on how many imports or exports could cross their borders.

Today, trade barriers have fallen in most parts of the world. The North American Free Trade Agreement (NAFTA) of 1994 ended trade barriers between the United States, Mexico, and Canada. This turned the entire continent into a free-trade zone. The General Agreement on Tariffs and Trade (GATT) cut or eliminated tariffs between 117 countries. Where entrepreneurs are free to trade voluntarily to as large a market as possible, their ability to find someone to buy their goods or services increases, as well as their ability to meet consumer needs.

Meanwhile, the Internet has made it much easier for businesses to sell to customers all over the world. Shipping, too, has become much faster and less expensive.

Society also benefits because free enterprise encourages competition between entrepreneurs. Someone who can make cookies that taste as good as Mrs. Fields Original Cookies, and sells them at a lower price, will eventually attract Mrs. Fields' customers. This will force Mrs. Fields to lower prices to stay competitive. Consumers will benefit because they will get to buy the same-quality cookies at a lower price.

On the flip side, free enterprise has some disadvantages. If a company fails, the employees become unemployed. Owners who have invested their financial resources in businesses may take a loss. Other companies or individuals may depend upon the products and services of a failed business and thus may lose customers or suppliers.

What Is a Small Business?

The public often thinks of business only in terms of "big" business—companies such as General Electric, ExxonMobil, Microsoft, McDonald's, and Nike. A small business is defined by the U.S. Small Business Administration's Office of Advocacy according to size. Companies having fewer than 500 employees and selling less than $5 million worth of products or services in a year, depending upon the industry, are generally considered "small" according to SBA standards. So, even a leading local employer may be considered a small business.

Most of the world's businesses are small businesses. A neighborhood restaurant or a clothing boutique is each an example of a small business. Surprisingly, the principles involved in running a large company, like Viacom, and a corner deli are the same. However, the operation of a small business is not the same as that of a large one. Most multimillion-dollar businesses in this country started out as small, entrepreneurial ventures. This is why entrepreneurship is often called the engine of our economy. It drives our economic creativity, giving rise to wealth and jobs, and improving our standard of living. It is no coincidence that the United States is one of the most entrepreneurial countries in the world and the richest.

Why Be an Entrepreneur?

Entrepreneurs put a great deal of time and effort into launching their own businesses. While establishing a business, an entrepreneur may also pour all his or her money into it. He or she may not be able to buy new clothes or a fancy car, go on vacation, or spend much time with family, until the business becomes profitable and starts generating cash.

If so much work and sacrifice are involved, why be an entrepreneur? The entrepreneur is working for the following rewards:

1. ***Control over Time.*** Do you work better at midnight than at 8 a.m.? If you start your own business, you will have control over how you spend your time by the type of business it is. Are you the kind of person who would rather work really hard for two weeks nonstop and then take a break? If you are an entrepreneur, you can structure your schedule to make this possible. You can also choose to hire other people to perform tasks that you do not like to do or are not good at, so you can stay focused on what you do best. Bill Gates liked to spend his time designing software. He hired others to manage Microsoft's operations and to market and sell its products. Many eBay entrepreneurs have carved out very flexible schedules for responding to orders, packaging, and shipping. Bricks-and-mortar retail stores, on the other hand, do not often afford such flexibility.

BizFacts

- There are 27.2 million businesses in the United States; approximately 99.9 percent of them are small companies with fewer than 500 employees.
- Small businesses in America have employed about half the country's private (non-government) workforce, hired 40 percent of high-tech workers, and created 60 to 80 percent of net new jobs annually over the last decade.
- Home-based businesses make up 52 percent and franchises compose 2 percent of small firms.
- Small businesses represent 99.7 percent of all companies with employees.
- Small firms constituted 97.3 percent of all identified exporters and produced 28.9 percent of the country's known export value in Fiscal Year (FY) 2006.

Source: Accessed from http://www.sba.gov on March 16, 2009.

2. ***Fulfillment.*** Successful entrepreneurs are passionate about their businesses. They are excited and fulfilled by their work. Entrepreneurs who are working to reach their full potential are rarely bored, because there is always plenty to do. If one facet of running the business is uninteresting to them, and they have the income to support it, they can hire someone else for that task.

   Social entrepreneurs who want to contribute to societal improvement find ways to do this while also earning profits. Founders of not-for-profits create enterprises to address societal needs that are important to them. Other entrepreneurs start lifestyle businesses that allow them to earn money while following their passion. For example, avid pilots may operate aviation-oriented businesses in which they can fly often, such as specialty delivery companies or teaching. Art lovers may open galleries, create art-rental businesses, or operate special art tours.
3. ***Creation/Ownership.*** Entrepreneurship is a creative endeavor. Entrepreneurs put time into creating something that they expect will survive and become profitable. Entrepreneurs own the businesses that they create and the profits that those businesses earn. *Ownership* is the key to wealth. Your goal is to find a business that will create a continuing stream of earnings. Eventually, you may be able to sell that company for a multiple of those earnings. That is how entrepreneurs create wealth. Many entrepreneurs, such as Bill Gore, the inventor of GORE-TEX fabric, start their own business after becoming frustrated or disillusioned in other roles, or having ideas rejected by an employer.
4. ***Control over Compensation.*** Entrepreneurs choose how and when they are paid. As owner of your company, you can decide to:
   - Pay yourself a **salary**—a fixed payment made at regular intervals, such as every week or every month. No matter how much time you put in, the salary remains the same.
   - Pay yourself a **wage**—a fixed payment per hour.
   - Take a share of the company's profit. As the owner you can pay yourself a portion of the business's profits. This kind of payment is called a **dividend**.
   - Take a **commission** on every sale you make. A commission is a percentage of the value of a sale. If you decide to pay yourself 10 percent commission, and sell an item for $120, your commission on the sale would be $12.

salary fixed amount of money paid to an employee at regular intervals.

wage fixed payment per hour for work performed.

dividend each stockholder's portion of the profit-per-share paid out by a corporation.

commission a percentage of a sale paid to a salesperson or employee.

5. ***Control over Working Conditions.*** As an entrepreneur, you can create a work environment that reflects your values. If you support recycling, you can make sure your company recycles. You will also evaluate your own performance. No one else has the power to fire you. If equality is vital, you may have an office with equal working spaces, no special privileges for managers, and few management layers.

Some of the greatest entrepreneurs in the world have dealt with problems growing up, such as extreme poverty, abuse, learning disabilities, and other issues. Sir Richard Branson, for example, had such severe dyslexia that he dropped out of high school. He became a successful entrepreneur, however, creating more than 200 companies—including Virgin Airlines, Virgin Galactic, and Virgin Records. The Virgin Group employs about 50,000 people in 29 countries with revenues of approximately \$20 billion.[3] Branson has a personal net worth of approximately \$4.4 billion, making him number 236 on the Forbes list of billionaires.[4] As an entrepreneur, he was able to create an environment in which he could succeed.

The Desire to Make Money Is Not the Only Reason to Start a Business

Starting a business is an opportunity, and like any opportunity, it should be evaluated by taking a careful look at the costs and benefits it offers. One thing is for certain, though, *the desire to make money, alone, is not a good enough reason to start one's own business.*

The financial rewards of owning your own business may not kick in until you have put in years of hard work. The desire to make money may not be enough to keep you going through the difficult early period. Most successful companies have been founded by an entrepreneur with a powerful and motivating dream, balanced by a strong work ethic and dedication.

[3]Virgin Group, http://www.virgin.com (accessed March 15, 2009).

[4]"The World's Billionaires," *Forbes*, March 5, 2008, http://www.forbes.com (accessed March 14, 2009).

Step into the Shoes...

Balloon Distractions, Inc.: Putting a New Twist on Entertainment

When Benjamin Alexander was a student at Rowan University in Glassboro, New Jersey, he earned spending money by working as a balloon artist. Today, he operates Balloon Distractions in Land O' Lakes, Florida, with approximately 200 independent contractors who are balloon artists. Alexander, who started the company in 2003, secures contracts with restaurants to provide balloon artists to amuse customers while they wait to be seated, or while they are seated and waiting for their food to be delivered.

Balloon Distractions provides its artists with a four-hour DVD training kit to teach them 25 shapes. The artists can recruit other artists, generally college students, and thereby become trainers. Artists book their restaurant locations online through the company's interactive Web site. These independent contractors work to earn tips plus bonuses.

Balloon Distractions uses entertainment skills Alexander developed during college, as well as selling skills learned in over 10 years as an automobile salesman and natural gas marketer. Alexander seized an opportunity and grew a business.

Source: Balloon Distractions, Inc. Web site at http://www.balloondistractions.com, accessed on February 7, 2010.

Entrepreneurs have said that they are not in business for the money so often that it has become a cliché, but, like most clichés, it is based on a degree of truth.

Definitions of Success—Monetary and Other

Today, the Millennial Generation (born between 1977 and 1995) has redefined success. It is more individualized than the traditional concept, and based upon factors beyond those of income and wealth. Business owners may start an enterprise to create a more environmentally friendly approach to a product or process, to provide jobs for a disadvantaged population, or to improve the mental or physical health of themselves or others. For these entrepreneurs, success might be measured by the ability to have an impact on the population they serve. Or, success may mean working to provide a lifestyle that permits a shortened work week or telecommuting. Recognition from peers and others could also be a goal. Financial success may be just one of many measures of achievement for an entrepreneur.

Taking the Long View

Successful entrepreneurs know that it is important to begin with the end in mind, so that they can always have a vision of where they want the organization to be at their personal exit point, even before they make the first sale. The daily tactical decisions you make will be affected by what you hope to create in the short *and* long term, so that a clear vision is vital. Some questions to ask yourself include:

- Are you planning to be active in the business until retirement? At what age will you retire? Who will take over then? A family member? A new owner?
- Do you plan to grow the business to a certain size or level of maturity and then sell it? If so, what is the target level? Are you looking at an initial public offering or a small private sale? Would you stay with the business after it was sold?
- Would you want to stay active for a given number of years? Then what would you do?

Taking the long view also means considering personal satisfaction, including conformance with individual values and ethics. Entrepreneurs make hundreds of choices and decisions every day. When you make everyday decisions, they can conform with your values and ethics or you can violate them to meet a customer need, provide an expedient or cost-effective solution to an immediate problem, or the like. For your long-term wellness and the benefit of those around you, it will be critical to keep your core values in the forefront. Consider the legacy you want to leave behind for your successors.

Benefits and Costs of Becoming an Entrepreneur

Even if you do have a clear vision that you believe will motivate you through the ups and downs of running a business, look closely at the costs and benefits of being an entrepreneur before you decide whether this is the life for you.

Benefits include:

- ***Independence.*** Business owners do not have to follow orders or observe working hours set by someone else.
- ***Satisfaction.*** Doing what you love to do, or turning a skill, hobby, or other interest into your own business can be highly satisfying.
- ***Financial Reward.*** Although income potential is generally capped for employees, entrepreneurs are limited only by their own imagination and tenacity. Entrepreneurs built most of our country's great fortunes. At the same time, many part-time, seasonal, and occasional entrepreneurs find ways to fund gaps in household income, pay for college, or support extraordinary expenses through entrepreneurship.
- ***Self-Esteem.*** Knowing you created something valuable can give you a strong sense of accomplishment. It can help you feel good about yourself.
- ***Contribution to Society.*** As a business owner, you decide how you can add value to your community and the wider world. The issues that you care about can be designed-in when you form your company.

Costs include:

- ***Business Failure.*** About one in five new businesses fails in the first eight years, although this is attributed to entrepreneurs not getting proper training.[5] Another third close because the entrepreneur becomes discouraged and gives up. Entrepreneurs risk losing not only their own money but also the financial investments of others.
- ***Obstacles.*** You will run into problems that you will have to solve by yourself. Your family and friends may actually discourage you, or not support your vision.
- ***Loneliness.*** It can be lonely and even a little scary to be completely responsible for the success or failure of your business.
- ***Financial Insecurity.*** You are not guaranteed a set salary or benefits. You may not always have enough money to pay yourself, particularly in the first 18 months of a new enterprise. You will have to set up and fund your own retirement fund.
- ***Long Hours/Hard Work.*** You will have to work long hours to get your business off the ground. Many entrepreneurs work six or even seven days a week, often for 12 hours or more per day. While you decide when to work, you may end up working many more hours as an entrepreneur than you would as an employee. Also, do not forget to examine the opportunities you will be giving up to start your own business. What are the next-best opportunities for your money and time? Some might include going to college or graduate school, or even working for someone else.
- ***Strain on Personal Relationships.*** Even with the strong support of family and friends, the inherent challenges of a small business can strain relationships to the breaking point.

Not everyone is cut out to be an entrepreneur. Entrepreneurs have to be able to tolerate a higher degree of risk and uncertainty than people who work steady jobs for established employers. With higher risk, however, comes the possibility of higher rewards.

[5] Linda Yu, "Self-Employment on Rise," *Metro* magazine, June 2004.

Cost/Benefit Analysis

Using a comparison of benefits and costs to make a decision is called **cost/benefit analysis**. It is a helpful tool because people tend to make decisions based upon emotions, not intellect, to evaluate the pros and cons. Strong emotion may overwhelm you to the point where you see only the benefits and not the costs of an action (or vice versa).

cost/benefit analysis a decision-making process in which the costs of taking an action are compared to the benefits.

Say you plan to buy a car. You might be overwhelmed by the idea of making such a large purchase, even if the benefits are greater than the costs. On the other hand, you might decide to buy a car at a cost that outweighs the benefits it will bring because you are temporarily blinded by a desire to own a really impressive vehicle. Making a list that includes the dollars and cents of the costs and benefits of your purchase is a concrete way to take the emotion out of the decision.

To turn an opportunity into a business you will have to invest both time and money. Before making this investment, think carefully about:

Costs. The money and time you will have to invest, as well as the opportunities you will give up, to operate the business.

Benefits. The money you will earn and the knowledge and experience you will gain.

Opportunity Cost

Cost/benefit analysis is incomplete without considering **opportunity cost**. This is the cost of your "next-best investment." Perhaps your goal is to become a composer who writes scores for movies. You get a full-time job at a local store for $400 a week to support yourself, so you can write and record music in the evenings that you hope to sell to producers, agents, or film companies.

opportunity cost the value of what must be given up in order to obtain something else.

You find, however, that whenever a producer or agent wants to meet with you, you cannot get out of work to go. You realize that, even though you are making $400 a week, you are missing some important opportunities. Perhaps it would be smarter to take a part-time job for $300 a week that would leave your mornings free for meetings. The opportunity cost of the $100 a week you will lose is made up for by the potential income from film-scoring jobs you are missing by not being free to see people in the business. If your first film-scoring job pays $5,000, for example, you definitely would have made the right decision to earn $100 a week less for a few months.

People often make decisions without considering the opportunity cost and then wonder why they are not happy with the outcome. Each time you make a decision about what to do with your time, energy, or money, think about the cost of the opportunities that you are giving up. Figure 1-1 presents a simple quiz that can help you decide whether you have what it takes to be an entrepreneur.

Avoiding Missteps

While experience is an excellent teacher, using knowledge, skills, and abilities to avoid errors, problems, and delays is much healthier. A savvy entrepreneur learns from the mistakes of others and appreciates the wisdom and experience of trusted advisors and mentors. Of course, it may be difficult to discern what advice is sound and what is likely to fuel further missteps.

Preparation and planning are keys to avoiding making mistakes. Thoughtful consideration of the entrepreneurship option is an excellent starting point. Thorough research and taking advantage of training and/or

Figure 1-1 *"Do you have what it takes?" quiz.*

Take the following quiz to learn more about yourself and whether you have what it takes to be an entrepreneur. Circle the answer that best represents how you feel.

1. You are at a party and a friend tells you that the guy in the expensive-looking suit recently invested in another friend's business. What do you do?
   a. Race over to him, introduce yourself, and tell him every detail of your business idea while asking if he would be interested in investing in it.
   b. Ask your friend to introduce you. Once introduced, you hand the potential investor your business card and politely ask whether you might be able to call on him sometime to present your business plan.
   c. Decide that it is probably not a good idea to bother the man at a party. After all, he is here to relax. Maybe you will run into him again somewhere else.
2. Your boss asks you to take charge of researching office supply stores and choosing the one that you think would be best for the company to use. What is your response?
   a. Yes! Finally, a chance to show the boss what you are made of—plus, you will be able to spirit a few of the supplies away for your own business.
   b. You are terrified; this is more responsibility than you really want. What if you make a mistake and cost the company money? You do not want to look bad.
   c. You are excited. This is a good opportunity to impress your boss and also learn how to compare and negotiate with suppliers . . . something you will need to do for your own business.
3. You are already going to school full time when you are offered a part-time job that is in the same field as the business you want to start when you graduate next year. What do you do?
   a. Take the job, after talking with your student advisor about how to juggle your schedule so it will fit, because you believe the experience and the contacts you will develop will be invaluable when you start your business.
   b. Take the job. In fact, you ask for extra hours so you can finally start making some real money. Who needs sleep?
   c. Turn down the job. School is hard enough without working, too. You do not want your grades to suffer.
4. You are offered a job as a survey-taker for a marketing firm. The job pays really well but will require you to talk to a great many people. What do you do?
   a. Take the job. You like people and this job will be a good way to practice getting to know what consumers want.
   b. Turn down the job. Just the thought of approaching strangers makes you queasy.
   c. Take the job so you can conduct some market research of your own by also asking the people you survey what they think about your business idea.
5. Your last job paid well and was interesting, but it required you to put in long hours and sometimes work on the weekends. What was your response?
   a. You put in the extra hours without complaint, but mainly because you felt that the rewards were worth it.
   b. You went a little overboard and worked yourself into a state of exhaustion; moderation is not your strong suit.
   c. You quit. You are strictly a nine-to-five person. Work is definitely not your life!
6. You are such a good guitar player that friends keep offering to pay for you to give them lessons. What is your response?
   a. You spend some money to run a six-week advertisement in the local paper, announcing that you are now available to teachat the same rate that established teachers in the area charge.
   b. You start teaching a few friends to see how it goes. You ask them what they are willing to pay and what they want to learn.
   c. You give a few friends some lessons but refuse to take any money.
7. Your best friend has started a business designing Web sites. He needs help because the business is really growing. He offers to make you a partner in the business even though you are computer-illiterate. What is your response?
   a. You jump in, figuring that you will learn the ropes soon enough.
   b. You ask your friend to keep the partnership offer open but first to recommend a class you can take to get your skills up to speed.
   c. You pass. You do not see how you can work in a business you know nothing about.

Analysis of the "Do You Have What It Takes?" Quiz

Scoring

1. a = 2	b = 1	c = 0
2. a = 2	b = 0	c = 1
3. a = 1	b = 2	c = 0
4. a = 1	b = 0	c = 2
5. a = 1	b = 2	c = 0
6. a = 2	b = 1	c = 0
7. a = 2	b = 1	c = 0

Figure 1-1 *"Do you have what it takes?" quiz.*

12 Points or More: You are a natural risk-taker and can handle a lot of stress. These are important characteristics for an entrepreneur to have to be successful. You are willing to work hard but have a tendency to throw caution to the wind a little too easily. Save yourself from that tendency by using cost/benefit analysis to carefully evaluate your business (and personal!) decisions. In your enthusiasm, do not forget to look at the opportunity costs of any decision you make.

6 to 12 Points: You strike an excellent balance between being a risk-taker and someone who carefully evaluates decisions. An entrepreneur needs to be both. You are also not overly motivated by the desire to make money. You understand that a successful business requires hard work and sacrifice before you can reap the rewards. To make sure that you are applying your natural drive and discipline to the best possible business opportunity, use the cost/benefit analysis to evaluate the different businesses you are interested in starting.

6 Points or Fewer: You are a little too cautious for an entrepreneur, but that will probably change as you learn more about how to run a business. You are concerned with financial security and may not be eager to put in the long hours required to get a business off the ground. This does not mean that you can not succeed as an entrepreneur; just make sure that whatever business you decide to start is the business of your dreams, so that you will be motivated to make it a success. Use cost/benefit analysis to evaluate your business opportunities. Choose a business that you believe has the best shot at providing you with both the financial security and the motivation you require.

technical assistance to bridge gaps in your preparation can make a world of difference.

Two of the best resources for keeping on track are mentors and advisors. Finding a committed business mentor with industry-specific knowledge and experience, broad general business experience, or both, is a worthwhile endeavor. If you can find a successful entrepreneur in your field, perhaps outside of your geographic area, having him/her as a mentor may prove invaluable. Many successful entrepreneurs will carve out time for promising newcomers. Unfortunately, becoming a mentor may be more of a commitment than your identified entrepreneur is willing or able to make. Perhaps he or she will become an advisor instead.

In addition to your paid professional advisors, such as attorneys and accountants, individual advisors or an advisory board can be the difference between success and failure. Even if you are forming a venture with a full slate of experienced technical and managerial professionals, the guidance of a carefully composed advisory board can provide valuable counsel and connections. Such a board might meet only once or twice a year to serve as a sounding board, share experiences, and help you avoid mistakes. During the times between meetings, advisors may also offer substantial assistance.

Of course, taking advantage of available courses in entrepreneurship, whether brief workshops, individual college courses, an entrepreneurial certificate program, or a degree program, can give you considerable advantage. The opportunity to learn from the experiences of others and to systematically explore entrepreneurship options and build skills is invaluable.

A well-prepared entrepreneur is more likely to stay on the path to success.

Entrepreneurial Options

Entrepreneurship extends beyond the traditional views of for-profit enterprises that are most commonly associated with it. There are many variations on entrepreneurship, and the opportunities are virtually limitless. Entrepreneurship may include for-profit enterprises that support the missions of not-for-profit organizations, businesses designed for social impact, and ventures that are environmentally oriented.

social entrepreneurship a for-profit enterprise that has the dual goals of achieving profitability and attaining social returns.

Social entrepreneurship has multiple definitions and forms, but in general it is commonly thought of as a for-profit enterprise that has the dual goals of achieving profitability and attaining beneficial social returns. Another view is that of taking an entrepreneurial perspective toward social problems.[6] Gregory Dees has created the following definition:

"Social entrepreneurs play the role of change agents in the social sector by:

- adopting a mission to create and sustain social value (not just private value),
- recognizing and relentlessly pursuing new opportunities to serve that mission,
- engaging in a process of continuous innovation, adaptation, and learning,
- acting boldly without being limited by resources currently in hand, and
- exhibiting heightened accountability to the constituencies served and for the outcomes created."

venture philanthropy a subset or segment of social entrepreneurship wherein financial and human capital is invested in not-for-profits by individuals and for-profit enterprises with the intention of generating social rather than financial returns on their investments.

green entrepreneurship enterprise activities that avoid harm to the environment or help to protect it in some way.

In this view, social entrepreneurship is less about profit than it is about social impact.

In addition, **venture philanthropy** is a subset or segment of social entrepreneurship. Financial and human capital is invested in not-for-profits by individuals and for-profit enterprises with the intention of generating social rather than financial returns. In some cases, venture philanthropy may involve the investment of capital in the for-profit, commercial part of a not-for-profit. In others, it may mean investing in not-for-profits directly, to encourage entrepreneurial approaches to achieve social impact.

Green entrepreneurship is another form of social entrepreneurship and can be defined as: "Enterprise activities that avoid harm to the environment or help to protect the environment in some way."[7] TerraCycle is an excellent example of green entrepreneurship. According to the Corporation for Enterprise Development (CFED), green entrepreneurship can

- create jobs and offer entrepreneurship opportunities;
- increase energy efficiency, thus conserving natural resources and saving money;
- decrease harm to workers' health;
- enable businesses to tap into new sources of local, state, and federal funding;
- take advantage of consumer preference for environmentally friendly goods; and
- preserve limited natural assets on which businesses and communities depend for business and quality of life.

Each of these alternative approaches offers opportunities for innovation and growth for the right entrepreneur.

Organically grown produce

[6] Gregory Dees, "The Meaning of 'Social Entrepreneurship'," May 30, 2001, *http://www.fuqua.duke.edu/centers/case/documents/dees_SE.pdf* (accessed December 2007). Used by permission.

[7] *Green Entrepreneurship. Corporation for Enterprise Development: Effective State Policy and Practice*, Volume 5, Number 2, April 2004, *http://www.cfed.org*.

How Do Entrepreneurs Find Opportunities to Start New Businesses?

In the twentieth century, Joseph Schumpeter expanded on Say's definition of entrepreneurship by adding that entrepreneurs create value "by exploiting an invention or, more generally, an untried technological possibility for producing a new commodity or producing an old one in a new way, by opening up a new source of supply of materials or a new outlet for products, by reorganizing an industry and so on."[8] This view emphasizes innovation as the key to entrepreneurship. Management expert Peter Drucker simplified this view to the essential core of creating a new business, taking on risk, and persevering in light of uncertainty.[9]

Schumpeter's definition describes five basic ways that entrepreneurs find opportunities to create new businesses:

Performance Objective 3

Find and evaluate opportunities to start your own business.

1. Use a new technology to produce a new product.
2. Use an existing technology to produce a new product.
3. Use an existing technology to produce an old product in a new way.
4. Find a new source of resources (that might enable the entrepreneur to produce a product more cheaply).
5. Develop a new market for an existing product.

Entrepreneurs Creatively Exploit Changes in Our World

Today's economists and business experts have defined entrepreneurship even more sharply. Drucker pointed out that, for a business to be considered entrepreneurial, it should exploit changes in the world. This is in alignment with Schumpeter's definition of entrepreneurship but explicitly takes it a step further . . . to take advantage of circumstances. These changes can be technological, like the explosion in computer technology that led Bill Gates and Paul Allen to start Microsoft, or cultural, like the collapse of Communism, which led to a great many new business opportunities in Eastern Europe.

Nothing changes faster than technology, which is defined as science that has been applied to industry or commerce. Not many years ago, there were no bar codes, no electronic scanners, and hardly anyone used e-mail or mobile phones. Today, even the smallest of organizations needs to use

[8]Joseph A. Schumpeter, *Capitalism, Socialism and Democracy* (New York: Harper & Row, 1942).

[9]Peter Drucker, *Innovation and Entrepreneurship: Practice and Principles* (New York: Harper Collins, 1985).

How Do Entrepreneurs Create Business Ideas?

1. ***They listen.*** By listening to others, entrepreneurs get ideas about improving a business or creating a new one. Create one business idea by listening. Describe how you got the idea.
2. ***They observe.*** By constantly keeping their eyes open, entrepreneurs get ideas about how to help society, about businesses to start, and about what customers need. Create a business idea by observing. Describe how you got the idea.
3. ***They think.*** When entrepreneurs analyze a problem, they think about solutions. What product or service could solve that problem? Create a business idea by thinking about a problem. Describe how you got the idea.

current technologies to be competitive. Smart entrepreneurs multiply their efficiency by taking advantage of the latest breakthroughs in business technology. To learn about what's new in technology, read current business and trade magazines and visit Web sites such as:

- The Business Technology Network, *http://www.techweb.com*.
- BusinessWeek Technology News, *http://www.businessweek.com/technology*.

Peter Drucker defined an entrepreneur as someone who "always searches for change, responds to it, and exploits it as an opportunity." Entrepreneurs are always on the lookout for ways to create opportunities from change.

Where Others See Problems, Entrepreneurs Recognize Opportunities

Here is a simple definition of an entrepreneur that captures the essentials: An entrepreneur recognizes opportunities where other people see only problems.

Many famous companies were started because an entrepreneur turned a problem into a successful business. An entrepreneur recognized that the problem was actually an opportunity. Where there are dissatisfied consumers, there are definitely opportunities for entrepreneurs.

Anita Roddick was an excellent example of an entrepreneur who started off as a dissatisfied consumer. She started The Body Shop International because she was tired of paying for unnecessary perfume and fancy packaging when she bought makeup, and she thought other women might feel the same way. Harlan Beverly is another problem solver. He realized that online gamers are frustrated by the lag time on response while playing their favorite online games and created products to address the problem. His BigFoot Networks has become an industry leader.

Train Your Mind to Recognize Business Opportunities

The first step in becoming an entrepreneur is to train your mind to recognize business opportunities. The next step is to let your creativity fly. Roddick suggested that you develop your entrepreneurial instincts by asking yourself such questions as

- What frustrates me the most when I try to buy something?
- What product or service would really make my life better?
- What makes me annoyed or angry?
- What product or service would take away my aggravation?

BizFacts

Entrepreneurship has proven to be an effective way for minorities and women to enter the business world.

- More than 4 million businesses were minority-owned in 2002, employing 4.8 million people and generating $694 billion in revenues.
- There were more than 9.2 million non-farm businesses owned by women (or co-owned equally with men), accounting for 40 percent of all U.S. companies.

Source: Accessed from http://www.sba.gov on March 16, 2009.

Entrepreneurs Use Their Imaginations

Businesses are also formed when entrepreneurs not only fume about products or services that annoy them but fantasize about products or services they would love to have in their lives. Jump-start your imagination by asking yourself such questions as

- What is the one thing I would love to have more than anything else?
- What would it look like? What would it taste like?
- What would it do?
- What innovative product or service idea have I been mulling over in my mind?
- What problem have I encountered in everyday life and thought: "There has to be a better way to do this?"

Consider posing these questions to friends and family members as well. You might hear about an opportunity you had not yet recognized.

An Idea Is Not Necessarily an Opportunity

Not every business idea you may have or invention you may explore is an opportunity. In fact, most ideas are not viable business possibilities. An opportunity has a unique characteristic that distinguishes it from an ordinary idea. An opportunity is an idea that is based on what consumers need or want and are willing to buy sufficiently often at a high enough price to sustain a business. A successful business sells products or services that customers need, at prices they are willing to pay. Many a small business has failed because the entrepreneur did not understand this. It is critical that the idea "has legs" for it to go on to success.

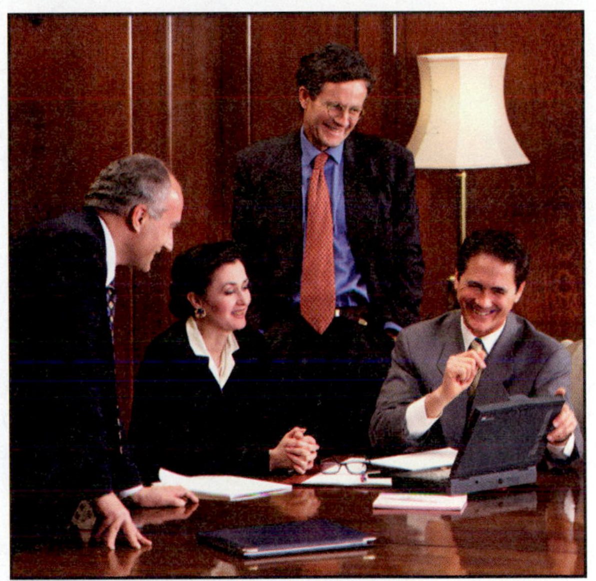

In addition, according to Jeffry Timmons, "An opportunity has the qualities of being attractive, durable, and timely and is anchored in a product or service which creates or adds value for its buyer or end user."[10]

[10]*New Venture Creation: Entrepreneurship for the 21st Century*, 5th ed. (New York: Irwin/McGraw-Hill, 1999), p. 7.

Entrepreneurial Wisdom...

A useful way to evaluate a business idea is to look at its Strengths, Weaknesses, Opportunities, and Threats (SWOT). This is called **SWOT Analysis**.

- *Strengths*—All the capabilities and positive points that the entrepreneur has, from experience to contacts. These are internal to the organization.
- *Weaknesses*—All of the negatives that the entrepreneur faces, such as lack of capital or training, or failure to set up a workable accounting system. These are internal to the organization.
- *Opportunities*—Any positive external event or circumstance (including lucky breaks) that can help the entrepreneur get ahead of the competition.
- *Threats*—Any external factor, event, or circumstance that can harm the business, such as competitors, legal issues, or declining economies.

Timmons defines a business opportunity as an idea, plus these four characteristics:

1. It is attractive to customers.
2. It will work in your business environment.
3. It can be executed in the window of opportunity that exists.
4. You have the resources and skills to create the business, or you know someone who does and who might want to form the business with you.

The window of opportunity is the length of time you have to get your business idea to your market. You might have a great idea, but if several other competitors have it, too, and have already brought it to the marketplace, that window of opportunity has been closed.

Remember, not every idea is an opportunity. For an idea to be an opportunity, it must lead to the development of a product or service that is of value to the customer.

Opportunity Is Situational

A problem is one example of an opportunity that entrepreneurs need to be able to recognize. A changing situation or trend is another. Opportunity is *situational*, meaning it is dependent on variable circumstances. There are no rules about when or where an opportunity might appear. Change and flux create opportunities.

Think about recent changes in computer technology. In the early 1990s, the conventional wisdom was that only the biggest telecommunications companies were going to be in a position to exploit the Internet and all the opportunities it had to offer. How could entrepreneurs compete with established, resource-loaded companies? The opposite has been true, however. Entrepreneurs have penetrated and, indeed, dominated the market for Internet-based services. Think of AOL, Google, and Yahoo! Each one is an entrepreneurial venture that left the telecom giants scrambling to catch up.

As Timmons has pointed out, it can take a huge corporation (think dinosaur) over six years to develop and implement a new business strategy. Entrepreneurs, in contrast, can dart in and out of the market like roadrunners. Successful entrepreneurs can "turn on a dime rather than a dollar bill."

The Five Roots of Opportunity in the Marketplace

There are "five roots of opportunity" that entrepreneurs can exploit.[11] Notice how similar these are to Schumpeter's definition of entrepreneurship.

1. **Problems** that your business can solve.
2. **Changes** in laws, situations, or trends.
3. **Inventions** of totally new products or services.
4. **Competition** If you can find a way to beat the competition on price, location, quality, reputation, reliability, or speed, you can create a very successful business with an existing product or service.
5. **Technological Advances** Scientists may invent new technology, but entrepreneurs figure out how to use and sell it.

[11]Adapted from the *Master Curriculum Guide: Economics and Entrepreneurship*, John Clow, ed. (New York: Joint Council on Economic Education, 1991).

Step into the Shoes...

Russell Simmons Makes Rap Happen

In the late 1980s, Russell Simmons was promoting rap concerts at the City University of New York. At the time, rap was considered a passing fad, but Simmons really loved it. Even though most record executives thought rap would be over in a year or two, Simmons truly believed it was a business opportunity. He formed Def Jam Records with fellow student Rick Rubin for $5,000. Within a year, they produced hit records by Run DMC and LL Cool J, and Simmons became a multimedia mogul.

Simmons took a chance on this opportunity because he felt that, if you personally know 10 people who are eager to buy your product or service, 10 *million* would be willing to buy it if they knew about it. Luckily, he was right about rap's popular potential, but he could have been wrong. That can be a problem with perceived opportunities—you may be passionate about something but there may not be enough consumer interest to sustain an actual business venture.

Simmons loved rap and hoped that other people would, too. That was the internal factor—he had the passion to sustain himself as he worked 24/7 to make his dream come true. As it turned out, music fans were a little bored with rock at that time, and looking for a fresh sound. Rap filled the bill. This was an external opportunity that happened to coincide with Simmons's internal commitment.

Integrating Internal and External Opportunities

It is helpful not only to be aware of the "five roots of opportunity" in the marketplace, but to think also about how we perceive opportunities ourselves. Opportunities fall into two classes: internal and external. An internal opportunity is one that comes from inside you—from a personal hobby, interest, or even a passion—or your organization, which could come in the form of the resolution of a problem, such as creating a viable product from scrap material, or the potential for a new product line.

An external opportunity, in contrast, is generated by a noticeable outside circumstance. External opportunities are conditions you notice that make you say to yourself, "Hey! I could start a great business from that!" For example, you see that people in your neighborhood are complaining about the lack of available day care, so you start a day care center. But what if you find out very quickly that two-year-olds get on your nerves? That can be a major drawback for external opportunities. Your idea may fill a market need, but you may not have the skills or interest to make it a successful business.

The best business opportunities often combine both internal and external factors. Ideally, a business that you are passionate about fills a huge need in the marketplace.

Establishing Strategies

Business success hinges upon the creation and application of profitable strategies to the work at hand. A **strategy** is a plan for how a business intends to go about its own performance and outdo that of its competition. Michael Porter created a "strategy framework" in his book, *Competitive Advantage*, which has held up well. This framework delineates cost leadership and differentiation as low-cost and product-uniqueness strategies. It also layers in the concept of focus strategies, which work in narrow market segments rather than broad markets. The illustration in **Figure 1-2** shows how each of Porter's Generic Strategies relates to the other.

strategy a plan for how an organization or individual plans to go about its own performance and outdo that of its competitors.

Figure 1-2 *Porter's Generic Strategies.*

Scope of Target	Strategic Advantage	
Market	**Product Uniqueness**	**Low Cost**
Industry-Wide (Broad)	Differentiation Strategy	Cost Leadership Strategy
Market Segment (Narrow)	Focus Strategy (Differentiation)	Focus Strategy (Low Cost)

Adapted from Michael Porter, *Competitive Strategy: Techniques for Analyzing Industries and Competitors* (Free Press, 1998).

A firm using a product-uniqueness strategy bases its competitive advantage on its ability to differentiate the firm's products and/or services from others in its competitive market space. Such factors as quality, availability, customer service, and the like, are critical to differentiation, as will be discussed in greater detail in the marketing chapters of this text.

If you choose to emphasize a low-cost approach, you will be using a cost-leadership strategy. This means that you are finding ways to reduce the costs of operations and management sufficiently to be able to "undercut" the pricing of your competition and are able to sustain a price advantage.

Another component of the Porter framework is that of a focus strategy. This line of attack narrows in and creates a laser-like focus on a particular market segment or group. Rather than strategically targeting an entire industry, you are finding a particular niche or subset of the customer base and focusing your marketing efforts on that niche. If you are able to find a sufficiently large niche to sustain your business, you can set the company apart from the competition, and can maintain the advantage. A focus strategy can work with differentiation and cost leadership.

Paths to Small Business Ownership

Not all business owners start their ventures from the ground up. Although the emphasis of this book is on starting and growing your own enterprise, the paths to business ownership are varied. You could buy an existing company, secure franchise rights, license or purchase critical technology or methods, inherit a company, or be hired as a manager.[12] There are pros and cons to each approach and it is worthwhile to give thought to each option. Note the possibilities in **Exhibit 1-1**.

Securing Franchise Rights

"A **franchise** is a legal and commercial relationship between the owner of a trademark, service mark, trade name or advertising symbol and an individual or group seeking to use that identification in a business."[13] For many people who want to own and operate a business, it is worthwhile to consider franchising as a path to business ownership. See Chapter 2 for a discussion of franchising as an entrepreneurial opportunity.

[12]Jerome A. Katz and Richard P. Green, *Entrepreneurial Small Business* (New York: McGraw-Hill/Irwin, 2008).

[13]U.S. Small Business Administration Workshop, "Is Franchising for Me?" *http://www.sba.gov/idc/groups/public/documents/sba_homepage/serv_sbp_isfforme.pdf* (accessed December 2007).

Exhibit 1-1 *Selected business entry options.*

	Start a Business	Buy an Existing Business	Secure a Franchise or License	License Technology
Customers	None	Established	None—but may have name recognition	None
Location	Needed	In place	Assistance possible	Needed
Management Control	Owner	Owner	Owner within terms of license	Owner within terms of license
Operational Control	Owner	Owner	Owner within terms of license	Owner
Marketing	Needed	In place (+/−)	Assistance possible. Rules absolutely.	Needed
Reputation	None	In place (+/−)	Should be. If not, why license?	Possible
Royalties/Fees	Not usual	Maybe	Ongoing	Likely
Financing	Needed	Prior owner may provide	Assistance possible	Needed
Disclosures	None	Buyer beware	UFOC and contracts	Agreement

Buying an Existing Business

A business purchase, or **acquisition**, might be a good way to jump-start your entry into small business ownership. There is both an art and a science to buying an existing business.

acquisition a business purchase.

The challenge is to do a complete, in-depth analysis of the opportunity, just as you would for a startup, with the added dimension of having an existing history, whether for better or for worse. Be wary of owners whose business seems to be too good to be true or who are overly eager to sell. Be thorough, whether you are buying an entire firm, a customer list, some or all assets, or taking on some or all debts. Done well, buying a business can be the starting point for success. Done poorly, buying a business can be more challenging and problematic than starting a new venture. See Chapter 3 for a more in-depth discussion.

Licensing Technology

One way to potentially shorten the product-development cycle and to access innovative technology would be to identify and *license* technology, that is, to enter into a contract to use it without purchasing the rights to own it. Whether you acquire such rights through a university, state economic development office, federal agency such as NASA, or an individual scientist/inventor, you can create a business based on technology transfer. Or, you may find that it makes more sense to purchase it outright or over time.

The MBA team of Bruce Black and Matt Ferris from the University of Georgia developed a business plan that garnered numerous competitive awards for the KidSmart Vocal Smoke Detector, which was created by an inventor and brought to market by them. The product is now available in major retail stores and on the Internet through the successor company, Signal One.

Before securing franchise rights, purchasing a business, or licensing technology, be certain to do your research thoroughly to understand what you are and are not buying and what your ongoing obligations (financial, operational, legal, and reporting) will be. Because these transactions are complex and can have significant financial and personal implications for you, it is important to invest in qualified legal and financial counsel before signing any agreements of this kind.

Do Not Take Unfair Advantage of Someone Else's Creativity

You would be upset if someone made money from your invention or artistic creation, so resist the urge to base your business on someone else's creative work. Not only is it unethical, it is against the law. Be sure that any business you start respects the intellectual property of others.

- Do not sell counterfeit knockoffs of popular brands.
- Do not take graphics, music, or content from the Web without permission and/or payment.
- Always know the source of the goods you buy from suppliers to avoid the risk of receiving stolen property.

The Many Faces of Entrepreneurship

Entrepreneurs are as diverse as the composition of the economy. They are of all ethnicities, races, religions, and every socioeconomic status. They enter into self-employment for a wide range of reasons and choose to continue as entrepreneurs or return to outside employment for just as many. There are women and minority entrepreneurs and young entrepreneurs in record numbers. Continuing an American tradition, there are also refugee and immigrant entrepreneurs.

This diverse and ever-changing pool of entrepreneurs is not filled with a single view of entrepreneurial success. Rather, the types of businesses formed are many, as well. In addition to full-time enterprises founded to maximize growth and wealth, there are firms that are started as part-time and small enterprises (microenterprises), "gazelles," artisanal and opportunistic enterprises, and others.

Gazelles

The classic entrepreneurial story is that of a single inventor or pair of inventors that develop a new, innovative technology or product in a garage, basement, or dormitory, lift themselves up by their bootstraps into a wildly successful business venture in virtually no time, take it public, and become incredibly wealthy in the process. This entrepreneurial stereotype is a description of a high-potential venture and its founders. **Gazelles** are companies that achieve an annual growth rate of 20 percent or greater, typically measured in the growth of sales revenue.

gazelle a company that achieves an annual growth rate of 20 percent or greater, typically measured by the increase of sales revenue.

They tend to be the exception rather than the rule for entrepreneurial ventures, but are a significant type of firm. Gazelles are financed by a combination of found resources with significant outside assistance. They rely heavily upon external financial support and counsel.

Microenterprises

microenterprise a firm with five or fewer employees, initial capitalization requirements of under $35,000, and the regular operational involvement of the owner.

Most businesses are founded as **microenterprises**, which are defined as firms with five or fewer employees, initial capitalization requirements of under $35,000, and have the regular operational involvement of the owner. In fact, over 60 percent of all U.S. firms have four or fewer employees, according to the U.S. Small Business Administration.[14] The Association for

[14]U.S. Small Business Administration, Office of Advocacy, 2006.

Enterprise Opportunity (AEO) estimates that the more than 24 million microenterprises in the United States account for 87 percent of all businesses and 18 percent of all private employment.[15]

Microenterprises are founded for a variety of reasons and are often more fluid than other types of businesses. These firms may be started to provide full-time or part-time employment for their owners. They may be intended as long-term enterprises and may or may not have the goal of growing larger. Or, they may be planned as only temporary ventures to provide income during periods of unemployment, or to supplement household finances for a particular purpose. **Lifestyle businesses** are microenterprises that permit their owners to follow a desired pattern of living, such as supporting college costs, or taking vacations. On the other hand, a microenterprise could make the difference between a family living in poverty and achieving economic stability.

lifestyle business a microenterprise that permits its owners to follow a desired pattern of living, such as supporting college costs, or taking vacations.

Mainstream Small Firms

These constitute the bulk of the small businesses in the public perception, in the press, and in community visibility. They are those that provide, or have the potential to provide, substantial profits to their owners. Mainstream small firms can be operated by founder-entrepreneurs, subsequent generations of family members, successor owners, or franchisees. They create many of the jobs noted by the U.S. Small Business Administration and employ the majority of American workers. Unlike many microenterprises, they are established with continuity and permanent wealth building in mind, and are more often registered with local, state, and federal agencies.

Making the Business Work Personally and Professionally

What makes a business work is not solely profitability and cash flow, although they are of course necessary. Each entrepreneur has his or her own goals and objectives for the business. As an entrepreneur, it will be up to you to determine how you want your business to be, and to make it happen.

A Business Must Make a Profit to Stay in Business

No matter how big or small, a business must make a **profit**, that is, a positive gain from operations after all expenses are subtracted. Most businesses do lose money initially because entrepreneurs have to spend money to set up operations and advertise to attract customers. If the business cannot make a profit and generate cash, eventually the entrepreneur will be unable to pay the bills and will have to close.

profit amount of money remaining after all costs are deducted from the income of a business.

Closing a business is nothing to be ashamed of, if you operate ethically and learn from the experience. In fact, most successful entrepreneurs open and close more than one business during their lives. If your venture is not making a profit after you have gotten it up and running, that is a signal that you may be in the wrong business. Closing it may be the smartest decision.

An entrepreneur may change businesses many times over a lifetime in response to changing competition and consumer needs.

[15]Association for Enterprise Opportunity, http://www.microenterpriseworks.org (accessed March 16, 2009).

Profit Is the Sign That the Entrepreneur Is Adding Value

Performance Objective 4
Explain how profit works as a signal to the entrepreneur.

Profit is the sign that an entrepreneur has added value to the resources he or she is using. Debbi Fields added value to scarce resources by creating something that people were willing to buy for a price that gave her a profit. In contrast, not making a profit is a sign that the entrepreneur is not using resources very well and is not adding value to them.

Profit Results from the Entrepreneur's Choices

trade-off the act of giving up one thing for another.

An entrepreneur's choices directly affect how much profit the business makes. For example, suppose, like Debbi Fields, you have a business selling homemade cookies. You might decide one week to buy margarine instead of butter because it is cheaper, even though the cookies may not taste as good made with margarine. This type of choice is called a **trade-off**. You are giving up one thing (taste) for another (money).

If your customers do not notice the change and continue to buy your cookies, you have made a good choice. You have conserved a resource (money) and increased your profit by lowering your costs. The increase in profit confirms that you have made the right choice.

If your customers notice the change and stop buying your cookies, your profit will decrease. The decrease in profit signals that you have made a bad choice. Next week you should probably go back to butter. The profit signal taught you that your customers were dissatisfied and the trade-off was not worth it. Every choice an entrepreneur makes is a trade-off.

Seven Rules for Building a Successful Business

Russell Simmons and Rick Rubin were successful in creating Def Jam because they instinctively applied the seven basic rules of building a successful business:

1. ***Recognize an Opportunity.*** Simmons believed that rap music was an untapped business opportunity.
2. ***Evaluate It with Critical Thinking.*** He tested his idea by promoting concerts and observing consumer reaction.

Entrepreneurial Wisdom...

Build Your Brain

Becoming a successful entrepreneur is all about making connections, those "Aha!" moments when you realize what your business opportunity is, or when you figure out how to do something better than the competition. Research indicates that mental exercise will help your brain become better at making such connections. Even the most erudite scientists recognize the value of activities that encourage brain cells to make new connections. Robotics engineer Hugo de Garis, who has worked on such projects as building an artificial brain for an artificial cat, plays classical piano every day before he sits down at the computer. "This helps to build my own brain," he told the *New York Times*.[16] Arnold Scheibel, head of the University of California–Los Angeles Brain Research Institute, suggests the following brain-builders:

- Solve puzzles.
- Play a musical instrument.
- Fix something; learn to repair cars or electrical equipment.
- Create art; write poetry, paint, or sculpt.
- Dance.
- Make friends with people who like to have interesting conversations.

---

[16] Nicholas D. Kristof, "Robokitty," *New York Times*, August 1, 1999.

3. ***Build a Team.*** Simmons formed a partnership with Rubin.
4. ***Write.*** Simmons and Rubin created a realistic business plan.
5. ***Gather Resources.*** Simmons and Rubin pooled their $5,000.
6. ***Decide Ownership.*** Simmons and Rubin formed a legal partnership.
7. ***Create Wealth.***

The Team Approach

Let's take a closer look at step 3: Build a Team. Alone, neither Simmons nor Rubin had enough money to launch a record label, but together they were able to do it. Their business was also helped by the fact that each knew different artists and had different contacts in the recording industry.

Everyone you know is a potential business-formation opportunity. Your friends or family members may have skills, equipment, or contacts that would make them valuable business partners. Perhaps you very much want to start a Web-site-design business because you know of companies in your community that want to put up Web sites. You are a graphic artist but you do not know how to use Web-site development programs. If you have a friend who has that knowledge, you might start a business together. Or maybe you would like to start a DJ business, but you only have one turntable or laptop computer. If you form the business with a friend, you can pool equipment. (When forming a business team, organize the venture so that everyone involved shares in the ownership and profits. People work much better when they are working for themselves.) Just be careful of jumping into business relationships with undue haste.

Now carry this idea a step further. Every person you meet is a potential contact for your business, just as you may be a valuable contact for theirs. Thinking this way will encourage you to *network*, or exchange valuable information and contacts with other businesspeople. Keep your business cards on you at all times and truly view every individual you meet as an opportunity for your business. Remember, though, that networking is a two-way street. See how you can help those that you meet rather than focusing only on how they can help you. The results can be nothing short of amazing.

Chapter Summary

Now that you have studied this chapter, you can do the following:

1. Explain what entrepreneurs do.
   - Entrepreneurs start their own businesses and work for themselves.
   - Entrepreneurs recognize opportunities to start businesses that other people may not have noticed.
   - Entrepreneurs shift economic resources from an area of lower productivity and into an area of higher productivity and greater yield. By doing this, they add value to scarce resources.
2. Describe how free-enterprise economies work and how entrepreneurs fit into them.
   - The free-enterprise system is based on voluntary exchange. Voluntary exchange is a trade between two parties who agree to trade money for a product or service. Both parties agree to the exchange because each benefits from the trade.
   - The free-enterprise system encourages entrepreneurs who use resources efficiently to satisfy consumer needs by rewarding them with profit.

3. Find and evaluate opportunities to start your own business.
   - The Five Roots of Opportunity are
     1. problems that your business can solve;
     2. changes in laws, situations, or trends;
     3. inventions of totally new products or services;
     4. *competition* (If you can find a way to beat the competition on price, location, quality, reputation, reliability, or speed, you can create a very successful business with an existing product or service.); and
     5. *technological advances.* (Scientists may invent new technology, but entrepreneurs figure out how to sell it.)
4. Explain how profit works as a signal to the entrepreneur.
   - Profit is the sign that an entrepreneur has added value to the scarce resources he or she is using.
   - Not making a profit is a sign that the entrepreneur is not using resources well and is not adding value to them.
5. A business opportunity is an idea plus these three characteristics:
   - It is attractive to customers.
   - It will work in your business environment.
   - It can be executed in the window of opportunity that exists.
6. Use cost/benefit analysis to make decisions.
   - Cost/benefit analysis is the process of comparing costs and benefits in order to make a good decision.
   - Cost/benefit analysis can be inaccurate without including opportunity cost. This is the cost of missing your next-best investment.
7. Use SWOT analysis to evaluate a business opportunity.
   - Strengths: All of the capabilities and positive points that the entrepreneur has, from experience to contacts. These are internal to the organization.
   - Weaknesses: All of the negatives that the entrepreneur faces, such as lack of capital or training, or failure to set up a workable accounting system. These are internal to the organization.
   - Opportunities: Any positive external event or circumstance (including lucky breaks) that can help the entrepreneur get ahead of the competition.
   - Threats: Any external factor, event, or circumstance that can harm the business, such as competitors, legal issues, or declining economies.

Key Terms

acquisition
capital
capitalism
commission
cost/benefit analysis
dividend
entrepreneur
free-enterprise system
gazelle
green entrepreneurship
lifestyle business
microenterprise
opportunity cost
product
profit
salary
service
social entrepreneurship
strategy
trade-off
venture philanthropy
voluntary exchange
wage

Entrepreneurship Portfolio

Critical Thinking Exercises

1. What would be the best thing about owning your own business? What would be the worst?
2. Identify three nonfinancial benefits of entrepreneurship that might be important to you. Write a paragraph about each.
3. If you were to start a business, what would be your opportunity cost? In other words, what is the next-best use of your time? How much money could you make working at a job, instead? The answer to this question will give you a rough idea of how to value your time when you start a business and have to figure out how much to pay yourself.
4. Describe an idea that you have for a business. Explain how it could satisfy a consumer need.
5. Explain how a business opportunity differs from a business idea.
6. Give an example of a change that has occurred or is about to occur in your area/neighborhood. Discuss any business opportunities this change might create.
7. List five business opportunities in your area/neighborhood and the need(s) each would satisfy. Note whether the opportunity you describe is internal, external, or a mix.

Key Concepts Questions

1. Define small business.
2. Explain how profit works as a signal to the entrepreneur.
3. Do you agree that it will probably take about three months for your business to start earning a profit? Why or why not? If not, how long do you expect it to take and why?
4. Describe three things you have learned about capitalism.
5. Visit the U.S. Small Business Administration for brochures and other materials. Find an office in your area or go to *http://ww.sba.gov.*

Application Exercises

Have a conversation with a friend or relative. Ask this person to tell you about which things he or she finds frustrating in the area/neighborhood. Write down these complaints.

Step 1: Generate at least three business opportunities from this conversation.

Step 2: Use the checklists below to evaluate your three business ideas as opportunities.

Step 3: Choose the best of the business opportunities and write a SWOT analysis for it.

Step 4: Create a cost/benefit analysis for starting this business. Use the analysis to explain why you would or would not actually start it.

Business Idea 1 ________________	Critical Evaluation	
Would it be attractive to potential customers?	Yes ______	No ______
Would it work in your business environment?	Yes ______	No ______
Is there a window of opportunity?	Yes ______	No ______
Do you have the skills and resources to create this business?	Yes ______	No ______
If you do not have the skills and resources to create this business, do you know someone who does and might want to create the business with you?	Yes ______	No ______
Business Idea 2 ________________	**Critical Evaluation**	
Would it be attractive to potential customers?	Yes ______	No ______
Would it work in your business environment?	Yes ______	No ______
Is there a window of opportunity?	Yes ______	No ______
Do you have the skills and resources to create this business?	Yes ______	No ______
If you do not have the skills and resources to create this business, do you know someone who does and might want to create the business with you?	Yes ______	No ______
Business Idea 3 ________________	**Critical Evaluation**	
Would it be attractive to potential customers?	Yes ______	No ______
Would it work in your business environment?	Yes ______	No ______
Is there a window of opportunity?	Yes ______	No ______
Do you have the skills and resources to create this business?	Yes ______	No ______
If you do not have the skills and resources to create this business, do you know someone who does and might want to create the business with you?	Yes ______	No ______

Exploring Your Community

Interview an entrepreneur in your community. Entrepreneurs are busy people, but most are willing to spend time talking with someone who is interested in what they are doing. Meeting over a meal might be the most efficient use of the entrepreneur's time. Before the interview, brainstorm 10 questions in the following four categories. If you can, tape the interview with the entrepreneur's permission. After the interview, be sure to write a thank-you note.

a. *Information gathering.* Open the interview with questions about the entrepreneur's family (any other entrepreneurs in it?) and educational and work background.
b. *About the business.* Next, ask questions about how the business was started. How did the entrepreneur recognize an opportunity and develop it?
c. *Running the business.* Ask about what problems came up as the business got underway and how they were solved.

d. ***Reflection.*** Ask the entrepreneur to reflect. What advice would he or she give to an aspiring entrepreneur? Has running a business been rewarding?

Exploring Online

Visit an Internet search engine, such as *http://www.google.com, http://www.yahoo.com, http://www.dogpile.com, http://www.AltaVista.com, http://www.BING.com,* or *http://www.MSN.com.* Search for one of the following sets of terms: business ideas, businesses for sale, or franchise opportunities. For the search that you selected, answer:

1. which search engine and term was used and
2. the number of matches ("hits").

Next, find a site that looks promising and answer these questions:

1. What is the Web site (URL and name)?
2. Who is sponsoring the Web site?
3. Is the Web site selling a product or information (as a primary function, not through banner ads)? If so, what?
4. Identify three businesses or ideas from the site, and state why they might or might not be viable opportunities.

Case Study Craigslist: Organic Entrepreneurial Opportunity

Craig Newmark's e-mail blasts to friends and coworkers morphed into one of the most popular sites on the Internet. Newmark was not planning to start a business at all when he began sending out e-mail blasts about San Francisco area events. In 1995, Newmark was a software engineer at Schwab and sent the e-mails for fun. The number of people on the list continued to grow until e-mail blasts were no longer viable, due to the number of recipients.

In 1999, Newmark moved into a full-time role in operating his start-up venture. Even the name was user-driven. Newmark had another name in mind, but people had been calling the blasts Craig's List, and the name stuck. Over time, Newmark developed a Web-based site that connected people for apartments, jobs, relationships, and more.

Craigslist generated an estimated $100 million in revenues in 2008. It generates in excess of 20 billion page views and has approximately 50 million unique visitors monthly. Driven by user demand, Craigslist has over 700 local sites in 70 countries. Yet, the company continues to operate out of a previously residential building in the Inner Sunset neighborhood of San Francisco.

Craig Newmark defies the rules of online business. Craigslist only charges fees for brokered apartment listings in New York City, job advertisements in 18 cities, and ads in its adult services category. The company relies upon word-of-mouth for advertising and trust for content. The site itself is relatively simplistic from a user perspective, consciously avoiding many of the leading Web-design dictates.

Newmark himself continues to serve as the company's customer service representative and founder. There is a team of about 30 that handles the balance of the company roles. In today's world, Craigslist could command considerably greater revenues and have even greater visibility, but Newmark has set his own goals.

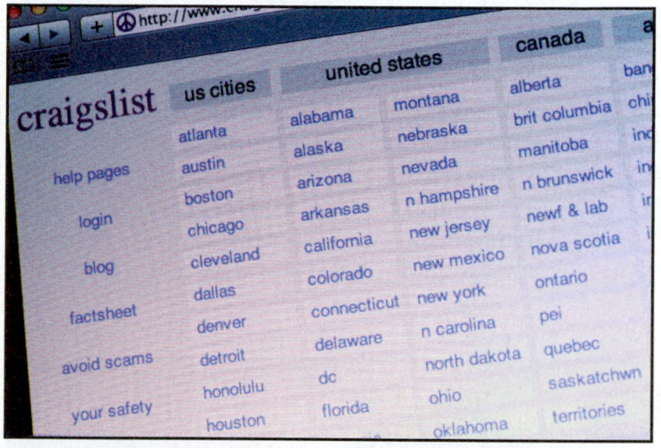

Case Study Analysis

1. What unmet needs of the customer, or conditions in the apartment hunting and job search processes, contributed to the success of Craigslist?
2. Do you think Craig Newmark thought through the Craigslist idea well enough before he launched the business?
3. How is Newmark's personality reflected in his company?
4. Is there a future for Craigslist? What might that future look like?

Case Sources

Brad Stone, "Revenue at Craigslist Is Said to Top $100 Million," *New York Times*, June 9, 2009, http://www.nytimes.com (accessed February 11, 2010).

Craigslist, http://www.craigslist.org (accessed February 10, 2010).

Craigslist.org site profile on Compete, http://siteanalytics.compete.com/craigslist.org (accessed February 11, 2010).

Case Study | Extreme Entrepreneurship

Extreme Entrepreneurship Education Corporation

Michael Simmons and Sheena Lindahl are both New York University (NYU) graduates (2005) who found their calling in entrepreneurship education. Michael, a management and marketing major, and Sheena, a communication studies major, formed Extreme Entrepreneurship Education Corporation (EEEC) as a limited liability corporation in 2003, headquartered in New York City. However, the story really began a number of years earlier when Michael was just 16.

Michael Simmons and Sheena Lindahl

Using the Internet to Start a Business

While attending high school, Michael and his friend, Calvin Newport, decided to start their own Web-development company, Princeton Web Solutions (PWS). For $80, they created their own Web site and submitted it to the online search engines. Only a few weeks later, they were hired to do their first project, for $1,000.

With each new project, the young men's confidence grew. They were able to make a profit and still stay competitive in the market by charging $75 per hour, about half the price of their competitors. The success of PWS led to public recognition in 2000, when *YoungBiz Magazine* rated the business as the #1 youth-run Web-development company in the United States.

After the dot-com market burst, many of PWS's potential clients disappeared. Michael used an online class scholarship, which he won from the National Foundation for Teaching Entrepreneurship (NFTE)—now the Network for Teaching Entrepreneurship—to learn more about running a business. The course also helped him overcome his fear of public speaking.

Sharing a Vision for Success

In college, Michael was inspired to write a book that he called *The Student Success Manifesto*.The book was intended to help students think in a whole new way while taking action toward reaching their goals. He explains:

> *I decided to write the book at the end of my freshman year when I realized, after my experience as an entrepreneur, that I had knowledge which could help my peers find passion, purpose, and prosperity in their own lives.*[1]

Through the Liberty Partnerships Program, Michael also got involved in teaching inner-city high school students about entrepreneurship. The Liberty Partnerships Program was established by the New York State Education Department to help prevent youths from dropping out of high school. Michael says:

> *I had certain perceptions going in, that were changed after I really experienced the influence [of the program] in an environment that was very different from the one I was raised in.*[2]

Attending NYU at the same time as Michael, Sheena shared his entrepreneurial mindset. At age 17, Sheena became financially independent from her parents, and paid her way through college. Sheena also honed her entrepreneurial and educational skills while working at GreenHills Ventures, a venture capital firm, and teaching at Project R.E.A.D., a nonprofit organization that seeks to raise the reading skills of inner-city elementary school children.

Together, Michael and Sheena founded the EEEC, which was dedicated to helping college students realize their dreams through entrepreneurship. They have also formed a life partnership as husband and wife, and as parents.

Making a Strategic Shift

At first, Michael and Sheena had intended to be publishers of entrepreneurial content. After publishing *The Student Success Manifesto*, they believed they were moving in the right direction. The profit per book unit was good, but they needed to sell a lot of units in order to make publishing profitable enough to support them full time.

To sell more books, Michael and Sheena began seeking bulk purchases from schools and other youth organizations. One marketing strategy included talking to groups of students when the schools purchased books. This tactic helped Michael and Sheena to realize that people would pay them to speak, whether books were purchased or not. So, they started charging for their speaking services.

One thing led to another. As more and more students expressed appreciation for the messages Michael and Sheena shared, the two of them explored ways to also include the stories of other young, successful entrepreneurs. Many ideas were discussed and rejected, but eventually the Extreme Entrepreneurship Tour (EET) was launched in 2006.

The EET is the first national collegiate entrepreneur tour in which students from all academic disciplines participate in half-day, campus-held events. A tour event can also be customized for a high school audience or local community members. The tour focuses on one of two themes: entrepreneurship, or "dream action." The content for a particular tour event can be customized to fit either theme.

Each tour event includes a successful young entrepreneur as the keynote speaker, exhibits, a workshop, speed networking, and a panel discussion with local entrepreneurs. An example of a typical event's program is illustrated on the EET Web site:[3]

Type	Who	Content	Time
Event Introduction	EET & School Representative	Intro to event, entrepreneurship, speakers, and corporate partners	3:00 – 3:15 p.m.
Inspirational Keynote 1	Successful Young Entrepreneur	"How they did it" story with lessons	3:15 – 3:45 p.m.
Workshop	EET Workshop, Facilitator, and Entrepreneur	Dream / idea creation with action plan and accountability.	3:45 – 4:45 p.m.
Networking Break / Exhibits			4:45 – 5:00 p.m.
Inspirational Keynote 2	Successful Young Entrepreneur	"How they did it" story with lessons learned	5:00 – 5:30 p.m.
Speed Networking		Attendees share their ideas with each other and partner up	5:30 – 5:45 p.m.
Networking Break / Exhibits			5:45 – 6:00 p.m.
Extreme Entrepreneurship Panel	EET Moderator, Students & Alumni, and Entrepreneurs	Panelists choose one to two questions to discuss and open up for other questions	6:00 – 7:00 p.m.

Operating the Tour

Running the tour involves a considerable investment of financial resources. For example, a customized 31-foot Winnebago transports the speakers and tour manager, EET banners, technical equipment, and registration setup equipment. For each event, there are at least three speakers, two of which are not EET employees, for whom there are expenses, including travel. EET provides pre-event support to event organizers, including conference calls and a point person to answer any questions.

Event organizers can visit the Web site to find templates for promotional posters and flyers, best practice information for participation, and information for pre-event setup. The schools are responsible for the promotion, event venue, refreshments, and the like. EET develops and prints an event program/workbook with speaker biographies, one semester at a time.

Extreme Entrepreneurship tour bus

A tour event is made financially possible through one or more sponsors that may include local companies and economic/workforce development organizations. In turn, student body participation and media coverage benefit the event sponsors by allowing them to connect with hundreds or even thousands of students in a positive way. Opportunities to create company awareness, foster brand or product loyalty, and do employee recruiting are some of the benefits sponsors can reap from a tour event.

Since the EET was started in 2006, over 80 schools have held an event, and that number keeps growing. Aside from Michael and Sheena, the staff has been mostly contractual. Revenues are based on fees charged to the host institution or organization, and event sponsorship.

The tour has won recognition for its excellence by receiving Northern Michigan University's 2007–2008 Program of the Year Award, and the 2008 Innovation Award from the National Association of Development Organizations.

Following Up Events with Action

After an EET event, students are able to continue benefitting from the experience by using JourneyPage, a virtual incubator for launching a business. JourneyPage is made up of tools and information that encourage personal accountability, allow students to continue relationships formed at a tour event, and provide access to entrepreneurial mentors.

For example, JourneyPage has a Web-based accountability tool that helps students reduce procrastination and maintain motivation and momentum. This is facilitated by goal tracking and partnering with other students who have similar aspirations. The accountability tool works in the following ways:

- Each member has an accountability partner.
- Each day, members enter their three most important business-related goals for that day.
- At the end of each day, a goal may be marked as completed, or it can be reset or delayed.
- Weekly scores are computed, based on goal completion. This data is tracked so that accountability partners and other friends using JourneyPage can see a member's progress.
- As a result, accountability partners and friends can offer feedback, encouragement, and coaching to their fellow members.

In addition to the accountability tool, JourneyPage provides content such as articles, audio, and video segments from tour keynote speakers, business and legal templates, resource lists and a searchable database, and a personal coaching program. After a student is accepted into the coaching program, he/she is provided with

- an initial one-hour consultation;
- daily e-mails in response to the goals being tracked with the accountability tool; and
- a telephone call each week to discuss difficulties the student may be having, and to help him/her make plans for the following week.

Although JourneyPage is available for personal use, it can also be licensed by schools and various development centers/agencies. In addition to JourneyPage, tour event content is available in a "Road Tour in a Box" package that consists of stories and lessons learned by successful young entrepreneurs.

Keeping the Business on Track

In order to stay on course and be successful, Michael and Sheena evaluate key performance indicators on a regular basis. Weekly measures center on budget versus actual performance. Calculations are primarily the number of students who attend the event, the student and host ratings of the event, and the budget performance. On a semester basis, the repeat customer percentage, the referral rate, the number of events, and the level of revenues are critical. Sheena explains,

> *We measure what is meaningful to our growth and what we can measure given our time and financial resource capacity.*

Michael and Sheena also formed a high-powered advisory board in 2007 that meets to review financial performance and work on specific issues. Sheena and Michael continue to keep their eyes on the key performance indicators so that they can keep on bringing the EET to colleges and universities nationwide.

Looking Back at the Planning Process

Some past ideas that were considered but rejected included creating young entrepreneur book lines, and applying the entrepreneurial mindset to various career book lines. However, looking back on how the EET evolved, Sheena points out that it was the gradual, small actions that put them in the position to create the tour, not excessive amounts of idea planning. The building of relationships with people in their market enabled Sheena and Michael to understand their customers' needs and wants. The tour business model best met those needs.

To gauge potential costs of running the tour, Michael and Sheena used the economics of one unit, and they tested their idea in the marketplace to find out whether they could sell it. In other words, they started slow by doing a scaled-down version of the program. For example, in the EET's first year, they did not use a tour bus. Based on her experience, Sheena suggests,

> *If you can try the business at some level without a huge investment, essentially doing mini-tests, you can see if things are working without taking a sizeable risk.*

Over the years, Michael and Sheena have created many formal business plans and executive summaries for competitions. Now, they mostly use PowerPoint presentation slides to help them build their internal business strategies. This less formal approach is simpler, makes it easy to adjust their plans, but still helps ensure that all the angles are considered.

Balancing Business and Family

Michael and Sheena find working together enjoyable. However, they do set limits and expectations to help minimize the stress of the business on their relationship. Specific times are set aside for work, family, and personal time. They also believe in the importance of communication. For example, if they are going out to dinner, they agree beforehand whether it will be a dinner to discuss business or just time to be together and have fun.

Investing in Yourself

When asked about the best way for college students to make more money, Michael replies,

> *I would definitely recommend that students invest their money in themselves and not in near-sighted whimsical things that they won't have around, won't help them succeed, tomorrow or ten years from now. When you invest the money you make in yourself, you receive compound interest and incredible returns.*[4]

Case Study Analysis

1. Prior to starting the EET, what types of things did Michael and Sheena do to help themselves build entrepreneurial knowledge/skills?
2. What motivated Michael and Sheena to start the EET?
3. How did Michael and Sheena determine that the EET was a sound idea? Did they use a feasibility analysis? What ideas did they discard before deciding on the EET?
4. What are the key messages that the EET delivers to prospective entrepreneurs?
5. Is the EET a business model that is conducive to franchising? Why or why not?
6. EET is a family business. How do Michael and Sheena address the issues of balancing the demands of the business with the family?

Case Sources

Extreme Entrepreneurship Education Corporation, http://www.extremee.org (accessed August 4, 2010).

Extreme Entrepreneurship Tour, http://www.extremetour.org (accessed August 4, 2010).

Liberty Partnerships Program, http://www.highered.nysed.gov/kiap/precoll/lpp/ (accessed August 4, 2010).

Used by permission of Extreme Entrepreneurship Education LLC.

---

[1]Kate Tobin, "NYU Student Writes Book For Entrepreneur Hopefuls," http://www.extremetour.org/press/youngmoney.html (accessed April 2009).

[2]Ibid.

[3]http://www.extremetour.org/about/event-format.php (accessed April 2009).

[4]Kate Tobin, "NYU Student Writes Book for Entrepreneur Hopefuls," http://www.extremetour.org/press/youngmoney.html (accessed April 2009).

Chapter 2

FRANCHISING

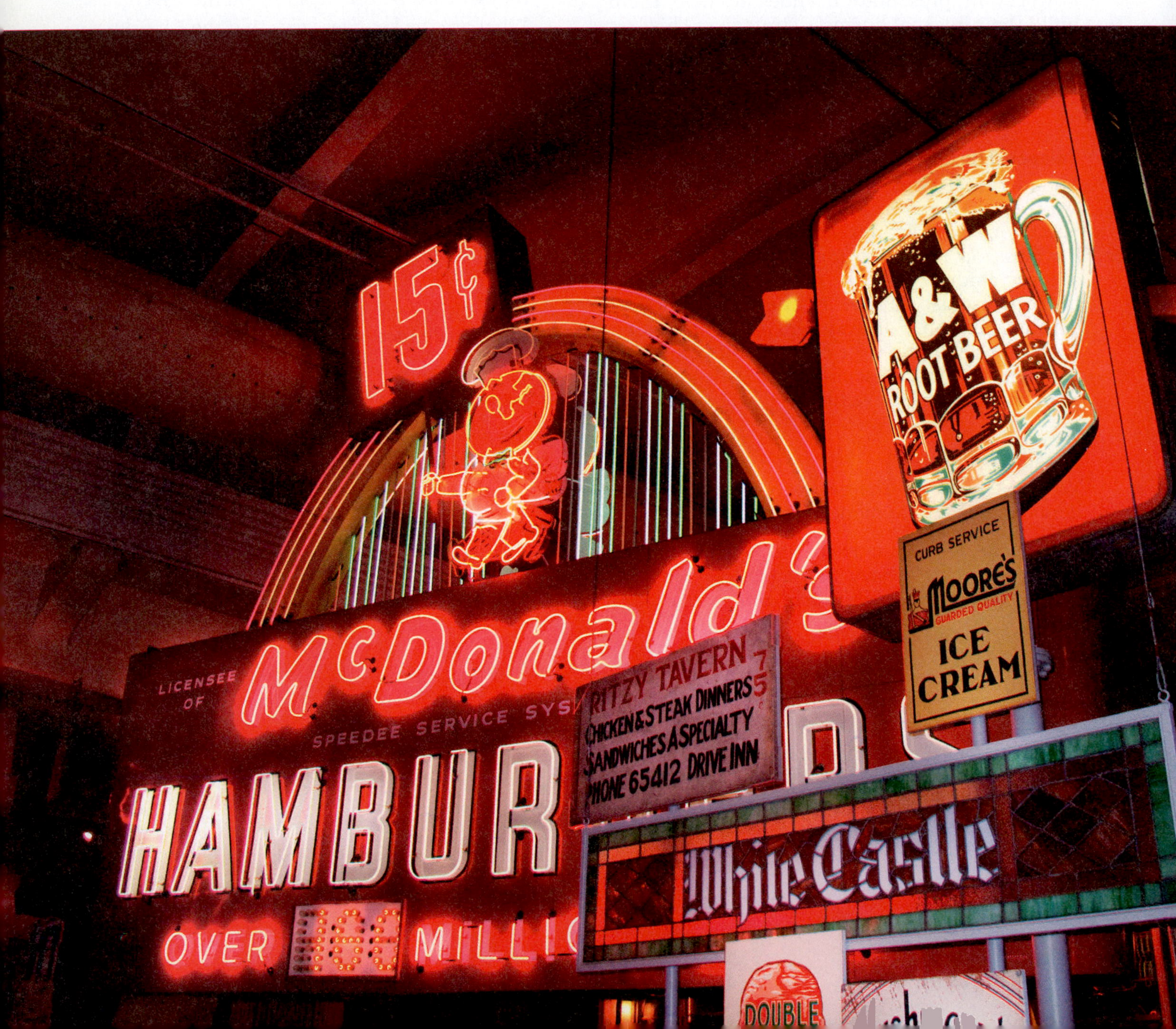

> **"The two most important requirements for major success are: first, being in the right place at the right time, and second, doing something about it."**
>
> —Ray Kroc, McDonald's Restaurants

In 1965, Fred de Luca was a 17-year-old high school graduate looking for a way to earn money for college when a family friend, Dr. Peter Buck, provided him with $1000 of start-up capital for a submarine sandwich shop.[1] With the opening of Pete's Super Submarines came the start of what has grown into a franchise operation with 30,800 franchised units in 89 countries,[2] generating total revenues in excess of $11 billion. The SUBWAY restaurant chain continues to be a privately held company with the original franchisor, Doctor's Associates Inc, with Fred de Luca as president. The company is a consistent leader in *Entrepreneur* magazine's annual listing of top franchises.

SUBWAY franchisees operate in traditional stand-alone units or in such nontraditional locations as convenience stores, shopping malls, and military bases. Franchisee candidates receive two weeks of classroom and on-site training and must pass a comprehensive examination before being accepted. With the initial franchise fee of $15,000, the costs of start-up range from just under $100,000 to over $200,000. The company offers equipment leasing and a franchise fee assistance program for minorities. It also offers loans to existing franchisees for relocation, expansion, and remodeling. Franchisees pay a percentage of weekly sales (approximately 4.5%) into an advertising fund and an additional 8% royalty on all sales, regardless of profitability. The company provides national and regional advertising. Franchises are being added continually.

Performance Objectives

1. Define and describe franchising.
2. Identify the positive and negative aspects of franchising.
3. Understand the structure of the franchise industry.
4. Recognize the legal aspects of franchising.
5. Learn how to research franchise opportunities.
6. Explore international franchising.

franchise a business that markets a product or service developed by a franchisor, typically in the manner specified by the franchisor.

Defining Franchising

Performance Objective 1

Define and describe franchising.

Whereas many individuals want to start their businesses from the ground up, others are happy to begin with a tested formula. Although there is no guarantee of success, for many, franchising is the best business start-up option.

A **franchise** is a business that markets a product or service developed by a franchisor, typically in the manner specified by the franchisor. It is also a legal and commercial relationship between the owner of a trademark, service mark, trade name, or advertising symbol and an individual or group wishing to use that identification in a business.[3] The franchise agreement determines the specific parameters of the relationship between the parties.

franchising the system of operating a franchise governed by a legal agreement between a franchisor and franchisee.

franchisor the person who develops a franchise or a company that sells franchises and specifies the terms and particulars of the franchise agreement.

franchisee the second party to the franchise agreement, the owner of the unit or territory rights.

Franchising is the system of operating a franchise governed by a legal agreement between a franchisor and franchisee. The **franchisor** is the person who develops a franchise or a company that sells franchises and specifies the terms and particulars of the franchise agreement. The **franchisee** is the second party to the franchise agreement and is the owner of the unit or territory rights. For

[1] Available at http://www.subway.com (accessed August 18, 2010).

[2] As of April 2009.

[3] Available at http://www.sba.gov/smallbusinessplanner/start/buyafranchise/ (accessed August 18, 2010).

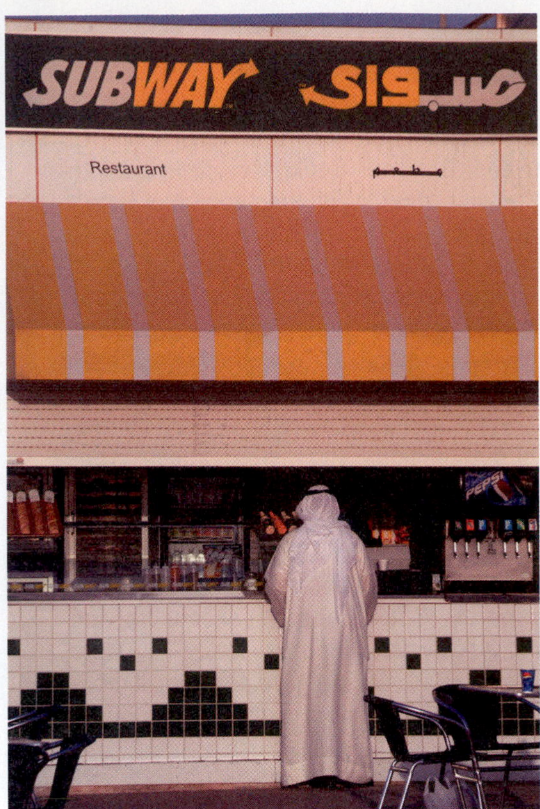

example, Liberty Tax Service (the franchisor) franchises tax-preparation businesses to local/territory owners (franchisees).

What Are the Types of Franchises?

All franchises involve legal agreements between the parties, and these are as varied as they are numerous. The types of franchises are defined by the Federal Trade Commission (FTC). However, the two main categories are

- Product and trade-name franchising, and
- Business-format franchising.

Product and trade-name franchising is the licensing of the product, or the production of the product, and the use of the trademark, logo, or other identity of the franchise. The franchisee usually sells products that are manufactured by the franchisor. It is essentially a supplier-dealer relationship with some level of exclusivity. In other cases, the franchisee sells products or services that are expected to meet the quality standards established by the franchisor. The operations of the business itself are at the discretion of the franchisee within the constraints of the agreement. For example, automobile dealerships are generally trade-name franchises.

product and trade-name franchising the licensing of the product or the production of the product and the use of the trademark, logo, or other identity of the franchise.

business-format franchising a form of franchising in which the franchisee secures the product and trade-name benefits but also the operating, quality assurance, accounting, marketing methods, and support of the franchisor.

master franchise a specific type of franchise that allows individuals and organizations to buy the right to subfranchise within a delineated geographic territory.

area franchise or **multiple-unit franchise** a type of franchise that gives the exclusive rights to open franchisee-operated units within specified areas.

Business-format franchising is a much broader and more extensive form of operation. The franchisee secures the product and trade-name benefits but also the operating, quality assurance, accounting, marketing methods, and support of the franchisor. Typically, this is the purchase of an entire business model and system, including access to management expertise. Some well-recognized business-format franchise systems include Krispy Kreme, Circle K, Pizza Hut, and Jani-King. Some unethical product and trade-name franchises will attempt to sell themselves as being business-format operations, making it particularly important to understand exactly what is being provided. To get a better idea of the range of legitimate franchises available, you may want to explore the franchise registry at http://www.franchiseregistry.com.

In addition to the two primary models described above, there are other variations on licensing and ownership structures offered. For example, there are **master franchises** that allow individuals and organizations to buy the right to subfranchise within a delineated geographic territory. Such franchises generally require the franchisee or area developer to take on additional franchisor responsibilities, such as providing training and support and recruiting the subfranchisees. Master franchises have higher initial franchise fees than those charged for a unit franchise with the same franchisor. It is typical for the master franchisee to form two companies, one for the operation of a primary, single franchise and another for expansion through subfranchisees.

Also, rather than purchasing a single unit, a franchisee may elect multiple-unit ownership, effectively blanketing one or more territories with the franchise brand. Such an **area franchise** or **multiple-unit franchise** gives the exclusive rights to open franchisee-operated units within specified areas.

Positive Aspects of Franchises

Entrepreneurs that want to start up with a formula for success may find numerous advantages in franchising, and you may be one of these entrepreneurs. The most significant advantage is the increased probability of success, given that franchise brands have positive track records and instant recognition in most communities. Some other advantages include training and financing assistance, purchasing power, advertising and promotional support, and operating guidelines and management assistance. Some factors to consider appear in **Exhibit 2-1**.

Performance Objective 2
Identify the positive and negative aspects of franchising.

Start-Up Assistance

Sound franchisors provide a significant quantity and excellent quality of start-up assistance to new franchisees, as well as ongoing education and support for established ones. In many cases, there is mandatory training and technical assistance before a franchise is granted. Some franchisors require examinations on the training content. Others require work experience with established franchisees. These forms of support are intended to foster franchisee success.

The FTC has specific requirements with respect to support that franchisors must provide, including

- one week of training to the franchisee and a manager,
- an operating manual for the franchise,
- ongoing support and assistance, and
- guidelines on audits.

Beyond the obligatory training and information, franchisors can provide other valuable start-up assistance. They may provide site-selection help to ensure that the location selected is likely to be successful. With business-format franchising, franchisees may have access to the entire package of components, making the start-up essentially a turnkey operation (a business that is ready to start immediately).

Exhibit 2-1 *Factors to consider before becoming a franchisee.*

1. **Franchisor success**—How many similar franchises are nearby? In total? How are they performing? What name recognition exists? What's its reputation? Ask franchisees and consumer protection agencies.
2. **Franchisor durability**—Determine the length of experience. Is this a long-term opportunity or a fad? Does the franchisor own any intellectual property?
3. **Franchisor financial health**—How healthy is the company? Financial statements should be in the disclosure documents. Be certain you understand them.
4. **Start-up investment**—What is the amount and what does it buy? Ask about all potential franchise costs. Be certain that ongoing costs and start-up costs are clear.
5. **Financing support**—Does the franchisor offer competitive financing? How much do you need until you reach positive cash flow? Do the financial projections under various conditions and know your options.
6. **Purchasing requirements**—Do you have to buy from the franchisor or its list of suppliers? Are there minimum purchases? Can you purchase from others? How does the pricing from the required suppliers compare?
7. **Term of the agreement**—What is it? What, if any, are the terms for selling the franchise rights to another operator? What are your renewal rights?
8. **Competition**—Are there any restrictions on how you can compete within your territory? Is there assistance to help you compete? What kind? What is the level of competition?
9. **Management fit**—Does the management style and level of control exerted by the franchisor fit for you? Is the loss of independence worth the potential gains?

In some cases, franchisors provide financing support, whether in the form of application assistance, agreements with third-party lenders, or direct financing. Hundreds of franchisors are certified through the U.S. Small Business Administration's Franchise Registry program (http://www.franchiseregistry.com), thereby streamlining the loan application process you and other prospective franchisees would encounter. Some franchises listed on the registry include AlphaGraphics, Cici's Pizza, Snap Fitness 24-7, and Jenny Craig.

The particular combination of start-up assistance and ongoing support provided by franchisors is a vital reason for opting to pursue a franchise rather than starting a venture from the ground up.

Instant Recognition

A strong advantage of purchasing a franchise is the instant name and brand recognition that a well-known and reputable franchisor has to offer. A new McDonald's franchise has the instant recognition that a new, stand-alone business, such as Michael's Magnificent Burgers, would not. With a franchise, the name and image are well established and widely understood. You purchase the use of the company's logo, trademark, and advertising, as well as the physical design, layout, and décor that ensure this recognition.

Purchasing Power

As a franchisee you will benefit from the purchasing power of the franchisor to get lower costs and favorable vendor service. Because franchisees are part of a potentially large group of customers for any one vendor, they have more clout with respect to pricing, delivery terms, and product quality. In addition, where custom-designed products or components are used, the costs of research, prototype creation, and testing are distributed among a far greater number of parties than for a stand-alone business. Any cost savings you realize will assist in offsetting ongoing franchise fees and may support greater profitability.

cooperative advertising fee a fee paid by franchisees to contribute to a shared advertising fund that is separate from royalty fees.

Advertising and Promotional Support

Advertising and promotional support is frequently included as part of the franchise opportunity and is crucial to brand identity and name recognition. Franchisees may pay a fee that is separate from the royalty fee, often called a **cooperative advertising fee**, to contribute to a shared advertising fund. Franchisors engage advertising and public relations firms to create strong, memorable, and effective national and regional advertising campaigns. They handle the national and regional media purchasing. Franchisors also provide you with templates and promotional materials for local use. The quality and quantity of advertising support is one of the most valuable aspects of franchising.

Many franchises have professional associations, which take an active role in determinations with respect to the cooperative advertising fund. They provide insight and feedback to the franchisor. Ideas may travel back and forth between franchisors and franchisees. For example, Ronald McDonald was created by a McDonald's franchisee and became one of the most recognized characters in the world.[4] At the same time, franchisors may decide to create promotions to boost their flagging revenues that have the effect of causing problems for franchisees. For example, a franchisor could promote a discounted price that succeeds in generating revenues, but insufficient profits. You may appreciate revenue generation but not at such a low price, because you will actually lose money after royalties are paid. Royalties are paid on top-line sales (gross revenues), not profits. Despite these challenges, advertising and promotional support is a combined effort.

Operating Guidelines and Assistance

Franchisors are required to provide operating manuals and training to their franchisees, which are valuable factors in success. In addition, ongoing operating training and assistance also increase the probability of positive franchisee performance. Further assistance with regulatory compliance, site selection and development, product research and development, and utilization of technology can all prove invaluable.

Some of the greatest challenges facing entrepreneurs are establishing and maintaining solid operations with structured quality assurance and sound financial record-keeping and human resources policies. Franchisees have the distinct advantage of benefiting from the years of experience and success of their franchisor, so that the learning curve is considerably less daunting. However, the start-up and ongoing assistance provided does not in any way guarantee your success.

Operating guidelines vary considerably in their breadth and depth. They may be as precise as the dimensions (with allowable tolerances) for food production, dress codes, and component specifications. They may

[4]Top 10 Advertising Icons of the Century, Advertising Age. Available at http://www.adage.com/century/ad_icons.html (accessed August 18, 2010).

Step into the Shoes . . .

Maritza Gonzalez and Noel Cruz—Kumon Math and Reading Center

Kumon Math and Reading Centers, a successful franchisor, had been providing supplemental academic support to students in Newark, New Jersey, public schools for four years, through the No Child Left Behind program, when Maritza Gonzalez and Noel Cruz opened a new center there. Maritza is a Kumon parent (that is, a parent of a child in the Kumon system), a product of Newark Public Schools, and a graduate of Montclair State University. For her, the opportunity to direct a Kumon Math and Reading Center is a chance to give back to the community. Noel Cruz headed up the No Child Left Behind program with Kumon and was an assistant principal at a charter school in Newark. Kumon is a 50-year-old after-school math and reading program with 26,000 centers in 45 countries (more than 1500 in the United States) and more than four million students globally.[5]

[5]See http://www.kumon.com/AboutUs/PressRoom.aspx (accessed June 23, 2009).

reach across all functions of the business. Or, they may be relatively broad and nonspecific. The nature and quality of operating guidelines as provided by the franchisor is essential to understanding the value of the franchise and the flexibility afforded the individual franchisee. What is needed and desired varies by franchisee and is based upon individual experience, desire for operating specifics and flexibility, and the cost of participation; however, most franchisors do not individualize franchise packages to accommodate individual needs. Franchisors have their manuals and methods, and that is what goes to new franchisees.

Record of Success

Any reputable franchisor can demonstrate a record of success that would provide a significant advantage for your business startup. In essence, the business formula has been tested and the product or service established. In addition to the name recognition afforded by the franchisor and the disclosure information that the franchisor must provide, you can and should explore the record of success of the franchisor and existing franchisees. An investment of time into online and other research on your part will identify the genuine track record of the franchisor. Strong franchisors have established multiple franchises, positive relationships with their franchisees, and show years of experience. They also have few, if any, legal disputes with franchisees and have garnered positive press reports. Such a record of success will bode well for a prospective franchisee, which will become a new component of the success equation.

Drawbacks of Buying a Franchise

Whereas purchasing a franchise has quite a few advantages, it is not without its drawbacks. Franchising is an excellent choice for many business startups, but it is not a good choice for many others. Franchising provides a higher probability of business success, but success is not guaranteed and is not without costs. Constraints on the creativity and freedom of the owner, high start-up and ongoing costs for franchise participation, and potential for termination of the agreement are all factors to be weighed. The quality and strength of the franchise brand and its program also matter.

Constraints on Creativity and Freedom

For the individual who wants to start a business to break away from the corporate mold and the rigors of a management and supervisory structure that restricted creativity and flexibility, franchising is unlikely to be the best

Global Impact...

Franchising Worldwide

Want to be an international mogul? Check out these Web sites:

International Franchising Opportunities—http://www.franchise-international.net/
World Franchising—http://www.worldfranchising.com

International Franchising's directory lists more than 1000 North American franchises that train and support franchisees overseas. It also provides contact information for consultants and attorneys specializing in international franchising. World Franchising lists the top 100 franchises worldwide, as well as the top 50 franchises that have fewer than 50 operating units.

option for a business startup. Franchisees are required to comply with franchise rules and processes, and autonomy is not a consideration. Products and services may not be altered, added, or dropped without franchisor agreement. In many instances, products or ingredients must be purchased from the franchisor or designated suppliers. Whereas the franchisor cannot require the individual franchisee to adhere to a pricing structure, purchasing requirements can lock in costs at higher than desired levels. The layout and design of the franchise outlet are often defined by the franchisor.

While the formula provided by the franchise guarantees brand recognition, eases the issues of start-up development, and ensures ongoing support, it removes the creativity and freedom that many entrepreneurs crave. You will have to decide whether the trade-off is worthwhile.

Costs

The costs of franchises vary significantly, depending upon the type of franchise, its brand recognition, popularity, and capacity to secure franchisees. Franchise costs are divided into initial franchise fees and ongoing fees. The typical franchisee can expect to pay start-up fees that range from about $3,300 for Jan-Pro, $950,200 to $1.8 million for a McDonald's outlet, or $161,000 to $1.4 million for a Circle K convenience store.[6] Ongoing costs generally include royalties of 1 to 12 percent (most are between 3 and 7 percent) of top-line revenues payable weekly or monthly, regardless of profitability or cash flow. In addition, cooperative advertising fees of 1 to 5 percent (or a flat fee) are payable periodically. Some franchisors require franchisees to spend a minimum amount on local advertising as well. Additional start-up cost considerations are the legal costs required for franchise agreement review, and any required plant, property, equipment, inventory, or marketing requirements. **Exhibit 2-2** includes some of the items that may be included as fees associated with franchises.

It is important that you understand and fully identify all of the costs so that you completely understand the legal obligations and the financial projections that reflect them. This is particularly true for the fees that are payable regardless of profitability or cash flow. Franchisors are focused on creating wealth for themselves. Good faith franchisors are also focused on the success of their franchisees, but a word to the wise is to be wary of franchisors that have a track record of high turnover among franchises and a reputation for "churning" their franchises for the fees. A quick search on the Internet will disclose such companies. Current required disclosures will reveal some of the legal issues as well.

Standards and Termination

Franchisors have standards and obligations that franchisees and prospective franchisees must comply with, initially and on a long-term basis. The start-up standards may include specific types of experience and skills, as well as net worth and liquidity requirements. The ongoing constraints typically are financial and performance based.

Each franchisor establishes specific experience requirements for new franchisees. Typically, these are based upon the type of franchise and experience with success and failure among franchisees. Some of the more established and successful franchisors require less education and experience prior to becoming a franchisee because of their highly developed and

[6] Source: http://www.entrepreneur.com (accessed February 22, 2009).

Exhibit 2-2 *Selected franchise fees and costs.**
Initial costs (categories will vary considerably)
Right to use the company name, trademark, or service mark (licensing fees)
Royalty fees
Training
Management assistance
Use of operations manuals
Signage
Insurance coverage (general liability, fire, inventory, burglary, worker's compensation, accident and health, use and occupancy, and possibly vehicle)
Advertising and promotion
Equipment
Furniture
Fixtures
Site selection assistance
Site purchase and preparation
Land lease, if not purchased
Construction or renovation
Initial inventory
Financing (initial costs plus interest)
Renewal of franchise
Transfer

* Must be disclosed in the Franchise Disclosure Document.

effective training programs. For example, Circle K, Jani-King, and Liberty Tax do not require specific industry experience but do want general business experience.

The financial requirements for becoming a franchisee depend upon the nature of the franchise and the type of franchise agreement. For example, home-based franchises have far lower net worth and liquidity requirements than retail establishments. Jan-Pro requires a net worth of $1000 to $14,000-plus, and liquid assets of greater than $1000 for franchisees who will expect to have a total investment of $3300 to $54,300.[7]

At the other end, Dunkin' Donuts requires a net worth of $1.5 million and liquid assets of $750,000, and is requiring a potential franchisee to commit to opening a minimum of five units.[8] Master franchisees and area franchisees (such as those associated with Dunkin' Donuts) must pay larger upfront fees and must have substantially greater net worth and liquidity than single-unit franchisees.

The ongoing compliance and performance standards and requirements of franchises also come with penalties and termination options for noncompliance. Franchisors may conduct periodic inspections, announced or unannounced, to evaluate compliance and conditions of the unit. Franchisees that stray from the company formula, fail to comply

[7]Accessed at http://www.entrepreneur.com on February 22, 2009.

[8]Accessed at http://www.dunkinfranchising.com on February 22, 2009.

with quality standards, or do not pay their fees are subject to termination and repurchase. Franchisors cannot afford to tarnish their brands with underperforming or noncompliant franchises. Also, they must produce revenue and earnings, manage their finances successfully, and are dependent upon the financial returns from their franchises for success.

The Structure of the Franchise Industry

Various forms of franchising have existed in the United States since the mid-1800s (beginning with the Singer Sewing Machine), with the industry evolving and growing over time. Most of the growth has occurred since the 1950s. A PricewaterhouseCoopers Study (2009) for the International Franchising Association reported 864,784 franchise establishments in the U.S. in 2008, with output of $839.2 billion and providing a total of more than 9.5 million jobs.[9] This is equal to about 8.1 percent of the private sector workforce and 5.3 percent of all payroll expenditures. The same study projects economic contributions of a significant multiple of this base.

Performance Objective 3
Understand the structure of the franchise industry.

The industry is led by several mammoth franchisors with thousands of franchisees worldwide. At the same time, there are numerous smaller franchisors with local and regional franchisees. *Entrepreneur* magazine publishes an annual issue devoted to franchising that provides insight into the industry. It is informative to compare the *Entrepreneur* rankings from year to year to understand whether companies in **Exhibits 2-3**, **2-4**, **2-5**, and **2-6** in the 2009 rankings for the Top 10 Franchises (same as Global Top 10), Top 10 Home-Based Franchises, Fastest-Growing Franchises, and Top 10 New Franchises, respectively, also appear in prior or subsequent years and where they rank.

Internet franchise a type of franchise company that does not depend upon physical location for the delivery of its products or services; rather, it is a "virtual" business.

In addition to the types of franchises described earlier, several other kinds have emerged and are growing in popularity. **Internet franchises**, such as We Simplify the Internet (WSI; http://www.wsimarketing.com) and Etsy.com have taken hold, as the World Wide Web has become ubiquitous. Internet franchises are franchise companies that do not depend upon physical location for the delivery of their products or services; rather, they are

9Accessed at http://www.franchise.org on February 22, 2009.

Exhibit 2-3 *Top 10 Franchises—2009.*

Name	Number of Franchises	Web Site
Subway	29,612	subway.com
McDonald's	24,799	mcdonalds.com
Liberty Tax Service	2,579	libertytaxfranchise.com
Sonic Drive-In Restaurants	2,768	sonicdrivein.com
InterContinental Hotels Group	3,498	ichotelsgroup.com
Ace Hardware Corporation	4,693	myace.com
Pizza Hut	10,239	yumfranchises.com
UPS Store, The/Mail Boxes Etc.	5,982	mbe.com
Circle K	4,085	circlek.com
Papa John's International Inc.	2,615	papajohns.com

Source: Excerpted from "Unconventional Thinking," *Entrepreneur®* magazine, January and February 2009, and reprinted with permission of Entrepreneur Media, Inc.

Exhibit 2-4 *Top 10 Home-Based Franchises—2009.*

Name	Number of Franchises	Web Site
Jani-King	12,980	janiking.com
Jan-Pro Franchising International Inc.	8,875	jan-pro.com
Servpro	1,420	servpro.com
ServiceMaster Clean	4,597	corporate.servicemaster.com
Snap-On Tools	4,318	snapon.com
Stratus Building Solutions	1,339	stratusclean.com
Matco Tools	1,480	matcotools.com
Jazzercise Inc.	7,578	jazzercise.com
Vanguard Cleaning Systems	1,175	vanguardcleaning.com
Bonus Building Care	2,119	bonusbuildingcare.com

Source: Excerpted from "Unconventional Thinking," *Entrepreneur®* magazine, January and February 2009, and reprinted with permission of Entrepreneur Media, Inc.

Exhibit 2-5 *Top 10 Fastest Growing Franchises—2009.*

Name	Number of Franchises	Web Site
Jan-Pro Franchising International Inc.	8,875	jan-pro.com
Subway	29,612	subway.com
Instant Tax Service	1,181	instanttaxservicefranchise.com
Stratus Building Solutions	1,339	stratusclean.com
Snap Fitness Inc.	701	snapfitness.com
Dunkin' Donuts	8,802	dunkinfranchising.com
Jazzercise Inc.	7,578	jazzercise.com
Bonus Building Care	2,119	bonusbuildingcare.com
Anytime Fitness	782	anytimefitness.com
Vanguard Cleaning Systems	1,175	vanguardcleaning.com

Source: Excerpted from "Unconventional Thinking," *Entrepreneur®* magazine, January and February 2009, and reprinted with permission of Entrepreneur Media, Inc.

Exhibit 2-6 *Top 10 New Franchises—2009.*

Name	Number of Franchises	Web Site
Instant Tax Service	1,181	instanttaxservicefranchise.com
Snap Fitness Inc.	701	snapfitness.com
Stratus Building Solutions	1,339	stratusclean.com
Chester's International	82	chestersinternational.com
HealthSource Chiropractic and Progressive Rehabilitation	195	healthsourcechiro.com
Goin' Postal	297	goinpostal.com
Senior Helpers	152	seniorhelpersfranchise.com
Oreck Clean Home Center	354	ownanoreckstore.com
Fast-teks On-site Computer Services	183	fastteks.com
Murphy Business and Financial Corporation	96	murphybusiness.com

Source: Excerpted from "Unconventional Thinking," *Entrepreneur®* magazine, January and February 2009, and reprinted with permission of Entrepreneur Media, Inc.

virtual businesses. Also, **conversion franchising**, wherein an existing stand-alone business or local chain becomes part of a franchise operation, has gained popularity. Another trend is **piggybacking** or **co-branding**, in which two franchises share locations and resources. Examples of this include Baskin-Robbins and Dunkin' Donuts. The franchising industry continues to expand and reach new entrepreneurs.

conversion franchising a type of franchising that is when an existing or stand-alone business or local chain becomes part of a franchise operation.

piggybacking or co-branding occurs when two franchises share locations and resources.

Franchising and the Law

Franchises are governed by state and federal laws and regulations. The Federal Trade Commission (FTC) is the primary government agency involved in oversight. The FTC primarily serves to protect the interests of franchisees by directing the disclosure rules for franchisors. The process and specific requirements have evolved significantly over the past century, with the most recent changes occurring in 2008.

Performance Objective 4

Recognize the legal aspects of franchising.

The **Franchise Disclosure Document (FDD)** has replaced the Uniform Franchise Offering Circular (UFOC) as the primary source of information for prospective franchisees regarding franchisors. It is registered with the FTC and must be organized into a common format so that prospective franchisees may more readily compare franchise opportunities. The FDD discloses the terms of the franchise relationship and any pertinent financial and legal issues affecting the franchisor, and must be provided by the franchisor a minimum of 14 days before the signing of a franchise agreement. As a practical matter, as a prospective franchisee, you should secure this document as early in the exploration and negotiation process as possible. The FDD includes such information as:

Franchise Disclosure Document (FDD) the primary source of information for prospective franchisees regarding franchisors.

- **Overview and background.** Company review and offer, background information on key personnel and directors, and disclosures of current and past litigation or bankruptcy.
- **Fees and costs.** All initial fees, all anticipated operating fees, and a table of the potential cost ranges for every part of the initial investment.
- **Contractual obligations.** Table of franchisee responsibilities with specific reference to the franchise agreement and the FDD, and an extensive list of franchisor obligations from pre-opening through ongoing operations. Also included are details about training programs and any required point of sale, advertising, or other required franchise systems. List of personal obligations of the franchisee.
- **Territory.** Terms regarding the limits of the protected territory that the franchisee will receive. This could be a very large area or very small. Or, there could be no protected territory. This has huge significance for the franchisee because franchisors have often put franchisees so close to existing ones that they compete with one another for business.
- **Financial performance.** Franchisor discloses the performance of franchisee units by providing statistical information with clearly stated assumptions and explanations of limitations. Prospective franchisees are best served by taking this data and carefully analyzing it to secure a better understanding of what is and is not stated, and to use it as a launching point for further research.
- **Data regarding existing units.** Table data regarding the existing units in the franchise system, and the units that have closed or transferred ownership, can assist in understanding success rates and "churn" by the franchisor.

- **Financial statements and contracts.** Past three years of the franchisor's audited financial statements and all contracts that the franchisee is required to execute. Contracts include the franchise agreement, and those for advertising co-op rules and conditions, real estate, personal guarantees, and territory development. Prospective franchisees should acquire legal and accounting review for these.
- **Termination, renewal, and transfer, and dispute resolution procedures.** Policies regarding exit strategies, including fees and restrictions, as well as rules regarding mediation and/or negotiation versus legal action are the best ways to understand the reality of costs, fees, requirements, and other conditions set by the franchisor. The refusal of a prospective franchisor to provide this information should be a red flag for any franchisee. Regardless of what a salesperson or franchise broker says to you, it is the FDD that is pertinent.

franchise agreement contract that determines the specific parameters of the relationship between the parties in a franchise.

In addition to the FDD, each franchisor and franchisee must enter into a **franchise agreement**, which is the legal document governing the specific franchise. Included in the franchise agreement are the following

- the term of the agreement or length of time the franchisor and franchisee agree to work together;
- standards of quality and performance;
- an agreement on royalties—usually a percentage of the franchisee's sales paid to the franchisor;
- a noncompete clause stating that, for instance, if you are licensing a McDonald's franchise, you cannot also own a Blimpie's;
- a "hold harmless" clause that may release the franchisor from specific actions or violations of state laws;
- integration clauses that may block the franchisee from suing the franchisor for misrepresentation or deception that occurred prior to the signing of the agreement;
- choice of venue or other provisions that require the franchisee to settle disputes with the franchisor in the franchisor's state;
- clauses regarding termination, renewal, and transfer of the franchise; and
- territories. Franchisors usually assign a territory in which an individual franchisee can do business. Within the assigned area, no other franchisee from that company will be allowed to compete.

As with any legal agreement, professional legal counsel skilled in this type of contract should be hired and engaged to fully explore the contents prior to signing it or paying any money to the franchisor. In addition, prospective franchisees may want to hire an accounting professional to provide a review of the franchise agreement and proposed business plan.

Steps for Franchise Selection

Performance Objective 5 Learn how to research franchise opportunities.

Deciding to purchase a unit franchise, or a master or area franchise, is a major decision that is best undertaken after complete due diligence. There are numerous steps involved in becoming a franchisee and it is important to pursue each. Skipping any one step, or not fully completing it, may create short-term and/or long-term barriers to success.

- **Self-reflection and engagement of core supporters.** Franchising is not for everyone who wants to enter into self-employment. Taking the time to reflect upon individual goals and objectives, as well as lifestyle and financial considerations, is vital. The SBA Web site (http://www.sba.gov) has a readiness assessment tool for franchise ownership. It should take about five minutes to complete and may provide valuable insights for prospective franchisees. Also, having the genuine, enthusiastic support of a core group of friends and family is critical to achieving and maintaining desired personal factors when deciding whether to buy a franchise or not.

- **Industry, type, geography, or brand selection, brand name, or business-format franchising.** If the outcomes of the reflection and analysis suggest franchising would be an excellent option for you, choosing the franchise will be the next step. Some individuals have a desire to be associated with a particular industry. Others would prefer a retail firm, a service company, a home-based organization, or the like. Still others have more interest in the geographic location of the franchise operation than the particular industry or type of business. Another set of prospective franchisees might have a particular franchise in mind, such as Insomnia Cookies, with the geographic location more flexible. For certain people, the greater flexibility of brand-name franchising is more desirable than business-format franchising. You can weigh these and other factors (such as the start-up franchise fee) to arrive at a set of guidelines for selection.
- **Research.** The decision-making process above will require some research, but it will be more focused on internal factors. With the results of this effort in hand, you can conduct further research to narrow the list of franchise choices to a manageable level before conducting in-depth analysis. The research need not be costly or complex, but it should be thorough enough to avoid traps and missteps at this early stage. A number of resources are listed in **Exhibit 2-7**.
- **Narrow the list of options.** The research should provide enough information to narrow the list of potential franchises down to a few. Now it is time to conduct in-depth research and hone in on the individual companies.
- **Make the broker decision.** Prospective franchisees can decide at any point whether or not to use a **franchise broker**, which is a third-party consulting company that prescreens prospective franchisees and matches them with franchisors. Broker and consultant fees are generally paid by the franchisors.
- **Visit franchise operator(s).** Before contacting the short list of franchise companies directly, those who are considering franchises with physical sites open to the public can strategically visit one or more units to observe them. Such visits are for information gathering and to observe such aspects as traffic flow, environment, quality of franchise décor and materials, management, and so forth. This is more akin to acting as a secret shopper than a formal visit. Try not to visit locations in your neighborhood, or in the immediate area where you would be operating.
- **Contact the franchisor.** You should request basic preliminary information from each franchise company. Typically, this information is available through a Web site or franchise development staff. The basic information will permit the screening of the small pool of franchise possibilities and narrowing it to one or two finalists. The steps from this point on will become intense and time consuming.
- **Perform due diligence on a specific franchise.** A franchise company will probably require completion of a qualification questionnaire,

Exhibit 2-7 *Resources for franchise research.*

Documents	
Franchise Opportunities Guide	Published semiannually. Available in print and online. http://www.franchise.org
A Consumer Guide to Buying a Franchise	Downloadable. http://www.ftc.gov
Web Sites	
www.entrepreneur.com/franzone	*Entrepreneur* magazine
www.franchisetimes.com	*Franchise Times* magazine
www.inc.com	*Inc.* magazine
www.money.cnn.com/magazines/moneymag/	*Money* magazine
www.worldfranchising.com	*World Franchising* magazine
www.franchise-update.com	*Franchise Update* magazine
www.franchise-international.net/	International franchising opportunities
www.franchising.com	Franchising opportunities
www.franchisehandbook.com	Franchise database
www.bison.com	Franchise information
www.FRANdata.com	Franchise information services
www.ifa-university.com	IFA University
Trade Associations	
International Franchise Association	www.franchise.org
American Association of Franchisees and Dealers	www.aafd.org
Trade Shows	
International Franchise Expo	Held in Washington, D.C., Los Angeles, and Miami—www.mfvexpo.com
National Franchise and Business Opportunities	www.franchiseshowinfo.com

which will enumerate your experience and financial qualifications. Once this is accepted, the franchise company will share its FDD, and you should analyze and understand it completely before moving forward. Calls to existing franchisees, possibly including a visit to the franchise company headquarters, will be important next steps. Internet research and Web buzz about a franchisor can also be taken into consideration, although these are best considered with a healthy dose of skepticism. Have people who are familiar with FDDs review it and other documents to check what you are looking at before agreeing to anything.

- **Explore financing options.** Each prospective franchisee will have a different personal financial situation. It is essential to know what your personal resources will be, from friends and family, financial institutions, private investors, and the franchisor. Identifying financial capacity can and should begin in the early-research phases.
- **Make a decision, negotiate the franchise agreement, and engage professional counsel.** The timing of this will depend upon the individual franchisee but is an essential step. The FDD and franchise agreement will be sufficiently complex that even the most sophisticated franchisee should engage legal and financial advisors.
- **Make it work!** The franchisor can provide the brand, the products, and even the system, but the franchisee has to make the business work.

Astute franchisees will take advantage of all the training and assistance they have received and will reap the benefits of being part of a successful franchise.

Exploring Global Franchising Opportunities

Performance Objective 6

Explore international franchising.

Franchising is a global phenomenon and opportunities abound in all areas of the world. It is common for franchisors to strategically identify countries or regions in which they plan to expand and to seek out franchisees in those areas. Some franchisors require the franchisees to be citizens of the countries in which they are developing franchises. Most franchisors prefer to expand through master franchises or area franchises rather than single units, selling franchise rights to large geographic areas or to entire countries. It is also common for franchisors to create joint ventures with existing firms in the markets they are entering.

Franchisors such as McDonald's and Intercontinental Hotels have been selling international franchises for decades. As of 2008, they have 12,283 and 824 international franchises, respectively.[10] Subway has 5,572 foreign franchises, and The UPS Store/Mail Boxes Etc. has 330 Canadian units and 1,191 other foreign units, according to *Entrepreneur.com*. Other franchisors have just begun to reach out beyond the borders of the United States. At the same time, franchisors from overseas have extended their reach beyond national borders to span the globe.

The decision to franchise globally is far more complex than addressing local and regional variations. Ethnic, cultural, and religious diversity compels variations in the business format and operations. For example, menus must be adjusted for dietary preferences and restrictions, uniforms may have to vary, advertising and promotion will be different, as will hours and cost structures. In addition, human resources issues and policies must be altered for governing law and custom. However, there are many lucrative and rewarding opportunities available for franchising around the world.

[10]Accessed at www.entrepreneur.com on February 22, 2009.

Chapter Summary

Now that you have studied this chapter you can do the following:

1. Define and describe franchising.
   - A franchise is a business that markets a product or service developed by the franchisor, typically in the manner specified by the franchisor.
   - Product and trade-name franchising is the licensing of the product or the production of the product and the use of the trademark, logo, or other identity of the franchise.
   - Business-format franchising takes place when the franchisee secures the product and trade-name benefits, and the operating, quality assurance, accounting, marketing methods and support of the franchisor.
2. Identify the positive and negative aspects of franchising.
   - Start-up assistance (+)
   - Advertising and promotional support (+)
   - Operating guidelines and assistance (+)
   - Record of success (+)
   - Constraints on creativity and freedom (-)
   - Costs (-)
   - Standards and termination (-)
3. Understand the structure of the franchise industry.
   - Large franchisors control most of the industry.
   - Types include Internet franchises, conversion franchising, and co-branding.
4. Recognize the legal aspects of franchising.
   - Franchise Disclosure Document (FDD) is essential.
   - State and federal regulations govern franchising.
   - A franchise agreement and other legal documents will be involved.
   - Use good legal counsel.
5. Learn how to research franchise opportunities.
   - Self-reflection and engagement of core support people.
   - Industry, type, geography, or brand selection and brand name, or business-format choice.
   - Research using available resources.
   - Narrow the list of options.
   - Make the broker decision.
   - Visit franchise operator(s).
   - Contact the franchisor.
   - Perform due diligence on the specific franchise.
   - Explore financing options.
   - Make a decision and negotiate the franchise agreement and engage professional counsel.
   - Make it work!
6. Explore international franchising.
   - Opportunities are available worldwide.
   - Decision is more complex than domestic franchising.

Key Terms

area franchise
business-format franchising
co-branding
conversion franchising
cooperative advertising fee
franchise
franchise agreement
Franchise Disclosure Document (FDD)
franchisee
franchising
franchisor
Internet franchise
master franchise
multiple-unit franchising
piggybacking
product and trade-name franchising

Entrepreneurship Portfolio

Critical Thinking Exercises

1. What are four positive aspects of franchising for a business startup? Why are they important?
2. What are some challenges faced by franchisees?
3. Describe the type of franchise that you might want to open.
4. Franchisees agree to pay a variety of fees to franchisors initially and in an ongoing manner. Describe these fees and why understanding their impact on profitability and cash flow is important to franchisees.

Key Concept Questions

1. Compare and contrast product and trade-name franchising and business-format franchising.
2. Explain why the Franchise Disclosure Document is critical to analyzing a franchise opportunity.
3. What, if any, trends in franchising suggest continued expansion of the industry? Contraction?

Application Exercise

Identify an industry or type of business that interests you. Select a community where you would like to locate such an organization (select a business that would have a physical presence). Find two competitors already in that market space and one franchisor that is not. Would it or would it not make sense to open a franchise in the community?

Exploring Online

1. Visit the Wahoo Fish Taco Web site at http://www.wahoos.com. What are the advantages of a Wahoo Fish Taco franchise according to the site? What franchise opportunities are available?
2. Visit the International Franchise Association Web site at http://www.franchise.org. Find a franchise organization that is unfamiliar to you. Find the following information about the franchisor:
   (a) When did it begin offering franchises?
   (b) How many company-owned units does it have?

(c) What are its initial financial requirements (start-up fee, net worth, liquid resources)?

(d) What type of franchisor is it (product or trade name or business format)?

If the information is not available on the International Franchise Association (IFA) Web site, try others from the list in **Exhibit 2-7**.

3. Visit http://www.Entrepreneur.com and find the most recent list of the top 10 franchises. Compare it with the list included in the text. What, if anything, has changed? Why do you think the change has occurred?

Case Study | Tim Lowder—Snap-on Tools®

During his career in the U.S. Navy, Tim Lowder found that he liked using Snap-on tools because of their high quality. Later, after retiring from the Navy, this factor influenced Tim's decision to buy a Snap-on franchise. Although becoming a first-time business owner was a little scary, Tim found that Snap-on's financial credit and business training programs made the process much easier. Tim "Da Tool Man" Lowder took advantage of Snap-on's Gateway Program, with a graduated buy-in process by building his equity for two years and then making the full investment to own his mobile store.

Snap-on, founded in 1920, was the first to develop a unique concept for making tools more productive. By manufacturing sockets that could "snap on" to different, interchangeable handles, what had been a one-piece wrench became a tool that could do the work of many types of wrenches. Snap-on now offers over 19,000 tool products. It was also named the #1 tool franchise and the #5 home-based franchise by *Entrepreneur*® magazine in 2009.

Tim operates his business from his home in Corpus Christi, Texas, but not in the way you might expect. Like the company's founders, today's Snap-on dealers take their products directly to their customers' businesses. Tim's "store" is a Snap-on truck that he uses to deliver, demonstrate, and sell tools. Every week, Tim visits an established list of customers provided by Snap-on.

Tim is thinking of expanding his business in the future by buying another Snap-on truck and hiring someone to run the second franchise for him. However, regardless of what business someone decides to start, Tim advises, "Don't go into it half-hearted. If you're going to do it, go ahead and commit to it and make it happen."[1]

Case Study Analysis

1. What type of franchise is Snap-on?
2. Using the Web sites listed under Case Sources, identify each of the following for a Snap-on franchise: franchise fee, net worth requirement, total initial investment, and ongoing royalty fee.
3. What are some of the distinctive advantages that would lead a franchisee to select a Snap-on franchise?
4. What might be some potential concerns about buying a Snap-on franchise?

Case Sources

Dane Carlson's Business Opportunities Weblog, http://www.business-opportunities.biz/2009/easing-into-business-ownership/ (accessed on August 18, 2010).

Entrepreneur® magazine's Web site franchise descriptions and ratings, http://www.entrepreneur.com/franchises/snapontools/282805-0.html.

Snap-on Franchise Web site, http://www1.snapon.com/franchise.

Snap-on Incorporated Web site, http://www1.snapon.com/corporate.

[1]Snap-on Incorporated, "From the Military to Snap-on," http://www1.snapon.com/franchise/owningaFranchise/militaryvideo.nws (accessed April 2009).

Case Study | Pietsch Siblings: Wahoo's Fish Taco® Franchisees

How Wahoo's Began

Before it became a successful franchise chain, Wahoo's was a small, Californian restaurant born from three brothers' craving for fish tacos. Growing up in Brazil and California, Wing Lam, Ed Lee, and Mingo Lee learned a lot about running a business by helping out in their family's Chinese restaurant. After discovering fish tacos while surfing in Mexico, the three brothers combined their knowledge of surfing culture and the restaurant industry into an entrepreneurial venture of their own.

When the first Wahoo's Fish Taco was opened in 1988, it was decorated with donated products from local surf businesses. The food was a combination of the Brazilian, Mexican, and Asian flavors and ingredients that the brothers loved. The restaurant quickly became popular because of its unique, fresh, and healthy food. Today, there are more than 50 Wahoo's franchise locations in California, Colorado, Texas, and Hawaii. One of these restaurants was started by three other siblings from the Pietsch family.

Wahoo's Comes to Hawaii

Wahoo's first Hawaiian franchise came about in a roundabout way. While working in Los Angeles for the Angels baseball team, Stephanie Pietsch met Wing Lam by chance, and a business friendship developed. Stephanie's brother Mike and sister Noel also liked the Wahoo's franchise concept. Born and raised in Honolulu, all three siblings thought a Wahoo's restaurant would do well in Hawaii's surfing-oriented culture.

To make a long story short, the Pietsches invited Wing and his brothers to Hawaii for a surfing trip and asked to be considered as franchisees. Even though the Pietsches' restaurant experience was limited, their knowledge of the local area, and Stephanie's extensive sports-marketing background, gave them an edge. The Pietsches opened their Wahoo's restaurant in 2006.

Wahoo's uses a very hands-on approach with its franchisees. The company provides mandatory training for approximately one month. Thereafter, communications continue via telephone and visits from Wing. Wahoo's open-door policy allows for plenty of give-and-take discussions between franchisor and franchisee. According to Mike Pietsch, "Franchising is a good way to get into business because there are systems already in place." Stephanie adds, "The franchise provides a support system so there's a resource for asking questions, training, and growing the business."[1]

Learning Valuable Lessons

The Pietsch-owned franchise was an immediate success, with customers lining up clear around the restaurant. "The first six months were a blur," Noel recalls. "We were doing better than we ever expected, but at a frantic pace."[2] After only five months, the Honolulu-based franchise became one of the top sales leaders for Wahoo's Fish Taco.

In the process, the owners learned many valuable lessons as they gained more experience. For example, keeping the restaurant staffed with quality employees was very difficult in Hawaii's tight labor market. During the first year and a half, almost the entire staff turned over about three times.

"Now," Noel says, "we are rarely hiring because we have a solid team of people who really want to be here and work hard at what they do." Stephanie adds, "We really learned to work on our efficiency. We're setting goals and controlling what we can, be it labor or food costs."[3]

Learning to improve their communication was another important lesson. Although they admit to having made mistakes, the Pietsches also feel they have learned how to make their business run smoother based on those experiences. They also schedule time to get together away from the restaurant to discuss how the business is working.

Marketing the Business

The Wahoo's franchise chain targets a particular customer mindset. This customer focus includes individuals who actually participate in extreme sports, such as surfing, skateboarding, and snowboarding. However, a much larger market segment is made up of those who simply want to live vicariously through others who are living a sports lifestyle.

Wahoo's encourages their franchisees to use regional sports and charity events, as well as other types of local grassroots opportunities, to help market their businesses. For example, the

Pietsches' restaurant sponsors many surfing and body-boarding events. Noel remarks, "We support the youth a lot because if we get them eating at Wahoo's, they'll do it the rest of their lives."[4]

To help grow their business, the Pietsch team opened a catering division. One promotional method they use involves taking food samples to the offices of local companies. The Pietsches also came up with an idea, endorsed by Wahoo's, for placing a lunch wagon at one of the local beaches. These two additional arms of the business help generate revenue but have lower overhead costs than adding an additional restaurant.

Wahoo's Franchise Information

If you are interested in opening a Wahoo's Fish Taco of your own, be aware that the company is looking for franchise candidates who have restaurant experience (in particular, multi-unit restaurant experience). However, as with the Pietsch siblings, applicants with other types of business backgrounds may be considered.

Wahoo's also prefers applicants with the financial means to potentially own and operate at least three restaurants in a particular geographical area. More than one restaurant provides the franchisee with a greater economy of scale. Because of Wahoo's national contracts with various vendors, larger volumes of ingredients can be purchased at a lower cost. In essence, the more fish tacos that are produced, the less expensive each one becomes, and so profits increase.

The initial franchise fee is $30,000 for the first restaurant and $25,000 for each additional one. The ongoing royalty fee is 5% of gross sales, paid weekly. Also, each franchisee must allocate 2% of gross sales for marketing and advertising. Wahoo's estimates that the cost of building a brand new restaurant will range between $540,000 and $715,000, depending on store location and size, materials used, and other local factors.

On advice from Wahoo's, a franchisee should provide his or her own start-up money, rather than borrow it. In the restaurant business there are seasonal ups and downs that affect cash flow. So, it is always best to have some available working capital to help avoid getting caught in a financial crunch.

In the end, however, money and experience are only part of a successful equation. To be a peak performer in the restaurant business, you have to love the work you do and know how to have fun doing it. That's the bottom line.

Case Study Analysis

1. Why did the Pietsches decide to purchase a Wahoo's Fish Taco franchise rather than start a restaurant on their own?
2. Name something the Pietsches could have done better to make their business startup go more smoothly.
3. What does the Pietsch-owned franchise do on an ongoing basis to maintain and grow success?
4. What type of a franchise is Wahoo's Fish Taco? What makes this true?

Case Sources

AsianLife Web site news article, http://www.asianlife.com/magazine/view/articles/id/645838631 (accessed August 23, 2010).

Hawaii Business magazine Web site news article, http://www.hawaiibusiness.com/SmallBiz/January-2009/Lessons-Learned-Wahoos-Fish-Tacos/index.php (accessed August 23, 2010).

Honolulu Star-Bulletin Web site news article, http://archives.starbulletin.com/2006/06/11/business/story01.html (accessed August 23, 2010).

MidWeek Web site news article, http://www.midweek.com/content/story/theweekend_coverstory/somethings_fishy_wahoos/ (accessed August 23, 2010).

Wahoo's Fish Taco Web site, http://www.wahoos.com.

[1]Susan Sunderland, *Something's Fishy @ Wahoo's*, http://www.midweek.com/content/story/theweekend_coverstory/somethings_fishy_wahoos (accessed August 23, 2010).

[2]Ibid.

[3]Jacy L. Youn, *Lessons Learned - Wahoos Fish Tacos*, http://www.hawaiibusiness.com/SmallBiz/January-2009/Lessons-Learned-Wahoos-Fish-Tacos/index.php (accessed August 23, 2010).

[4]Ibid.

Chapter 3

FINDING OPPORTUNITY IN AN EXISTING BUSINESS

"I have found no greater satisfaction than achieving success through honest dealing and strict adherence to the view that, for you to gain, those you deal with should gain as well."

—Alan Greenspan, Former Chairman of the Federal Reserve Bank

Many businesses succeed through the entrepreneurial effort of owners that were not the founders. Charles R. Walgreen, Sr., became a store owner in 1901 when he purchased a pharmacy from Isaac Blood in Chicago for $6000.[1] Walgreen had worked at the store as a pharmacist and was not satisfied with the quality or customer service there, or at pharmacies in general. (He had worked in drugstores since he was a teenager.) However, he saw value in taking over a business that was already in existence, and started with one that he knew well. Walgreen saw that the neighborhood was thriving, but the store was struggling. It did not take long for Walgreen's innovative approach to store layout and merchandising to reap rewards. He opened a second store in 1909 and, by 1916, he had incorporated nine stores as Walgreen's Inc.

Not content to rest upon his success, Walgreen's "shook up" the soda fountain portion of the pharmacy business in 1922 with the invention of the malted milkshake, which was a revolutionary product and boosted sales phenomenally. By 1926, Walgreen had opened his 100th store in Chicago, and the company went public the following year. Twelve years later, Walgreen's transitioned the presidency to the founder's son, Charles Walgreen, Jr., illustrating business growth through acquisition, a public stock offering, and generational transfer. This leadership change was followed by continued expansion that resulted in Walgreen's becoming the nation's largest self-service retailer by 1953.

Walgreen's continued to grow and successfully transferred the presidency to the third generation in 1969. The company reached the $1-billion sales mark in 1975 and opened its 1000th store in 1984. Charles Walgreen, III, retired in 1999 but remained on the Board of Directors. As of 2009, Walgreen's is the second largest drugstore chain in the country, with 6000 stores including 76 outlets coming in through an acquisition in 2006 and another 100 added in 2007. Also, Walgreen's acquired the Take Care Health Systems, adding clinics to its business mix.

Walgreen's is a classic example of entrepreneurial success through acquisition and internal growth.

[1]*Source:* Walgreen's corporate Web site, http://www.walgreens.com, accessed on March 17, 2009.

Performance Objectives

1. Understand the potential benefits of buying a going concern.
2. Identify potential drawbacks of purchasing a business.
3. Learn how to identify and evaluate purchasing opportunities.
4. Learn how to determine the value of a business.
5. Learn how to negotiate and close the deal.
6. Recognize joining a family business as an entrepreneurial pathway.

Many entrepreneurs, like Charles Walgreen, Sr., elect to purchase a going concern rather than starting a business "from scratch." Others decide to apply their entrepreneurial talents to existing family-owned businesses that they buy. Both approaches are potential pathways to success through opportunities found in already existing businesses. Approximately 750,000 businesses change ownership each year, demonstrating the popularity of this option. **Exhibit 3-1** provides insights into the number of business starts and closures per year, which illustrates that the number of businesses changing ownership is greater than the number started *de novo*.

Reasons to Buy an Existing Business

Performance Objective 1

Understand the potential benefits of buying a going concern.

Becoming a successful entrepreneur is a process that can be simplified and accelerated by purchasing an operating business. Entrepreneurial risk can be reduced and potential bargains may be available. However, buying an existing business could also be a route to ownership that is fraught with pitfalls. This is truly a case of *caveat emptor*—let the buyer beware. However, the well-prepared shopper can find the right business to buy.

Quicker, Easier Start-up

A successful existing business has already leapt over many of the hurdles that would be encountered by a start-up venture. The issues of location, customer development, product or service delivery, and supplier relationships, among others, have been addressed. By acquiring existing relationships and operations, you can save much of the time and effort required to put these into place. Employees can be a particularly valuable part of an acquisition, as they bring institutional memory and relationships to the new owner. In many cases, the seller will also agree to remain in the business for a predetermined length of time to assist in the transition.

Of course, the full benefits of these assets will be realized only if they are truly represented. For example, employees will have to stay with the firm and cooperate with the new owner to provide the value expected. Customer, supplier, and financial-institution relationships need to be positive and healthy. If these conditions are met, you may be many steps ahead of the game by purchasing the right business.

Exhibit 3-1 *Starts and closures of employer firms, 2003–2007.*

Category	2003	2004	2005	2006	2007
New Firms	612,296	628,917	644,122	640,800e	637,100e
Closures	540,658	541,047	565,745	587,800e	560,300e
Bankruptcies	35,037	34,317	39,201	19,695	28,322

e = SBA Office of Advocacy estimate.

Source: U.S. Dept of Commerce, Bureau of the Census; Administrative Office of the U.S. Courts; U.S. Dept. of Labor, Employment and Training Administration, http://www.sba.gov, accessed March 17, 2009.

Reduced Risk

Entrepreneurs that carefully consider the best fit for themselves, and perform a thorough search and careful research, can significantly decrease the risk of failure through an acquisition. The majority of small businesses that change owners are still in business five years later, about double the rate of start-up survival.

Stepping into an existing business can reduce risks associated with uncertainties and unknowns. Start-up businesses face multiple risks, primarily those of not finding a sufficient market and not being able to operate profitably. By buying a going concern, you can take advantage of the established customer base and the systems that are in place to generate cash flows and profits. Whereas past success does not ensure future success, it does increase the likelihood that a business will be profitable.

Bargain Potential

Whereas bargain hunting is not likely to be your primary motivation in purchasing an existing business, it is possible to buy a going concern for less than it would cost to start a similar company. In some cases, a business may be losing money according to its books and records but reveal a solid cash-flow opportunity when examined closely. Or, there may be waste and poor management that can be improved upon to gain value. By the same token, an overly eager seller, or a price that sounds too good to be true, may be a sign that the opportunity actually *is* too good to be true. This is another example of why solid research and due diligence is so critical to a purchasing decision.

Your Knowledge Can Be Beneficial

If you find a business for sale that you already understand, it can jump-start the ownership process. It may be that you work in the same industry or type of firm. Or, perhaps this type of company is a supplier to or a customer of your current company. Maybe you have transferable skills from prior experience that fit.

You can have an understanding of a business from skills attained in your volunteer activities, or as a stay-at-home parent or caregiver, rather than through employment experience. Or, you can seek out employment in the type of company you want to purchase, so that you will have operating experience in advance. For example, buying a restaurant without ever having managed one is often a recipe for disaster.

Of course, if you have an opportunity to buy the business where you work, you may have an advantage. In this case, you may already know the positive and negative aspects of the business and can make a more informed decision. Be careful, though, because your perspective as an employee may be limited or biased.

In any event, if you have or can build an understanding of the type of business you are buying, you will make a more informed purchase decision and reduce your learning curve.

Potential Pitfalls of Buying an Existing Business

Whereas an existing business can provide a hedge against entrepreneurial risk, there are numerous hazards in purchasing a going concern. Typically, you will have to secure more capital to buy a business than to start one up

Global Impact...

Buying Ownership in a Business You Understand—Globally and Locally

Theresa Rogers has a passion for wine. She has taken that passion, and her extensive knowledge of the industry, and has been applying it to Horseneck Wine and Liquors since she purchased the company in 1989. Rogers was studying Hugh Johnson's *Pocket Encyclopedia of Wine* at the age of 19, and secured a job as a salesperson in the Fine Wine division of Heublein, for all the five boroughs of New York, first as a commissioned salesperson and then managing a sales force. From there, Rogers worked with a small company to build a brand called Bollini Chardonnay, the first Italian Chardonnay to be marketed across the United States that cost less than $10 per bottle. Rogers built the brand to 30,000 cases in a three-year period in all the major markets. She then went to work for the Empson Company, the first Italian exporter of the finest Italian wines, such as Gaja. Rogers works with Angelo Gaja, from Piedmont, to develop his brand as the top of the Italian Barbarescos and Barolos. Rogers bought her first store in 1986 and sold it in 2005. She purchased Horseneck as her second store.

Horseneck Wines and Liquors, in Greenwich, Connecticut, has grown from a $500,000 wine shop into a firm having one of the largest collections of fine and rare wines in the state, with $5 million in annual sales.[2] Rogers took an existing business and built upon its potential by plowing her profits back into the company and creating market opportunities. She established her networks and customer base through contributions to charity events, giving wine-tasting parties, and building relationships with local retailers and restaurateurs. As with any wine store, Horseneck sells a range of international wines and spirits. But they go one step farther, working to create the largest collection of Bordeaux, Burgundies, and Italian wines in Connecticut. Rogers started with an existing business and truly made it her own.

because you are paying for the established customer base, supplier relationships, and skilled employees. Another pitfall that can be fatal is the potential for being misled, whether intentionally or not, regarding the true condition and viability of the firm. Yet another is electing to take ownership of a company built in the mold of the previous owner and finding that it is not a good fit for you. Still another frequent issue is that a company's existing customers often are no longer customers after the sale. The customers of a company before it is sold do not necessarily remain so afterwards, in which case revenues will be lower than anticipated. These dangers can be avoided, or at least minimized, by carefully researching every aspect of the organization, its customers, suppliers, and employees, as well as the financial reports and tax returns. Outside counsel regarding the accounting and legal issues involved is strongly recommended. Again, due diligence and thoughtful deliberation are essential ingredients to a business purchase.

Performance Objective 2

Identify potential drawbacks of buying a business.

Investment Requirements

Buying an existing business will require gathering the financial resources needed to complete the transaction and operate successfully. When you start a business from scratch, you will have to build your own customer base, create your brand, hire employees, and develop a supply chain. When you buy a business, this work has been done for you, but the individual who did all that—the owner—will need to be compensated for it, raising the financing requirements.

Buying Someone Else's Problems

Whereas buying a business has many advantages that may translate into market benefits, you will also take over its challenges and problems. Some

[2]*Entrepreneur* magazine, February 2009, p. 33.

of these challenges may be obvious and are among the reasons that you saw value in buying the business in the first place. Others may be well hidden and need digging to discover. Undisclosed issues might include

- dissatisfied customers, suppliers, employees, or creditors;
- plant and equipment obsolete, inefficient, or in need of costly repairs;
- lack of innovation or failure to keep up with market trends;
- obsolete or overvalued inventory and/or accounts receivable; and
- patents no longer valid and in force (this can be found out through the U.S. Patent and Trademark Office).

These are types of issues that can catch you off guard, cost you your investment, and bring a lot of heartache. Be very deliberately diligent in understanding exactly what you are getting and not getting.

Business Is Not a Good Fit

Whereas it is important to find a business that meets the prospective buyer's financial, industry, and other criteria, none of those factors will matter if it does not fit well with personality, lifestyle, and work-environment requirements. It is easy to get caught up in the excitement of the purchase, but a business that is a poor fit at the owner level will soon become a burden, no matter how outwardly successful it may be or become. You need to "keep your eyes on the prize" and remember that the prize includes lifestyle factors that are important to you.

Examples of poor fits abound. For example, if you are very hands off as a manager, and you buy a business that requires you to get out onto a production floor and roll up your sleeves whenever someone is out, or you have to be "chief cook and bottle washer," you may rapidly learn to resent the business. If you like to work late at night but need to be present during traditional retail store hours, you will be exhausted and unhappy, at least until you can afford to comfortably adapt your schedule.

Finding and Evaluating Available Businesses

The process of finding and evaluating available businesses is similar to that of identifying a business to start or franchise to buy. The first step is to carefully evaluate your personal goals and objectives and the support of those closest to you. Through an iterative process, you can determine your focus and gather data accordingly. Once you have identified one or a few prospective sellers, the critical stage will be due diligence followed by negotiation and closing the deal.

Performance Objective 3

Learn how to identify and evaluate purchase opportunities.

Step into the Shoes . . .

A Sweet Schedule

Andrea Dashiell started Honeecakes Bakery in 2004, when she was a student at Suitland Senior High School in Forestville, Maryland. She took orders and produced homemade pound cakes, pies, and pastries around her school schedule, initially as part of her involvement with the Network for Teaching Entrepreneurship (NFTE). Now a full-time college student living two hours away, Andrea continues to operate Honeecakes Bakery through online and telephone ordering, while working around her class schedule. By electing to have a virtual storefront rather than a physical retail site, Andrea has continued her business and furthered her education on her terms.

Source: Courtesy of Honeecakes Bakery.

Sources of Existing Businesses

Sources of leads to available businesses abound. The challenge is identifying the sources most suited to your individual goals and objectives, and sifting through the potentially overwhelming amount of data to find the pertinent information for decision making. At first, your search may be very broad, much as it could be for a franchise opportunity. After thoughtful evaluation of your decision-making criteria and priorities, it should be possible to narrow the search to businesses meeting your industry, geography, size, life-cycle, profitability, and other criteria. **Exhibit 3-2** lists a number of sources for leads regarding businesses for sale.

business broker a company or individual that buys and sells businesses for a fee.

In addition to the do-it-yourself sources noted above, there are **business brokers** that buy and sell businesses for a fee, in essence serving as a matchmaker. These brokers may have a small portfolio of businesses that they are selling, or they may be part of a regional, national, or international network of brokers. Their income is based upon their ability to close a sale, so be wary of any broker that seems overly aggressive. The International Business Brokers Association, Inc. is the largest association in the industry, so check with them, and you may also want to check with your local Better Business Bureau, and with the broker's references, before paying any fees or entering into an agreement. As with any contractual relationship, proceed with due caution and understand what you realistically can gain through the process.

Exhibit 3-2 *Sources of leads on businesses for sale.*

Type/Source	Resource/Opportunity
Direct Inquiry/Networking	
Current employer	Opportunity to purchase the business or referral to available businesses
Current commercial customers and suppliers	Opportunity to purchase the business or referral to available businesses
Competitors	Opportunity to purchase the business or referral to available businesses
Friends and family	Networks with leads to businesses for sale
Solicitation	
Direct mail	Using a limited mailing to targeted companies and/or individuals seeking leads
Advertising—local and regional publications, business magazines and newspapers, trade publications. (See *SRDS Business Publications* for a list of trade journals.)	Advertisements of businesses for sale and/or placing an advertisement for a purchase. Trade publications can be particularly useful when searching for a particular type of company.
Internet	
BizBuySell—www.bizbuysell.com	Sends registered users e-mail alerts regarding businesses for sale
Craigslist—www.craigslist.org	Free listing service for sellers and buyers
Businesses for Sale—www.businessesforsale.com	Paid listings of thousands of businesses for sale
Business Broker Net—www.businessbroker.net	Classified advertising for buyers and sellers
BizQuest—www.bizquest.com	Searchable paid listings of businesses for sale
Merger Network—www.mergernetwork.com	Matching qualified-buyer members with sellers
Start-Up Journal—www.startupjournal.com	*Wall Street Journal* publication

However you identify a business to buy, it is crucial to have others on your team (or at least, on your side) who know what they are doing with respect to the business you are considering. It is even better if they have done this before. Having access to resource people that have also started and operated a business can help.

Due Diligence—Reality Versus the Story

The process of searching for and identifying a business to buy can be an exhilarating and emotional time. It is also a time when rational thought and clear, well-developed research and analysis will be critical to success. It is easy to fall in love with the idea of owning a business and overlook the pitfalls and problems. Thus, **due diligence**, which is the exercise of reasonable care in the evaluation of a business opportunity, is vital. You have to sift through the story that the seller and/or broker is telling you to discover the reality of the situation. Whether there is unintentional failure to disclose the full and true nature of conditions, or there is deliberate fabrication of information, the burden is on the buyer to identify the issues. Unlike the Franchise Disclosure Document, there is no standard, federally regulated disclosure required, so discovery is up to the buyer and his/her attorney and accountant.

due diligence the exercise of reasonable care in the evaluation of a business opportunity.

Due diligence requires that the buyer acquire a broad range of information about the business, starting with the background information from the seller and through personal observation. Today, a quick scan of the Internet for information on the company and/or owner can provide ready access to information such as customer satisfaction/dissatisfaction, press coverage, and legal issues. Outside parties can provide a more complete picture of the firm. For example, bankers, suppliers, employees, and customers may provide realistic assessments and data. However, inconsistent or conflicting information, refusal to provide contact names, or hesitancy to open up to questions are all signs of potential problems and should be heeded.

If you want to truly understand a potential acquisition, information from stakeholders can prove invaluable. Internal documents, financial audits, and other information from the owners are critical to the process, but input from suppliers, customers, and employees is crucial to creating a complete picture. It is perfectly appropriate to request lists of current and former suppliers, customers, and employees, both satisfied and dissatisfied, to interview. You are likely to get more of the truth about the business from its stakeholders. However, you have to be very careful to avoid disclosing the potential sale if the current owner is protecting that information.

Part of the due diligence process should be to identify the real reason that the owner is selling. Whereas people may offer such explanations as retirement, illness, relocation, or change of heart, the real answer may be something else and less benign. Common undisclosed reasons to sell a business are

- lack of sufficient cash flow;
- unprofitability;
- difficulty in finding and retaining necessary staff;
- loss of exclusive franchise rights;
- pending changes in zoning or traffic patterns;
- changing industry or market conditions that will limit growth potential;
- entrance of new competitors;
- desire to start a new, competitive business in a better location; and
- pending or active litigation.

By completing the due diligence process, a prospective buyer may find that none of these negative circumstances exists and will feel comfortable making the purchase. However, it is better to find out about any potential pitfalls in advance, and to address them, than to receive unpleasant surprises after the purchase is final.

You can expect to receive information from a business broker and are well within your rights to request whatever information you require to make your decision. Sellers may be hesitant to disclose too much information to potential buyers, because of concerns about competitive issues or the potential damage of disclosure should the sale not go through. They may require a signed **nondisclosure agreement**, a legal document enumerating the type of information that is to remain confidential.

nondisclosure agreement a legal document enumerating the type of information that is to remain confidential.

The prospective buyer can and should request full disclosure of all aspects of the business that pertain to its potential success. **Exhibit 3-3** lists the records of information a buyer should request and review during due diligence. These are highly sensitive data for a business owner and may not be readily made available. Recognize that you have to be able to access any organizational documents, contracts and leases, financial statements, and tax returns to even consider purchasing a business. The more of the other items that you can review, the better, particularly if you sense or observe something that may be problematic.

With this information in hand, you can work with skilled professionals, such as attorneys and accountants, to piece together a more realistic view of the business opportunity.

Determining the Value of a Business

The valuation of a business is a combination of art and science, and ultimately a matter of arriving at a price and set of terms that both the buyer and seller find acceptable. For a public company, valuation is the worth of

Exhibit 3-3 *Records and information for a prospective buyer to review.*

- Financial statements, audited if available, for the previous three to five years
- Tax returns for the previous three to five years
- Bank deposit tickets for the past two years
- Employee records and turnover history for five years
- Ownership/shareholder structure and agreements, with any changes, for five years
- Statements of the business capital structure and assets, including nature of ownership
- Description of the products/services offered, with pricing and promotional materials
- Statements of condition of machinery, equipment, and physical plant, including any appraisals (followed by physical inspection)
- Inventory records (followed by physical inspection)
- Contracts, liens, leases, and other legal agreements
- Patents and records of patent-protection maintenance
- Other intellectual property protection, such as trademarks, copyrights, and sales marks
- Description of the technology in use, including computer software and dates of upgrades
- Disclosure of pending and active litigation, zoning, and regulations, as well as recently completed litigation
- Customer lists and sales records
- References from both satisfied and dissatisfied customers
- Supplier lists and references
- Credit and collections history in summary form and by account
- Statement of anticipated material changes
- Noncompete agreements

the stockholders' equity. For a going concern with audited financials, the determination can be based upon projected earnings and cash flows. For other going concerns, the process is more complex because the quality and reliability of the financial information is less certain. The primary methods of valuation are asset valuation, earnings valuation, and cash flow valuation.

Performance Objective 4

Learn how to determine the value of a business.

Asset valuation is a method that analyzes the underlying value of the firm's assets as a basis for negotiating the price. The four most common standards are

asset valuation a method that analyzes the underlying value of the firm's assets as a basis for negotiating the price.

1. ***Book value.*** Starting with the value of assets reported in the books and records of the firm as a reference point, the actual value will depend upon its accounting practices, such as allowances for losses and depreciation.
2. ***Adjusted book value.*** This takes into account any of the discrepancies identified in the calculation of book value, and looks at the actual market value versus the stated book value. Intangible assets are often excluded in this method.
3. ***Liquidation value.*** This is a determination of the net cash that could be obtained through disposing of assets via a quick sale, with liabilities either paid off or negotiated away. It also includes the cost of liquidating. Neither buyers nor sellers are particularly interested in establishing a price based upon liquidation, but it does establish a "floor," or minimum value, for the firm.
4. ***Replacement value.*** This is the determination of the cost of newly purchasing the assets, as would be required to start up the firm. This is also used more as a point of reference than as a pricing option.

Earnings valuation is a method that assesses the value of the firm based upon a stream of earnings that is multiplied either by an agreed-upon factor (the capitalization factor) or by the Price/Earnings ratio (for a publicly traded company). As with any methodology of this nature, the challenge is how to determine the variables. Three ways of looking at earnings are

earnings valuation a method that assesses the value of the firm based upon a stream of earnings that is multiplied either by an agreed-upon factor (the capitalization factor) or by the Price/Earnings ratio (for a publicly traded company).

1. ***Historical earnings.*** Start with the value of earnings reported in the books and records of the firm over multiple years. This can then be adjusted for items that will distort earnings, such as salaries of family members, or depreciation. Historical earnings can be valid if future earnings can be reasonably projected as a result.
2. ***Future earnings under current ownership.*** This considers additional information that is available above and beyond historical earnings, such as economic changes, the competitive environment, and new products and services that have been introduced.
3. ***Future earnings under new ownership.*** This is a determination of the projections that you make according to the changes you plan to implement. This may be the upper limit of what you are willing to consider.

In addition to determining which type of earnings to use, valuation will depend upon which measure of earnings is selected. Will it be before or after taxes? Will it be earnings before interest and taxes (EBIT), or operating income? Which one is selected may make a significant difference in the valuation. It is traditional to use the after-tax earnings value without extraordinary items. However, if the new owner will have a different financing structure, using EBIT may be best. Ultimately, a price must be negotiated to the satisfaction of both the buyer and seller.

cash flow valuation a method of calculating the worth of a business by using projected future cash flows and the time value of money.

Another method of arriving at the worth of a business is to calculate the **cash flow valuation**, using projected future cash flows and the time value of money to arrive at a figure. This requires assessing the future expectations of cash flows from the business and applying financial calculations to arrive at the current value. It is less likely to be used for an entrepreneurial venture, but may be considered as an option.

Whatever value is calculated through the quantitative methods above, the final price should also reflect nonfinancial variables. While performing due diligence, you gathered information regarding the market space; the competitive environment; the legal and regulatory status of the firm; and any pending changes in the physical environment or labor situation, or need for investment in plant, property, or equipment. The value of customer goodwill must also be factored into the price, and the competitive and legal environments also have a role in the pricing. The offer price and the maximum amount you are willing to pay should encompass all of the factors you have identified. This price will have to be tempered by what you can afford.

Negotiating and Closing a Purchase

Performance Objective 5 Learn how to negotiate and close the deal.

Once you complete your research, perform due diligence, and decide that you would like to purchase a particular business, it is time to negotiate the final price and terms of the sale and close the transaction. Whereas it is the objective of both parties in the negotiation to reach an agreement, their respective goals are very different. As the buyer, you are working to secure the best price possible, to reduce your initial investment capital costs and maximize returns. The seller is working to recoup as much money as possible through the sale. Remember, the price you pay should be no greater than you determined in advance. It is better to have invested the time and resources and then walk away from a deal that is not the right fit, than to pursue it and find that you cannot reach your goals.

When determining the price and terms of the sale, it is essential to clearly establish what is being purchased—assets only or the business as a whole. An asset sale reduces the buyer's liability because the outstanding debts and any undisclosed or unknown liabilities remain the seller's responsibility. In a whole business sale, the buyer acquires all the assets and liabilities of the company, known or unknown. You may also complete a purchase of the whole business and address the liability issue through an indemnification clause in the sales contract.

In addition to the stated price of the business, the terms of the sale will be a major factor. Will the previous owner hold a note payable on all or part of the purchase price? Under what repayment terms? Is there a noncompete agreement restricting when and where the seller can open the same kind of business? Is the seller remaining with the business for a specified amount of time to perform particular duties? Sometimes a seller may want a quick sale and wish to cut all ties. In other situations, there may be tax advantages to having a different structure. This needs to be clearly spelled out in the sales contract.

All of the terms and conditions should be agreed upon, with appropriate professional counsel for all parties, prior to the formal closing date. You should clearly understand all legal agreements and have them either drawn up or reviewed by your legal counsel. The investment in professional advice prior to the sale can be crucial. Once the closing is complete, you will have signed a number of important legal documents, including a bill of sale, any financing contracts, and other agreements. You will now be the owner of an operating business!

Buying into a Business over Time

One option that may permit a current owner to separate from a company gradually, receive a stream of payments, and support customer loyalty is purchasing a business over time. You may create such an arrangement in a variety of ways. Typically, the future owner joins the existing company with gradually increased responsibility and equity. This permits time to more fully understand the existing operation while the owner is still present and active, and allows for a smoother transition. As with any purchase agreement, it must be carefully structured to protect all parties.

Family Business as an Entrepreneurial Opportunity

Much has been written about startups, franchises, and business acquisitions as entrepreneurial paths. Joining a **family business**, a firm that has two or more members of the same family managing and/or working in it, and that is owned and operated for the benefit of that family's members, can present an opportunity for entrepreneurial success as well.

family business a firm that has two or more members of the same family managing and/or working in it, and that is owned and operated for the benefit of that family's members.

Whether it is the second generation or the tenth, there may be significant room for innovation, growth, and wealth building. For example, when Alan Levin became president and CEO of Happy Harry's Discount Drugs in the late 1980s, to fill a void left by the unexpected death of his father, Harry, he began an adventure that led to expansion from a handful of stores to 76 outlets 20 years later, when he sold the firm to Walgreen's. Clearly, Alan had found entrepreneurial opportunity in a family business. There was ample opportunity for fostering entrepreneurial energy and talent.

Performance Objective 6

Recognize the joining of a family business as an entrepreneurial pathway.

With a family business, much like the acquisition of any going concern, there is a chance to build upon its strengths and to turn around problematic aspects. The greatest difference is that the changes will benefit the family and not only the buyer. A sound core business can provide a solid foundation for growth and expansion. If you join a family business in which your insights and energy are appreciated and supported, you can be part of the team that has built upon prior success. If the family business is floundering, perhaps suffering from sales decline, cash flow challenges, or other factors that threaten its viability, you can bring a fresh perspective and an additional skill set to the firm.

As with participating in any venture, and perhaps even more so because of the family aspect, you should proceed with your eyes wide open when joining a family business. Your role and the roles of others in the company should be clearly defined, as should your compensation and participation in profits and ownership. How you will work with one another should be discussed frankly to prevent miscommunications that can lead to permanent breakdowns in family relationships. To the extent that it is viable, conduct your due diligence as if you were purchasing a business from an unrelated party, but recognize

Step into the Shoes

Putting Spring into a Third-Generation Business

Brothers Tom and David Walker grew up at Oregon Mattress Company in Newburg. Their grandfather founded the company in 1932, and their father operated it into the 1990s. Tom and David worked with their father for a number of years to expand the business and enhance its overall viability. They moved from producing under the Lady Americana label to Restonic, a well-respected national brand, and Sleep E-Z, their own brand.

Late in 2009, Oregon Mattress opened two retail stores featuring mattresses produced in its Portland-area factory. The BedCo Mattress Superstores are located in Lake Oswego and Beaverton.[3] The Walkers saw an opportunity to increase their share of the local market through direct retail sales of locally produced mattresses, including hard-to-find custom sizes and shapes, and their signature round beds. Now, as the fourth generation of Walkers joins Oregon Mattress Company, the firm is bouncing back in a weak economy.

Source: Courtesy of Oregon Mattress Company.

that the very process of exploring the opportunity must be carried out with family relationships in mind.

Perhaps the notion of joining a family business has been appealing from a very young age. Perhaps it is best to experience working in other businesses or fields of endeavor and turning to the family business later. Perhaps you will be drawn into the business because of a family emergency or tragedy. Regardless of the point of entry or reason, your best entrepreneurial opportunity may lie within the family business.

Chapter Summary

Now that you have studied this chapter you can do the following:

1. Understand the potential benefits of buying a going concern.
   - Startup can be quicker and easier.
   - Reduced risk results from the established business structure and relationships.
   - The potential to identify and purchase a business at a bargain price exists.
2. Identify potential drawbacks of purchasing a business.
   - The current owner may fail to disclose negative information regarding the firm's condition.
   - The business may be a poor fit for the buyer.
   - Pitfalls may be avoided through a thorough due diligence process and use of qualified professional counsel.
3. Learn how to identify and evaluate purchase opportunities.
   - Identify personal goals and objectives to create the best match.
   - Use the many resources available to identify prospective purchases.
   - Perform due diligence to secure the most complete and accurate information.
4. Learn how to determine the value of a business.
   - Use asset, earnings, and/or cash flow valuation methodologies to arrive at a range of potential prices.
   - Consider the spectrum of nonfinancial factors in the price.
   - Arrive at offer and maximum price before entering the negotiations.

[3]Nick Peterson, "Oregon Mattress Co. Goes Retail," *The Times*, December 11, 2009.

5. Learn how to negotiate and close the deal.
   - Recognize the mutual goal of making the transaction happen, despite differing individual goals.
   - Negotiate a price and set of terms that is satisfactory to all parties.
   - Hold a formal closing and complete all legal documents with the support of qualified legal and accounting counsel.
6. Recognize the joining of a family business as an entrepreneurial pathway.
   - A family business may have the potential to foster entrepreneurial energy and talent.
   - A sound core business provides a solid foundation for future success.
   - A floundering family business offers a chance to turn around the company and benefit the entire family.
   - Sometimes an entrepreneurial opportunity is right in front of us; we just have to recognize it.

Key Terms

asset valuation
business broker
cash flow valuation
due diligence
earnings valuation
family business
nondisclosure agreement

Entrepreneurship Portfolio

Critical Thinking Exercises

1. What are four reasons to purchase a business rather than start up a new one?
2. Describe the type of business that you would consider buying. Why did you choose it?
3. What are some red flags that you might discover during due diligence?
4. How can entering a family business be a path to entrepreneurial success?

Key Concept Questions

1. Define due diligence and list some of the information to gather and analyze during the process.
2. Explain three ways that businesses can be valued.
3. Describe the potential problems in buying a business.

Application Exercise

You have been considering going into business for three years and have saved $10,000 toward this dream. Since graduating from college two years ago, you have worked full time at a bank as a credit analyst and part time at a bookstore. These jobs have given you some perspective on financial services and retail trade. Now, you are ready dig in and find a business to buy or start.

1. How will you decide what type of business to own (industry, geography, lifestyle, technology, etc.)?
2. Why would you (or would you not) weigh the option of buying a business?
3. Identify three possible sources of information on businesses for sale and find two possibilities from each. List the information that is provided on these six businesses.
4. Select one of the businesses and explain why it interests you as a possible investment.

Exploring Online

1. Perform a search of business brokers through an Internet search engine of your choice. What are the first five listings (excluding the sponsored links)?
2. Visit one of the Internet resources listed in **Exhibit 3-1**. Search for businesses for sale. Look at convenience stores, auto repair shops, or restaurants. Answer the following:
   (a) Which site and business type did you select?
   (b) How many businesses were listed for sale in your category?
   (c) Were there categories of businesses under the main search category? If so, what were they?
   (d) Examine one of the businesses for sale and record the information provided.

Case Study | A Family Affair

From as long as Deanna could remember, she had helped her mother in The Pantry, a small but successful bakery and restaurant that was known for unique desserts and pastries. When she was young, she helped clean tables in the small customer-seating area. As she grew older, she helped take phone orders and worked at the bakery counter.

Although succession plans were never discussed, Deanna had always planned to work full time in the business after college, and eventually take over the company management when her mother retired. Deanna's mother and father had divorced when Deanna was very young, and because she was an only child, there were no other siblings to take control of the company. If Deanna did not assume ownership, the business would have to be closed or sold to an outsider.

In 1999, Deanna went off to college to study restaurant management. She enjoyed being away from home more than she had anticipated and did very well in her courses. She also became aware of other career opportunities in the food industry that she had never before considered. She realized that she would gain valuable experience by working for other companies before she returned to her mother's business.

At about the same time, however, Deanna's mother remarried. Her new husband had two daughters of his own, aged 16 and 17. Because employee turnover at The Pantry was always a concern, Deanna's mother was more than happy to have his daughters work in the business part time while they were in high school.

To Deanna, though, this was a cause for concern. Now that she had stepsisters, the ownership of The Pantry was not necessarily hers when her mother retired. She was concerned that, if she accepted a position with another company after college, her mother might interpret that as a lack of interest in The Pantry. Once, when she was home during a spring break, she tried to initiate a conversation about the future of the business. Her mother's response was, "I'm only 45 now, and I'm not going to retire for a long time. So don't worry about it."

Deanna also realized that, in the future, if her mother and stepfather gave equal ownership to all three daughters, this would result in her owning one-third, whereas the two stepsisters together would own two-thirds. If the relationship did not work well, she would always be outvoted. She would not have control of the business, and even under the best of circumstances, this was not appealing.

Case Study Analysis

1. If you were in Deanna's position, what would you do?
2. Identify options that Deanna's mother and stepfather could consider rather than dividing business ownership equally among the children.
3. How could this business serve to provide entrepreneurial opportunities for Deanna?

Case Source

Peggy A. Lambing and Charles R. Kuehl, *Entrepreneurship*, 4e (Upper Saddle River, NJ: Pearson Education, Inc., 2007), p. 263.

Case Study | Krispy Kreme Doughnuts®

Prospects and Risks in Buying a Business

The history of Krispy Kreme Doughnuts illustrates some of the potential opportunities and pitfalls that can result from buying an existing business. Since its beginning, Krispy Kreme has been bought and sold several times, with both successful and disastrous outcomes.

Building on a Secret Formula

The ongoing success of Krispy Kreme started with a unique formula, still in use today. In 1933, Ishmael Armstrong bought a doughnut shop, a special recipe for yeast-raised doughnuts, and the name "Krispy Kreme" from Joe LeBeau, a French chef originally from New Orleans. Armstrong started producing doughnuts using that secret formula in his shop in Paducah, Kentucky. He also hired his nephew, Vernon Rudolph, to help with the production process and to sell the doughnuts from door to door.

Because of the tough economic times during the Great Depression, Armstrong couldn't sell enough doughnuts from the shop in Paducah to be profitable. So he and Rudolph left Kentucky and went to the larger city of Nashville, Tennessee. There, he opened another doughnut shop, hoping that the new location would produce greater sales.

Not much later, in 1935, Armstrong sold his doughnut shop in Nashville to Rudolph's father, Plumie, and moved back to Kentucky. With the help of his sons, Vernon and Lewis, Plumie Rudolph ran not only the Nashville store but opened two others—one in Charleston, West Virginia, and another in Atlanta, Georgia.

Continued Growth and Success

Even though the family doughnut shops were successful, Vernon Rudolph wanted his own store. In 1937, he and two of his friends took some doughnut-making equipment and the special recipe and drove to Winston-Salem, North Carolina. They used their last $25 to rent a small store on Main Street. They borrowed the ingredients needed to make their first batch of doughnuts, which they sold to local grocery stores. In a short time, the three young men had made enough money to pay back the grocer who had loaned them the ingredients.

Rudolph began to notice how the smell of hot, fresh doughnuts coming out of the fryer caused people to loiter outside the bakery. So, he cut a hole in the outside bakery wall and began selling doughnuts through a window for 25 cents per dozen. Although the main portion of his sales continued to be wholesale customers, such as grocery and convenience stores, Rudolph did not want to ignore the retail trade.

Over the next 10 years, Rudolph opened shops in seven more cities. Krispy Kreme was trademarked in 1946 and incorporated in 1947. Also in 1947, the company licensed its name to people it termed "associates." Agreeing to buy the special doughnut mix from Krispy Kreme, and to follow its operating standards, these franchisees opened their own doughnut stores.

By 1960, Krispy Kreme had come to be recognized by its red, green, and white logo and the shops' green-tiled roofs. A coffee bar also became a standard feature at all Krispy Kreme outlets. Most shops had a small glass window that allowed customers to look inside the kitchen and get a partial glimpse of the doughnuts being made.

The Wrong Fit

Krispy Kreme continued to prosper, growing to over 60 stores in the southeastern United States by 1973, when Vernon Rudolph died. Three years later, the company was sold to Beatrice Foods of Chicago, a very large conglomerate that included dairy, meat, grocery, candy, and other food-related companies.

Krispy Kreme's small-town business model did not fit with Beatrice Food's big-business approach. The new owner focused primarily on raising profits and decided that the way to do so was to make major changes. For example, Krispy Kreme's logo was redesigned in an attempt to modernize it. In an effort to bring in new customers at slow times during the day, other foods were added to the menu, including soups, sandwiches, and biscuits. But this increased shops' operating costs without increasing customer numbers.

Perhaps worst of all, the original doughnut recipe was altered in an effort to cut costs and improve revenue margins. Those decisions almost ruined Krispy Kreme. The customer's experience and the unique taste of the doughnuts were no longer the focus. According to Scott Livengood, one of Krispy Kreme's CEOs in later years:

> *Our soul is in the doughnut business, and Beatrice just didn't get that.*[1]

Getting Back on Track

In 1982, a group of some 20 frustrated Krispy Kreme franchisees pooled their resources to buy back Krispy Kreme from Beatrice Foods. What they didn't have in savings, they borrowed, and purchased the company for $22 million. They restored the doughnut formula and business model used in former years. However, the leveraged buyout created a large debt that kept the company from growing much over the next 10 years.

In the late 1980s and early 1990s, Krispy Kreme's new owners studied consumer research, both past and present, to help identify the heart of the Krispy Kreme brand. Although some of the research was formal, a lot of information was gathered through spontaneous discussions with customers. Over and over, the business's owners heard stories about happy memories eating hot doughnuts with friends and family.

As a result, Krispy Kreme expanded the idea of allowing customers to peek inside the kitchen by developing a theater-like atmosphere in many of the stores. Instead of a small window, glass walls were built around the production area. Customers were now able to see the entire doughnut-making process. When the "Hot Doughnuts Now" neon sign was turned on outside, it signaled to customers that fresh doughnuts were being made, so they could come in to watch.

Earning a Place in History

By the early years of the new century, Krispy Kreme had nearly 300 retail stores that together produced over 2 billion doughnuts annually. Today, the company continues to grow, opening new stores all over the world in addition to the United States—Canada, Mexico, the United Kingdom, the Philippines, Japan, Australia, and the Middle East.

Krispy Kreme executives have learned from mistakes made in the past by their predecessors. Instead of rushing to implement new plans before the time is right, each potential new geographic location is carefully studied to make sure its market will support a full-scale doughnut operation. Krispy Kreme's management also spends time checking out sites for the individual stores. In addition, potential franchisees and employees are thoroughly screened. Those selected are required to maintain meticulous standards, to ensure consistent product quality.

Even though these business strategies are time consuming, Krispy Kreme's successful comeback since the Beatrice Foods ownership has proved that this approach works well. In fact, the company is now an official part of American history. In 1997, after 60 years in business, Krispy Kreme was inducted into the Smithsonian Institute's National Museum of American History.

Case Study Analysis

1. What mistakes did Beatrice Foods make after purchasing Krispy Kreme? Why wasn't Krispy Kreme a good fit for Beatrice?
2. What opportunity did the franchisees see in buying back Krispy Kreme rather than starting a new company from scratch?
3. Describe several business lessons that can be drawn from Krispy Kreme's history.
4. Krispy Kreme started as a family business. How has that influenced the operation of the company?
5. Identify three questions you would have asked Ishmael Armstrong while performing due diligence for the potential purchase of Krispy Kreme Doughnuts. List three questions that you would ask today if you were considering becoming a Krispy Kreme franchisee.

Case Sources

Kirk Kazanjian and Amy Joyner, *Making Dough: The 12 Secret Ingredients of Krispy Kreme's Sweet Success* (Hoboken, NJ: John Wiley & Sons, Inc., 2004).

Krispy Kreme Doughnuts Web site, http://www.krispykreme.com.

Smithsonian Institute National Museum of American History Web site, Archives Center, Krispy Kreme Doughnut Corporation Records, http://americanhistory.si.edu/archives/d7594.htm (accessed May 2009).

[1]Kirk Kazanjian and Amy Joyner, *Making Dough: The 12 Secret Ingredients of Krispy Kreme's Sweet Success* (Hoboken, New Jersey: John Wiley & Sons, Inc., 2004), p. 84.

Chapter 4

THE BUSINESS PLAN: ROAD MAP TO SUCCESS

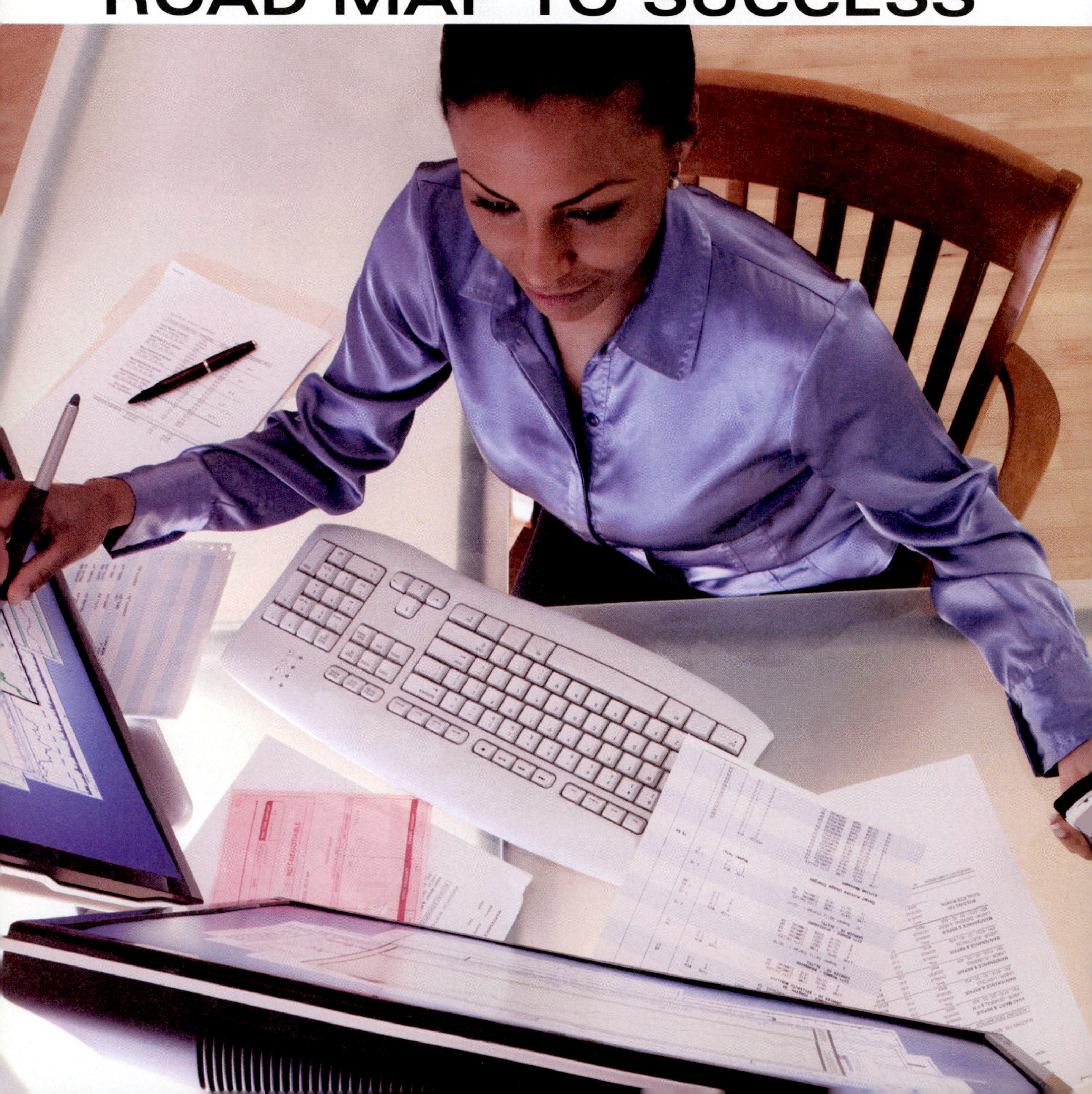

"If you don't know where you are going, any road will get you there."

—Lewis Carroll, English author

Great business ideas can grow into great businesses, or they can wither away from neglect or unfavorable environments. One thing that successful businesses have in common is a sound idea and an entrepreneur who has a plan for turning the idea into reality.

Many people dream about opening a retail store. Some people dream about owning *several* retail stores. Still others start with a single store and grow the enterprise into thousands of stores. That is what happened with Donald and Doris Fisher, the founders of Gap Inc. In 1969, the Fishers, at the time of Woodstock, the Vietnam War, and the moon landing, started a small retail store in San Francisco. Don Fisher stated, "I created Gap with a simple idea: to make it easier to find a pair of jeans. We remain committed to that basic principle."[1]

Gap Inc. continues providing store experiences that are pleasant for the customer and offer a broad selection of fits and styles. The company has expanded to include the Old Navy, Banana Republic, and Piperlime brands. There are more than 150,000 employees worldwide in more than 3100 stores. In fiscal year 2008, Gap Inc. had revenues of $14.5 billion. Doris Fisher and her son Bob continue to serve on the Gap's board of directors. The company has come a long way from its origins while maintaining a strong, consistent focus.

Performance Objectives

1. Know what a feasibility analysis is and when to create one.
2. Know what a business plan is and how to describe it.
3. Explain the various purposes for a business plan and the audience for it.
4. Understand the components of a business plan.
5. Be able to demonstrate proper development and formatting of a business plan.

[1] Available at *http://www.gapinc.com/public/About/about.shtml* (accessed March 14, 2009).

Feasibility Analysis: Does My Idea Work?

feasibility analysis a study to assist in making the "go/no go" decision based upon a close examination of product/service, market, industry, and financial data in a sufficient degree of detail to ensure confidence in the results.

Performance Objective 1

Know what a feasibility analysis is and when to create one.

The time and energy involved in generating and exploring business ideas can be extensive, with the SBA reporting that, for many entrepreneurs, the process can take years. With that sort of investment, it is an advantage to filter out the ideas that are viable from those that are not. A **feasibility analysis** will assist in making the "go/no go" decision based upon a close examination of product/service, market, industry, and financial data in a sufficient degree of detail to ensure confidence in the results. This is an excellent precursor to committing the time and resources to planning the implementation of the business, and then presenting it for financing after the creation of a comprehensive business plan. The feasibility analysis essentially tests a business concept for viability in three areas:

1. product and/or service feasibility,
2. market and industry feasibility, and
3. financial feasibility.

This test of feasibility presumes business desirability and that you are interested in this particular business in this industry.

Analyzing Product and/or Service Feasibility

Entrepreneurs are often described as committed to their business idea. They take on an almost religious zeal, and essentially fall in love with the concept of the product or service, creating a fantasy of what the business will be. Conducting a product or service feasibility analysis serves the dual purpose of determining whether production of the product or delivery of the service is possible at a profit, and whether customer demand is sufficient. Without affirmative answers to both these queries, success will be elusive at best.

A product or service is only worthwhile pursuing if it can be produced and delivered at a profit in an ongoing manner. For example, scientists develop innovative technologies in their laboratories that can significantly outperform any technology that is commercially available. Some entrepreneurs may want to introduce products that embody the next big technology, and move down the path toward securing financing and establishing marketing strategies, only to find out that the production cost would lead to an unreasonable retail price and the volume of production would be too low to serve the target market. In order to avoid such unwelcome surprises, you can create the production design for your product and create a working model, called a *prototype*, fabricated for testing by laboratories and prospective customers. Services can also be tested for timeliness and cost of delivery.

Determining whether a product appeals to prospective customers and whether the appeal will translate into sales will be vital to assessing feasibility. Subsequent chapters of this text will address specific sources of information that you can use to determine feasibility. These sources can be direct from the targeted customer base (primary), or through already existing research (secondary).

It is important to perform this feasibility study in order to avoid wasting valuable resources. An amazing product or innovative service would not necessarily translate into enough sales to sustain your business.

If the results of the feasibility analysis are negative, it is time to seriously rethink the product or service and its fit in the marketplace. Inconclusive or positive results on the product or service itself can be considered with the balance of the feasibility analysis to decide whether or not to proceed to the business-plan stage.

Analyzing Market and Industry Feasibility

Evaluating the targeted market and industry is essential to determining the viability of a business idea. Just as a seed will grow in fertile soil and wither away in barren earth, business ideas will take hold or fail based largely upon the market and industry in which they are launched. This segment of a feasibility analysis examines the attractiveness of the proposed industry and the opportunity to find strategic, defensible niches. Later chapters will provide good resources for conducting such analysis in greater detail.

One tool that is particularly valuable for industry feasibility analysis is the "five forces" model created by Michael Porter of Harvard University, which focuses on the competitive intensity of a market.[2] The model is designed to assess the overall industry competitiveness level in which closely related or similar products and/or services are sold. You would create a separate model for each proposed line of business. **Figure 4-1** provides a visual summary of the model.

It is the interaction of the forces that creates the industry environment, and the attractiveness of participating in it, for a given business. The five industry forces identified by Porter[3] are essentially:

1. competitor rivalry,
2. barriers to entry,
3. threat of substitutes,
4. supplier power, and
5. buyer power.

[2]Adapted from Michael Porter, "How Competitive Forces Shape Strategy," *Harvard Business Review*, March/April 1979, pp. 137–145.

[3]Ibid.

Figure 4-1 *Porter's Five Forces Analysis.*

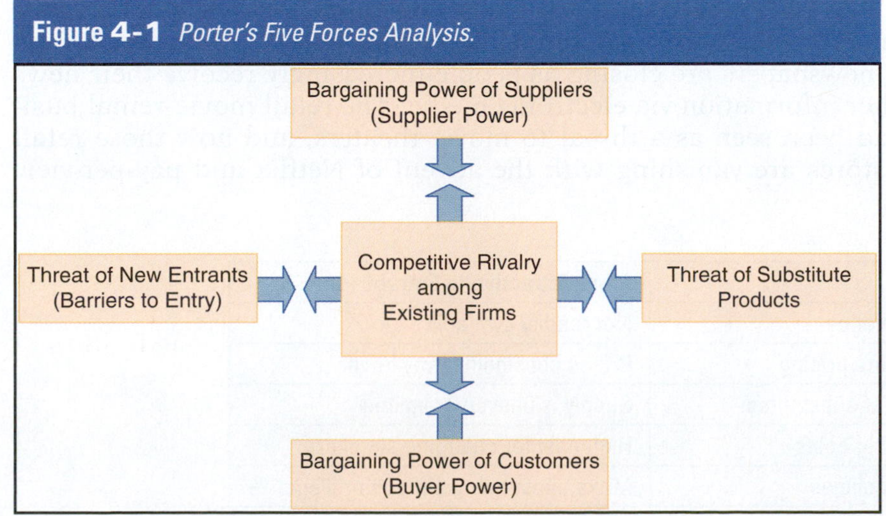

Competitor Rivalry

The degree of rivalry among existing competitors is generally the strongest force in an industry. Some industries are more aggressive and competitive than others, and you will want to know how your business would perform in the existing environment. For example, look at the number of Chinese restaurants in a large city, or the competitive environment for power companies. Key aspects include

Factor	More Attractive to Entrant
Number of firms	Larger or fewer than five
Size of firms	Varied
Industry size/trend	Growing rapidly
Differentiation	Differentiation matters

Barriers to Entry

The threat of new entrants into an industry will be greater, the larger the number of new entrants. As an entrant, you want the barriers to be low. As an established firm, you will want them to be high. Once you enter, you want the barriers to be high enough so that others cannot do the same. For example, it is relatively easy to start a landscaping company, so competitors range from the neighborhood teenager with the family mower to larger companies with more expensive equipment and many employees.

Factor	More Attractive to Entrant
Capital requirements	Low for entry
Cost advantage	Not based upon company size
Economies of scale and/or scope	Minimal or absent
Switching costs	Low cost for changing suppliers
Brand loyalty	Customer resistance to change is low
Distribution channels	Established, but open
Public policies	Do not impede entry; may facilitate entry

Threat of Substitutes

The level of threat posed by alternative products and services that may provide benefits to industry customers matters to a potential entrant. For example, newspapers are closing as people increasingly receive their news and other information via electronic media. The retail movie-rental business had been seen as a threat to movie theaters, and now those retail rental stores are vanishing with the advent of Netflix and pay-per-view movies.

Factor	More Attractive to Entrant
Convenience	Not readily available
Substitute pricing	Prices not significantly lower
Supply of substitutes	Supply is uneven or limited
Switching costs	High cost for changing suppliers
Public policies	Make substituting difficult or illegal

Supplier Power

The less power and control the suppliers of raw materials, components, and labor have over competitors, the more attractive the industry. Where there are a few powerful suppliers, new entrants will have little flexibility and control, both of which they need.

Factor	More Attractive to Entrant
Brand reputation	Not critical
Substitutes for supplies	Commodities, easy substitution
Switching costs	Relatively low
Impact of individual supplier on costs	Small portion of overall costs of finished products

Buyer Power

This force is similar to that of suppliers, but on the demand side. The larger and more diverse the customer base, the less dependent competitors in an industry will be on particular customers. Where customers are many, they can exert control to force prices downward, quality upward, and margins to the floor. Generally, the more a company is recognized for being the low-price leader in its industry, the more it applies pressure on its suppliers, and has the power to get what it wants.

Factor	More Attractive to Entrant
Buyer size	Variable
Number of buyers	Large number of buyers
Product importance	Not a large part of the costs of finished goods
Delivery demands	Restricted geographic area
Switching costs	Relatively high
Product differentiations	More differentiation, fewer commodities
Information availability	Hard for customers to compare features and prices

As you examine the industry in relation to each business idea, it will become easier to determine the attractiveness of the industry. To further analyze the information, you can create a table listing each factor and assign a weight to each, to come up with a quantitative analysis of the competitiveness in each industry.

Once you have selected the industry, it is time to find a defensible target or set of targets that you can claim and protect. You can design a successful focus strategy to foster business success if you have identified a niche of sufficient size to permit profitability. Identifying this niche and the potential growth of the segment is an excellent precursor to completing financial feasibility analysis.

Analyzing Financial Feasibility

Having completed the product or service feasibility analysis, and also one for the market and industry, you can complete the process by assessing the financial viability of your business idea. This analysis does not need to be detailed. At this point, addressing capital requirements, revenues, costs, and earnings should suffice.

The amount of start-up capital required will be a function of the size and type of organization you are starting. For example, a business that is bringing a patented technology to market by assembling components manufactured by other companies will have lower capital costs than one that manufactures and assembles the parts. Some businesses require very little start-up capital (less than $35,000), whereas others might require millions of dollars before making a single sale. A complete financial feasibility analysis will forecast and incorporate such costs.

An entrepreneur can assess feasibility better with a reasonable projection of revenues, based upon anticipated pricing and volume. Using industry-comparable data, particularly any growth statistics for similar firms, can help to make such estimates valid. There is often a temptation to be either overly optimistic or overly pessimistic at this stage, so tempering these extremes with solid data can be significant.

Finally, cost factors should be calculated and returns on investment projected. The earlier analysis of the product or service viability feeds directly into this calculation. By understanding projected costs and offsetting them against revenues, profit projections are possible. With these projections in hand, you can evaluate the return on the capital invested to make a "go/no go" decision.

The outcome of the feasibility analysis will be to show whether the business idea can be a profitable venture with a sufficiently large return on investment. This is a step in the filtering and selection process that narrows and focuses the business idea so that it can be further developed in a business plan, or set aside for a stronger concept.

What Is a Business Plan?

business plan a document that thoroughly explains a business idea and how it will be carried out.

Performance Objective 2

Know what a business plan is and how to describe it.

By the time you complete this book, you will have written a **business plan** that you can use to design, start, and operate your own venture. A business plan is a document that thoroughly explains a business idea and how it will be carried out. The plan should include the following:

- the story of what the business is and will be,
- all costs and a marketing plan,
- description of how the business will be financed, and
- an estimate of projected earnings.

The foremost reason to write a business plan is to organize your thoughts *before* starting a business. Many of the entrepreneurs mentioned in this book wrote a business plan before they made a single sale. However, many, if not most, businesses are started based upon a concept in the founder's head. Writing a business plan is a daunting and time-consuming process. Even though creating a plan is a best practice, many entrepreneurs do not elect to create one, often to their detriment. In fact, a well-written plan will guide you every step of the way as you develop your business.

Why Do You Need a Business Plan?

Whether you are planning a microenterprise with virtually no start-up costs, or a multimillion-dollar venture, you will find a business plan an essential tool. No serious professional investor will agree even to see you unless you have put together a comprehensive, convincing business plan. A plan can also help you determine on paper whether your business is viable before you make mistakes in the real world, so that you can adjust accordingly. It will force you to analyze markets and opportunities in realistic terms before you attempt to secure financing. The business plan is vital to current and proposed businesses as a guide to operations and direction, which can be modified as the organization evolves.

Writing a Business Plan Early Will Save You Time and Money

Performance Objective 3

Explain the various purposes for a business plan and the audience for it.

While you work on your plan, you will also be figuring out how to make your business successful. Before you serve your first customer, you will have answered every question you can think of. How much should you charge for your product or service? What exactly *is* your product or service? What is one unit of sale? What will your costs be? How are you going to market your product or service? How and where will you sell it? Figuring all this out in advance will save you time and money.

The business plan can be a front line of defense against a poor idea. In fact, "If your proposed venture is marginal at best, the business plan will show you why and may help you avoid paying the high tuition of business failure. It is far cheaper not to begin an ill-fated business than to learn by experience what your business plan could have taught you at a cost of several hours of concentrated work."[4]

If you start your business without a plan, these kinds of questions can overwhelm you. By the time you have completed the exercises in this book, though, you will have answers, and you will be able to chart a road map for your own business! You can use the Biz Builder online tools to create a professional plan, and a Microsoft PowerPoint presentation that will emphasize the highlights of your strategy.

Several software packages on the market are designed to help you write a business plan, including

- Tim Berry's Business Plan Pro® (Palo Alto Software, *http://www.BusinessPlanPro.com*). There is also a Social Enterprise Edition available.
- Linda Pinson's Automate Your Business Plan for Windows (Out of Your Mind and into the Marketplace, *http://business-plan.com/automate.html*).
- Biz Plan Builder (JIAN, *http://www.BizPlanBuilder.com*).
- Business PlanMaker Professional (Individual Software, Inc., *http://www.individualsoftware.com*).

These software packages and their sample business plans will provide guidance in developing your own unique design. Be wary of creating a cookie-cutter plan and falling into the trap of using the data and financial projections of sample plans. In the end, a business plan must be the creation of the individuals who will operate the business.

In addition, by using the Web, you can save some time and money by presenting your business plan to several investors at a time, no matter where they are located. With a presentation program like PowerPoint, you can broadcast your presentation in real time over

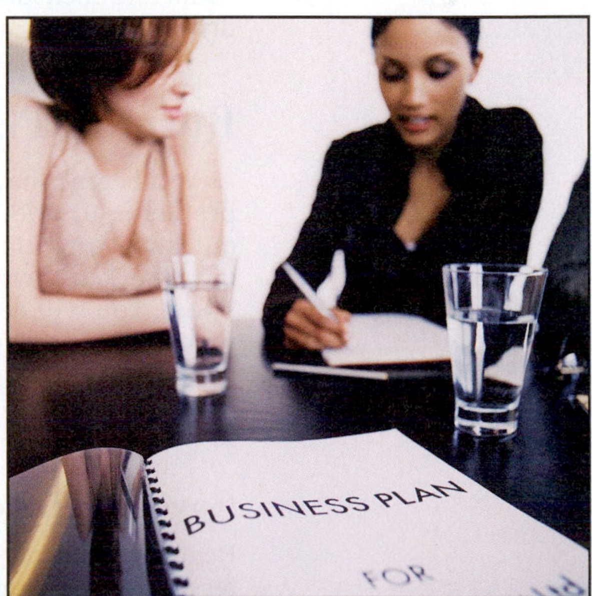

Writing a business plan will allow you to address all angles of your business idea. (© Getty Images-Stockbyte)

[4]Joseph R. Mancuso, *How to Write a Winning Business Plan* (Englewood Cliffs, NJ: Prentice Hall, 1985), p. 44.

the Web, or send it electronically to interested parties. With proper technology, you can also include audio to accompany the presentation. Whereas it is always preferable to make a presentation in person, this can be an effective way to present your business plan to investors at their convenience. Remember, though, that proper nondisclosure agreements are an absolute necessity because business plans are valued property of their developers.

Your Business Plan Is the Key to Raising Capital

As mentioned, bankers and other potential investors will refuse to see an entrepreneur who does not have a business plan. You may have a brilliant idea, but if it is not written out, people will be extremely unlikely to invest in your business or loan it money.

A well-written plan will show investors that you have carefully thought through how you intend to make your business profitable. The more detail you offer investors about how their money will be used, the more willing they will be to invest. The financial projections should be realistic and attainable. Your plan should be so thoughtful and well written that the only question it raises in an investor's mind is: "How much can I invest?"

The Business Plan Is an Operations Guide

Whether or not you need to raise capital, a business plan is a vital tool for guiding the internal operations of your business. Business owners and managers increase the probability of success by taking the business plan in their heads and committing it to paper. The transition may be bumpy because the process of writing a coherent plan will require answering difficult questions. However, the process of developing the plan will generate an increased clarity of vision, mission, and goals for the entire team. With your business plan as your benchmarking tool, you can compare your company's progress to your stated plan. You can also use the business plan as a point of reference when it seems you are going off track, or becoming distracted from your goals. The presence of financial and operational goals and measures, as well as mission and vision statements, can feed a drive for success and motivate a team to excellence.

Business Plan Components

Performance Objective 4
Understand the components of a business plan.

As you begin a new enterprise, you can find a seemingly endless variety of problems to address and questions to answer. Such a situation could quickly overwhelm you if you don't have a plan. However, by the time you have worked through all of the steps of a business plan, you will have answers. You will develop a love for the business, rather than being in love with the idea of the business and having unrealistic expectations. The order of the components of a plan can vary somewhat, but there are elements common to all. An outline of one kind of business plan is illustrated in **Exhibit 4-1**.

Cover Page and Table of Contents

Begin the plan as you intend to continue it. The cover page should be professional, neat, and attractive. It should provide the name of the business and the principals, the date, contact information, and any confidentiality statement. The table of contents should be sufficiently detailed so an investor or manager can easily find a section, but not so detailed that it takes up pages of the plan.

Exhibit 4-1 *Business plan outline.*

Cover Page
Table of Contents
1.0 Executive Summary
2.0 Mission, Vision, and Culture
3.0 Company Description
4.0 Opportunity Analysis and Research
- 4.1 Industry Analysis
- 4.2 Environmental Analysis
- 4.3 Competitive Analysis

5.0 Marketing Strategy and Plan
- 5.1 Products/Services
- 5.2 Pricing
- 5.3 Promotion
- 5.4 Place

6.0 Management and Operations
- 6.1 Management Team
- 6.2 Research and Development
- 6.3 Physical Location
- 6.4 Facilities
- 6.5 Inventory, Production, and Quality Assurance

7.0 Financial Analysis and Projections
- 7.1 Sources and Uses of Capital
- 7.2 Cash Flow Projections
- 7.3 Balance Sheet Projections
- 7.4 Income Statement Projections
- 7.5 Breakeven Analysis
- 7.6 Ratio Analysis
- 7.7 Risks and Assumptions

8.0 Funding Request and Exit Strategy
- 8.1 Amount and Type of Funds Requested
- 8.2 Exit Plan
- 8.3 Milestones

Appendices
- Resumes
- Sample Promotional Materials
- Product Illustrations/Diagrams
- Detailed Financial Projections

Executive Summary: A Snapshot of Your Business

The executive summary has to be compelling and comprehensive. It may be the only part that many people will read. It is the hook that either reels in potential investors or loses their attention. If a reader doesn't fully understand the business concept and the purpose of the plan from the executive summary, the rest of the plan is likely to remain unread. So, the executive summary must encapsulate the story of the business clearly and concisely, propose the funding request, and inspire enthusiasm for the possibility of success.

This section should be written last and limited to one or two pages. It should answer the who, what, when, why, and how questions for the business. Who will manage the business? What will it do and what is the owner asking for in the plan? When will the proposed plan be implemented? How will the business succeed? Done well, the reader will have a light bulb moment and be eager to read the rest of the plan.

Mission and Culture: Your Dreams for the Organization

mission a concise communication of strategy, including a business definition and explanation of competitive advantage.

mission statement a brief, written statement that informs customers and employees what an organization's goal is, and describes the strategy and tactics to meet it.

vision a broader and more comprehensive perspective on an organization than its mission; built on the core values and belief systems of the organization.

culture the beliefs, values, and behavioral norms of an organization.

Each company has the opportunity to create its own unique mission, vision, and culture. The founding team can determine how to strategically use the company's competitive advantage to satisfy customers. Culture can be shaped according to the environment and the manner of treating employees, customers, and other stakeholders that the owner(s) model and support. The **mission** of your business, expressed in a mission statement, is a concise communication of strategy, including your *business definition* and *competitive advantage*. The function of a **mission statement** is to clarify what you are trying to do, and it can provide direction and motivation to those who are involved in the business.

A clearly stated mission statement not only tells your customers and employees what your business is about, but can also be a guide for every decision you make. It should capture your passion for the business and your commitment to satisfying your customers. The mission statement should be limited to 40 or 50 words, to encourage clarity and conciseness.

The **vision** for your business is broader and more comprehensive, painting the big picture of what you want your organization to become. It is built on the core values and belief systems of the organization. It is typically shorter than the mission statement, with a loftier perspective.

The **culture** of an organization, whether intentionally or unintentionally created, is largely defined by its leadership. You can build a culture for your company by making the beliefs, values, and behavioral norms explicit and intentional. A business's culture has many components, including norms for risk-tolerance and innovation, orientation with respect to people, team-formation and outcomes, attention to detail, and communication. Whether you want a free-thinking, aggressive company with informal communications or a structured, formal organization with formal communications, you will set the standards and be the role model for your organization's culture.

Global Impact...

Upcycling Waste Internationally—TerraCycle, Inc.

In 2003, John Szaky's TerraCycle won a business plan contest from Carrot Capital for $1 million in seed capital. But the venture capital firm wanted TerraCycle to drop its environmental focus, and Szaky turned down the offer. It was a critical decision that later helped the business achieve its competitive advantage.

One innovation was implemented when TerraCycle ran out of money to buy bottles in which to sell the fertilizer. They decided to use recycled soda bottles, to package the worm waste. This concept grew into the production of other green products. TerraCycle converts unrecyclable packaging waste to upcycled products. Pencil holders made from Kool-Aid packets, tote bags made from Capri Sun drink pouches, and backpacks made from Clif Bar wrappers are just a few examples. TerraCycle calls this process turning branded waste into sponsored waste.

Today, more than one hundred TerraCycle products are sold in large retail chains, including Home Depot, Whole Foods, Wal-Mart, and Target. The concept has spread to the United Kingdom, Brazil, Mexico, and Canada, with the greatest impact in the United Kingdom. By working with groups in each country, TerraCycle has the potential of becoming the icon that represents upcycled waste.

Sources: TerraCycle, Inc., *http://www.terracycle.net* (accessed January 20, 2010) and Tom Szaky, *Revolution in a Bottle* (New York: Penguin Group, Inc, 2009).

Company Description—Background and Track Record

If the company is already established, is a franchise, or is the reincarnation of a previous business, there will be a history to share with the reader of the plan. The business description does not need to be long. It should simply provide the background for understanding the rest of the plan. It should include summary information about the company's founding, its progress, and its financial success.

If this is a start-up venture, this section should describe briefly the background story of the company, explaining what you have done thus far and why you have done it. The legal form of the business (i.e., sole proprietorship, corporation, LLC, partnership) should also be noted.

Opportunity Analysis and Research—Testing Ideas

The opportunity analysis and research section will provide the credible data and information to determine and demonstrate the market viability of your proposed business on paper, and perhaps in the field, before you start. It should be a clear description of why the business presents an excellent opportunity, based on sound research and logic. Entrepreneurs often either put little time and attention into this section, or they ignore any data that do not agree with their view of the opportunity. This can prove to be a fatal flaw in business planning. A well-researched opportunity analysis can help to move your business to the head of the line for financing.

The **industry analysis** will provide the broad context for your business plan. It will deal with such factors as industry definition, industry size and growth (or decline), product and industry life cycle, and any current or anticipated legal or regulatory concerns. Determining industry structure, including geographic distribution, business size of member firms, concentration of power, and rates of failure, is also important. For example, the failure rate of restaurants is notoriously high and should be addressed in a business plan for a restaurant concept. This is also the place to discuss how you will track industry developments on an ongoing basis.

industry analysis a critical view of industry definition, industry size and growth (or decline), product and industry life cycle, and any current or anticipated legal or regulatory concerns.

The **environmental analysis** addresses the roles of the community, region, nation, and the rest of the world as they relate to your business. Whether or not demographic and family changes are working in your favor could mean adjustments for the business. Changes in technologies and economic conditions might radically alter your plans. Examples of this could include the aging of the baby boomer generation or the prevalence of computer technology.

environmental analysis a review that addresses the roles of the community, region, nation, and the rest of the world, as they relate to a business.

The opportunity analysis should include a **proof of market** investigation that will provide evidence of a market opportunity for your organization. This should identify market size, both in terms of dollars and units. There have to be enough customers who will purchase your products or services in sufficient quantity at a high enough price, and often enough, for your business to be sustainable.

proof of market an investigation that provides evidence of a market opportunity.

Next, this analysis should describe your **target market** segments, which are groups that are defined by common factors such as demographics, psychographics, age, or geography. For example, your target market segment for a gospel club may be African American Christians between 18 and 25 years of age living in the Detroit metropolitan area. Discuss the size of your target market and the market share that would be attainable. This is also where you can describe your 10 identified customers (remember Russell Simmons's comment).

target market the groups that are defined by common factors such as demographics, psychographics, age, or geography are of primary interest to a business.

A **competitive analysis** is the next important component of the opportunity analysis. This should compare your organization with several

competitive analysis research that compares an organization with several direct and indirect competitors by name in a manner that is meaningful to targeted customers.

direct and indirect competitors by name, and include comparisons that would be meaningful to customers. The format of a competitive analysis can vary significantly, but it must make clear where your competitive strengths and weaknesses are and where there are holes in the competitors' businesses. Factors to compare may include but would not be limited to location, product selection, market share, product or service quality, experience, advertising, pricing, finances, capacity, hours, size and skill of workforce, and reputation. It is often most effective to create a chart or table to show this.

Marketing Strategy and Plan: Reaching Customers

marketing mix the combination of the four factors—product, price, place, and promotion—that communicates a marketing vision.

marketing plan a statement of the marketing goals and objectives for a business and the intended strategies and tactics to attain them.

A description of how you will reach your customers and your anticipated sales volume brings the opportunity and research discussion to the bottom line of sales. Your **marketing mix** will be the combination of the four factors (the Four P's) that form your competitive advantage, also known as *core competency*—product, price, promotion, and place. As you choose the elements of your **marketing plan**, always keep your vision in mind. What is the benefit your product or service is providing to customers?

- ***Products/Services.*** The product or service should meet or create a customer need. The distinctive features and benefits of the product or service must be clearly stated. Remember, the packaging is also part of the product. Your customer may throw away your packaging but that does not mean it is unimportant. If you are introducing an innovative technology, the value of the innovation to customers warrants explanation here.
- ***Pricing.*** The product or service has to be priced such that target customers will buy it, and the business will make a profit. Price should reflect your vision, strategy, and policy. It has to be right. For example, if you are marketing a luxury item, a relatively low price might not send the right message to your target customer. Highlight competitive advantages such as quality, credit terms, warranty type and length, service, and innovativeness that support the pricing.
- ***Promotion.*** Promotion consists of advertising, publicity, and other promotional devices, such as discount coupons or giveaways. Publicity is free, whereas advertising is purchased. The description of your promotional plans should be specific with respect to the methods used, the time line for implementation, and the budget. Often this section is further divided into advertising, public relations and publicity, and direct marketing. **Advertising** consists of paid promotion through media outlets, such as broadcast or cable television, the Internet, radio, magazines, and newspapers. **Public relations** consists of community activities that are designed to enhance your organization's image. **Publicity** is free notice in the media presented as news. **Direct marketing** includes telemarketing, direct mail, in-person selling, and other personalized marketing. Remember to include samples of your promotional materials in the appendices of your plan, if possible.
- ***Place.*** This is the venue from which you will sell and distribute your product. Your selling location should be where consumers in your target market do their shopping. Where should you go to bring your product or service to the attention of your market? If you are selling a luxury item, you will need to place it in stores or on Web sites that are visited by customers who can afford it. Included in *place* is your selection of a type of sales force (i.e., independent, company, single line, or

advertising paid promotion through media outlets.

public relations community activities that are designed to enhance an organization's image.

publicity free promotion.

direct marketing a method that includes telemarketing, direct mail, in-person selling, and other personalized marketing.

multiline), any geographic definition of your market, and all channels of distribution. Are you going to sell directly to consumers, work through wholesale distributors, be Web-based, or sell at retail?

Management and Operations: Making the Plan Happen

The people you hire and the processes that you plan to implement will be an essential part of your business plan. This is where the rubber meets the road in the planning process.

The management team is often the deciding factor for financial support of a business. Moreover, with all other factors being equal, a strong management team will be successful in business, and a weak one will fail. The team must be composed of an effective balance of members with technical expertise (i.e., engineering, marketing, accounting, and operations), experience in the field, as well as life experience. Briefly discuss the current and proposed management team and reference their resumes in the appendices.

It can also be worthwhile to add an organizational chart representing the company as it is proposed in the near term and with growth. In addition, descriptions of key roles and responsibilities, and the compensation rates and structures for each, will need to be included.

If your business will be involved in **research and development**, this section should describe it. Include the state of development, such as prototype, testing, or commercialization. Any patents, patents pending, or other intellectual property should be discussed with the limits or law (not losing protection) and the stage of commercial readiness.

The description of the physical location is similar to the discussion of *place* in the marketing mix but with the emphasis on logistics and workforce readiness. Describe the desired physical location(s) of the organization and the rationale. For example, if you require a concentration of highly skilled scientists, you might want to locate near a university with a strong science orientation, or near other firms with similar labor-pool

Step into the Shoes...

Crushing the Competition

Bigfoot Networks, Inc., 2005 Global Champion, MOOT Corp

Harlan Beverly describes himself as having been "an extreme hardcore PC gamer" since he was a child. He is also someone who was frustrated by the in-game lag he experienced when playing online PC games. Harlan returned to college for an MBA at the University of Texas (UT) at Austin so that he could acquire the knowledge and skills to start a company using Network Acceleration technology. He had filed 19 patents related to this technology while working at Intel. Along the way, he partnered with Michael Cubbage and Robert Grim to start Bigfoot Networks.

Bigfoot has won numerous awards, including the 2005 Global Championship in the MOOT Corp competition, and the 2005 Fortune Small Business Startup Competition. They have developed both software and hardware products to reduce lag in game servers and PCs. Their flagship product is the Killer network interface card (NIC) that is powered by LLR technology (patent pending). They received $4 million in venture capital funding in 2006.

The management team was formed at UT Austin and entered in numerous business plan competitions before launching the venture from an incubator. The company has since created innovative technology to provide solutions to online gamers and the makers of online games. Bigfoot Networks has created an innovative, exciting venture from their business plan.

Sources: "Bigfoot Networks Receives $4 Million Investment from Venio Capital Partners to Accelerate Online Games," February 2006, *http://www.mootcorp.org/Bigfoot%20Funding.asp* (accessed December 2007).
John Callahan, Bigfoot Networks Interview, *FiringSquad*, March 21, 2006, *http://www.firingsquad.com/features/bigfoot_networks_interview/*.
Bigfoot Networks, Inc., *http://www.killernic.com* (accessed December 2007).

requirements. Local wage rates and community support are other factors to discuss. In addition, geographic proximity to customers and/or suppliers or distributors may be a critical site factor. Other aspects to consider are business-friendly laws and courts, tax rates and structures, school systems, overall quality of life, and environment.

The facilities required for the success of your enterprise should be discussed in sufficient detail. You should describe the building according to its type and size, and equipment should be specified and "costed out" (details can be included in the appendices). If you know that you require production, warehousing, showroom, and office space, you can describe each. This is where you can discuss your plans to lease or purchase property and equipment, and any tipping points for going from lease to purchase. Remember that it isn't financially prudent to buy a building when you could just rent a small incubator space to get started. Nascent entrepreneurs often immediately want to buy their own facilities and brand new equipment. In reality, leasing space and equipment reduces required start-up capital and can provide greater flexibility.

The production methods and inventory control systems that you plan to use will be critical to your success. Even if you are in a service enterprise, you will have supply issues to address in terms of staffing, logistics, and materials. The business plan is an opportunity to set inventory control systems, production processes, and quality assurance methods. You can highlight any technological innovations that will enhance the company's competitive position. What to include will vary considerably, but the identification of your choices and methods of measurement is essential.

Financial Analysis and Projections: Translating Action into Money

The financial section of the business plan will be the numerical representation of all that you wrote previously. This section should demonstrate organizational viability in financial terms. Commercial lenders in particular will often go directly from the executive summary to the financials before reading anything else. If the numbers make sense, they may look at the rest of the plan. If not, your plan may well land in the trash basket. Your financial estimates should be as realistic as you can make them. Don't pad the numbers. It is not in your best interest to create unrealistic expectations, to delude yourself and your business associates, or to have potential investors or lenders reject your projections as pie-in-the-sky. You are likely to show initial losses, and you should be up front about this. The financials should match both the general market and the other information you provided throughout the business plan. Investors can sense overblown numbers and will react accordingly.

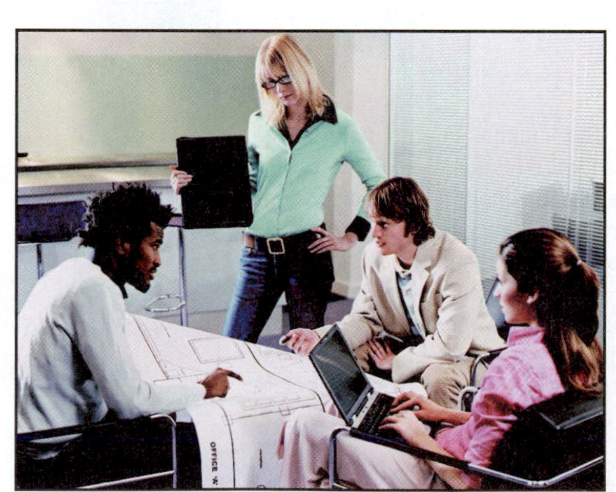

The facilities and equipment for your business should be discussed in detail with the entire management team. (© Digital Vision/Getty)

- ***Sources and Uses of Capital.*** This section is the numeric representation of the start-up costs plus a verbal description of capital requirements. It states where you expect to obtain your financial support and how you will use the funds. When securing bank or community-development financing, your lender may require you to draw down (take in incremental amounts) funds in accordance with your list of costs. It is essential to make the list as complete and accurate as

Exhibit 4-2 *Start-up costs.*

Item	Cost	Estimate/Actual
Start-Up Expenses		
Accountant Fees	$300	Estimate
Expensed Equipment	900	Actual
Financial Institution Fees	350	Estimate
Identity Set/Stationery	750	Estimate
Insurance	2,200	Estimate
Legal Fees	3,000	Estimate
Licenses/Certificates/Permits	550	Actual
Marketing Materials	4,400	Estimate
Payroll (with taxes)	5,500	Estimate
Professional Fees—Other	300	Estimate
Rent	1,200	Actual
Research and Development	200	Estimate
Travel	3,200	Estimate
Utilities	200	Estimate
Web Fees	8,000	Estimate
Other	1,500	Estimate
Total Start-Up Expenses	**$32,550**	
Start-Up Assets		
Cash Balance for Starting Date	$10,000	Actual
Equipment	41,800	Actual
Furniture and Fixtures	21,975	Actual
Leasehold Improvements	5,200	Estimate
Machinery	3,700	Actual
Rent Deposit	1,200	Actual
Signage	6,000	Estimate
Utility Deposit	400	Actual
Other	1,500	Estimate
Total Start-Up Assets	**$91,775**	
Total Start-Up Requirements	**$124,325**	

possible. It is a sad day for everyone when an entrepreneur's credit and cash are completely exhausted just short of the start-up point. A sample start-up cost list is shown in **Exhibit 4-2**.

- ***Cash Flow Projections.*** The **cash flow statement** shows cash receipts less cash disbursements over a period of time. Creating your cash flow projections for three years will bring financial potential and risks into clear focus for you and your stakeholders. Don't be alarmed to see negative numbers on your first couple of efforts at this. However, if the numbers truly do not work, it might be time to reconsider your business approach, or the basic concept, rather than simply manipulating the numbers to achieve satisfactory results on paper.

cash flow statement a financial statement showing cash receipts less cash disbursements for a business over a period of time.

In a start-up business, cash flow is likely to be negative at various points, such as the early months or in certain seasons. A business cannot survive long with negative cash flow, so it must increase cash coming in (revenues, loans, equity investments, and the like) and/or reduce the amount of cash going out (expenses, equipment purchases, debt repayment, and so forth). Remember, be realistic about these

Exhibit 4-3 *Cash flow calculations.*

Starting Cash	(+)
Cash In from Operations [Sales]	(+)
Cash Out from Operations [Cost of Goods Sold, Expenses, Taxes]	(−)
Cash In from Investing [Equity Infusions, Earnings on Investments]	(+)
Cash Out from Investing [Equipment Purchases, Repaying Investors]	(−)
Cash In from Financing [Loans]	(+)
Cash Out for Financing [Repayment of Debt]	(−)
Ending Cash Balance [Starting Balance for Next Period]	(=)

projections. Be careful of significantly increasing your revenue projections solely to improve the numbers. If you add debt, account for its interest and principal repayment in future periods. When you have finished your business plan, it should never show a negative cash balance at the end of a period, because negative cash means you are overdrawn in your accounts, and projecting overdrawn accounts in a business plan, or operating that way, is hardly a best practice. You may very well have suffered losses that are reflected on your income statement, but the ending cash balance cannot be negative. **Exhibit 4-3** shows how cash balances are calculated.

balance sheet a financial statement summarizing the assets, liabilities, and net worth of a business.

asset any item of value.

liability a business debt.

net worth the difference between assets and liabilities.

owner's equity net worth.

income statement a financial document that summarizes income and expense activity over a specified period and shows net profit or loss.

profit and loss statement (P&L) an income statement.

- ***Balance Sheet Projections.*** Your three years of projected **balance sheets** will provide snapshots of your business at specific points in time, such as the last day of a month, quarter, or year. Balance sheets show the business's **assets** (what you own), **liabilities** (what you owe), and **net worth** or **owner's equity**. These statements provide insights into your financing strategy and overall business health. **Exhibit 4-4** shows a rudimentary balance sheet format.

Assets = Liabilities + Owner's Equity

- ***Income Statements for Three Years.*** An **income statement** or **profit and loss statement (P&L)** summarizes income and expense activity over a specified period, such as a month, quarter, or year,

Exhibit 4-4 *Balance sheet summary format.*

Balance Sheet for XYZ Company
As of (Month) (Day), Year

Assets	**Year 1**	**Year 2**	**Year 3**
Cash	$____	$____	$____
Accounts Receivable	____	____	____
Inventory	____	____	____
Capital Equipment	____	____	____
Other Assets	____	____	____
Total Assets	**$xxxxx**	**$yyyyy**	**$zzzzz**
Liabilities			
Short-Term Liabilities	$____	$____	$____
Long-Term Liabilities	____	____	____
Owner's Equity	$____	$____	$____
Total Liabilities & Owner's Equity	**$xxxxx**	**$yyyyy**	**$zzzzz**

Figure 4-5 *Income statement summary format.*

Income Statement for XYZ Company
For the Year Ending December 31, Year

	Year 1	Year 2	Year 3
Net Sales Revenue (+)	$______	$______	$______
Cost of Goods Sold (−)	______	______	______
Gross Profit (=)	$______	$______	$______
Operating Expenses (−)	$______	$______	$______
General Expenses (−)	______	______	______
Other Expenses (−)	______	______	______
Net Income before Taxes	$______	$______	$______
Taxes	$______	$______	$______
Net Income	$______	$______	$______

and shows *net profit* or *loss*. Generally, start-up enterprises suffer losses for several months or even a few years, depending on the type of business. You can show initial losses in your statements, but they must be comparable to industry norms, and you must have cash to cover any shortfalls. The projections that you provide should clearly be your best estimate and based on the detailed breakdown of sales, pricing, cost, and other data contained in your plan. It is helpful to show best case, worst case, and expected scenarios for income. Be careful to avoid ski-slope projections, which add projections linearly, with profitability occurring suddenly in either year three or five. A simple example of an income statement is shown in **Exhibit 4-5**.

- ***Breakeven Analysis.*** This calculation will determine your organization's **breakeven point**, that is, when the volume of sales exactly covers the fixed costs. Calculating the breakeven point will help demonstrate whether there is a viable market for your business. For example, if there are 1500 students in a school and you must sell 2500 yearbooks to reach breakeven, you know that it is time to reconsider your plan. Breakeven is calculated as

breakeven point when the volume of sales exactly covers the fixed costs.

$$\frac{\text{Fixed Cost (\$)}}{\text{Gross Profit per Unit (\$)}} = \text{Breakeven Units}$$

- ***Ratio Analysis.*** In order to understand your business performance relative to your industry peers, you can use ratio analysis. A business plan should include standard ratios: gross profit, quick, current, debt, collection period, receivable turnover, inventory turnover, net profit on sales, net profit to assets, and net profit to equity. One of the best ways to interpret your calculated ratios is to compare them with others in your industry via the Risk Management Association (RMA) Annual Statement Studies, which you may access at a library or purchase online for specific industries (*http://www.rmahq.org*). If you use Business Plan Pro, industry ratios will be available when you calculate them for your business plan. By comparing your business from one period to another and looking at the industry norms, you can adjust the way you will operate, or you can explain why you are outperforming your industry through your competitive advantages, or underperforming because of specific circumstances.

- ***Risks and Assumptions.*** All businesses take risks and make their projections based on assumptions. In order for your plan to be realistic, you will need to state your assumptions and known risks explicitly. You will have done some of this in your SWOT analysis; this section pertains to the financial projections. For example, you can include the per-unit costs and volume projections, anticipated tax and benefits rates, and other calculated and projected values. You can also articulate the risks of implementation delays, cost overruns, lower-than-expected sales, industry price wars, and so forth. As with the other sections in your plan, this should be balanced and realistic, not overstated or underplayed.

Funding Request and Exit Strategy: The Ask and the Return

Your business plan should explicitly state the amount of funds you need in accordance with the financial projections you provide. Whether the need is $500 or $50 million, the reasoning for the request will have to be clear and compelling. Then, you should identify the type of financing you require or are requesting and include your own financial contribution and that of any partners or co-owners, the amount of debt (loans) you will need to take on, and the percentage of equity (ownership) you want to retain. This is where you state the financing terms that you want, including rates, repayment periods, and the like. Recognize that this is part of a negotiation process and that the request should be very carefully structured. If you intend to sell shares of stock in a corporation or are forming a business partnership, legal counsel will be essential so that you do not violate federal regulations and laws, or create an improper agreement. The importance of your ask cannot be overemphasized. Business plan readers need to know what you want.

The exit strategy is the way in which you and/or your investors expect to leave the company someday in a planned and orderly way. For investors, this might mean a buyout plan for their equity, or an **initial public offering (IPO)** when the company goes public, that is, puts itself on the stock exchange. It could mean the sale of the business when certain benchmarks are met, or at a predetermined point in time. It could mean having you give up day-to-day operations according to a succession plan. Lenders and investors will want to know how they will recoup their investment and earn enough profit to warrant the risk they are taking.

initial public offering (IPO) first offering of corporate stock to investors on the open (public) market.

Any business plan is only as strong as its implementation schedule. Therefore, the schedule or timetable of *milestones* (goals) that you include will be important to your business and your stakeholders. By establishing realistic deadlines for the completion of activities, you demonstrate knowledge and understanding of the necessary tasks. You can use PERT or GANTT charts, techniques that will be described in the final unit of this book, or any structured method that details the starting and ending dates of tasks and enumerates the resources needed and the responsibility of personnel. Using a software tool such as Microsoft Project or Excel can make this process easier to manage.

Appendices: Making the Case in Greater Detail

The appendices will provide you with an opportunity to strengthen your business plan with examples and details that are not critical for inclusion in the main portions. This is the place to add management resumes, sample promotional materials, and illustrations or diagrams of products and packaging. In some cases, the detailed financial projections appear in the appendices. Each appendix should be numbered and placed in the plan according to the order of reference in the text. The appendices should be listed in your table of contents.

Business Plan Suggestions

As you put together your business plan, there are a number of guidelines and suggestions that can help you get the most value for your time and effort. These will make the plan look more professional, easier to read, and more likely to be thoughtfully considered. In fact, you will find it easier to refer back to your business plan if it is clear, concise, visually appealing, and well organized. For the plan you should

Performance Objective 5

Be able to demonstrate proper development and formatting of a business plan.

- ***Write for your audience.*** Whether the plan is for an internal (you and your team) or an external (lenders and investors) audience, it will need to address issues and concerns in language your readers will understand. They need to see that this business is something they want to be on board with (if company personnel) or that it satisfies a market need (if potential investors).
- ***Show that you have skin in the game.*** No matter who the audience is, they will want to know that you are emotionally, intellectually, and financially invested in the business.
- ***Be clear and concise.*** Simple, direct language written without too many adjectives or unnecessarily complex terminology is best. Even for highly technical sections, the business plan should avoid jargon and repeated references made through acronyms and initials. This includes writing in a pompous (self-important) way. Keep it simple. Readers know that explaining a complex subject in a clear, concise manner requires a thorough understanding of the subject. Depending on your audience and the type of business, your plan should be from 15 to 40 pages long, including appendices.
- ***Use current data and reports for your industry.*** This is important to validate that you are being realistic and have truly done your research. If you are out of step with current and anticipated conditions, the assumptions that you make for your financial and market performance are likely to be inaccurate and unrealistic.
- ***Choose a voice and stick with it.*** It is best to write your business plan in the third person (not the first-person—"I" or "we") to give it an objective tone. Be careful not to switch back and forth between voices.
- ***Use a consistent, easy-to-read format.*** Choose a format and use it consistently throughout the plan. For example, using 1-inch margins, double spacing, and a serif font (such as Times New Roman) will make the document easy to read.
- ***Number and label.*** Number pages, figures (drawings, illustrations, photos), and tables, and refer to each in the text by title and number to make it easy for the reader to understand and find sections of the plan. Each figure or table should be numbered sequentially, and should be given a heading.
- ***Present it professionally.*** A professional business plan on high-quality paper with a neat, attractive cover, cover page, and professional binding will go a long way in impressing the reader. A dirty, dog-eared, or unbound business plan will probably not even be read. An overly fancy, elaborate plan bound like a book, with four-color glossy illustrations, may cause the reader to wonder why you have gone to such

unnecessary expense, suspecting that you are either wasteful or are perhaps camouflaging an unsound plan with bells and whistles.

It is a good idea to have others look at your business plan before you circulate it to potential investors. If you can get relatively objective friends, colleagues, or family members to read the plan as early as the first draft, you can probably get valuable feedback and ideas for improvement. If you need assistance with spelling and grammar, or any other aspect of the format, this is the time to get it. It is also a good time to use any community resources that may be available to you, such as Small Business Development Centers (SBDCs) or Rural Entrepreneurship Centers.

Presenting Your Business Plan

A written business plan is only one component of the business-planning process. It may open the door for a presentation to potential investors (stakeholders). Or it may be the leave-behind document that is meant to remind the investors of your presentation. In either case, the presentation of the road map for your venture, whether live, Web-based, or in some other form, is your opportunity to convey your business concept to a particular audience and then to have an interactive discussion regarding your proposal.

Business plan presentations may be formal or informal, and you may have anywhere from a few minutes to a couple of hours for the complete presentation and discussion. Presentations to venture capitalists may be limited to as little as 5 to 20 minutes. Regardless of the setting or audience, your presentation should be articulate, well thought out, organized, rehearsed, polished, and professional. As you work on plans for your enterprise, it is a good idea to work on an **elevator pitch** that quickly conveys to the listener in an engaging way what you are proposing and why he or she should be interested. This quick spiel should take 15 to 30 seconds (the duration of an elevator ride). It is often more challenging to boil the business plan down to its essentials than to make a full exposition. For a formal presentation, an attractive multimedia presentation, free from errors, excessive animation, and other distractions is advisable. Some venture presentation tips are given in **Exhibit 4-6**.

elevator pitch a 15 to 30 second presentation that conveys in an engaging way what a business is proposing and why the listener should be interested.

Business plan and pitch competitions provide advantages and disadvantages. Certainly, the preparation for competition is an excellent opportunity to put a deadline on the creation of a plan, and the presentations are opportunities to hone presentation skills and strengthen the concept. Also, competitions may provide significant cash prizes and access to venture capital. However, business plan competitions are time consuming and can prove a distraction from making progress on the business. Some competitions have team guidelines that do not conform to the actual business team, so the competitors on the team will have varying levels of interest and commitment, creating tension and conflict. Even if you win a competition, you may not want to accept the prize if the terms and conditions are not acceptable. Your time might be better spent elsewhere. Weigh the pros and cons before investing the time and effort.

Business Plan and Venture Competitions

Numerous business plan and venture-funding competitions are held each year for young people, undergraduate students, graduate students (primarily MBAs), and nonstudent professionals. Many business schools and classes hold internal competitions and then advance winners to regional, national, and even international events. Prizes may range from $500 to

Exhibit 4-6 *Venture presentation tips.*

Timing	• Be prompt and ready to start on time. • Use the entire time allocated and use it productively.
Audience	• Know your audience and tailor the presentation accordingly. • Establish rapport with the audience.
Presentation Style	• Dress appropriately and maintain a professional demeanor. • Be enthusiastic, but not artificial or arrogant. • Use proper pronunciation and language.
Presentation Contents	• Create a "hook" to capture the audience quickly. • Hit the highlights without going into excessive detail. • Keep it simple by emphasizing key points and avoiding technical jargon and acronyms that will lose your audience's interest. • Use visual aids, such as slides and sample or prototype products, to reinforce your message without distracting from it. • Emphasize the benefits of the opportunity so that they are absolutely clear to the audience. • Conclude with a "Thank You."
Follow-Up	• Expect and prepare for questions. Be thoughtful and positive in your responses. • Contact each audience member to move toward your goals.

Source: Adapted from Thomas W. Zimmerer and Norman M. Scarborough, *Essentials of Entrepreneurship and Small Business Management*, 5th ed. (Upper Saddle River, NJ: Prentice Hall, 2007).

financing and professional services packages worth millions. A list of regional, national, and international competitions for undergraduate and graduate students can be found in **Exhibit 4-7**.

Chapter Summary

Now that you have studied this chapter, you can do the following:

1. Know what a business plan is and describe it:
   - a road map to success,
   - a history and a plan for an organization, and
   - meeting the needs of various audiences.
2. Explain the various purposes of a business plan and the audiences for it.
   - A business plan is used by entrepreneurs to organize their thoughts before starting a business and to determine business viability.
   - It can be used to raise money from investors and lenders. Almost always, bankers and other potential investors will refuse to consider funding an entrepreneur who does not have a business plan.
   - It can help guide the operation of the business.
3. Understand the components of a business plan.

   The parts of a business plan include a cover page; table of contents; executive summary; mission, vision, and culture; company description; opportunity analysis; marketing strategy and plan; management and operations; financial analysis and projections; funding request; and exit strategy.

Exhibit 4-7 *Business plan and venture competitions for undergraduate and graduate students.*

Competition	Host/Sponsor	Web Site
Camino Real Venture Competition	University of Texas at El Paso	caminorealcompetition.org
Cardinal Challenge Business Plan Competition	University of Louisville	business.louisville.edu
CEO Best Elevator Pitch Competition	Collegiate Entrepreneurs, Organization	www.c-e-o.org
Conquest	Birla Institute of Technology & Science, Pilani, India	www.celbits.org/conquest
Emerging Business Leaders Summit (EBLS) Business Plan Competition	Minority Business Development Agency	www.medweek.gov
FGV Latin Moot Corp Competition	Fundacäo Getulio Vargas, Säo Paulo, Brazil	Latinmootcorp2.fgv.br
Global MOOT Corp Competition	University of Texas at Austin	www.mootcorp.org
Global Social Venture Competition	University of California at Berkeley, London Business School, Columbia University, Indian School of Business, Thammasat University	www.gsvc.org
IBK Capital Ivey Business Plan Competition	University of Western Ontario	www.iveybpc.com
Idea to Product Competition (I2P)	University of Texas at Austin	www.ideatoproduct.org
International Business Plan Competition	University of San Francisco	www.usfca.edu/IBPC/
McGinnis Venture Competition	Carnegie Mellon University	www.mcginnisventurecompetition.com
Nascent 500	Ball State University	www.bsu.edu/entrepreneurship/nascent500
New Venture Championship	University of Oregon	www.oregonnvc.com
New Ventures World Competition	University of Nebraska at Lincoln	www.cba.unl.edu/outreach/ent/bpc
OFC Venture Challenge	Clark Atlanta University	www.ofcvc.org
Rice Business Plan Competition	Rice University	www.alliance.rice.edu/alliance/RBPC.asp
Spirit of Enterprise MBA Business Plan Competition	University of Cincinnati	www.uc.edu/ecenter/
Stuart Clark Venture Challenge	University of Manitoba	www.umanitoba.ca
Thammasat Asia Moot Corp Competition	Thammasat University, Thailand	www.asiamootcorp.org
The John Heine Entrepreneurial Challenge	Queensland University of Technology, Australia	www.johnheinechallenge.org
Uniandes Moot Corp Business Plan Competition	Universidad de los Andes, Colombia	Mootcorp.uniandes.edu.co
Utah Entrepreneur Challenge	University of Utah	www.uec.utah.edu
Venture Challenge	San Diego State University	www-rohan.sdsu.edu/dept/emc/
Wake Forest Elevator Corp.	Wake Forest University	www.mba.wfu.edu
West Virginia Statewide Collegiate Business Plan Competition	West Virginia University	www.be.wvu.edu/bpc/

Sources: Compiled and updated from www.Mootcorp.org and Mark Cannice, "Getting in on the University Business Plan Competition Circuit," *Entrepreneur*, October 19, 2009.

4. Be able to demonstrate proper development and formatting.
   A solid, viable business plan that is sloppy and filled with errors may be rejected on that basis alone. The business plan should be well organized, neatly presented, and written in correct English.

Key Terms

advertising
asset
balance sheet
breakeven point
business plan
cash flow statement
competitive analysis
culture
direct marketing
elevator pitch
environmental analysis
feasibility analysis
income statement
profit and loss statement (P&L)
industry analysis
initial public offering (IPO)
liability
marketing mix
marketing plan
mission
mission statement
net worth
owner's equity
proof of market
public relations
publicity
target market
vision

Entrepreneurship Portfolio

Critical Thinking Exercises

1. Shawn is creating a business that provides advertising on public restroom stall doors. He is funding the project from his personal savings of $5000 and does not expect to use any outside financing. Should he create a business plan? Why or why not?
2. Charity and Devon are planning to license technology from NASA that would make it impossible to accidentally lock a child in a car. The technology is complex, and the market analysis and financial assumptions take up a lot of pages. The two women have written an 80-page business plan. Explain your concerns about the length of the plan in light of the chapter text.
3. What factors make the difference between a good business plan and an excellent one? (Hint: Use the chapter data and rules from competitions.)
4. Visit an Internet shopping site such as the Home Shopping Network (*http://www.HSN.com*) or QVC (*http://www.QVC.com*). Select five products that are being sold that you find interesting or unusual. Make a list of the products and your explanation of the market opportunities they reflect.
5. How does the following statement apply to business plans? Errors of omission can sometimes be greater than errors of commission.

Key Concept Questions

1. Explain why the executive summary is the most important section of any business plan.
2. One mistake entrepreneurs make in their business plans is that of only including an income statement. What other financial statements should be incorporated and why?
3. Print your assignment with 1-inch margins, double spaced, using 12-point Times New Roman. Then, print the same document with 0.8-inch margins, single spaced, using the 10-point Arial typeface. Which is easier to read? Why? How does this relate to business plans?
4. Name three categories of investors/lenders that might have an interest in your business plan.
5. How can spending time researching and writing a business plan save an entrepreneur time and money in the short and long term?
6. Why is it important to identify a business's culture from the beginning?

Application Exercises

Visit or call (visit after calling) an entrepreneur in your community to discuss business plans.

a. Ask whether he or she wrote a business plan before starting the business. Since then?
b. If he or she did write a plan, for what has it been used?
c. If he or she did not write a plan, why not?
d. Did the owner have any assistance in writing or reviewing the plan?
e. If so, what was the source of assistance?

Exploring Online

Find a business plan on the Internet (not on the Business Plan Pro disk). Examine it to see whether it follows the guidelines provided in this text. Use a highlighter to mark the sections of the plan that are present. Then, make a list of missing or incomplete sections. Indicate how it does/does not follow the rules for formatting and content. Is the plan viable? Why or why not? Would you invest in it? Why or why not?

In Your Opinion

If an entrepreneur presents a business plan that an investor believes is deliberately vague and has provided inflated financial statements, what should that investor do?

FASTSIGNS—Finding Opportunity in Technology

Small Business School **video clip titles are in red**

Gary Salomon, cofounder and Chairman of the Board

This business began on the back of a paper napkin at a breakfast discussion. Gary Salomon had seen the way a computer could make high-quality signs in hours, instead of the days required for traditional production. He jumped at the opportunity to build a business offering this service internationally. Today, the company he founded in 1985 in Dallas, Texas, FASTSIGNS, is America's leading sign company and has over 550 locations worldwide.

The typical FASTSIGNS is located in a strip shopping center, making it easily accessible to attract both business and consumer sales.

MAKE THE OLD NEW

Salomon did his research and knew that the sign industry does $5.5 billion in U.S. sales annually. He also learned that the temporary sign business is a niche that big companies weren't interested in. The old-fashioned, hand-done methods were too expensive for people who just want to stick a sign in their yard announcing, "Garage Sale Today."

Keep Your Eyes Open to Spot Opportunity

Salomon saw the technology he now uses while he was making a sales call for the first company he owned. He struck a deal with the inventor and with vision and sweat equity, he now dominates the marketplace. There are two ways to look at the word, "owns." You can own something in the legal sense, meaning you have the patent or copyright to a product or idea, which entitles you to use the courts to stop others from profiting from your invention. Another way to look at this word is in the light of the marketplace. If the marketplace thinks of you when they think of a product or service, you *own* it.

Buy Someone Else's Idea

FASTSIGNS acquired the legal right to use the technology because the inventor only wanted to use it in his one location. Salomon wanted to take the idea international. He recognized that the technology was not being fully exploited by the inventor, and negotiated a deal to get access. There were multiple ways for Salomon to do this. He could have paid a fee for usage, he could have made the inventor a part owner of the company, or he could have bought out the inventor.

Often inventors are reluctant to do these things because they think that the idea is everything. However, as veteran entrepreneur, Bill Tobin, told the *Small Business School,* the idea is two percent of the success of a business. Certainly a business needs the right idea at the right time, but to exploit the idea, to deliver it to customers who are happy to pay for it, a business has to have what Salomon brought to FASTSIGNS . . . vision, money, and the drive to develop sales and marketing.

Salomon not only owns the technology he uses, the growth and sales of FASTSIGNS tells us that he owns the mindshare of consumers. From the beginning, FASTSIGNS has been the leader in its niche as measured by locations and sales. You have to own an idea legally to grow a business. It's even better if you can own the business from the marketplace point of view, as does Salomon.

Put Skin in the Game

Gary Salomon and his partners, Steve Mailman and Bob Schanbaum, put together about $40,000 by pooling their own savings and by getting a small bank loan to open up the first FASTSIGNS store. They decided if this one location generated $15,000 per month in sales within the first year, they would go forward with the idea to grow using a franchise model. Starting a business is difficult, and money flows out before it flows in, so Salomon kept his job for ten months and used his paychecks plus savings to take care of his personal bills.

CREATE A NEW BREED OF OWNERS

Salomon could see by operating the first FASTSIGNS himself exactly what needed to be done to make profits. He codified all of his activities and created systems so that he could then teach others to do exactly what he had done. This effort prepared him to grow the business by selling franchises. Each initial franchise fee fuels the home office with cash, and the monthly fees support all of the marketing and training provided by the home office to each owner in the field. These revenues reduce the need for external financing.

Just as Salomon targeted his service to a small niche of the sign business, he targeted his franchise sales efforts. He never tried to find every person who was thinking they wanted to own a business. From the beginning, he reached out to sell franchises to engineers, CPAs, experienced managers, and even bankers, because people with these types of backgrounds thrive on systems. They find comfort in knowing precisely how someone else achieved success.

The general pool of people who want to own their own business is heavily weighted with the type of person who wants to act independently and create one's personal rules. These folks can be renegades and too creative to be happy following a system laid out by someone else. Salomon saved time and money by determining in advance who would make the best owner of a FASTSIGNS franchise.

FASTSIGNS franchisee

Let Go to Grow

Small Business School taped a FASTSIGNS corporate meeting and found that Salomon focused on listening. He told me that when he was running the first store he could keep his finger on all the activities, and with just four to five employees he knew what every person on the payroll was accomplishing. Now he has to listen to and give a lot of authority to managers.

Salomon said, "When you have a staff of 75–80 you've got to work through people, and you've got to make the shift from being an entrepreneur to being more of an organized business. That's a threshold that I had a great deal of difficulty with coming through many years ago. I finally decided to stop meddling with what they were doing.

"In the beginning I had to keep everything in my head and after a while it became evident that while that fed my ego it didn't allow the people that I had hired, put in place, and paid a decent wage to be able to be fulfilled by what they were doing. Because you put people in place you have to let them do their job properly. The more people we attracted over time the more I was looking for the areas that I was not really the best at. I'm great at ideas, I'm great at marketing, and I'm great at sales. But when it comes to the day-in-and-day-out activities of management, that's not my bailiwick."

Check Your Ego at the Door

By admitting to his weaknesses, Gary Salomon cleared a hurdle most owners either don't try to jump over, or they try and fail. He was able to stop doing and start leading. He said, "I try to keep things as simple as possible. Basically, I try to have people get the feedback they need in order to be as productive as possible and I try to reward accordingly. I think the bottom line is I don't have much of an ego. I'm not really interested in as much being right as I am interested in having the best result or the best solution, and if it's not my idea, I really don't care. I'd rather it just be, you know, the best idea.

"When you have that attitude, people aren't afraid of giving you an opinion, because they know they're not going to be shot down. And as a matter of fact, you know, while I sometimes have some excellent ideas, I'm sometimes shown the door, in a manner of speaking, as to how unreasonable that idea might be. But what it does is, is it fosters the ongoing embracing of ideas coming from other people, because they know that it's going to be considered, and that we mean it.

"So, you know, does that necessarily mean that you always get the right solution to a problem? No. But at least people aren't afraid of offering it. And I think that, you know, compensation is a part of keeping good, quality folks, but it's not really the top item. It's creating an environment where people feel like they can make a difference, and that they're being listened to."

Salomon leads people by laying out the plans in writing, then giving them the freedom to succeed or fail. He doesn't depend upon a big personality to win people over to his side. Gary Salomon found a technology with promise and used his leadership skills and abilities to form a team that took advantage of the technology to develop a market.

Case Questions

1. How did Gary Salomon exploit an opportunity to start FASTSIGNS?
2. What are some of the keys to Salomon's success with FASTSIGNS?
3. How did the founders finance the start-up of FASTSIGNS?
4. How was FASTSIGNS's growth financed?
5. Why would an inventor sell the rights to an idea?
6. Why do you think people might enjoy working for Salomon in the corporate office?

Case prepared by Hattie Bryant, creator of *Small Business School*, the television series made for PBS and Voice of America, http://SmallBusinessSchool.org

UNIT 2

WHO ARE YOUR CUSTOMERS?

Chapter 5

CREATING BUSINESS FROM OPPORTUNITY

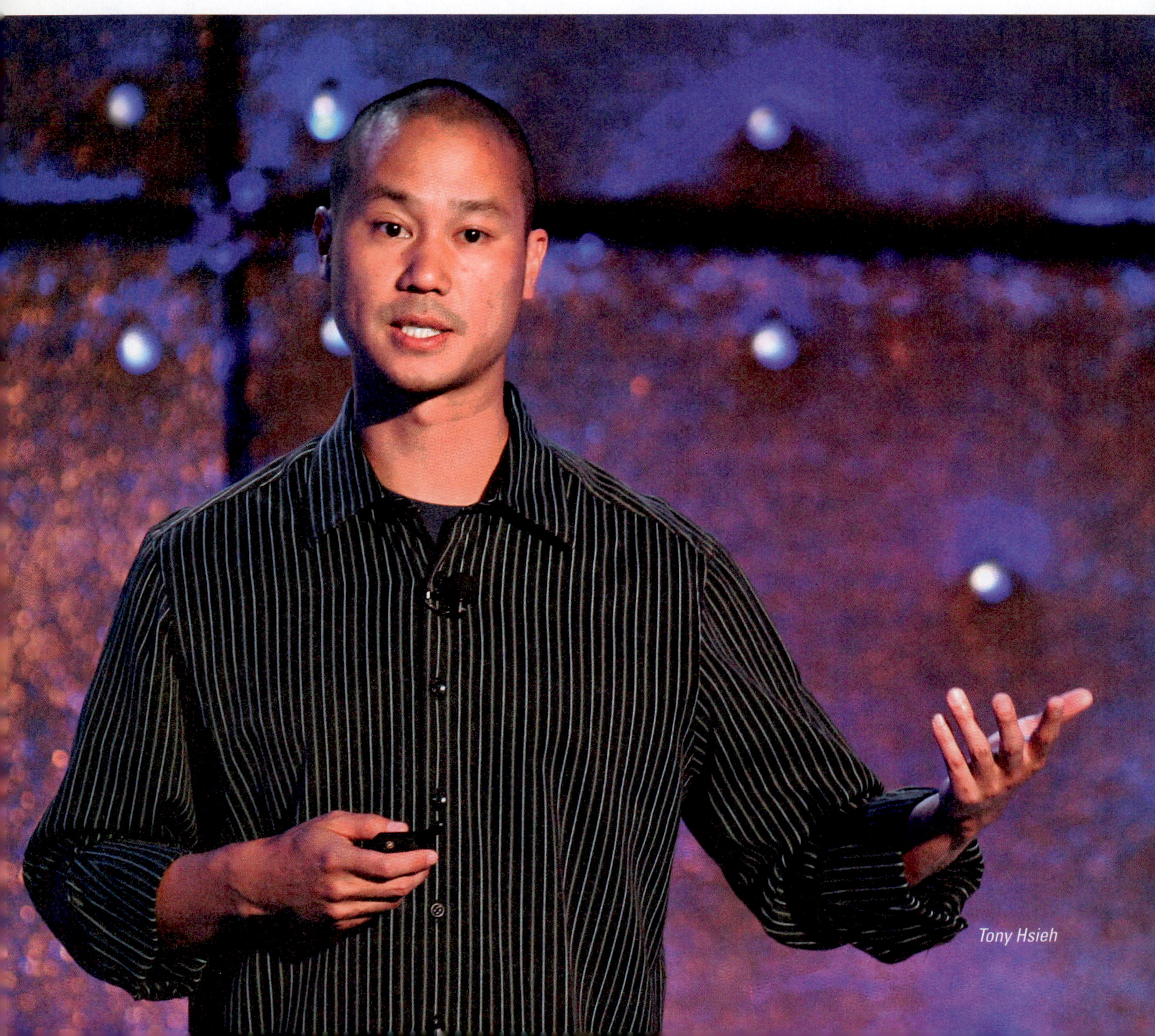

Tony Hsieh

> **"Problems are only opportunities in work clothes."**
>
> —Henry J. Kaiser, American industrialist

Entrepreneurs find and take advantage of opportunities that others don't recognize or cannot access the resources to exploit. When Zappos.com founder Nick Swinmurn became frustrated by looking for shoes in a mall and online, he saw an opportunity to create an online megastore with a multitude of sizes, styles, and colors. Swinmurn was three years out of college when he launched Shoesite.com, with $150,000 in 1999. Within a month, he relaunched as Zappos.com. In 2000, Tony Hsieh of Venture Frog Incubators saw the opportunity in Zappos, investing $1.1 million and joining Swinmurn. The company thrives on providing the best selection and service with a focus on the "wow" factor. Zappos.com carries more than 1100 brands, stocks more than 3 million shoes, employs more than 1300 people, and has annual revenues in excess of $1 billion.[1]

Performance Objectives

1. Define your business.
2. Articulate your core beliefs, mission, and vision.
3. Analyze your competitive advantage.
4. Perform viability testing using the economics of one unit.

Apple and the Personal Computer

market a group of people or organizations that may be interested in buying a given product or service, has the resources to purchase it, and is permitted by law and regulation to do so.

In 1943, IBM's founder Thomas Watson said, "I think there is a world market for about five computers." A **market** is a group of people or organizations that may be interested in buying a given product or service, has the resources to purchase it, and is permitted by law and regulation to do so. When Watson made his statement, computers were forbiddingly large and expensive machines that only the government, universities, and a few giant corporations could afford. That was the market for computers at the time.

By the 1970s, however, a few people were talking about creating personal computers. These enthusiasts were outside of mainstream thinking. One such visionary was Stephen Wozniak, who had landed his first job at Hewlett-Packard, then as now, a major company. He was also attending meetings of the Homebrew Club, a Palo Alto-based group of electronics hobbyists. Wozniak was determined to build a small, personal computer to show the club members, using existing technology. He believed that there was a much larger market for hobbyist computers than IBM and Hewlett-Packard thought. Tandy, Hewlett-Packard, and IBM all had personal computers on the market, but not of the sort Wozniak envisioned.

Wozniak offered Hewlett-Packard a chance to codevelop his small computer. The company was not focused on desktop computing, and the technology did not fit within its computer or calculator strategies, so they turned him down. Wozniak's friend Steve Jobs also was interested in the technology, and set out to sell some hobbyist computers. Jobs sold 100 circuit boards to a local start-up computer shop, and then Wozniak, Jobs, and three helpers soldered together components in the garage of Jobs' home in Cupertino, California.

[1]Zappos.com, Inc., http://www.zappos.com (accessed February 12, 2010).

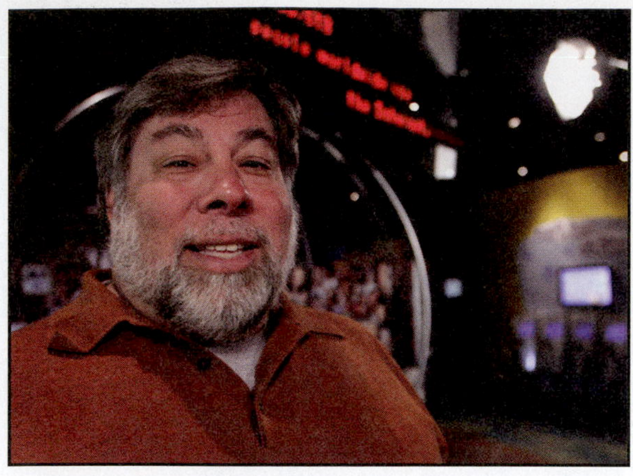

Apple cofounder Stephen Wozniak.

Wozniak worked on his design concepts until he created the Apple II, which could display pictures and text and is now considered one of the great achievements in the computer industry. Jobs, meanwhile, searched for an investor. Finally, after being turned down by friends and family, he found Mike Markkula, who also saw the possibilities of Apple. Markkula agreed to invest $80,000 in the company in return for a significant share of equity. He also put together Apple's business plan and worked to secure additional investors. This is a classic demonstration of entrepreneurs recognizing opportunities that others do not see.

By 1984, Apple had sales of $1.5 billion, and over $42 billion in fiscal year 2009. Wozniak and Jobs recognized an opportunity that led to a product that satisfied the needs of an enormous market that the giants of the industry did not recognize.

Business Definition

In order to operate a successful enterprise, you will need to be able to provide a complete company description. This description should include the need for your product or service that is either unsatisfied by the current players in the market or is something you can provide better, differently, or more economically.

Before you can start a business, you must define it in several dimensions. The *business definition* answers three questions: who, what, and how?

1. **Who** will the business serve? In other words, who are the potential qualified customers in the market for your product or service? They may not currently recognize a need for your specific product or service, but they are in the market for the products or services of your competition.
2. **What** will the business offer the customers? What is the complete bundle of products or services your enterprise will provide? This should address not only the tangible product or intangible service but the benefits it will bring. For example, a mattress store sells "restful sleep" rather than just mattresses.
3. **How** will the business provide the products or services it offers? What are the primary actions and activities required to conduct this business? All businesses must produce a product or service, sell it to a customer, deliver it, and receive payment. This part of the business definition includes the primary activities of
   - buying or developing or manufacturing the product;
   - identifying its potential qualified customers and selling the product to them;
   - producing and delivering the product or service; and
   - receiving payment.

Performance Objective 1 Define your business.

A solid business definition has three elements:

1. ***The Offer.*** What will you sell to your customers? That is called your *offer*, and includes exactly which products and services you will bring to the market and how you will price them. For example, you will provide online and telephone fitness consulting service for an initial four-week period at $25 per week, or eight weeks at $20 per week.

2. ***Target Market.*** Which segment of the consumer market are you aiming to serve? As discussed in Chapter 4, this is your *target market.* Defining your target market in a way that will help you identify potential customers is an important factor in achieving success. This definition must be precise enough so that you can identify a viable market for the business and focus your marketing efforts. A target market of every adult in the United States is clearly too broad and unfocused. A market of every member of Congress from the state of Rhode Island (three individuals) would be too narrow.
3. ***Production and Delivery Capability.*** How will you provide your offer to your targeted customers? This includes how to perform the key activities required to produce the product or service, deliver it to your customers, and ensure that they are satisfied.

Apple began as a manufacturing business, making a product. There are four basic types of businesses:

1. **Manufacturing** produces a tangible product and sells it, either through distributors or directly to end customers.
2. **Wholesale** buys in bulk from manufacturers and sells smaller quantities to retailers.
3. **Retail** sells individual items to consumers.
4. **Service** sells an intangible product to businesses or consumers.

manufacturing making or producing a tangible product.

wholesale buying in bulk from manufacturers and selling smaller quantities to retailers.

retail selling individual items to consumers.

What Sort of Organization Do You Want?

Each organization has the opportunity to create a unique mission, vision, and culture that are supported by its core values. The founding team can determine how to use the company's competitive advantage to satisfy customers. Culture can be shaped according to the environment and how employees, customers, and other stakeholders are treated—an example that is set by the entrepreneur (owner).

Performance Objective 2

Articulate your core beliefs, mission, and vision.

Your Company's Core Values

When you start your own company, what beliefs will you use to guide it? These are the **core values** of your business. Core values include the fundamental ethical and moral philosophy and beliefs that form the foundation of the organization and provide broad guidance for all decision making.

Examples of the core values of a business might be

- "At Superior Printing, we engage in business practices that affect the environment as little as possible."
- "At Sheila's Restaurant, we believe in supporting local organic farmers."

core values the fundamental ethical and moral philosophy and beliefs that form the foundation of the organization, and provide broad guidance for all decision making.

Exercise

Imagine you are Nick Swinmurn of Zappos.com. On a separate sheet of paper, define your business:

1. Who will the business serve?
2. What will the business offer? What are the products (or services) the business will sell?
3. How will the business provide the products or services it offers? What are the primary actions and activities required to conduct this business?

Core values will affect business decisions. The owner of Superior Printing, for example, will choose ink that is less harmful to the environment over a cheaper ink that is more harmful. Superior Printing may also have a paper-recycling program, to minimize its paper consumption. The owner of Sheila's Restaurant will buy fruits and vegetables from local organic farmers. Your core beliefs will affect everything, from the cost of materials to the prices you charge and how you treat customers. For additional examples of core values, see **Exhibit 5-1**.

Your Company's Mission Is to Satisfy Customers

The mission of your business, expressed in a *mission statement*, is a concise communication of your purpose, business definition, and values. The function of a mission statement is to clarify what the business is trying to do in the present, but it can provide direction and motivation for future action through a clear and compelling message.

As noted in Chapter 4, a well-crafted mission statement will not only tell your customers and employees what your business is about but can (and should) be a guide for every decision you make. It should capture your passion for the business and your commitment to satisfying your customers. A mission statement should be limited to 40 or 50 words to compel clarity in concept and expression. The mission statement should address the following topics: target customers; products and services;

Exhibit 5-1 *Core values.*

Tyson Foods Inc.

Based on our heritage of more than 65 years, these are the core values that we strongly believe in (listed in alphabetical order):

- *Brand Excellence*
- *Commitment, Fun and Opportunity*
- *Environmental, Food Safety and Team Member Safety Responsibility*
- *Family and Social Responsibility*
- *Innovation*
- *Integrity*
- *Market and Customer Focus*
- *Self-leadership and Learning*
- *Teamwork*

Dow AgroSciences

To ensure the prosperity and well-being of Dow AgroSciences employees, customers and shareholders, cumulative long-term profit growth is essential. How we achieve this objective is as important as the objective itself. Fundamental to our success are the core values we believe in and practice.

- *Employees are the source of Dow AgroSciences success. We communicate openly, treat each other with respect, promote teamwork, and encourage personal initiative and growth. Excellence in performance is rewarded.*
- *Customers receive our strongest commitment to meet their needs with high quality products and superior service.*
- *Products are based on innovative technology, continuous improvement, and added value for our customers and end users.*
- *Our conduct demonstrates a deep concern for human safety and environmental stewardship, while embracing the highest standards of ethics and citizenship.*

DuPont Company

Safety, concern and care for people, protection of the environment and personal and corporate integrity, are this company's highest values, and we will not compromise them.

Exhibit 5-2 *Mission statements.*

Nike—*Crush Reebok.*

Walt Disney—*To make people happy.*

W.L. Gore & Associates—*Our products are designed to be the highest quality in their class and revolutionary in their effect.*

Slumber Parties, Inc.—*We seek to empower women at every stage of life through our products, demonstrations and careers. To achieve this goal, we offer women the opportunity to become more confident and satisfied in all aspects of their lives.*

DuPont—*Sustainable Growth: Increasing shareholder and societal value while reducing our environmental footprint*

Dell Computers—*With the power of direct and Dell's team of talented people, we are able to provide customers with superb value; high quality; relevant technology; customized systems; superior service and support; and products and services that are easy to buy and use.*

markets served; use of technology; importance of public issues and employees; and focus on survival, profitability, and growth.

Here is an example of a mission statement for the Most Chocolate Cake Company:

> *The Most Chocolate Cake Company will create the richest, tastiest, most chocolaty cakes in our area. They will be made from the finest and freshest ingredients with our own special frostings and fillings. Baked to order and individually decorated for that special occasion, they will make any event as special as our cakes!*

The Most Chocolate Cake Company's mission statement defines the business and its competitive advantage, the core of its strategy. Examples of mission statements from a range of organizations appear in **Exhibit 5-2**.

Your Company's Vision Is the Broader Perspective

The *vision* for your business is broader and more comprehensive than its mission, painting a picture of the overall view of what you want your organization to become in the future, not what it is at the moment. It is built upon the core values and belief systems of the organization. It should energize your people, and they should embrace it with enthusiasm and passion. This means that the vision has to be compelling across the organization. It has to matter. Employees need to be empowered to fulfill the vision. Examples of vision statements for various organizations appear in **Exhibit 5-3**.

Your Company's Culture Defines the Work Environment

The culture of an organization is largely shaped by its leadership. *Culture* is the core values of the organization in action. Leaders of a company build a particular culture by making the beliefs, values, and behavioral norms explicit and intentional. Culture includes factors such as risk tolerance and innovation; orientation with respect to people, teams, and outcomes; attention to detail; and communications norms. Organizational culture is learned by members of the team in a number of ways, including anecdotes, ceremonies and events, material symbols, and particular use of language. For example, at General Electric, stories of Jack Welch are legendary. At Hewlett-Packard there was the Hewlett-Packard Way, based on anecdotes passed down from employee to employee. Those who work in small enterprises often see the top management daily and take their cues directly

Exhibit 5-3 *Vision statements.*

Caterpillar—*Be a global leader in customer value.*

McDonald's—*Our vision is to be the world's best quick service restaurant experience. Being the best means providing outstanding quality, service, cleanliness, and value, so that we make every customer in every restaurant smile.*

General Motors—*GM's vision is to be the world leader in transportation products and related services. We will earn our customers' enthusiasm through continuous improvement driven by the integrity, teamwork, and innovation of GM people.*

Bimbo Bakeries USA—*To be the baking leader in the United States through quality, freshness, service and the building of our brands.*

DuPont Company—*Our vision is to be the world's most dynamic science company, creating sustainable solutions essential to a better, safer, healthier life for people everywhere.*

Cargill—*Our purpose is to be the global leader in nourishing people. We will harness our knowledge and energy to provide goods and services that are necessary for life, health and growth.*

because there are very few or no layers between them. As enterprises become larger, leaders frequently take on larger-than-life roles through stories.

Ceremonies can make a significant difference in a company's culture. Are there regular recognition events for innovation? Does the company invite family members to events throughout the year? Is there a birthday celebration for each employee? Are years of service recognized? Material symbols come in many shapes and forms. At the Wilmington, Delaware, headquarters of Legacy MBNA America, the values of the company appear on every archway, and handprints of the employees make colorful wall art in some buildings. At any business, reserved parking spots and special privileges for certain employees send a message to everyone. Are these spaces for top executives? Expectant mothers? Are office sizes determined by pay grade? Finally, language tells a lot about the culture. Is everyone on a first-name basis with everyone else? Are some people addressed informally and others not? Is the language around the company in general formal or informal? Is communication respectful?

These and many other factors are all part of the culture of an organization. Culture should be crafted to follow core beliefs and support the mission and vision of the business.

The Decision Process

Translating opportunity into success can and has happened in literally millions of different ways. Each business has a different story. However, there are three primary routes in the deliberate-search process to identify opportunities:

- The entrepreneur looks for business opportunities through a process of identification and selection, beginning with self-developed (or group-developed) ideas.
- The entrepreneur uses essentially the same process but starts with research on hot businesses or growth areas.
- The entrepreneur has an idea for a product or service and searches for a market.

In each case, a decision is made based on personal values and thinking. Whereas each ultimately funnels the procedure down to a business concept, the processes are repeated, often with many ideas being considered before a viable picture emerges. The first two options are market driven, and the third is product driven. Entrepreneurs do better looking to the market(s) of

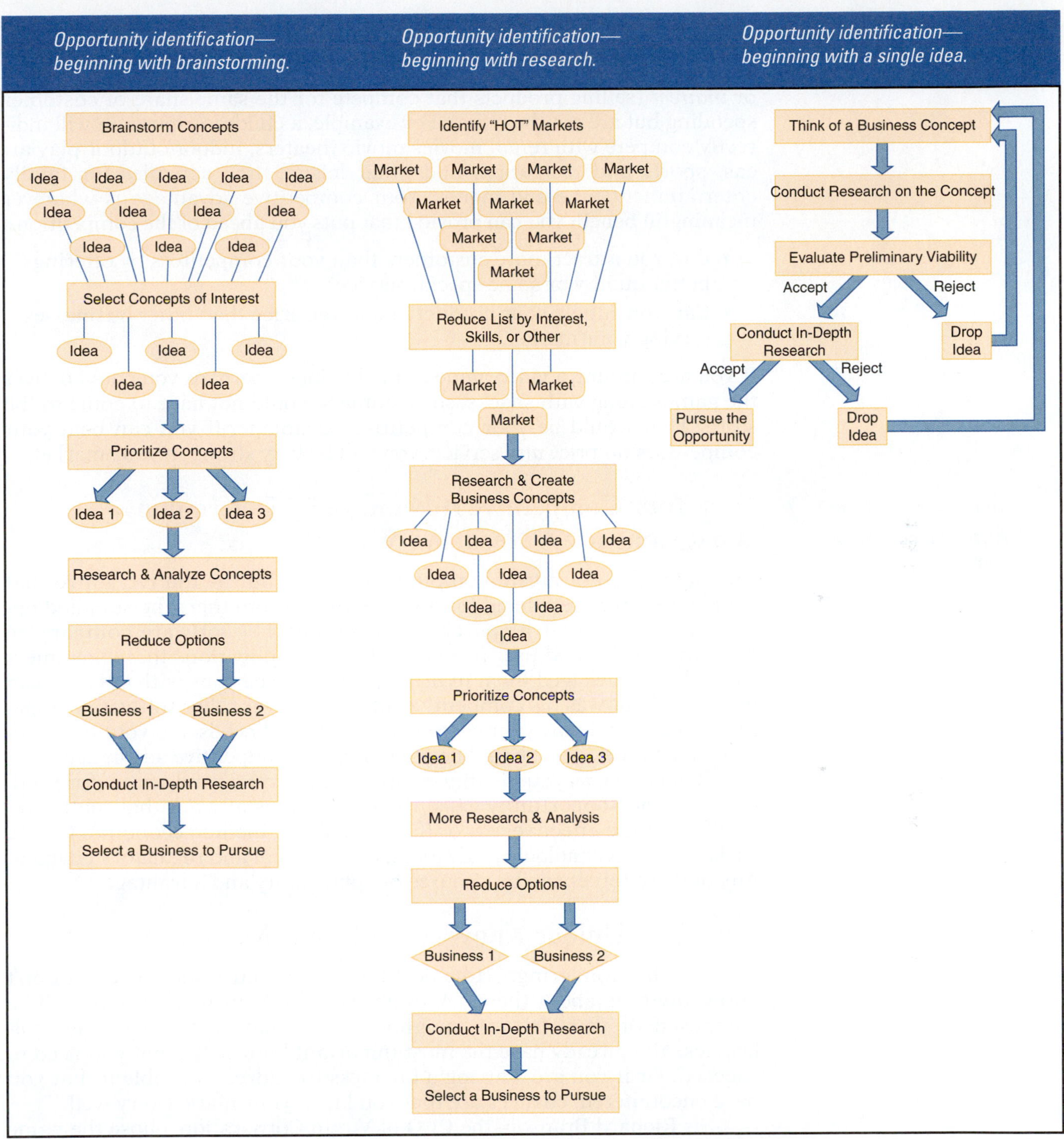

interest, rather than creating a product and then trying to find a customer base. You can do this all alone, but it is best to work with others who will provide honest, constructive feedback.

Your Competitive Advantage

For your business to be successful and to fulfill your mission and vision, you will need a strategy for beating the competition. This is your *competitive advantage,* or core competency. It is whatever you can do better than the competition that will attract a sufficient number of customers to your business so it can succeed. The competitive advantage must be *sustainable* in order to create long-term viability. Your competition is defined by your target market and can be *direct* (selling the same or similar products to the same market) or *indirect* (selling products that compete for the same share of customer spending but are not the same). For example, a children's museum will indirectly compete with rental movies/movie theaters, indoor/outdoor play areas, sports and recreation, and other leisure-time activities for family entertainment time and money. Your competitive advantage is whatever meaningful benefit you can provide that puts you ahead of the competition.

- Can you attract more customers than your competitors by offering better quality or some special service?
- Can you supply your product at a lower price than other businesses serving your market?

If you are running a video game rental business, perhaps you could deliver the games along with snacks, so customers would not have to come to the store. That would be your competitive advantage. If you can beat your competitors on price *and* service, you will be very strong in your market.

Performance Objective 3

Analyze your competitive advantage.

Find Your Competitive Advantage by Determining What Consumers Need and Want

Bill Gates did not invent computer software, but he did recognize that people were frustrated and intimidated by it. From there, he supplied operating systems that he purchased from another software company to IBM, and he created user-friendly software applications that consumers wanted and packaged them in bright, attractive cartons with easy-to-read manuals. That was his competitive advantage over other software companies. When you know your customers' wants and needs and your competitors' capabilities, you should be able to find a competitive advantage.

Remember, as you identify environmental trends and search for product or service-opportunity gaps, there are forces at work that matter regardless of the effectiveness of the idea. These include economic forces, social forces, technological advances, and political and regulatory changes. Any of these forces can be a source of opportunity and advantage.

You Have Unique Knowledge of Your Market

You may be wondering: "How do I figure what customers need? I don't know anything about them." Actually, you do. Your market may well be composed of your friends, neighbors, classmates, relatives, and colleagues. You already have the most important knowledge that you need to succeed. Or if you are starting a business to address a problem that you have encountered, chances are that you know your market very well.

Sir Richard Branson, the CEO of Virgin Corporation, chose the name "Virgin" for his company because it reflected his total inexperience in business. His empire, which includes Virgin Megastores, Virgin Atlantic Airways, and Virgin Mobile, began as a tiny discount mail-order record company, which he started at age 19 after he had dropped out of high school. "I realized I'd be hopeless at studying," Branson told *Woman's Journal* magazine in 1985. "So I quit to do something I knew I could do and which interested me." Branson knew his market—other young people who were into music—very well. Then, he learned about the other markets that he entered.

How will you know if a business idea is going to be successful? You cannot have a guarantee, but your market will tell you a lot about your chances. The answer will come in the form of the signal called *profit*.

Step into the Shoes...

SoftTribe Founders See That Tropical Tolerance Is Needed for Software in Ghana

Hermann Chinery-Hesse and Joe Jackson saw an opportunity in the need for software that has tropical tolerance when they cofounded SoftTribe in 1991. The company develops software, taking into consideration the unique requirements of the Western African social and business environment. According to their partner, Microsoft, "The SoftTribe software is practical and resilient, functional under conditions of intermittent connectivity, power fluctuations, low bandwidth, and operators who, as a rule, are less familiar with computing than in some other parts of the world."[2]

Chinery-Hesse has been called the Bill Gates of Ghana for his success in building this company and for his desire to "spark an entrepreneurial revolution in Africa by bringing e-commerce to the most remote corners of the continent."[3] SoftTribe is the largest software company and is a Microsoft partner to permit its expansion having found opportunities in sub-Saharan Africa.

You can learn a lot about the potential for success well ahead of starting your enterprise through customer and market research, in addition to competitive analysis.

The Six Factors of Competitive Advantage

Competitive advantage comes from one (or a combination) of six factors:

1. ***Quality.*** Can you provide higher quality than competing businesses?
2. ***Price.*** Can you offer a lower price on a sustained basis than your competition?
3. ***Location.*** Can you find a more convenient location for customers?
4. ***Selection.*** Can you provide a wider range of choices than your competitors can?
5. ***Service.*** Can you provide better, more personalized customer service?
6. ***Speed/Turnaround.*** Can you deliver your product or service more quickly than the competition?

Is Your Competitive Advantage Strong Enough?

When deciding whether or not your business concept is viable, it will be essential to determine your competitive advantage and whether it is strong enough. According to Jeffry Timmons,[4] a successful company needs the following:

- ***To sell to a market that is large and growing.*** The market for digital cameras is a good example. New products are being marketed to meet the demand, such as printers that turn digital photos into prints with digital photo frames.
- ***To sell to a market where the competition is able to make a profit.*** It will be interesting to observe what happens in the market for hybrid cars. Right now the jury is out as to whether the companies manufacturing them can make a profit, so most automakers are not yet entering the field. There may not be a sufficiently large market at present to make entry worthwhile.

[2]"Taking African Business Global," Microsoft Unlimited Potential, http://www.microsoft.com/unlimitedpotential/ (accessed January 13, 2010).

[3]Max Chafkin, "Meet the Bill Gates of Ghana," *Inc.*, October 1, 2008, http://www.inc.com/magazine/20081001/ (accessed January 13, 2010).

[4]Jeffry A. Timmons, *New Venture Creation*, 6th ed. (New York: McGraw-Hill/Irwin, 2003).

Entrepreneurial Wisdom...

A new business usually will require time before it can turn a profit. Federal Express, in fact, suffered initial losses of a million dollars a month! But if you are not making enough money to stay in business, that is the market speaking. It is telling you that your business is not satisfying consumer needs well enough. Do not take it personally. Many famous entrepreneurs opened and closed a number of businesses during their lifetime.

Henry Ford failed in business twice before the Ford Motor Company was a success. If you want to be a successful entrepreneur, start growing a thick skin and decide right now that you intend to learn from failures and disappointments. Do not let them get you down. Most importantly, learn from them, so that you do not make the same mistakes again.

barriers to entry the factors that contribute to the ease or difficulty of a new competitor joining an established market.

- ***To sell to a market where the competition is succeeding but is not so powerful as to make it impossible for a new entrepreneur to enter.*** Microsoft has been taken to court several times by competitors who argue that it is so big that new software companies cannot enter the market. **Barriers to entry** are the factors that contribute to the ease or difficulty of a new competitor joining an established market, and they cannot be so high that market entry and success are not possible.
- ***To sell a product or service that solves problems consumers may have with the competition (such as poor quality or slow delivery).*** This is how FedEx beat its competition—the Flying Tigers, the U.S. Postal Service, and United Parcel Service (UPS)—when it entered the package-delivery market with its guaranteed overnight service.
- ***To sell a product or service at a competitive price that will attract customers.*** UPS fought back by offering a less-expensive overnight delivery service than FedEx's.

In addition to the above, it is also necessary to:

- understand the needs of your customers;
- have a sustainable competitive advantage or multiple advantages; and
- deliver a product or service that meets your customers' needs at the right price.

Checking Out the Competition

One useful exercise is to learn everything you can about particular competitors, especially those that have earned the respect of the marketplace. Try to identify the sources of their competitive advantage. Look at their Web sites. Conduct Internet searches. Track their advertising and promotion, including print, broadcast, Internet, and sponsorships. If they are retailers, shop their stores or have your friends and family do so. Get to know them, but do not do anything unethical or illegal to obtain information. You will also need to keep an eye on your competition *after* you have started your business, because new factors might undermine your competitive advantage.

Today's entrepreneurs, even those starting very small ventures, may face competition from far beyond their neighborhoods because customers can go shopping on the Web. Most entrepreneurs are *optimistic*. Optimism is a trait that goes with entrepreneurship, so they tend to get excited about the Web's potential customer base. What they often do not consider is that, "The world already is selling to their customers—aggressively and seamlessly."[5] Therefore, get online yourself and conduct a thorough search of your industry. You may find that there is literally a world of opportunity or, conversely, that the world is full of competitors.

[5]Fred Hapgood, "Foreign Exchange," *Inc.*, June 1997.

To determine whether you have a competitive advantage that will enable you to outperform your closest and strongest competitors, ask these questions:

- ***Competitive offers.*** How does your offer compare with those of your leading competitors? What are the key features of each?
- ***Unique selling proposition.*** Based on that comparison, what is your **unique selling proposition (USP)**, the distinctive feature and benefit that sets you apart from your competition? This will require a comparison of offers and identifying what is unique about yours. What is it about your offer that your competitors cannot or will not match?
- ***Cost structure.*** What is different about your business activities and the cost of doing business, compared to the competition? Overall, are you at a cost advantage or disadvantage?

unique selling proposition (USP) *the distinctive feature and benefit that sets a company apart from its competition.*

To be successful, you must have a USP that will attract customers to buy from you. Second, you must have a cost structure that is sufficiently advantageous so that, when all of your costs are deducted from your revenue, you will have sufficient profit left over. If you can achieve a cost advantage or at least minimize any cost disadvantage, this will help you achieve a profit. This profit is your reward for operating a successful business.

The Most Chocolate Cake Company

There are a number of ways to highlight your competitive advantage and to identify opportunities. In this example, Amy makes and sells chocolate cakes. She chose this product because she loves chocolate, and she enjoys baking cakes. She decided to make the most chocolate cakes possible. From this decision, she came up with the concept for her product and the name of her business, The Most Chocolate Cake Company.

Amy's target market was the segment of the public that loved chocolate cakes but did not have the time or interest in baking them. Because cakes are usually purchased for special occasions, our entrepreneur believed she could charge a good price, at least as much as a bakery store cake.

She decided she would make the cakes special by

- using the finest ingredients (quality);
- personalizing each cake through expert custom-decorating (selection); and
- baking the cakes to order, so they would be fresh for the event (quality).

Amy bakes her cakes at home in her specially designed commercial kitchen, which makes them literally homemade, and thus reduces the cost

Business Definition Question	The Most Chocolate Cake Company
1. ***The Offer.*** What products and services will be sold?	Chocolate cakes for special events at a price competitive with neighborhood stores.
2. ***Target Market.*** Which consumer segment will the business focus on?	People who love chocolate and those who want a special cake for a special event.
3. ***Production Capability.*** How will that offer be produced and delivered to those customers?	Homemade and baked to order to ensure freshness, using high-quality ingredients.
4. ***Problem Solving.*** What problem does the business solve for its customers?	Specialty cakes of top quality made-to-order.

of producing them. She is not renting commercial space or paying a staff. Of course, the flip side of baking at home is that her production is limited. Also, she may have to take time to deliver each cake, depending on local zoning regulations regarding retail trade.

The chart on page 117 shows how Amy answered the key questions about business definition.

The chart below addresses competitive differences for the Most Chocolate Cake Company.

Competitive Advantage Question	Competitive Advantage
1. ***The Offer.*** What will be better and different about the products and services that will be sold?	Most Chocolate will use more and higher-grade chocolate; better ingredients in general, especially in frostings and fillings; will have personalized decorations; and will be freshly baked to order.
2. ***Target Market.*** Which consumers should be the focus of the business to make it as successful as possible?	People who love chocolate and those who want a special cake for a special event.
3. ***Production and Delivery Capability.*** What will be better or different about the way that offer is produced and delivered to the customers?	Homemade and baked to order to ensure freshness, using highest-quality ingredients.

Our entrepreneur is betting that her more chocolaty cake with its special frosting and decoration, as well as its freshly homemade quality, will be successful in the marketplace. This is her USP. She hopes it will be a source of competitive advantage, along with the cost advantage of baking the cakes at home. Based on this analysis, she has determined how she wants to make her offering better and different from those of her competitors.

Another approach to the analysis is to compare your business concept with the competitors that you have identified through your research. A simple comparative table is a good way to display this. The table should include each of the six factors of competitive advantage. Plus, if there are particular features that you want to highlight, or specific aspects of the six factors, adding them to the table will make them more prominent. These ratings can be done solely by you, your team, through market research techniques, or however you think you can get the most unbiased responses.

There are many ways to construct this type of competitive analysis table. **Exhibit 5-4** shows ratings of excellent, good, moderate, fair, and poor for each factor with each competitor. This makes competitive advantages and weaknesses readily apparent. However, it does not yield an overall rating.

The chart in **Exhibit 5-5** is an example of a more quantitative approach to competitive analysis. First, based upon industry data or quality customer research, each factor is assigned a weight according to its importance to the company's target customers, with the total of all factors equaling 1.00. For example, *quality* could be weighted 0.20, *location* weighted 0.10, with other factors adding up to 0.70 if customers are very concerned about the quality of the product and whether they can buy it on the Internet. Second, each competitor should be rated on an odd-numbered scale, such as 1 to 5, with 1 being lowest and 5 being highest, on each factor. For example, the Most Chocolate Cake Company could rate a 5 on quality and 2 on selection, whereas the supermarket could rate 2 on quality and 5 on location. Third, to calculate a weighted score, each rating should be multiplied by the associated weight to obtain a total. For example, if quality is rated 0.20 and Most Chocolate's quality is rated 5, the weighted value is 1.00. Looking

Exhibit 5-4 *Comparative analysis—qualitative—The Most Chocolate Cake Company.*

	Most Chocolate Cake Company	Mega Super Market, Inc.	Average Bakery Co.	Fancy Bakery, LLC
Quality	Excellent	Fair	Fair	Excellent
Price	Fair	Good	Moderate	Poor
Location	Moderate	Excellent	Moderate	Good
Selection	Fair	Moderate	Good	Moderate
Service	Excellent	Fair	Moderate	Fair
Speed/Turnaround	Good	Excellent	Moderate	Fair
Specialization	Excellent	Poor	Fair	Moderate
Personalization	Excellent	Moderate	Good	Excellent

Exhibit 5-5 *Comparative analysis—quantitative—The Most Chocolate Cake Company.*

		Most Chocolate Cake Company		Mega Super Market, Inc.		Average Bakery Co.		Fancy Bakery, LLC	
	Wt.	Rating	Wtd. Rating	Rating	Wtd. Rating	Rating	Wtd. Rating	Rating	Wtd. Rating
Quality	0.20	5	1.00	2	0.40	2	0.40	5	1.00
Price	0.10	2	0.20	4	0.40	3	0.30	1	0.10
Location	0.10	3	0.30	5	0.50	3	0.30	4	0.40
Selection	0.15	2	0.30	3	0.45	4	0.60	3	0.45
Service	0.10	5	0.50	2	0.20	3	0.30	2	0.20
Speed/Turnaround	0.05	4	0.20	5	0.25	3	0.15	2	0.10
Specialization	0.20	5	1.00	1	0.20	2	0.40	3	0.60
Personalization	0.10	5	0.50	3	0.30	4	0.40	5	0.50
Total	1.00	XXXXX	**4.00**	XXXXX	**2.70**	XXXXX	**2.85**	XXXXX	**3.35**

across the competitors at scores on individual factors can yield insights into areas of strength or vulnerability. Finally, all the weighted values for each company should be totaled and an overall rating calculated. By looking at the ratings, it becomes apparent who the strongest and weakest competitors are, and a company can address the results of the analysis.

Competitive Strategy: Business Definition and Competitive Advantage

Your business will only succeed if you can offer the customers in your market something more, better, and/or different from what the competition is doing. Your competitive advantage (core competency) is essential and, once you establish it, your business decisions will start to fall into place. Every advertisement, every promotion, even the price of your product and the location of your business should be designed to get customers excited about your competitive advantage.

competitive strategy the combination of the business definition with its competitive advantage.

Your **competitive strategy** combines your business definition with your competitive advantage. A competitive advantage must be *sustainable,* meaning that you can keep it going. If you decide to beat the competition by selling your product at a lower price, your advantage will not last long if you cannot afford to continue at that price. Small business owners should realize that price alone is not likely to work as an advantage in the long run. A larger business can almost always beat you on price because it can buy larger quantities than you can, and therefore probably receive a greater discount from suppliers.

Being able to temporarily undercut the competition's prices is not a competitive advantage. Being able to *permanently* sell at a lower price because you have discovered a cheaper supplier *is* a competitive advantage. Being able to develop and maintain proprietary product or service features and benefits is another approach to finding a sustainable advantage.

Strategy versus Tactics

tactics the specific ways in which a business carries out its strategy.

Your **strategy** is the plan for outperforming the competition. Your **tactics** are the ways in which you will carry out your strategy.

If you plan to open a bookstore, how will you compete with the chain outlet in the neighborhood? This competitor buys more books and will receive higher discounts from wholesalers. So you probably will not be able to compete on price. How else could you attract customers? Perhaps you could make your bookstore a kind of community center, so people will want to gather there. What tactics could you use to carry out this strategy?

- Hold poetry readings and one-person concerts to promote local poets and musicians.
- Create special-interest book-discussion groups.
- Offer free tea and coffee.
- Provide comfortable seating areas for conversation and reading to encourage customers to spend time in your store.
- Set up a binder of personal ads as a dating service.

If your tactics attract enough customers to make a profit, you will have found a strategy for achieving a competitive advantage.

To find a competitive advantage, think about everything your business will offer. Examine your location, product, design, and price. What can you do to be different, and better in some way, than the competition?

Feasibility Revisited: The Economics of One Unit as a Litmus Test

Once you have chosen a business idea and determined your competitive advantage, you should make a preliminary analysis to determine whether the business can be financially viable. In other words, can you provide your product or service at a price that will cover your costs and provide you with a profit? Wozniak and Jobs were able to set up business in an office once they secured Markkula's investment in Apple. This gave them a better environment to develop and introduce the Apple II, which provided them operating profits. Before investing considerable time, effort, and money on your business concept, you can use what you learned from your competitive analysis to make a preliminary assessment of the financial opportunity. There is considerably more financial analysis to be done before opening your doors, but this is a good point at which to do an evaluation.

Performance Objective 4 ›

Perform viability testing using the economics of one unit.

Entrepreneurs use profits to pay themselves, to expand their businesses, and to start or invest in other businesses. Therefore, every entrepreneur needs to know how much **gross profit** (price minus cost of goods sold) the business will earn on each item it sells. To do this, entrepreneurs calculate the **economics of one unit of sale (EOU)**, which will tell you how much gross profit is being earned on each unit of the product or service that you sell.

gross profit total sales revenue minus total cost of goods sold.

economics of one unit of sale (EOU) the amount of gross profit that is earned on each unit of the product or service a business sells.

Defining the Unit of Sale

Begin with the **unit of sale**, which is the basic unit of the product or service sold by the business. Entrepreneurs usually define their unit of sale according to the type of business. For example,

unit of sale the basic unit of the product or service sold by the business.

Manufacturing. One order (any quantity; e.g., 100 watches)
Wholesale. A dozen of an item (e.g., 12 watches)
Retail. One item (e.g., 1 watch)
Service. One hour of service time (e.g., one hour of lawn-mowing service) or a standard block of time devoted to a task (e.g., one mowed lawn)

If the business sells a combination of differently priced items (such as in a restaurant), the unit of sale is more complicated. The entrepreneur can use the average sale per customer minus the average cost of goods sold per customer to find the economics of one unit of sale. The formula would be as follows:

Average Sale per Customer − Average Cost of Sale per Customer = Average Gross Profit per Customer

A business that sells a variety of items may choose to express one unit of sale as an average sale per customer (see **Exhibit 5-6**).

Cost of Goods Sold and Gross Profit

To get a closer look at one unit of sale, entrepreneurs analyze the **cost of goods sold (COGS)** of one unit. These are

cost of goods sold (COGS) the cost of selling one additional unit of a tangible item.

- the cost of materials used to make the product (or deliver the service) and
- the cost of labor directly used to make the product (or deliver the service).

Exhibit 5-6 *Unit of sale as a combination of different items.*

UNIT OF SALE AND ECONOMICS OF ONE UNIT OF SALE			
Type of Business	**Unit of Sale**	**Economics of One Unit of Sale**	**Gross Profit per Unit**
1. Retail & Manufacturing	One item (e.g., one tie)	\$7 − \$3 = \$4	\$4
2. Service	One hour (e.g., one hour of mowing a lawn)	\$20 − \$10 = \$10	\$10
3. Wholesale	Multiple of same item (e.g., one dozen roses)	\$240 − \$120 = \$120	\$120
4. Combination	Average sale per customer minus average cost of goods sold per customer (e.g., restaurant meals)	\$20 − \$10 = \$10	\$10 average gross profit

Exhibit 5-7 *Economics of one unit of sale versus total gross profit.*

	Economics of One Unit (EOU)	Total Gross Profit for 12 Units (@ $10 per Unit Sold)
Price Sold/Revenue	$20	$240 (12 × $20)
− Cost of Goods Sold	−$12	$144 (12 × 12)
Gross Profit	$8	$96 (12 × 8)

cost of services sold (COSS) the cost of selling one additional unit of a service.

For a product, the cost of direct labor used to make the product plus the cost of materials used are the COGS. The equivalent for a service business, the **cost of services sold (COSS)**, are the cost of the **direct labor** used to produce the service plus the cost of the delivery of the service.

The cost of goods sold can be thought of as the cost of selling "one additional unit." If you buy watches and then resell them, your COGS per unit is the price you paid for one watch. Once you know your COGS, you can calculate gross profit by subtracting COGS from revenue (see **Exhibit 5-7**).

Your Business and the Economics of One Unit

The economics of one unit of sale is a method for seeing whether your business idea could be profitable. If one unit of sale is profitable, the whole business is likely to be. On the other hand, if one unit of sale is *not* profitable, then no matter how many units you sell, the business will never be successful. Let's use **Exhibit 5-7** as an example.

Say you have a simple business selling decorative hand-blown wineglasses that you buy from a local artist wholesale for $12 each and resell to friends for $20 each. The cost of goods sold for each wineglass is the wholesale price of $12 (gross profit = $8).

You buy a dozen glasses for $12 each wholesale. Your unit of sale is one glass. Your cost of goods sold is $12 per unit, assuming you have no direct labor cost.

You sell all the glasses at $20 each. Here is how you would calculate your gross profit.

Total revenue = 12 glasses × $20 selling price = $240
Total cost of goods sold = 12 glasses × $12 purchase price = $144
Total gross profit (contribution margin) = $96
$240 revenue − $144 COGS = $96

Total Revenue − Total Cost of Goods Sold = Total Gross Profit

You made a gross profit of $96.

For a manufacturing business, one unit might be one pair of sneakers. The costs would include **direct labor**, the money paid to the people who make the product (sneakers, in this example), and the supplies, such as fabric, rubber, and leather (see **Exhibit 5-8** on following page).

The manufacturer makes a gross profit of $3 for every pair of sneakers sold. That may not seem like much, but manufacturers sell in *bulk*. In other words, a manufacturer might sell several million pairs of sneakers per year.

The economics of one unit also applies to wholesale, retail, and service businesses. Assume the wholesaler buys a set of one dozen pairs of sneakers from the manufacturer for $180 and sells them to a retailer for $240 (see **Exhibit 5-9** on following page).

Exhibit 5-8 *Economics of one unit, manufacturing.*

ECONOMICS OF ONE UNIT (EOU)			
Manufacturing Business: Unit = 1 Pair of Sneakers			
Selling Price per Unit:			**$15.00**
Labor Cost per Hour:	$4.00		
No. of Hours per Unit:	2 hours	$ 8.00	
Materials per Unit:		4.00	
Cost of Goods Sold per Unit:		**$12.00**	12.00
Gross Profit per Unit:			**$ 3.00**

Exhibit 5-9 *Economics of one unit, wholesale.*

ECONOMICS OF ONE UNIT (EOU)	
Wholesale Business: Unit = 1 Dozen Pairs of Sneakers	
Selling Price per Unit:	**$240.00**
Cost of Goods Sold per Unit:	**180.00**
Gross Profit per Unit:	**$ 60.00**

Exhibit 5-10 *Economics of one unit, retail.*

ECONOMICS OF ONE UNIT (EOU)	
Retail Business: Unit = 1 Pair of Sneakers	
Selling Price per Unit:	**$35.00**
Cost of Goods Sold per Unit:	**20.00**
Gross Profit per Unit:	**$15.00**

Exhibit 5-11 *Economics of one unit, service.*

ECONOMICS OF ONE UNIT (EOU)		
Service Business: Unit = 1 Hour		
Selling Price per Unit:		**$50.00**
Supplies per Unit (hair gel, etc.):	$ 2.00	
Labor Costs per Hour:	25.00	
Cost of Goods Sold per Unit:	**$27.00**	**27.00**
Gross Profit per Unit:		**$23.00**

The retailer pays the wholesaler $240 for one dozen pairs of sneakers. The retailer's COGS, therefore, is $20 ($240/12 for the shoes only; the retailer does not add direct labor). The store sells one pair at a time to customers for $35 (see **Exhibit 5-10** above).

Here is the economics of one unit for a hair stylist who charges $50 per cut (see **Exhibit 5-11** above).

The Cost of Direct Labor in the EOU

Janet has a business designing handmade bookmarkers. Her unit of sale is one bookmarker. Below is additional information about Janet's business:

- She sells 40 bookmarkers per week to a bookstore in her neighborhood.
- Her selling price is $4.50 each, including an envelope.
- Her costs are 80¢ per card for materials (construction paper, glue, and paint) and 20¢ each for the envelopes, for a total of $1.00 each.
- On average, it takes her one hour to make six bookmarkers.
- Janet pays herself $9 an hour.

The direct labor for each bookmarker is $1.50 ($9/6). Janet wisely realizes that she must include the cost of her labor in the EOU. See how she did this in **Exhibit 5-12**.

Janet's gross profit is $2 per bookmarker sold. Assuming no other expenses, she will keep this as owner of the business. She also earns $1.50 per bookmarker by supplying the labor, thus ending up with a profit of $3.50 per bookmarker.

Now, think back to Amy of the Most Chocolate Cake Company and perform a similar analysis.

- Amy takes an average of two hours to bake a cake.
- It costs $5 for the ingredients for an average cake.
- Amy pays herself $15 an hour.
- The price of an average cake is $40.

This yields a gross profit of $5 per cake. With the gross profit of $5 and the $30 she paid herself, Amy ends up with $35 per cake. Assuming she does not have to deliver the cakes, this may be sufficient for her. If she needs to earn more, she will have to charge more, work faster, work more hours, or decrease the costs. These may or may not be realistic options.

Hiring Others to Make the Unit of Sale

Janet realizes that if the bookstore wants to order more bookmarkers, or she can sell them to additional bookstores, she will not have enough time

Exhibit 5-12 *EOU example, Janet's company.*

ECONOMICS OF ONE UNIT (EOU)		
Manufacturing Business: Unit = 1 Bookmarker		
Selling Price per Unit:		**$4.50**
Materials:	$1.00	
Labor:	1.50	
Cost of Goods Sold per Unit:	**$2.50**	**2.50**
Gross Profit per Unit:		**$2.00**

to make them all herself. To solve this issue, she hires a friend to make the bookmarkers for $9 per hour. Although the EOU stays the same, Janet will have more time to look for new opportunities for her business. Her income from the business will now come solely from the gross profit, which is currently $2 per unit.

Amy can produce about 20 cakes during a 40-hour workweek and 30 cakes in 60 hours. That means she can earn $600 to $750 per week, or between $31,200 and $39,000 per year before taxes, without allowing for vacation or sick days. There would be an additional $100 to $150 in gross profit per week before other expenses are figured. Assuming Amy can sell 20 to 30 cakes per week at $40 each, she will have a maximum income of about $46,800.

Amy knows that she will have other expenses, so $40,000 is more realistic. Like Janet, Amy wants to earn more than that per year, so she, too, could add employees if the market would support greater volume. If she paid her employees $15 per hour (the minimum living wage in some areas in 2004), she would need to sell 8000 cakes per year to make her $40,000. That is 154 cakes per week, requiring perhaps seven full-time bakers. This would not be possible in her home kitchen.

However, we have to be sure that Amy is not comparing apples to oranges when making the analysis. With more people, the tasks could be delegated so that it took only one hour per cake, bringing the gross profit to $20 each. If Amy could also get better pricing on ingredients because of increased volume, the gross profit would be even higher. At $20 per unit gross profit, Amy would need to sell only 2000 cakes per year, or 39 per week. That could be accomplished with two full-time bakers. As a home-based business, that would be more realistic.

Amy, like any entrepreneur, has to decide what is realistic, what is achievable, and what her goals are.

Going for Volume

Janet meets a bookstore supply wholesaler. He offers to buy 2000 bookmarkers if Janet can deliver them in one month and sell them for $3.50 each, $1 less than she had been getting. This would reduce her gross profit but offer more revenue. Three questions immediately came to mind:

1. ***Can I produce the 2,000-unit order in the required time frame?***
   After doing some calculations, Janet realized that if she hired 10 people each to work 35 hours a month, she could deliver the order in time. Janet convinces 10 people to take on the one-month commitment by offering $12 per hour.

Exhibit 5-13 *EOU example, Janet's company with employees.*

ECONOMICS OF ONE UNIT (EOU)		
Manufacturing Business: Unit = 1 Bookmarker		
Selling Price per Unit:		**$3.50**
Materials:	$1.00	
Labor:	1.50	
Cost of Goods Sold per Unit:	**$2.50**	**2.50**
Gross Profit per Unit:		**$1.00**

Exhibit 5-14 *Gross profit projection, Janet's company with employees.*

GROSS PROFIT PROJECTION (BASED ON EOU)		
Janet's Total Gross Profit		
Revenue ($3.50 × 2,000 bookmarkers):		**$7,000.00**
Materials ($1 × 2,000):	$2,000.00	
Labor ($2.00 × 2,000) :	4,000.00	
Cost of Goods Sold:	**$6,000.00**	**6,000.00**
Gross Profit:		**$1,000.00**

2. ***If I lower the price to $3.50 for each bookmarker (instead of $4.50), will I still make an acceptable gross profit per unit?***
   To answer this question, Janet created a chart (see **Exhibit 5-13**) and realized that her new gross profit per unit would be $1. Let us look at the EOU if she factors in her labor at $12 per hour, or $2 per bookmarker.
3. ***How much in total gross profit will I make from the order?***
   To answer this question, Janet created another chart (see **Exhibit 5-14**) and realized that her total gross profit would be $1000.

Janet concluded that $1000 in gross profit was much better than earning $80 a week in gross profit, plus $60 a week for her labor (what she earned making the bookmarkers herself each week at a selling price of $4.50). Even though the wholesaler was asking for a lower selling price, her total revenue, and therefore her total gross profit, would be much higher. When Janet realized that she could deliver the order in the required time and make $1000, she accepted the offer.

Five breakthrough steps entrepreneurs can take are

1. calculating the unit of sale,
2. determining the economics of one unit of sale,
3. substituting someone else's labor,
4. selling in volume, and
5. creating jobs and operating at a profit.

currency money that can be exchanged internationally.

foreign exchange (FX) rate the relative value of one currency to another.

At first, an entrepreneur can be part of his or her own economics of one unit. If you start making (manufacturing) computers in your garage, like Steve Jobs and Stephen Wozniak did when they started Apple, you should include your labor on the EOU worksheet.

Global Impact...

Selling Your Product around the World

Through the Internet, even a very small business run by one person can reach customers internationally. What if a customer from Germany contacts you through your Web site and wants to buy your product in euros, the currency of much of Europe? **Currency** is money that can be exchanged internationally. In the United States, the currency is the dollar. In Japan, it is the yen. In Mexico, it is the peso.

The **foreign exchange (FX) rate** is the relative value of one currency to another. It describes the buying power of a currency. The foreign exchange rate (FX rate) is expressed as a ratio. If one dollar is worth 1.25 euros, to calculate how many euros a certain number of dollars is worth, multiply that number by 1.25.

$$\$5 = \$5 \times €1.25 = €6.25$$

How would you figure out how many dollars €6.25 is worth? Simply divide €6.25 by 1.25 to get $5.

Tip: There are currency converters available online, such as at http://finance.yahoo.com/currency?u.

Over time, though, Jobs and Wozniak made enough profit to hire others to manufacture the computers. Jobs and Wozniak took themselves out of the economics of one unit so they could be the creative leaders of the company. And, by lowering prices, they were able to sell millions of units.

Chapter Summary

Now that you have studied this chapter, you can do the following:

1. Define your business.
   - Identify the four basic types of business.
     - Manufacturing makes a tangible product.
     - Wholesale buys in quantity from the manufacturer and sells to the retailer.
     - Retail sells to the consumer.
     - Service sells an intangible product to the consumer.
2. Articulate your core beliefs, your mission, and your vision.
3. Analyze your competitive advantage.
   - Your competitive advantage is whatever you can do better than the competition that will attract customers to your business.
   - Find your competitive advantage by thinking about what consumers in your market need. You have unique knowledge of your market.
4. Perform feasibility analysis by calculating the economics of one unit of sale.
   - The EOU is the basis of business profit.
   - Entrepreneurs use profits to pay themselves, expand the business, and start or invest in new businesses.
   - The entrepreneur chooses how the unit is defined:
     - One item (unit).
     - One hour of service time (if the business is a service business).
     - If the business sells differently priced items (such as in a restaurant), use the average sale per customer as the unit. The average would be total sales divided by the number of customers:

       Total Sales/Number of Customers = Average Unit of Sale

   - To get a closer look at the costs involved in figuring one unit, entrepreneurs analyze the cost of goods or services sold (COGS or COSS) of a unit.
     - The cost of materials used to make the product (or deliver the service).
     - The cost of labor used to make the product (or deliver the service).
   - Once you know your cost of goods sold, you can calculate gross profit. Subtract total COGS from your total revenue to get your gross profit.

     Revenue − COGS = Gross Profit

Key Terms

barriers to entry
competitive strategy
core values
cost of goods sold (COGS)
cost of services sold (COSS)
currency

economics of one unit of sale (EOU)
foreign exchange (FX) rate
gross profit
manufacturing
market
retail
tactics
unique selling proposition (USP)
unit of sale
wholesale

Entrepreneurship Portfolio

Critical Thinking Exercises

1. Use the following charts to define a business you would like to start, and analyze your competitive advantage.

Business Definition Question	Response
The Offer. What products and services will be sold by the business?	
Target Market. Which consumer segments will the business focus on?	
Production Capability. How will that offer be produced and delivered to those customers?	
Problem Solving. What problem does the business solve for its customers?	
Competitive Advantage Question	**Competitive Difference (USP)**
The Offer. What will be better and different about the products and services that will be sold?	
Target Market. Which segments of consumers should be the focus of the business to make it as successful as possible?	
Production and Delivery Capability. What will be better or different about the way the offer is produced and delivered to those customers?	

		Your Company		Competitor Number 1		Competitor Number 2		Competitor Number 3	
	Weight	**Rating**	**Weighted Rating**	**Rating**	**Weighted Rating**	**Rating**	**Weighted Rating**	**Rating**	**Weighted Rating**
Quality									
Price									
Location									
Selection									
Service									
Speed/Turnaround									
Specialization									
Personalization									
Total	1.00	xxxxx	________	xxxxx	________	xxxxx	________	xxxxx	________

2. Are there customers for your business in other countries? How do you plan to reach them?
3. Describe any international competitors you have found who may be able to access your customers. How do you intend to compete?
4. Describe three core values you will use to run your own company.
5. What are three of the concepts that a mission statement should contain and why?
6. Write a mission statement for your business.

Key Concept Questions

1. Gross profit is the profit of a business before which other costs are subtracted?
2. What is the average unit of sale for the following businesses?
   - Business 1: A restaurant that serves $2100 in meals to 115 customers per day.
   - Business 2: A record store that sells $1500 worth of CDs to 75 customers per day.
3. For the following business, define the unit of sale and calculate the economics of one unit:

   Sue, of Sue's Sandwich Shoppe, sells sandwiches and soda from a sidewalk cart in a popular park near her house. She sets up her cart in the summers to earn money for college tuition. Last month she sold $1240 worth of product (sandwiches and sodas) to 100 customers. She spent $210 on the sandwich ingredients and buying the sodas wholesale. Her unit is one sandwich ($4) plus one soda ($1).
4. When Stephen Wozniak and Steve Jobs envisioned a computer in every home, computers were large, expensive machines. They were only available to the government, universities, scientists, and very large companies. What technology currently available today to only a few people can you envision meeting a need for many consumers in the future?
5. Is there a service presently available to only a few consumers? Or one that is not available yet? Write about a service that you can imagine eventually becoming very popular, and the need(s) it will meet.
6. If the FX rate between the U.S. dollar and the Japanese yen is 1:119, how many yen will it take to equal $20?
7. If the FX rate between the Japanese yen and the euro is 189.35:1, how many yen will equal 10 euros?

Application Exercises

You own a small record label. You sell CDs through your Web site for $15, including shipping and handling. You get an offer from someone who owns a record store in Germany who would like to sell your CDs. He wants to buy them at $10 each and sell them for €30. He says his profit from each sale would be €12 and he will split it with you. Assuming the exchange rate between the dollar and the euro is $1 = €2:

a. How much profit would you get from the sale of each CD in the German store?
b. How much is that profit in dollars?
c. Is this a good business opportunity for you? Why or why not?
d. If the FX rate between the dollar and the euro falls to $1 = €1 would this still be a good business idea for you? Why or why not?

Exploring Online

1. Use the Internet to research suppliers for a business you would like to start. Describe the business and list the URL, e-mail, phone and fax, and street address for five suppliers you located via the Internet.
2. Visit *http://www.download.com* and find three shareware programs that would be of value to you as an entrepreneur.

Case Study Ibtihaj "Ippy" Amatul-Wadud—Ippy's Islamic Fashions

Although she didn't know it at the time, Ippy Amatul-Wadud laid the foundation for a future business when she began learning how to sew at age 10. Using the sewing machine her mother bought for her, Ippy eventually became a good seamstress. Ippy began using her skills to make her own clothes because there were no local stores that sold apparel for Muslim women and girls. If she, her mother, and four sisters wanted to buy appropriate Islamic clothing, they had to travel from Springfield, Massachusetts, where they lived, to New York or New Jersey.

As a teenager, Ippy began participating in an after-school E.Y.E. class sponsored by the Springfield Technical College's Entrepreneurial Institute. As its name implies, the E.Y.E. (Excellence in Youth Entrepreneurship) program teaches entrepreneurial knowledge and skills to young people. This program uses the nationally acclaimed Network for Teaching Entrepreneurship (NFTE) curriculum. High school and college-aged students in the Greater Springfield area who are interested in learning how to create a business plan or start a business are invited by outreach workers from local high schools to contact the Entrepreneurial Institute.

Ippy realized that she could create a business that would solve a resource problem for Muslim girls such as herself. To make a long story short, she wrote a business plan that won second place in the Entrepreneurial Institute's regional YES! Business Plan Competition. Her plan also placed third in NFTE's New England Regional Business Plan Competition. And that wasn't all. Ippy later became a finalist in *BusinessWeek* magazine's 2008 "America's Best Young Entrepreneurs" annual competition.

Working from her home, Ippy sews custom-made clothing, primarily for Muslim women and girls in the U.S. For apparel worn outside the home, she sews long, loose dresses, and scarves for covering the head, neck, and ears. She also makes a traditional outfit, called a *salwar kameese,* which is often worn at parties inside the home.

In the beginning, Ippy did not spend money to advertise her business. Customer interest spread by word-of-mouth, and networking became a means for generating more sales. From there, she began making plans for expansion via a Web site, and eventually a storefront. Ippy believes that it's important for entrepreneurs to dream big, and she hopes someday to be able to sell worldwide.

Case Study Analysis

1. How did Ippy identify her market?
2. What knowledge, skills, and abilities did Ippy have before starting her company? What start-up costs did Ippy have?
3. Why might *BusinessWeek* have named Ippy as a finalist for "America's Best Young Entrepreneurs"?
4. Ippy participated in a program that helped her turn her sewing talent into a business. What type of assistance was it? Who provided it?

Case Sources

AllBusiness.com, Inc. Web site article, "Area Dressmaker Fills Need," http://www.allbusiness.com/company-activities-management/company-structures/11876739-1.html.

Bloomberg Businessweek Web site article, "America's Best Young Entrepreneurs: Class of 2008," http://images.businessweek.com/ss/09/10/1009_alums_roundup/14.htm.

Springfield Technical Community College's Entrepreneurial Institute Web site, http://www.stcc.edu/ei/.

Case Study | Honest Tea

Seth's Problem: "I Was Thirsty!"

Seth Goldman likes to say that his business got started because he was thirsty. A natural-born athlete, Seth was always searching for a satisfying drink to quench his thirst after a tough workout. While there were plenty of sports drinks and sodas he could buy, not to mention water, none of these options ever appealed to him. So he started to experiment.

A Hobby Evolves into a Business Idea

After he graduated with an MBA from Yale, Seth began concocting fruity beverages in his kitchen as a hobby. But he was not satisfied. One day he decided to call his old business school professor, Barry Nalebuff, to discuss the problem. Nalebuff had just returned from India, where he had been studying the country's tea industry. He explained that beverage companies that purchased their raw materials from Indian tea plantations did not use whole tea leaves in their manufacturing. Instead, they took whatever was left over after the quality leaves had been packaged and used for other products, such as tea bags. Seth and Barry had a hunch that they were circling in on an opportunity. Even better, Barry had already come up with a name for a company that would make beverages using top-of-the-line tea leaves. The company would be called Honest Tea. Seth loved the name and what it represented. He hung up the phone and resolved to continue his experiments by brewing tea leaves in his kitchen until he came up with the perfect product.

That was in 1998. Today, Honest Tea sells 30 different kinds of bottled iced teas as well as a growing line of bagged and loose teas. In 2001, the company generated $1.9 million in sales; in 2002, this had increased to $3.2 million. Seth is aiming for a 75-percent growth rate each year, and the company seems to be on track to accomplish this. So, how did Seth do it? How did this drink hobbyist succeed in competing with big-time beverage companies?

Honest Tea's Competitive Advantages

Seth has worked hard to define the company around the features that make Honest Tea stand out from the competition. In Seth's own words, "Given that this is a highly competitive market, the most important factor in our favor is that we offer a differentiated product. A company like Coca-Cola is a thousand times our size. What we are offering is a very strong brand that is consistent with what is in the package and very meaningful to customers." Ironically, in February of 2008, Coca-Cola bought 40 percent of Honest Tea for $43 million.

For example, Honest Tea is the only bottled tea company whose products are all 100 percent USDA organic certified. What does this mean and why does it matter? When an item is labeled "USDA organic," it confirms that certain pesticides and other toxic chemicals have not been used in growing or producing it. Increasingly, consumers, particularly the health-conscious, are seeking out organic goods in the marketplace.

Honest Tea also uses up to two-thirds less sugar in its teas compared with its competitors, such as Snapple and Arizona. Seth likes to say that his teas are "lightly sweetened." This feature appeals to consumers who care about their health and diet.

Socially Responsible Business

The "honest" part of Honest Tea extends beyond using organic ingredients. Seth goes to great lengths to educate customers about the company's ethical and socially responsible business practices. For example, Honest Tea purchases peppermint leaves for its "First Nation Peppermint" iced tea from a woman-owned herb company on the Crow Indian reservation in Montana, where the unemployment rate is a staggering 67 percent. By purchasing peppermint leaves from this supplier, Honest Tea is promoting economic activity in a location where many suffer from poverty and joblessness. A percentage of the revenue from the sale of this product is donated to nonprofit organizations that help at-risk Native American youth.

Seth wants customers to know that, when they buy Honest Tea, they are also doing something good for the community. As Seth puts it, "A commitment to social responsibility is central to Honest Tea's identity and purpose. The company strives for authenticity, integrity, and purity in our products and in the way we do business."

Staying in the Game

The beverage market is highly competitive, but Honest Tea appears to be thriving because it is delivering a differentiated product that customers feel good about buying, and it uses organic ingredients. Comparable brands like Snapple, Lipton, and Arizona iced teas may cost 25 to 50 cents less per bottle, but do not offer the same quality and promised health benefits. However, some high-end tea purveyors, such as Tazo iced and loose teas, sold exclusively at Starbucks and other retail locations, may pose a threat to Honest Tea in the long run. In order to stay in the game, Seth needs to continue to enhance and market the features that make Honest Tea a specialty product.

Case Study Analysis

1. What are Honest Tea's competitive advantages?
2. Brainstorm a list of Honest Tea's competitors. What are the competitive advantages of their products?
3. Look at the list you generated of Honest Tea's competitive advantages. Which is most important to you as a consumer and why?
4. Given what you already know about Honest Tea's business philosophy and practices, if you were Seth's business advisor, what additional competitive advantages would you encourage him to develop?
5. What does it mean for a company to engage in "socially responsible business practices"?
6. Assume the following prices of a 16.9-oz. (500 ml) bottle of the following iced-tea products:

   - Snapple = $1.89
   - Arizona Iced Tea = $1.95
   - Honest Tea = $2.39

   Would you be willing to pay between 25 and 50 cents more to purchase an Honest Tea beverage because you know that the company engages in socially responsible business practices and uses organic ingredients? How much are these features worth to you and why?

Case Sources

Honest Tea, http://www.honesttea.com.

Brian Duchovnay, "A Boston Tea Party: Seth Goldman of Honest Tea Visits HBS," *Harbus News,* February 23, 2004, www.harbus.org.

Jon Goldstein, "Honest Tea's Best Policies," *Baltimore Sun,* August 5, 2003.

Net-Impact Success Story: Seth Goldman. "Member Success Stories," http://www.net-impact.org.

EXPLORING YOUR MARKET

"In my factory we make cosmetics, but in my stores we sell hope."

—Charles Revson, founder of Revlon cosmetics

The original McDonald's was a modest burger restaurant in San Bernardino, California, owned by brothers, Maurice and Richard McDonald. Ray Kroc was a 52-year-old salesman of Multimixer milkshake machines, and the McDonald brothers' restaurant was his best customer. When Kroc received an order from the McDonald brothers for eight Multimixers, enough to make 40 milkshakes at once, he had to learn more about the operation and its market.

What Kroc found was that the McDonald brothers had hit upon a unique value proposition that drew customers from miles around. The restaurant combined three factors:

1. fast, friendly service;
2. consistent quality in its burgers, shakes, and fries; and
3. low prices.

The McDonalds had found the magic formula for fast-food success. They knew they could expand their business beyond the several outlets that they had, but they both hated to fly and wanted to stay locally focused. In 1955, Kroc offered to form a partnership to create identical McDonald's restaurants around the country. In 1961, Kroc bought out the brothers for $2.7 million, but he strictly adhered to their original recipes and value proposition. Kroc wanted every McDonald's customer, from Anchorage to Miami, to eat an identical product. According to Bill Bryson's history of McDonald's, *Made in America,* Kroc "dictated that McDonald's burgers must be exactly 3.875 inches across, weigh 1.6 ounces, and contain precisely 19 percent fat. Big Mac buns should have an average of 178 sesame seeds." Today, there are more than 31,000 McDonald's outlets in more than 100 countries.

Performance Objectives

1. Explain how marketing differs from selling.
2. Understand how market research prepares you for success.
3. Choose your market segment and research it.
4. Position your product or service within your market.

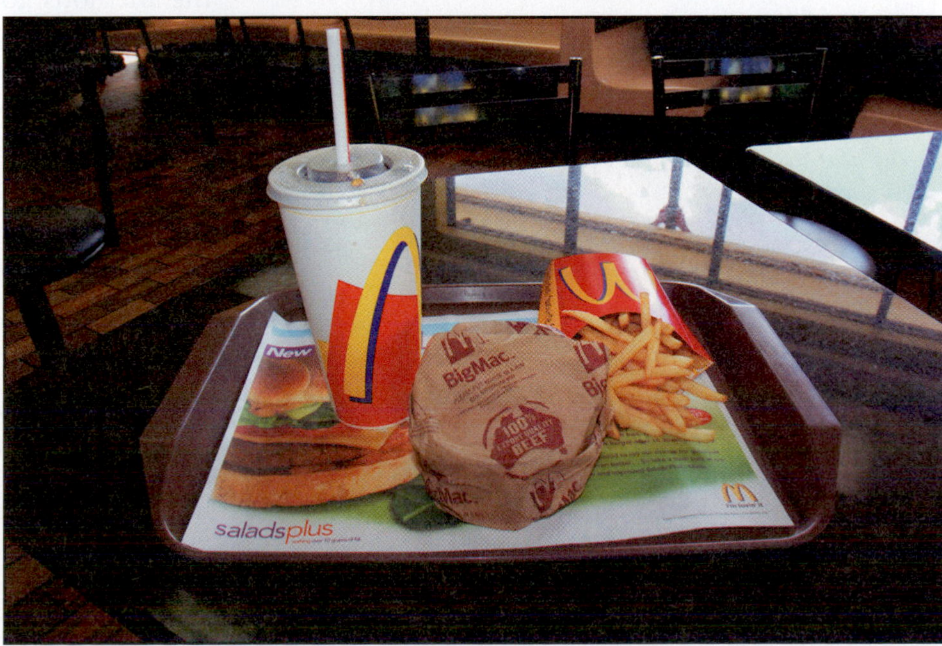

McDonald's has a formula for success.
(© Doug Steley A/Alamy)

Markets and Marketing Defined

A market, as defined in Chapter 5, is a group of people or organizations that may be interested in buying a given product or service, can afford it, and can do so legally. A market is identified by attitudinal, behavioral, demographic, and other characteristics.

marketing the development and use of strategies for getting a product or service to customers and generating interest in it.

Marketing is satisfying the customer at a profit.[1] Marketing is the business function that identifies these customers and their needs and wants. Through marketing, the name of your business will come to mean something clear and concrete in the customer's mind. As an entrepreneur, your current and future customers should always be your top priority.[2] Above all, marketing is the way a business tells its customers that it is committed to meeting their needs. Marketing should constantly reinforce your competitive advantage.

Performance Objective 1

Explain how marketing differs from selling.

Nike sells athletic shoes. It puts them in stores where consumers can buy them. But Nike also *markets* athletic shoes. Nike creates advertisements and promotions designed to convince customers that Nike sneakers will inspire them to *Just Do It.* You can choose sneakers from many companies, but Nike hopes you will feel inspired by its marketing to seek out and buy its brand.

A Business That Markets Versus a Market-Driven Business

Do not make the mistake of treating marketing as an isolated business function rather than the engine that drives all business decisions. Most experts agree that, to be successful, a business must develop its marketing vision first and then use it as the basis for all subsequent decisions.

Market Research Prepares You For Success

Performance Objective 2

Understand how market research prepares you for success.

Whether you have a product or service that you want to market, or are searching for a market opportunity and are creating a product or service to fill that need, research can help you succeed. Your research can be conducted at the level of the industry, the market segment, or the individual consumer. Whereas the questions you ask will be very different at each level, the methods for answering them are similar.

The Nike "swoosh"—a logo recognized worldwide. (Sandy Feisenthal, Corbis Bettmann)

Research Your Market *Before* You Open Your Business

Large corporations spend a great deal of money on market research before they introduce a product or service. They need to get it just right. Take a lesson from the big companies. Do not begin until you have researched your market thoroughly. Be open to criticism. It is not always pleasant to hear, but it will be valuable. Criticism can help you fine-tune your business.

[1]Adapted from Philip Kotler and Gary Armstrong, *Principles of Marketing*, 9th ed. (Upper Saddle River, N.J.: Prentice Hall, 2001).
[2]Ibid.

Exercise

On a separate piece of paper,

1. give an example of a company that you believe operates as a market-driven organization, and why you think so; and
2. give an example of a company that functions as an organization that markets.

Types and Methods of Research

How you conduct your research will be very important in determining whether it is reliable and valid. Clearly, you do not want to make business decisions based upon partial or incorrect information. The quality of your research defines the quality of the answers to your research questions. If you do not already know how to perform research, be certain to learn how to generate reliable and valid data before embarking upon a research project. Using incorrect or invalid research can lead to dangerously wrong answers to research questions, resulting in wasted resources, poor performance, and even business failure.

You or a market research firm (or a group of students) can carry out two types of research. **Primary research** is conducted directly on a subject or subjects. **Secondary research** is carried out indirectly, through existing resources. For example, if you conducted 100 interviews with students on a campus, it would be primary research. If you examined a study on those students conducted by someone else, it would be secondary. Often, primary research is expensive and time-consuming to conduct. However, if you want to test a product or idea, it can be your best option.

primary research a type of research conducted directly on a subject or subjects.

secondary research a type of research carried out indirectly, through existing resources.

Bear in mind that, when you design a market-research survey, the method you use will affect the answers you get. A combination of primary and secondary research will generally be best, and for each type of research there is a set of methods that you can select to fit your needs. These are tools that can aid you in determining the viability of your business concept and/or product. The number of options is seemingly endless. Which methods to use will depend upon your level of analysis (individual, market, industry, and so forth), your research questions, and the time and money you can devote to them. Remember, it is better to do your research and discover that you should revamp your plans than to skip this step, ignore the results, and find out only through an expensive failure in the marketplace.

Getting Information Directly from the Source: Primary Research

When you need to ask questions specific to your product or service, or need to observe how people act or react, it is best to conduct primary research. Primary research methods include

- ***Personal interviews.*** Interview individuals in person, using either question guides that have flexibility, or structured, step-by-step surveys. For example, you could interview students in your school or consumers in a shopping area.
- ***Telephone surveys.*** Personal interviews not conducted in person. When your customer base will not be strictly local, you can reach more people via telephone. However, in the United States, telephone surveys are regulated, so you have to be careful to comply with the

laws and regulations. Also, with the increasing usage of cellular telephones, land lines are decreasing in popularity, and samples may be skewed because older populations have the majority of the existing land lines.

- ***Written surveys.*** These can be administered via the postal service or by e-mail. There are numerous survey programs available on the Internet that can simplify this process. One is Survey Monkey (*http://www.surveymonkey.com*), which creates neat, written surveys online. The survey questions should be clearly stated, easy to understand, and relatively short.
- ***Focus groups.*** If you want to get information that is generated through guided group discussion, you can use focus groups. There are facilities designed specifically for conducting focus groups, or you can simply find a quiet space with adequate facilities.
- ***Observation.*** By watching, you can observe patterns of interaction, traffic patterns, and volume of purchases that will help you understand your prospective customers and your competition. Secret shoppers (people who are hired to shop a store) fall in this category. Also, attending an event, such as a trade show or professional meeting, is an opportunity to observe and learn. Make certain you do this ethically and legally.
- ***Tracking.*** It can be useful to track advertisements, prices, and other information through the media. You can compile this data to see pricing and promotion patterns, as well as the marketing strategies, of your competitors.

Getting Information Indirectly: Secondary Research

When you want to learn about your industry, competition, or markets, secondary research may be your best option. Some of these methods are

- ***Online searches.*** By using search engines such as Google, Yahoo! Search, Dogpile, Ask.com, Live Search, and Excite, you can find stories, historical records, biographical information, and statistics. Be wary of sources when using Internet data, as the facts may not always be accurate. Many of them use information contributed by users, and this data may not be verified or reliable.
- ***Database searches.*** Public databases such as the U.S. Census (www.census.gov) are available to you via the Internet. Such sources can provide you with extensive consumer and business information, and some industry reports. **Exhibit 6-1** is a screen shot of a Census page. You can visit the U.S. Securities and Exchange Commission's EDGAR Database to find publicly traded companies in your industry.

  You can use proprietary databases at a university or public library to find articles and books about your market. Interestingly, much of the information available on businesses, populations, markets, and the like is not available through Internet search engines. Libraries sign up for databases that are available only through (relatively costly) paid subscriptions. They also have services to provide certain journal and magazine articles for downloading or printing. For example, you can secure financial data through Hoover's subscription information services, articles from JSTOR or ABI/INFORM databases, and industry comparables from Risk Management Associates on a fee basis. Even viewing articles from the *Wall Street Journal* can require a paid subscription.

Exhibit 6-1 *Census data.*

United States and states - Home health care services, Table 1. Selected Industry Statistics for th... Page 1 of 1

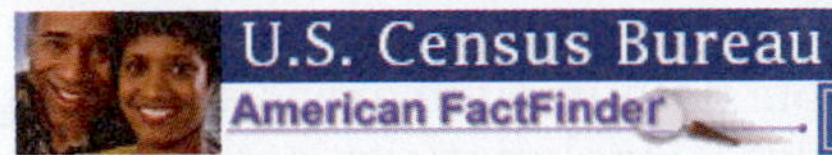

Main Search Feedback FAQs Glossary Site Map Help

Home health care services

NAICS: 621610

Table 1. Selected Industry Statistics for the U.S. and States: 2007

[NOTE. Data based on the 2007 Economic Census and the 2007 Nonemployer Statistics. For information on confidentiality protection, sampling error, nonsampling error, and definitions, see Survey Methodology. Data in this table represent those available when this report was created; employer and nonemployer data may not be available for all NAICS industries or geographies. Data in this table are subject to employment- and/or sales-size minimums that vary by industry.]

Geography	Number of establishments	Number of employees	Annual payroll ($1,000)	Sales, shipments, receipts, or revenue ($1,000)	Nonemployer Number of establishments	Nonemployer Sales, shipments, receipts, or revenue ($1,000)	2007 population estimate
United States	(r)22,975	(r)972,791	(r) 23,373,475	(r)46,174,331	N	N	301,621,157
Alabama	423	13,011	355,117	756,080	N	N	4,627,851
Alaska	41	1,732	35,606	50,138	N	N	683,478
California	2,341	56,251	1,724,312	3,575,223	N	N	36,553,215
Colorado	282	13,530	321,077	594,989	N	N	4,861,515
Connecticut	235	15,305	451,262	807,103	N	N	3,502,309
Delaware	44	2,126	68,047	137,058	N	N	864,764
District of Columbia	27	1,835	39,559	67,455	N	N	588,292
Georgia	543	16,554	454,692	960,141	N	N	9,544,750
Hawaii	65	2,872	68,463	120,117	N	N	1,283,388
Idaho	131	3,155	70,309	136,468	N	N	1,499,402
Kentucky	224	6,755	232,449	569,028	N	N	4,241,474
Louisiana	575	15,995	418,448	870,415	N	N	4,293,204
Maine	126	5,308	125,346	239,455	N	N	1,317,207
Maryland	292	8,548	260,959	516,607	N	N	5,618,344
Massachusetts	477	21,321	659,614	1,283,325	N	N	6,449,755
Mississippi	256	7,196	208,528	497,109	N	N	2,918,785
Montana	70	2,019	36,258	73,299	N	N	957,861
Nevada	170	4,646	124,500	247,911	N	N	2,565,382
New Hampshire	96	4,206	106,488	198,819	N	N	1,315,828
New Jersey	537	34,883	848,764	1,494,002	N	N	8,685,920
New Mexico	138	6,466	135,201	243,558	N	N	1,969,915
New York	944	144,246	3,444,280	6,432,091	N	N	19,297,729
North Carolina	1,067	43,154	808,238	1,559,896	N	N	9,061,032
Ohio	993	46,744	1,051,297	2,065,541	N	N	11,466,917
Oregon	178	4,574	143,902	377,065	N	N	3,747,455
Pennsylvania	774	33,622	963,647	1,875,883	N	N	12,432,792
Rhode Island	67	4,571	114,136	209,787	N	N	1,057,832
South Carolina	237	10,025	226,321	478,973	N	N	4,407,709
Tennessee	465	14,404	435,930	1,031,242	N	N	6,156,719
Utah	153	5,110	155,271	376,066	N	N	2,645,330
Vermont	42	2,345	57,662	99,920	N	N	621,254
Virginia	523	18,633	441,868	825,367	N	N	7,712,091
Washington	300	11,136	294,518	566,998	N	N	6,468,424
West Virginia	104	3,061	80,304	163,178	N	N	1,812,035
Wyoming	42	442	10,933	26,197	N	N	522,830

Source: U.S. Bureau of the Census, 2007 Economic Census

D: Withheld to avoid disclosing data for individual companies; data are included in higher level totals.
N: Not available or not comparable.
Q: Revenue not collected at this level.
r: Revised.
S: Withheld because estimate did not meet publication standards.
s: Sampling error exceeds 40 percent.
X: Not applicable.
Z: Less than half the unit shown.
Additional symbols

http://factfinder.census.gov/servlet/IQRTable?_bm=y&-ds_name=EC0700A1&-NAICS2007=62... 7/12/2010

Also, reference librarians will assist you in your research, so that you use your research time more effectively.

- ***Industry associations, chambers of commerce, and public agencies.*** These types of organizations frequently collect demographic and statistical data on and for their members or constituents. They issue publications that contain valuable data in such areas as pricing trends, productivity, cost structures, legal matters, economic and environmental topics, and statistics. This kind of information is sometimes extremely expensive to gather but can be of great value to a start-up enterprise.
- ***Review of books and records.*** Although it is rare to have the opportunity, if you can examine records (or even journals or research notes) that are pertinent to your business, you may gain valuable insights. This is particularly true if you are practicing due diligence with a view to buying a business.
- ***Competitor Web sites.*** Look for annual reports, which are available to the public and reveal marketing and other information about a company. Annual reports provide information for benchmarking and include industry insights. In addition, check out company blogs and newsletters. It is amazing what you can find if you just look!

Market Research Helps You Know Your Customer

Performance Objective 3

Choose your market segment and research it.

market research is the collection and analysis of data regarding target markets, industries, and competitors.

Before you can put a marketing plan in place and deliver a competitive advantage to your customers, you will need to find out who your customers *are* or *can be*. **Market research** is the process of finding out

- who your potential customers are,
- where you can reach them,
- what they want and need,
- how they behave, and
- what the size of your potential market is.

Through market research, business owners ask prospective customers questions. President Woodrow Wilson once stated, "I not only use all the brains that I have, but all that I can borrow."

If you actively listen to what your customers are telling you and engage them in discussion, you can learn a lot about them. Whether your customers are private consumers or other businesses, you will want to get into their minds and find out what they really think about such subjects as

- your product or service,
- the name of your business,
- your location,
- your logo and branding materials,
- your proposed prices, and
- your promotional efforts.

If you listen to your customers and talk to them, you can learn a lot.

Market research helps you get a fix on who your customers are by answering such questions as

- How old are they?
- What kind of income do they earn?
- What are their hobbies and interests?
- What is their family structure?
- What is their occupation?
- What is the benefit your product or service offers that would best attract them?

The ideal customer should be at the center of your marketing plan. This profile will guide every marketing decision you make. If your target customer is affluent, for example, you might decide to price your product fairly high to reflect its quality. If your target market is more middle income, you might choose a strategy of lower prices to beat the competition.

Do You Know 10 People Who Love Your Product? You May Have a Winner!

Not everybody has to like your product. What's important is that some people love it—a lot. As we have seen, Russell Simmons started one of the first rap record labels, Def Jam Records, and became a multimillionaire. His perception was that if you personally know 10 people who love your product, you could have a winner.

What if you conduct your market research and learn that you do not have a winner? Is your business concept dead? Only the one you thought of first! Think positively; this is an opportunity to develop an even better idea.

Customer Research

You will want to find out everything you can about your ideal customers. What do those individuals eat, drink, listen to, and watch on TV? How much do they sleep? Where do they shop? What movies do they like? How much do they earn? How much do they spend?

A large corporation might hire a consulting firm or advertising agency to conduct market research, or may have its own marketing division. Small business owners can and should conduct market research, too. This can vary from a simple survey of your friends and neighbors that can be carried out in a day, to detailed statistical studies of a large population.

Several of the methods described above are well suited to learning about your prospective customers. If you already have a customer base, you should be learning from them, too. A few examples follow:

- ***Surveys.*** Well-designed surveys ask people directly, in interviews or through questionnaires, what they would think about a product or service if it were available. Your marketing survey should ask about
  - product or service use and frequency of purchase;
  - places where the product is purchased (the competition!) and why consumers like to purchase from these businesses; and
  - business names, logos, letterheads—everything that will represent your business in a customer's or potential customer's mind.

  Make sure your marketing surveys also gather specific information about consumers that will help you understand them better:
  - interests and hobbies,
  - reading and television-watching habits,

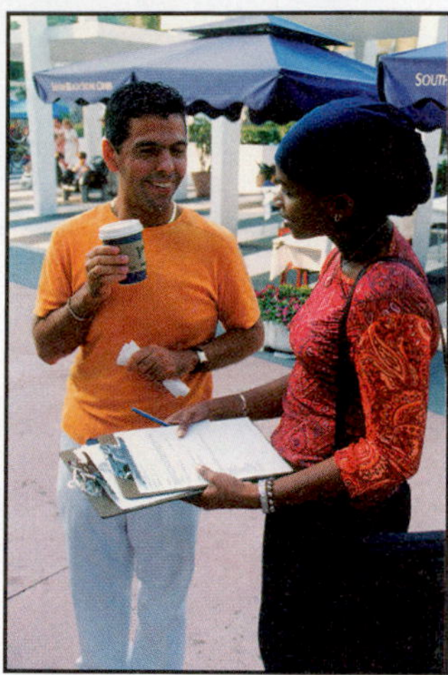

Woman conducting a market survey about banking habits with pedestrians at the Lincoln Road Mall in Miami Beach. (© Jeffrey Greenburg/Photo Researchers, Inc.)

- educational background,
- age,
- occupation,
- annual household income,
- gender, and
- family size and structure.

- ***Focus Groups.*** Another way to survey people about a product or service in development is to hold focus-group discussions. A focus group is composed of perhaps 10 to 12 people who meet screening criteria, such as being users or prospective users of a particular product. The group is typically led by a facilitator, trained in market research, who asks questions about the product or service. The resulting discussion is usually videotaped or audiotaped for later analysis. Competing communications companies, such as AT&T and Verizon, regularly hold focus groups to stay current with how consumers feel about their respective services or to determine how they will react to new calling plans or promotions.
- ***Research Reports.*** Market research firms are paid by other companies to gather information. Academics and other researchers study consumers and their purchasing and consumption patterns. The federal government can also provide statistics on consumers, from the census and other data it gathers. These sources can provide statistics on the following:
  - age;
  - annual income;
  - ethnic or religious background;
  - gender;
  - geographic location (zip code, census tract, electoral district);
  - interests;
  - occupation;
  - type of dwelling—single-family home, condominium, townhouse, or apartment (rental or owned); and
  - spending and savings patterns.

demographics population statistics.

Market research companies keep records of the typical consumer in a given area. They can then provide statistics based on age, occupation, geographic location, income, or ethnic/religious background. Market researchers also delve into consumers' hobbies and interests, and whether they own or rent their homes. Statistics dealing with the behavior of groups of people are called **demographics**.

Many kinds of statistics are available from the U.S. Government Printing Office. The latest edition of *The Statistical Abstract of the United States* is available online and provides 1400 statistical tables.

Industry Research: The 50,000-Foot Perspective

Industry research focuses not on individual consumers, but on a segment of business as a whole. It provides a broader perspective and shows trends, new and emerging opportunities, and industry norms. If you want to start a record label, you will need to know how the recording industry is doing. Is it growing? Are people buying more CDs this year, or fewer? Who are the major consumers of CDs? Which age group buys the most recordings? What kind of music is selling?

To make the best use of industry data, you will have to correctly identify your industry and examine it. The codes of the North American Industry Classification System (NAICS), or Standard Industrial Classification (SIC), are generally used as industry identifiers. Once you have the NAICS code (six digits), you can readily search many sources of data. You can find NAICS and SIC codes at the library in the *North American Industrial Classification System: United States, 2007* (NTIS, 2007) and the *Standard Industrial Classification Manual, 1987* (NTIS, 1987), respectively. You can also find your NAICS code online at the U.S. Census Web site (*http://www.census.gov/epcd/naics02/*), in which you will enter a keyword and then narrow your selections until you find the best fit for your organization.

Once you have identified your industry, you can perform data searches to find relevant statistics and reports. Some places to look include the Standard and Poor's *Industry Surveys*, the U.S. Census Web site (*http://www.census.gov*), Wetfeet.com (*http://www.wetfeet.com/asp/industries_atoz.asp*), and BizMiner (*http://www.bizminer.com*). The census data will include the number of firms, revenues, number of paid employees, and more. In many cases, there are industry reports available on the Census site. There are numerous other sources as well. Once you identify them, you can answer such questions as

- What is the scale (size) of the industry, in units and dollars?
- What is the scope (geographic range) of the industry? Is it local (city or neighborhood only), regional (covering a metropolitan area or state), national, international (present in two or more countries), or global (everywhere)?
- Is it a niche industry or does it reach a mass market?
- What does industry and firm profitability look like?
- What trends are occurring in the industry? Is it growing? Declining? Stagnating?
- What is the structure of the industry? Is it highly concentrated, with a few companies controlling it? Is it highly fragmented, with a lot of competition?
- What competition is in the market space and what are they doing? Do an industry SWOT analysis to visualize this.

The methods to use for industry research overlap with those for customer research to some extent, but they reach further. Some methods to try include

- ***Interviews.*** Perhaps you can find people in the industry (staff) or who study the industry (stock analysts, professors, economic development professionals) who will share insights and data.
- ***Observation.*** This might include visiting public tours of industry facilities, trade meetings, and so forth.
- ***Tracking.*** Keeping track of industry advertisements and reports could help. For example, you may want to start a financial services company, so tracking interest rates is vital.
- ***Written sources for statistical data.*** Such statistics can be found in a variety of written sources, including those mentioned earlier. Check out the Internet Public Library at *http://www.ipl.org/div/subject/browse/bus82.00.00/*. For industry and firm profitability, try online services for a fee, such as Risk Management Association (RMA) or BizMiner. Or use free library resources, such as *RMA Annual Statement Studies: Financial Ratio Benchmarks*.

- ***Books and articles.*** Surprisingly, there are books and articles about almost any business topic that you can imagine. If your library doesn't have what you need, you might be able to acquire it through interlibrary loan.
- ***Competitor Web sites.*** As noted previously, annual reports often include excellent descriptions of companies within an industry, and their respective operating environments.
- ***Trade associations and chambers of commerce.*** Virtually every industry has at least one professional or trade association. You can search online by industry plus the word *association* to find them. Or, you can look in Gale Publishing's *Directory of Associations* at a library. The American Society of Association Executives gateway (*http://www.asaecenter.org*) has an online list of members, and you can find association magazines and journals at *http://www.mediafinder.com*.

By taking the time to research and understand your industry, you can be more successful in your own business. Plus, you will know a lot more about your field.

Ford and Chrysler each spent millions on market research before producing, respectively, the Mustang and the minivan. It was worth millions of dollars to these companies to determine if the public wanted these automobiles because it was going to cost tens of millions to produce them.

Make Market Research an Integral Part of Your Business

Market research is not something you only do once. Make it an ongoing part of your operations. Just as your tastes and desires change as you learn about new ideas and products, so do those of your customers. By continuing to survey your customers as your business develops, you will stay current with their needs and how they feel about your product. You can provide customers with prepaid response cards, conduct in-store surveys, or conduct telephone surveys, depending upon your business. By carefully reviewing your customer purchasing and contact history, you can target your surveys for maximum effectiveness.

Global Impact . . .

Cell Phones in the Sauna?

The Finnish telecommunications company Nokia is tremendously innovative. The company has been codeveloping a device that will enable people to make payments for anything, from a bar tab to a bank loan, using their cell phones. But when a reporter from *Wired* magazine asked a Nokia spokesman if anyone was working on making heatproof cell phones, so Finns could take them into the sauna, where they spend a significant amount of time, the spokesman fixed the reporter with a look of disdain and explained, "In sauna, we do not even want to hear Bach." (*Wired,* "Just Say Nokia," by Steve Silberman, September 1999).

When you know your market, you will know how to reach the people in it. This is why it is so important to take the time to conduct market research before you open your business. You may be impatient to get started, but do not do so until you have come to know your market intimately.

New global opportunity? (© Corbis Super RF/Alamy)

How Customers Decide to Buy

How will you figure out who the potential customers are for *your* business? It is critical to understand not only who is in your target market, but how they will purchase your product (or service).

Step One. If you have developed a product or service, ask yourself what consumer need it will serve. Arm & Hammer turned this marketing question into a gold mine by developing its simple baking-soda powder into toothpaste, air and carpet fresheners, and deodorants.

Step Two. Think about who might actually buy your product. Remember that the people who use a product are not always the purchasers. Mothers generally buy children's clothes, so, if you are making children's playsuits, they should offer features/benefits that appeal to mothers. They could be marketed as very easy to clean, for example.

Step Three. Analyze the buying process that will lead customers to your product.

1. ***Awareness.*** The customer realizes a need. Advertising is designed to make consumers and business customers aware of potential needs for everything from dandruff shampoo to office supplies to automobiles.
2. ***Information Search.*** The customer seeks information about products that could fulfill the need. Someone looking for a multivitamin might pick up a brochure on the counter of the local health food store, or simply look on the shelves of a supermarket. A retailer might search a business-to-business phone directory for sign companies.
3. ***Evaluate Alternatives.*** Once information is gathered on a single product, the customer may want to examine alternatives before making a purchasing decision. The individual looking for a multivitamin might check out what's available in the health food store, and compare the price and content with the more commercial brands found in the local supermarket or drug store. The business owner might get several quotations on business signs that she needs.
4. ***Decide to Purchase.*** The first purchase is really a test; the customer is trying your product to see how well it performs (or testing the quality of your service).
5. ***Evaluation of Purchase.*** If your product or service is satisfactory, the customer may begin to develop loyalty to your business and tell others about it, as well. Now, how can you keep this customer for life?

Owning a Perception in the Customer's Mind

More valuable to McDonald's than all the Big Macs it sells every year is the perception it owns in the minds of its customers—that every time they patronize a McDonald's, they will eat food that tastes exactly the same as at every other McDonald's, that the prices will be reasonable, and that the service will be friendly and fast.

For Burger King to compete with McDonald's, it had to fight for a mind share of the fast-food customer. Burger King opened its attack with "Have It Your Way," which targeted McDonald's mass-manufacturing approach to making hamburgers. It followed up with "Broiled, not Fried" and "The Whopper Beats the Big Mac."

It is almost impossible to topple an established leading brand in a market. Burger King's executives wisely decided that their goal was to be a strong number two. As number two, you try to create a new category (broiled instead of fried hamburgers, for instance) rather than attempting to take over the competitive advantage of the number one company in the market. Avis lost money for 15 years because it tried to overtake Hertz. The company finally accepted its number two position and turned it into a competitive advantage through its advertising campaign: "We Try Harder!"and became very profitable.

You do not have to be number one to be successful; discover a competitive advantage and attack the market by creating a new category in the customer's mind. Domino's Pizza found a competitive advantage by delivering orders in less than 30 minutes. That one marketing insight created a hugely successful company.

Features Create Benefits

There is a subtle, but important, difference between the benefits and the features of a product. The features are facts. The features of a drill might include its hardness and sharpness, but the benefit is that it makes a hole. The feature of a Teflon coating on a pan creates the benefit of easy cleaning. The essence of selling is showing how and why the outstanding features of your product or service will benefit customers. Smart marketers always emphasize benefits, not features, because consumers will buy what solves their problems or makes their lives more pleasant.

Home Depot: Teaching Customers So They Will Return

Home Depot's marketing vision is not just to sell tools and materials but to teach people how to use them to improve their homes and lives. The company's marketing vision focuses on what its customers need Home Depot products to do.

Successful companies are not built on one-time sales but on repeat business. The owners of Home Depot have calculated that a satisfied customer is worth more than $25,000 in sales over the customer's lifetime. Bernie Marcus, one of Home Depot's founders, has said, "All of our people understand what the Holy Grail is. It is not the bottom line. It is an almost blind, passionate commitment to taking care of customers."

Home Depot's multimillion-dollar insight was that its customers not only needed the products it sold but they also needed help in using them.

BizFacts

Minority business owners (often defined to include women) should contact local corporate offices and ask about minority purchasing programs, or find the local office of the National Minority Supplier Development Council (*http://www.nmsdcus.org*) or government diversity agency. Many companies and most government agencies are committed to buying up to 25 percent of their supplies and services from minority-owned businesses.

Needs, Wants, and Demands

Home Depot is meeting its customers' needs for help with home improvement, not just tools. What are needs, really, and how do they differ from desires (wants) or demands?

- ***Needs.*** Northwestern University Professor Philip Kotler's classic marketing textbook defines human needs as "states of felt deprivations."[3] Meeting a customer need is solving a problem or helping someone achieve comfort.
- ***Wants.*** Kotler defines wants as "the form taken by human needs as they are shaped by culture and individual personality."[4] Wants are objects that will satisfy a need. "I'm hungry; I want a hamburger," a New Yorker might say. "I'm hungry; I want jerk chicken," a Jamaican might say. Essentially, wants are needs with individual preferences.
- ***Demands.*** Demands, according to Kotler, are wants backed by buying power. A poor student might translate hunger into a demand for a Big Mac, whereas a successful lawyer might transform his hunger into a demand for a steak dinner. People demand the products and services that best satisfy their wants within the limitations of their resources.

The most successful companies pay close attention to consumer demands. They constantly observe their customers, survey them, and analyze their wants, needs, and demands. They hire people to look for customer needs that might be going unfulfilled. This is all part of customer analysis, one step in developing a marketing plan.

Which Segment of the Market Will You Target?

Marketing strategies are focused on the customer, and a business has to choose which customers to target. Almost certainly, your product will not be needed by everyone. You will have to figure out which segments of the market to target.

There is a huge market for home repair, including professional carpenters and builders. Home Depot's competitive advantage would not be strong in the market segment composed of professionals, in which the distribution channels are strong and well established. A **market segment** is composed of customers who have a similar response to a certain type of marketing. Home Depot chose to market primarily to the nonprofessional, private individual.

market segment a group of consumers or businesses that have a similar response to a particular type of product or service.

In the cosmetics industry, one segment reacts positively to luxuriously packaged, expensive brands. Another is most responsive to products that claim to reduce signs of aging. Another's primary concern is (reasonable) price. A company that recognizes these market segments and chooses one to concentrate on will do better than a business that tries to sell its cosmetics to every adult female in the country.

It is difficult to target very different segments of a market simultaneously. Volvo, for example, has established a reputation as a safe, family car. It targets parents with young children. Volvo would have a difficult time also trying to market a two-seat convertible sports car to young adults who are concerned more with style and speed than safety.

[3]Philip Kotler and Gary Armstrong, *Marketing: An Introduction* (Upper Saddle River, N.J.: Prentice Hall, 1997), p. 6.
[4]See Kotler and Armstrong, *Marketing*, p. 7.

Successful Segmenting: The Body Shop

The Body Shop is a good example of the success that can result from choosing the right market segment. Founder Anita Roddick disliked paying for expensive packaging and perfuming when she bought cosmetics. She was also annoyed by the extravagant claims made by many cosmetics companies and by the high prices of their perfumes and lotions. Price became an integral part of the image for many products. A brand called Joy, for example, was marketed as the most expensive perfume in the world.

Roddick saw an opportunity to create a different line of cosmetics. She would use natural products that would be packaged inexpensively and marketed without extravagant claims. As she said in her book, "It is immoral to deceive a customer by making miracle claims for a product. It is immoral to use a photograph of a glowing sixteen-year-old to sell a cream aimed at preventing wrinkles in a forty-year-old."[5]

Roddick tapped into a segment of the cosmetics market that had been neglected, and her business grew explosively as a result. Her success proves that selling an honest product honestly can be the best marketing strategy of all.

But what if Roddick had found that there were very few women interested in natural cosmetics? If she had determined this before starting, then she could have changed her segmentation strategy. If not, her business would not have survived, because even though the cosmetics market is large, her segment would have been too small to support her venture. As *The Ten-Day MBA* author Steven Silbiger points out, "The easiest mistake to make is to believe that your *relevant* market includes the total sales of your product category."[6]

It is possible to go after a small, niche segment, but then your price would have to be high enough to make a profit, and the customers would have to buy often enough to keep your business going. Jaguar and Rolls-Royce each sell far fewer cars than Honda or Ford, but at much higher prices. Jaguar and Rolls target the luxury segment of the car market.

Applying Market Segmentation Methods

Marketers have developed four basic ways to segment:

- ***Geographic.*** Dividing a population by location.
- ***Demographic.*** Dividing a population based on a variable such as age, gender, income, or education. For business customers, variables such as sales volume and number of employees could matter.
- ***Psychographic.*** Dividing a population by psychological differences, such as opinion (conservative versus liberal) or lifestyle (sedentary versus active).
- ***Behavioral.*** Dividing the market by purchase behaviors that have been observed, such as brand loyalty or responsiveness to price.

Say you want to make and sell hacky sacks on your college campus. Twenty thousand students attend the college. To which students will you direct your marketing? If 50 of the 200 students surveyed are interested in buying your hacky sack, you can expect that approximately 5000 students of the 20,000 would represent your total potential market. Which segments of that market should you target?

[5]Anita Roddick, *Body & Soul, Anita Roddick Tells the Story of the Body Shop, Inc.* (New York: Crown Publishers, 1991).
[6]Steven Silbiger, *The Ten-Day MBA* (New York: William Morrow, 1993), p. 31.

Step into the Shoes . . .

How Thomas Burrell Became a Leader in Marketing to African Americans

To market a product or service to a specific market segment, you must research what the people who comprise it want. In the late 1960s, major corporations became more conscious of the potential clout of African American consumers but were unsure how to market to them.

In 1971, Thomas Burrell opened one of the first black-owned advertising agencies in the United States. By 1972, Burrell had convinced McDonald's that Burrell Advertising could help the huge company expand into the African American market. Burrell came to be the fastest-growing and largest black-owned advertising agency in the United States.

Burrell Advertising has created more than 100 commercials for McDonald's. Other Burrell clients have included Coca-Cola, Ford Motor, Johnson Products, Schlitz Brewing, Blockbuster Entertainment, Procter & Gamble, Jack Daniel Distillery, Polaroid, Stroh Brewing, and First National Bank of Chicago.

Burrell himself could probably quote the demographics of the African American market off the top of his head. He has combined his company's thorough market research with his own personal experience as an African American male to create powerful appeals to the targeted market. Burrell describes his marketing philosophy as "positive realism." He adds, "We wanted to make sure the consumer understood the advertiser was inviting that consumer—that black consumer—to participate as a consumer of their product. Black consumers have not felt they were being extended an invitation."

Thomas Burrell, founder of Burrell Advertising.

If your company has very limited resources, you might choose to target only one segment. A large company might decide to appeal to the entire market by designing a product tailored for each segment. Gap Inc., for example, has three product lines—Old Navy, Gap, and Banana Republic—each priced for and tailored to a segment of the sportswear market.

You could use any of the four segmentation methods listed previously:

- ***Geographic.*** You could decide that your market is everyone who lives within two miles of the campus.
- ***Demographic.*** You could decide to focus on health-minded students.
- ***Psychographic.*** You could decide to market to individuals who like rock music.
- ***Behavioral.*** You could decide to market to individuals who buy Frisbees or play soccer.

One way to gauge your market would be to interview a sample of 200 students with a structured survey, showing them the product and asking such questions as

- Do you play Frisbee?
- If so, how often do you play?
- Do you own a hacky sack?
- Would you be interested in purchasing this hacky sack, if it were available?
- How much would you pay for this hacky sack?
- How many of these hacky sacks would you buy per year?
- What suggestions do you have to improve this hacky sack?

Once you have chosen your market segment, you can really fine-tune your market research, because you now have to focus only on these customers—not on every potential customer in your market. Collecting data from the people in your market segment can be fun as well as financially rewarding. Here are a few questions you can adapt to your own product or service:

1. Do you currently use this type of product?
2. What brand(s) of this product do you currently use?
3. Where do you buy it? Please be specific about the source, such as the name and location of the store, a direct marketing representative, or a Web site.
4. How much do you pay for it? (Probe for size and price, if appropriate.)
5. How often do you buy it?
6. Would you buy our product/service?
7. How much would you be willing to pay for it?
8. Where would you shop for it?
9. How would you improve it?
10. Now that you have seen/tasted/felt/smelled this product, who do you consider to be its closest competitor?
11. Is our product/service worse or better than those of our competitors? Please explain.

The Product Life Cycle

product life cycle (PLC) the four stages that a product or service goes through as it matures in the market—introduction, growth, maturity, and decline.

You will also need to analyze where your market is in its **product life cycle (PLC)**. The PLC is the set of four stages that a product or market goes through from its beginning until its end. **Figure 6-1** illustrates two product life cycles.

1. ***Introduction.*** Your product or service is in the invention and initial-development stages. It is new to the market and is essentially unknown, so you will need to introduce it to potential customers, who may be curious about your product but not familiar with it. Marketing at this stage will require education and testing with price and presentation. Some tinkering with the design or technology may also be required. When the personal home computer was first

Figure 6-1 *Product life cycle.*

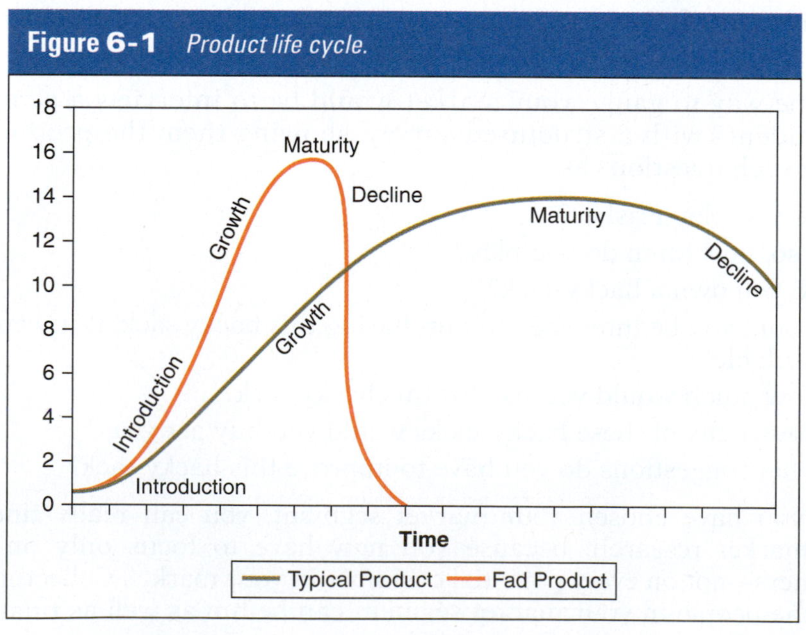

introduced, Apple's marketing was focused on convincing consumers how easy it would be to use. Apple used the same strategy in the introduction of the iMac.

2. ***Growth.*** Once you achieve success in introducing your product or service to the marketplace, your organization will grow and attract attention from your competition, as well as perhaps attract new entrants in the field. Attracted by your growth in sales, competitors now start entering your market, or more strongly defend their market spaces, so efforts at this stage will have to focus on communicating your competitive advantage to consumers. Customer purchases increase dramatically and you have reached a mass market.
3. ***Maturity.*** At this stage, consumers have become knowledgeable about both you and your competitors. The market has become relatively crowded, and there is no more growth as your product or service is currently offered. Advertising will need to focus on promoting brand loyalty. Stability of profits now depends more on cost strategies as demand becomes relatively flat.
4. ***Decline.*** At this point, your competitive advantage has eroded, and sales and profits are declining. New developments will be necessary to revive the market's interest.

Product life cycles are applicable in different ways. For example, the Pet Rock, essentially a small stone that people were to pretend was a pet, had a very short life cycle. Such fad items attain popularity quickly and mature and decline equally rapidly. Other products, such as prescription drugs, will have longer life cycles because of patent protection, high market-entry costs, and their medical necessity for certain population groups. Ideally, you will look at the overall life cycle of a market to determine where your product or service will fit.

It is important for you to understand where each product or service is in the PLC. See **Figure 6-1** on the previous page for an illustration of the PLC of a normal product and for a fad item. It is important to have a continuous flow of new products, so that your organization as a whole is not on the decline. For example, if you owned a pharmaceutical company, you would want to introduce new products well before the existing ones reached maturity/decline, so that there would be continuity in revenue. You would also want to find new uses for existing drugs, to extend their life cycles. For example, AstraZeneca's Seroquel was initially approved for schizophrenia, and was used off-label for bipolar disorder. To extend Seroquel's life cycle, AstraZeneca sought U.S. Food and Drug Administration (FDA) approval for the additional use. This is far less costly and quicker than developing a new brand-name drug.

For services, the life cycle is essentially the same as for products. However, extending the life cycle can be easier for a service than for a product. Starting a new cycle could be as simple as modifying the delivery process.

In addition, if you are considering acquiring an existing business, it is critical to understand where in the PLC its products and services are. Are they all toward the end of their life cycles? Mixed? At the beginning? This will dramatically affect the future value of the company.

Is Your Market Saturated?

Figuring out where your product is in the PLC will tell you whether your market is close to saturation. In other words, have all 3 million people in your market already bought a competitor's product? Nokia, for example, has a 39 percent share of the global market of $1.1 billion in mobile phones.[7] But that market is nowhere near saturation. Meanwhile, Nokia introduced its Short Message Service (SMS), which allows e-mail messages to be sent between mobile phones in Finland. SMS quickly became Finnish teenagers' favorite way to communicate. Observing how quickly the technology spread among Finnish teenagers gave the Nokia management ideas about how they would market SMS in the 140 countries where they sold cell phones.

Market Positioning: Drive Home Your Competitive Advantage

Performance Objective 4

Position your product or service within your market.

positioning distinguishing a product or service from similar products or services being offered to the same market.

After deciding which market segments to target, an entrepreneur will need to figure out what position the company should try to occupy in those segments. *Position* is defined by Philip Kotler as "The place that the product occupies relative to competitors in consumers' minds."[8] The goal of market **positioning**, therefore, is to distinguish your product or service from others being offered to the market segments you have targeted. You can do that by focusing on your competitive advantage. "Have It Your Way," Burger King promised, driving home its competitive advantage—that at Burger King you can specify exactly how you want your hamburger prepared and garnished.

As you can see from the Burger King example, positioning involves clearly communicating your competitive advantage to the consumer and demonstrating how your product/service is different. Your goal is to position your product/service clearly in the mind of your target market as the brand that provides that difference. Try using the following format to develop a positioning statement for your business:

> (Your business name/brand) is the (competitive industry/category) that (provides these benefits, or points of difference) to (audience/target market).

Here is an example: (Microsoft) is the (leading U.S. software producer) that (provides affordable computer solutions) to (American businesses).

By the time you have completed the four steps of your marketing plan, you will know your potential customers, your competitors, and your market intimately. It is a lot of work but well worth it. Make a commitment to let marketing drive your business decisions, and you will greatly increase the odds that your business will be successful.

Developing a Marketing Plan

Now that you understand how marketing should permeate your business, you are ready to develop a plan for introducing your product to your market. The marketing plan, as discussed in Chapter 4, can serve as a stand-alone document or be part of a complete business plan. Either way, it should be a functioning, evolving part of your business. We began with customer analysis because, before you can develop a marketing vision, you will need to know who your customers are and what they want.

Q: Why does a customer go to a hardware store to buy a drill?

A: Because she needs to make a hole.

---

[7] Mark Landler, "Nokia Pushes to Regain U.S. Sales in Spite of Apple and Google," *The New York Times*, December 10, 2007.

[8] Adapted from Kotler and Armstrong, *Principles of Marketing*, 9th ed. (Upper Saddle River, N.J.: Prentice Hall, 2001).

The *hole* is what the customer needs, not the drill. If the hole could be bought at the hardware store, the customer would not bother with the drill.[9] If you are marketing drills, therefore, you should explain to the customer what good holes they make! If someone invents a better hole-maker, drill manufacturers will soon be out of business.

Your marketing plan must include an understanding of prospective customers and their wants, needs, and demands. It should also identify and analyze market segments. The plan should incorporate industry research and trend analysis. It will state your market-positioning approach. In short, a marketing plan looks at all aspects of the market space for your enterprise, from the broadest perspective to the narrowest.

Chapter Summary

Now that you have studied this chapter you can do the following:

1. Explain how marketing differs from selling.
   - Marketing is the business function that identifies your customers and their needs and wants.
   - Through marketing, the name of your business comes to mean something clear and concrete in the customer's mind. Above all, marketing is the way a business communicates its competitive advantage to its market.
2. Understand how market research prepares you for success. Market research is the process of finding out who your potential customers are, where you can reach them, and what they want and need.
   - Getting the information directly from the subject: primary research.
     - Personal interviews
     - Telephone surveys
     - Written surveys
     - Focus groups
     - Observation
     - Tracking
   - Getting information indirectly: secondary research.
     - Online searches
     - Books and articles
     - Trade associations, chambers of commerce, public agencies
     - Review of books and records
     - Researching customers and industries
3. Choose your market segment and research it.
   - Before you can develop a marketing vision for your business, you will need to know who your customers are and what they want.
     1. A market segment is composed of consumers who have a similar response to a certain type of marketing.
     2. Segmentation methods:
        a. *Geographic*. Dividing a population by location.
        b. *Demographic*. Dividing a population based on a variable like age, gender, income, or education.

[9]Special thanks to Joe Mancuso for this concept.

c. *Psychographic*. Dividing a population by psychological differences such as opinion (conservative versus liberal) or lifestyle.
d. *Behavioral*. Dividing the market by observable purchase behaviors such as brand loyalty or responsiveness to price.

4. Position your product or service within your market.
   - The goal of market positioning is to distinguish your product or service from others being offered to the same market segments. You can do that by focusing on your competitive advantage.
   - Use the following format to develop a positioning statement for your business: (Your business name/brand) is the (competitive industry/category) that (provides these benefits, or points of difference) to (audience/target market).

Key Terms

demographics
market research
market segment
marketing
positioning
primary research
product life cycle (PLC)
secondary research

Entrepreneurship Portfolio

Critical Thinking Exercises

1. Step One: Consumer Analysis

Describe the typical consumer your business plans to target.

Attribute	My Customer
Age	
Income	
Education	
Hobbies	
Other	

What need do you plan to satisfy for this consumer? ___________

2. Step Two: Market Analysis
   - How large is the total market for your product or service? How did you arrive at this figure?
   - Which segment of this market do you intend to target? Why? How large is the segment?
   - Describe your segmentation method. Why did you choose this method?
3. Choose five people from your market segment to research with a survey. Write 10 questions in a yes-or-no format and ask the survey participants to frame their responses on a scale of one to four, or design your own range. Also ask five open-ended questions (questions that cannot be answered with a yes or no).

Key Concept Questions

1. Which four factors should market research include and why?
2. Write a positioning statement for your business.
3. Describe where you think your product or service is in the product life cycle.
4. Read and interpret the chart in **Figure 6-2**.
   a. Which single provider has the largest market share? What is the percentage?
   b. What share do the two largest suppliers enjoy together?
   c. How much bigger is IBM's share than Apple's?
   d. If there are approximately 100 other smaller makers of personal computers, about how much market share would each have on average?

Figure 6-2 *Global PC market share.*

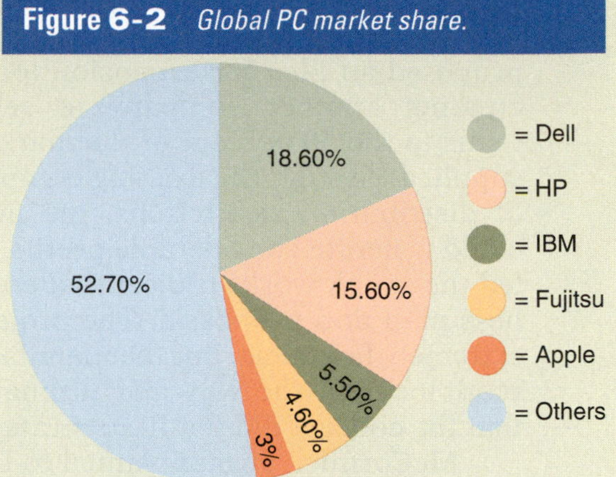

5. Research can give you a great deal of information, but you will have to use your math skills to make it more useful. For example, imagine you are interested in opening a dog care service, and you have gathered the following facts:
   - In 2000, the U.S. Census Bureau estimated that there were 2.67 people per household.
   - According to your city's public records, the population of your community is 80,000.
   - The *U.S. Pet Ownership & Demographics Sourcebook*[10] estimates that the number of dog-owning households in a community equals 0.361 multiplied by the total number of households.
   - The *Sourcebook*[11] also estimates that the number of dogs in a community equals 0.578 multiplied by the total number of households—or 1.6 multiplied by the number of dog-owning households.

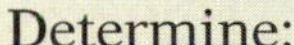

Determine:
   a. The number of dog-owning households in your community.
   b. The number of dogs in your community. Round your answers off to the nearest whole number.

Application Exercises

Order a sandwich at three different fast-food restaurants; then answer the following:

1. Did you observe any differences in how the employees handled your order? Describe them.
2. Describe what you believe to be the marketing vision of each restaurant based on what you observed. Write a positioning statement for each restaurant.
3. Analyze the market for each restaurant, using the four methods of market-segmentation analysis: geographic, demographic, psychographic, and behavioral.
4. Where do you think each restaurant is in the product life cycle?

Exploring Online

Go online and conduct an industry-wide search for competition for your business. Create a profile of the competition (this may be written using a word-processing program or shown as a graph using Excel). It should include minimum and maximum prices, minimum and maximum ordering times, and any other information you feel is pertinent.

[10] 2007 American Veterinary Medical Association, Schaumburg, IL.
[11] Ibid.

Case Study | American Electrical: Understanding the Market Sparks a New Venture

Entrepreneur Tom McCormick was the vice president of sales for an $800 million global manufacturer of electrical components when he proposed an idea for expansion to his boss. By creating another company to sell accessory items to the 50 percent of the market not being supplied through the existing company because of distribution restrictions, the manufacturer could generate considerable profits. McCormick led the skunk works project that created a business plan and proposals. The projections were extremely favorable, but the manufacturer threw roadblocks in the way and ultimately decided that the concept did not fit its strategy.

McCormick always wanted to have his own business; as he says, "I talked about it constantly to the point where some close friends made fun of me!" He had sold T-shirts while in college, met with business brokers, and networked. When the business proposal was rejected by his employer, McCormick decided that it was time to take the business plan and run with it. He says, "I knew where my first 100 sales were going to be and I had already researched who and how." He found suppliers, starting with one in Germany, and hired a graphic designer to produce two short product catalogs. In July of 1997, he took $60,000 from his retirement fund and founded American Electrical, Inc. (AEI).

Today, McCormick's company generates approximately $3 million per year in sales and has three full-time employees; it operates out of a 5000-square-foot office/warehouse in Richmond, Virginia. American Electrical imports electrical and electronic controls from 10 companies, primarily in Europe, for the industrial controls marketplace in the United States. Tom McCormick took his business plan and turned it into a successful venture.

Tom McCormick, American Electrical, Inc.

Case Study Analysis

1. In what areas of the market did McCormick do research before starting his business?
2. What research methods would you recommend for AEI today? Name three specific sources of information.
3. How did McCormick identify AEI's market? Name the segmentation method and the segment they chose.
4. What is the role of marketing in McCormick's business?

Case Study | Russell Simmons, Hip-Hop Entrepreneur

Russell Simmons turned off his cell phone and took a rare moment to admire the view from his fourteenth-floor office in midtown Manhattan. At 47, Simmons knew he had a lot going for him. As the president of Rush Communications, he sat at the helm of a constellation of successful enterprises, including a record label, a clothing line, a philanthropic arts foundation, and a multimedia production company. Lately, he had been thinking about how to leverage his influence as a hip-hop mogul to inspire young people to get involved in social issues such as voter registration and education reform. Yet, when he was growing up in Hollis, Queens, in the 1960s and 1970s, Simmons never could have imagined that his life would have turned out like this.

Russell Simmons, media mogul.

Window of Opportunity

Early on, Simmons decided that he wanted to make his own way in the world. His father had been a teacher, and his mother worked as a recreation coordinator. Both enjoyed stable jobs, but Simmons was not driven by a need for security. He wanted to live a fast-paced life and call his own shots. In 1977, Simmons, who never liked school very much, enrolled at the City College of New York as a sociology major. That year, something happened that permanently changed the course of his life. He went to hear a rap artist named Eddie Cheeba perform and was amazed to see how the rapper had cast a spell over the audience with his freestyle rhymes. In Simmons's own words:

> *Just like that, I saw how I could turn my life in another, better way. . . . All the street entrepreneurship I'd learned, I decided to put into promoting music.*[12]

At that time, rap and hip-hop were underground musical styles, but Simmons set out to change this. He believed that rap music had the potential to reach a larger audience, and so he teamed up with another aspiring rap producer, Rick Rubin. Rubin had built a recording studio for rap artists in his New York University dorm room. Together, they decided to transform Rick's studio into a viable record label. By 1985, Def Jam Records was officially underway.

Def Jam experienced its first surge of success when it scored a hit with Run DMC's remake of the Aerosmith classic, "Walk This Way." Bridging the worlds of rock and rap music turned out to be a stroke of genius. Simmons and Rubin singlehandedly introduced a whole new market of mostly white, suburban, heavy-metal music fans to hip-hop. Suddenly, Run DMC was being featured on MTV, and rap was no longer an underground fad.

Marketing Insight: Authenticity Matters

Simmons learned an important lesson from Run DMC's success. He realized that these artists had gone to the top of the charts because they had remained true to their street style and musical origins. Whereas Run DMC may have popularized wearing gold chains, branded sneakers, and name-plate belts among suburban teenagers, these were the fashions that its core audience of urban youth had already embraced. Simmons understood that being perceived as authentic was key to making it in his segment of the music industry.

[12]Russell Simmons, *Life and Def: Sex, Drugs, Money + God* (New York: Crown Publishing, 2002).

You have to tell the truth. It endears you to the community. The [people] can smell the truth, and they're a lot smarter than the people who put the records out.[13]

Simmons knew how to market his product, and his ability to promote rap music and the hip-hop lifestyle was influenced by how close he was to it.

Simmons has maintained this philosophy of "keeping it real" throughout his business career. It permeates everything he does and is even reflected in his preference for wearing Phat Farm sweatshirts instead of Brooks Brothers suits. Since those early days, Simmons has gone on to launch many other business ventures, which are all geared toward the same target market: urban teens and young adults. This market has the power to influence the tastes and preferences of other consumers.

Simmons's Empire Grows

In 1999, Simmons sold his stake in Def Jam records to Polygram Records for over $100 million. He has since focused his energies on developing the various entertainment, fashion, and multimedia companies that make up Rush Communications. Simmons's business goals have evolved from promoting hip-hop music to developing new products and services for the urban youth market.

Simmons also began using his status as a taste-maker and hip-hop entrepreneur to influence public debate about political issues. In 2002, he organized a youth summit in New York, featuring hip-hop artists such as Jay-Z and Alicia Keyes. When Simmons put out a call to action over the airwaves, over 20,000 students showed up at New York's City Hall to protest the mayor's proposed cuts to the education budget. Simmons has demonstrated that he has the skill and sophistication to market ideas as well as products and services. He continues to sit at the helm of Rush Communications, where he keeps his radar attuned to new opportunities in the marketplace.

[13]Jennifer Reingold, "Rush Hour," *Fast Company* magazine, no. 76, November 2003.

Case Study Analysis

1. Why do you think Russell Simmons has been successful?
2. Describe the target market that Simmons is trying to appeal to in all of his business ventures. What does this target market value?
3. Simmons grew up surrounded by hip-hop music and culture. In what ways did this give him an advantage in the marketplace? How might his insider's knowledge also function as a limitation?
4. Brainstorm a business idea that you could pitch to Russell Simmons that would be appropriate for Rush Communications. What market research would you need to conduct in advance to assess whether or not your idea had the potential to be successful?
5. Russell Simmons invested $5000 to start Def Jam and then later sold his business to Polygram Records for $100 million. Calculate Simmons's return on investment (ROI).

Case Sources

Jennifer Reingold, "Rush Hour," *Fast Company* magazine, no. 76, November 2003.

Russell Simmons, *Life and Def: Sex, Drugs, Money + God* (New York: Crown Publishing, 2002).

Nicole Miller Company

***Small Business School* video clip titles are in red**

BE WILLING TO BUCK THE SYSTEM

Nicole Miller

In 1982, Nicole Miller and Bud Konheim noticed that in department stores the trendy dresses were found in the junior department, while the well-made dresses were in the missy department. Nicole and Bud were working together at a large clothing manufacturer, and they began discussing the need for dresses that were trendy and well made. With the blessing of their employer, Nicole and Bud started a new company to fill what proved to be an enormous niche in women's fashion. Every product starts at Nicole's sketch pad, and today her designs generate $82 million in annual sales.

Create a Win/Win

The startup was smooth because Nicole and Bud essentially took one division of the large manufacturer and spun it out into what is now Nicole Miller. Bud kept his role as manager, and Nicole maintained her role as designer. At the request of their former employer, they sold off the inventory owned by the old company, then launched their new line selling to the same customers.

According to Bud, "Day one was a change of name as far as the customers went. We had a three-week period that my employer was paying the salaries and wishing me well, we had our sales people informing all of the customers that everything they had on order was going to be shipped as of June 1, 1982—they were going to get their shipments on time, just the way they ordered them—but the name on the label was going to be Nicole Miller. And they were going to get an invoice from Nicole Miller and they were going to pay Nicole Miller. We were just switching the names. Everybody went along with it because all they wanted was the merchandise—it was fine. In our first month we shipped $600,000. It was lucky in a way, but we had prepared for the luck. It was like—we gave luck a chance to happen."

When Bud started selling the new Nicole Miller label, the buyers were uncertain about the placement of these hybrid dresses. The combination of trendy and well-made did not fit neatly into their existing merchandising. The dresses were too trendy for the missy department and too expensive for the junior department. As a veteran dress salesman, Bud knew how to ease their concerns and, even more importantly, he had a relationship with the buyers that he had formed over years, selling for the old company. They trusted him. What appeared to be success right out of the chute actually happened because Nicole and Bud started a business that grew out of their extensive experience plus recognition of a market opportunity.

SELL HAPPINESS

Nicole told me that her goal is to create timeless designs and her customers tell me that Nicole has succeeded. I wear Nicole Miller designs and have had some of them for 10 years. Customers I met in the Nicole Miller

Case prepared by Hattie Bryant

shop in La Jolla, California, told me they were anxious to find something they loved from Nicole Miller because they knew they would be wearing it for years. Yet, the designs are fresh enough to fulfill the initial mission of creating trendy, well-made clothes.

In addition to creating stylish yet timeless clothing, Nicole and Bud committed to making the price affordable. Designer labels at one time were out of reach for the average American woman, but Nicole Miller changed this by finding just the right mix of design, fabrication, and cost of manufacturing.

As clichéd as it may sound, Bud says, "We sell happiness. The dress has to be hip, well made, and priced so the woman has a smile on her face when she leaves the store." The style, the craftsmanship, and the price all combine to make the customer feel as if she is wearing more than she paid for. Nicole has to be looking for new fabrics and creating new designs while Bud is monitoring the competition and keeping a sharp eye on costs.

Keep Manufacturing at Home

According to the Fashion Center Web site New York City's Garment District is comprised of 18.4 million square feet, extending from Fifth to Ninth Avenues and from 35th to 41st Streets, in zip code 10018.[14] More than 100,000 people work here and the Nicole Miller Company is proud to say that their clothing is made, from idea to finished product, in New York City. Nicole and Bud enjoy doing business close to home because they are veteran New Yorkers. They know its Fashion District and the people who run the businesses that support the making of clothing in New York. On top of that, they know their customers.

Having the garments sewn a few blocks from their office makes quality assurance more manageable for the general product lines. Also, about one-third of Nicole Miller's clothing revenues come from its bridal collections, and quality assurance is particularly critical for bridal gowns. When a woman selects a Nicole Miller gown and/or bridesmaid dress, it is custom sewn. Bridal salons take measurements and send them in to New York, where the gowns are sewn when the orders are received. This type of business would be considerably more difficult to manage if the sewing were done elsewhere. By keeping the entire process in New York, the turnaround time can be less than one week.

Also, Nicole Miller does not mass-produce any one item. Its strategy depends upon fresh designs every month, with those items produced in small lots, sent to the stores, and sold. Once those items are gone, there is no reordering. Nicole Miller is already producing the next new thing.

This company is not interested in competing head-to-head with the mass market chains and large manufacturers. It is interested in serving its niche of loyal repeat customers and new ones that they attract. Those customers do not want to see what they are wearing on someone else. By controlling quantity and quality, Nicole Miller keeps customers happy. And, as Bud says, Nicole Miller's core product is happiness.

STUMBLE INTO MILLIONS BY TAKING ADVANTAGE OF OPPORTUNITIES

There is an old saying, "Make lemonade out of lemons," and this is what Nicole did when she thought she had selected a dress fabric that flopped. She told me, "We just made ties as a joke out of a fabric that was not

[14]Fashion Center Business Improvement District (BID) Web site at http://www.fashioncenter.com (accessed on August 23, 2010).

selling when we put it out there as a dress. Sometimes the best things that happen are flukes." The tie collection led to her handbags, eyeglass cases, socks, and other items. Today, the licensing of her designs for these specialty products generates half of the company's revenue. This is another example of finding and exploiting an opportunity.

Break with Tradition

In a cost-cutting effort, Bud decided Nicole Miller would stop participating in the major New York fashion shows. His rationale was that the expense of participation, and to get the press to write about Nicole Miller's hot items from the shows, was more about name recognition than closing sales. To get the attention of the press, the company would have to design outrageous garments, which would never sell to real customers. He calculated that they never got a strong return on their investment for participation.

Because no one store ordered her entire collection every month, Nicole debated with Bud, opining that, without the fashion shows, no one would ever see her entire collection. To address that concern, she suggested that they open their own shop, which would be the place for everyone in New York to see every piece in every collection. It worked. The store even made money.

When this first boutique was running smoothly, Bud and Nicole knew they could continue to grow with department store orders and with their own chain of boutiques simultaneously. There are presently 15 company-owned shops and 15 licensed locations. Taking on the task of operating retail stores on top of creating, manufacturing, and marketing Nicole Miller clothing has been satisfying for both Bud and Nicole. The small shops present the right image to customers. The image they strive for is that they are unique and they provide warm service, fashion-savvy salespeople, and custom gowns for brides. The shops say to the customer, "We are small and you are very important to us."

See the Work as a Circle

Bud thinks of the business process as a circle. He put his thoughts on a chart that everyone in the company can see. The chart makes it clear that he views each person as adding an equally valuable part to the whole. He does not see himself or Nicole at the top, sending down instructions. He envisions the work flowing through the creation to the sewing to the shipping to the selling teams, and he does not step in unless there is a problem.

Bud is the CEO, and he is ultimately responsible for the success of the business. He is the one who takes on all of the headaches. He has even said, "I get paid for taking Excedrin. I tell everybody that I want to hear the bad news. The good news will take care of itself. Give me the bad news because that is what I am here for." However, his quick smile and warm personal-communication style telegraph to the organization that he is a team player, not lone wolf.

He says, "I don't tell it, I sell it." This means that he works hard to get the employees to move along in his direction, but he takes the time to engage them in the process and gain their agreement. That's what he means by selling. Bud is continually selling ideas to his team. If they refuse to buy what he is selling, he will adapt when it makes business sense.

Growing Is Harder Than Anticipated

Nicole told me, "I have to say about this business, that it only gets harder. When you start out a business it is all so simple—there is one person that does this and one person that does that and one person that does that. And then before you know it, there are like a hundred people and five of them are doing this and you don't know what people are doing anymore. And you are saying, 'How did we manage when we just had one person in this position?'" Growth has not been a painless process for Nicole Miller. The entire team has had to learn to adapt and grow with the company.

Nicole Miller and Bud Konheim consider themselves fortunate to have found each other and lucky that they have been able to stay partners. Nicole is a sensitive artist, whereas Bud is a bundle of energy and optimism. They respect each other so much, and have made the division of labor so clear, that no matter how large the challenge facing them, together they have always found a way to work through it and ultimately profit. When I asked Bud what he thought about the future, I laughed when he said, "The end game is, come to my funeral."

Case Analysis

1. What was the opportunity that Nicole Miller and Bud Konheim observed?
2. How did the founders manage to launch a company and see $600,000 in sales the very first month?
3. Can a company's pricing strategy really be about selling happiness?
4. Why did this dress design and manufacturing company open its own store?
5. Why does the company sew their clothes in New York City when they could get them sewn cheaper in Asia?
6. Would you like to work for Bud Konheim? Why or why not?

Case prepared by Hattie Bryant, creator of *Small Business School*, the television series made for PBS and Voice of America, (http://SmallBusinessSchool.org).

UNIT 3

INTEGRATED MARKETING

Chapter 7

DEVELOPING THE RIGHT MARKETING MIX AND PLAN

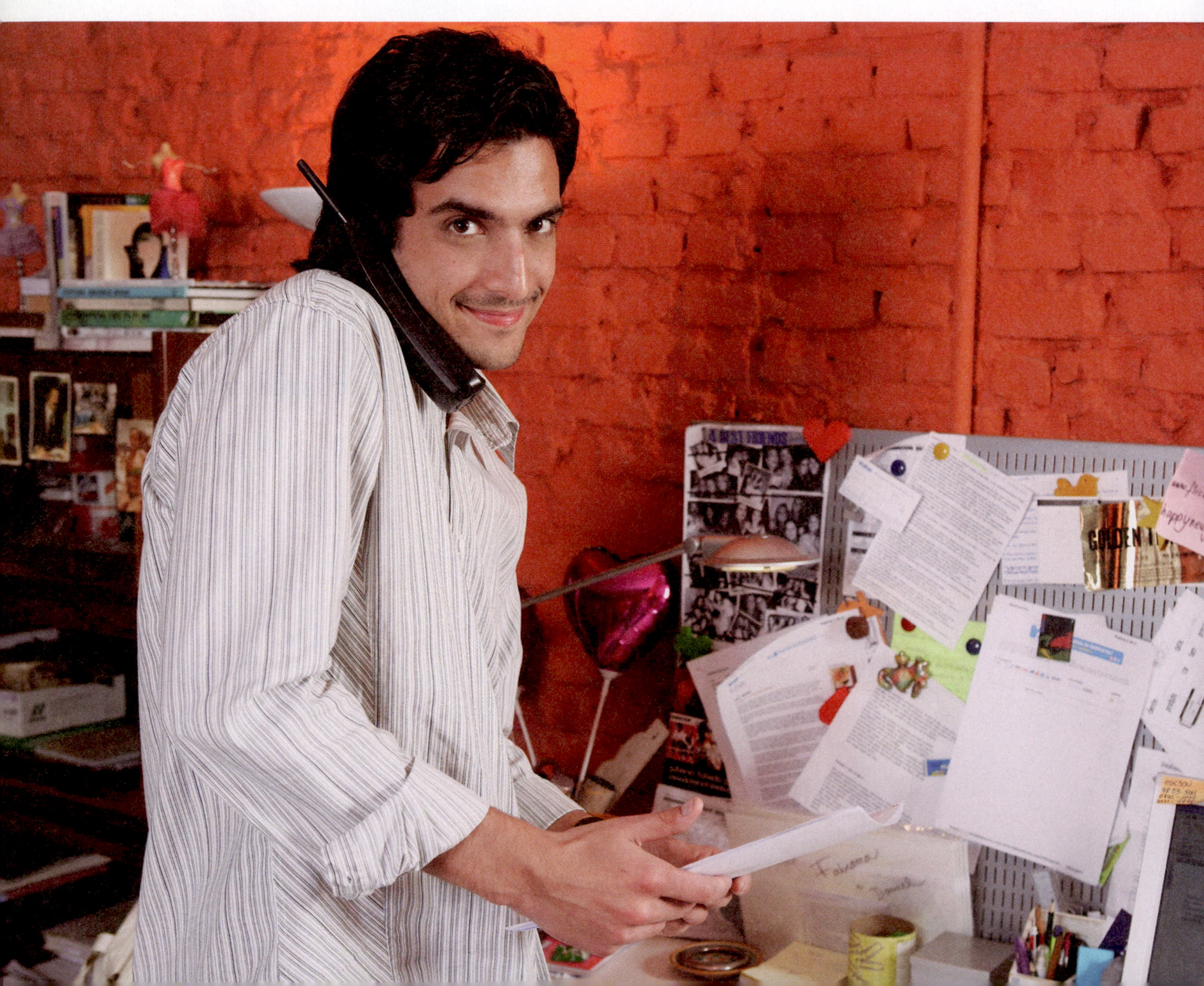

"I found that if you give the consumer a snapshot where he could see himself as he really is and the way he wants to be portrayed, people really respond to it."

—Thomas Burrell, founder, the Burrell Communications Group

All of BMW's marketing, from the price of the cars to the advertisements in magazines catering to people who buy expensive things, is designed to remind customers that it makes luxury automobiles. If BMW lowered the price of a sedan, would that damage the customer's belief in BMW's market position as a provider of luxury cars? This is the question that working through the next step of the marketing process will help answer. BMW illustrates the importance of getting the marketing mix—product, price, place, and promotion—right. Without an effective combination of these elements, your business is likely to fail.

Performance Objectives

1. Combine the four P's—product, price, place, and promotion—into a marketing mix.
2. Choose the attributes of your product or service.
3. Determine the mix of promotion to use for your business.
4. Find a way to add the fifth P, philanthropy, to your business.
5. Understand the importance of a marketing plan.
6. Identify the critical components of a marketing plan.
7. Use breakeven analysis to evaluate your marketing plan.

BMW positions its products as luxury purchases.

The Four Marketing Factors

The four P's, referred to on the previous page, together will communicate your marketing vision and competitive advantage to your customer:

- product,
- price,
- place, and
- promotion.

Performance Objective 1

Combine the four P's—product, price, place, and promotion—into a marketing mix.

If you tweak one P, you will have to pay attention to how it affects the others. If you raise your price, for example, are you now still selling the product in the right place? Or will you need to move to a location that will put you in contact with consumers willing to pay the new price? Where will you promote your product at the higher price? Will you have to take out ads in different magazines or newspapers to reach these more affluent consumers?

As you choose the elements of your marketing plan, always keep your vision in mind. What is the benefit your product or service is providing to consumers?

- ***Product.*** The product (or service) should meet or create a customer need. The product is the entire bundle, such that the packaging is also part of the product. Your customer might not be consciously aware of your packaging, but that does not mean it is unimportant. Starbucks revolutionized the American coffee shop partially by introducing Italian names for the different serving sizes.
- ***Price.*** Generally, a product has to be priced low enough so the public will buy it and high enough for the business to make a profit. Price should also reflect your marketing vision. If you are marketing a luxury item, a relatively low price might confuse the consumer, who will be led to wonder about its quality.
- ***Place.*** The location where you choose to market your product, whether a retail storefront, in a customer's home, on an online storefront, or from a cart on the street, must be where customers who will want or need it shop. Selling bathing suits on a beach in Alaska in February is not going to fill a customer need. Where should you go to bring your product or service to the attention of your market? If you are selling a luxury item, you will need to place it in stores that are visited by consumers who can afford it.
- ***Promotion.*** Promotion is the development of the popularity and sales of a product or service through advertising, publicity, or other promotional devices, such as discount coupons or giveaways. Publicity is notice that is free, whereas advertising is purchased. If a newspaper writes an article about your business, it is publicity. If you buy an ad in that newspaper, you are advertising.

Product: What Are You Selling?

Steve Jobs and Stephen Wozniak were in their early twenties in California when Jobs sold his Volkswagen minibus, and Wozniak sold his Hewlett-Packard calculator, to raise the $1,300 that started Apple. They soldered together the circuit boards with three other friends to fill their first substantial order.

Jobs made sales calls to every computer store in the area with their one sample machine, and finally convinced a small start-up store in Mountain

View to order 50 circuit boards. The owner agreed to pay Apple $548 for each, and then had to add the remaining components.

Jobs and Wozniak had one month to build the 50 circuit boards, but they did not have the money to buy the necessary parts. Using the order, though, the partners found a supplier that was willing to give them $25,000 worth of parts on 30-day credit. They started building the circuit boards. By the end of the month, they had built 100 and delivered 50 to the store in Mountain View. They paid the supplier on the twenty-ninth day. Apple has come a long way since then.

Your business, no matter how humble its beginnings, may have the potential to grow into a multimillion-dollar company, so it is important that you think through every step of its development. How you define and refine your product or service will have a tremendous impact on your ability to grow.

Create Your Total Product or Service Concept

A *product* is something that exists in nature or is made by human industry, usually to be sold, whereas a service is *intangible*—work, skills, or expertise provided in exchange for a fee. Your product will be defined by its physical attributes (e.g. size, color, weight, shape), its performance characteristics (e.g. speed, strength, efficiency, durability), as well as its pricing, branding, and delivery. It is the total package that people are buying. A dirty stone glued onto a piece of cardboard with a scrawled, handwritten price and sold by a kid on the street would be a much different product from a "pet rock" (a real fad product in the 1970s) that has been cleaned, polished, placed in a nest of attractive packing material in a box, and displayed in an upscale retail store.

Performance Objective 2

Choose the attributes of your product or service.

A parallel exists for services. Think about a one-person cleaning service in which the individual arrives in an old, battered van and appears tired and unkempt, and compare that image with neatly dressed, uniformed personnel that arrive in a new vehicle (with the name of the company on the side of the truck) to work as a team. Retail service businesses sell directly to the end consumer, but there are also service businesses that have only wholesale or manufacturing business customers.

The selection of your product or service and its branding will be a critical part of your marketing mix.

Focus Your Brand

The key to building a successful brand is to focus tightly on the primary benefit you want customers to associate with your business. Marketing expert Al Ries explains that the most successful businesses *focus* their marketing, so that they come to own a category in the customer's mind.[1] You want to own a benefit the way Volvo owns safety or Federal Express owns guaranteed overnight delivery.

Even entertainers can become a brand. Oprah Winfrey is among the most recognized and wealthiest celebrities in the world today. She is the head of a global media empire, and a philanthropist.[2] From her roots in Nashville radio, Winfrey has become a media mogul, with such well-recognized names as *The Oprah Winfrey Show; O, The Oprah Magazine; O at Home; Oprah & Friends Radio*; Harpo Films, and Oprah.com.[3]

[1]Al Ries, *Focus: The Future of Your Company Depends on It* (New York: HarperCollins, 2005).
[2]Information available at *http://www.oprah.com* (accessed July 9, 2009).
[3]*The Oprah Winfrey Show* and *Oprah & Friends* are registered trademarks of Harpo, Inc. *O, The Oprah Magazine* and *O at Home* are registered trademarks of Harpo Print LLC.

Oprah Winfrey, philanthropist and media mogul.
(AP Wide World Photos. Used by permission).

Ford's Costly Failure: The Edsel

One of the most notorious examples of a product whose failure was caused by lack of focus is the car Ford introduced in 1958, the Edsel.

Ford tried to include every kind of gadget and design element the company thought consumers might possibly want in a car. They also manufactured multiple models at varying prices that overlapped some Ford and Mercury models, thus confusing the public as to which brand was a step up from which. The goal seemed to be to try to appeal to everyone, but Ford soon learned that trying to appeal to everyone appealed to almost no one. The Edsel had no outstanding benefit that could be clearly marketed. In addition, consumers didn't really like the way the car looked. In the first year, some 63,000 Edsels were produced when sales had been estimated at 200,000 cars.

Even millions of dollars of promotion will not make consumers buy a product they do not want. Ford spent more money on advertising the Edsel than had ever been spent on one line of cars. Three years and $350 million later, Ford pulled the plug on the Edsel.

Ford's Focus on Success: The Mustang

Ford learned from the Edsel mistake, however. When it introduced the Mustang in 1964, it focused very clearly on a target market of people from 20 to 30 years old who wanted a powerful car. Everything about the car, from its design to the colors it came in, was focused on appealing to young drivers. The marketing described the Mustang as "for the young at heart." Only one model was offered. The Mustang was a huge success.

Interestingly, Ford tried to offer some luxury and four-door versions of the Mustang a few years later. Sales dropped, probably because the brand had started to lose focus. The Mustang remains one of Ford's stronger sellers.

Global Impact...

Social Gaming Worldwide

Social gaming online has become an international phenomenon, and Zynga Game Network Inc. has ruled that world with around 65 million daily users, as of the end of 2009. Whereas the popularity of specific games—such as FarmVille, Mafia Wars, and Zynga Poker (Texas Hold'em)—has waxed and waned, CEO Mark Pincus and his team have continued to focus on developing the right marketing mix, and are planning to stay ahead of the curve.

Pincus suggests in an interview, "When we think about next year, we know we have to double down on social, it needs to be more about real user interaction and communication inside of gaming experience. Today, it's very hard to communicate with friends in FarmVille, but people talk about it at the bar, in dorms, on Facebook, and everywhere else. In 2010, they should talk about it in FarmVille."[4] This change will bring players around the globe closer together.

[4]Eric Eldon, "Interview with Zynga CEO Mark Pincus on Social Gaming in 2010," *Inside Social Games*, December 29, 2009, http://www.insidesocialgames.com/2009/12/29/ (accessed January 13, 2010).

How to Build Your Brand

You can build your own brand by following these steps:

- ***Choose a business name that is easy to remember, describes your business, and helps establish mindshare,*** which is the degree to which *your* business comes to mind when a consumer needs something that your product or service could provide.
- ***Create a logo that symbolizes your business to the customer.*** A **logo** (short for *logotype*) is an identifying symbol for a product or business. A logo is printed on the business's stationery, business cards, and flyers. When a logo has been registered with the U.S. Patent and Trademark Office to protect it from being used by others, it is called a **trademark**, which is any word, name, symbol, or device used by a manufacturer or merchant to distinguish a product. The Nike swoosh is an example of a logo. So are the McDonald's golden arches.

  A company uses a trademark so that people will recognize its product instantly, without having to read the company name or even having to think about it. Rights to a trademark are reserved exclusively for its owner. To infringe on a trademark is illegal.

logo short for logotype, a company trademark or sign.

trademark any word, name, symbol, or device used by an organization to distinguish its product.

- ***Develop a good reputation.*** Make sure your product or service is of the quality you promise. Always treat your customers well. You want people to feel good when they think of your brand or hear it mentioned.
- ***Create a brand personality.*** Is your brand's personality youthful and casual, like the Gap? Safe and serious, like Volvo? Customers will respond to brand personality and develop a relationship with it. Personality will reinforce your name and logo.
- ***Communicate your brand personality to your target market.*** What type of advertising will best reach your target market? Where should you put flyers? Which newspapers or magazines does your target market read?

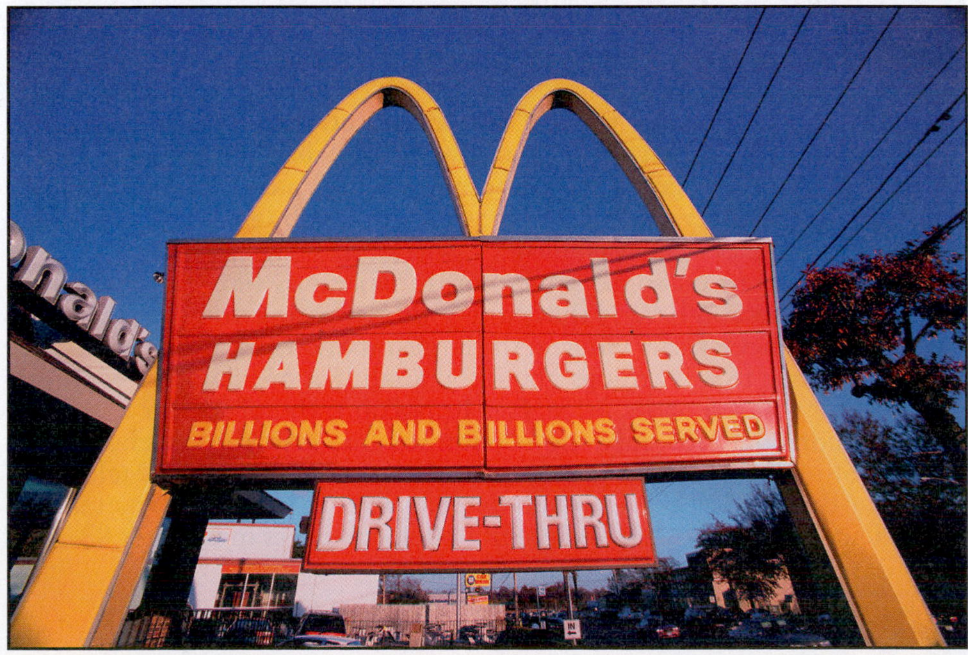

The world's best-known trademark, McDonald's golden arches.
(© James Leynse/CORBIS SABA. Used by permission.)

Laurel Touby, entrepreneur.

Step into the Shoes...

Trademarking a Domain

In 1998, Laurel Touby purchased the domain name *www.hireminds.com* for her online job listings network for New York City journalists and editors, but she failed to apply for a trademark. By 1999, Touby had a thriving site. She was charging publishers looking for writers and editors $100 per ad, and her clients included many national publications.

However, Touby got a phone call from a recruiter for Boston computer companies informing her that she had purchased all the domain names around Touby's and was applying for the trademark to her domain name, as well. As your company grows, or if you are starting an online business, you may want to purchase a domain name for your Web site(s).

The domain name is the first part of the URL; it ends in ".com" for a commercial business, ".org" for a not-for-profit, or ".net" for a network. Check out InterNIC, *http://www.internic.net,* where you can register a domain name. If you do purchase a domain name, seriously consider spending an additional $200 to have it trademarked. The U.S. Patent and Trademark Office will award the trademark to whichever business can prove it used the domain name in trade first.

Always present yourself and your business in such a way that people will have confidence in your product or service. Anything that harms your reputation will damage your sales and profits. Anything that boosts your reputation will have a positive impact on your business.

Here are seven things you can do to build and maintain your brand and its reputation:

1. provide a high-quality product or service,
2. maintain the highest ethical standards,
3. define your product or service clearly—*focus*,
4. treat your employees well,
5. make all your advertisements positive and informative,
6. associate your company with a charity, and
7. become actively involved in your community.

Price: What It Says about Your Product

As reported by author Jay Conrad Levinson, a study of consumers in the furniture industry found that price came ninth when they were asked to list factors affecting their decision to make a purchase.[5] Quality was the number two influence on buying patterns, and confidence in the product was number one. Service was third.

Although your customers may not think exactly like those who buy furniture, the lesson here is that simply undercutting your competitors' prices will not necessarily win you the largest market share. For one thing, consumers tend to infer things about the quality or specialness of a product or service based on its price. It is important, therefore, for entrepreneurs to consider not only the economics but also the psychology of pricing. Studying the pricing strategies of your competitors will tell you a lot about the importance of psychological pricing in your market. A detailed discussion of pricing and credit policies appears in Chapter 8.

[5]Jay Conrad Levinson, *Guerrilla Marketing Attack* (Boston: Houghton Mifflin, 1989).

Place: Location, Location, Location!

Regarding place, the type of business you are running will influence your choice of location and your distribution system for reaching out from that place to your customers. For a retail business, site location is the key to attracting customers. Ideally, you will want your store or business to be where your market is. This is why you did the work of consumer and market analysis to figure out who your customers were. You should know where they shop. Your goal is to find a location you can afford that is also convenient for your potential customers.

Wal-Mart has done an efficient job of choosing locations that were ideal for attracting its potential customers, yet underserved by similar retailers. Wal-Mart was the first mass-merchandise store to choose locations in rural and semirural markets. This strategy has been so successful that other stores now seek to be located near a Wal-Mart.

Of course, the Internet has made it possible for an entrepreneur to start a retail business out of his or her home and reach customers all over the world. This has led to the belief that online stores can forgo the expense of renting a location that caters to foot traffic. As the old saying goes, however, you can lead a horse to water, but you can't make him drink. How do you get your customers to your site and then induce them to buy? If you are going to start a retail business online, you must figure out how you will attract customers to your Web site (*market* the site).

For nonretail businesses, the key to location might be cost or convenience rather than proximity to the market. Wholesale businesses that require a great deal of storage space do best in areas where rent or property costs are low, where there is space for large commercial buildings, and where their trucks and vans have easy access to roads and highways.

The Internet is making it easier for people who provide services—such as graphic or Web-site design, writing/editing, or accounting—to start businesses at home. Communication with clients is easy via e-mail, and the overhead costs are certainly minimal. On the other hand, working at home requires discipline and a tolerance for isolation. If you are the sort of person who would not be happy spending your workdays by yourself, it is probably not for you.

philanthropy a concern for human and social welfare that is expressed by giving money through charities and foundations.

Promotion: Advertising + Publicity

Performance Objective 3

Determine the mix of promotion to use for your business.

Promotion is the use of advertising and publicity to get your marketing message out to your customers. Advertising, as discussed in Chapter 4, is paid promotion that is intended to generate increased sales of your product or service. Examples of advertising include television commercials, billboards, and magazine ads. Publicity is free mention of a company, person, event, product, or service in media, such as newspapers and magazines or on radio or television. Chapter 9 will go into the topics of advertising and promotion in more detail, including the topics listed in **Exhibit 7-1** below.

The Fifth P: Philanthropy

There is a long, proud connection in the United States between entrepreneurs and **philanthropy**, a concern for human and social welfare that is expressed by giving money through charities and foundations. A **foundation** is a **not-for-profit organization** that manages donated funds, which it distributes through grants to individuals or to other nonprofit organizations that help people and social causes.

foundation a not-for-profit organization that manages donated funds, which it distributes through grants to individuals, or to other nonprofit organizations that help people and social causes.

not-for-profit organization an entity formed with the intention of addressing social or other issues, with any profits going back into the organization to support its mission.

Exhibit 7-1 *Advertising and promotion options.*

Promotion Methods		
Advertising specialties	Coupons	Public speaking
Banner ads	Direct mail	Samples or demonstrations
Billboards	Directories	Signs
Blogs	Flyers	Special events
Broadcast media	Networking	Sponsorships
Brochures	Newsletters	Telemarketing
Business cards	Print media	Toll-free numbers
Catalogs	Promotional clothing	Web sites

Performance Objective 4

Find a way to add the fifth P, philanthropy, to your business.

Many philanthropic organizations in the United States were established by entrepreneurs. As a business owner, you have a responsibility to help the communities you serve. The people and causes you choose to support should be those that matter to you. Your philanthropy may also generate positive publicity because you can choose to promote your giving. For this reason, marketing experts sometimes consider philanthropy as the fifth marketing P.

The Bill and Melinda Gates Foundation is one of the world's largest charitable organizations, with over $33 billion in capital. This money comes from the personal wealth they earn from Microsoft. As a private foundation, it is required by the federal government to give away 5 percent of the fair market value of its assets every year (this is usually less than the earnings on the fund's investments). The Gates Foundation provides a great deal of money annually (about $1.65 billion, based on a $33 billion fund) to other charities. These in turn use the money for social and community programs that the Gates Foundation supports, such as those relating to education and health care.

You can be philanthropic even if you have very little money to donate. You can give your time in volunteer work for an organization you believe in. If you know how to paint a house, or if you have some carpentry skills, you could contribute your efforts to help build homes for an organization such as Habitat for Humanity, which provides affordable housing for low-income families. If you love animals, volunteer at your local animal shelter.

Cause-Related Marketing

cause-related marketing marketing inspired by a commitment to a social, environmental, or political cause.

Cause-related marketing—marketing inspired by a commitment to a social, environmental, or political cause—is an easy way to work philanthropy into your business. You could donate a fixed percentage of your profits (perhaps 1 or 2 percent) to a particular charity, and then publicize this in your marketing materials. Or you could donate something from your business. If you own a sporting-goods store, you could donate uniforms to the local Little League team.

Encourage your employees to participate in charitable work, too. Volunteerism is a great way to improve morale and make a difference. AT&T pays its employees to devote one day a month to community service.

Gaining Goodwill

Many entrepreneurs try to make a difference in their communities by giving money and time to organizations that help people. Microsoft, for example, made it possible for the National Foundation for Teaching Entrepreneurship

Entrepreneurial Wisdom…

Be sure to obtain videotapes of any mention you receive on television. There is no more powerful sales tool than a video that includes a story, however brief, on your business.

(NFTE; now the Network for Teaching Entrepreneurship) to develop an Internet-based entrepreneurial curriculum, BizTech. Microsoft has donated both money and computer-programming expertise to this project.

Why would Microsoft do this?

- First, Bill Gates and other Microsoft executives believe in NFTE's mission and want to help youth learn about business. The Internet-based program makes it easier to teach entrepreneurship to greater numbers of young people around the world.
- Second, Microsoft gains publicity and **goodwill**, which is composed of intangible assets, such as reputation, name recognition, and customer relations. Goodwill can give a company an advantage over its competitors.

goodwill an intangible asset generated when a company does something positive that has value.

Not-for-Profit Organizations

Not-for-profit organizations are those whose purpose is to serve a public or mutual benefit rather than to accrue profits for investors. The Internal Revenue Service classifies nonprofits under section 501(c)(3) in the tax code. These corporations are tax-exempt. This means they do not have to pay federal or state taxes, and they are neither privately nor publicly owned. Essentially, a board of directors controls the operations of a 501(c)(3) nonprofit.

Such well-known institutions as the Boys and Girls Clubs of America, the YMCA, the Girl Scouts, the Red Cross, and Big Brothers/Big Sisters are all examples of nonprofits. Their founders were social entrepreneurs and, although they did not earn large sums of money personally, and could not have sold their organizations at a profit, they received great satisfaction and made a difference. Wendy Kopp of Teach for America, and Michael Bronner of Upromise, described in the following section, are two examples of social entrepreneurs who founded innovative and successful nonprofit organizations.

Teach for America and Upromise

Founded in 1990 by Wendy Kopp, Teach for America recruits recent college graduates to become public school teachers. The organization has trained some 28,000 young teachers, and placed them in two-year teaching positions in under-resourced schools where they will impact approximately 500,000 students annually.

Step into the Shoes…

The Body Shop's Campaigns

One of the strongest examples of cause-related marketing by an entrepreneur is the late Anita Roddick's The Body Shop—a chain of cosmetic and skin-care product stores. The company has run media campaigns on causes ranging from saving whales to preserving the rain forest, and each campaign has had the same result: It has attracted customers in droves. In 1990, they set up The Body Shop Foundation, which funds projects in areas such as education, environmental conservation, and domestic violence.

Roddick (who passed away in 2007) once estimated that The Body Shop gained about $4 million per year in publicity from its various campaigns for solving social and environmental problems.

Anita Roddick, founder of The Body Shop.

Michael Bronner, a former marketing executive who became a social entrepreneur, started Upromise in 2001. Bronner felt strongly that the cost of sending a child to college had become much too expensive for most families. He believed that there needed to be a better way of helping families save money for higher education.

Bronner developed the idea that a portion of the money that families already spent on popular goods and services, such as groceries and toys, could go into a college savings account for their children. Upromise works with thousands of organizations such as Sprint, Dell, Century 21, and Expedia.com. Every time one of the over 10 million members makes a purchase from one of these companies, a percentage automatically goes into a special college savings account.

What Entrepreneurs Have Built

Many philanthropic organizations in this country were created by entrepreneurs who wanted to do good works with some of the wealth they had earned. Entrepreneurs have financed great museums, libraries, universities, and other important institutions. Some foundations created by famous entrepreneurs (in addition to the Gates Foundation) include the Rockefeller Foundation, the Coleman Foundation, the Charles G. Koch Foundation, the Ford Foundation, and the Goldman Sachs Foundation.

Some of the most aggressive entrepreneurs in American history, such as Andrew Carnegie, have also been the most generous. In 1901, after a long and sometimes ruthless business career, Carnegie sold his steel company to J. P. Morgan for $420 million. Overnight, Carnegie became one of the very richest men in the world. On retiring, he spent most of his time giving away his wealth to libraries, colleges, museums, and other worthwhile institutions that still benefit people today. By the time of his death, in 1919, Carnegie had given away over $350 million to philanthropic causes.

You Have Something to Contribute

You may not have millions of dollars to give to your community—yet. But there are many ways you can be philanthropic that will help others, get your employees excited, and create goodwill in your community:

- Pledge a percentage of your profits to a nonprofit organization you have researched, believe in, and respect. Send out press releases announcing your pledge.
- Become a mentor to a younger entrepreneur. Help that individual by sharing your contacts and expertise.
- Volunteer for an organization that helps your community. Find out how you can serve on its board of directors, or fill another vital role.
- Sell your product to a charity that you support at a discount. The charity can then resell it at full price to raise money.
- When you give it some thought, you will realize that you have a lot to give. Remember, making a contribution does not necessarily mean giving money. You can donate time, advice, and moral support.

These days, customers have access to a lot of information about what companies do with their money. Make sure you are always proud of your business. Choose to support causes that are important to you and that make business sense, too. Philanthropy will strengthen your relationship with your customers because it goes beyond the sale and into what is truly important in everybody's life.

Developing a Marketing Plan

Performance Objective 5

Understand the importance of a marketing plan.

The marketing plan can be a stand-alone document or the section of a business plan that identifies the organization's marketing strategy and tactics to create a comprehensive statement of how it will secure and retain its customers. In either case, the plan will include a clear discussion of the product (or service), price, promotion, and channels of distribution for the company, and a detailed description of the competition and target market. The marketing plan clarifies how you will sell your products or services and where you fit into the competitive landscape. According to Kuratko and Hodgetts, the roles of the marketing plan include:[6]

- convincing skeptical investors that your plan has merit,
- using and disclosing market studies,
- identifying the target market for the organization,
- evaluating the competition,
- demonstrating the pricing strategy, and
- detailing the advertising plan.

Performance Objective 6

Identify the critical components of a marketing plan.

Either a stand-alone marketing plan or one incorporated into a business plan will include the same market-analysis information. The stand-alone plan should also include a *situation analysis*; financial projections and information; an implementation time line or plan; and methods for evaluating success and assuring it, as well as any supplemental supporting materials. **Exhibit 7-2** shows the components of each type of plan.

[6]Donald F. Kuratko and Richard Hodgetts, *Entrepreneurship: A Contemporary Approach,* 5th ed. (Mason, Ohio: Southwestern Publishing, 2000).

Exhibit 7-2 *Marketing plan components.*

Component	Stand-Alone Plan	Business Plan Section
OPPORTUNITY ANALYSIS	✓	
Industry Analysis	✓	
SWOT Analysis	✓	
Environmental Analysis	✓	
Competitive Analysis	✓	
MARKETING ANALYSIS	✓	✓
Overall Market and Target	✓	✓
Goals and Objectives	✓	✓
Marketing Strategy	✓	✓
Product/Service	✓	✓
Pricing Strategy	✓	✓
Promotion Strategy/Plan	✓	✓
Place/Distribution	✓	✓
Philanthropic Plan	✓	✓
Future and Contingency Plans	✓	✓
FINANCIAL PROJECTIONS	✓	
IMPLEMENTATION TIME LINE	✓	
MEASUREMENT	✓	
SUPPLEMENTAL MATERIALS	✓	

As with business plans as a whole, marketing plans should be organic documents that are reviewed and revised on a regular basis, to keep them timely and useful.

Marketing Analysis

The analysis of the market is the heart of the marketing plan. This brings together the various strategic and tactical components of the marketing efforts into a single comprehensive section. It is essential that the template for the sales plan include the five P's of marketing. The product, price, promotion, place, and philanthropy are detailed here. Wrapped around the core marketing strategy and selling plan are the descriptions of the overall market and the specific target market for the company, the marketing goals and objectives, and any future and contingency plans. Future plans could include a discussion of planned research and development as well as any growth designs, whether through product line expansion, additional channels of distribution, or by other means. Contingency plans show how your organization will react to moves by your competitors or other changes in the marketplace. They will diagram strategies and options that you will use to address these changes, and demonstrate your understanding of the need to be prepared for change in a competitive landscape.

Marketing as a Fixed Cost

Let's say you want to launch a new software program. You have researched the consumer environment, pinpointed your market segment, and determined your marketing mix. You are now ready to implement a marketing plan that will get your vision out there. There is one more question: Can you afford your marketing plan?

Marketing is part of your business's fixed costs. Marketing should not be budgeted as a percentage of sales but rather as money that is needed to drive sales. As you remember, fixed costs are those that do not vary with sales; they can be remembered as USAIIRD (utilities, salaries, advertising, insurance, interest, rent, and depreciation). There are also variable costs, such as commissions, that vary with sales. For a business to survive, though, it must be able to cover its fixed costs. Most fixed costs, such as rent, insurance, and utilities, are hard to cut back if your sales are slow.

Marketing costs are more flexible. They fall into the category of advertising and may also show up under salaries, if you hire a marketing consultant or full-time marketing staff. They will be a critical component in determining your company's breakeven point and its viability.

Calculate Your Breakeven Point

Performance Objective 7

Use breakeven analysis to evaluate your marketing plan.

The question is this: Can you sell enough units to pay for your marketing plan? The breakeven point, as discussed in Chapter 4, is the moment at which a business has sold enough units to equal its fixed costs. If you estimate that your market is approximately 3 million people, but you have to sell 5 million units just to cover the cost of your marketing, the plan is not viable.

This is why calculating the breakeven point will tell you if your marketing plan will work. It shows whether or not you can cover your fixed costs with the number of units you plan to sell. If not, the one place you can cut costs in your marketing plan. However, you should do this with care.

David is an artist who supports his painting career by creating unique tank tops with airbrushed designs. The shirts are very popular with the young women in Manhattan's East Village, and David sells the shirts each weekend at a flea market on East 4th Street. Let's say he buys eight dozen (96) tank tops for $576. He airbrushes them and sells them all at the weekend flea market for $1152. David considers one tank top his unit of sale. The cost of goods sold (COGS)—without labor—would be calculated as $576/96 = $6, with selling price per unit $1152/96 = $12.

- How much did each tank top cost David? $ _________ This is his cost of goods sold (COGS).
- How much did he charge for each tank top? $ _________ This is his selling price per unit.
- David's unit of sale is one tank top.
- David's cost of goods sold is $6.
- David's selling price is $12.

$12 (Selling Price per Unit) − $6 (Cost of Goods Sold per Unit)
= $6 (Gross Profit per Unit)

- David's gross profit per unit is $6 per tank top.

Next, David needs to take a look at his fixed costs. Let's say he spends $150 a month on renting his space at the flea market and $30 monthly on flyers (advertising). His monthly fixed costs are $150 + $30 = $180. How many tank tops does he have to sell to cover his fixed costs? Use the following formula:

$$\frac{\text{Fixed Cost}}{\text{Gross Profit per Unit}} = \text{Breakeven Units}$$

$$\frac{\text{Fixed Cost: \$180}}{\text{Gross Profit per Unit: \$6}} = 30 \text{ Breakeven Units}$$

David needs to sell 30 tank tops to cover his fixed costs. David typically sells about 20 tank tops each weekend, so in one month he can expect to sell

20 Units × 4 Weekends = 80 Units

David can definitely afford to spend $30 per month on flyers. He could even afford to add another expense to his marketing plan, such as getting business cards printed or setting up a Web site, from which customers could order shirts and find out where he will be selling each weekend, as his specific location varies.

We do need to recognize that David did not include any labor cost, because he paid himself from the profits. If David were to add in $3 per shirt of labor costs, his COGS would rise to $9, and his gross profit per unit would drop to $3. His new breakeven point would be 60 units. Additionally, any payment for the time it took to sell the shirts would come out of the profits.

Breakeven Analysis of a Restaurant

Here is a breakeven analysis from a chicken restaurant in Florida called Mary Ann's.

Typically, a customer at Mary Ann's buys a bucket of chicken for $8 and a drink for $2, so the average sale per customer is $10. Therefore, a business unit is defined as a $10 sale. The cost of goods sold for each unit is $3.50 for the chicken and $0.50 for the drink, so the cost of goods sold is $4.00 per unit.

Mary Ann's fixed costs for a month are

Utilities	$1000
Salaries (indirect labor)	$3000
Ads	$1000
Interest	0
Insurance	$1000
Rent	$2000
	$8000

The restaurant is open on average 30 days per month.

To figure out how many units Mary Ann's has to sell each month to break even, divide the gross profit per unit into the monthly fixed costs.

$$\text{Gross Profit per Unit} = \text{Unit Price } (\$10) - \text{COGS } (\$4) = \$6$$

$$\text{Breakeven Units} = \frac{\text{Monthly Fixed Costs } (\$8000)}{\text{Gross Profit per Unit } (\$6)} = 1333 \text{ Units}$$

Because the store is open 30 days per month, to break even Mary Ann's has to make 45 average sales per day:

$$\frac{1333 \text{ Units}}{30 \text{ Days}} = 44.43 \text{ (45 Units per Day)}$$

Breakeven is the point at which fixed costs are recovered by sales, but no profit has yet been made. Once you have determined your breakeven point, the next question in the analysis is, "Can my business reach breakeven in its relevant market?" In the previous example, can Mary Ann's reasonably expect to break even and sell 45 buckets of chicken a day? The answer to this question for your business venture will be in the market research you have conducted to get to this, the last step in creating a marketing plan. You should know the answer. If not, you must conduct further research until you can confidently gauge whether or not you can afford your marketing plan. Revising your plan is another option, of course.

Breakeven analysis is a good tool for examining all your costs and should be performed frequently. It is especially important after you have completed your marketing plan and before you open your business, to see if your plan is realistic.

Chapter Summary

Now that you have studied this chapter, you can do the following:

1. Combine the four P's—product, price, place, and promotion—into a marketing mix.
2. Determine the attributes of your product or service.
3. Choose where and how to advertise your business.
   - Promotion is the use of advertising and publicity to get your marketing message out to your potential customers.
   - Publicity is free mention of your business—in newspapers or magazines or on radio or television.

- An advertisement is a paid announcement that a product or service is for sale. Examples of advertising include television commercials, billboards, and magazine ads.

4. Decide how your business will help your community philanthropically.
   - Philanthropy is the giving of money, time, or advice to charities in an effort to help solve a social or environmental problem, such as homelessness, pollution, or cruelty to animals.
   - You can be philanthropic even if you have very little or no money to donate. You can donate your time by volunteering for an organization that is doing work you want to support.
5. Understand the importance of a marketing plan:
   - convincing skeptical investors that your plan has merit,
   - using and disclosing market studies,
   - identifying the target market for the organization,
   - evaluating the competition,
   - demonstrating the pricing strategy, and
   - detailing the advertising plan.
6. Identify the critical components of a marketing plan:
   - opportunity analysis,
   - marketing analysis,
   - financial projections,
   - implementation time line,
   - measurement, and
   - supplemental information.
7. Use breakeven analysis to evaluate your marketing plan.
   - Breakeven is the point at which a business sells enough units to cover its costs.
   - Breakeven analysis tells you if your marketing plan is viable. It shows whether or not you can cover your fixed costs with the number of units you expect to sell. If not, the one place you can cut costs is in your marketing plan.

Key Terms

cause-related marketing
foundation
goodwill
logo
not-for-profit organization
philanthropy
trademark

Entrepreneurship Portfolio

Critical Thinking Exercises

1. Describe how a product or service will fit into and complement your marketing mix.
2. Explain how pricing tells a story about your product.
3. Where do you plan to locate your business? Explain.
4. How do you plan to include philanthropy in your marketing mix?

5. Use the following chart to describe your marketing mix.

	Your Business
Product	
Place	
Price	
Promotion	
Philanthropy	

6. Use computer software to create a logo for your business. Do you intend to trademark your logo? Explain.

Key Concept Questions

1. Brainstorm five creative ways for a small business with a very low budget to advertise and promote its products or services using the latest developments in communications and Internet technology.
2. Visit a shopping mall on a major online Internet server. List three advantages and three disadvantages of opening a Web site for your business at an online server's shopping mall.
3. Explain why breakeven is such a critical concept for any organization.

Application Exercise

1. Visit a library (public or university) and locate its reference section. What resources can help you to open a business like The Daily Perc? Identify at least six such resources.
2. Use the following chart to describe the basics of your marketing plan section.

Component	What Will You Include?
OPPORTUNITY ANALYSIS	
Industry Analysis	
SWOT Analysis	
Environmental Analysis	
Competitive Analysis	
MARKETING ANALYSIS	
Overall Market and Target	
Goals and Objectives	
Marketing Strategy	
Product/Service	
Pricing Strategy	
Promotion Strategy/Plan	✓
Place/Distribution	✓
Philanthropic Plan	✓
Future and Contingency Plans	✓
FINANCIAL PROJECTIONS	✓
IMPLEMENTATION TIME LINE	✓
MEASUREMENT	✓
SUPPLEMENTAL MATERIALS	✓

Exploring Online

Find out how much it would cost to run a banner ad on the personal start pages (the pages subscribers see when they log on) for the following online services: AOL, Google, Panix, and Yahoo!

AOL Banner Ad Price: $____________________
Google Banner Ad Price: $____________________
Panix Banner Ad Price: $____________________
Yahoo! Banner Ad Price: $____________________

Case Study | 23andMe

Recent years have seen an explosion in genetic research and the use of DNA technology. 23andMe, founded in 2006 by Linda Avey and Anne Wojcicki, helps each customer understand his or her unique genome, made up of 23 pairs of chromosomes. 23andMe's Personal Genome Service winner of TIME magazine's 2008 Invention of the Year award, gives people data about their ancestry, including possible predispositions for dozens of diseases and health conditions. Individuals are also given the chance to help advance genetic research. According to Avey:

> *We're generating information that not only gives you an idea of what your risks are, but it's prognostic information, too.*[1]

The basic service may be purchased on the company's Web site for a one-time fee of $399 plus shipping costs. A collection kit is shipped to the customer, who sends a saliva sample to 23andMe. Several weeks later, the customer can view the results online. By participating in this service, 23andMe's customers can provide data for a genetic research initiative with the Parkinson's Institute in Sunnyvale, California.

In the fall of 2008, 23andMe dropped its basic price from $999 to $399, to help increase customer demand. At that time, Avey indicated that lower costs for mechanisms used to scan genomes helped to make the price reduction feasible. 23andMe's primary competition, Navigenics, and deCODE genetics, charged about $2500 and $1000, respectively, for similar services. Avey explained:

> *It's really more about getting the price down to a point that is more affordable. If that was what was holding [customers] back, this will be a better price for them to get involved.*[2]

When 23andMe reduced its price, the chief executive of Navigenics, Mari Baker, commented that cheaper does not always mean better. Baker admitted that her company's costs were much greater than 23andMe's new price. Avey pointed out that the lower price not only makes genetic information accessible to more individuals, it simultaneously helps to find more answers to genetic-risk problems. Referring to the research database 23andMe is building, Avey said:

> *It's all about numbers and having as many people enrolled as possible.*[3]

23andMe is located in the Silicon Valley, a region in the San Francisco Bay area known for its technological firms. 23andMe now stands alongside many other high-tech businesses, such as Microsoft, Apple, and Intel, as part of Silicon Valley's history of entrepreneurial innovation. 23andMe is funded in part through prominent health-science and technology companies, angel investors, and venture capital firms, listing Google, Inc., Genentech, Inc., and New Enterprise Associates on its promotional information. In short, 23andMe brings medical technology to individual consumers at a price designed to encourage purchase, and thereby increase genetic data.

Case Study Analysis

1. What is the product/service offered by 23andMe?
2. What could 23andMe's new pricing structure suggest about its brand? In other words, what risk(s) did 23andMe take when it cut its basic price in half?
3. What role does company location likely play in 23andMe's marketing strategy?
4. List factors to include in a breakeven analysis for 23andMe. Suggest the company's strategy for achieving a breakeven point.
5. How has 23andMe woven philanthropic attitudes into its business? Name some specific ways in which the company could incorporate philanthropy further into its marketing mix.

Case Sources

23andMe, Inc. Web site, *https://www.23andme.com*.

Entrepreneur magazine's Web site article, *DNA: The Next Dotcom?*, *http://www.entrepreneur.com/magazine/entrepreneur/2009/february/199580.html*.

New York Times Web site article, *DNA Profile Provider Is Cutting Its Prices*, *http://www.nytimes.com/2008/09/09/business/09gene.html*.

Silicon Valley Web site, *http://www.siliconvalleyonline.org*

[1]Dennis Romero, *DNA: The Next Dotcom?* http://www.entrepreneur.com/magazine/entrepreneur/2009/february/199580.html (accessed June 2009).
[2]Andrew Pollack, *DNA Profile Provider Is Cutting Its Prices*, http://www.nytimes.com/2008/09/09/business/09gene.html (accessed June 2009).
[3]Ibid.

Case Study | Malia Mills Swimwear

When 38-year-old Malia Mills decided to launch her own swimwear company, she set out to do much more than just sell high-end bathing suits. Mills wanted to inspire a beauty revolution that would fundamentally change the way that women felt about themselves. Before she became an entrepreneur, Mills had worked in the fashion world as a designer for established apparel companies. Mills (a native of Hawaii) saved the money for her start-up investment by working for many years as a waitress in New York City. She started Malia Mills Swimwear in 1991.

The slogan of Mills's business is "Love Thy Differences," and Mills is passionate about encouraging all women, regardless of age, weight, or body type, to feel good about themselves and to celebrate their uniqueness. In Mills's world, if a woman does not like the way she looks in a swimsuit, it is the suit that has to change, not the woman. As she explains, "We are passionate about inspiring women to look in the mirror and see what is right instead of what is wrong."

Apparel for all body types.

The Polaroid Project

If you walk past the Malia Mills Swimwear flagship store in New York's SoHo, the first things you will notice are the photographs in the window. Instead of showcasing fashion models, the window display features a collage of Polaroid pictures of customers wearing her signature swimwear. According to Mills's sister, Carol, who manages the store, "We've had so many customers walk in off the street because of those photographs. People are thrilled to see actual women in all colors, shapes, and sizes wearing our suits." This Polaroid project actually began as an offbeat idea thought up by a summer intern on a particularly slow sales day. Mills liked the idea of using photographs of her customers because it resonated with the core mission of her business.

Place Matters: Setting the Right Tone

To create a comfortable environment for her customers, Mills has constructed her stores to look and feel like cozy lounges. She herself always hated trying on bathing suits in department stores under the glare of unflattering fluorescent lights. In her boutiques, the lighting is soft, and dressing rooms are located in the back so that the customers will not feel exposed to other shoppers. She provides free bottled water so that they can feel relaxed and at home. Sales associates are always on hand to assist with finding the appropriate suits. Mills does not believe in a one-size-fits-all design philosophy. People's bodies do not come in packages of small, medium, and large. Accordingly, her tops are sized like lingerie, and bottoms come in sizes 2 to 16. All pieces are sold as separates, which allows customers to mix and match across different style and fabric options, as well as size.

The Price/Production Connection

Malia Mills's suits are priced at the high end of the swimwear market. A bikini top or bottom will cost somewhere between $130 and $165, and one-piece suits run an average of $325. This pricing scheme reflects some of the choices Mills has made as an entrepreneur about how her suits are produced. For example, she chooses to manufacture in New York City instead of outsourcing production to Asia or elsewhere, where labor costs are lower. According to Mills, "It costs us much more per unit to sew our suits locally but supporting our community is worth it. The women (mostly) who sew our suits do so with extra care—we visit them often and they know how important quality is to us."

Mills chooses to import the fabrics she uses from Europe and she typically buys them in small quantities, which is more costly, so that her designs stay fresh. Mills also pays a premium to the fabric mills that custom-dye her materials in unique colors and this also contributes to the bottom line of her manufacturing costs. Her suits are so well made that she sometimes worries about undercutting herself in the marketplace. If the average woman owns two or three bathing suits, and a Malia Mills suit can last several years, it could take a long time for a customer to seek a replacement.

Smart Selling Requires Trial and Error

Early on, Mills sold her suits wholesale to department stores, but she found that this strategy did not fit well with her core mission. Mills's suits got lost on the racks next to other brand-name apparel, and the salespeople did not understand how to answer customers' questions about the unique features of her product, such as how they are sized differently from other swimsuits. So, eventually Mills decided to sell directly to the consumer. Maintaining control over the sales process has allowed Mills to stay true to her mission of providing women with an enjoyable and empowering experience, purchasing swimwear that fits in a relaxed environment.

Promotions: Getting the Word Out

Over the years, Mills has been successful in generating PR. Her company has been profiled in major publications such as *The New York Times*, *Sports Illustrated*, and *Harper's Bazaar.* It has helped to have celebrities such as Madonna wearing her suits, especially when they are photographed in public. Recently, Mills began purchasing advertising for the first time in local print media. She is doing this as an experiment to see if it has a noticeable impact on generating new customers. In the meantime, the growth of Malia Mills Swimwear continues to be propelled by word of mouth and customer loyalty. Each day, the business connects with passersby who are lured into the store by the Polaroid photographs of ordinary women wearing her bathing suits. Once these women walk in off the street, there is a pretty good chance that they will walk out as customers.

Case Study Analysis

1. Describe the unique features of Malia Mills's product.
2. Malia Mills Swimwear is not inexpensive. Why do you think customers are willing to pay a premium for her suits?
3. The case mentions that Malia Mills Swimwear is currently experimenting with paid advertising. If you were in charge of marketing for the company, how would you assess whether or not it was cost-effective to continue purchasing advertising?
4. What kind of environment is Malia Mills trying to create in her stores? Why is this important?
5. Besides her own boutiques, specialty stores, and through the Internet, what might be some additional sales venues for Malia Mills Swimwear to consider exploring?
6. Why was the "Polaroid project" a successful promotional venture?
7. Imagine a scenario in which Malia Mills Swimwear hired you as a media consultant. Answer the following:
   - Come up with a cause-related marketing strategy for the company.
   - Describe three strategies for the company to pursue in obtaining media coverage.

Case Sources

Malia Mills Web site, *http://www.maliamills.com.*

"Chic to Chic—Turn Style into Sales with a Clothing-Design Company," by Pamela Rohland, *Business Start-Ups* magazine, December 1999, *http://Entrepreneur.com/article/0,4621,231846,00.html.*

Chapter 8

PRICING AND CREDIT STRATEGIES

"The price of success is hard work, dedication to the job at hand, and the determination that whether we win or lose, we have applied the best of ourselves to the task at hand."

—Vince Lombardi, legendary football coach

When John Warnock and Chuck Geschke left Xerox PARC in the Silicon Valley to form Adobe in 1982, they knew that they had created a valuable product in Adobe PostScript. Little did they know that they would "democratize information," as Guy Kawasaki states on the Adobe Web site.[1] Adobe's Acrobat Reader and Portable Document Format (PDF) have become ubiquitous. The publicly traded company has grown to $3.58 billion in revenues (FY 2008) and 7335 employees.[2] Yet, Acrobat Reader is free through the company's Web site, and PDF, the de facto standard internationally for document sharing, is also available free of charge. It is pre-installed on the computers of the top 10 manufacturers.

Adobe's primary customer segments are knowledge workers and enterprises, creatives and designers, high-end consumers, and partners and developers. They fuel the company's revenue stream. The company's pricing strategy is very clear. As consumers download Adobe Reader, Flash Reader, Media Player, and other products, they fuel the demand for the professional, high-end consumer products of the company. The free products drive demand for Adobe's profitable products.

Performance Objectives

1. Understand the relationship between price and overall strategy.
2. Describe various pricing strategies.
3. Calculate markups from manufacturer through the consumer.
4. Explore the role of trade credit in pricing.
5. Consider discounts, incentives, and other price adjustments.

[1]Guy Kawasaki, Streaming Web video accessed from http://www.adobe.com on March 27, 2009.
[2]Adobe Web site at http://www.adobe.com, accessed on March 27, 2009.

Pricing: Image, Value, and Competition Together

price the amount that a seller requires in exchange for the use of a product or service, or transferring its ownership.

Customers frequently judge the quality and value of a product or service based upon its **price**, which is simply the amount that a seller requires in exchange for the use of a product or service, or transferring its ownership. Pricing strategy is more than the calculation of what to charge based upon costs and desired profitability. It is about gaining market positioning for advantage and the psychology of pricing. New entrepreneurs often assume they should sell their product or service at the lowest price they can afford, regardless of the message they are sending to customers, and their competitors' capacity to underprice them. Sometimes, however, consumers assume that a low price indicates low quality.

Performance Objective 1

Understand the relationship between price and overall strategy.

The relationship between price and strategy should be straightforward and clear. A high quality product that is priced "too low" for example, may become suspect in the eyes of consumers. They may question the hidden flaws in the product, or their judgment of its quality when the price is lower than the *perceived* quality. Or, they may not perceive the quality at all. The matrix in **Figure 8-1** illustrates the conventional pairing of price and quality dimensions.

Strategies and Tactics for Effective Pricing

Pricing strategy is not a one-size-fits-all proposition. As you define the marketing strategy for your company, including your target market(s), competitive advantages, and overall marketing mix, the range of appropriate pricing strategies emerges. For example, an exclusive, highly specialized product targeted toward upscale consumers would logically be priced at a premium. However, at its point of introduction, it may have to be priced in line with the competition until it is established as the market leader. At the same time, mass-market products may be priced at a lower level. There are multiple factors to be considered when creating your pricing strategy, as illustrated in **Exhibit 8-1** and discussed in the balance of this chapter.

Performance Objective 2

Describe various pricing strategies.

Figure 8-1 *Price and quality dimensions.*

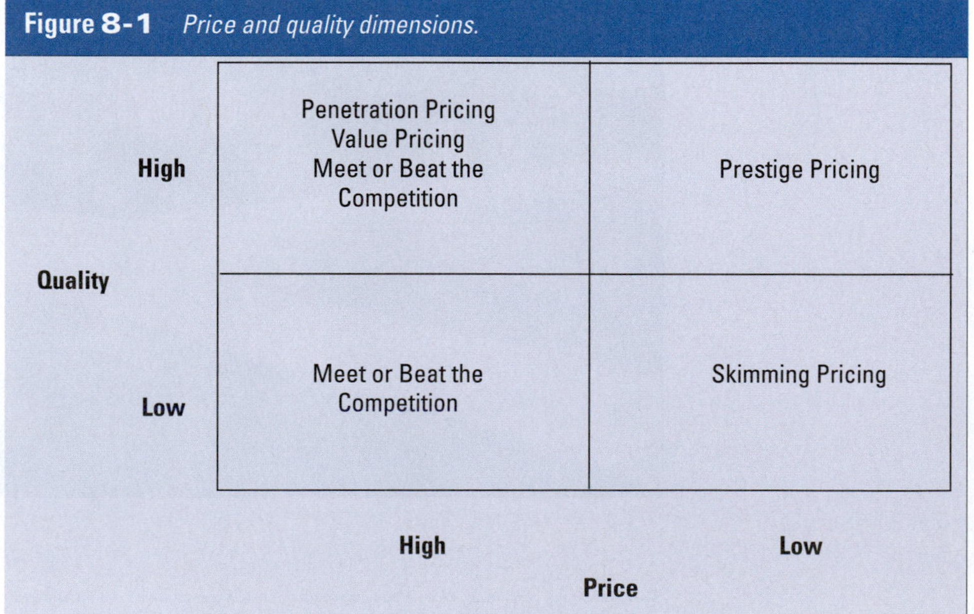

Exhibit 8-1 *Eight steps to better pricing.*
1. Assess what value your customers place on the product or service.
2. Look for variations in the way customers value the product.
3. Assess customers' price sensitivity.
4. Identify an optimal pricing structure.
5. Consider competitors' reactions.
6. Monitor prices realized at the transaction level.
7. Assess customers' emotional response.
8. Analyze whether the returns are worth the cost to serve.

Source: Robert J. Dolan, "How Do You Know When the Price Is Right?" *Harvard Business Review*, September–October 1995.

The particular pricing strategies that are commonly used are described below:

Value Pricing Strategy

One popular strategy is value pricing, which is offering "more for less" by underscoring a product's quality, while at the same time featuring its price. Value pricing is not just price-cutting. It means finding the balance between quality and price that will give your target customers the value they seek. Value pricing began in the 1990s as a reaction to the glitzy eighties, when marketers used high prices to pitch luxury and extravagance. Companies like Wal-Mart and Procter & Gamble have effectively shifted to value pricing. This strategy requires a delicate balance, to avoid customer confusion and mixed marketing signals.

Prestige Pricing Strategy

When a firm sets high prices on their products or services to send a message of uniqueness or premium quality, it is using a **prestige pricing** strategy. For this to be effective in the long run, the product must fulfill the image and sustain it.

prestige pricing the pricing strategy in which a firm sets high prices on their products or services to send a message of uniqueness or premium quality.

Cost-Plus Pricing Strategy

The **cost-plus pricing** method is one of the most commonly used pricing strategies; you take your cost and add a desired profit margin. It is the simplest cost to calculate, once your complete costs are known and your desired rate of return is established. However, it fails to take marketing vision and market conditions into consideration. For example, the competitive environment is neglected, as is the value of the product or service to your targeted customers. **Markup pricing** is a cost-plus pricing strategy in which you apply a predetermined percentage to a product's cost to obtain its selling price. Markup pricing is described in greater detail later in this chapter.

cost-plus pricing takes the organization's product cost and adds the desired markup.

markup pricing a cost-plus pricing strategy in which you apply a predetermined percentage to a product's cost to obtain its selling price.

Penetration Pricing Strategy

Penetration pricing offers a low price during the early stages of a product's life cycle to gain market share. Japanese companies employed this method to dominate consumer electronics markets. Toyota deliberately priced the Prius at about $3000 below cost to secure a leadership position in the emerging market for hybrid automobiles in the United States. The

penetration pricing a pricing strategy that uses a low price during the early stages of a product's life cycle to gain market share.

risk with penetration pricing is that, once you start at a low price point, it is often difficult to increase your price, or to depend upon cost savings to increase profitability.

Skimming Price Strategy

skimming prices strategy seeks to charge high prices during the introductory stage when the product is novel and has few competitors to take early profits and then to reduce prices to more competitive levels.

The **skimming prices strategy** is the opposite of penetration strategy because it seeks to charge high prices during the introductory stage when the product is novel and has few competitors to take early profits and then to reduce prices to more competitive levels. This strategy recognizes that competition and product maturity may erode the firm's capacity to maintain the pricing later. RCA used this strategy when it introduced color television in the 1960s.

Meet-or-Beat-the-Competition Pricing Strategy

It is common for service businesses to use a meet-or-beat-the-competition pricing strategy, which entails constantly matching or undercutting the prices of your competition. Airlines tend to compete intensely by lowering their ticket prices. The more you can show that your business is different from your competition, however, the less you will have to compete with your price. When Sir Richard Branson started Virgin Atlantic Airways, he offered massages and individual videos at each seat. His marketing emphasized how much fun it was to fly on Virgin. This strategy was successful, even though Virgin did not always offer the lowest fares.

Follow-the-Leader Pricing Strategy

follow-the-leader pricing a pricing strategy that is similar to a meet-or-beat-the-competition strategy but uses a particular competitor as the model for pricing.

A **follow-the-leader pricing** strategy is similar to a meet-or-beat-the-competition but with a particular competitor as the model for pricing. Typically, the leader is a dominant firm in the industry and controls a substantial portion of market share.

Personalized Pricing Strategy

personalized pricing a dynamic pricing strategy in which the company charges a premium above the standard price for a product or service to certain customers who will pay the extra cost.

The **personalized (dynamic) pricing** strategy is one in which the company charges a premium above the standard price for a product or service to certain customers, who will pay the extra cost. Personalized pricing is particularly applicable when the product or service is highly valued by certain customers, perhaps for its performance, importance to the production process, or for outstanding delivery or service aspects. Such pricing works only when products are not easily compared, and customers are not likely to communicate with one another.

Variable Pricing Strategy

variable pricing strategy provides different prices for a single good or service.

Many businesses use this type of strategy, often without conscious recognition of it. So that they can offer discounts, credit terms, and price concessions to their customers, firms use a **variable pricing strategy**, which sets different prices for a single product or service.

Price Lining Strategy

price lining the process of creating distinctive pricing levels.

In addition to selecting among the specific pricing strategies described above, you may want to create distinctive price levels for your merchandise. **Price lining** is the process of creating graded pricing levels. For example, Sears carries "good, better, best" product lines in its paint products and prices them accordingly.

Pricing Varies by the Type of Firm

Manufacturers, wholesalers, retailers, and service businesses have different types of pricing conventions based upon the nature of the firm and the particular industry and customers that it serves. Some pricing strategies are broadly used in one field and avoided in another. It is critical to understand the pricing conventions in your particular type of business, and to decide proactively how you will apply it.

As noted in the previous section, markup pricing is commonly used as a form of cost-plus pricing. It is used from manufacturing through retail. Whereas it is laden with drawbacks, markups are relatively easy to understand, to calculate, and are broadly used. Depending upon whether you manufacture, distribute, or retail your products, or perform a combination of these functions, you will have to keep end price and industry markups in mind. If you are a manufacturer, you can work backwards from the target retail price to determine what your cost has to be in order to maintain the usual and customary markups along the chain. The manufacturer and retailer typically double their costs to determine a selling price. A wholesaler usually marks up by about 20 percent to figure the selling price, because the wholesaler is only providing a service (stocking the manufacturer's product) for the retailer. If the wholesaler were to charge too high a price, the retailer might try to buy directly from the manufacturer and eliminate the middleman. **Figure 8-2** shows how a dollar of manufacturing cost gets marked up to yield $4.80 at retail.

Performance Objective 3
Calculate markups from manufacturing through consumers.

There can be other links in this chain besides these four. A manufacturer may have to buy raw materials or manufactured parts to make the product. There may be other middlemen, such as agents, brokers, or other wholesalers between manufacturer and wholesaler or between wholesaler and retailer. Whereas the distribution links and prices vary, pricing strategies can be distributed as suggested in **Exhibit 8-2**.

Pricing Techniques for Manufacturers

Manufacturers often have difficulty in determining the best price to charge for their products. If they are producing parts or assemblies for use in further manufacturing processes, they face different pricing challenges from those manufacturers selling to wholesalers or directly to consumers. In any case, it is common for manufacturers to set list prices for standard products and to discount from the list using volume discounts, credit terms, and various other incentives. For job shop or custom products, pricing is arrived at through a quotation process. Producers that want to supply the military and

Figure 8-2 *Structure of markups.*

Manufacturer $1.00 Manufacturer's Cost × Markup Factor → $2.00 Manufacturer's Price
Wholesaler $2.00 Wholesaler's Cost × Markup Factor → $2.40 Wholesaler's Price
Retailer $2.40 Retailer's Cost × Markup Factor → $4.80 Retailer's Price
Consumer $4.80 Consumer's Cost

Exhibit 8-2 *Pricing strategies by business type.*

Pricing Strategy	Manufacturing	Wholesale	Retail	Service
Cost-Plus	x	x	x	x
Follow-the-Leader	x		x	x
Meet-or-Beat-the-Competition	x	x	x	x
Penetration			x	x
Personalized			x	x
Prestige			x	x
Skimming	x			x
Value			x	x
Variable	x	x		

Note: Any of the strategies can be applied to any industry, but these are more common.

other government entities also have to provide quotations, through competitive bidding processes. In each case, the challenge is to charge according to the firm's established strategy and to secure sufficiently profitable and sustainable revenues.

Pricing Techniques for Wholesalers

As the connector between manufacturers and retailers, wholesalers must price very carefully, so that they add value to the distribution process and are not skipped over in the chain. Often, wholesalers operate on smaller margins, serving as the combiner to make it possible for retailers to purchase from multiple manufacturers simultaneously, while buying fewer products than they would have to buy from each manufacturer. Plumbing supply wholesalers, for example, carry broad and deep inventories so that their plumbing-contractor customers can purchase in small quantities as they need materials, or can order in larger quantities for projects.

Pricing Techniques for Retailers

Just as manufacturers and wholesalers must carefully balance pricing strategy with the competitive environment and customer needs, retailers must price right to survive and thrive. Because many entrepreneurs sell a variety of items at different retail prices with different wholesale costs, it would be time-consuming to try to figure an acceptable markup for each item. Instead, retailers use percentage markup that should be based upon the competitive environment. Every item in a gift shop, for instance, could be marked up 50 percent.

$$\text{Wholesale Cost} \times \text{Markup \%} = \text{Markup}$$

If you know the markup and wholesale cost of an item, you can figure the markup percentage using this formula:

$$\frac{\text{Markup}}{\text{Wholesale Cost}} \times 100 = \text{Markup \%}$$

Let's say a gift shop buys cards for \$2 each from the wholesaler and sells them for \$3 each.

$$\text{Markup} = \$3 - \$2 = \$1$$

While preparing her monthly income statement, if the gift shop owner finds that she is not generating enough profit, she can raise her markup percentage slightly to try to increase revenue. Or she can try to find a cheaper wholesale supplier to lower costs. All pricing should ultimately be customer focused.

Keystoning—The Retailer's Rule of Thumb

Retailers who buy goods wholesale and resell them in stores sometimes keystone, or double, the cost of goods sold, as a rule of thumb for estimating what price to charge. If you buy cell phones for $22 each from a wholesaler, for example, selling them at $44 each in your store will probably cover your costs and provide you with an acceptable profit.

Keystoning is a good way to estimate a price but should not be the only method. If you are selling hacky sack balls that cost $4, consider selling them for $8. When pricing, however, the entrepreneur must always be sensitive to the market and to what competitors are charging. Perhaps you could sell the hacky sack balls for $9 and make greater profits, or maybe the market will not support $8, and you have to decide whether to sell for less. As a retailer, you should not rely solely upon keystoning because it could result in underpricing and leaving profits behind, or overpricing and lost business.

As part of the retail strategy, building sale prices, promotions, and other discounts into the pricing strategy and structure is critical to business success. Whatever pricing approach you take, it has to be synergistic with the overall strategy of the firm. If you want to be the best fine-dining establishment in your metro area, the pricing has to match with the service, décor, location, menu, and total dining experience. At the same time, you have to be careful not to price yourself out of the market by charging so much that you do not have sufficient sales for business continuation.

When creating your retail business concept, consider which pricing strategy best suits your business model. You may be able to support prestige or personalized pricing. You may want to use penetration or skimming pricing. Or, you may use price lining to reach multiple price points and targets simultaneously.

Pricing Techniques for Service Businesses

Service businesses can use the strategies that manufacturers, wholesalers, and retailers use to create prices, with the exception being that the labor cost is the primary product cost. Services can be priced at a premium or discount and can have tailored prices for specific customers. The cost factors that service businesses should consider, above and beyond the obvious competitive environment, are the labor employed, the materials used to deliver the service, overhead costs, and desired profit levels. Unlike retailers, who can readily use keystone prices based upon the price of merchandise, service businesses need to have reliable and accurate costing information to even set approximate prices (although competitive pricing may be a good starting point, too). Often, charges are based upon an hourly labor rate because labor is the primary cost component. For example, a management consulting price may charge a rate equal to three to five times the full-wage costs of the consultants.

An example of a common service can be found in a computer installation and repair service, Computer Associates. The company estimates its cost-per-hour by examining its total fixed and variable expenses minus material divided by the hours worked.

$$\text{Total Cost per Hour} = \frac{\text{Fixed Costs} + \text{Variable Costs} - \text{Materials}}{\text{Hours}}$$
$$= \$292{,}700/8{,}920 = \$32.81/\text{hr.}$$

If Computer Associates wants to use cost-plus pricing, it must add an allocation for profits. So to obtain the hourly price, the owners use

$$\text{Price per Hour} = \text{Total Cost per Hour} \times \frac{1}{(1 - \text{Net Profit Target})}$$

In this case, they are targeting a 60% profit rate, so that

$$\text{Price per Hour} = 38.21 \times 31/(1 - 0.60)4 = \$38.21 \times 2.5 = \$95.53/\text{hr.}$$

For each job, the hourly rate should be multiplied by the number of hours of labor and added to the materials cost, plus a markup on materials. Using the Computer Associates example yields the following:

Cost of Services (15 hours × $95.50/hr.)	$1432.50
Cost of Materials	$200.00
Markup on Cost of Materials (70%)	$140.00
Total Service Price	$1772.50

Entrepreneurs in service businesses have to be wary of pricing properly. Particularly for those who transition away from being paid an hourly wage as a service technician, there is a fear of overcharging and not getting the work. This may well be a case where customers truly believe "you get what you pay for," and will pay the higher price in exchange for the perceived better-quality option. A local furniture repairman found that he was able to increase his fee threefold, and he continued working the same number of hours with substantially higher margins.

Pricing Principles

market clearing price the particular price at which the supply of products and/or services matches the demand for them.

At the root of all pricing decisions is the need to reach the market attractively and to attain **market clearing prices**, which are prices at which the supply of products and/or services matches the demand for them. If prices are too high, the supply will exceed demand, leaving excess inventory. If prices are too low, there may be shortages of products. If shortages are persistent or stock-outs are problematic, customers may seek alternate or substitute products, leading to the permanent loss of customers.

elastic demand customer demand changes significantly upward or downward when the price of a product changes.

inelastic demand the type of demand which does not change in a significant way when prices change.

The amount of flexibility that you have in pricing your products or services depends upon the demand elasticity of your customers. If you have **elastic demand**, customer demand changes significantly upward or downward when the price of a product changes. Purchases that are considered to be discretionary, or luxury, items tend to have elastic demand. **Inelastic demand**, on the other hand, is demand that does not change in a significant way when prices change. This is often the case for necessity products such as food and gasoline. Consumers will adjust their consumption, but not radically, when prices change for these items.

Extending Credit to Customers

Regardless of whether you are a business-to-business company or a business-to-consumer company, you will probably be asked to extend credit to your customers. By extending credit, you are making your product or service more accessible to many more people. As credit has become more readily available, consumers have often come to expect credit cards to be readily accepted, and vendors are expected to give payment terms. As a retailer, whether with a physical storefront, virtual storefront, or both, you should consider accepting credit and debit cards. They are ubiquitous and customers expect to be able to pay retailers by this method.

The Costs and Benefits of Credit

Extending credit has costs and benefits to all types of organizations. It brings benefits in the form of greater purchasing by customers to build firm revenues and growth. American consumers have become accustomed to being able to make purchases, ranging from a cup of coffee to major appliances, on credit cards. They don't expect to have to save the full price of a home or an automobile before purchasing it. Business owners expect to be able to establish credit terms with their vendors. Businesses that don't offer credit options may lose customers to the ones that do.

The benefits of offering credit are offset to some degree by the potential and realized costs. The decision to extend credit is one that affects pricing and financial performance. Whether you extend credit directly to your customers or you work through a third-party vendor, you need to recognize that your cash flow will be slowed and your prices will be reduced. Credit can be extended directly through installment credit for consumers and through trade credit for companies. It can be provided indirectly, through the acceptance of credit cards such as MasterCard, VISA, American Express, and Discover. The specific costs are discussed in greater detail below.

Types of Credit

Credit may be extended as consumer credit or trade credit, according to the type of customer. Businesses selling to consumers can extend consumer credit through credit cards or installment loans. Businesses selling to other businesses extend trade credit.

Step into the Shoes . . .

Fixing General Motors by Focusing the Brand

When Alfred Sloan took over the management of General Motors in 1921, the product line was a mélange of automobile divisions and overlapping price ranges:

Chevrolet:	$795	to	$2075
Oakland:	$1395	to	$2065
Oldsmobile:	$1445	to	$3300
Scripps-Booth:	$1545	to	$2295
Sheridan:	$1685		
Buick:	$1795	to	$3295
Cadillac:	$3790	to	$5690

Sloan replaced this with an overall, stepped pricing strategy. A customer could move up the "automobile ladder" as personal finances improved:

Chevrolet:	$450	to	$600
Pontiac:	$600	to	$900
Oldsmobile:	$900	to	$1200
Buick:	$1200	to	$1700
Cadillac:	$2000	to	$3700

Alfred Sloan, General Motors.

It took 10 years for General Motors to surpass Ford using this strategy, but once it did, it could not be stopped. GM held close to 50 percent of the American market for over half a century.

Credit Cards

These can be issued directly by a merchant or through a third party. Store or merchant credit cards are issued to customers by the firm as a means of building loyalty and as a marketing effort. Often, cardholders are eligible for special discounts and store events or can accumulate points toward rewards, all of which drive the customer back into the store or onto an online store front. For example, Kohl's department stores offer charge customers exclusive monthly discounts. Talbot's offers multiple levels of credit cards, with points accumulating based upon purchases and rewards for predetermined purchasing volumes. Private-label cards may be carried by the merchants themselves, but are generally issued by a mainstream financial institution that manages the credit cards for a fee.

merchant card services financial systems to permit acceptance of major credit cards.

For smaller companies, such private-label cards are not financially viable, and they choose to establish **merchant card services**, systems to permit the acceptance of major credit cards from financial services institutions or other vendors. With such services, they can usually accept both MasterCard and VISA. Usually, Discover Card and American Express are established as additional services. In order to acquire merchant card services, retailers and others have to apply and provide their credit information. Also, there are start-up fees ranging from about \$50 to \$200 dollars, an equipment fee of about \$250 to \$1500, and other miscellaneous fees. Ongoing fees include an interchange fee of \$0.25 to \$0.75 per credit transaction, and a discount rate (fee) of 1 to 6 percent of each purchase. There are also monthly statement fees of \$4 to \$20 per month, and other fees, depending upon the servicer.

For home-based businesses, and others that cannot or do not wish to obtain merchant status with credit card companies, there are third-party firms that fill the gap, particularly for Internet retailers. These firms do not customarily charge monthly fees or set-up fees but do have a per-transaction fee and a fee based upon the purchase price. PayPal is the most widely recognized and used of these services.

Installment Credit

installment credit loans to be paid back in installments over time.

There are small businesses that directly extend **installment credit**—or loans to be paid back in installments over time—to their customers. Typically, the customers are purchasing large-ticket items such as used cars, bedding, and furniture that the consumers want/need to finance over time. Some firms build business relationships with finance companies and/or banks for this purpose.

If a company has sufficient capital to provide its own installment payment programs and can assume the risk, it may earn significant revenues on the interest from financing. Customers who receive such credit must pay principal and interest over the life of the loan. Small business owners retain an ownership interest in the purchased item as collateral on the loan (e.g., the car title), so they can reclaim (repossess) the merchandise if the customer fails to adhere to the loan terms. Many of the smaller used car dealers who promise credit to all customers use this type of financing as a primary source of revenue, sometimes selling the same vehicles many times to many different people, and repossessing them. You should determine how this type of credit arrangement fits within your ethics, and the laws of your area, before pursuing such a strategy. The decision to extend installment credit is a business decision the risks and rewards of which need to be weighed.

Trade Credit

Providing credit directly to customers is usual and customary business practice for manufacturers and wholesalers. Orders may be released with a range of different credit terms. For example, if the product is custom-made or the credit risk is high, it may be sold on cash-in-advance (CIA) terms, requiring prepayment from the customer before either shipping or production. If the customer is new or has credit issues, product may be shipped with cash-on-delivery (COD) terms, requiring the delivering party to collect payment in full, perhaps in the form of a cashier's check or the like, prior to completing the delivery. Other credit is extended in terms of the day payment is due, such as 30, 60, or 90 days. If you want to add an incentive for early payment, a discount can be added, as in the example of 2/10, net 30—which means a 2 percent discount is offered for payment within 10 days, or full payment within 30 days.

Credit's Impact on Pricing

Performance Objective 4

Explore the role of trade credit in pricing.

Any type of credit offered to a customer reduces the amount of funds received and/or delays their receipt. In order to price objectively, the costs of extending credit must be fully incorporated into the pricing decision. For example, the credit-card processing fees can reduce the amount received from an individual sale by about 10 percent. Unfortunately, customers do not typically view the cost of the credit card usage as a discount, and usually are unwilling to pay extra for it. (However, some universities do charge a fee for tuition payments made by credit card.) So, the credit card costs are reductions in earnings for the firm. The same is true for any prompt or early payment discounts offered to trade customers. Installment credit may either increase or decrease, depending upon its structure and the quality of the credit. Also, payment terms mean waiting longer for your funds, such that you may need to incur borrowing costs of your own, or have negative cash flow impacts.

Managing the Credit Process

The decision to extend credit is part of the pricing decision and the financial analysis of the business. If the decision is to retain the credit-granting process within the firm rather than transferring the risk to a third party for a fee, a process should be established well ahead of granting credit. This process should make an objective analysis of whether the buyer can and will repay the debt and when he/she will do so. The analysis also should determine how, if at all, you can compel repayment in the case of delinquency or default.

Global Impact...

Raw Material Prices Challenge Manufacturers

When the price of crude oil rises, much of the world feels the pain. Manufacturers using crude oil in their production are affected. When copper prices rise, the effects are also felt worldwide. Volatile raw material costs in one place can have huge ripple effects upon costs and prices globally. Whereas labor costs frequently are perceived to be a primary driver of manufacturing costs, the impact of changing raw material costs may also be quite significant, particularly when they are extremely volatile. Manufacturers must control raw material costs to create sustainable profits.

Manufacturers have to buy smarter, explore alternate materials, and evaluate their ability to increase prices to their customers. Manufacturers purchase materials sourced globally to attain the most favorable pricing, making any changes in pricing a global issue. Thus, a price increase in crude oil in Saudi Arabia has ripple effects on Main Street U.S.A.

Source: Jill Jusko, "Rethinking Raw Materials," IndustryWeek.com, August 1, 2006, http://www.industryweek.com (accessed on March 29, 2009).

A credit application is an excellent starting point for consumer- and trade-credit analysis. A well-designed credit application will request the following information for trade credit:

- Contact name, telephone numbers, fax, and e-mail
- Full business name and aliases (DBA)
- Complete street address (a P.O. Box is not sufficient)
- Date and state of incorporation, if applicable
- Date founded
- Employer identification number (EIN) or Social Security Number
- DUNS number (from Dun and Bradstreet), if applicable
- Full legal name and complete contact information for any owners of 10% or more with ownership percentage noted
- Names and contact information for three or four supplier references
- Name and contact information for commercial bank reference
- Financial resources, revenues, debt position, and other pertinent information
- Amount of credit and payment terms requested
- Estimated annual purchasing volume of the company
- Financial statements or tax returns as appropriate to the amount of credit requested
- Signature line, giving legal permission to acquire credit information

For consumer credit, similar information is needed, including full information on any co-signers and a listing of other creditors (such as credit cards, auto loans, home mortgages).

Note above that, depending upon the nature of your business and the amount of credit requested, you may require business financial statements, audits, and/or tax filings. Similar documents can be requested from consumers. However, remember that the credit process is part of your sales and marketing and customer service efforts. There is a fine line between requesting the information that you need to make a credit decision and overburdening and annoying the customers to the point of losing them. Ask only for what you need and will use in making the credit determination, rather than that which it would be good to know.

Sources of Credit Information

The best indicator of future performance is past performance. This truism is particularly applicable with respect to credit. The first and best source of credit information is your customer's credit history and an explanation of any irregularities in it. Credit applicants with poor credit history should be given an opportunity to provide a letter of explanation, and you can decide whether they have taken responsibility for the problems or are denying responsibility and blaming others. Bankers and other lenders know that customers who have taken responsibility for credit issues make far better customers than those who refuse to do so. This is sometimes called taking a stand of responsibility versus the stand of a victim. If you decide to take a risk on people and/or companies with less than perfect credit, it is vital to understand your risk.

Consumer credit histories are available through consumer credit agencies, particularly Experian, TransUnion, and Equifax. Business credit information may be available through Dun and Bradstreet (D&B; http://www.dnb.com), customer financial statements, as well as other suppliers and industry professionals. Bankers may also be a resource. The fees associated with securing credit information should be considered in your costs of doing business. Remember to be objective about the information that you obtain, and filter out biased or subjective data from objective analysis. At the same time, proceed with caution when red flags begin to appear.

Aging of Receivables

If you decide to extend credit to customers, you will need to track and manage repayment of the *accounts receivable* that you generate. The most critical element of this process is to get into the habit of timely billing and consistent, effective collections. When your firm grows, these procedures need to be formalized and practiced to maximize cash flow. As will be discussed in Chapter 15, setting up a receivables aging schedule and carefully monitoring your carrying costs is important to your company's overall financial health, and to calculating prices and costs.

Credit Regulation

State and federal laws govern the process of securing credit information and the disclosure of credit terms and conditions. These protections have been created for the benefit of consumers to shield them from unscrupulous lenders. Before you create your credit policies, application forms, and processes, obtain the appropriate legal information. It is beneficial to have your credit documents and procedures reviewed by legal and accounting professionals to ensure that you are starting off correctly.

Discounts, Incentives, and Other Price Adjustments

The final price that customers pay can be reduced by discounts from list prices and incentives. Some price adjustments, in addition to cash discounts and accounts receivable carrying costs, are

- order size (quantity) discounts,
- annual/quarterly/monthly volume discounts or bonuses,
- dealer and distributor discounts,
- promotion discounts and bonuses,
- merchandising discounts,
- cooperative advertising and marketing allowances,
- product or product-line rebates,
- exception discounts, and
- freight/shipping allowances.[3]

Performance Objective 5
Consider discounts, incentives, and other price adjustments.

These price adjustments could come through any number of areas of the company and can vary widely from customer to customer, not necessarily according to a particular strategy, such as volume. The same product could have a broad range of prices and you might be surprised to see the differences. Michael Marn and Robert Rosiello have created methods for understanding pricing structures within a firm.[4] The **pocket price** is

pocket price the portion of full price that remains after all pricing factors are deducted.

[3]Michael V. Marn and Robert L. Rosiello, "Managing Price, Gaining Profit," *Harvard Business Review*, September–October 1992.
[4]Ibid.

Figure 8-3 *Pocket price waterfall for a manufacturer.*

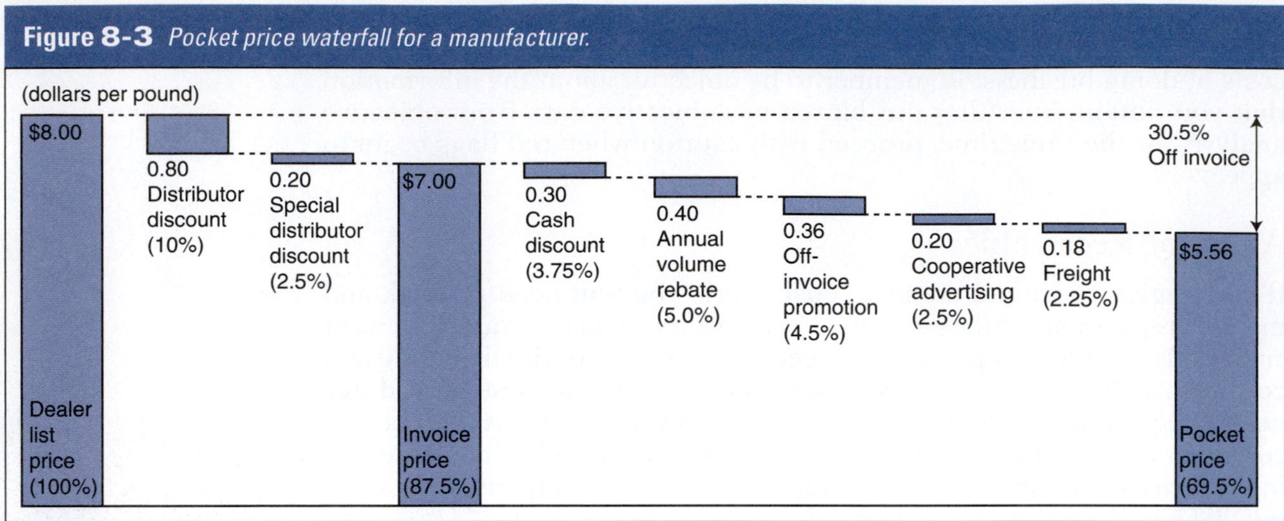

what remains after all pricing factors, such as discounts and allowances, are deducted from lists or invoices to reach the final prices. The "pocket price waterfall" is a visual representation of this concept. **Figure 8-3** illustrates the pocket-price-waterfall concept for a manufacturer.

In addition to looking at the pocket price waterfall, managers may explore the range of prices at which the same product or service is sold to different customers. The pocket price band shows the range of prices for a given unit volume of a particular item at a given point in time.[5] **Figure 8-4** illustrates a pocket price band.

If you are establishing pricing for new products or markets, you can keep tighter control by looking at the price more holistically with a view toward the list, intermediate, and pocket prices. Regardless of the age or maturity of the firm, understanding where prices can be eroded, and establishing and maintaining policies and procedures to ensure that prices are well-managed, is a best practice. Remember to make changes or establish adjustments to pricing based upon the factors that matter most to your customers. Get the most for your investment.

[5]Ibid.

Figure 8-4 *Pocket price band.*

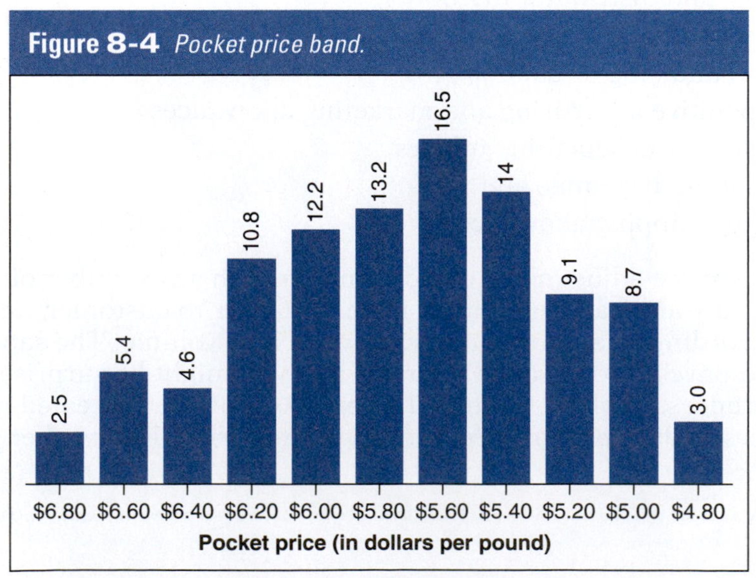

Chapter Summary

Now that you have studied this chapter you can do the following:

1. Understand the relationship between price and overall strategy.
   - Pricing positions the product or service.
   - Pricing strategy should match firm strategy.
   - Following a logical process can lead to better pricing.
2. Multiple pricing strategies are available to businesses.
   - Value pricing—offering more for less.
   - Prestige pricing—setting a high price to convey high quality or uniqueness.
   - Cost-plus pricing—applying a factor to calculated costs.
   - Penetration pricing—charging lower initial prices to capture market share.
   - Skimming pricing—charging higher initial prices.
   - Meet-or-beat-the-competition pricing—just what it says.
   - Follow-the-leader pricing—using a competitor as a model for your pricing.
   - Personalized (dynamic) pricing—charging different prices as the market will bear.
   - Price lining—setting a range of pricing levels.
3. Determine markups.
   - Manufacturers and retailers often double their cost, which is called keystoning.
   - Wholesalers often add 20 percent.
   - Service firms may use cost plus a markup on hourly and materials costs.
4. Explore the role of trade credit.
   - Credit can increase both revenues and costs.
   - Consumer and trade credit options include credit cards, installment debt, and trade credit.
   - The decision to extend credit is part of the pricing decision and financial analysis.
   - Credit applications and information should be carefully compiled and analyzed from a variety of sources.
   - Federal and state regulations apply.
5. Discounts, incentives, and price adjustments.
   - These adjustments reduce the final price that customers pay and need to be considered. Some adjustments include
     - order size (quantity) discounts,
     - annual/quarterly/monthly volume discounts or bonuses,
     - dealer and distributor discounts,
     - promotion discounts and bonuses,
     - merchandising discounts,
     - cooperative advertising and marketing allowances,
     - product or product-line rebates,
     - exception discounts, and
     - freight/shipping allowances.[6]
   - The pocket price waterfall and pocket price band assist in analysis.

[6]Michael V. Marn and Robert L. Rosiello, "Managing Price, Gaining Profit," *Harvard Business Review*, September–October 1992.

Key Terms

cost-plus pricing
elastic demand
follow-the-leader pricing
inelastic demand
installment credit
market clearing price
markup pricing
merchant card services
penetration pricing
personalized pricing
pocket price
prestige pricing
price
price lining
skimming prices strategy
variable pricing strategy

Entrepreneurship Portfolio

Critical Thinking Exercises

1. Meet with a partner and discuss the pros and cons of the following pricing strategies: value pricing, keystoning, cost-plus, penetration strategy, skimming strategy, and meet or beat the competition—for each of your respective businesses. Present your recommendations for each other to the class.
2. What costs and benefits are there to offering trade credit? How can a small firm ensure that it controls the costs?
3. What is the relationship between price and image? Why is it important?

Key Concept Questions

1. Define cost-plus pricing. Why is it used so frequently? What are the drawbacks associated with using it?
2. What is penetration pricing? Can you think of an example of a company that has used penetration pricing to introduce a new product? What firm is it and what is the example?
3. What is the relationship between pricing and competition?
4. How can a pocket price waterfall assist a business?
5. What is meant by 15/10 net 45? What is the impact on the seller's pocket price when a customer takes advantage of this?

Application Exercises

1. Using the markups described in the chapter, calculate the price at each link in the distribution chain for a blouse that cost the manufacturer $4.75 to make:
   Manufacturer's cost: $__________
   Manufacturer's price: $__________
   Wholesaler's cost: $__________
   Wholesaler's price: $__________
   Retailer's cost: $__________
   Retailer's price: $__________
2. Create a pocket price waterfall for Creative Toy Manufacturing's (CTM) new electric yo-yo. The list price is $5.50 each with a minimum order of 12 dozen. The standard dealer discount (off invoice) is 50% and the

order discount is 3% for orders of more than 20 dozen. There is a special promotion of $0.10 each off of invoice. The payment terms are 2/10 net 30. Because CTM is encouraging customers to advertize the electric yo-yo, there is a 5% cooperative advertising allowance for dealers. Customers are being offered a rebate of $0.50. What is the pocket price for CTM?

Exploring Online

1. Perform an Internet search on either a product or service comparable to what you plan to market, or one that you personally own. Attempt to find at least three sites that sell it.
   a. List the applicable price point, including all discounts, allowances, and promotions, plus any shipping and handling required.
   b. Are there more or less than three prices available? Why do you suppose this is?
   c. Explain any challenges you had in performing the steps in this exercise. What do they tell you about the product or service? The companies selling them?
2. Visit the PayPal Web site (http://www.paypal.com) and one of the following: Intuit Payment Services (http://www.payments.intuit.com), eCommerce Exchange (http://www.ecenow.com), Merchant Accounts Express (http://www.merchantexpress.com), or Charge.com. Make a chart comparing the charges and requirements for merchants with each.

Case Study | Credit Policies—Harold Import Company

If you like to cook, have ever purchased a gourmet cooking item, or ever shopped in a gourmet kitchen store, chances are you have a Harold Import Company (HIC) product in your kitchen. Since its start in 1957, HIC has sold over 20 million pieces of porcelain dinnerware worldwide.

When Harold Laub launched HIC, it became the first company to import the 10.25-inch white coupe dinner plate into the United States from Japan. But that was only the beginning. Soon, HIC was importing a wide range of white porcelain items that included bakeware as well as dinnerware. When Harold's wife, Mildred, joined the company in 1962, she helped expand the business further, with imports of kitchen gadgets.

Today, HIC distributes over 3500 house ware, gourmet food, and kitchen products from 25 different countries, including the original 10.25-inch white coupe dinner plate. HIC is still run by members of the Laub family, who continue to diversify the product lines while maintaining high quality.

As a standard procedure, HIC asks each new customer to fill out a form containing basic company information. Items on this form include mailing, shipping, and e-mail addresses; contact names and telephone numbers; the type of business and its resale tax identification number; and the customer's desired method of payment.

If the customer wishes to establish an account with terms of net 30 days, a credit application must also be completed. This form requires the contact information for three vendors from whom the customer has previously purchased goods.

Harold Import Company calls each of the provided trade references to find out the customer's payment history. If responses are positive, an HIC account with credit is set up. The credit limit is determined by a combination of factors. For new customers, HIC staff looks at the amount of credit that the customer is requesting and the amount of credit their references currently provide. HIC staff makes a determination based on those two numbers and their level of comfort with the customer. However, if feedback indicates late payments, then HIC asks the customer to provide banking information. In these questionable cases, the customer may pay with a credit card or send a prepayment, which is almost always a company

check. By using this process, HIC is able to provide multiple payment options to potential buyers while keeping risk at a minimum.

For established customers, the credit limit is typically 40 percent of their yearly sales volume. The reason for this level is that if HIC's customer fails to pay its obligation, on average, HIC's loss is limited to its expected profit. If an established customer needs credit beyond the 40 percent, the HIC staff looks at it on an individual basis and makes the determination based on factors that include payment history, frequency of ordering, length of time as a customer, and general creditworthiness within the industry.

Case Study Analysis

1. What types of credit does HIC offer?
2. What types of general information does HIC ask all new customers to provide?
3. Describe the process used by HIC to evaluate credit risk and to determine an acceptable means of payment.
4. In general, what are the pros and cons for HIC to offer credit options?

Case Sources

Harold Import Company Web site, http://www.haroldimport.com.

Case Study Texas Jet—Premium Pricing for Premium Service

***Small Business School* video clip titles are in red**

LEAD WITH SERVICE AND TURN TIME INTO AN ASSET

Texas Jet is a gas station for airplanes. However, owner Reed Pigman doesn't use today's gas station as a model for thinking about his business. He uses the Ritz Carlton Hotel chain as his guide. Reed says, "The people who fly and ride in private planes are the same people who stay at a Ritz Carlton or other luxury hotels. That means they don't compare us to the corner gas station, they compare us to the luxury service they get when they travel."

Reed's business operates 13 hangars totaling more than 225,000 square feet and supplies two-thirds of the fuel at Meacham Field, located in Fort Worth, Texas. Private aircraft depend upon a network of fueling stations that are called fixed-base operations (FBO), and Texas Jet is one of the best in the world, according to *Professional Pilot* magazine and *Aviation International News*.

In 2009 and 2010, Texas Jet was named the number one FBO by the pilots surveyed. *Professional Pilot* named Texas Jet number one because Texas Jet is a place the pilots enjoy while they are waiting for their customers to return. More significantly, the pilot's customer is given the red-carpet treatment.

There is a very demanding supply chain within these operations, with high levels of expectations regarding customer service. The pilot is the customer of Texas Jet, and the passengers are the customers of the pilot. Although a few pilots own their planes, most are the full-time employees of the companies that owns the planes, and often the passengers are their key executives. Passengers could also be individuals who have a fractional ownership in a private airplane, who have chartered an airplane, or who are just paying for an empty leg. Everyone is a choice customer and all expect top-quality customer care and attention to detail.

Texas Jet sells jet fuel and support services for the private airplanes. When the pilots prepare a flight plan, the destination FBO is part of the plan. They have to buy fuel and there are choices with respect to which FBO they select. Whereas the pilots may spend extended time at the FBO's facility, the passengers generally spend very little time there. However, the few minutes the passenger does spend there are critical to the pilot's success.

I saw Texas Jet employees literally throwing out a red carpet for the passengers to step on. This is going on while the pilot is checking gauges and shutting things down. The pilot chose Texas Jet and gets the credit for the red-carpet treatment, while taking care of matters in the cockpit. It is a special touch, and excellent service. Reed says, "The pilots want to know when they pull up on our ramp that we will take care of the boss in the back of the airplane. We will handle every request with a smile."

Texas Jet arranges for the ground transportation to pick passengers up right at plane side and, if they need food on the airplane, that is handled too. While the passengers are taking care of business or social obligations in Fort Worth, the pilots have a place at Texas Jet to sleep, work out, eat, relax, visit with other pilots, watch TV, send e-mails, check the weather, and work on flight plans.

The day I was there, it was cold outside, but the pilots received a warm welcome. There were freshly baked cookies and hot apple cider in the lobby to make them feel at home. Did your mother ever have cookies for you when you came home from school? When you opened the door, did you smell the sweetness in the air before you saw the cookies? Reed understands that pilots have to spend a lot of time away from their families and his goal is to make Texas Jet an extended family for every pilot who buys fuel from him.

Also, there are always fresh apples in a bowl at Texas Jet. They look good, they smell good, they taste good, and they are good for you. This brings up the old adage that my mom used to repeat, "An apple a day keeps the doctor away." There is a little child inside all of us and, without smothering, great companies find ways to mother their customers. At Texas Jet, employees ask the pilots simple questions like, "How is your day going?" By being genuinely interested in their customers as people, not just as pilots who buy fuel, the Texas Jet team turns their customers into friends and family.

PRICE IT HIGH

Excellence pays. Reed charges more for fuel than his competitors, and at the same time he sells two-thirds of all the fuel purchased in his market. Texas Jet recognizes what many small business owners learn the hard way, that having the lowest price and building a stable, long-lasting company can be opposing goals. Reed says, "It took me a while to realize that I've got to charge a fair price for the fuel I sell. I stopped letting myself get beat up by people that would say, 'Boy, I got fuel just the other day that's 30 cents cheaper than what you're selling it.' I've got to make a margin so I can keep the best people here and so I can reinvest in the business."

In addition to the red carpet, apples, hot apple cider, and cookies, Texas Jet provides covered parking, crew cars, so the pilots don't have to rent a car if they want to leave Meacham Field, air-conditioning units to keep the inside of the planes cool while they are on the ground in the hot Texas sun, the snooze room, the TV room, work-out equipment with showers, and an office with Internet access. All of these facilities and services increase the costs for Texas Jet, but they also justify the higher cost of fuel and provide reasons for the customers to return. They provide competitive advantages that increase the value of Texas Jet's products and services.

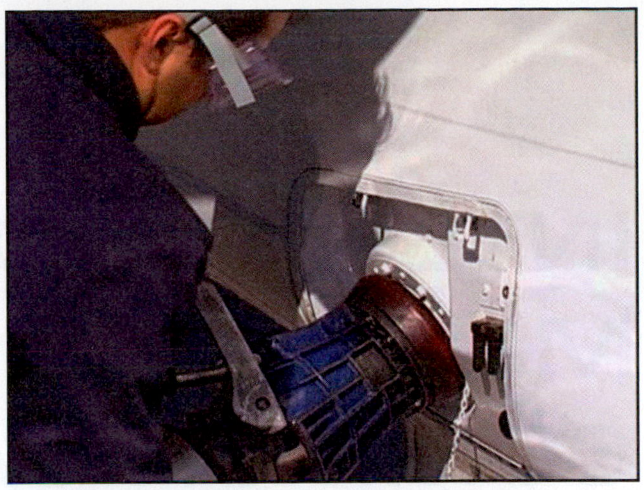

There are 4000 fixed-base operators in the United States, and Texas Jet has been in the top 10 over and over again. Reed is too humble to say that he can't learn from others who run FBOs, but when you are the best in your own field, you have to go outside of it for inspiration. Reed now looks to the hospitality industry for service-improvement ideas. He wants to know how a five-star hotel and a white-tablecloth restaurant take care of customers. He has learned that getting to the top was hard, but staying at the top is the greater challenge.

Case Analysis

1. What is an FBO and who are its customers?
2. What makes Texas Jet special?
3. Why has Texas Jet won so much recognition?
4. What is the Texas Jet pricing strategy?
5. Does Texas Jet think of itself as a fueling station?

Case prepared by Hattie Bryant, creator of *Small Business School*, the television series made for PBS and Voice of America, http://SmallBusinessSchool.org.

Chapter 9

INTEGRATED MARKETING COMMUNICATIONS

"Many a small thing has been made large by the right kind of advertising."

—Mark Twain, American author

Marketers strive to create images that customers recognize and associate with their products and services. Leo Burnett Company, a Chicago-based agency, leads the pack in terms of creating advertising icons. *Advertising Age* magazine selected the top ten icons based upon effectiveness, longevity, recognizability, and cultural impact.[1] Do you recognize them?

1. The Marlboro Man
2. Ronald McDonald
3. The Jolly Green Giant
4. Betty Crocker
5. The Energizer Bunny
6. The Pillsbury Dough Boy
7. Aunt Jemima
8. The Michelin Man
9. Tony the Tiger
10. Elsie the Cow

The Marlboro Man.

Performance Objectives

1. Define integrated marketing communications and its components.
2. Conduct promotional planning and budgeting.
3. Understand advertising and advertising management.
4. Identify and evaluate media.
5. Discuss sales promotion.
6. Explore alternative marketing options.
7. Analyze database and direct-response marketing opportunities.
8. Incorporate e-active marketing.
9. Describe publicity and public relations.

Use Integrated Marketing Communications for Success

Performance Objective 1

Define integrated marketing communications and its components.

Marketing communications promotes your business to your current and prospective customers and those who influence the purchasing and sales decisions. All communications include an originator or source, a specific message (overt and/or subliminal), a channel for dissemination, and a target or receiver. By integrating your communications, you can maximize the impact of your communications resources, primarily as expended for promotion.

Promotion has expanded beyond advertising, sales promotions, and personal selling to include database marketing, sponsorships, direct marketing, alternative marketing, e-active marketing, and public relations. Promotion should be based upon an organization's strategic marketing plan and is meant to create a unified communications program. Promotional tools, applied well, get your marketing message out to your customers. *Advertising*, as discussed in Chapter 4, is paid promotion that is intended to support increased sales of your product or service. Examples

[1]http://adage.com/century/ad-icons.html (accessed March 2009).

Entrepreneurial Wisdom . . .

Take advantage of resources available to learn more about target markets.

www.claritas.com	Consumer geodemographic information
www.adage.com	Advertising statistics, trends, and examples
www.strategicbusinessinsights.com	Values and lifestyles (VALS) psychographic segmentation
www.iVillage.com	Target information—Web site for women
www.targetmarketnews.com	Target information—African Americans
www.hispaniconline.com	Target information—Hispanics
www.planetout.com	Target information—gays and lesbians

of advertising include television commercials, billboards, and magazine ads. *Publicity* is free mention of a company, individual, event, product, or service in media such as newspapers and magazines, or on radio and television stations.

Reinforce the Company's Unique Selling Proposition

Your unique selling proposition (USP) becomes valuable to your organization when it is successfully communicated to your target customers and should motivate purchasing and repeat purchasing decisions. Integrated marketing communications frame the USP in multiple media to reach targeted audiences and communicate the salient information, evoke emotional responses, and create effective, favorable impressions. A unique selling proposition that is not successfully communicated is worthless. A unique selling proposition that is successfully communicated can be priceless.

Promotional Planning

Performance Objective 2
Conduct promotional planning and budgeting.

Vast quantities of promotional effort bombard businesses and consumers daily, and frequently create unwanted clutter and noise. They also reflect opportunities for quality customer contact. The challenge for businesses is to determine the best opportunities, and to create promotions that effectively cut through the clutter and noise, engage the attention of prospective customers, and generate profitable sales. Successful promotions are the result of solid planning. For promotional planning to be integrated within your organization, all of the company's components need to have meaningful roles in the planning process.

Create a Promotional Strategy Using Promotions Opportunity Analysis

promotions opportunity analysis a process that includes research into target markets and the promotional strategies to reach them.

The **promotions opportunity analysis** is a process that includes research into target markets and the promotional strategies to reach them. It is critical for you to learn as much as is practical about your target audience(s) so that you can create effective strategies for communicating messages that are heard, understood, and yield the desired results.

According to Kenneth Clow and Donald Baack,[2] the five steps of promotions opportunity analysis are

1. conduct a communications market analysis,
2. establish communications objectives,
3. create a communications budget,
4. prepare promotional strategies, and
5. match tactics with strategies.

In previous chapters, you learned how to conduct competitive and environmental analysis through the use of the SWOT method, among others. A communications market analysis is similar, but based specifically on a communications perspective. The areas to be examined include opportunities, competitors, target markets, customers, and product positioning.[3] When looking for opportunities, organizations ask key questions, such as

- Are there customers that the competition is ignoring or not serving?
- Which markets are heavily saturated and have intense competition?
- Are the benefits of our goods [or services] being clearly articulated to the various customer market segments?
- Would there be opportunities to build relationships with customers using a slightly different marketing approach?
- Are there opportunities that are not being pursued, or is our brand positioned with a cluster of other companies in such a manner that it cannot stand out?[4]

With the promotions opportunity analysis complete, you can establish communications objectives. These objectives will be needed to guide strategy, budgeting, implementation, and measurement of promotional efforts. An organization may have a single objective, or simultaneous multiple aims. These objectives should be derived from marketing goals, such as return on investment, sales, or profits and should be clearly spelled out and measurable. **Exhibit 9-1** lists some common communications objectives.

Exhibit 9-1 *Communications objectives.*

- Develop brand awareness and image
- Provide information
- Increase category demand through persuasion
- Change customer beliefs or attitudes
- Enhance purchasing actions
- Encourage repeat purchases
- Build customer traffic
- Enhance company image
- Increase market share
- Reinforce purchasing decisions

[2]Kenneth Clow and Donald Baack, *Integrated Advertising, Promotion, and Marketing Communications*, 4th ed. (Upper Saddle River, N.J.: Prentice Hall, 2010).
[3]Ibid.
[4]Ibid., p. 92.

Karmalogy beads from Zorbitz.

Step into the Shoes . . .

Robin Sydney—Zorbitz, Inc.: A Line of Products Worn by A-List Stars

Could a 19-year-old take $100 in cash and a $5 pile of rocks and create a multimillion-dollar business? Robin Sydney and her mother, Marian, did just that when they created SunRocks, which later became Zorbitz. Sydney sought out a mentor. She found the marketing genius behind VISA and Reebok. The women also learned about retail and wholesale from the owner of one of the largest gift stores in Los Angeles. For Sydney stumbling upon Chinese feng shui jade good-luck charms while conducting research on another idea, led to selling bead bracelets to Whole Foods Markets and becoming the top-selling gift product in that company's southern Pacific market. Zorbitz has grown with the addition of Karmology Bead Bracelets, which combine lucky karma beads with powerful gemstones to help bring good luck, good karma, and everything people want in their lives.

Zorbitz emphasizes the healing qualities of their products (e.g., love, health, wealth, and miracles), the A-list stars that wear their products (e.g., Ashlee Simpson, Halle Berry, Paris Hilton, and Freddie Prinze, Jr.), and the charitable contributions they make worldwide. So in this case, $100 in cash and $5 in rocks, considerable creativity, and promotional savvy can add up to more than $2.5 million in annual sales.

Source: Zorbitz Web site at http://www.zorbitz.net and "California Teen Creates Million Dollar Idea . . . And Zorbitz Takes Off," *Los Angeles Cityzine*, December 20, 2007, http://www.la.cityzine.com/2007/12/20 (accessed May 20, 2009). Courtesy of Zorbitz, Inc.

Determine a Promotional Budget

The creation and careful control of a promotional budget is essential to marketing success. A well-structured budget based upon the promotions opportunity analysis, promotional objectives, and an effective strategy will support measurement and control. These in turn will foster improved performance. There is no single correct way to determine your promotional budget. However, there are several methods that can be used in combination:

- percentage of sales method,
- competitive spending method,
- excess funds approach, and
- objective and task method.

Percentage of Sales

Percentage of sales is a common way for calculating the aggregate budget amount. It is the simplest to use because the budget is derived either from the prior year's sales, or anticipated sales. The percentage to be used is best taken from a comparable industry but may be whatever you want to employ.

The percentage of sales method of budgeting is preferable to not establishing a promotional budget, but suffers from several drawbacks. This approach seems counter-intuitive to the promotional needs of an organization, because you spend less when you most need promotion—when sales are low. You spend more when you are selling more. Also, this technique may not take competitive spending into account, and does not consider your overall strategy.

Competitive Spending

Competitive spending is another way to set a promotional budget. It entails researching your competition to determine their level of spending. This may be as simple as investigating financial-statement studies, or as complex as attempting to track and cost out all of their promotional activities. This meet-the-competition method is often used in highly competitive markets, in which the objective is to prevent market-share loss.

Although knowing what your competitors are doing and spending is a good practice in general, setting your budget based upon theirs is not optimal. This benchmarking implies that you can make a complete assessment, that competitors are spending the right amount of money, and that this would also be the correct amount for you to spend. The competition may be spending based upon a percentage of sales method, according to their excess funds, or even based upon which media and advertising salespeople they like. In other words, competitors may not be using the best methods to create their promotional budgets, so copying what they do could easily be ineffective.

Excess Funds

The excess funds approach to promotional budgeting means determining what is left over, or what you can afford after other expenses are calculated and allocating funds based upon the results. This is among the least strategic of the budgeting methods because it is completely internally driven. Whereas better than having no budget at all, using excess funds is not recommended. This is a particularly poor option for start-up companies and businesses in periods of rapid growth because there are rarely excess funds to spend at the very times when promotional efforts are most needed.

Objective and Task

The objective and task method is to budget expenditures according to the specific strategies and tactics developed to reach promotional objectives. This entails building a budget based upon what you have determined is needed to be successful. In order to create this type of budget, management enumerates the objectives for the year, and the budget required to reach them. The more specific you can be about measurable objectives, and the specific media and methods to be used, the stronger the focus of your efforts will be, and the more effective your budget can be as a guide and control.

There is no single perfect method of establishing a promotional budget because there is both art and science involved. As an entrepreneur, using the best aspects of each method is your best bet. Rather than determining what you can easily afford, estimate what you would ideally spend, and decide how much you could invest to accomplish your goals and objectives. Know where you plan to spend the funds and how you will monitor and control them. This budget should support your strategy and tactics, but not control them so tightly that you cannot take advantage of opportunities if they arise.

The Advertising Advantage

The topic of advertising and advertising management has a certain glamour about it. The popular media have portrayed advertising as a fast-paced, highly creative, fun, and lucrative career choice. At the same time, advertising itself has often been shown to be false, manipulative, deceitful, and coercive. For some, it is something to be avoided whenever possible. Others embrace it and enjoy wearing branded clothing, promotional T-shirts, caps, and the like, and watch the annual Super Bowl more for the television advertisements than for the football. It does not matter where you fall personally in this spectrum. It is important to determine the best, most effective method of advertising for your business to reach your prospective and current customers—to run a successful company. This is where advertising management becomes critical.

As with any aspect of your business, advertising has specific objectives that make it an integral component of the marketing mix. Advertising aids the marketing effort by creating brand awareness and reinforcing the

Figure 9-1 *Advertising expenditures by industry.*

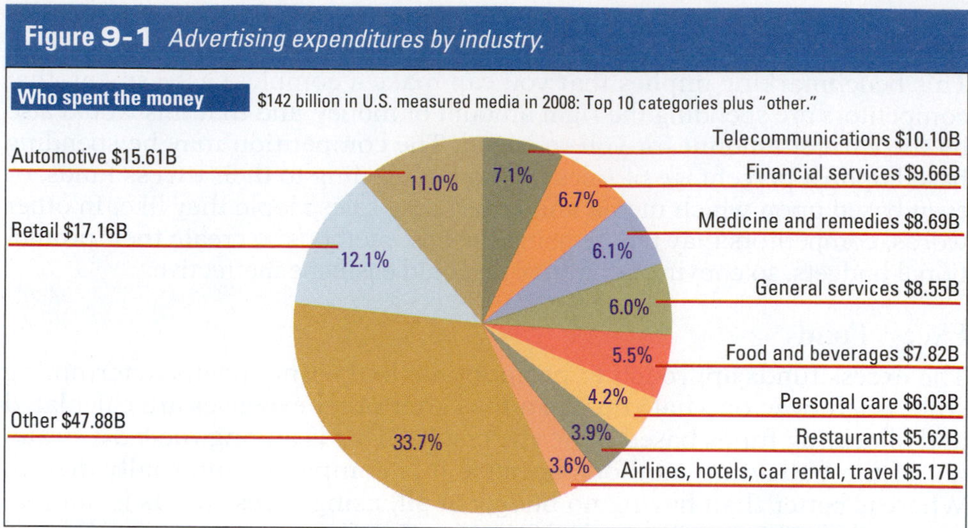

Source: WPP's TNS Media Intelligence (www.tns-mi.com). Spending based on TNS's IB measured media. Numbers rounded. Categories are aggregated from TNS classifications by Ad Age DataCenter. See "Total U.S. Advertising Spending by Category" in AdAge.com/June09 for deeper data.

purchasing decision. The objectives of advertising and its management reflect those of promotion, and successful advertising will achieve them all:

- build brand and image,
- provide information,
- persuade,
- stimulate action, and
- reinforce the purchasing decision.

Performance Objective 3

Understand advertising and advertising management.

Advertising builds brand recognition and creates a positive image. For example, General Mills's Lucky Charms brand cereal and Malt-O-Meal's Marshmallow Mateys are essentially the same products, with slightly better nutritional value in Marshmallow Mateys; but Lucky

Figure 9-2 *Advertising expenditures by media.*

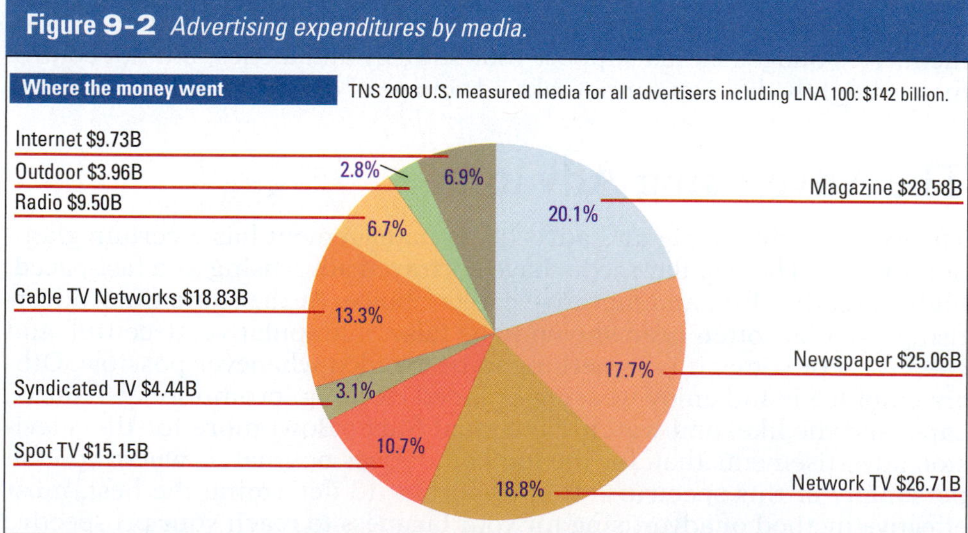

Source: WPP's TNS Media Intelligence (www.tns-mi.com). Spending based on TNS's IB measured media. Numbers rounded. Magazine includes consumer, Sunday, local, business-to-business and Spanish-language. Newspaper includes local, national and Spanish-language. Radio includes network, national spot and local. Internet is display advertising only (and so excludes paid search and broadband video). See "Total U.S. Advertising Spending by Medium" in AdAge.com/June09 for deeper data.

[5]Pricing and nutritional information from Malt-O-Meal Web site, http://www.malt-o-meal.com (accessed May 13, 2009).

Charms have significantly greater advertising and brand recognition and command a higher average price per pound ($3.17 versus $2.20).[5] Advertising can work for your company, too.

Advertising Agencies and Freelancers

Business owners have the option of creating their own advertising, and purchasing the media in which to advertise. They also can hire advertising agencies or freelance artists. Which option is best will depend upon a number of factors, including

- size of the company and its advertising budget;
- in-house capacity, including time and talent; and
- owner preferences.

It is important to remember that the advertising should be part of an integrated approach and is the paid component of that approach. As such, it must convey the desired message to the targeted customers to secure the desired outcomes. Once a management team has taken the time and effort to develop an integrated marketing strategy, measurable goals and objectives and a budget, following up with solid implementation will be essential. Regardless of how a company manages its advertising, this follow-through is vital.

For a company that does not have internal advertising expertise, selecting an advertising agency or a freelancer (or group of freelancers) can be a valuable investment, but the fees associated with an agency or freelancer must be weighed against the returns to be gained. A good agency will do much more than create concepts and purchase advertising space. It will partner with your company to ensure the integration of your strategy and the advertising, strengthening what you have created and increasing its effectiveness. A full-service agency will be able to provide creative thinking, advertising and packaging design, public relations, and media placement. Freelancers provide a range of services—with some supplying designs based upon your concepts, and others covering the range of services of an agency but through a single individual. Often, freelancers will specialize in a single aspect of integrated marketing, such as advertising design, packaging design, public relations, or event planning. The challenge for a business owner is determining how much advertising support to buy and whether the quality available is what is needed.

For franchisees, much of the advertising support is part of the package of services that are purchased as part of the franchise agreement, with the quantity and quality of materials and assistance dependent upon the terms of that agreement. The best franchisors purchase and manage the national and regional advertising, perhaps with the guidance of a franchisee committee, and let the individual franchisees decide on local options. Franchisors may provide the advertising designs and materials or the guidelines, reducing the need to engage a full-service agency at the local level.

Often, suppliers, trade associations, or the media themselves can provide free or reduced-cost services, as well. For many years, Leggett and Platt, a manufacturer supplying the mattress industry, had an in-house agency that provided design services, including logos, brochures, advertisements, and the like for its customers, saving literally thousands of dollars in costs. Trade associations, such as the milk industry, with its "Got Milk?" campaign, provide support to their members. In some cases, they offer logos and seals of approval, or membership marks, to include in advertisements, which lend credibility to the individual advertiser. For example, the Better Business Bureau logo is often used for this purpose. Media companies may provide design services as part of the cost of placing an advertisement. With all of these options, it is critical that you be certain the message conveyed by the media is consistent with your strategy and image.

Types of Advertising

institutional advertising provides information about an organization, rather than a specific product, and is intended to create awareness about the firm and enhance its image.

product advertising is designed to create awareness, interest, purchasing behavior, and post-purchase satisfaction for specific products and services.

Advertising is not a one-size-fits-all proposition; rather, it comes in so many forms and options that the types of advertising seem to be limitless. However, there continue to be two primary kinds: institutional advertising and product advertising. **Institutional advertising** provides information about an organization rather than a specific product, and is intended to create awareness about the firm and enhance its image. This advertising is exemplified by the Bank of America ads that focus on the company as the "bank of opportunity" rather than promoting particular financial products. Such advertising is designed to build general credibility and recognition for specific products or services. **Product advertising** is designed to create awareness, interest, purchasing behavior, and post-purchase satisfaction for specific products and services. Typically, small, entrepreneurial companies expend their advertising resources on product advertising. For example, they may want to promote the sale of a particular item, or a store-wide sale.

Institutional and product advertising are not mutually exclusive. For example, all advertisements placed by an organization might include a tag line or feature that extols a virtue of the firm such as local ownership, length of time in business, quality of workmanship—while at the same time promoting a particular product or service. Or, ads that are more "evergreen" (of longer duration), such as those in directories or on promotional items, may be more institutional, whereas those that are less durable (e.g., daily or weekly newspaper ads) can focus on products. How you decide to promote your organization and products should be defined by your strategy, your industry, available options, and your budget.

Media Planning and Buying: Focus on Your Customer

An effective advertisement for a business typically concentrates on the benefit the product or service provides the customer. This is why it is important that you carry through your consumer

analysis. You will need to know who your customers are and what their lifestyle is in order to know how to effectively reach them. It is valuable to know and understand the media habits of people in your target market. What are their media reading, viewing, and listening patterns? What appeals to them? What doesn't? If you are advertising a snowboarding trip, it would be a waste of money to take out an ad in a magazine featuring tropical vacations. By visualizing and knowing your customer, you will avoid wasting money in outlets in which the audience won't be interested in your product or service. Combine this common-sense approach with solid research to maximize advertising effectiveness.

The Media

There are many places to advertise and publicize your business. These are referred to collectively as *the media*, which includes broadcast and print categories as well as outdoor advertising and the Internet. The trick will be to choose the most effective outlets for your advertising dollars, which may be quite limited. Your **media strategy** is the identification of the media you will use and the creative decisions involved. It should be based upon the marketing analysis. Once a media strategy is developed, a **media schedule**—spelling out the particular media vehicles to be used, the volume of usage, and the timing—becomes important.

Critical factors to consider when purchasing media are reach and frequency, as well as cost per *impression*. **Reach** is defined as the number of components in your target audience (people, businesses, households) that will be exposed to the advertising during a given period. **Frequency** is how often they will be exposed to it during a particular time frame. For example, a daily newspaper may reach 500,000 people one time. A directory may reach two million people 12 times a year. In addition to reach and frequency, businesses can consider gross ratings points, based upon opportunities to see. **Opportunities to see (OTS)** is the cumulative number of exposures in a given time period, usually four weeks. For example, if you place four ads on a TV show that is televised twice a week, you will get 32 OTS in a four-week period (four ads per show × two shows per week × four weeks). **Gross ratings points (GRP)** are calculated by multiplying the media vehicle's rating (reach) by the OTS, or number of insertions, to measure the intensity or impact of a media plan.

An important consideration in advertising is the "waste." If you wanted to reach 25- to 35-year-old working women with children in San Francisco, you would consider advertising in the *San Francisco Chronicle*. There would be a lot of waste, but it might be the best choice available to you. When you calculate the cost per impression (cost of the advertising divided by the number of times people see it), you will see if it makes sense. Sometimes it might be more logical to purchase advertising in a smaller, more targeted publication. At other times, the opposite could be true. The process of purchasing media may include multiple parties. The **media planner** is the person that creates a media plan with a specific advertising schedule. A **media buyer** purchases time/space and negotiates pricing and scheduling details. This individual works with the media sales representatives. In a small advertising firm, the same individual may do planning and buying. Or, you may do this yourself. Remember, regardless of how it is done, advertising should not be random or infrequent. It needs to be regular and well planned.

- ***Broadcast Media.*** Communication outlets that use air space, including radio and television, make up the broadcast media. Advertising often can be purchased, or publicity garnered, for your business from local as well as national media outlets.

Performance Objective 4

Identify and evaluate media options.

media strategy the identification of the media a business will use and the creative decisions involved.

media schedule spells out the particular media vehicles to be used, the volume of usage, and the timing.

reach the number of components in a target audience (people, businesses, households) that will be exposed to the advertising during a given period.

frequency how often individuals will be exposed to an advertisement during a particular time frame.

opportunities to see (OTS) the cumulative number of exposures in a given time period—usually four weeks.

gross ratings points (GRP) are calculated by multiplying the media vehicle's rating (reach) by the OTS, or number of insertions, to measure the intensity or impact of a media plan.

media planner the person that creates a media plan with a specific advertising schedule.

media buyer the person who purchases time/space and negotiates pricing and scheduling details.

- ***Television.*** Even though TV advertising rates are comparatively high, television can be an effective media option. An entrepreneur with a new business can sometimes negotiate discounted rates, or get free mention (publicity), if he/she has a good story. If you have a product or service that would benefit from TV or radio advertising, consider going with a media-buying service instead of purchasing it yourself, to avoid paperwork and confusion. Media-buying services are granted the same 15 percent discount as advertising agencies, but they often return 10 percent of the savings to you, the advertiser, keeping 5 percent as their fee. You can find media buyers in the Yellow Pages.

  The nature of TV advertising has changed significantly from the medium's early days, when there were only three channels and limited programming. The number of channels has grown tremendously and the availability of TiVo, DirecTV, videos, and other options has changed the impact of television advertising. With the targeted audiences for cable channels, advertising can be more focused. At the same time, the sheer number of viewing options, and the capability of the viewer to skip over the advertisements completely means that effectiveness can be hard to measure.
- ***Radio.*** Radio advertising is sold in a variety of ways, with prices based upon the length of your ad, the time of day it will run, and its duration and frequency. Radio stations can provide you with sophisticated data regarding their listeners, so that you can more readily determine whether there is a good fit with your target market. University and local community radio stations often do not carry advertising but may be willing to mention a new business venture that has an interesting or unusual angle. As with TV, radio advertising has changed over the years. The recent advent of satellite radio, and the ability to play music without ads, has had an impact as well but, according to the annual RADAR report from the Radio Advertising Bureau (RAB), the weekly audience for radio was over 235 million in 2008, totaling 92% of all U.S. consumers.[6] The RAB Web site (http://www.RAB.com) includes a business survey derived from the U.S. Department of Commerce, and other data that indicates when it is most important to advertise (by months) for 40 categories of businesses.
- ***Print Media.*** Newspapers, magazines, and directories are examples of print media. It is not always the largest, most well-recognized newspaper or magazine that would be best for your business. In fact, you may find that community newspapers or lifestyle publications are better targeted, more economical, and more effective. A year-long study of newspaper advertising determined that a potential customer needs to see an ad at least nine times before the marketing message penetrates.[7] In addition, the study found that, for every three times a consumer sees an advertisement, he or she ignores it twice. This indicates that a consumer will have to see your ad 27 times before actually buying something.

  If you take out a newspaper ad that will appear three times a week, therefore, commit to running it for nine weeks at the very least. The most common advertising mistake entrepreneurs make is to give up too soon. One gauge of how effective a particular advertising medium will be for your business is to observe it for a while and see whether your competitors use it regularly. If they do, they are probably seeing a good return on their investment, so you

[6]Arbitron, RADAR 100, March 2009, http://www.rab.com/public/marketingGuide/rabRmg.html (accessed May 23, 2009).
[7]Conrad Levinson, *Guerrilla Advertising* (Boston: Houghton Mifflin, 1994).

Figure 9-3 A print ad has five parts.

may, too. Remember, print media has suffered as electronic media has grown exponentially. Be certain to request independent confirmation of subscriber and readership data provided by media representatives, to confirm the accuracy of their claims.

It is important to use effective design for all of your print advertising and to reinforce your brand each and every time. **Figure 9-3** is an example of a print advertisement that incorporated the five main parts of a print ad: a headline, the deck (subhead), copy (text), graphics (photos or drawings), and your company logo with any tagline.

- ***Newspapers.*** Newspapers may be published daily, weekly, or at less frequent intervals. They can be community-based, local, regional, national, or international, and with a focus on news, finance, or any other topic. For a retail store serving a radius of five miles or fewer, a weekly community newspaper could be ideal. For a major investment bank, *The Wall Street Journal* would possibly be the best choice. A religious bookstore may find the best fit in the local diocesan weekly. In addition to geographic scope, and related to it, circulation can range from several hundred to millions. With the widespread use of the Internet, many newspapers also have online editions.

  The number of advertising options in newspapers is large and changes frequently. Classified advertising and display advertising are common features of newspapers. However, what varies is how they can be placed. Many newspapers now create special editions or special-interest advertising sections, to be inserted in the newspaper or distributed separately. For example, a local Gannett publication has periodic inserts such as "Prime Life," "Celebrations," parenting, camp programs, home sections, and the like. Each of these is directly targeted to a particular demographic, lifestyle, or other segment, and includes pertinent advertising and editorial content.

  There is an entire category of nonsubscription publications made available at targeted distribution points. These publications, often in newspaper format, include parenting publications, entertainment guides, home and real estate advertising, ethnic publications, natural foods and nutrition publications, and so forth. Some of them include stories about their advertisers, or invite advertisers to submit stories.

Newspapers have the advantages of being highly flexible with significant credibility. You can place ads such that they change frequently. Readers pay attention to the articles that they read and have sufficient interest in the ads that advertisers can put more information in them. The disadvantages of newspapers include difficulties in targeting, as well as a short shelf life. Also, if you want to run a national campaign, the buying process is cumbersome.

- ***Magazines.*** Publications classified as magazines offer highly segmented markets and are targeted by those interests. Because readers are often subscribers, there is high audience interest and this increases attention to advertising. If your business has a precisely defined target, there may be magazines that are ideally suited for inclusion in your marketing mix. This is particularly true for business-to-business marketing because business and trade journals can reach target customers very effectively.

  Magazines differ from newspapers as advertising media primarily because of their longer shelf life. Subscribers may read through the magazine several times, yielding multiple exposures. Moreover, magazines may be passed along to others, such as with trade journals, or be left in a common area where people may read them, such as a doctor's waiting room. In addition, magazines have higher-quality printing and more options. Scratch-and-sniff ads, fold-outs, cut-outs, and other unusual presentations offer enhanced marketing advantages.

  There are several drawbacks associated with magazines. Clutter can be problematic, particularly with magazines that have more pages of advertising than editorial content. Lead times of up to six months can make it difficult to make changes, and the long shelf life can mean that messages may survive beyond the advertisers' intentions, in the case of volatile or highly competitive industries.
- ***Directories.*** Telephone books, and directories with membership lists from professional associations or chambers of commerce, are examples of directories. They can be an excellent source of customer leads and good advertising venues. They tend to have a long shelf life and may be referred to repeatedly. You may use professional directories, in particular, if you can clearly identify professional associations or organizations that have members in your target audience. Advertisements and listings in directories should focus more on institutional advertising, due to the longer-term nature of the medium.
- ***Outdoor Advertising (Out-of-Home Advertising).*** Billboards are the most commonly recognized type of outdoor advertising. They are almost always in highly visible locations and use short, punchy copy that motorists can grasp at a glance. There are other forms of outdoor advertising, such as signs on park benches, stadium-fence ads, and the like. The nature of outdoor advertising has changed with the advent of technological innovations. For example, animated videos are projected in Times Square in New York through the use of LED technology. The pie chart in **Figure 9-4** shows the distribution of outdoor advertising revenue for its providers, according to the major product categories of billboards, transit, and street furniture.

Billboard advertisements have the advantage of long life (contracts are generally one month or more), and the ads can be quite spectacular because of their scale. Commuters are exposed to the ad multiple times as they travel past it, twice a day. However, billboards have short exposure time unless traffic is particularly heavy and slow, or there is a traffic signal or stop sign that causes motorists to pause.

Figure 9-4 *2009 outdoor advertising revenue by major product category.*

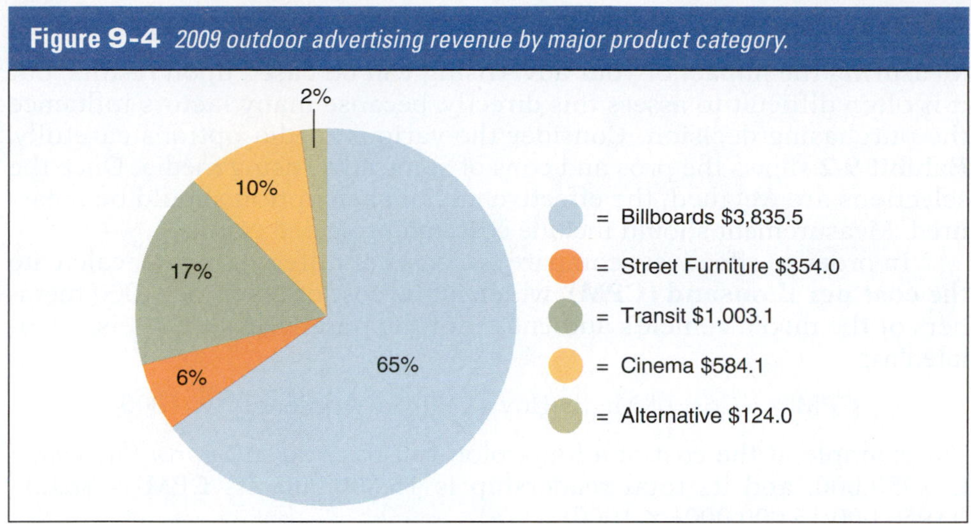

Source: Courtesy of Outdoor Advertising Association of America.

Mobile billboards (a truck covered with advertising) will travel specified routes or park in desired locations to provide highly targeted advertising on a relatively grand scale. These are being banned in some cities, and challenged on the basis of environmental impact and risk of distracting drivers.

Billboards are most commonly used to advertise for local services and amusements (e.g., eating places, insurance agencies, banks, hotels, motels, resorts, and grocery stores); real estate; communications; public transportation, and for media advertising. According to the Outdoor Advertising Association of America Web site (http://www.oaaaa.org), outdoor advertising expenditure is four percent of the total U.S. media expenditures. So, depending upon your business type, marketing objectives, and budget, outdoor advertising could be a viable option.

Billboard advertisement.

Advertising Measurement: Beyond Reach and Frequency

Measuring the impact of your advertising will be based upon results, but it is often difficult to assess this directly, because many factors influence the purchasing decision. Consider the various media options carefully. **Exhibit 9-2** shows the pros and cons of some advertising media. Once the selections are weighed, the effectiveness of each option should be measured. Measurement should include cost and projected results.

cost per thousand (CPM) the cost of reaching 1000 members of the media vehicle's audience.

cost per rating point (CPRP) a measure of the efficiency of a media vehicle to a company's target market, calculated by dividing the cost of the media buy by the vehicle's rating.

In order to effectively compare the costs of different media, calculate the **cost per thousand (CPM)**, which is the cost of reaching 1,000 members of the media vehicle's audience (not the purchaser's). CPM is calculated as:

$$\text{CPM} = (\text{Cost of Media Buy (\$)/Total Audience}) \times 1000$$

For example, if the cost of a four-color, full-page ad in *Sports Illustrated* is $950,000, and its total readership is 15,000,000, its CPM is $63.33 ([$950,000/15,000,000] × 1000).

The CPM calculation makes it possible to compare media, but it does not consider the advertiser's target market explicitly, and that target market might be significantly smaller than the total readership. The **cost per rating point (CPRP)** is an additional measure of the efficiency of a media vehicle to a company's target market. It is calculated by dividing the cost

Exhibit 9-2 *Pros and cons of selected advertising media.*

	Pros (Advantages)	Cons (Disadvantages)
Television	Low CPM Highly targeted with cable High intrusion value High reach and frequency potential Message is immediate	High cost for ad campaign Clutter Short life of advertising message High production costs Long lead time
Radio	Relatively low cost Short-term commitment Short lead time Message is immediate Promotes recall Mobility (radios travel with people)	Auditory only Clutter—information overload Short life of advertising message Low attention Local nature
Newspapers	Geographic targeting Short lead time Flexibility and credibility More copy potential Direct response possible	Expense may be high Demographic targeting is limited Short shelf life Declining readership Waste Poor-quality production
Magazines	Targeted reader interest High color/production quality Direct response possible Long shelf life	Lack of immediacy Exposure dispersed over time Longer lead times High cost
Internet	Targeting potential Moderate cost Global reach Relatively short lead time	Not ubiquitous Banner ads feed-click through to full ads
Outdoor Media	Repeat exposures Geographic selectivity Moderate CPM High-impact, dramatic ads possible	Limited message size Limited demographic selectivity Initial design and production costs Short exposure time

of the media buy by the vehicle's **rating** (the percentage of the company's target market exposed to a TV show or print ad):

rating the percentage of the company's target market exposed to a TV show or print ad.

CPRP = Cost of Media Buy ($)/Vehicle's Rating

It is important to recognize that a media vehicle may have a low CPRP but also only reach a small part of the company's target market. In order to address whether an ad in a specific media vehicle will effectively reach a company's target market, the "weighted"(or demographic) CPM can be calculated as

Weighted CPM = (Ad Cost ($) × 1000)/Actual Audience Reached

For example, *Sports Illustrated* has a standard CPM of $63.33, and you want to reach the professional athletes who read it, so you use research that shows 10,000 of *Sports Illustrated*'s readers are in this category. The weighted CPM would be ($950,000 × 1000) / 10,000, or $95,000, which would not seem to be the most efficient expenditure of funds to reach professional athletes. Once the weighted CPM is calculated, you can compare it to other potential media choices to make a buying decision.

All of this information can be valuable in deciding which media to select. When combined with your advertising message and design, you can create a complete program. The key is to spend just sufficient funds to reach the target audience as frequently as needed to achieve your advertising objectives.

Marketing Materials Should Reinforce Your Competitive Advantage

All promotional items for your business should reflect and reinforce your marketing vision, which in turn will reinforce your competitive advantage. They should include the name of your business, your logo, and a slogan, if you have one. All your business materials, in fact—such as order forms, invoices, and receipts—should also reflect and reinforce your business's competitive advantage.

You will have a much stronger impact if all your business materials are tied together with a strong, coordinated image. This should extend beyond your logo into the format, font style, colors, and look of your materials. As you create your stationery and business cards (identity set),

Global Impact . . .

Naked Communications

The first British Invasion may have been the arrival of the Beatles in 1964, but the second seems to have come in the form of a global communications firm, Naked Communications, which arrived in the United States with considerable attention and interest. Naked Communications is a global organization with offices in London and New York. Clients include Honda, Minute Maid, Nokia, Boots (the U.K.'s largest pharmacy chain), and ad agencies such as BBDO, Lowe, and Leo Burnett. Naked Communications is neither an advertising agency nor a traditional media planning firm, and it chose a name that conveyed the company's approach to integrated marketing, stripping the concept bare and then working to find the best promotional path.

The team at Naked believes that the right approach to advertising is to gather all the people who have brand responsibility together and work toward an answer to the question, "What's the right message communicated in the right way through the right channel in order to effectively reach the right consumer?"[8] Global business requires global communications and organizations to support them. Naked Communications does just that.[9]

[8]Danielle Sacks, "Is Mad. Ave. Ready to Go Naked," *Fast Company*, http://www.fastcompany.com/magazine/99/naked.html (accessed December 19, 2007).
[9]www.nakedcomms.com (accessed July 2009).

advertisements, publicity pieces, and brochures, the consistency of your image will help to convey your competitive advantage. If it is done well, your image will be in alignment with your strengths, and you will be positioned for success. If this is done poorly, you will lack credibility, which can then harm, if not destroy, your chances of success.

Good marketing materials serve three functions:

1. Creating them will organize your business thinking.
2. They will enable you to teach others in your company about the business.
3. They will enable you to go into the marketplace and sell your product or service with confidence.

Collateral Materials: Print and Multimedia

Advertising can get people interested in your business but, before they buy, prospects will often want more information. Depending upon your business, brochures will enable you to provide that information and turn interest into a sale.

At the bottom of every print ad you run, offer to send a brochure. When you mail the brochure, include a personal letter thanking the prospective customer for requesting it. If you do not hear back in a few weeks, send a follow-up note. You are establishing one-on-one contact with someone you did not know before, the kind of personal connection that can lead to a sale. The brochure could actually close the sale itself, by providing a toll-free number to call.

Whether you use print, audio, or video brochures will depend on your budget and your business. Here are some suggestions from Jay Levinson's *Guerrilla Advertising*:[10]

- ***Print brochures*** should fit into a standard envelope, make ordering simple, and connect the contents closely with your advertising.
- ***Audio brochures*** can work when visuals aren't necessary to sell your product or service, and should run between 10 and 20 minutes. Many motorists have CD players in their cars and are good candidates for audio brochures.
- ***Video brochures*** should run between 5 and 10 minutes and describe your business both verbally and visually. If your business has ever been profiled on a television show, you've already got the centerpiece of your video brochure!
- ***Flyers*** are one-page ads you can create on a computer, or even by hand (if you have artistic talent). Fax your flyer to the customers on your mailing list; photocopy and distribute it at church functions, sporting events, under windshield wipers, or hand them out on the street. Flyers can also include discount coupons.
- ***Newsletters*** have become easy to produce for distribution by e-mail and in hard copy. Be certain to include interesting and useful information in an attractive, well-designed format. Remember, it will need to interest your target market in terms they understand.
- ***Business cards*** should include the name, street address, and other contact information (phone and fax numbers, e-mail address, and Web site) of your business, as well as your own name and title.

[10] Levinson, *Guerrilla Advertising*, 1994.

A card can also include a short catchy phrase or motto, such as *For Sound Advice* if you are operating a stereo-repair business. Always carry some cards with you to hand out to potential clients and contacts.

- ***Signs.*** One of the simplest ways to gain recognition is to use effective signage. Take advantage of opportunities to post visible signs. Signs should be clearly written, grammatically correct, and visually appealing. Also, be certain that your sign placement is legal, so that you are not forced to remove signs and/or pay fines. Your signs can be temporary or permanent and can be stationary or mobile. Consider all your options in light of your marketing strategy. Keep it simple and show your brand!

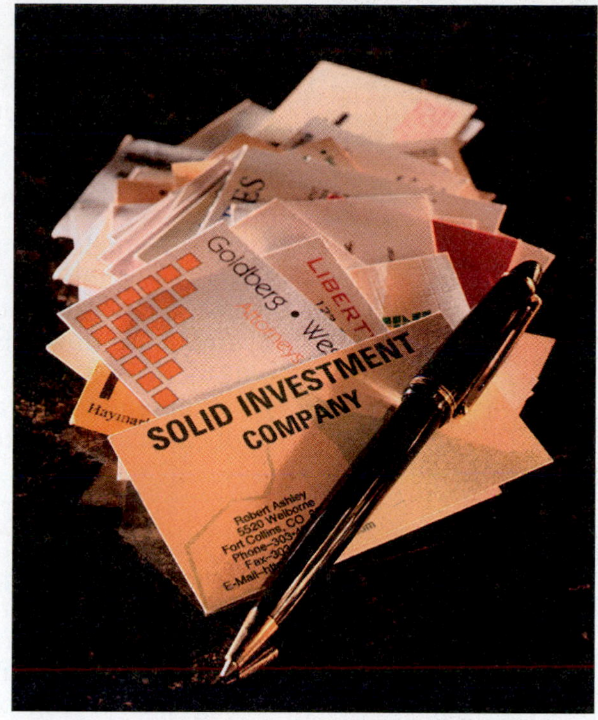

Business cards carry your message and image. (© Don Farrall/Getty Images)

Sales-Promotion Solutions

Sales promotions provide another set of tools to add to the mix. Various efforts to increase sales volume by specified levels, which either reward purchases or provide discounts, can be effective for both consumer and business-to-business marketing. Sales-promotion solutions do not have to be complex or sophisticated in order to work. In fact, it is best if they are simple and easily understood. If an incentive program is difficult to figure out, customers may simply not bother to participate, because it isn't worth the trouble. **Exhibit 9-3** identifies some common types of sales-promotion methods.

Performance Objective 5

Discuss sales promotion.

When to Use Promotional Tools

Promotional tools are best used when the strategy calls for a highly targeted, time-limited boost in response. They can be excellent tools for encouraging new product trials and for raising seasonal performance. They should always be part of the overall marketing strategy and budget. Contests and sweepstakes are a way of securing product engagement and, potentially, repeat sales (e.g., for a game that requires collecting game pieces). Coupons require the customer to actively seek

Exhibit 9-3 *Sales-promotional tools.*

Consumer	Business-to-Business
Coupons	Incentives
Contests and Sweepstakes	Contests
Refunds and Rebates	Refunds and Rebates
Sampling	Sampling
Premiums	Allowances
Tie-ins	Trade Shows
Bonus Packs	

out your product on the shelves or to contact you for the product or service. *Sampling* brings the product or service message to life for the customer through experience. Bonus packs and tie-ins lead to a trial of additional products.

Advertising Specialties

The strategic inclusion of advertising specialty items can be an effective sales-promotion tool. Freebies are always a draw with customers, but do not disappoint them with gifts that look and feel cheap. The best give-aways are those that are useful, such as pens, on which prospective customers will see your business name and contact information. Visit wholesalers, or search online to investigate discount prices on quantities of calculators, watches, pens, or other appropriate items.

Trade Show Exhibits

The use of trade show exhibits is a proven promotional strategy for business-to-business companies and can also succeed for certain types of consumer marketing. This is one of the best forms of experiential marketing, because it lends itself to having prospective customers engaged in trying out your products, or having services demonstrated. Whereas the cost of trade-show space, a professionally designed booth, transportation, and other related expenses can be relatively high, the opportunity to have impact can make it worthwhile. This is particularly true for business-to-business marketing that can be achieved at targeted professional conferences. There is often no more efficient way to reach so many potential customers so efficiently with a consistent message. Tsnn.com reports that there are 15,000 trade shows, exhibitions, public events, and conferences each year. The keys to successful trade show promotion include preparation, booth training for all staff, quality exhibits, careful goal setting, and consistent efforts to reap the benefits of the investment.

Mall Carts or Kiosks

For many seasonal businesses, or businesses that are working to create full-scale retail operations, mall carts or kiosks may prove effective. Signing a multiyear lease for a retail store is not likely to make sense for a seasonal business such as a Christmas or Halloween operation. Sometimes such businesses can find vacant retail spaces to rent for just a season, or they can partner with others to rotate in and out of a store. In other situations, they can create a business model of changing seasonal inventory and focus. However, for many business owners, these options are not practical or desirable and having a temporary retail location is preferable. Also, if you are working on a retail concept and want to try out the idea, products, prices, and so forth, a temporary location is a good opportunity to test-drive your business before investing in longer-term, more costly retail space. Such a trial run may also provide you with sales and marketing data that will assist you in attracting financing. For an investment of $1500 to $10,000 plus inventory and rental fees, you could be up and running.

Alternative Marketing

Performance Objective 6

Explore alternative marketing options.

The marketing approaches described above have been practiced for many, many years and are considered to be tried-and-true methods to promotion. However, marketing has evolved with changing times and technology to include more recent forms. The following is a discussion of some of the alternative forms of marketing in use today.

Guerilla Marketing

J. Conrad Levinson coined this term in 1984 with his book of the same title, meaning original, unconventional, and inexpensive small-business strategies. Since then, **guerilla marketing** has expanded to encompass other kinds of unconventional strategies—such as viral marketing, buzz marketing, word-of-mouth advertising, and grassroots marketing. The notion is to find creative, surprising ways to get your message to your target market without spending a fortune.

guerilla marketing original, unconventional, and inexpensive small-business strategies.

Buzz Marketing

Buzz marketing is another name for word-of-mouth marketing. It can occur naturally (*organic buzz marketing*) or can be jump-started by the organization (*amplified buzz marketing*). It is one of the most effective forms of promotion available, because people are sharing their excitement and enthusiasm about a product or service with others who trust and value the advice. By giving your customers an outstanding experience, you are encouraging organic buzz marketing. If you can created *amplified* buzz marketing, it will boost recognition and marketing still further.

buzz marketing another name for word-of-mouth marketing.

Product Placement/Branded Entertainment

The use of product placement in television, movies, and other scenarios is another good promotional tool. Such placements reach consumers on a more subconscious level and do not contain an overt sales pitch. When the movie *E.T.* hit the theaters, Reese's Pieces were included as a product placement, and they continue to be associated with the movie decades later. The quantity of in-show brand appearances during an average hour of prime-time network television programming was just short of eight minutes during the fourth quarter of 2008, with an average of almost fourteen minutes during unscripted reality programming and just about six minutes per hour during scripted programs.[11] Today, there are firms that focus on locating

[11]TNS Media Intelligence press release, May 4, 2009.

and negotiating product placements. Two such companies are Creative Entertainment Services (acreativegroup.com) and GameShowPlacements.com (for game and cable shows). Depending upon your product, it may be worthwhile to pursue placement possibilities.

Lifestyle Marketing

In order to successfully market their brands, companies are striving to align them with consumer needs, interests, desires, and values, and to apply lifestyle marketing with knowledge of consumer behavior. This form of marketing reaches beyond the traditional demographic approaches to engage customers based upon how they live.

In-Store Marketing

There are numerous options for carrying out in-store marketing, whether in your own space or in stores where your product is sold. For example, signage, shelf placement, sampling, and "edutainment" can all play roles. Which ones are best will depend upon your marketing strategy.

edutainment combining education and entertainment to make a more lasting impression upon the audience.

- ***Samples or Demonstrations.*** Offer samples of your product to potential customers who pass by your business. Or take samples to a high-density location, such as a park or town square. If you are selling a service, consider demonstrating it outdoors or in a mall (get permission first). When you open your business, you can give away samples of your product to encourage customers to tell their friends about it. Many large businesses, such as BJ's Wholesale Club and Sam's Club, make extensive use of sampling and edutainment to encourage purchases. **Edutainment** is combining education and entertainment to make a more lasting impression upon an audience. You might use this method to show the originality of your product and engage prospective customers to learn about it.
- ***Point-of-Purchase and Shelf Placement.*** These opportunities include the complete visual component of your in-store placement, such as packaging, any couponing with shelf placement, and special display units. By putting products where prospective customers will be drawn to them visually, you are increasing the chances of purchase. Well-designed point-of-purchase materials can make a huge difference in sales.

Other Media Venues

In addition to the methods and media described above, there are a number of other media venues worth noting. These options should also be considered in your media planning. See **Exhibit 9-4** for examples of other media venues.

Exhibit 9-4 *Other media venues.*

Ambient Advertising	In-Door Advertising	Other Advertising
Parking Lots	Movie Theaters	Carry-Out Menus
Tunnels	Video Games	Shopping Bags
Escalators	Bathroom Stalls	Advertising on Clothing
Benches (Bus Stops)	Commercial Trucks	Brochure Racks
	Airline In-Flight	

Database and Direct-Response Marketing

Performance Objective 7
Analyze database and direct-response marketing opportunities.

The use of databases has been integral to the advertising and promotion discussion above with respect to data research and analysis, but its value can far exceed that. Through the use of selected databases, you can create communications that are highly targeted and customized, thereby increasing your impact and effectiveness. At the same time, marketing efforts that engage your customers and have direct-response mechanisms can build your customer base and foster customer loyalty. It is less costly to maintain repeat customers than to generate new ones. Thus, the emphasis of database marketing is to identify customers and build loyalty. The primary focus is on relationship-building rather than sales.

Data Collection, Coding, and Mining

In order to be successful in data marketing, you must have quality data. The data that you need consists of information, such as

- Customer names and mailing addresses
- E-mail addresses
- Any customer profile or preference data
- Purchasing and returns history
- Web-site visiting information (from cookies on company site)
- Customer survey results
- History of contacts, including calls and correspondence
- History of promotional contacts and responses
- Additional data and data analysis from external sources

Data should be collected at each point of interaction, without being intrusive or annoying to the customer. Remember to update addresses through the U.S. Postal Service or another service provider at least once annually, because 20 percent of the U.S. population moves each year. Updating e-mail addresses is important for the same reason.

lifetime value the profit earned from a particular customer or customer segment.

RFM analysis the creation of a three-digit score for each customer based upon recency, frequency, and monetary values.

data mining a computer program to analyze and sort the data, to identify your best existing customers and model those who might become excellent customers.

Coding the data that you have collected is an essential step toward analyzing and using it to its maximum effectiveness. With proper coding, you can create marketing campaigns and personalize communications programs. You can calculate the profit earned from a particular customer or customer segment, which is known as **lifetime value**. The calculation of lifetime value is generally figured in one-year increments over, say, three or five years. Another measure is **RFM analysis**, which is the creation of a three-digit score for each customer based upon *recency* (date of most recent purchase), *frequency* (number of purchases over a specific time period), and *monetary value* (dollars spent on company products within a period). The method you use can be one of these, or a different coding method that you design and find meaningful.

Once data is collected and coded, you can use **data mining**, a computer program to analyze and sort the data, to identify your existing customers, and model those who might become excellent customers.

Marketing Communications Driven by Databases

Database information and analysis can fuel your market-driven communications to cross-sell customers, tailor promotions, and to project future purchases. By making effective use of these database options, you can personalize your approach to customers, create greater engagement and loyalty, and build sales and repeat purchases. Typically, such programs take the form of e-mail, telemarketing, or direct mail, more often with customer permission, rather than unsolicited or through loyalty/frequency programs. Related to your database marketing will be direct-response marketing, which markets products directly to customers and prospects through direct mail, catalogs, the Internet, and other media.

E-mail Marketing

Targeted customers may opt in to e-mail marketing programs for reasons such as a chance to win a sweepstakes, access specific content, or because they are existing customers and want e-mail offers and updates. Kohl's department stores solicit customer e-mail addresses with the promise of advance notice of sales and a $5 coupon. Once you secure the permission to e-mail, ensure that the program is successful both for you and your customers by having a plan that reinforces the incentive to participate. Also, remember to provide your customers with opt-out choice and keep track of what does and does not work.

Direct Mail

Consumers and business-to-business customers can be targeted with direct mail, and you can use this method with internally generated or purchased lists. It is vital to target the mailing according to the customers on the list—understanding whether list members have a previous purchase history or not and what is of interest to them can make a world of difference. Direct mail can be targeted and results can be measured through response rates. Direct mail is an excellent method of getting customers to your Web site. However, direct mail suffers from the clutter created by the volume of direct-mail offers received by consumers, and by the potentially high cost of producing and mailing materials. **Exhibit 9-5** lists reasons for the use of direct mail.

Catalogs

Even with the growth of online shopping, catalogs represent a viable direct-response marketing option. They are low pressure and can direct

Exhibit 9-5 *Direct mail opportunities: When you think of your use of mail advertising, what applications come to mind?*

New customer acquisition	53.8%
Customer communication	53.2%
Building brand awareness	51.2%
Generating sales	50.7%
Generating leads	43.2%
Building customer loyalty	40.1%
Driving store traffic	31.1%
Building customer confidence	26.6%
Other	6.7%

Source: "Recent Research—2009 Marketing in a Down Economy," from Advertising Age Custom Publishing, March 30, 2009. Copyright 2009 *Advertising Age.* Used by permission.

readers to Web sites for purchases. When you have built a list of 10,000 names, it might be time to pay for a color catalog, because then the price of printing per catalog will be sufficiently low. You can produce a two-color catalog economically with even fewer names.

Coupons

Another form of direct mail that you might want to consider is coupons. You can send out discount (price break) coupons as an incentive to first-time customers, or offer discounts for a limited time. This will encourage people to try your product or service. There are businesses that package coupons (card packs) from multiple companies into a mailer and send it to a targeted audience. You can save money by piggy-backing on their targeting.

Infomercials and Direct-Response Commercials

Both of these methods use paid television advertising to prompt direct purchases. Infomercials are typically one-half hour in length and play on cable television late at night. Direct-response commercials may be found on any channel. They are often 60-second spots that encourage viewers to "call now," with prompts of a toll-free number or Web site, or both.

Telemarketing

Companies use in-bound and out-bound telemarketing to support their sales and marketing efforts. Once you have compiled an extensive database of customers, you can use it to invite them to events or sales. You can also purchase lists. Be careful that you adhere to rules and guidelines with regard to telemarketing, and that you respect "Do not call" requests. Sometimes it is worthwhile to hire professional telemarketers. In-bound telemarketing can be highly effective. You can cross-sell or up-sell customers that have called you for a variety of reasons.

E-Active Marketing

Performance Objective 8
Incorporate e-active marketing.

Internet advertising has grown with the expansion and adoption of Internet technology. Not only have entrepreneurs and major corporations come to include online advertising and promotion as a regular part of the media mix, entire industry segments have evolved to serve the interactive

Figure 9-5 *Desired online social tools: "How interested are you in each of the following from your favorite brand, store, or service provider?"*

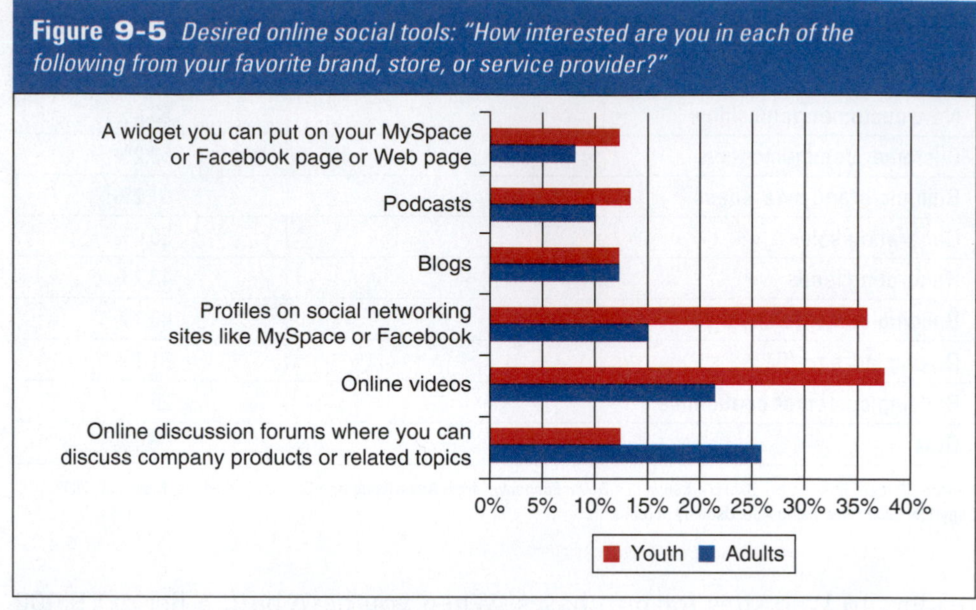

Base: U.S. online adults, age 18 and older, and U.S. online youth, ages 12 to 17.
Sources: North American Technographics Media and Marketing Online Survey, Q2 2008; North American Technographics Youth Online Survey, Q2 2008; Forrester Research, Inc., The Social Tools Consumers Want from Their Favorite Brands, report prepared by Josh Bernoff, April 16, 2009, http://blogs.forrester.com/a/6a00d8341c50bf53ef01156f827e11970c-pi (accessed May 21, 2009).

media field. The number of advertising opportunities is seemingly infinite, ranging from Google to little-known sites. Businesses can elect to use display advertising in the form of banner ads, pay to raise their visibility within search engines, or partner with other online companies to obtain mention and have customers directed to them. They can use social media, blogs, and e-mail. These options continue to expand and evolve at a rapid pace. When the two major components of Internet marketing, e-commerce and interactive marketing, combine, **e-active marketing** results. You can make the best use of e-active marketing approaches by marrying them with your offline efforts to create a unified approach to marketing. **Figure 9-5** shows the level of interest in various types of information from businesses.

e-active marketing when the two major components of Internet marketing—e-commerce and interactive marketing—combine.

E-Commerce

The provision of an electronic storefront and/or other forms of electronic commerce is one way of implementing your marketing strategy, as discussed in Chapter 6.

Interactive Marketing

According to John Deighton of Harvard University, interactive marketing is the ability to address the customer, remember what he/she says, and address that same customer again in a way that illustrates that his/her information has been remembered.[12] Whereas interactive marketing is not necessarily online marketing, the collection of customer information and communicating with them is facilitated by the Internet. An excellent example of the use of interactive marketing is Amazon.com, which collects user information to make purchase recommendations.

[12]John A. Deighton, "The Future of Interactive Marketing," *Harvard Business Review* 7, no. 6 (November–December 1996, 151–160).

Online Advertising

This typically takes the form of banner advertisements on Web sites. These can be highly targeted, based upon the online habits and interests of consumers. Such ads can be purchased directly from the owners of the Web sites on which you wish to advertise, or through brokers who purchase online advertising for specific target markets. For small, local businesses with a Web site, it may be possible to work in partnership with other companies that sell complementary products to create click-through opportunities for their customers to visit your site, and vice versa. This type of advertising includes pay-per-click (PPC), wherein firms bid on keywords that they would expect their potential customers to use to search for their goods and services, so that they can appear in the search return results as "sponsored ads" and thus become considerably more visible. With this type of advertising, you only pay when someone clicks on your ad.

Brand Spiraling

Integrating a company's conventional offline branding strategy with its Internet strategy can be accomplished through **brand spiraling**, which is companies using conventional approaches through print and broadcast media to drive traffic to their online sites. Once customers are guided to their online sites, the companies take advantage of Internet interactivity and learn more about them. The companies then use this knowledge to further refine their products and sales and marketing tactics. They also can use e-mail addresses and other information to reach customers in additional ways. The brand spiral is a continuous learning and changing process for a company—it assists in reaching and influencing customers through online and offline tactics.

brand spiraling integrating a company's conventional offline branding strategy with its Internet strategy by using conventional approaches to drive traffic to its online sites.

Blogs

A **blog** (short for Web log) is a journal that appears on the Internet periodically (perhaps daily) and is intended for the public. **Blogosphere** is the term used for all the blogs on the Internet. Businesses provide blogs, often written by their owners, to create a personal connection with the customers. These are only effective if the information is kept interesting and timely and customers are led to the sites by other promotions. Some blog-hosting services include:

blog (short for Web log) a journal that appears on the Internet periodically (perhaps daily) and is intended for the public.

blogosphere the term used for all the blogs on the Internet.

Blogger	www.blogger.com
LiveJournal	www.livejournal.com
Twitter	www.twitter.com (microblogging)
TypePad	www.typepad.com
Vox	www.vox.com
WordPress	www.wordpress.com
Xanga	www.xanga.com

Online Social Networks

The number and variety of online social networks has grown phenomenally in recent years, and is expected to continue to do so in the near future. Social networks such as Facebook, MySpace, and LinkedIn, as well as those for interest-specific niches (e.g., Flickr, imeem, BlackPlanet, Classmates.com, Goodreads, and MyHeritage), continue to evolve, as new and different uses emerge. Advertising opportunities on these networks are more complex than those on Web sites with banner ads. For many social networks, advertising and promotion are either banned or taboo. Some users create subtle promotion through what are essentially scripted conversations on these sites. These "undercover" or deceptive marketing efforts are intended to appear as if they happened naturally, and are referred to as **stealth marketing**.

stealth marketing undercover, or deceptive, marketing efforts that are intended to appear as if they happened naturally.

Recent research by the Internet Advertising Bureau in the United Kingdom addressed the methods for maximizing results from social networking: "The IAB research found that exclusive content, which appeals to 28% of social networkers, and genuine interest in the message, which attracts 37%, are the keys to a positive response from consumers on social networks. And because only 5% say they actively dislike messages from brands, there are big opportunities for marketers who can hit the right notes."[13] In addition to online social networking, the option of **mobile social networking**, the updating of social-network sites via mobile handsets, is increasing. This means that users are accessing the information at all times and at any location.

mobile social networking the updating of social-network sites via mobile handsets.

Consumer-Generated Advertising

This can include campaigns in which the company solicits advertisements from customers. You can ask your customers to create videos, stories, print advertisements, and the like, generally through a contest or promotion, to fuel your advertising programs. Such advertising creates authenticity and credibility in a way that company-generated advertising cannot. Consumer-generated media (CGM) also comes in a variety of forms that are not specifically solicited by companies, such as message-board posts, blogs, forum commentary, and the like. Consumer-generated advertising can generate enthusiasm and engagement as well as increased loyalty.

Viral Marketing

Interactive marketing options have been expanded through technology to include **viral marketing**, a term coined by Tim Draper of Draper Fisher Jurvetson. Viral marketing is defined as the process of promoting a brand, product, or service though an existing social network, typically an online network such as MySpace or Facebook, in which a message is passed from one individual to another—much as a virus spreads. A viral campaign can be an e-mail or a video that may include hyperlinked promotions, advertisements, games, online newsletters, and so forth. There has to be a reason for people to tell others about the message or pass it along, such as entertainment value, uniqueness, or potential financial reward.

viral marketing the process of promoting a brand, product, or service though an existing social network, where a message is passed from one individual to another—much as a virus spreads.

In August of 2007, with a budget of $150,000, TuitionBids.com's agency, Fanscape, created a viral marketing campaign targeted at 16-to 24-year-old high school and college students and their parents, with the intention of creating buzz and awareness of the company and to drive sales leads.[14] The strategy used was to "surround and deliver [the] target audience with valuable information." They used a multifaceted approach that "fused online Content and Promotional Integration programs, Social Media techniques, dedicated emails from Fanscape's proprietary database, a pay-per-click (PPC) campaign, and display ad buys to create as many relevant touch points with the target audience as possible." This included an e-mail to 100,000 members of the Fanscape database. The results included "32 million branding impressions with over 40,000 clicks, 150 WOM

[13]Emma Hall, "How to Get the Most Out of Social Networks and Not Annoy Users," *Advertising Age*, April 27, 2009, p. 30.
[14]WOMMA Web site http://www.womma.org. Case study available at http://www2.fanscape.com/tuitionbids/omma0808.html (accessed May 18, 2009).

placements, 26 editorial placements for over 2 million unique views, 8 contests, adding another 3 million unique views, a 25% open rate on the Fanscape email (well above industry averages)." Tuitionbids.com had a 6.4% conversion rate, which is about three times the industry average.

By creatively generating interest in and excitement about your story, or an aspect of your business, you can work to create a viral campaign. Kristen Smith, Executive Director of WOMMA, suggests the following six ways to keep people talking about your company and your products:[15]

1. Listen, speak, listen some more.
2. Be transparent and disclose.
3. Evaluate ROI continually.
4. Spread the word, not the manure.
5. Encourage an enterprise-wide WOMM.
6. Employ online and offline WOMM.

Publicity Potential

Generating Publicity

Performance Objective 9

Describe publicity and public relations.

Publicity, sometimes referred to as public relations (PR), as discussed in Chapter 4, and is defined by the Institute of Public Relations as, "[T]he planned and sustained effort to establish and maintain goodwill and mutual understanding between an organization and its public." Always save any publicity you receive. Frame and display articles prominently in your place of business, and make copies to send or hand out when it is appropriate. Each item of publicity has enormous value. Consumers give publicity credibility because it is not paid for.

Publicity is very important for a small business, which often has a negligible advertising budget. To get publicity, you will need to mail or fax a pitch letter and a press release to the magazine, newspaper, TV station, or radio station you hope to interest.

pitch letter correspondence designed to explain the story behind the press release, and why it would be interesting and relevant to the media outlet's readers, listeners, or viewers.

press release an announcement sent to the media to generate publicity, and states the "who, what, when, where, and why" of a story.

A **pitch letter** sells the story. It tells the person reading it why he or she should be interested in your business. A **press release** is an announcement sent to the media to generate publicity, and states the "who, what, when, where, and why" of a story. A pitch letter allows you to explain the story behind the press release, and why it would be interesting and relevant to the media outlet's readers, listeners, or viewers.

Before mailing or faxing a pitch letter and press release, call or e-mail the outlet and ask to whom you should direct the material. Say something like, "My name is Jason Hurley, and I'm a young entrepreneur with a downtown delivery/messenger service. I'd like to send WKTU a press release about the commitment we have just made to donate 10 hours of free delivery service per month to Meals on Wheels for seniors. To whom should I direct a press release?" Sometimes you can find this information on the Internet.

Get to know the print, radio, and television journalists pertinent to your business, so you can get publicity. The most effective way to get notice for your business is to contact the reporters yourself. You might be tempted to hire a professional publicist, but many reporters are bombarded by these people and would rather hear directly from you. Dedicate a block of time to send e-mails and make phone calls pitching your business and explaining

[15] Kristen Smith, "Six Ways to Leverage Word-of-Mouth," March 1, 2009, http://www.womma.org (accessed May 17, 2009).

why your story is worth covering. Be totally honest and build positive relationships. The type of reporting you want will develop most often because the writer comes to care about your story and sees it as interesting and important. Once you establish rapport and credibility with reporters, they are likely to call you for stories, insights, and comments.

Press releases can generate positive reports and stories about your business in newspapers, magazines, and on radio stations. For newspapers, make sure you send the release about a month before the event you are promoting. Follow up with a phone call two weeks later, and then one week after that (a week before the occasion). The precise timing will depend on the media outlet and its publication or broadcast schedule.

Telling the Story

Younger entrepreneurs can have an advantage here because relatively few young people start their own businesses. The print, radio, and television journalists in your area may want to hear about you.

Bear in mind, however, that reporters are looking for stories that will interest their readers. It is fine to send out a press release announcing the opening of your business, but be aware that it will not be a story until it is up and running. There is no point sending out a pitch letter and press release until you are actually in business and have a story to tell. The fact that your business is open, however, doesn't necessarily translate into a story of interest to reporters. You have to make the connection:

- Who are you and what has happened to you or what have you done that would make you and your business an interesting story?
- Did you have to overcome any obstacles in order to start your business?
- What about your product or service is unique? Is it something your community really needs?
- When is a specific event taking place that is newsworthy, or of interest for a story?
- Where are you locating the business or where is the event or activity occurring?
- How has your business changed you and helped members of your community?

Always answer the basic questions of who, what, when, where, why, and how for reporters. Answers to these questions will help them determine whether your story might be of interest to their readers or viewers. Reporters are very busy people, so keep your answers to these questions tight and concise. Try to find one focus or angle for your story. What's the "hook"?

Sample Press Release

As we have said, in order to tell your story in a press release or to a reporter, you will have to answer the six basic questions: who, what, when, where, why, and how. Who are you; what did you do; and when, where, why, and how did you do it?

A press release must provide contact information (name, phone, e-mail, and Web site) and answer the six questions (see **Figure 9-6**).

Figure 9-6 *Sample press release.*

DOGFISH HEAD COLLABORATES WITH 3 BREWERS, BATALI & BASTIANICH ON NYC BREWPUB

Fri, 02/19/2010 - 11:54am — mariah

The International Craft Brewing Renaissance Taken to New Heights

FOR IMMEDIATE RELEASE

February 20, 2010

Four well-known brewers are joining forces with Mario Batali, Joe Bastianich, and Italian food emporium Eataly to open a brewery-pub on a New York City rooftop with breathtaking views of the Flatiron and Empire State Buildings.

The four breweries collaborating on this project include two Italian craft brewers—Teo Musso, Brewmaster of Birrificio Le Baladin and Leonardo Di Vincenzo of Birra del Borgo, and two Italian–American craft brewers—Sam Calagione of Dogfish Head Craft Brewery and Vinnie Cilurzo of the Russian River Brewing Company.

The first floor of the building at 200 5th Avenue will house Eataly, an epic Italian specialty foods market, and multiple restaurants that pair gourmet foods with artisanal beers and wines. Additionally, there will be an 8,000-square-foot rooftop brewery and restaurant operated by B&B Hospitality's, Mario Batali, and Joe Bastianich.

The rooftop bar and restaurant will house a copper-clad brewing system. The idea is to create an artisanal, old-world Italian craft brewery that just happens to be located on a rooftop in Manhattan, says Dogfish Head's Sam Calagione. The four brewers are working together on recipes for Eataly's house beers. Those beers will feature Italian and American ingredients. The beers will be unpasteurized, unfiltered, naturally carbonated, and hand-pulled through traditional beer engines for the most authentic and pure presentation. The four individual brewers will also occasionally brew beers under their own names on site. The rooftop restaurant project will pair artisanal, rustic, homemade beers with the artisanal, rustic cooking of Chef Mario Batali. Additional Italian and American regional craft beers will be served both at the rooftop bar and in the downstairs restaurants.

Craft beer sales continue to gain traction in America and around the world. With all the diversity, complexity, and food-compatibility of world-class wine at a fraction of the price, the craft-beer segment enjoys continued growth in a challenging economy.

The four consulting brewers met in Boston this week to brew the first test batch of Eataly beer, an English Mild fermented with Italian chestnut powder (photos above). Plans call for Eataly New York to open in late summer 2010.

More from the brewers . . .

"Eataly is the representation of the earth, its products and an example of real Italian taste. The brewery will surely be a fusion of Italian and Italian/American styles and I am very happy to make this journey with this fantastic group!"—Teo Musso, Brewmaster, Birrificio Le Baladin.

"In 2006 I went to the Slow Food Salone del Gusto in Italy. Upon meeting many Italian craft brewers, I was not only impressed by the quality of their beer, but their passion for brewing as well. It was at that time I learned how great Italian craft beer was! To now collaborate with two of the most dynamic Italian craft brewers, along with my friend Sam Calagione, at Eataly New York will not only be a lot of fun, but very educational as well."—Vinnie Cilurzo, Brewer/Owner, Russian River Brewing Company.

"Eataly Brewery will be a great fusion of the well-known Italian gastronomic culture and our rising beer culture with the taste and the creativity of the American craft beer movement. This may well be the craziest and most amazing brewery in the world."—Leonardo Di Vincenzo, Brewmaster, Birra del Borgo.

"While the Italian craft brewing renaissance started later than ours here in the States, they have quickly made up for lost time with world-class artisanal beers. Both Dogfish Head and Russian River have pushed the boundries of beer, particularly those that pair well with food, for many years. We are looking forward to working with our Italian Brewing Brethren, Mario Batali, Joe Bastianich, and the folks at Eataly to further strengthen the bond between world-class beer and world-class food in the most beautiful setting for a brewery I have ever seen."—Sam Calagione, President/Founder, Dogfish Head Craft Brewery.

Follow Up a Press Release

Follow up your press releases with phone calls and e-mail. Try to reach the journalists directly. Be polite but persistent. Do not wait for a newspaper or radio station to return your call; call again (but do not make a pest of yourself)—they receive many press releases every day.

As we have said, save all publicity you receive to show potential customers. Publicity has enormous value because it can attract more publicity and more customers. Remember, it has greater credibility for consumers than advertising, which you will have paid for.

Public Relations

In addition to publicity, you can build positive public relations for your company through involvement in the local community and in local, national, and international professional and business organizations that pertain to your business. Some ways of doing this are with special events, sponsorship, networking, and public speaking.

Special Events

Hold contests, throw parties, or put together unusual events to attract attention and customers. Contests and sweepstakes can gather valuable names for your mailing list. Or, participate in special events yourself to gain publicity for your business through effective networking with other participants.

Sponsorships

Sponsoring a local sports team is a great way to involve your business in the community and meet potential customers. Sponsorships are a way of advertising. Just be certain that the audience for the event fits into your target market.

Networking

Networking, as discussed in Chapter 1 with respect to effective selling, is the exchange of information and contacts. When done efficiently and courteously, networking can serve as an excellent promotional vehicle.

Public Speaking

Taking advantage of opportunities to address members of your target audience as a guest speaker or paid professional can build your credibility and attract recognition and customers. You have the added weight of the sponsoring organization behind you, when you are a guest speaker.

Chapter Summary

Now that you have studied this chapter you can do the following:

1. Define integrated marketing.
    - Communications strategies, tactics, and other components should be integrated for maximum effectiveness.
    - Integrated communications may involve advertising, promotions, personal selling, database marketing, direct marketing, alternative marketing, e-active marketing, and public relations.
    - Your integrated communications should reinforce your brand and your unique selling proposition.

2. Conduct promotional planning and budgeting.
   - Promotional planning determines the best opportunities for quality, and effective customer contact.
   - All parts of your organization should be involved.
   - Complete a promotions opportunity analysis to create a promotion strategy.
   - Establish communications objectives.
   - Create a promotional budget to accomplish the objectives.
3. Understand advertising and advertising management.
   - Advertising objectives include
     - Building brand and image
     - Providing information
     - Persuading
     - Stimulating action
     - Reinforcing a purchasing decision
   - Determine if and when to use an advertising agency or freelancer.
   - Take advantage of assistance from media companies, trade associations, and suppliers.
   - Decide which advertising will be institutional and which will be product advertising.
4. Identify and evaluate media options.
   - The customers' interests and benefits should be the focus of media decisions.
   - Develop a media strategy and schedule tied to the overall marketing strategy.
   - Work with a media planner and buyer or internally to assess your options based upon an analysis of anticipated media effectiveness.
     - Broadcast media include television and radio.
     - Print media include newspapers, magazines, and directories.
     - Outdoor advertising primarily consists of billboards.
     - Internet advertising is a key part of e-active advertising.
   - Plan measurement into your media decisions.
   - Collateral materials should reinforce the company's competitive advantage.
5. Discuss sales promotion.
   - Encourage customers to buy more frequently through promotional tools.
   - It is best to use promotional tools for highly targeted, time-limited increases in response.
   - Advertising specialties will remind customers of your business or product.
   - Trade show exhibits can provide high engagement and impact.
   - Mall carts and kiosks may be effective for seasonal or start-up businesses or for product trials.
6. Explore alternative marketing options.
   - Guerilla marketing is unconventional, creative marketing that can get your message to your target market.
   - Buzz marketing gets the story of your business and/or products out through word of mouth.
   - Product placements and branded entertainment are more subtle ways to gain exposure.

- Lifestyle marketing engages customers according to their needs, interests, desires, and values and considers their behaviors.
- Samples and demonstrations, point-of-purchase materials, and shelf placement are forms of in-store marketing.
- Other, often unexpected, media venues can also have an impact.

7. Analyze database and direct-response marketing opportunities.
   - Use databases to create highly targeted, customized communications.
   - Design and implement the data-collection plan to maximize value.
   - Code and analyze the data to extract information and target it.
   - Create communications based upon the databases.
8. Incorporate e-active marketing.
   - E-commerce options can increase sales.
   - Use interactive marketing to collect consumer information and communicate with them via the Internet.
   - Include online advertising—typically banner ads—on Web pages to reach targeted customers.
   - Brand spiraling can be of value as it integrates your offline and online branding strategies.
   - Maintain blogs as journals for public reading on the Internet.
   - Online social networks such as Facebook, MySpace, and BlackPlanet present opportunities to create targeted messages.
   - Support consumer-generated advertising and media to fuel your promotional programs.
   - Viral marketing campaigns can spread the word about a company, product, or service rapidly and effectively.
9. Describe when and how to use publicity and public relations.
   - Use press releases and pitch letters to generate publicity for your business.
   - The pitch letter tells the reader why he or she should be interested in your business, product, service, or event.
   - The press release tells the who, what, when, where, why, and how of your story.
   - Build customer relations through special events, sponsorships, networking, and public speaking.

Key Terms

blog
blogosphere
brand spiraling
buzz marketing
cost per rating point (CPRP)
cost per thousand (CPM)
data mining
e-active marketing
edutainment
frequency
gross ratings points (GRP)
guerilla marketing
institutional advertising
lifetime value
media buyer
media planner
media schedule
media strategy
mobile social networking
opportunities to see (OTS)
pitch letter
press release
product advertising
promotions opportunity analysis
rating
reach
RFM analysis
stealth marketing
viral marketing

Entrepreneurship Portfolio

Critical Thinking Exercises

1. Identify a well-known public figure and discuss his/her brand. How has this individual enhanced this brand? How has he/she damaged it?
2. Brainstorm five creative ways for a small business with a very low budget to advertise and promote its products or services using the latest developments in communications and Internet technology.
3. Why does viral marketing have such success potential? How can a viral marketing campaign work against a company?
4. What role should the unique selling proposition play in a company's advertising strategy?

Key Concept Questions

1. Name four common marketing objectives. Explain why they are important.
2. What are the types of communications budgets? What is the best method of budgeting?
3. Identify the parts of promotions opportunity analysis planning.
4. The examples provided in the Entrepreneurial Wisdom section of this chapter include several sites targeted to specific ethnic, demographic, or lifestyle groups. Select three of the Web sites listed there and answer the following:
   a. What types of marketing messages can you find on the site?
   b. How do the messages differ from one another?
   c. How are the messages the same?
   d. How might you use the information on these Web sites to assist in creating integrated marketing communications plans?
5. How can entrepreneurs stretch their advertising budgets? Name at least five ways.
6. What are some benefits of using marketing databases for small businesses?

Application Exercises

1. Answer the questions that follow and use them to write a press release for your business.
   a. What was your life like before you began the study of entrepreneurship?
   b. Were you having any problems in school or at home?
   c. What have you learned about business that you did not know before?
   d. What is the best thing about running your own business? What obstacles have you had to overcome to get your business going?
   e. Has running your own business changed how you are doing in school? Has it changed how you get along with your family?

f. Are you more involved in your community since you started your business?
g. How has your business changed your life? What would you be doing if you were not an entrepreneur?
h. If you could give one piece of advice to students who were thinking about starting a business, what would it be?
i. What are your goals for the future?

2. Use your press release to write a pitch letter for the opening of your business.
3. Create a chart like the one below to describe your marketing plan in detail. If you do not have a business concept, create a plan for a religious bookstore in a location that you specify. Include each media supplier, if possible, and delete the types that you are not expecting to use.

Company Name: ____

Media Type or Promotional Method	Name of Outlet(s) (list each separately)	Target Market	Budget ($)	Objective(s)
Newspaper				
Magazine				
Directory				
Television				
Radio				
Outdoor				
Internet				
Brochures				
Flyers				
Newsletters				
Business Cards				
Signs				
Sales Promos				
Advertising Specialties				
Trade Shows				
Carts/Kiosks				
Alternative Marketing				
Other Media				
Direct Response				

Exploring Your Community

1. Visit three independently owned businesses (not on the Internet) that are in the same industry. Identify the target market for each (demographic, lifestyle, and the like). Note the various advertising and promotional methods in use at the business location. Search online for a company Web site. Ask the store owner or manager where they advertise and whether they create press releases. Report back on the results.
2. Obtain ad rates from two local radio stations, a local newspaper, and a cable television channel.

Media	Advertising Rates	Reach
Radio ______	______	______
Radio ______	______	______
Newspaper ______	______	______
Cable ______	______	______

Exploring Online

1. Select either your own company or an entrepreneurial venture that interests you. Find three similar businesses on the Internet and select the two best sites. What features make them attractive? Why did you think they were better than the third site? How would you distinguish your own site?
2. Find out how much it would cost to run a banner ad on the "personal start" pages (the pages subscribers see when they log on) for the following online services: AOL, Google, Panix, and Yahoo!

AOL Banner Ad Price: $______

Google Banner Ad Price: $______

Panix Banner Ad Price: $______

Yahoo! Banner Ad Price: $______

Case Study

Dr. Farrah Gray: Young Millionaire, Entrepreneur, and Philanthropist

Most six-year-olds have not begun to dream of entrepreneurship. Most 14-year-olds only dream about being millionaires. Most 21-year-olds are in the early stages of their work lives or in college. None of this was true for Dr. Farrah Gray.

At age six, young Farrah (who was born in 1984) was selling products door-to-door from his home in the South Side of Chicago. He was a self-made millionaire by age 14. He received an honorary doctorate at the age of 21.

Farrah Gray is a master of promotion, inspiration, and entrepreneurship. He has achieved more before the age of 25 than most people do in their entire lives. The National Urban League named him one of the most influential black men in America. He is a syndicated columnist, writing for the National Newspaper Publishers Association, reaching 15 million readers in 200 weekly newspapers. He serves as an AOL money coach and has been featured on the Dream Team of Financial Experts in *O, The Oprah Magazine*. He is a professional speaker on topics that include financial management, creativity, personal development, and leadership. He has been featured thousands of times in print and on broadcast media.

Dr. Gray has created numerous business ventures, fulfilling his dream of becoming a 21st-century CEO. These include a mail-box franchise, prepaid phone cards, an interactive teen talk show, and Farr-Out Foods. As a 12-year-old, he was inspirational as the cohost of Las Vegas-based *Backstage Live*, which was simulcast to 12 million people weekly. He is the author of two books, *Reallionaire: Nine Steps to Becoming Rich from the Inside Out* and *Get Real, Get Rich: Conquer the 7 Myths Blocking You from Success*, and is the editor-in-chief/publisher of *Prominent* magazine.

While enjoying this spectacular success, Dr. Gray's commitment to philanthropy also emerged early and continues to flourish. When he was eight, he cofounded the Urban Neighborhood Enterprise Economic Club (U.N.E.E.C.) on Chicago's South Side. He later created New Early Entrepreneur Wonders (NEEW) Student Venture Fund to engage and encourage at-risk young people to find legal sources of entrepreneurial income. This was followed by the establishment of the Farrah Gray Foundation, which supports scholarships for students at historically black colleges and universities (HBCUs) and promotes youth entrepreneurship. He is a spokesman for the National Marrow Donor Program, and the National Coalition for the Homeless.

Dr. Farrah Gray is an extraordinary example of a successful young entrepreneur and philanthropist.

Case Study Analysis

1. Clearly, Farrah Gray is a master of integrated promotion. List the promotional methods he has used and why he may have selected each.
2. What is the most interesting part of his story for you? Why?
3. The Farrah Gray Foundation serves as a vital part of Gray's activities. Explain how it is important.
4. If you were going to meet with Farrah Gray, what would you want to discuss and why?

Case Sources

The Farrah Gray Web site at *http://www.drfarrahgray.com*. The Farrah Gray Foundation Web site at *http://www.farrahgrayfoundation.org*.

Case Study | eHarmony

***Small Business School* video clip titles are in red**

TURN A SMALL IDEA INTO A BIG ONE

Forty-three percent of all people over age 18 in the United States are single. In my interview with Dr. Neil Clark Warren, the founder of eHarmony, I was surprised when he told me, "Most singles yearn to find the right person and to have a good marriage."

In 1993, Dr. Warren wrote *Finding the Love of Your Life* and, in 1995, Greg Forgatch joined him to launch a company offering seminars based upon the principles in Warren's book. The two opened their second business, eHarmony.com, in 2000. Today, the service is being used by 20 million paying customers. After some tweaking of the platform, Dr. Warren's company has been a major player in the multimillion dollar online matchmaking business since its launch, and was bringing in $700 million in revenue when the *Small Business School* taped the eHarmony story.

One major difference between a business that stays small and one that grows is market potential. Dr. Warren spent 35 years as a marriage counselor being frustrated because he could not help enough of the couples fix their marriages. He started thinking about what he could do. Rather than working on a small scale and in a relatively ineffective way with couples who should never have gotten married in the first place, Dr. Warren figured he could truly help people if he could show them how to find the right person to marry.

At first glance, it seems like a subtle shift. Dr. Warren is still in the marriage business. He had a hunch that marriages fail mostly because of poor selection of partners, so he started the rigorous process of doing his own scientific study. He did "autopsies" on 512 marriages. From that, he concluded there was an opportunity for him, but at that time he did not know the magnitude of the opportunity. When making a living as a private counselor, Dr. Warren was limited by time. By leveraging his intellectual property to the Web, his primary market became the 93 million single Americans who are over 18 and have Internet access. Because of its Web-based design, the service is global. *Online Dating Magazine* estimates that more than 20 million people a month visit online dating services. The eHarmony service has captured a significant portion of the market.

Dr. Neil Clark Warren, founder of eHarmony.

CHARGE MORE AND DEMAND MORE THAN YOUR COMPETITION

Although it is a market leader today, eHarmony was late to enter the online matchmaking business. This gave its founders a chance to learn from others, and as a result it developed a unique product with a distinctive competitive advantage. eHarmony was and may still be the most expensive service in its market, and it requires that the customer spend more time on the site before being matched and meeting other singles, particularly at the initial sign-up point. Taking time to complete the first evaluation has been key, because Dr. Warren had already determined that, offline, people rush into dating relationships too quickly. eHarmony slows down the getting-to-know-you stage and demands substantial information and commitment at the time a person pays for the service.

FIND AN ADVERTISING STRATEGY

"If you build it, they will come" was not working for eHarmony. The site was up and running. Some singles were signing up. Dr. Warren's reputation was established and, due to his best-selling book, he had a bit of a following; however, the paying customers were not getting enough matches so everyone was discouraged.

The founders were ready to quit, but they decided to try advertising on the radio. That first radio campaign, which cost the company just a few thousand dollars, worked. After that early success, eHarmony's advertising budget gradually rose to

$20 million by 2004. The company had found a medium that worked for them and they have grown and refined it to enhance its effectiveness.

The first president of eHarmony, Greg Forgatch, told me, "In early 2002 we started looking at radio. It's easy and it's not too expensive. It's a matter of cracking the code. We built 13 different radio spots. Some of them never reached the air.

"In September 2002 we launched a radio ad that popped. Here's what's amazing—the same ad has been running for over 16 months. It had some legs. It's working. It started:

> Hi, my name's Sarah and I met my husband on eHarmony.com.
>
> Hi, my name's Debbie and I met my husband John on eHarmony.com.
>
> Hi, I'm Cindy and I met my husband Bill on eHarmony.com.

"Right there we positioned ourselves as building marriages—giving people hope that they can develop a lasting relationship. It wasn't about dates and quantity and guys with great jobs and cute girls.

"Then Dr. Neil Clark Warren comes on. He has a special voice, credibility, and a meaningful message. We closed with another gal talking about her husband. Then we figured out we needed to give people more than hope. We needed to give them a free personality profile. That was a wonderful direct-response tool. We had a call to action. Write this down and get the free profile. We tried some agencies but Neil wrote the best eHarmony ad ever written."

There were four parts to this successful campaign. First, it used real customers, not actors, who speak about their experience in their own words. Second, it used Dr. Warren, because his is the voice of authority on the subject of marriage and online dating. Third, it repeats the name of the company four or five times. And fourth, it offers a call to action that is obviously hugely attractive to singles.

The team at the *Small Business School* completed the free eHarmony profiles ourselves, so that we could tape the process for the television production. None of us were legal prospects for eHarmony, because we were married. However, we can report that, once a person takes the free offer made in the ads, eHarmony has a friendly but what we would call a "hard-sell" follow-up e-mail protocol.

After eHarmony saw success with radio advertising, it took the same winning formula and made TV commercials, starting in 2004. At first they featured successful matches and some commentary from Dr. Warren. However, eHarmony is no longer using Dr. Warren in their ads. He is still the chairman of the board but no longer involved in the day-to-day operations. The ads are bringing in thousands of prospects a day, but eHarmony still has to work hard to convert them to paying customers.

Case Analysis

1. What are some of the steps that led to creating eHarmony?
2. What advantages did eHarmony have because it was not the first entrant into the online dating market space?
3. What disadvantages might there be as a late entrant into a market? Did eHarmony experience any or all of these? Which ones?
4. Why did Greg Forgatch believe that eHarmony's first radio ad worked so well?
5. What key advertising concepts has eHarmo247ny applied?

Case prepared by Hattie Bryant, creator of *Small Business School*, the television series made for PBS and Voice of America, http://SmallBusinessSchool.org

Chapter 10

MARKETING GLOBALLY

"Opportunities multiply as they are seized."

—Sun Tzu,
author, military strategist

The world's largest package delivery service started out in the basement of a home in Seattle, Washington, in 1907. At the age of 19, James E. (Jim) Casey borrowed $100 from a friend and partnered with Claude Ryan to form the American Messenger Company. The company's messengers delivered packages, ran errands, brought food from restaurants, and carried notes and baggage. Deliveries were generally made on foot or via bicycle. The competition was intense, but Jim used his experience at other companies, and strong policies, to support his slogan of "best service and lowest rates" to succeed.[1]

When technology changed with the proliferation of telephones and automobiles, the American Messenger Company adapted and became Merchants Parcel Delivery. The company readjusted its focus as the result of a merger with a competitor, and shifted from messages to packages. The use of brown as a signature color began in 1916. In 1919, the company expanded to Oakland, California, and became United Parcel Service (UPS).

UPS expanded across the country, first through ground services and then with air delivery as well. The company was the first to offer air delivery via privately operated airlines, in 1929. With the onslaught of the Great Depression, the air service was dropped late in 1929 (and resumed in 1953). For many years, UPS needed federal and state authority, respectively, to move packages across state lines and within individual states. Permission to serve the 48 contiguous states was granted in 1975. UPS was the first national delivery service.

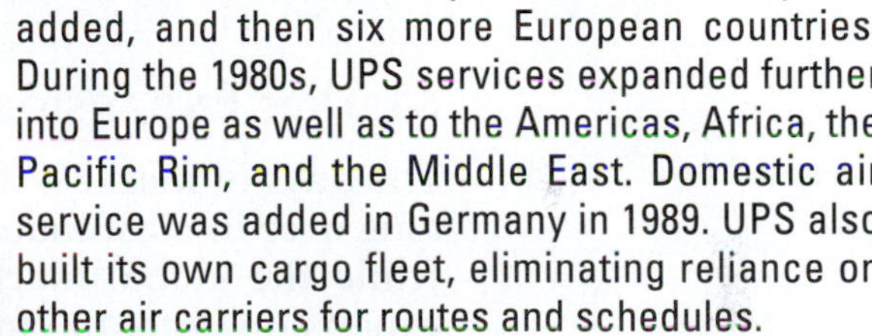

Sixty-eight years after its founding, UPS entered international markets by adding package and document air service to Canada; a year later, Germany was added, and then six more European countries. During the 1980s, UPS services expanded further into Europe as well as to the Americas, Africa, the Pacific Rim, and the Middle East. Domestic air service was added in Germany in 1989. UPS also built its own cargo fleet, eliminating reliance on other air carriers for routes and schedules.

Over time, UPS has become a leader in global supply-chain management, managing logistics and distribution with movements of goods, information, and funds. International expansion has come from both acquisitions and internal growth. For example, UPS entered the China market through a joint venture, and then bought out the partner company in 2005. By purchasing Challenge Air, UPS became the largest express and air-cargo carrier in Latin America. The company has also made acquisitions in Poland and the United Kingdom. UPS has grown within its industry to become a $36-billion leader in facilitating commerce worldwide.

Performance Objectives

1. Identify the reasons for ventures to market globally.
2. Understand the various strategic options for global ventures.
3. Explore the challenges to international trade.
4. Learn about the types of support that are available for global ventures.
5. Describe regional trade agreements that influence global trade.

[1]UPS International Web site, http://www.ups.com (accessed May 29, 2009).

Reasons to Market Globally

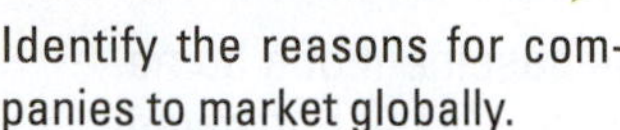

Performance Objective 1

Identify the reasons for companies to market globally.

In today's world, global marketing is not just for a few select, huge multinational firms. It is an option, and can be a necessity, for businesses of all sizes. With the advent and explosion of the World Wide Web, and the ease of communications and transportation across political and economic borders, the reasons for global marketing are more compelling today than ever before. These reasons include: the expansion of markets, increasing access to resources, reductions in costs, and competitive advantages that are specific to individual localities. A small, home-based business in Michigan can have an Internet presence that is a leader in sales in Mali, using merchandise made of components from Mexico. A not-for-profit in the United States can acquire products from Afghanistan that creates jobs and opportunities for women in villages there, and can then sell the products to affluent Americans. A plumbing manufacturer in rural America can have fixtures designed in Argentina, the parts manufactured in Taiwan, and then assemble them at its headquarters for shipment to anywhere in the world.

A small business started today can be born global, with the intention of operating across geographic and political borders from the beginning.[2] This can mean including global expansion in future plans, or starting out with international strategies. However, a company may want to wait until it is more established to venture into the global marketplace, or it might be forced to do so by economic realities. In any case, international marketing opportunities are available to companies of all sizes.

Market Expansion

The days of markets being limited primarily to a local customer base are long over in most industries. The U.S. market has over 300 million people, while the global market is approximately 7.1 billion, presenting huge expansion potential for many companies.[3] Small businesses account for 97 percent of the country's identified exporters, so you would be in good company as an entrepreneur. Whether your domestic customer base is too small to permit desired growth, too crowded with competitors to achieve sales and profitability goals, or the global marketplace is simply a better strategic fit, you can strategically expand your market—possibly exponentially—by becoming a global marketer. Done well, you can develop a competitive advantage that will position you for long-term viability and success.

The opportunity to grow your business by accessing new markets can prove to be strong motivation for seeking international possibilities. Much discussion centers on the so-called BRIC countries—Brazil, Russia, India, and China—as forces in world markets, due to their huge populations. India and China alone account for over 2.5 billion of the world's people, or 37 percent. Brazil and Russia, with their immense quantities of natural resources, have enormous potential for growth as well. In 1997, Jeffrey E. Garten of Yale identified the "Big Ten Emerging Markets,"[4] with the list of countries being modified in 2005.[5] **Exhibit 10-1** shows some market data

---

[2]Gary A. Knight and S. Tamar Cavusgil, "Innovation, Organizational Capabilities, and the Born-Global Firm," *Journal of International Business Studies*, vol. 35, no. 2, March 2004, pp. 124–141.
[3]U.S. Small Business Administration, *Breaking into the Trade Game: A Small Business Guide to Exporting*, Fourth Edition, 2008.
[4]Jeffrey E. Garten, *The Big Ten: Big Emerging Markets and How They Will Change Our Lives* (Cambridge, Mass.: Basic Books, 1997).
[5]"Emerging Markets: Beyond the Big Four," *Business Week*, December 26, 2005, http://www.businessweek.com/pring/magazine/content (accessed June 14, 2009).

Exhibit 10-1 *Big ten emerging markets.*

	Population 2009 Estimate	2008 Wealth (GDP per Capita)	Economic Growth 2007–2008 (GDP)
World	6,790,062,216	10,400	3.8%
Brazil	198,739,269	10,100	5.2%
China	1,338,612,968	6,000	9.8%
Egypt	83,082,869	5,400	6.9%
India	1,166,079,217	2,800	6.6%
Mexico	111,211,789	14,200	1.4%
Poland	38,482,919	17,300	4.8%
Russia	140,041,247	15,800	6.0%
South Africa	49,052,489	10,000	2.8%
South Korea	48,508,972	26,000	2.5%
Turkey	76,805,524	12,000	1.5%

Source: U.S. Central Intelligence Agency, *World Fact Book.* Updated May 13, 2009. Available online at http://www.cia.gov/library/publications/the-world-factbook/, accessed June 8, 2009.

regarding the Big Ten, and **Figure 10-1** provides a map highlighting these countries. Depending upon your specific business, there may also be other countries that would be logical entry points for you.

For many years, a major reason to export goods to foreign markets for U.S. companies was to extend their product life cycle. Products that were approaching maturity or market saturation in domestic markets could be introduced abroad and begin a whole new life, continuing to be profitable for years beyond their domestic life span. With the advent of sophisticated communications technology, and the overall shortening of product life cycles, this purpose has been eroded although not eliminated. Products may be adopted in multiple locations simultaneously or with little lag time.

Figure 10-1 *Big ten emerging markets.*

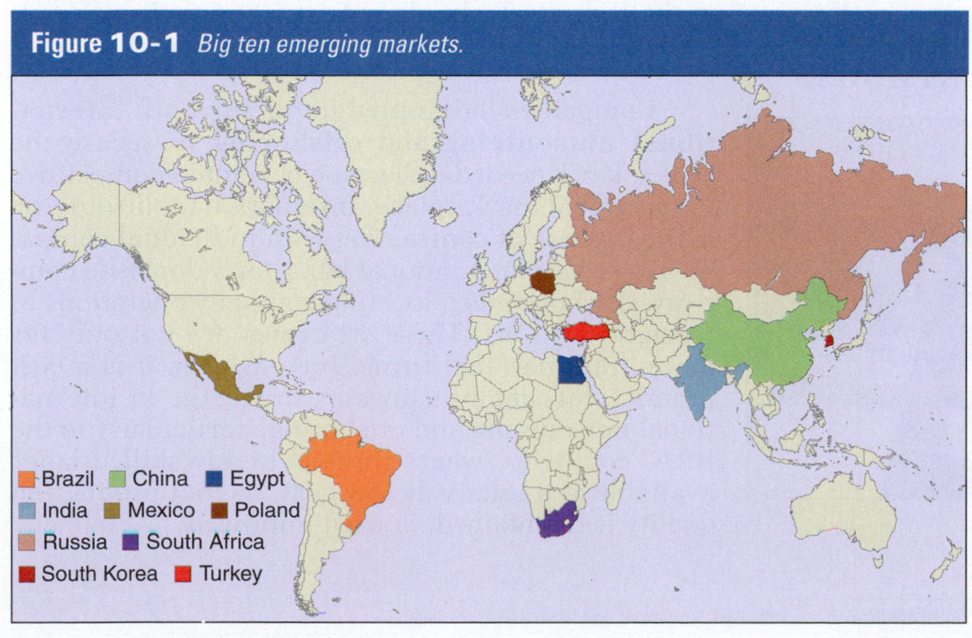

Intellectual property, products, and technologies can be a critical part of global market expansion, because they create unique, highly specialized opportunities. Certainly, ideas are generated around the world, and you can work to identify those resources to develop domestic and international markets. Perhaps a scientist in Ukraine has developed a revolutionary medical product but cannot bring it to market, and you have the knowledge, skills, and resources necessary to do so. You could source the idea in Ukraine, produce the product in East Asia, and sell it in the United States and elsewhere. Also, your product could be so highly targeted and expensive that the domestic market simply would not be large enough to sustain your business, and international expansion was necessary. Finally, you could have a product that has caught on rapidly in the United States that also has demand overseas, but it is likely to be a fad rather than have an extended life cycle. In this case, you might want to go global to take advantage of the opportunity.

Access to Resources

Global markets offer expanded access to raw materials, intellectual property, human capital, and other resources that companies need and want. For example, if you are creating cutting tools using lasers and diamonds, diamond mines simply do not exist everywhere. You will have to go to the international market to acquire industrial diamonds. However, this should not be a problem; the sourcing of raw materials internationally is a long-established business practice.

A more recent practice is that of acquiring human capital resources globally. The reasons may be a scarcity of qualified, skilled labor in domestic markets, the prohibitively high cost of local labor, or both. For example, the Disney International Program works with colleges and universities throughout the United States to partner with programs worldwide that bring student interns to Walt Disney World in Orlando, Florida, where they earn college credit while learning about hospitality and tourism. Another example is WuXi AppTec Company, Ltd., which is based in Shanghai, China, and is an integrated research and development services company that outsources scientists in pharmaceuticals, biotechnology, and medical devices. WuXi has been recognized for five consecutive years on the Deloitte Technology Fast 500 Asia Pacific list, has U.S. operations, and is now traded on the New York Stock Exchange (NYSE: WX).[6]

international outsourcing the process of contracting with individual companies to secure international labor for a domestic company.

offshoring relocating company operations to foreign locations.

Companies have opted to pursue both **international outsourcing** and **offshoring** to secure the skilled labor needed to become or remain competitive in the global marketplace. International outsourcing is the process of contracting with individual companies to secure international labor for a domestic company. Offshoring is relocating company operations to foreign locations. These strategies are not only for large, multinational firms. Increasingly, it is a best practice for small businesses to engage in international outsourcing and offshoring, particularly in the BRIC countries, where there is highly skilled labor available at a relatively low cost, so that production quality is maintained, or even improved.

A telephone call center in India.

[6]WuXi AppTec Web site, http://www.wuxiapptec.com (accessed June 9, 2009).

Entrepreneurial Wisdom . . .

There are numerous Web sites with valuable information on countries and trading that may be excellent sources of specific resources, provide opportunities for cost reduction, or represent a treasured customer base. Among these are

Country Reports	U.S. Department of State	www.state.gov/countries
Country Risk Assessment	EXIM Bank	www.exim.gov/tools/country/country_limits.html/
Directory of Export Management Companies	Federal International Trade Association	fita.org/emc.html
Export Portal	U.S. Department of Commerce	www.export.gov
Guide to Exporting	U.S. Small Business Administration	www.sba.gov
Guide for Commercial Importers	International Trade Council	www.usitc.gov
World Fact Book	U.S. Central Intelligence Agency	https://www.cia.gov/library/publications/the-world-factbook/index.html

Gauri Nanda is a young entrepreneur who considered licensing her product when she graduated from MIT, where she designed the product in the Media Lab.[7] However, Gauri wanted greater control and elected to have it made offshore, through a Hong Kong manufacturer she found on Alibaba.com, a lead site for Chinese companies. Gauri's Clocky is a miniature robot alarm clock that makes quirky sounds and movements and is sold online and through boutiques at $50 apiece. During the first year, 9000 Clockys were sold. The use of a Hong Kong manufacturer permitted Gauri and her company, Nanda Home, to compete in the U.S. consumer electronics market.

Cost Reduction

Much has been researched and written about the cost advantages of global ventures. Stories of customer service operations for U.S.-based companies in Bangalore, India, abound. For many years after World War II, *Made in Japan* indicated cheaply made, inferior goods, but the quality of Japanese automobiles has long been widely recognized. Today, medical tourism has become a new market, with people traveling internationally to undergo less costly health-care procedures, such as plastic surgery in Brazil or eye surgery in India. Foundries and factories have been moving offshore for many years to attain cost savings. Businesses have become international ventures in order to reduce costs such as raw materials, labor, and production overhead. They may also achieve cost reductions through market expansion, as they reach economies of scale and efficiencies through experience.

For many companies, these cost reductions have been attained by locating a facility abroad, or by securing raw material or manufacturing suppliers in foreign markets. In the 1980s, Speakman Company, a well-established manufacturer of faucets and shower heads, found that the costs of domestic production were becoming prohibitive, and they located foundries in Asia, and developed a new technology in South America, to reduce costs. The company continued to assemble the final products in the United States, while realizing substantial savings in materials and labor. However, these material savings do not always translate into overall cost savings if the cost or difficulties in transporting the goods is too great.

[7]Max Chafkin, "Case Study #1: The Reluctant Entrepreneur," *Inc.* magazine, July 2007, http://www.inc.com (accessed June 7, 2009).

For example, a U.S. mattress manufacturing firm realized that it could acquire springs at a lower price in the global marketplace, but the cost of transportation would offset the gains.

Location-Specific Advantages

The world has many interesting locations with unique combinations of human, natural, and financial resources. These natural resources include minerals, agricultural crops, and petroleum. Location-specific human resources include skilled artisans—such as the silversmiths of the Andalucía region of Spain, the carpet weavers in Iran, and the technical skills of Indian software engineers. In order to take advantage of these location-specific resources, companies must reach across borders and either import products, acquire human capital, or create their own locations. Just as American cities and states have designated industrial and business zones, and granted special tax incentives to attract commerce, foreign governments create incentives for investors to stimulate growth and employment. These may include tax advantages and favorable legal and regulatory environments. For example, Qatar has become one of the fastest-growing economies in the world because of its government's strategic decision to create the Qatar Financial Centre (QFC), and to support it with Education City. QFC has attracted the operations of many of the world's leading financial companies to this small country on the Arabian Peninsula. In order to entice targeted firms, Qatar has established a highly favorable business-tax rate and provided significant investment support.[8]

Other businesses, both small and large, have chosen to locate outside their home countries for proactive and defensive reasons. In order to secure or maintain major customers, a physical presence in their locality is sometimes required. Customers want and demand the availability of a local representative, if not a physical plant or distribution center. When Speakman Company assembled their shower heads in the United States, and had their representatives in Italy, Germany, the United Kingdom, and Australia market them to commercial contractors there, those customers insisted that there be a ready supply of products on the spot, without the delay of shipping from the United States. Rather than shipping as needed for projects, Speakman had to find physical distribution points in those countries. Companies will often elect to create a presence rather than lose a customer.

Whether it is to take advantage of location-specific resources or special incentives, or to create or preserve customer relationships in specific locations, you can identify and secure global marketing advantages by recognizing and strategically acting upon such opportunities.

Improving Quality Levels

Global marketing is also driven by a desire to improve quality levels for a company's products or services. Consumers and business customers in different countries and regions have varied quality standards. The Japanese are widely recognized for their exacting product demands; thus Japan may be an excellent choice as a partner where product-quality standards are particularly tight. The range of options for attaining such quality extends from direct purchase, to locating in the country, to acquiring raw materials and components. The cachet of a Swiss watch, exotic Kenyan or Costa Rican coffee, or a German chef's knife exists because of an established reputation for quality. Small businesses can capitalize on such quality advantages to reach world-class levels in the global marketplace.

---

[8]Qatar Financial Centre Authority Web site, http://www.qfc.com.qa/output/ (updated April 20, 2009; accessed June 8, 2009).

Strategy Options for Global Ventures

Your decision to market globally is one that should include considering the multiple strategy options available to you: importing, exporting, franchising, forming strategic alliances, and locating abroad. Which options, if any, are right for you will be unique to your business.

Performance Objective 2
Understand the various strategic options for global ventures.

Importing

Importing is the sale of products produced in a foreign country to customers in your home country, and it can be a successful strategy across a broad array of business types and sizes. If you find a product abroad that either cannot be satisfactorily produced at home, or is simply better-positioned as an import, you may want to become an importer. Alternatively, you may decide to import products or components to take advantage of the cost and/or quality factors discussed earlier.

importing the sale of products produced in a foreign country to customers in your home country.

Because of intense price competition at the global level, you may have to import to remain competitive. Domestic costs may just be too high for business success in markets in which price outweighs other factors for customer advantage, making the import of less costly components, agricultural products, or finished goods a necessity. Whereas companies like Nicole Miller Ltd. may be able to continue production in New York City, many firms in the fashion industry have switched to importing products, largely for cost reasons. Importing requires specific skills and knowledge to achieve planned quality levels and cost savings, so you may have to make considerable changes in your business model to succeed. However, small firms can be nimble and may be able to take advantage of import opportunities and secure a significant advantage in the market. Also, if you design your organization to be a global business from the start, importing may be a core strategy and skill that will bring success.

Importing is a highly regulated, complex process that requires research, commitment, and cultural competency. Clearly, the Internet has made searching for some suppliers easier, but many will not have an Internet presence, or may not have English-language skills. You may have to put forth considerable effort to meet people where they are, rather than where you want them to be, in terms of readiness and interest. For example, that fantastic village filled with amazing craftswomen in the Andes may create beautiful, marketable textiles that no other company is importing to the United States, but the route from their looms to your customers may be treacherous, literally and figuratively. You need to do your research and establish your target costs. You also must become intimately familiar with and sensitive to cultural and ethnic traditions, so that you can be effective in your interactions with foreign businesses and their people. A keen understanding of your rights and responsibilities with respect to importing laws and regulations, combined with the right relationship with intermediaries, is essential to importing success.

There is a well-developed system of trading through international brokers and dealers that will manage almost every aspect of the importing process, but ultimately the importing company must pull together all of the components. Foreign embassies, consulates, and the National Customs Brokers and Forwarders Association of America (http://www.ncbfaa.org) are good sources of information on importing options and the companies that can facilitate the process. Whether you find the supplier at a U.S. trade show, an international trade fair, online, through a sales representative, a friend, or while on a vacation or buying trip, you will need to determine the fit of the foreign business with your markets and its capacity to deliver

Daniel Uribe, Lazer Bearings.

Step into the Shoes . . .

Keeping Sales Rolling: Daniel Uribe, Lazer Bearings

For skateboarding fanatic Daniel Uribe of Torrance, California, the moment for turning his passion into a business occurred in 2007 while still in high school. He founded Lazer Bearings, after contacting manufacturers via the Internet to save money on ceramic bearings, and realized that he could create a profitable business. Daniel took Third Place at Smith/Barney/NFTE's National Youth Entrepreneurship Challenge.

Daniel sells high-performance silicon-nitrate ceramic bearings for skateboards and rollerblades. He markets to consumers and businesses and sells the benefits that are vital to each. Features he identifies are that his ceramic bearings are lighter and harder than others. They are extremely smooth and resistant to contamination, and thus Lazer Bearings are faster, more durable, and less likely to clog. Quality bearings may reduce injuries, too. By sourcing his ceramic bearings from China rather than Switzerland, Daniel provides an equal-quality product at a lower price, permitting retailers to approximately double their profits. Daniel worked with his manufacturer to ensure that the design was precisely what he wanted to market. Daniel researched the field thoroughly when he developed his business plan. Daniel Uribe and Lazer Bearings are keeping sales rolling.

products and/or services of consistent quality in a timely fashion at a stable, profitable price.

Exporting

exporting the sale of goods or services produced domestically to foreign customers.

One of the most traditional methods of entering the global marketplace is through **exporting**, or selling goods or services produced domestically to foreign customers. Higher growth rates and lower failure rates are reported among companies that export, compared to those that do not.[9] The U.S. government is committed to supporting the export of goods and services around the globe. Entrepreneurial ventures can enter the international marketplace with relatively low risk and at relatively low cost. For most businesses, it is not necessary to locate abroad or even open a satellite office, so the capital and human-resource investments are minimized. For some companies that take advantage of technology, the incremental costs of exporting are primarily shipping and tariffs, so that they can profitably market globally by charging higher prices to cover these expenses. If products, labeling, and packaging do not have to be modified, and if incremental costs can be covered, exporting can be a successful business strategy. **Exhibit 10-2** identifies some of the advantages and disadvantages of exporting.

Companies that are interested in exporting have many resources available for the exploration of their options, including World Trade Center affiliates, international trade-lead services, trade intermediaries, and trade missions. World Trade Center affiliates and other resources can provide assistance tailored for exporters in their localities. International trade lead for potential exporters and importers are available from a multitude of sources. They may consist of searchable international opportunities, company directories, electronic marketplaces, and the like. These lead sources may be free, or require paid membership. They may focus on a particular country or region, such as TradeIndia, or Australia on Display, or they may be global, such as the International Business Forum, Bidmix.com, or the World Bank FundLine. The Federation of International Trade Associations (http://www.fita.org) and the U.S. Commerce Service (http://www.export.gov) can provide extensive lead information.

[9] Howard Lewis III and J. David Richardson, *Why Global Commitment Really Matters!* (Washington, D.C.: Institute for International Economics, 2001).

Exhibit 10-2 *Advantages and disadvantages of exporting.*

Reasons to export (advantages) include

- enhance competitiveness,
- increase sales and profits,
- gain global market share,
- reduce dependence on existing markets,
- exploit corporate technology and know-how,
- extend sales potential of existing products,
- stabilize seasonal market fluctuations,
- enhance potential for corporate expansion,
- sell excess production capacity, and
- gain information about foreign competition.

A business may be required to (disadvantages)

- subordinate short-term profits to long-term gains,
- hire staff to launch the export expansion,
- modify products or packaging,
- develop new promotional material,
- incur added administrative costs,
- dedicate personnel for traveling,
- wait longer for payment,
- apply for additional financing, and
- obtain special export licenses.

Source: U.S. Small Business Administration, *Breaking into the Trade Game: A Small Business Guide to Exporting*, Fourth Edition, 2008.

Trade intermediaries serve as contract distributors of products between countries, and have extensive trading networks and contacts. Such intermediaries simplify the exporting process so that the exporter can focus on doing what it does best: making the product. They minimize the costs and risks of entry into global markets. **Exhibit 10-3** identifies several such intermediaries. Another excellent preliminary way to find global market opportunities is to participate in a **trade mission**, an international trip taken by government officials and businesspeople to promote exports or to attract investment. Such a mission might be sponsored by a state government (economic development office), trade group, federal agency, or foreign government. A trade mission will generally require that each participating business pay its own costs, plus a share of the overall mission costs.

trade intermediary organization that serves as a contract distributor of products traded between countries.

trade mission an international trip by government officials and businesspeople organized to promote exports or to attract investment.

U.S. companies that are successful exporters span a multitude of industries and come from across the nation. The Pampered Chef, Ltd., founded in 1980 by Doris Christopher with $3000 borrowed against her husband's life insurance policy, markets in the United States, Canada (1996), the United Kingdom (1999), Germany (2000), and Mexico (2009) through a direct sales force of over 60,000 independent consultants, and serves 12 million customers.[10] The Pampered Chef markets to customers through home parties that include demonstrations of some of the 300 or so high-quality kitchen tools offered in a cooking-show format that is tailored to individual locations.

Numerous small business exporters are recognized by the U.S. Small Business Administration, and in business and trade publications. A sampling

[10]The Pampered Chef, Ltd. Web site, http://www.pamperedchef.com (accessed June 14, 2009).

Exhibit 10-3 *Selected trade intermediaries.*

Confirming house (buying agent)	These companies are agents of foreign firms that are paid a commission to locate U.S. products at the lowest possible price. They may include government agencies or quasi-governmental companies and can be involved in purchasing missions to the United States.
Export agents, merchants, or remarketers	These commissioned sales representatives carry multiple noncompeting product lines for manufacturers in international markets. These agents operate under their own names and maintain their identities. They do not offer all of the services of EMCs (see below), including the financial and advertising support. The export agent is most effective when you are not planning to establish your own export department, are entering a new foreign market, or are introducing a new product. You give up marketing and promotion control of your products and carry the risk that your future sales will be adversely affected.
Export management company (EMC)	It provides global sales expertise and serves as the exclusive export department for noncompeting companies, often in a particular industry or sector. Most operate on buy-and-sell agreements with domestic companies so that small businesses acquire a global presence and international exposure at relatively low cost and with limited resources. EMCs can work as your global marketing department with proven, established access to markets and in-depth knowledge of foreign trade. Expect to pay them on either a commission basis (approximately 15 percent on industrial goods and 10 percent on consumer goods) or via a discount on goods they buy from you.
Export trading company (ETC)	EMCs and ETCs are similar in their capacity to act as your global marketing department to support the export of goods and services. They can take title to the products, as well. Some ETCs are operated by producers, and may include competitors. The U.S. Office of Export Trading Company Affairs (OETCA) in the Department of Commerce promotes the creation and success of export intermediaries and issues them trade certificates of review.
Piggyback Marketing	Rather than entering a foreign market on your own, you may be able to work with another manufacturer or service company that will distribute your product or service. Such a situation can occur when a U.S. company needs to supply a variety of products, and has to secure them from multiple vendors.

Source: "Selected Trade Information" from U.S. Department of Commerce: *A Basic Guide to Exporting,* 1998, prepared by Unz & Co., http://www.unzco.com/basicguide/ (accessed June 13, 2009).

of such recognition is exemplified by the 2009 *Commercial News USA* Exporter of the Year awardees, which are shown in **Exhibit 10-4**.

It is worthwhile to note that exports need not be limited to products or agricultural goods. Exports also include services that can be provided to customers abroad. As shown in **Exhibit 10-5**, the types of services demanded have expanded from the traditional service exports to include types of technical and business expertise.

Exporting may be well supported and present excellent potential for entrepreneurs, but it also has significant challenges and financial costs. Finding the right trading partners, overcoming information, language, cultural, financial, and governmental barriers—and coping with volatile political and economic conditions—require persistence and research. Grasping the complex cost structures to determine profitable pricing means considering a multitude of variables that are unique to international markets. **Exhibit 10-6** identifies a number of exporting costs above and beyond labor and materials. In addition, the requisite product changes and disclosures that involve financial costs and loss of intellectual property advantages may be obstacles to address. The good news is that many small businesses have found success through exporting. According to the SBA, "70% of all U.S. exporters have 20 or fewer employees."[11]

[11]U.S. Small Business Administration Web site, http://www.sba.gov/services/ (accessed June 13, 2009).

Exhibit 10-4 *Exporters of the Year, 2009.*

Industry Category	Company Name	Hometown	Brief Description
Medical/Scientific Products and Equipment	Bio-Med Devices	Guilford, CT	Manufactures and markets critical-care and transportable respirators, ventilators, air-oxygen blenders, monitors, breathing circuits, and accessories.
Environmental	Bio-Microbics, Inc.	Shawnee, KS	Manufactures wastewater and storm-water treatment systems.
Building/Construction Equipment/Hardware	Cemen Tech	Indianola, IA	Manufacturer of columetric concrete equipment.
Commercial Food-service Equipment	Greenfield World Trade, Inc.	Ft. Lauderdale, FL	Supplies equipment and related services, including design consultation, export documentation, warehousing, and parts.
Industrial Equipment Services and Supplies	Industrial Motion, Inc.	Mooresville, NC	Provides spare and replacement machine parts to U.S. companies with manufacturing facilities abroad, from warehouses and offices in Shanghai, Singapore, Delhi, and Chennai.
Consumer Goods	Lifetime Products, Inc.	Clearfield, UT	Design and manufacture of lifestyle products such as outdoor furniture, storage sheds, backyard play systems, and sports equipment.
Electrical/Electronics	Matthews Studio Equipment, Inc.	Burbank, CA	Manufactures hardware and lighting-control devices for the motion picture, television, photographic, and theatrical-production industries.
Agriculture	Meyer Industries	Midvale, ID	Manufactures and markets pest control for residential and commercial use, including the Rodenator.
Business Services	Access USA Shipping d/b/a MyUS.com	Bradenton, FL	International package-forwarding services including parcel receiving, storing, and consolidation.
Health, Beauty, and Fashion	NOW International	Bloomingdale, IL	Serves the natural products industry with dietary supplements.
Franchise	Sign-A-Rama	West Palm Beach, FL	Provides comprehensive sign and graphics services.
Automotive	Treatment Products Ltd.	Chicago, IL	Manufactures and markets automotive appearance products.

Source: Exporter of the Year 2009, from "Twelve Companies Named Exporters of the Year by ThinkGlobal," from *Commercial News USA* (Official Export Promotion Magazine of the U.S. Department of Commerce), February 2009, http://thinkglobal.us/exporteroftheyear/2009/ (accessed June 9, 2009). Used by permission.

Exhibit 10-5 *Service exports.*

Most Common Service Exports	More Recent Service Exports Demanded
Travel	Business, Technical, and Accounting
Transportation	Advertising
Financial	Engineering
Entertainment	Franchising
Health Care	Consulting
Telecommunications	Public Relations
	Testing
	Training

Source: U.S. Small Business Administration, *Breaking into the Trade Game: A Small Business Guide to Exporting*, Fourth Edition, 2008.

Exhibit 10-6 *Exporting costs: above and beyond material and labor.*

Export Packaging	Bunker Surcharge	Bank Collection
Container Loading	Courier Mail	Cargo Insurance
Inland Freight	Tariffs	Telex
Truck/Rail Unloading	Forwarding	Demurrage
Wharfage	Export Documentation	Import Duties
Handling	Consular Legalization	Ocean Freight
Terminal Charges	Bank Documentation	Dispatch

Source: U.S. Small Business Administration, *Breaking into the Trade Game: A Small Business Guide to Exporting*, Fourth Edition, 2008.

You too can succeed as an exporter with excellent planning and superior execution.

Strategic Alliances

Perhaps a strategic alliance involving two or more firms, in which each partner provides a particular set of skills or resources, is the best way for an entrepreneur to reach global markets. Such alliances may be technology-based, production-based, or distribution-based. International strategic alliances involve partners from at least two countries, one of which is a local partner in the targeted geographic location—for example, the various alliances formed by domestic and foreign airlines, such as the Star Alliance, established in 1997 as the first of its kind. With 20 members, including U.S. Airways, Lufthansa, Singapore Airlines, South African Airways, and THAI, Star Alliance permits each to have more efficient in-country transit. By combining the foreign company's language, cultural, sociopolitical, and market knowledge with the capacity and skills of other alliance partners, all companies can reduce their risks and improve their potential rewards. The shared risks and rewards foster greater collaboration and trust than is normally developed in a conventional supplier-customer relationship, thereby creating increased opportunities for success.

Global Impact . . .

Finding Foreign Partners

Large corporations often maintain foreign operations, or have relocated because of lower costs or other market advantages. Changes in technology have made it easier than ever for small companies to benefit from such cost savings, too. UPS, FedEx, and others are all competing for your international shipping business. You can also ship larger products by boat. Ocean freight is slower but much less expensive. The World Wide Web, electronic mail, and teleconferencing have made the world smaller, so that entrepreneurs can find opportunities globally. For example, locating an overseas manufacturing partner could turn your idea into a profitable business.

The following resources can help you find foreign partners:

1. The CIA's *World Factbook* at *http://www.cia.gov/cia/publications/factbook* includes information such as
   - How much the average worker earns per year
   - How much education the citizens have
   - What languages are spoken
2. Locate foreign companies on foreign search engines. Find "International Search Engines," or "[your country of interest] Search Engines," to get connected.
3. Foreign countries have embassies in Washington, D.C., and consulates in the larger cities. They can be good starting points for making international business connections.

International Licensing

When importing and exporting are not viable options, international licensing may create a valuable revenue stream by selling the rights to use patents, copyrights, trademarks, products, processes, or technology. Licensing is a way to secure rights to a product or process that you want to develop and market domestically. Or, on the other hand, you can grant a license (as the licensor) to a foreign company (the licensee) and earn royalties. **Royalties** are fees paid to a licensor by a licensee based upon production or sales of the licensed product. An example of international licensing is Peter Paul Mounds and Almond Joy candies, which are brand names owned by Cadbury Schweppes, a British food and beverage company, and are manufactured and marketed in the United States by Hershey Foods. At the same time, Sunkist (RJR Nabisco) foods are licensed to Morinaga in Japan for distribution there.[12]

royalties fees paid to a licensor by a licensee based upon the production or sales of a licensed product.

If you own intellectual property, proprietary products, specialized technology, or substantial brand recognition, international licensing may be a good fit. There may be greater potential value in licensing technology or intellectual property than in exporting or direct foreign investment, especially when the competitive nature of the international market is unfavorable or unfamiliar. With foreign licensing, market entry is faster, simpler, and less costly. Also, where import quotas or tariffs might make a market too restricted, a license can help to avoid both. Licensing can also reduce transportation costs and avoid restrictive laws and practices.[13] Cosmederm Technologies Inc. (http://www.cosmederm.com), a California company, has secured worldwide patent and trademark protection for its COSMEDERM-7 and Cosmederm products for dermatologists and other skin care industry providers, and is working with British pharmalicensing.com to access foreign markets. According to the licensing Web site, "The rationale for licensing is the enhancement of brand image without having to develop and produce a new product . . . legal protection."[14]

Licensing is a relatively straightforward way to enter global markets, although, as with any contractual relationship, the licensing agreement must be carefully constructed. If licensing requires disclosure of too much proprietary product or competitive information, the licensee may act in bad faith and become a competitor. Another risk is that of the licensee not producing to company standards, or otherwise damaging the brand.

International Franchising

In Chapter 3, it was made clear that international franchising can be an excellent option for those who want to become franchisors or franchisees. For some established franchisors, there are territories that they are making available globally, typically by country or region.

[12]Dennis R. Henderson, Ian M. Sheldon, and Kathleen N. Thomas, "International Licensing of Foods and Beverages Makes Markets Truly Global," *Food Service Review*, September–December 1994.
[13]Ibid.
[14]Web site for pharmalicensing.com, http://www.pharmalicensing.com (accessed June 9, 2009).

This opens up opportunities for franchisees from those regions and countries, as well as for American companies seeking to establish franchise locations outside the United States. Usually, some legal relationship with local owners is required, and the laws vary widely from place to place. International franchising has grown considerably during the past 30 years, to the point where it is a major export industry. As domestic markets become cluttered, with limited room for growth among franchises, international franchising presents an opportunity to increase sales and profits.

International franchises vary with respect to consistency of products and services relative to the United States-based franchisor. Just as there are regional variations on the menus of domestic franchises, products and services may be adapted to suit customers in international markets. Foreign consumers may want to purchase food from McDonald's, but they expect to see traditional American fare along with products specifically created for their palates and in accordance with custom. So, franchisors often offer products and services that are identical with their flagship brand offerings, as well as those tailored to the consumers in a given market.

International Facilities

You may not want to establish a new venture or a franchise in an international location; rather, you may find significant value in creating a facility abroad for an existing business. Whether you establish such a facility to more efficiently and effectively serve customers in a particular geographic area, or to produce goods or components more cost effectively, international facilities can present significant opportunities. For many entrepreneurial ventures, establishing a foreign sales office or a production facility may be frustrating, too expensive, and overly complex. In countries with weak infrastructure or corrupt bureaucracies, the process can be difficult to navigate even with assistance. At the same time, if you plan to enter and grow in the global marketplace, locating a physical office or plant in a target market can be lucrative.

The initial impetus for locating a sales office or plant abroad is often cost savings. This can be because costs in the United States are prohibitive and those in the other country are significantly lower, or because an established international customer base warrants a sales office, distribution center, or production facility close to the customers. Establishing such an operation should be a strategic decision, based upon a realistic assessment of the costs and benefits of locating abroad. It is important to fully understand the business and political environment before moving forward, so that the full potential can be realized.

Challenges to International Trade

Performance Objective 3

Explore the challenges to international trade.

Entering and succeeding in international trade is not without its challenges, but overcoming those challenges can lead to global entrepreneurial success. Recognizing sources of potential difficulties and planning to meet and overcome them is the key to success. Global marketing has inherent risks from external factors, such as the economic and political risk of each foreign location and the world as a whole, as well as internal factors of organizational capacity. Successful global marketers are well informed about trade conditions and geopolitical affairs. They also make the internal preparations required to manage an international customer and/or supplier base.

Economic Risk

When a company begins to trade outside its home country, it assumes **economic risk**, which is the possibility that changes in the economy of the country where it does business will cause financial or other harm. Factors such as the inflation rate, availability of financial resources, and the like, can work in favor of a global company or can work against it.

economic risk the possibility that changes in the economy of a country where it does business will cause financial or other harm.

Prudent global entrepreneurs learn all that they can about the economy of the countries where they intend to do business, and stay current with respect to changes where they are active. They also work with merchants and agents that can help to minimize economic risk, due to their knowledge and experience in the markets. In addition, the U.S. Export-Import Bank (Ex-Im Bank) provides information about the economic and political risk of a given country, and has an export credit insurance program to protect against failure of repayment by foreign customers for political or commercial reasons.

One specific risk facing global entrepreneurs is the exchange rate. The rate of exchange can change favorably or unfavorably for a business transaction in the interval between ordering and payment, sometimes radically altering the profitability of the transaction. For a firm located abroad and operating in terms of the local currency, this can pose particularly serious problems. Imports or exports can insulate themselves from rate changes by trading in U.S. dollars, and by using financing strategies known as currency hedging. By trading in U.S. dollars, the business shifts exchange-rate risk to its trading partner.

Political Risk

As you might expect, there is also **political risk** in global marketing, the possibility of a country's political structure and policies negatively impacting a foreign company transacting business inside its borders. To minimize this risk, it is critical that you carefully assess the political environment of the host country to understand the laws and leadership, particularly if they are undergoing radical change. The relative stability or instability of the government will largely define the political risk. While researching potential trade areas, it is critical to understand the overall sociopolitical environment, as well as the specific laws and regulations pertaining to your business field. Political aspects to evaluate include

political risk the possibility of a country's political structure and policies impacting a foreign company transacting business in its geopolitical borders.

- The attitude of the government toward foreign companies and/or foreign investment, including direct foreign investment. Is it welcome or unwelcome?
- The political structure of the host nation and its stability. Is the current leadership solidly entrenched or is a regime change imminent?
- The anticipated actions/reactions from the host government. How, if at all, will they support, challenge, or prevent your operations?
- Any potential points of conflict, or friction between the planned venture and the national interests of the host country. What are the potential problems?

Examples of political challenges are for a country to ban all exchange of goods with the United States, the prohibition of foreign direct investment, or a government seizure of foreign assets. More subtle, but equally dangerous, are regulations requiring full disclosure of product information that strip away the intellectual property protection enjoyed in the United States that will reveal trade secrets.

Organizational Capacity

Any overseas marketing effort will always be more complex than operating in your home market. It requires a serious commitment of time and effort and can stretch organizational capacity to the limit. International participation, whether through imports, exports, strategic alliances, international licensing or franchising, or direct foreign investment, is complex and requires juggling many simultaneous activities. **Exhibit 10-7** shows specific issues to be considered during the decision to export that may apply to global marketing in general.

Exhibit 10-7 *Management issues in the decision to export.*

Management Objectives

- What are the company's reasons for pursuing export markets? Are they solid objectives (e.g., increasing sales volume or developing a broader, more stable customer base) or are they frivolous (e.g., the owner wants an excuse to travel)?
- How committed is top management to an export effort? Is exporting viewed as a quick fix for a slump in domestic sales? Will the company neglect its export customers if domestic sales pick up?
- What are management's expectations for the export effort? How quickly does management expect export operations to become self-sustaining? What level of return on investment is expected from the export program?

Experience

- With what countries has business already been conducted, or from what countries have inquiries already been received?
- Which product lines are mentioned most often?
- Are any domestic customers buying the product for sale or shipment overseas? If so, to which countries?
- Is the trend of sales and inquiries up or down?
- Who are the main domestic and foreign competitors?
- What general and specific lessons have been learned from past export attempts or experiences?

Management and Personnel

- What in-house international expertise does the firm have (international sales experience, language capabilities, etc.)?
- Who will be responsible for the export department's organization and staff?
- How much senior management time (a) should be allocated and (b) could be allocated?
- What organizational structure is required to ensure that export sales are adequately serviced?
- Who will follow through after the planning is done?

Production Capacity

- How is the present capacity being used?
- Will filling export orders hurt domestic sales?
- What will be the cost of additional production?
- Are there fluctuations in the annual work load? When? Why?
- What minimum-order quantity is required?
- What would be required to design and package products specifically for export?

Financial Capacity

- What amount of capital can be committed to export production and marketing?
- What level of export-department operating costs can be supported?
- How are the initial expenses of export efforts to be allocated?
- What other new domestic development plans are in the works that may compete with export plans?
- By what date must an export effort pay for itself?

Source: "Management Issues in the Decision to Export," from U.S. Department of Commerce: *A Basic Guide to Exporting*, 1998; prepared by Unz & Company, http://unzco.com/basicguide/ (accessed June 13, 2009). Used by permission of Unz and Company.

Effective communication is critical to global marketing success. Communication with customers must be effective, linguistically and culturally. In order to drive such contact, internal teams must communicate well, often across languages and cultures. As a global competitor, you have to be highly responsive to inquiries, so that prospective customers are not lost because of lack of diligence.

Cultural and linguistic dissimilarities between employees of different countries can be a source of inspiration and learning, as well as possible friction and miscues. Flexibility, tolerance, and acceptance become particularly important. Management approaches that are effective in a home market may be ineffective elsewhere, and hiring practices, compensation, hours, holidays, and benefits may be radically different.

In addition to human-capital stresses, financial-capital issues abound. Of particular concern is the financial impact of currency fluctuations and the company's capacity to manage them. Another set of concerns centers on the movement of funds out of foreign countries, and to maintaining adequate cash flows. Organizational capacity may be strained because of financial requirements and constraints.

All areas of a small company will be tested by global expansion, so that the marketing, accounting, operations, and legal spheres are also affected. The marketing aspects—research and analysis, market adaptation, product modification, pricing, distribution channels, and promotion—will all demand attention. International accounting standards and practices vary widely, with any foreign operation needing to comply and integrate with that country's standards and practices. Even for businesses that export or import, addressing currency conversion can be problematic. Operating issues include the ability to understand and interpret international rules and regulations, and to successfully implement production and distribution. Finally, global marketing exponentially increases the legal issues facing the business—including customs, tariffs, and taxes domestically, and intellectual property, local laws and regulations, and trade barriers abroad.

Global marketing may test the limits of any entrepreneurial venture. However, entrepreneurs need not go it alone. There are numerous free and fee-based services to supplement their internal capacity. For many, going global can be a key to success.

Legal and Regulatory Barriers

The number of laws and regulations facing global marketers eclipses that of purely domestic companies, because each country or group of countries has its own unique set of laws and regulations. Barriers to trade include tariffs, quotas, embargoes, and dumping, as well as political and business barriers. Understanding and navigating these obstructions can be a significant challenge for many small companies.

Tariffs

Governments impose **tariffs**, which are taxes or duties on goods and services imported into a country, thereby increasing the cost of the imports. Tariffs are intended as *protectionist* measures, to weaken competition for comparable domestic products and services. The United States imposes tariffs on thousands of goods, and U.S. Immigration and Customs Enforcement is responsible for implementing more than 400 statutes and has personnel in 50 offices overseas.[15] When importing, you will need to include

tariffs taxes or duties on goods and services imported into a country.

[15]United States Immigration and Customs Enforcement Web site, http://www.ice.gove/pi/topics/ (accessed June 14, 2009).

tariffs in your costing calculation. When exploring export markets, remember to account for any tariffs levied by those countries to determine your potential price competitiveness.

Quotas

quotas limits created by countries on the specific amounts of products that can be imported into them.

As an alternative to tariffs, some countries create limits on the amounts of specific products (such as cheese or wine or automobiles) that can be imported. Such limits are called **quotas**, and effectively ration imported goods and thus protect domestic producers from foreign competition. Countries may impose and lift quotas at will, and it is critical for small firms to be mindful of changes.

Embargoes

embargo the total prohibition on imports of all or specific products from one or more nations.

Taken to the extreme, quotas become embargoes. An **embargo** is the total prohibition on imports of all products from a particular nation, or of specific products. Unlike tariffs and quotas, embargoes may have purposes beyond economic ones, such as political, health, environmental, or other motives. Political embargoes are commonly used by the United States government to express dissatisfaction with the political policies of other nations. Health reasons for embargoes may include restricting agricultural imports to prevent the spread of disease. The United States has placed embargoes on all goods from Cuba, Iraq, North Korea, among other countries for political reasons, and has banned imports of certain produce, plants, and animals for health reasons.

Dumping

dumping when companies price products below cost and sell large quantities in foreign markets.

Some companies price products below cost and sell large quantities in foreign markets through a process called **dumping**. Domestic firms can be harmed because their prices are undercut. As a protectionist measure, many countries have enacted antidumping laws. In the United States, such a statute is the U.S. Antidumping Act. Companies may file complaints under this law and must prove that they suffered direct harm, and that the prices being charged in the United States are lower than those in the dumping company's home country.

In addition to the above, countries have various regulations regarding such things as labeling, packaging, and certification. For example, France requires GMO-free certification, warranting that a food product is free from genetically modified ingredients. Ingredient disclosures and nutrition information on foods vary radically from country to country. Product warnings and other information also vary. All of these factors should be researched, assessed, addressed, and taken into account in planning to avoid costly errors.

Cultural and Ethnic Considerations

Much has been written about the importance of understanding the cultural norms in global markets, and adapting to them in order to successfully conduct international trade. The values, perspectives, beliefs, and norms shared by a group of people constitute its *culture*.

What is an acceptable business practice in one country can be considered rude and inappropriate in another. For example, the Japanese have a different sense of personal distance from Americans, such that Americans may feel uncomfortable when Japanese colleagues seem to invade their personal space. By the same token, in many countries, including Japan, business is transacted through personal relationships first, often with the bulk of interaction time spent on seemingly social chatter. In other cultures, the business interaction is a more formal process, with protocols for exchanging business cards, greeting one another appropriately, and only then discussing business.

Business considerations also extend to marketing promotions, quality expectations, and the importance of personal relationships. Marketing approaches that work in the United States may be ineffective or even offensive elsewhere, so that it is important to work with experienced, successful marketers when exporting. Also, your Web site may need to be available in multiple languages and be translated not just literally, but with any necessary idiomatic adjustments. The long-famous case of the Chevrolet Nova being sold in Mexico without a name change is a classic faux pas. *No va* in Spanish means "it doesn't go," which is not a promising name for an automobile. Each culture also has its norms for personal relationships and face-to-face meetings. Whether you can rely upon telephone and electronic media, or will have to meet personally will depend upon the culture. You should be aware of the protocol around hierarchy as well, so that you do not offend a customer or supplier by not having someone they perceive as of at least equal ranking working with them. Finally, quality expectations need to be made clear so that there is no misunderstanding through faulty communications.

Becoming sensitive to cultural norms and being careful to avoid violating them is important to engaging in international markets. A good way to guarantee failure is to ignore cultural customs. A path to success includes understanding and honoring the culture of those with whom you do business.

Support for Global Ventures

Entering the global marketplace is not for the faint of heart, but it also doesn't have to be a solo expedition.

There are a wide variety of resources available to support entrepreneurial ventures with global interests. Services include

- readiness assessment,
- market research, analysis, and planning,
- consulting/counseling,
- training and education programs,
- publications,
- databases,
- trade missions,
- trade shows,
- partner search, and
- financing.

Resources are offered both online and in person through a range of federal, state, and local agencies, as well as trade associations and other not-for-profits, and commercial organizations.

Market Research, Analysis, Planning, and Readiness

Performance Objective 4

Learn about the types of support that are available for global ventures.

As with any business startup or expansion, market analysis, readiness assessment, and planning are critical steps to entering global markets. Of particular concern to small firms preparing to go global is finding the right international markets and creating a marketing plan. There are numerous organizations and agencies that will help with finding existing data on markets, laws, and regulations. Some information sources are listed in **Exhibit 10-8** and others are distributed throughout this chapter.

Before entering a market in any way, you should either rely upon the expertise of the trade intermediary that you have carefully identified and researched, visit the country in question, or both. If you cannot make a personal visit, learn as much as you can from both official and unofficial sources, such as from Americans who currently do business in the country, as well as directly from its citizens. Also, keep up with markets through publications such as *World Trade Magazine* (http://www.worldtrademag.com) and *International Trade Forum* (http://www.tradeforum.org).

Some organizations that assist small businesses also provide readiness-assessment services. These services can help you determine what you need to do to be prepared for global marketing. For example, you may have a product that is viable from a market perspective, but you may need to address packaging and compliance issues before exporting it. By assessing readiness, you can avoid costly mistakes and position your company for international success.

Exhibit 10-8 *Information resources for international trade.*

United States Department of Commerce

- International Trade Administration (ITA): advice and information.
- Export portal (http://www.export.gov): information about federal export programs, services and staff.
- United States and Foreign Commercial Services (US&FCS or the Commercial Service)—trade specialists available through e-mail in 69 cities with Export Assistance centers, and in 70 countries:
    - access through export assistance centers or at http://www.buyusa.gov;
    - specialists organized by industry;
    - information regarding foreign markets, agent/distributor services, and trade leads; and
    - counseling on business opportunities, trade barriers, and overseas prospects.

Small Business Development Centers and SCORE

- Services are supported by the U.S. Small Business Administration (SBDCs) and state, local, and private resources and is affiliated with colleges and universities.
- Counseling, training, and research assistance.
- Programs on international business development.

United States Export Assistance Centers (USEACs)

- Designed as a single point of contact to exporters for federal export promotion and finance programs.
- Readiness-assessment services.
- Referral to how-to-export programs.
- Market-entry programs:
    - Industry and country profiles,
    - Help with finding distributors,
    - Identifying tariffs and regulatory requirements,
    - Assistance with financing, and
    - How to get paid.

District Export Councils (DECs)

- Sponsored by ITA, with 51 councils and 1800 volunteers.
- Volunteers assist small businesses in entering the global marketplace.
- Often found through local Commercial Service or Export Assistance Centers.

Source: U.S. Small Business Administration, *Breaking into the Trade Game: A Small Business Guide to Exporting,* Fourth Edition, 2008.

Customer and Partner Identification and Relationship Building

Once target markets are identified through the market-analysis and planning process, specific leads need to be generated, customer contacts initiated, and customer relationships built. The number of Web sites that are designed to assist in identifying trade leads is large and growing. The Federation of International Trade Associations' list of no-fee (free) sites alone contains 89 listings. A selection of free Web sources from that list appears in **Exhibit 10-9**. These sites offer leads for importers and exporters, with some geared toward specific regions or nations. In addition to the free leads, there are fee-based services that will develop leads for you.

In addition to the lead sources, the various providers of counseling and assistance can offer contacts, and you can pursue your own networking to identify prospective customers and/or partners. As noted previously, trade missions put together by governmental and nongovernmental organizations also provide opportunities for travel to countries of interest, to explore international options. Plus, trade intermediaries can handle much of the initial marketing and communications for you, and will work with their networks of contacts.

Once you establish these relationships, it will need to be a high priority for you to maintain and grow them. It will be much more difficult to sustain a relationship with a firm that is literally halfway around the world than with one that is a mile away. You can work with the advisors and build a network with other global marketers to establish a plan for supporting customer relationships.

Exhibit 10-9 *Selected no-fee international trade-lead Web sites.*

Name of Service	Web Site URL	Description
U.S. Commercial Service e-Market Express	www.buyusa.gov/eme/	Trade leads and international market reports of U.S. exporters in selected industries.
FITA/Alibaba Marketplace	www.fita.alibaba.com	Partnership between FITA and Alibaba.com featuring exporters from China.
Real-Time Taiwan Trade Exchange	www.manufacture.com.tw	Trade lead listings.
WebBusinessDataBank	www.wbdb.net	Web site for posting offers to buy and sell on the Web.
ExportersUS	www.exportersus.com	Trade leads for import and export with the U.S.
Foreign Trade Online	www.foreign-trade.com	Trade leads and other resources.
Importers.com	www.importers.com	Trade-lead listings.
Trade Feeds	www.tradefeeds.com	Aggregator of trade leads from Alibaba.com, Biztee.com, EC21.com, Importers.com, Toboc.com, and 01wholesale.com.
United Nations World Trade Point Federation ETO System	www.tradepoint.org/index.php	Trade leads from the World Trade Point Federation
Global Trade and Technology Network	www.usgtn.net	GTN is a U.S. Agency for International Development (USAID)-sponsored marketplace for the transfer of technology and services.
eMarket Services	www.emarketservices.com	Not-for-profit project funded by the trade promotion organizations of Australia, Denmark, Holland, Iceland, Italy, New Zealand, Norway, Portugal, Spain, and Sweden.

Source: The Federation of International Trade Associations, *Really Useful Links for International Trade*, http://fita.org (accessed June 9, 2009).

Financing

For many small businesses, a significant barrier to global marketing is not being able to access financial resources. The usual sources of business financing, including customer-based, are not available for exporting and other international trade endeavors. However, commercial banks, alone or in cooperation with the U.S. Small Business Administration, as well the Export-Import Bank and trade intermediaries, have financing products available to support global trade. These forms of assistance include letters of credit, export loan programs, and international trade loans.

Letters of Credit

letter of credit a financing instrument that is usually issued by a bank on behalf of its customer that promises to pay a certain amount of money once specific conditions are met.

A commercial **letter of credit** is a financing instrument that is issued by (usually) a bank on behalf of a customer, serves as a promise to pay a certain sum of money once specific conditions are met. It is used for financing the movement of goods internationally. The letter of credit adds the reputation and resources of the financial institution to that of the customer. Letters of credit are only as good as the bank that issues them.

Each letter of credit is customized for the particular circumstances and is valid for a single transaction. Such letters are particularly valuable for exporters because they know that they will be paid, as long as the letter-of-credit terms are met.

A standby letter of credit provides credit from the issuing bank for transactions not involving the movement of goods. Standby letters of credit are irrevocable once issued, making it much like a bank guaranty.

Working Capital Loan Program (EWCP)

The EWCP is a loan-guaranty program offered to commercial banks by the SBA to encourage lending to businesses that generate export sales and need working capital.[16] Banks can make loans of up to $2 million for working-capital purposes to companies exporting goods from the United States, and the SBA will provide a 90-percent guaranty as a credit enhancement, up to $1.5 million it has the same 90-percent guaranty for amounts over $1.5 million through a co-guaranty program with the Export-Import Bank of the United States. Loans are typically made for 12 months and interest rates are set by the lenders. EWCP borrowers must have been in business for a minimum of one year (waivers are possible) and meet SBA eligibility and size requirements. There is not a content requirement for the government, but exports must be shipped and titled from the United States. Shipments to embargoed nations are excluded. Collateral requirements include the receivable generated by the sale and the export-related inventory. EWCP loans can be reissued annually.

Export Express Loan Program

In this SBA guaranty program, lenders use their own credit underwriting and documentation and receive expedited review and response (24 hours or fewer) from the SBA. The program is for loans and lines of credit up to $250,000 that are available for "manufacturers, wholesalers, export trading companies and service exporters."[17] Lenders obtain an 85-percent guaranty for loans of up to $150,000, and loans from $150,000 to $250,000 get a 75-percent guaranty. Interest rates are set by the lenders, as are collateral requirements. Loans are set with differing maturities, depending

[16]U.S. Small Business Administration Web site, http://www.sba.gov (accessed June 13, 2009).
[17]Ibid.

upon their purposes. The SBA Web site's list of permitted export development activities includes

- standby letters of credit,
- foreign trade-show participation,
- translation of marketing materials,
- general lines of credit,
- transaction-specific needs for export orders, and
- real estate, and equipment to produce exports.

Export Express loans come with technical assistance for exporters from the SBA's Export Assistance Centers and other agency resources, such as Small Business Development Centers (SBDCs) and the Service Corps of Retired Executives.

International Trade Loans

The International Trade Loan program from the SBA is for exporters and for companies that have been adversely affected by imports, and is intended to improve the borrower's competitive position. The program operates through SBA lenders and permits a higher SBA-guaranteed portion ($1.75 million versus $1.5 million) than with a regular SBA 7(A) loan. The maximum gross loan amount is $2 million, and the interest rate is determined by the lender. Collateral requirements for SBA International Trade Loans include a first-lien position or first mortgage on the property or equipment being financed, with additional collateral used to reach the full value of the loan, if possible. This loan is designed for financing long-term fixed assets, and working capital cannot be part of the loan. Maturities vary from 10 to 25 years.

Ex-Im Bank's Export Working Capital Program

This program is designed to facilitate exports by providing pre-export financing through commercial lenders with a guarantee from the Export-Import Bank.[18] Exporters must have at least one year of operating history, a positive net worth, and must be located in the United States. The goods to be exported must have a minimum of 50 percent U.S. content and must be shipped from the United States, and any services sold need to be performed by U.S.-based personnel. The Ex-Im Bank normally provides a 90-percent guaranty and has no minimum or maximum amount—but the portion of the contract to be borrowed depends upon the nature of the loan or the collateral offered. Loans are generally for one year but can extend up to three years. According to the Ex-Im Bank Web site, "Exporters may use the guaranteed financing to

- purchase finished products for export;
- pay for raw materials, equipment, supplies, labor and overhead to produce goods and/or provide services for export;
- cover standby letters of credit serving as bid bonds, performance bonds, or payment guarantees; and
- finance foreign receivables."

In addition, the Ex-Im Bank has short-term, multibuyer export-credit insurance, which U.S. exporters that have working capital loans can purchase at a discount.

[18]Export-Import Bank of the United States Web site, http://www.exim.gov (accessed June 14, 2009).

Export Medium-Term Delegated Authority Program

This program provides guarantees to commercial banks for the foreign buyers of U.S. exports, to reduce the risks for U.S. banks and to allow U.S. companies to compete globally. Selected commercial banks can offer 180-day to five-year loans, with guarantees given without prior federal approval as of 2009. These loans are made to foreign purchasers of U.S. capital goods, and the lender shares the risk with the Ex-Im Bank by retaining 10 percent of the risk. Transactions benefitting a small business exporter or supplier require lower commercial bank risk.[19]

Ex-Im Bank's Loan Guarantee

The Loan Guarantee program enhances export capacity by guaranteeing financing to creditworthy international buyers of U.S. exports, and covers 100 percent of political and commercial risks without a limit on transaction size. The financing is primarily intended for the purchase of U.S. capital equipment and services, but can also be available for software and certain other fees and expenses of the business, as detailed by the Ex-Im Bank. The level of Ex-Im Bank support depends upon the value of the goods or the portion of U.S. content, and the buyer must make a 15-percent cash payment to the exporter. Repayment terms are generally 5 to 10 years.

Trade Agreements Influence Global Marketing

Performance Objective 5

Describe regional trade agreements that influence global trade.

Regional Trade Agreements (RTAs) are designed to facilitate trade on a regional basis, generally including tariff cutting and trade regulations between signatory nations.

Many countries and regions have established trade agreements, laws, and tariffs, which affect global trade. As noted previously, tariffs, quotas, and embargoes are various forms of trade barriers erected by individual countries. There are also trade agreements among and between countries that establish the rules of the game. Depending upon where you want to trade, these agreements may have a direct impact on your international efforts. Even if you are not planning to become a global marketer, you may find that these and other agreements will affect your domestic competitive environment.

Regional Trade Agreements (RTAs) focus on removing barriers at the border by reducing tariffs to increase market access between signatory

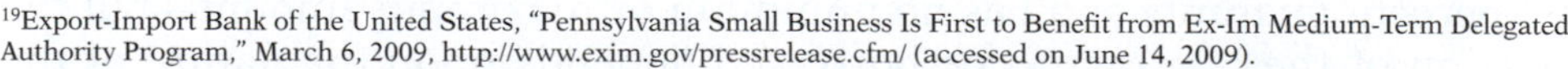

[19]Export-Import Bank of the United States, "Pennsylvania Small Business Is First to Benefit from Ex-Im Medium-Term Delegated Authority Program," March 6, 2009, http://www.exim.gov/pressrelease.cfm/ (accessed on June 14, 2009).

Figure 10-2 *Payment risk diagram.*

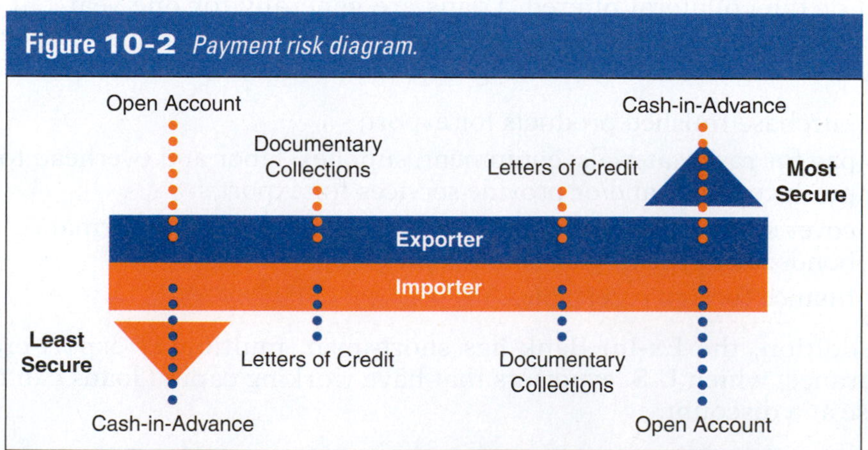

Source: U.S. Department of International Trade Administration, Trade Finance Guide 2008, http://www.export.gov (accessed August 24, 2010).

nations. RTAs are designed to facilitate trade on a regional basis, generally including tariff cutting and often including complex regulations regarding trade between participating countries. Among the more sophisticated RTAs, there are rules on competition, labor, investment, and the environment. A total of almost 400 RTAs are expected to be implemented by 2010, with 90 percent being **Regional Free Trade Agreements (RFTAs)** and partial-scope agreements.[20] RFTAs go a step farther by simplifying commercial regulations and reducing tariffs to zero (or very low levels) to eliminate trade barriers between them, without establishing a common trade policy for nonmembers. According to the World Trade Organization (WTO), "The surge in RTAs has continued unabated since the early 1990s."[21] The WTO provides cautionary comments with respect to RTAs because such agreements are inherently discriminatory, and the ultimate net impact may not be positive. Of particular concern is the membership of countries in multiple RTAs. Some of the most significant RTAs are described below.

Regional Free Trade Agreements (RFTAs)
Regional Trade Agreements that simplify commercial regulations and bring tariffs toward zero for member states.

European Union (EU or EC)

The European Union is a political and economic confederation formed in 1993 that has addressed foreign and security policy, created a central bank, and adopted a common currency (the euro). The member nations of the EU are Austria, Belgium, Bulgaria, Cyprus, Czech Republic, Denmark, Estonia, Finland, France, Germany, Greece, Hungary, Ireland, Italy, Latvia, Lithuania, Luxembourg, Malta, Poland, Portugal, Romania, Slovak Republic, Slovenia, Spain, Sweden, The Netherlands, and the United Kingdom.

European Free Trade Association (EFTA)

The European Free Trade Association was founded in 1960 with its stated premise as "Free trade as a means of achieving growth and prosperity amongst its Member States as well as promoting closer economic cooperation between the Western European Countries."[22] The member states are Iceland, Liechtenstein, Norway, and Switzerland.

North American Free Trade Agreement (NAFTA)

The North American Free Trade Agreement is a trilateral accord established in 1994 to support free trade between Canada, Mexico, and the United States. This agreement created the world's largest free trade area. Much has been written and debated about the positive and negative impacts on labor costs, markets, and the like, and you may find that NAFTA directly or indirectly affects your competitive circumstances and opportunities.

Southern Common Market (Mercosur)

Mercosur is a regional association formed in 1991 between Argentina, Brazil, Paraguay, and Uruguay that permits free transit of goods and services between them, eliminates customs rights and nontariff transit restrictions, and sets a common external tariff and trade policy regarding nonmember states.[23] Mercosur moved from free trade to a common market, which permits the free movement of labor and capital across borders.

[20]World Trade Organization Web site, http://www.wto.org/english/tratop_e/region_e/region_e.htm (accessed June 14, 2009).
[21]Ibid.
[22]European Free Trade Association Web site, http://www.efta.int (accessed June 14, 2009).
[23]Southern Common Market, http://actrav.itcilo.org/actrav-english/telelearn/global (accessed June 15, 2009).

Association of Southeast Asian Nations (ASEAN) Free Trade Area (AFTA)

The establishment of the AFTA was almost complete in 2009, with member countries progressing in lowering intra-regional tariffs in accordance with the Common Effective Preferential Tariff (CEPT).[24] Most tariffs on CEPT products have been lowered to 0 to 5 percent, and the members have agreed to work on nontariff barriers. The member states are Brunei, Darussalam, Cambodia, Indonesia, Laos, Malaysia, Myanmar, the Philippines, Singapore, Thailand, and Vietnam.

Common Market of Eastern and Southern Africa (COMESA)

This defines its role as "promoting regional economic integration through trade and investment."[25] COMESA's mission is to "Endeavor to achieve sustainable economic and social progress in all member states through increased cooperation and integration in all fields of development particularly in trade, customs and monetary affairs, transport, communication and information technology, industry and energy, gender, agriculture, environment and natural resources."[26] The formation of a free trade area through the removal of tariff and nontariff barriers, including coordination of trade statistics, customs procedures, and management systems was COMESA's first goal. A free trade area was established with 14 members. Formation of a Customs Union with a common external tariff was anticipated for 2009. A full monetary union with a common currency and central bank is the next priority. The member states of COMESA are Burundi, Comoros, Democratic Republic of the Congo, Djibouti, Egypt, Eritrea, Ethiopia, Kenya, Libya, Madagascar, Malawi, Mauritius, Rwanda, Seychelles, Sudan, Swaziland, Uganda, Zambia, and Zimbabwe.

One topic in particular to analyze when considering global marketing is whether any U.S. trade agreement provides you with a competitive advantage, or whether any country with which you want to trade is a member of an RTA. The Office of the U.S. Trade Representative, in the Executive Office of the President, has an online resource center (http://www.ustr.gov/countries-regions/) that provides information on RTAs, including primary imports and exports and RFTA status. This analysis could dramatically alter your cost structure and present a greater opportunity for global marketing success.

[24]Association of Southeast Asian Nations Web site, http://www.asean.org (accessed June 14, 2009).
[25]Common Market of Eastern and Southern Africa Web site at http://www.comesa.int (accessed June 14, 2009).
[26]Ibid.

BizFacts

Duties are assessed under many agreements, including

- North American Free Trade Agreement (NAFTA),
- Generalized System of Preferences (GSP),
- Caribbean Basin Initiative (CBI),
- Andean Trade Preference Act (ATPA),
- U.S.–Israel Free Trade Area Agreement,
- U.S.–Jordan Free Trade Area Agreement,
- Compact of the Free Association (FAS),
- African Growth and Opportunity Act (AGOA), and
- U.S. Caribbean Basin Trade Partnership Act (CBTPA).

Chapter Summary

Now that you have studied this chapter you can do the following:

1. Understand the reasons to market globally.
   - Expanding market opportunities.
   - Acquiring access to resources that are scarce or more competitive.
   - Reducing materials, labor, and other costs.
   - Taking advantage of resources specific to a location.
2. Articulate the primary strategic options for global ventures.
   - Importing goods and services to the home market.
   - Exporting goods and services to global markets.
   - Creating and managing strategic alliances with global partners to improve performance.
   - Licensing products and processes to attain the maximum benefits of intellectual property.
   - Franchising on an international scale to increase business opportunities and enter new, profitable markets.
   - Operating international facilities to supply regional customers or provide parts or inventory to other operations.
3. Recognize the factors that challenge and impede global marketing.
   - Economic risk threatens financial stability and success.
   - Political risk poses threats to global ventures as regime changes, changes in laws, and cultural norms may have profound negative impact.
   - Organizational capacity for global marketing, in the form of human and financial capital, may limit success.
4. Explain the types of support available to global firms.
   - Assistance with market analysis and planning is offered to provide advantages in the global economy.
   - Customer relationship building is fostered through networks of support services.
   - Financing for exporting can be obtained through credit guarantees.
5. Describe regional trade agreements that influence global trade.
   - Regional Trade Agreements and Regional Free Trade Agreements are designed to facilitate trade between signatory nations.
   - The United States has agreements with many nations that facilitate trade.

Key Terms

dumping
economic risk
embargo
exporting
importing
international outsourcing
letter of credit
offshoring
political risk
quotas
Regional Free Trade Agreements (RFTAs)
Regional Trade Agreements (RTAs)
royalties
tariffs
trade intermediary
trade mission

Entrepreneurship Portfolio

Critical Thinking Exercises

1. How do trade agreements affect trade barriers? What can this mean to small business?
2. Why are cultural competency and sensitivity important for participants in the global marketplace?
3. How can emerging markets provide opportunities for entrepreneurial ventures?
4. What contributions can trade intermediaries make for small firms?

Key Concept Questions

1. Describe the four principal drivers of global business participation for small business.
2. What are the basic challenges facing global companies? How can small business address them?
3. What types of support are available to entrepreneurial ventures for global expansion?

Application Exercise

Identify two ways that globalization may affect your business or a business with which you are familiar. What are the positive and negative aspects of each?

Exploring Online

1. At the U.S. Department of Commerce's export Web site (http://www.export.gov), find the Trade Events category and click on it. Using the menus and search tool, find trade missions and trade events in biotechnology or hotel/restaurant equipment that are scheduled over the next 12 months. Select one trade event and note its location and date. Indicate the price for registration and any special requirements. How would you decide whether this is a worthwhile event for a company?
2. Visit the *World Fact Book* (http://www.cia.gov/cia/publications/factbook) and find a profile of one of the Top 10 Emerging Markets. Identify two products or services to import from that country, or to export to it, and answer the following:
   a. Why would these products or services be suited to this country?
   b. What steps would you take to import or export them?
   c. What sources of support might you access? Why?
   d. What challenges would you expect to encounter?

Case Study | Luggage Concierge

Every year, millions of bags are mishandled by U.S. airline companies. Luggage Concierge alleviates this problem by shipping luggage to and/or from customers' travel destinations. Customers benefit from faster and easier airport check-ins, fewer worries about late or lost luggage, and the freedom from hauling their bags around. This is especially helpful when traveling with odd-shaped or oversized luggage, such as skis and golf bags.

Luggage Concierge's shipping service is initiated by visiting their Web site or calling their toll-free telephone number. The customer provides the addresses where the luggage is to be picked up and where it is going. The number of pieces, as well as their sizes and shapes, are also given. This information, the type of service (one-way or round trip), and the delivery speed determines the price.

Next, Luggage Concierge sends the customer a Welcome Packet with instructions and shipping labels. One of the company's Luggage Coordinators schedules pick-up times for the luggage and tracks the shipment to ensure proper arrival and return. To add to customers' peace of mind, complimentary insurance covering each bag's contents is included in the price.

Luggage Concierge has many strategic business partners, including credit card companies (such as MasterCard and American Express), resorts and hotels (such as Caesars Palace and Marston Hotels), cruise and travel businesses (such as Crystal Cruises and CouTour Travel), shipping companies (such as UPS and DHL), and more. For example, as part of the alliance with Crystal Cruises, Luggage Concierge provides a dedicated, 24/7 telephone line for passengers. Crystal's repeat customers also get a 20% discount on luggage shipments to and from the cruise ships.

When they made an alliance with UPS International in 2009, Luggage Concierge was able to expand their shipping services to 220 worldwide destinations, more than any of its competitors. The "Wheels Up Customs Clearance" that this partnership provides allows Luggage Concierge's customers to have their luggage delivered to most countries within eight business days. Customers can also know where their luggage is at all times, thanks to real-time tracking capability.

Case Study Analysis

1. What reason to market globally (as noted in the chapter) does the Luggage Concierge and UPS alliance serve? Explain.

2. Luggage Concierge has created a number of strategic alliances with domestic and global partners.
   a. What is the rationale for Luggage Concierge's decision to create alliances rather than expanding on its own?
   b. Identify three of these partnerships and the value of global alliance for each party.
3. How do customers benefit from the alliance between UPS International and Luggage Concierge?
4. What are some of the challenges that Luggage Concierge would have likely faced in becoming a global marketer that UPS can handle for them?

Case Sources

Associated Content Web site article, "Luggage Shipping Companies Allow Travelers to Fly Light," http://www.associatedcontent.com/article/333035/luggage_shipping_companies_allow_travelers_pg2_pg2.html?cat=3.

Cruise Diva Web site article, "Cruise Travel: Take the LUG Out of Luggage," http://cruisediva.blogspot.com/2007/10/cruise-travel-take-lug-out-of-luggage.html.

Luggage Concierge Web site, http://www.luggageconcierge.com.

Thomson Reuters Web site article, "Luggage Concierge Announces Alliance with UPS International," http://www.reuters.com/article/pressRelease/idUS164378+18-May-2009+BW20090518.

Case Study | Lourdes "Chingling" Tanco, MIDA Trade Ventures, Inc.

A Global Seafood Legacy

Chingling Tanco has traveled the world to bring success to her companies, MIDA Trade Ventures, Inc. and MIDA Food Distributors, Inc. Started in the Philippines, these sister companies are in the seafood trade business. MIDA Trade acts as the buying agent, whereas MIDA Food focuses on the distribution of frozen seafood at home and abroad.

MIDA Trade was the first company to export seafood from Indonesia to the United States. The strong, international business network that Chingling and her team have built over the past 20 years helps to keep MIDA at the top of its industry. Many market segments are served, including restaurants, cafeterias, hotels, resorts, and even private households.

MIDA has offices across Southeast Asia in the Philippines, Indonesia, Vietnam, and Singapore. As many as 200 different kinds of seafood are stocked by MIDA Food, including a wide variety of fish, mollusks (clams, oysters, mussels, and scallops), crustaceans (shrimp, lobsters, and crabs), and cephalopods (squid, cuttlefish, and octopus).

MIDA Food also distributes value-added products in which the seafood has been prepared in some manner. For example, items include portioned entrees and appetizers, which are created in marinated, breaded, smoked, and sauced versions. In addition, MIDA has a division for canned seafood.

MIDA distributes seafood internationally.

In the Beginning

Before she became an entrepreneur, Chingling earned an economics degree from Bryn Mawr College in Pennsylvania. After graduating, she worked for a business that traded feed and fertilizers in the United States and Asia. When the company was bought by ConAgra Foods in 1985, Chingling became involved in shrimp trading. At that time, ConAgra owned Singleton Seafood, the largest shrimp processor in the United States. The following year, ConAgra sent Chingling to Indonesia to manage a joint-venture trading company.

In 1990, Chingling was reassigned to the Philippines. Very soon afterward, she decided to create her own company. MIDA Trade Ventures was born to be a global buyer for ConAgra and Singleton Seafood. MIDA continued to grow, adding new clients in the United States as well as in Europe, Australia, and northern Asia.

In the late 1990s, an economic crisis caused seafood prices in the Philippines to skyrocket. Seafood stock was also becoming harder to find in the Philippines. Chingling found a way to turn those problems into an opportunity, by importing tuna from Indonesia and selling it directly to Filipino restaurants. The initial cargo sold fast, and MIDA Trade made a profit. As a result, Chingling launched MIDA Food Distributors in 1997, with its own trucks and cold-storage. MIDA Food was soon distributing frozen seafood to more than 1000 local hotels and restaurants.

Today, MIDA Trade and MIDA Food continue to work as a successful team, supplying seafood to both local and international markets. Chingling's vision enabled her to turn her background knowledge and experience into an entrepreneurial success story.

Keys to Global Success

The MIDA companies pride themselves as seafood specialists. With Chingling's leadership, the following strategies have helped create and maintain a thriving business:

Hire the right people for the job, and train them well. MIDA employs a multicultural group of people with degrees in many areas, including economics, custom brokerage, microbiology, industrial engineering, fisheries, food technology, and more.

MIDA also provides on-the-job training and continuing education to ensure its employees excel at their jobs. MIDA Food's staff have been certified by the Aquaculture Certification Council. The term "aquaculture" refers to the cultivation or farming of marine and fresh-water animals and plants.

Know your customers/markets. MIDA recognizes that knowing its clients means understanding their laws and cultures, as well as their product needs and expectations. MIDA staff travel extensively to develop and maintain customer relationships. This includes attending international trade shows and conferences to stay on top of market trends. MIDA is also a member of multiple professional seafood associations, and it subscribes to many seafood-related publications.

Provide high-quality products, consistently. Supplier assessment and quality control are two main areas to which MIDA pays a lot of attention. For example, MIDA buys only from seafood producers who can provide high-quality products in adequate volumes, maintain strict food-safety standards, and use ethical practices. A seller's financial stability and ability to provide products in a timely and efficient manner are also important. MIDA freezes fresh seafood only in plants, which are certified to export to the United States, Japan, and Europe. Deliveries are made promptly, and products must be kept at a specific temperature.

Be actively responsible. MIDA regularly inspects processing plants to assess how well its suppliers are complying with environmental and social responsibilities. Environmental issues include proper water disposal, mangrove destruction/replanting, and practicing sustainable aquaculture practices. Social responsibilities include preventing child labor and meeting minimum wage standards. In addition, Chingling serves on the Fisheries and Aquaculture Board of the Philippines.

Provide excellent service, from beginning to end. MIDA's customer service starts with supplier negotiations in an effort to obtain the best prices and highest-quality products for their clients. MIDA also handles all logistical issues. This means monitoring customer deadlines, taking care of all contractual and shipment paperwork, following various countries' packaging and labeling requirements, using only reputable shipping companies, and overseeing the loading of all cargo. Customer service is concluded by confirming that the cargo has been received and making sure the customer is happy.

Case Study Analysis

1. How has Chingling used her education and prior work experience to support the success of MIDA?
2. MIDA is based in the Philippines, a country that is a member of a Regional Trade Agreement (RTA). Which RTA is it? How might this affect the business dealings of the company?
3. What are MIDA's marketing advantages?
4. If a MIDA customer in the United States wished to export North Atlantic Salmon to the Philippines through MIDA, what sort of financing option might be of value for the transaction?
5. MIDA has a commitment to ensure that international sanitation standards are followed and the processing plants comply with environmental and social responsibility issues. How is this accomplished and what issues are specified?

Case Sources

MIDA Food Distributors, Inc. Web site, http://www.midafood.com (accessed August 24, 2010).

MIDA Trade Ventures, Inc. Web site, http://www.midatrade.com (accessed August 24, 2010).

Singleton Seafood Web site, http://www.singletonseafood.com/History/history.html (accessed August 24, 2010).

Courtesy of Mida Trade Ventures.

Chapter 11

SMART SELLING AND EFFECTIVE CUSTOMER SERVICE

"The secret of success is to have a self-seller, and if you do not have one, get one."

—William C. (Billy) Durant, founder of General Motors

From 1878 to 1886, in Flint, Michigan, William Durant, invariably called "Billy," started a variety of entrepreneurial ventures in the fields of insurance, real estate, and construction. None of them took off. He had yet to find his self-seller. When he was 25, however, Durant hitched a ride to work and noticed that his friend's new horse-drawn buggy rode more smoothly than any other he had been in. The friend explained that the buggy had a new kind of spring. Durant was so impressed that he decided he wanted to own the company that made it.

Durant learned that the buggies were made by the Coldwater Road Cart Company. The very next day, Durant went to the owner and made a deal to buy the business for $1500 and insisted that the sale include the patent for the springs. The transaction was completed in two days. This first of many deals exemplified Durant's business philosophy: "Decide quickly, make your pitch, nail down the details, and do not worry about the money."

Durant was serious about the money aspect. When he closed the deal on Coldwater, he did not have the $1500, but he did not let that deter him. He borrowed $2000 from his local bank and had two sample buggy carts made from the leftover $500. He rode one to a county fair in Madison, Wisconsin. The cart sold itself, and within a week he had orders for 600 of these vehicles. By 1893, his original $2000 investment had grown to $150,000. By 1901, his company was the largest buggy manufacturer in the country. Then Durant turned his attention to the fledgling automobile industry. In 1904, he took over the Buick Motor Company, which eventually became General Motors.

Performance Objectives

1. Explain the importance of selling based upon benefits.
2. Use the principles of selling to make effective sales calls.
3. Know how to make a successful sales call.
4. Analyze and improve your sales calls.
5. Provide excellent customer service.
6. Define customer-relationship management and understand its value.

Selling Skills Are Essential to Business Success

Personal selling is dealing with a potential customer face to face and trying to convince him or her to make a purchase. Salespeople often become successful entrepreneurs because they learn to listen to what the customer needs and wants on a daily and personal basis.

Some great American entrepreneurs (in addition to Durant) who started out in sales are

- Ray Kroc, founder of McDonald's, as we saw in Chapter 1, was selling milkshake machines when he was inspired to turn the McDonald brothers' hamburger restaurant into a national operation.
- Aristotle Onassis was a wholesale tobacco salesman before becoming a multimillionaire in the shipping business.

- King C. Gillette was a traveling salesman when he invented the safety razor.
- W. Clement Stone started out selling newspapers at the age of six before going on to build a great fortune in the insurance industry.
- Mary Kay Ash was in direct sales for 25 years before she cofounded Mary Kay Cosmetics with her son.

Selling Is a Great Source of Market Research

If a customer is dissatisfied, it is often the salesperson who hears the complaint. In that sense, selling is a constant source of valuable market research. Depending upon the business you start, when you start it, you will probably not be able to hire a sales staff. You will be the sales staff.

Even if you have never sold any product in your life, you can develop into a fantastic salesperson. In fact, you already have a lot of practice selling. Everyone tries to persuade (sell) others to agree to something or to act a certain way. Being face to face with customers and trying to sell your product may make you uncomfortable. But if you think of rejections as learning experiences and opportunities for continuous market analysis, you will look forward to sales encounters throughout your entrepreneurial career.

The Essence of Selling Is Teaching

The creative art of selling is teaching the customer how the features are benefits. Inexperienced salespeople make a common mistake: they think telling the customer about the features of a product will sell it. But remember, a customer who buys a drill does not need a drill; the customer needs to make a hole.

The essence of selling is teaching how and why the outstanding features of your product or service will benefit your customers. Durant succeeded by showing that a new type of spring (feature) made riding in his buggy carts more comfortable (benefit).

The Principles of Selling

Performance Objective 1

Explain the importance of selling based upon benefits.

Every entrepreneur has to be able to identify the benefits his or her product can provide, and make an effective sales call. Entrepreneurs sell constantly, not just to customers but to potential investors, bankers, and people they want to hire. Commit the following selling principles to memory

BizFacts

Many salespeople earn a *commission*, a percentage paid on each sale. A salesperson making a 10 percent commission selling cars, for example, would earn $1000 after selling a $10,000 car.

$$.10 \times \$10{,}000 = \$1000$$

Entrepreneurs can use commissions to motivate sales staff. When you are starting out and cannot afford to pay sales representatives full-time salaries, you can offer commissions instead, because they get paid as you get paid and earn more as they sell more.

and you will be on your way to becoming a successful salesperson. These principles apply to any product or service:

Make a Good Personal Impression

When selling your product or service, prepare yourself physically. A salesperson must be clean and well dressed; it is important to dress appropriately for your customer base. If you are selling oil to gas station owners, do not wear $800 suits—but dress professionally. Some suggest that, for sales calls, your business card should not identify you as president or owner, so your prospects can talk with you more easily. This would depend upon who you are meeting, so use common sense.

Performance Objective 2
Use the principles of selling to make effective sales calls.

Know Your Product or Service

Understand its features and the benefits they can create. It is your chance to teach the customer about the product or service. Explain the benefits without overselling. Do not try to share everything you know, however, as that is likely to be too much information. You don't want to alienate or bore the customer.

Believe in Your Product or Service

Good salespeople believe in what they are selling and feel good about selling it. If, during this stage, you begin to feel that your product or service does not measure up to your personal standards, reconsider selling it. Your business will fail if you do not believe it is of the quality and value that you promise. Always be on the lookout for ways to improve your product, or develop a better one.

Know Your Field

Invest in understanding the industry and your competition. Read the trade literature. Learn about your competitors. Buy their products or try their services and compare them with yours. If possible, experience a call from one of your competitor's salespeople. This could be a gold mine of information. Study the strengths and weaknesses of your competitor's product or service; your sales prospects may inquire about them during your own calls and you should be prepared.

Know Your Customers

Be thorough in your customer analysis. What are their needs? How does your product or service address them? Understand what makes them tick. Use resources such as the Internet to get publicly available background information, and access any other resources that you can.

Prepare Your Sales Presentation

Know ahead of time how you want to present your product or service. Identify the key points you believe are important to this particular customer. Jot them down on a note card. Study it. Put it away. Practice the sales call. Role play. Know how to overcome objections.

Think Positively

This will help you deal with rejections you may experience—before you make your first sale. Many people do not realize how mentally strong you have to be to conduct sales calls. One entrepreneur went on 400 calls for his import-export firm before he closed a sale of more than $1000. But this experience made him a much better salesperson.

Keep Good Records

Have your record-keeping system, including invoices and receipts, set up before you go on your first sales call. Use a database system to keep records of your sales calls, and to remind you of appropriate follow-up actions. This will be the start of your customer-relationship management process.

Make No Truly Cold Calls

Unless you are doing door-to-door sales, or retail sales, your prospect meetings should be "warm" calls. You can send an introductory letter, e-mail, or postcard so that the customer will know why you want to make the call. Or, better yet, try to get a personal introduction, or referral, so that the prospect feels more comfortable with you from the start.

Make an Appointment

People will be more likely to listen when they have set aside time to speak with you, whether by phone or in person. They will be less than receptive if you interrupt their day unannounced.

Treat Everyone You Sell to Like Gold

Joe Girard is a car salesman who has been dubbed "The World's Greatest Salesman" 12 times by *The Guinness Book of Records.* In his book, *How to Sell Anything to Anybody,* Girard states his Law of 250 as follows: "Everyone knows 250 people in his or her life important enough to invite to the wedding and to the funeral." He goes on to explain, "This means that if I see 50 people in a week, and only two of them are unhappy with the way I treat them, at the end of the year there will be about 5,000 people influenced by just those two a week."[1] Obviously, if each person you sell to influences 250 others, you cannot afford to alienate even one sales prospect! (However, this does not mean that you keep trying to sell beyond rejection.)

The Sales Call

A sales call is an appointment with a potential customer to explain or demonstrate your product or service. During the sales call, you will want to do the following:

- make the customer aware of your product or service,
- make the customer want to buy that product or service, and
- make the customer want to buy it from *you.*

Electronic Mail, Blogs, and Newsgroups

Performance Objective 3

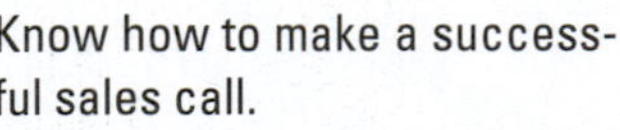

Know how to make a successful sales call.

In today's technology-savvy environment, there are multiple methods for communicating with sales prospects. Among these options are electronic mail, newsgroups, and blogs. Which, if any, is best-suited to your business

[1]Joe Girard, *How to Sell Anything to Anybody* (New York: Warner Books, 1986), p. 48.

will require careful consideration on your part. Electronic mail (e-mail for short) is defined as correspondence sent via the Internet. **Newsgroups** are online discussion groups focused on specific subjects. In addition, social networking services such as Facebook, MySpace, and Twitter afford means of frequent communications.

newsgroup an online discussion group focused on specific topics or interests.

Sending e-mail or posting messages on newsgroups or blogs can help contact sales prospects and keep in touch with customers you already have, but you must use these methods carefully. In the physical world, you can look for sales prospects by distributing flyers or by calling people from a list. Using e-mail or newsgroups in a similar fashion can result in your e-mail box being jammed with "flames"—or hate mail. Most newsgroups do not appreciate receiving unwanted advertisements, called **spam**, and members may respond angrily.

spam unwanted Internet advertisements or e-mails.

If done correctly, becoming involved in a newsgroup or social network can lead to qualified prospects. Let's say you sell photographic supplies and you hear about an interesting newsgroup for photographers. Do not blitz it with ads. Instead, before posting any messages, **lurk** for awhile, meaning that you just read messages and get a feel for the discussions taking place without participating. Once you are comfortable, try posting a message. For example, see the text in **Exhibit 11-1**. Because this is not a sales pitch, no one in the newsgroup should take offense, and your message may attract potential sales prospects to your Web site.

lurk reading messages and getting a feel for discussions on a Web site, newsgroup, or the like without participating in the online conversation.

Prequalify Your Sales Calls

Before calling to make an appointment for any sales call, identify and list your **prospects**, the people/organizations that may be receptive to your sales pitch. Include everyone you can imagine, but then go through it carefully and ask:

prospect a person or organization that may be receptive to a sales pitch.

- Is this individual in my market?
- Does he/she need my product?
- Will my product/service remove a problem or source of "pain," or improve the individual's life?
- Can he/she afford it?

If the answer to any of these questions is "no," making a sales call on that person will probably be a waste of time for both of you. People spend money to buy things they want or need. If your product or service helps, that is great. If not, do not hesitate to move on to consider the next

Exhibit 11-1 *Message to a newsgroup.*

This week's discussion on the advantages of the new Nikon mini-camera was very interesting. I'm in the photography-supply business and am looking for interesting items to add to my Web site. I have already posted articles from Advanced Photography magazine and tips from some of my clients. Does anyone have any other ideas for useful information that I could post? Thanks!

Sandra Bowling
PhotoSupply Online
http://www.photosupply.com
E-mail: photosupply@AOL.com
The Photographer's Source for Supplies and Advice

prospect (sometimes called a "suspect" until the call is qualified). Asking such questions is called *prequalifying* a sales call. Invest the time it takes to get your prospect list organized and analyzed. Abe Lincoln's famous saying applies here, "If I had ten hours to chop down a tree, I'd spend nine sharpening my axe." Remember, you can purchase or develop lists of potential customers and conduct research.

Focus on the Customer

During each call, focus on one thought: What does the customer need? Visualize your product or service fulfilling that need. If you believe in your product or service, and there is a good fit, you will be able to see this without any problem. In general, focusing on listening to the potential customer will help you overcome self-consciousness. If you actively listen and probe, the customer will tell you what is personally important, either directly or indirectly. A feature that creates a benefit in your mind may be meaningless to one prospect but extremely important to another. Pay attention.

Mental visualization will help you perform better when you are in the actual situation. Practice the sales call in your mind, visualizing how you want it to go, but be prepared to deviate from that vision. Visualization will enlist your subconscious mind in the sales process, instinctively providing you with subtle verbal and body-language cues that can convince a customer to buy from you. You will be better prepared and more comfortable in your role.

The Eight-Step Sales Call

Whereas each sales call will be as different as the people involved in it, there are eight steps to follow to make them more successful.

1. ***Preparation.*** Prepare yourself mentally and through organization. Think about how the product/service will benefit this specific customer. Have the price, discounts, all technical information, and any other details "on the tip of your tongue," or at your fingertips. Be willing to obtain further information if your customer should request it. Visualize the sales call in your mind until it goes smoothly and successfully. Jot down a few key probing questions and points you think will help. Bring the appropriate materials, samples, and data with you.
2. ***Greeting.*** Greet the customer politely and graciously. Do not plunge immediately into business talk, unless you know from prior experience or your network of contacts that your customer prefers to do so. Take the time to know the prospect's style and be sensitive to it. The first few words you say may be the most important. Keep a two-way conversation going. Maintain eye contact, and keep the customer's attention. Remember that the customer is first and foremost a human being with whom you can make a connection. The more you can learn about his/her family, hobbies, interests—anything to help develop a genuine relationship—the better your chances of eventually securing a sale. However, avoid being perceived as nosy or overly personal—by remaining genuine. The best salespeople keep records on their customers with all sorts of information, to remind them of details for future conversations and to follow up over time. Sales may depend upon the characteristics and benefits of the product or service, but customers buy from people they know and like when they have a choice. They usually have a choice.

3. ***Showing the Product/Service.*** Personalize your product or service by pointing out the benefits for this particular customer. Use props and models (or the real thing) where appropriate. If possible, demonstrate the product or service to showcase its unique selling proposition in a way that will be meaningful for this customer.
4. ***Listen to the Customer.*** Begin with the customer's needs in mind and be wary of making assumptions about these needs. If you listen actively and probe carefully, you can learn the challenges he or she is facing and tailor you sales pitch according. After you pitch your product or service once, sit back and let the customer talk about it. This is how you will get your most valuable information. Neil Rackham, the author of *SPIN Selling,* had his consulting firm, Huthwaite, analyze more than 35,000 sales. He discovered that in successful calls it was the buyer who did most of the talking.[2]
5. ***Dealing with Objections.*** The best, most effective way to deal with objections is to prevent them from being raised. Address the known objections in a positive light before the customer raises them. During the listening phase, you will hear other objections to your product or service. Always acknowledge objections and handle them. Do not pretend you did not hear, overreact, or be afraid to listen. A famous real estate entrepreneur, William Zeckendorf, said, "I never lost money on a sales pitch when I listened to the customer." Do not hesitate to tell the absolute truth about any negative aspect of your product or service. Each time you admit a negative, you gain credibility in the customer's mind. However, be careful to not overemphasize a flaw or complain about the product or service.
6. ***Closing the Sale.*** Review the benefits of your product or service. If negatives have come up, point out that, at this price, the product or service is still an excellent buy. Narrow the choices the customer has to make. Close the sale, if it is time to do so. Do not overstay your welcome. Stop while you are ahead. An important rule of thumb: If a customer says no three times, you still have a chance. If he/she says it the fourth time, it really means no. If the answer *is* no, take it gracefully. Remember that the sales cycle for your product or service is a critical factor here. Some sales take months or even years to close. A "no" today is not necessarily a "no" forever. You will learn to tell the difference.
7. ***Follow-up.*** Make regular follow-up calls to find out how the customer liked the product or service. Ask if you can be of any further help. If the customer has a complaint, do not ignore it. Keeping the customer's trust after the sale is the most important part of the whole process.

   A successful business is built on repeat customers. Plus, every time you talk to a customer you are deepening your friendship. Your best sales prospects in the future are people who have already bought something from you. Keep them posted on the progress of your business by sending postcards or flyers.
8. ***Ask for References.*** Ask your customers to refer you to other potential customers. Try to set up a system that encourages others to send sales prospects your way. Offer discounts, gift certificates, or other incentives to those who refer people to you, for example. Give customers a few business cards to pass on to their friends.

[2]Neil Rackham, *SPIN Selling* (New York: McGraw-Hill, 1996).

Three Call Behaviors of Successful Salespeople

Neil Rackham, during his research, discovered that successful salespeople exhibit certain "sales-call behaviors."[3] He concluded that there are three steps that lead to more sales:

1. ***Let the customer talk more than you do.*** According to *SPIN Selling,* "The more your customer talks, the more you will learn about their needs, which puts you in a better position to offer them the most customized and most helpful solutions." Encourage your customers to talk to you about their situations and problems. As they talk, they will begin to understand their own needs better and realize the importance of solving the problem.
2. ***Ask the right questions.*** How do you get customers to talk to you? Rackham notes that you have to ask the right questions. If your sales calls are leaving you with little information and few sales, you are not asking the questions that uncover your customers' needs. Again, instead of focusing on selling your product, focus on listening to your customer. Try to draw him or her out. Be an active listener. You need to correctly understand the problem *before* suggesting that your product or service provides a solution.
3. ***Wait to offer products and solutions until later in the call.*** First, let your customer talk. Second, once you have the customer talking, ask the right questions to help uncover the problem. Now you are ready to offer your product or service as a solution to this problem. As Rackham writes, "You cannot know what solution to offer if you do not uncover customer needs and decision criteria first. For example, if you spend your time with the customer talking about how quiet your machine is, and noise is not a factor your customer cares about, you've wasted your time (and theirs)."[4] You cannot offer a valuable solution until you know what problem the customer needs to solve.

Analyze Your Sales Calls to Become a Star Salesperson

Every sales call is an opportunity to improve your selling skills—even if you did not make a sale. The star salesperson analyzes each call by asking

- Was I able to get the customer to open up to me? Why, or why not?
- Did I do or say anything that turned the customer off, or was offensive, or caused him/her to disbelieve me?
- Which of my questions did the best job of helping the customer focus on his/her challenges? How can I ask better questions?
- Was I able to make an honest case for my product/service being the one that could solve the customer's problem?
- Did I improve my relationship with this person during the call?

Rackham's research shows that, unless you analyze your selling at this level of detail, you will miss important opportunities for learning and improving your selling skills.

Turning Objections into Advantages

Performance Objective 4

Analyze and improve your sales calls.

Getting the customer to open up may lead to your being told things you may not want to hear about your product or service. These objections, however, can be valuable sources of marketing data. Sales expert Brian Tracy recommends writing down the objections and comments that customers make about your product. He believes that all objections fall into

[3] Rackham, *SPIN Selling*, p. 110.
[4] Rackham, *SPIN Selling*, p. 84.

one of six categories and suggests making a list of every objection you have ever heard, and then grouping them under the following headings:

1. price,
2. performance,
3. follow-up service,
4. competition,
5. support, and
6. warranties and assurances.[5]

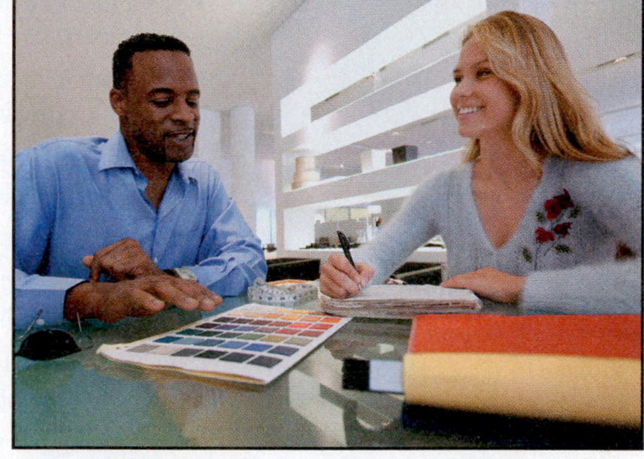

Direct selling experience can be a great foundation for an entrepreneur.
(©Digital Vision/Getty Images)

Once you have listed the objections under these headings, take a close look at them. Try to rephrase each set of objections in a single question of 25 words or less.

Work on developing objection-proof answers to each of these questions, answers that are backed by proof, testimonials from customers, research, and data comparing your product with the competition's. If you make the effort to do this, you will learn to appreciate hearing objections. More importantly, you may be able to head off objections before they arise.

- You will have well-prepared responses, backed by written documentation; and
- if you do hear a new objection for which you have not developed a response, you will be excited about the opportunity to address it.

Use Technology to Sell

Where appropriate and applicable, use the latest advances in technology to sell your product, help your customers understand and use it, and stay in touch with them. Some examples include

- a multimedia demonstration or presentation of your product;
- a Web site that customers can visit for updates and product facts, to share ideas, and to find technical data;
- using e-mail, blogs, and social networking to stay in touch with customers;
- webinars and audio conferences to educate and introduce;
- digital planners and calendars and sales and contact management software to keep prospect lists organized and log sales calls and customer information; and
- personal digital assistants (PDAs) and other technology to place orders and secure immediate responses to customer inquiries.

[5] Brian Tracy, *Be a Sales Superstar: 21 Great Ways to Sell More, Faster, Easier in Tough Markets* (San Francisco: Berrett-Koehler Publishers, 2003), p. 84.

Global Impact . . .

Keep an Open Mind

Your business may be small but do not forget that, via the Internet, you can participate in an exciting global economy. The more you travel and learn about other cultures, the more effective business leader you will become. The best entrepreneurs are tolerant and open-minded. They are curious about other countries, other cultures, and other ways of life, because these are all interesting and potential sources of business.

Perhaps there is a product you will discover on a backpacking trip in Europe that you can profitably import into the United States. Perhaps there is a consumer need you will find while reading about Panama online that you can meet by exporting your product there. Once you realize you are a citizen of the world, the sky is the limit for your career as an entrepreneur.

BizFacts

Kay Keenan and Steve Smolinsky are the consummate networkers. They have written a book on the topic highlighting material covered in their *Conversation on Networking.* Following are some of the tips from their book:

- It's a lot more fun to be with upbeat people. Negative stories shove people away . . . Positive stories bring them closer.
- If you go to an event or meeting with someone, split up. It improves your chances of meeting interesting people.
- Only if you're dead is it okay to say "nothing" when asked, "What's new?"
- Go early (to an event) and study the nametags on the registration table.
- Strong relationships are a two-way street.
- Learn to appreciate silence in a conversation. You can often see people thinking, but you rarely can hear their brain working.
- If you don't ask, you don't get. That means referrals, as well as most other things.
- Being comfortable with yourself leads to being comfortable with others.
- Carry your own nametag with you. Wearing a nametag is a great conversation starter, and your name will always be spelled correctly!
- A wonderful meeting not followed up is like having a winning lottery ticket and not cashing it in.

Source: Kay Keenan and Steven Smolinsky, *Conversation on Networking: Finding, Developing, and Maintaining Relationships for Business and Life* (Birchrunville, Pa. Forever Talking Press, 2006).

All the technological concepts used to identify customers through market research can be instrumental in selling to your segment of the market.

The One-Minute Sales Call

Believe it or not, it is a challenge for most people to pay attention to someone for more than a minute. You will do best if you keep the core of your sales calls under a minute. Write down your sales pitch, and practice delivering it to friends or relatives. Time yourself. You will be surprised at how fast a minute can go by. You cannot practice your sales pitches enough. Spending time planning a call is better than agonizing over why a call failed.

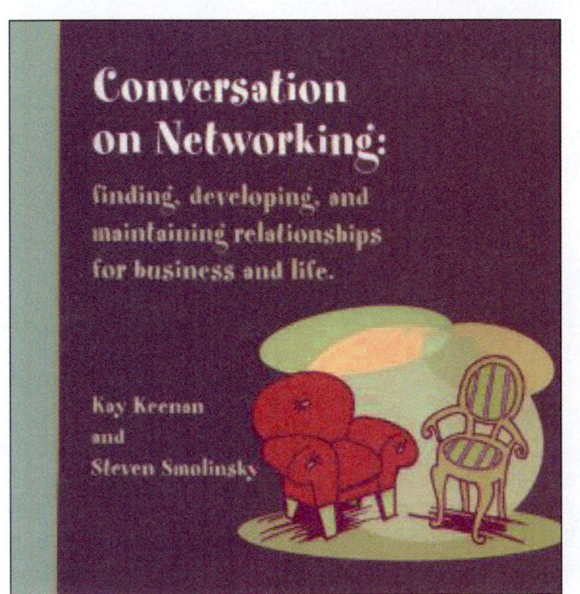

Conversation on Networking *provides insightful information on networking effectiveness.*

Here is an example to get you started. Let's say you make baby food from organic fruits and vegetables. You are trying to convince the owner of Johnson's General Store to buy your products. Remember, you need to build in places to engage the customer in the conversation, and this should be tailored to the specific challenges disclosed previously.

Hello, Mr. Johnson. Thank you for agreeing to see me today. I'm excited about this product and think you and your customers will be, too.

I brought you a jar of our baby applesauce. It is nicely packaged, don't you think? (pause) We hand-decorate each jar. It makes a nice gift for new or expectant parents. The eye-catching ribbons will be sure to attract your customers.

We use only organic fruits and vegetables, no sugar, and very little salt. Our label explains that some babies are sensitive to the additives and dyes found in certain commercial baby foods. These may give sensitive babies headaches or upset stomachs. Our food is very gentle on the baby's stomach, and that makes the parents' lives much easier!

I understand your concern that our product costs twenty-five cents more per jar than the brands you presently stock. According to recent industry research, baby-food customers will pay up to 50 percent more for high quality and for knowing that their babies are protected from harmful additives or high levels of sugar and salt. Also, because we add very little water to our product, customers actually get more food for the money than some of the less-expensive brands.

I really think you could start a local trend by stocking our baby food, Mr. Johnson. There has been a shift in the market toward healthy food for adults, and those adults are also looking for healthy baby food. Our products combine an eye-catching look with healthy ingredients that new parents and their friends and relatives will not be able to resist. How many jars would you like to order to start with?

Successful Businesses Need Customers Who Return

Making a sale to a customer is actually only the first step in your relationship with this individual. Your real goal is not the first sale, but to develop repeat business—customers who will buy from you over and over again. Successful companies are built on repeat business. As we noted earlier, the founder of Home Depot has calculated that one satisfied customer is worth more than $25,000 in sales over a lifetime.

Customer Service Is Keeping Customers Happy

Performance Objective 5

Provide excellent customer service.

customer service everything a business does to keep the customer happy.

Customer service is everything you do to keep your customers happy, especially *after* they've bought something. It includes maintaining and repairing the product or service once it has been sold, and dealing with customer complaints. Many businesses do not take the time or effort to provide excellent customer service. Smart entrepreneurs understand, however, that investing in customer service is likely to have a high return, because it retains customers and minimizes their dissatisfaction.

Here are some suggestions that may work for your business:

- Know your customers by name.
- Deliver the product or service on time, every time.
- Help customers carry their purchases to their vehicles.
- Suggest a less expensive product, if it will meet the customer's need, or offer a recommendation to a source of a product that you do not sell if it is what they want and you cannot offer a substitute.
- Provide a full refund to any customer who is dissatisfied.
- Take time to listen politely and with empathy to complaints.
- Provide a toll-free customer-assistance phone line that is easy to use.
- Offer product or service information of interest to customers in a nonthreatening manner.

Smart entrepreneurs pay close attention to their customers. They constantly ask questions and analyze their needs. They train their employees to look for customer needs that might be going unfulfilled. The most successful entrepreneurs become customer-service experts. Excellent customer service, combined with smart selling and a product that offers a unique competitive advantage, will lead to success.

T. Scott Gross.

Step into the Shoes . . .

Positively Outrageous Service

T. Scott Gross is a motivational speaker and management training consultant who has operated in both the entrepreneurial and corporate worlds. He was the national director of training for the Church's Chicken chain, and became a Church's franchisee in 1985.[6] Gross was fortunate to be able to use his earnings from speaking and consulting to keep the restaurant in business. He and his staff quickly learned that running the restaurant by the book simply was not sufficient. That led to the concept of Positively Outrageous Service (POS).

How much service is enough? How good does it need to be? For Gross and his team, it was not enough just to satisfy customers. Businesses should delight and astound them.[7] He describes POS as, "[T]he story you can't wait to tell . . . unexpected service delivered at random . . . It is a memorable event and is so unusual that the customer is compelled to tell others."[8]

Gross tells the following story:

"In the borderline bizarre category is our now-famous drive-through wind-shield-washing service. It was my response to a suggestion by my brother, Steve, our manager, that we should do 'something outrageous.' Now, while a Church's employee wielding a spray bottle attacks their windshields, I handle the microphone and the other half of the fun: "Good afternoon. Thanks for choosing Church's. As soon as that tubby guy gets out from in front of your car, pull up to the window for the best lunch you've had all day. No, on second thought, when he gets in front of your car, pull on up!" If a woman customer jokes that we should clean the car's interior, too, I might say: "Oh, madam, we aren't going to do insides. But if you come through tomorrow, we're going to try our hand at hair styling, and on Saturday, we're going to take a shot at dentistry!" The result is almost always a customer who is laughing when he or she reaches the pickup window. Doing the unexpected for our customers has earned us a reputation as a fun place to do business, where you can count on getting treated well."[9]

Positively Outrageous Service

- is random and unexpected: the element of surprise is part of its power;
- is out of proportion: it's an extravagant gesture that catches attention;
- involves the customer personally: it's an invitation to play that personalizes the service; and
- creates positive word of mouth: more powerful than advertising, POS generates its own buzz.[10]

Could providing Positively Outrageous Service fit into your business?

The Costs of Losing a Customer

Have you heard the expression "The customer is always right?" There will be times when a customer may get angry at you, complain, or make demands that you believe are unreasonable.

In *Customer Service: A Practical Approach,* Elaine Harris describes four costs of losing a customer:[11]

1. ***Loss of current dollars.*** These are the funds the customer was spending at your business.
2. ***Loss of jobs.*** Harris describes an advertising agency that lost one client because of a lack of courtesy and follow-through by the agency. Losing that client forced the owner of the business to close the office, putting 50 people out of work.
3. ***Loss of reputation.*** Remember Joe Girard's Law of 250. Do you really want to send a person away unhappy? One unhappy customer can keep many people away from your business.
4. ***Loss of future business.*** Once the customer is gone, so is the hope of any future purchases by that customer.

6T. Scott Gross, "'Outrageous Service Keeps Them Laughing—Getting the Customer Involved in Surprise Services Brings Satisfaction and Sales Increases," *Nation's Business*, 1992. Gale Group, 2004, http://findarticles.com/p/articles/mi_m1154/is_n3_v80/ai_11921694/print (accessed August 31, 2010).
7T. Scott Gross, *Positively Outrageous Service: How to Delight and Astound Your Customers and Win Them for Life*, 2nd ed. (Chicago: Dearborn Trade Publishing, 2004).
8Ibid.
9Gross, *Positively Outrageous Service*.
10Available at http://www.tscottgross.com (accessed August 31, 2010).
11Elaine Harris, *Customer Service: A Practical Approach* (Upper Saddle River, N.J.: Pearson Education, Inc., 2003).

Use your self-control to stay polite, even when a customer is getting angry. Do your best to find a solution that will send him/her away satisfied, and diffuse any lingering ill will. Your effort will protect your business and may even earn you a customer for life. Often, if you simply ask, "What will it take to make you a satisfied customer?" you will find that the customer will pause and suggest a reasonable solution to the situation.

Customer Complaints Are Valuable

You may not enjoy hearing a customer complain about your product or service, but a complaint is full of valuable information that probably no one else will tell you, and you do not have to pay for it. Listen closely to learn what your customers need and want:

- Always acknowledge complaints and criticism and deal with them. Never pretend that you did not hear a negative comment. If the customer *perceives* a problem, it *is* a problem.
- Do not overreact to negative comments and, above all, do not take them personally.
- Always tell the truth about any negative aspect of your product or service. When you admit a negative, you gain the customer's trust. However, this is different from complaining about your own product, the vendor, or your customers. You need not emphasize any weaknesses but should acknowledge them when asked and offset them with benefits.

Remember, a successful business is built on repeat customers. When you listen to a customer, you are building a relationship. You are encouraging loyalty to your business.

The Better Business Bureau

If you have a business and treat a customer poorly, he or she may report you to the local Better Business Bureau (BBB). The BBB is a nonprofit organization, composed of for-profit and nonprofit organizations that

Customer service is everything you do to keep the customer happy.
(©Studio M, The Stock Connection)

publishes reports about the reliability, trustworthiness, and performance of businesses and charities. You may want to consider the value of becoming a BBB-accredited organization. The BBB bases much of its reporting on complaints submitted by customers. Think about that when you are tempted to ignore a customer's request, or to lose your temper. Even if you believe you are in the right, you could damage your business's reputation.

An angry customer can make you feel angry, too. It is crucial that you and your team members stay calm when dealing with a customer who is upset. Ask the customer to explain the situation, and do not interrupt. This will provide time for him/her to vent and then calm down. If you show that you are willing to listen, you will probably defuse much of the irritation.

If the customer is using profanity, however, say something like "I understand your frustration, but I'm not comfortable with the way you are expressing it. Let's find a solution for you."

Elaine Harris provides a list of words to use and words to avoid when dealing with customers[12] (see **Exhibit 11-2**).

Customer Relationship Management Systems

customer relationship management (CRM) company-wide policies, practices, and processes that a business uses with its customers to generate maximum customer satisfaction and optimal profitability.

One approach to securing and sustaining customers is to implement a **customer relationship management (CRM)** system, which is the company-wide policies, practices, and processes that a business uses to manage its interactions with customers to generate maximum customer satisfaction and optimal profitability. CRM is a deliberate program of guidelines for excellence in customer service and relationship management designed to ensure positive interactions and encourage repeat purchases and referrals. All of the sales and customer service skills and best

[12]Harris, *Customer Service*.

Exhibit 11-2 *Words matter; smart customer service.*

Words to Use	Words to Avoid
Please	Cannot
Yes	Never
May I	Do not
Consider this	You have to
Do	Do not tell me no
Let's negotiate	Will not
Will	Not our policy
Thank you	Not my job
You	Profanity
Us	Vulgarity
Appreciate	Problem
Can	Sorry
Use customer's name	Endearments (honey, sweetie, etc.)
Would you like	We'll try
Opportunity	Haven't had time
Challenge	I do not know
Regret	Hang on for a second

practices introduced in this chapter can be components of a customer relationship management system. CRM can be very simple, such as methods for greeting and treating customers, to very sophisticated, such as using state-of-the-art technology to provide highly targeted customer information and analytics.

CRM affirms that customer service is an aspect of marketing. Marketing brings a customer to your business, but it does not stop there. Once the customer is inside your door or on the phone, the treatment should be consistent with your marketing. If your competitive advantage is speedy service, make sure your employees move quickly. If your advantage is a cozy, easygoing environment, make sure each customer is warmly welcomed and made to feel at home. Your customer service must reinforce your overall marketing plan. Through a well-designed and executed CRM system, you are reinforcing and building marketing effectiveness.

Why Does CRM Matter?

Customer relationship management can be the component of your business that makes it a sustainable entity. The costs of securing new customers are invariably significantly higher than the costs of keeping a repeat customer. According to the Customer Service Institute, 65% of a company's business comes from existing customers, and it costs five times as much to attract a new customer as it does to keep an existing one satisfied.[13] *Losing* a customer is even more expensive. According to Technical Assistance Research Programs Institute (TARP) Worldwide's recent word-of-mouth (WOM) survey, "42% of consumers who hear about a positive product experience will buy that product for the first time and another 21% of those consumers will buy more. The effects of positive WOM mirror those of negative WOM as 42% of consumers who hear of a negative WOM stop buying that product and 14% buy less. However, consumers with negative experiences provide more detailed explanations through more channels than those who have positive experiences."[14]

When you know the purchasing patterns and interests of a customer, you can make informed decisions about the products, services, and promotional offers that will be of interest and result in additional sales. With CRM, you can focus on optimal interactions with customers during all types of transactions (i.e., purchases, returns, ordering, inquiries, and complaints), as well as building on and using data regarding customer behavior to foster positive transactions.

Because customer service is also a valuable source of market research, CRM supports market research for companies that employ it. Market research should not end once you open your business. Each customer can be a valuable source of information. Some easy ways to collect market research as part of your customer service for retail businesses include

- Providing a short survey on a stamped postcard with every item purchased, or a Web site with a survey and reward on every receipt. Or include a survey that can be redeemed for a discount on the next item purchased.

[13]Customer Service Institute of America Web site, http://www.serviceinstitute.com/CCSM.htm (accessed June 23, 2009).

[14]"Consumer Word of Mouth Changes Buying Habits 60% of the Time, TARP Worldwide Poll Finds: Men and Senior Citizens Most Likely to Complain," Press release. TARP Worldwide, February 12, 2008, http://www.tarp.com/news_wom_poll.html (accessed June 23, 2009).

- Asking selected customers to fill out a longer survey—again, offering a discount or prize drawing as an incentive.
- Always asking, and have your employees ask, standard questions when completing a sale, such as "Do you have any suggestions on how we could improve our product?" or "Were you satisfied with the service you received today?" or "Were you able to find everything that you wanted?"

Components of CRM for the Small Business

CRM has consistent components that may be incorporated across business types and sizes. It reaches across the marketing, sales, and service functions of a business to create positive customer experiences. **Exhibit 11-3** shows the Solution Map of CRM as described by SAP, the top seller of CRM systems. In the case of businesses that purchase highly sophisticated software, these components are part of the software solution, but for companies with less complex operations and fewer resources, many of these functions can be carried out without software applications beyond basic record keeping, with simple databases, contact management software, and industry-specific systems.

The SBA Web site (http://www.sba.gov) offers a perspective on customer service, and customer relationship management in general, relating it to the axiom inherent in the Golden Rule, "Do unto others as you would have them do unto you," and stating, "Companies of all sizes are realizing that their strongest selling point can sometimes boil down to treating customers as they would like to be treated—or better."[15] The message is getting through. According to John Goodman, president of TARP, "In the past few years, companies began to realize that service was really a competitive factor, and began to view it as an integral part of their product."[16] It is often in the area of service and CRM that a small business can outclass its larger competitors, so that customers may spend more to buy from them because of the service differential.

[15]U.S. Small Business Administration Web site, http://www.sba.gov (accessed June 20, 2009).
[16]Ibid.

Exhibit 11-3 *SAP Solution Map for CRM.*

Marketing	Sales	Service
Marketing Resource Management	Sales Planning and Forecasting	Service Sales and Marketing
Segmentation and List Management	Sales Performance Management	Service Contracts and Agreements
Campaign Management	Territory Management	Installations and Management
Real-Time Offer Management	Accounts and Contacts	Customer Service Support
Lead Management	Opportunity Management	Field Service Management
Loyalty Management	Quotation and Order Management	Returns and Depot Repair
Communication Promotion	Pricing and Contracts	Warranty and Claims Management
	Incentive and Commission Management	Service Logistics and Finance
	Time and Travel	Service Collaboration, Analytics, Optimization

Source: SAP Web site, http://www.sap.com/solutions/business-suite/CRM/businessmaps.epx (accessed June 20, 2009, as submitted). SAP Solution Map for CRM courtesy of SAP AG.

The SBA offers three Golden Rules for small businesses with respect to CRM.

- Golden Rule 1: Put the customer first.
- Golden Rule 2: Stay close to your customers.
- Golden Rule 3: Pay attention to the little details.

The SBA offers further advice on the components of customer care that they translate into five rules. These rules are part of the essential components of successful CRM.

1. ***Conduct your own survey.*** Profit from the ideas, suggestions, and complaints of your present and former customers. Talk and meet with your customers. Ask questions. Learn their attitudes, what they want, and what they dislike.
2. ***Check employees' telephone manners periodically.*** This link is particularly important for small businesses because bad telephone handling can undermine other constructive efforts to build a profitable enterprise.
3. ***Rules such as prompt answering and a cheerful attitude of helpfulness are of critical importance.*** Have someone whose voice is unfamiliar play the role of a customer or prospective customer, preferably a difficult one.
4. ***Make customer service a team effort.*** Use group meetings, memos, posters, and in-house publications to build customer consciousness throughout the organization. Continually drive home the crucial rule that getting and holding customers requires team play; invite employees' ideas.
5. ***Extend your efforts after hours.*** It's the friendly feelings people have that draw them to you and your business. Take advantage of the relaxed atmosphere of social occasions, or a neighborly chat over the back fence, to turn friends into customers or to reinforce the loyalty of existing ones.[17]

How Technology Supports CRM

The general conception of CRM is that it is technology used to build and maintain customer relationships. Certainly, as noted, the use of computer technology can have a significant role in CRM, but the system should be inclusive of all forms of relationship management, from greeting a customer on the phone, in-person, or even on the home page of your Web site, to the use of sophisticated software systems. With CRM, customer interactions with all parts of the company are unified and customer information is tracked, analyzed, and used to improve customer satisfaction and business profitability. Specialized CRM software is available to companies large and small. **Exhibit 11-4** shows the top vendors of CRM software. The total expenditures for CRM in 2007 were $8.1 billion.[18]

It truly is not necessary to invest in a sophisticated CRM software system to use technology to benefit your customer relationships. You can purchase a database package to create significant gains. A **database**

database a collection of information that is generally stored on a computer and organized for sorting and searching.

[17]Ibid.
[18]"Gartner Says Worldwide Customer Relationship Management Market Grew 23 Percent in 2007," Press release, Stamford, CT: Gartner, Inc., July 7, 2008, http://www.gartner.com/us/crm (accessed June 20, 2009).

Exhibit 11-4 *Worldwide vendor revenue estimates for total CRM software (millions of U.S. dollars).*

Company	2007 Revenue	2007 Market Share (%)
SAP	$2,050.8	25.4
Oracle	$1,319.8	16.3
SalesForce.com	$676.5	8.4
Amdocs	$421.0	5.2
Microsoft	$332.1	4.1
Others	$3,289.1	40.6
Total	$8,089.3	100.0

Source: Gartner, Inc., *Dataquest Insight: Customer Relationship Management, Worldwide, 2007,* http://www.gartner.com (accessed June 19, 2009). Data updated periodically by Gartner.

is a collection of information that is generally stored on a computer and organized for sorting and searching. Create a database on your computer to collect any information you obtain from customers, either by using a package such as Microsoft Access, or via a specialized customer software system for your industry. Your database should include every customer you have ever had, as well as potential customers: friends, family, and other contacts. The database should include contact information (i.e., name, e-mail address, phone and fax numbers, and mailing address); any preferences or pertinent personal information (e.g., sizes, birthdays, family, hobbies, memberships); and purchase and payment history. Also, include any contact information, such as when the contact was made, who was involved, what type of contact it was (i.e., in person, telephone, text, social network, or e-mail), and a note about the topics of discussion and any appropriate follow-up. Design the database and start collecting this information from the beginning, and you will be ahead of the game when you are ready to make sales calls or send out marketing material.

As your database grows, you can make it more sophisticated by organizing it by region, customer interest, or any number of other variables, and send out targeted e-mails. If you sell gourmet sauces, for example, your notes could tell you whether a customer is interested in hot sauces or dessert sauces. When you add a new hot sauce to your product line, you will know whom to target with an e-mail announcement introducing it, possibly with a special offer. Use the resources available to you to maximize your culture of focus on the customer, and a strong customer-relationship management.

Exercise

Contact your phone company, either by phone or through Internet research, to find out how to set up an 800 number for your business, so customers can call toll free. Some long-distance providers offer special discounts to small-business owners. AT&T has a program called Small Business Advantage.

How much will an 800 number for your business cost?
Did you find any special discounts?

Chapter Summary

Now that you have studied this chapter, you can do the following:

1. Explain the importance of selling based upon benefits.
   - Features are the qualities of a product or service.
   - Benefits are what the product or service can do to fill customer needs.
   - Customers purchase based upon perceived benefits.
2. Use the principles of selling to make effective sales calls.
   - Make a good personal impression.
   - Know your product or service.
   - Believe in your product or service.
   - Know your field.
   - Know your customers.
   - Prepare your sales presentation.
   - Think positively.
   - Keep good records.
   - Make an appointment.
   - Treat your customers like gold.
3. Know how to make a successful sales call.
   - Use technology to assist you.
   - Prequalify your leads, so that you are making the best use of your time and theirs.
   - Focus on the customer, not on the product or service.
   - Incorporate the eight-step sales call.
4. Analyze and improve your sales calls.
   - Was I able to get the customer to open up to me? Why, or why not? Did I do or say anything that turned the customer off?
   - Which of my questions did the best job of helping the customer zero in on his/her problem?
   - Was I able to make an honest case for my product/service being the one that could solve the customer's problem?
   - Did I improve my relationship with this individual during the call?
5. Provide excellent customer service.
   - Customer service is everything you do to keep your customers happy, especially after the sale. It includes maintaining and repairing the product or service once it has been sold, and dealing with customer complaints.
   - A successful business is built on repeat customers.
6. Define customer relationship management and understand its value.
   - Identify the key components of CRM.
   - Recognize that CRM can be simple to complex, and that you can incorporate technology into it to obtain higher value.
   - Use CRM to tailor your products, services, and promotions to customers to yield increased profitability.

Key Terms

customer relationship management (CRM)
customer service
database
lurk
newsgroup
prospect
spam

Entrepreneurship Portfolio

Critical Thinking Exercises

1. Describe the features of each product listed below and then create a benefit statement for each that you would use as selling points.

   Product

   wristwatch with daily-events calendar

   milk-free chocolate

   vegetarian dog food

   personal lie detector
2. Create a customer profile database for your business containing at least 20 data fields. Which five questions would you ask every customer?
3. Describe a business that you deal with as a customer. Describe the customer service at this business. What do you like (or dislike) about it? How could it be improved?
4. List five things you intend to do in your business to offer superior customer service.
5. Identify five specific sales-call prospects for your business. Prequalify them using these questions: (1) Is the prospect in my market? (2) Does he/she need my product/service? (3) Will my product/service remove a problem or source of "pain," or improve the individual's life? (4) Can he/she afford it?
6. Have you created any marketing materials for your business? If so, have three friends and a mentor (someone older whom you respect and who can give you good business advice) look at your materials and give you feedback. Write a memo listing their suggestions and what you plan to do to improve your marketing materials.
7. Write a one-minute sales call for the product (or service) your business will be selling. Try your pitch out on a partner and write down his/her objections. Rewrite your pitch to incorporate these criticisms. Try your pitch again. Repeat this process until you think you have a strong sales call.

Key Concept Questions

1. Explain Joe Girard's Law of 250 in your own words, and give examples from your own life.
2. Why is customer service an extension of marketing?
3. Give three reasons why you think it is important to keep collecting market research even after you have opened your business.
4. What do you expect your personal look to be when you start selling your product/service, and why?
5. What sources of information can you use to develop a customer profile?
6. List three ways you intend to provide superior customer service.
7. Create a company signature for your business e-mail. Keep it under eight words.

Application Exercises

1. Develop a one-minute sales pitch for three items that you are wearing. Try out the pitch for each on a partner. Have your partner help you time the pitches to one minute. Do the same for your partner.
2. Write a memo to your partner discussing his/her sales calls and how they could be improved. Use the eight steps of a sales call in the text as your guide when analyzing your partner's efforts.
3. Arrange to receive a sales pitch from a competitor in the business field that you intend to enter. After the presentation, write down your objections to purchasing the product/service. Use Brian Tracy's method to categorize your objections and then phrase them in a single question composed of 25 words or less. Be conscious of doing this ethically.

Exploring Your Community

1. Visit three businesses in your community and take notes on your experience as a shopper. Write a memo comparing the customer service at each. Include such information as the following: Were you greeted when you came in? Did anyone offer to help you? If you bought something, were you given a survey? What differentiates the best firm from the worst in terms of customer service?
2. Interview an entrepreneur about the type of CRM he/she uses. Discuss customer service and complaint handling in particular. Summarize the interview in a short paper.

Case Study

Kay Keenan and Steve Smolinsky–Conversation on Networking

In late 2004, Howard Weisz had a problem. As a long-time member of the Mid-Atlantic Consultants (MAC) Network, he had agreed to organize a program on networking for the group. As the date approached, Howard realized that he really didn't want to moderate this event. His solution was to ask Kay Keenan, founder of Growth Consulting, to present the program. Kay had previously worked for Howard before she became a well-known speaker and consultant on networking.

Kay felt there should be more than one presenter, because the topic was networking. So, she created a panel of volunteers from the MAC members. Steven Smolinsky, founder of Benari LTD, volunteered even though he did not know Kay. Later, Steve received a call from Kay telling him that all the other panelists had cancelled, so it was just going to be the two of them. They decided to use a conversational approach that involved the audience. Thus, Conversation on Networking was born.

During the program, the audience reacted with incredible enthusiasm, interest, and participation. Afterwards, testimonials flowed in as attendees discovered rapid results from using the skills they had learned. Word spread fast, and many requests were made for a repeat session. Because of further demand, Kay and Steve responded by taking the show on the road. Since that time, numerous public and private events have been held around the country.

As the name implies, Conversation on Networking is a fully interactive program about how to effectively meet people, and how to develop those contacts into long-term relationships. Kay and Steve recognize that there is no single, correct answer to a networking issue, because appropriate advice is dependent on each particular situation. As a result, the discussions that occur between the presenters and the attendees focus on real, everyday issues that people have experienced.

To further customize their advice, Kay and Steve provide forms that an attendee may complete before or after an event. This information is used to create a report with individualized feedback. The goal of the program is to help participants obtain immediate results after leaving a Conversation on Networking event.

Steve Smolinsky and Kay Keenan of Conversation on Networking.

In addition to events, Kay and Steve use many other ways to share their experiences and ideas. The Conversation on Networking Web site includes basic information about services and events, networking tips, short video clips, links for e-mailing Kay and Steve, and a link to Steve's blog. You can sign up to receive a newsletter as well as purchase their book, and/or a DVD, via the Web site. Customer testimonials are also posted online. The newsletter and blog often mention readers and clients, giving an extra boost to the networking information that is shared.

Case Study Analysis

1. How does Conversation on Networking reinforce the importance of selling based upon benefits?
2. List three things that Kay and Steve have done that you could adopt to help build business relationships.
3. What principles of selling do Kay and Steve employ to sell Conversation on Networking?
4. How do Kay and Steve support their customers and colleagues, and utilize customer referrals?

Case Sources

Conversation on Networking Web site, http://www.conversationonnetworking.com.

Kay Keenan and Steven Smolinsky, *Conversation on Networking: Finding, Maintaining, and Developing Relationships for Business and Life* (Birchrunville, Pa.: Forever Talking Press, 2006).

Case Study | Off-Centered Ales—On Target Sales: Dogfish Head Craft Brewery

One look at Dogfish Head Brewery's Web site (*http://www.dogfish.com*) or a few minutes in the presence of the business's founder, Sam Calagione, and it is apparent that sales and customer service are key components of this company's success. Sam and Mariah Calagione opened Dogfish Head Brewings and Eats (DFH) at Rehoboth Beach, Delaware, in 1995. Since then, Dogfish Head has expanded to include a 103,000-square-foot brewery and a small distillery, with 50 distributors in 25 states. There are also DFH Alehouses in Gaithersburg, Maryland, and Falls Church and Chantilly, Virginia. DFH has been on the Inc. 500 list of fastest-growing companies in the United States, and is the fastest-growing small brewery.

Sam Calagione of Dogfish Head.

Sam became fascinated with craft brews when he worked in a New York City restaurant that featured microbrews. In *Brewing Up a Business*, he writes, "I first decided to open my brewery when I was 24 years old . . . I worked as a brewer's assistant as I wrote my business plan . . . I made pilot batches of beer and developed recipes and brand names." Sam and Mariah wanted to create a successful brewpub, rather than a stand-alone beer-production facility, so that they would have direct interaction with customers. As the Web site reports, "We quickly got bored brewing the same things over and over—that's when we started adding all sorts of weird ingredients and getting kind of crazy with the beers!" By serving the results in the brewpub, DFH could modify and improve them based on customer response. This customer focus has been central to DFH from its inception.

Dogfish Head offers "off-centered ales for off-centered people," creating brews for hardcore "beer geeks, wine people and foodies." They market brews with creative names and ingredients and interesting back stories, whereas the objective continues to be designing unique and enticing beers. For example, *Midas Touch* is "an ancient Turkish recipe using the original ingredients from the 2700-year-old drinking vessels discovered in the tomb of King Midas himself." *Raison D'être*, which was voted "American Beer of the Year" in 2000 by *Malt Advocate*, is a deep mahogany ale brewed with beet sugar, green raisins, and Belgian yeast. The DFH flagship beverage is *60 Minute IPA*, a heavily hopped India Pale Ale. DFH's *90 Minute Imperial IPA* has been described by *Esquire* as "perhaps the best I.P.A. in America." DFH sells its 30-plus styles of ale and a half-dozen types of spirits. They are known for their quality, distinctive, extreme brews using nontraditional ingredients with stronger flavor and higher alcohol content. They also are priced significantly higher than those of the largest brewing companies.

The DFH way of doing business is to understand that selling is all about finding out about your customers' needs, and delivering products and services to meet these needs, exceeding customer expectations. Sam learned about the market by making a point of spending time to "get out and meet your brand through the eyes of the world . . . In the case of the beer business that means I spend time with my distributors, retailers, and my customers."[1] He and the DFH team continue to do so. All DFH team members are passionate and knowledgeable about the company and its products, and this passion attracts and retains customers. Sam writes, "If you take the time to roam constructively, you will learn a tremendous amount about your company and its place in the competitive environment. You will be able to gauge your company's successes and failure through the eyes of your customer."[2]

[1]Sam Calagione, *Brewing Up a Business* (Hoboken, N.J.: John Wiley and Sons, Inc., 2005).
[2]Mariah Calagione of DFH.

Sam articulates his view of customer service and selling, "Always remember that you are your customers and your customers are you. To treat them any differently than you would expect to be treated just because you are the seller and they are the buyer would be a mistake . . . In business large and small, loyal customers are earned from trust, respect, and the consistent quality of products and services based on personal values." A dedication to people and respect for them is a priority for DFH.

Dogfish Head focuses on education as the pathway to sales, eschewing advertising campaigns. Sam writes, "Knowledge gives the customer the power to make a decision; the quality of the experience gives them the power to decide if the experience was worth the price." The company spends approximately 20 percent of its advertising budget on samples and tastings for customers and prospective customers. DFH only advertises in beer publications, and in local Delaware publications for the brewpub. They focus their funds on ingredients and innovative equipment and let respected third parties speak for them. The accolades continue to accumulate. International beer expert Michael Jackson has dubbed Dogfish Head "America's most interesting and adventurous small brewery."

The sales force is actively involved in the establishment of revenue goals and the creation of the budget. The sales managers work with the 50 distributors to establish the forecast for the coming year's sales volume and mix. This information is compiled to inform the creation of the budget. The sales team agrees to the final budget, so that they are clearly attuned to the relationship between the budget and their commissions and bonuses. The goals are clear, and exceptional performance is rewarded.

Every team member is a salesperson at DFH. Everyone must know the difference between DFH products and those of competitors and needs to understand why DFH's are better. They have to have basic knowledge of the company, its philosophy, and its products. Team members are given opportunities to walk in the shoes of their colleagues by experiencing different roles within the company. They can build a more robust picture of the entire organization and become more passionate and knowledgeable about DFH. Sam encourages creating a "sales-centric" mentality.

It is easy to understand why DFH has been so successful.

Case Study Analysis

1. Through which channels does Dogfish Head sell its products?
2. According to Sam Calagione, what does education have to do with sales?
3. What are the roles of the customers of DFH?
4. How do members of the sales force participate in goal setting?
5. Why is sampling an important part of the sales process for DFH?
6. What is the relationship between the sales strategy for DFH and its pricing strategy?

Case Sources

Dogfish Head Brewery Web site at http://www.dogfish.com.

Sam Calagione, *Brewing Up a Business: Adventures in Entrepreneurship from the Founder of Dogfish Head Craft Brewery* (Hoboken, N.J.: John Wiley and Sons, Inc., 2005).

Sam Calagione and Marnie Old, *He Said Beer, She Said Wine* (New York: DK Publishing, 2008).

Sam Calagione as told to Nitasha Tiku, "The Way I Work: Dogfish Head's Sam Calagione," *Inc.*, July 1, 2009.

Ken Done Studios

http://www.done.com.au/
http://www.kendone.com/

Small Business School **video clip titles are in red**

DO WHAT WORKS

Ken Done is Australia's most recognized modern artist. Since 1975, he has painted nearly every day. From his massive body of work has sprung an enterprise that employs more than 100 people. He has galleries in London, New York, and other locations, where his paintings are sold. Customers may purchase swimwear, sportswear, and accessories—all designed by the Ken Done studios, at boutiques and online. At its peak, sales were in excess of 100 million AUD—with most revenue coming from licensed products.

Ken spent 16 years in the advertising industry in London, New York, and Sydney. This uniquely prepared him to be a working artist who would avoid the starving stage that so many painters struggle through. Like most successful entrepreneurs, Ken paid his dues by working for others. Then he had a gut feeling that he could make his own idea work financially. When he left his secure job in New York City at the advertising agency giant J. Walter Thompson and returned to his country to make his way as a fine artist, he did not expect to attain the success he has today.

While sitting with Ken in one of his galleries in Sydney, he told me, "This is an accidental business. To get into the businesses that we're in at the moment, it was surprising in the sense that from my first exhibition, even though I'd been painting all my life—for my first exhibition when I was 40, I made 12 T-shirts to give to the press to remind them of that particular show. And, look, they liked them so much that people wanted more.

"It's a very straightforward exercise, isn't it? If you make something and it's well priced and people like it, almost inevitably you realize you can make some more. And in this sense—I mean, I'm a painter. That's how I spend all my time. But the concept of repeating the singular effort or taking one part of a piece of design and multiplying it is essentially, you know, what business, I suppose, is about."

Done's paintings can be translated into multiple media, ranging from the original art that is sold in galleries, to prints sold online, and tote bags, watches, swimwear, cover-ups, and T-shirts sold in retail stores and online.

Ken didn't intend to sell T-shirts; he intended to sell paintings. The T-shirts were a marketing stunt that changed his life. Fortunately, his wife, Judy, had worked as a fashion designer. Combining their backgrounds and talents, the two have built a company that started with Ken's paintings and grew as Judy applied the art to clothing and accessories.

Since the art press liked his T-shirts so much, the demand exceeded his supply; he printed more, and he didn't give them away. He sold them for $12 each. Even though his profits were slim on this first item, he knew he was on to something that he never would have thought of on his own. By being open to what his potential customers might buy, he launched a solid business.

Giving away the T-shirts to people who could talk up his paintings was a perfect integrated marketing idea. In "Web speak," this is called viral marketing. Ken wanted the art press to say good things about his exhibition, so that customers with the resources to buy would find their way to his gallery and buy his paintings. Regardless of what the art press wrote about that first exhibition, they talked about the T-shirt; creating that word-of-mouth marketing (buzz)—what every business craves. The press reaction and subsequent spread of news about Ken Done's work is an excellent example of viral marketing. Ken has relied heavily upon viral marketing and direct sales, as well as his Web site, to keep his brand successful. Just as the use of the T-shirts to capture the attention of the press was creative and innovative, the marketing of Ken Done's art in its various forms uses creativity and innovation to reinforce the brand and extend its markets.

If Ken had spent his exhibition marketing budget on champagne and hors d'oeuvres, some might think, "This is the right kind of marketing. He is serving high-end refreshments to sell his expensive paintings." With the benefit of time, we can see that there was probably nothing he could have done better than making those T-shirts from his own designs that captured the spirit of his paintings.

Ken said, "I made 12 T-shirts. People liked them so much, I made 12 more. Those 12 sold very quickly, so suddenly I thought—because that original T-shirt—it was a blue drawing on white—I think made this giant mental leap of thinking, 'Let's do one white on blue.' Suddenly, there are two. It's a choice. It's a product range. So from having a choice of two to a number of shops and licensing arrangements, that's just, you know, like a game. But you have to make something that people want."

Over time, Ken and his team have developed an approach to their markets that relies heavily upon physical locations and word-of-mouth for its promotion, with less than 5 percent of revenues devoted to advertising. The product mix is divided between T-shirts and seasonal apparel (40%), women's fashion (20%), swimwear (15%), children's products (10%), accessories (10%), and artwork (5%). Ken Done products are priced for the midmarket, with different products playing different roles. For example, the bread-and-butter items are priced competitively, while maintaining solid margins. Other products are sold to set the pitch of the retail environments, and priced accordingly.

SELL BEAUTY

Beauty is the brand, and plenty of art critics snub Ken Done, but he sticks to his core belief. He told me that photographers and film makers are so good at showing us the sad, dark side of the world that he does not want to compete on that level. Ken Done's world is color. The stunning sea, sand, sky, flora, and fauna of his country never bore him.

In addition to painting, over the years he has taken on projects that align with his brand. From 1988 to 1999, Ken created the cover art for a Japanese fashion and lifestyle magazine, and I had a chance to see for myself that this work made him a star in Japan. While I was in the gallery with Ken, a couple of Japanese women came in, and they could not believe their eyes. They had no idea that he would be in the gallery; and to them, he was bigger than Elvis. Well, maybe they have never heard of Elvis, but I could tell that they were overwhelmed. I offered to take their picture with the artist, and they were most grateful.

Ken is one of just 13 artists who have created a BMW Art Car; he redesigned the restaurant at Sydney's Powerhouse Museum, and created the official logo for the Sydney 2000 Olympic Games. Not content to only build his own business, he has worked to define his country. According to the publishers of the book, *Ken Done: The Art of Design*, Mr. Done has not only built his own business, he has created an image of Australia.

SIGN CONTRACTS ONLY WITH THOSE WHO DON'T NEED ONE

To protect his brand, Ken pulled out of lucrative contracts with large American department stores. He had licensed his art to handbag, shoe, and clothing manufacturers, but he was not happy with how the final product evolved in the hands of others. And, they made a request that he simply refused to grant.

He told me, "We had to work in Neiman Marcus, in Bloomingdale's, in Macy's. And that arrangement was good. It was fine. But we started to lose control in a sense that because it was often going into colder parts of America and they wanted more winter clothes. They want brown. They said, 'Brown's very important in Chicago.' I said, 'I'm playing golf. I don't care whether brown's in Chicago.' I'm not putting it down, it's just that America's like this huge ball; it's really, really, really hard to get it rolling. And once it starts to roll, it's incredible—and it was just too much for us. And the clothing wasn't looking exactly like our stuff. So we decided at that point in time we would cut out all wholesaling and all licensing, and we cut our business by 50 percent in one hit, because we couldn't control it."

He got out of the contract by picking up the phone and telling the person who handled the American business, "I'm not going to do it anymore." Fortunately, Ken understands that you should not sign a contract with a person who won't let you out of it. Business owners enter into a lot of agreements with customers, suppliers, and employees. Contracts are a way of documenting these agreements. They ensure that the understanding of the parties regarding performance and compensation is the same on both sides. We use contracts to protect ourselves, to manage business risk. However, a contract is only as good as the people who sign it. Ken Done had a relationship with his American partner, and there were no hard feelings or lawsuits when Ken needed to reign in his product line and quit the American market.

CHANGING CHANNELS TO MAINTAIN BRAND INTEGRITY

Ken Done has changed his channels of distribution several times, to maintain brand integrity and to take advantage of opportunities—or address threats. Oscar Done, Ken's son and Done managing director, reports that the company gained international recognition through licensing agreements in Australia, the United States, and Japan. The upside was the wide distribution and increased brand recognition. The downside was the loss of control, and the receipt of licensing fees rather than the usual product margins. The company was unhappy with the licensing arrangements and changed its course. Later in the '90s, Done-branded products were sold only in company retail stores, with no distributors or licenses.

The focus on company-owned retail stores in Australia worked well leading up to the 2000 Sydney Olympics. Done was an official Olympic supplier, and benefitted greatly from tourism. However, the tourism was severely impacted after the September 11, 2001, tragedy and the SARS virus. Revenues declined, and fixed costs escalated.

Ken Done once again entered into a licensing agreement in the early 2000s; this time focusing on swimwear and resort wear. The company created a network of sales agents across the United States to promote the premium Done products. Distribution reached approximately 200 stores, including a number of high-end retailers. Oscar explains, "While this did deliver new channels of distribution, it was very laborious, and we faced the unpredictable challenges of currency values, market regulation and logistics that virtually made it a profitless exercise at the end of the day, if we were to remain price competitive. We needed to develop a more robust infrastructure in the U.S. which meant further investments of time and money." Ultimately, management decided that they did not wish to pursue that route and retrenched.

In order to focus on the company's strengths in design, Done has downsized to two boutique retail shops in Sydney, and a comparatively narrow product range.

Ken Done paintings sell for $30,000 to $50,000 U.S. dollars, and you can buy a T-shirt from his Web site for $20. I don't think he will ever retire, as the last thing he said to me was, "I wanted to work this morning. I want to work every day."

Case Analysis

1. How does Ken Done incorporate the Four P's into a creative, effective, integrated marketing effort?
2. What is the product mix that Ken Done's enterprises have developed?
3. How are his products distributed (through what channels)?
4. Take a look at Done retail stores on the Internet. Set the pricing to USD and browse through the Web site. What pricing strategy is employed by the company?
5. Discuss the company's global marketing.
6. What was Ken Done's first marketing effort?
7. What was the result of this effort?
8. How does Ken Done extend his brand?

Case prepared by Hattie Bryant, creator of *Small Business School*, the television series made for PBS and Voice of America, http://SmallBusinessSchool.org.

UNIT 4

SHOW ME THE MONEY: FINDING, SECURING, AND MANAGING IT

Chapter 12

UNDERSTANDING AND MANAGING START-UP, FIXED, AND VARIABLE COSTS

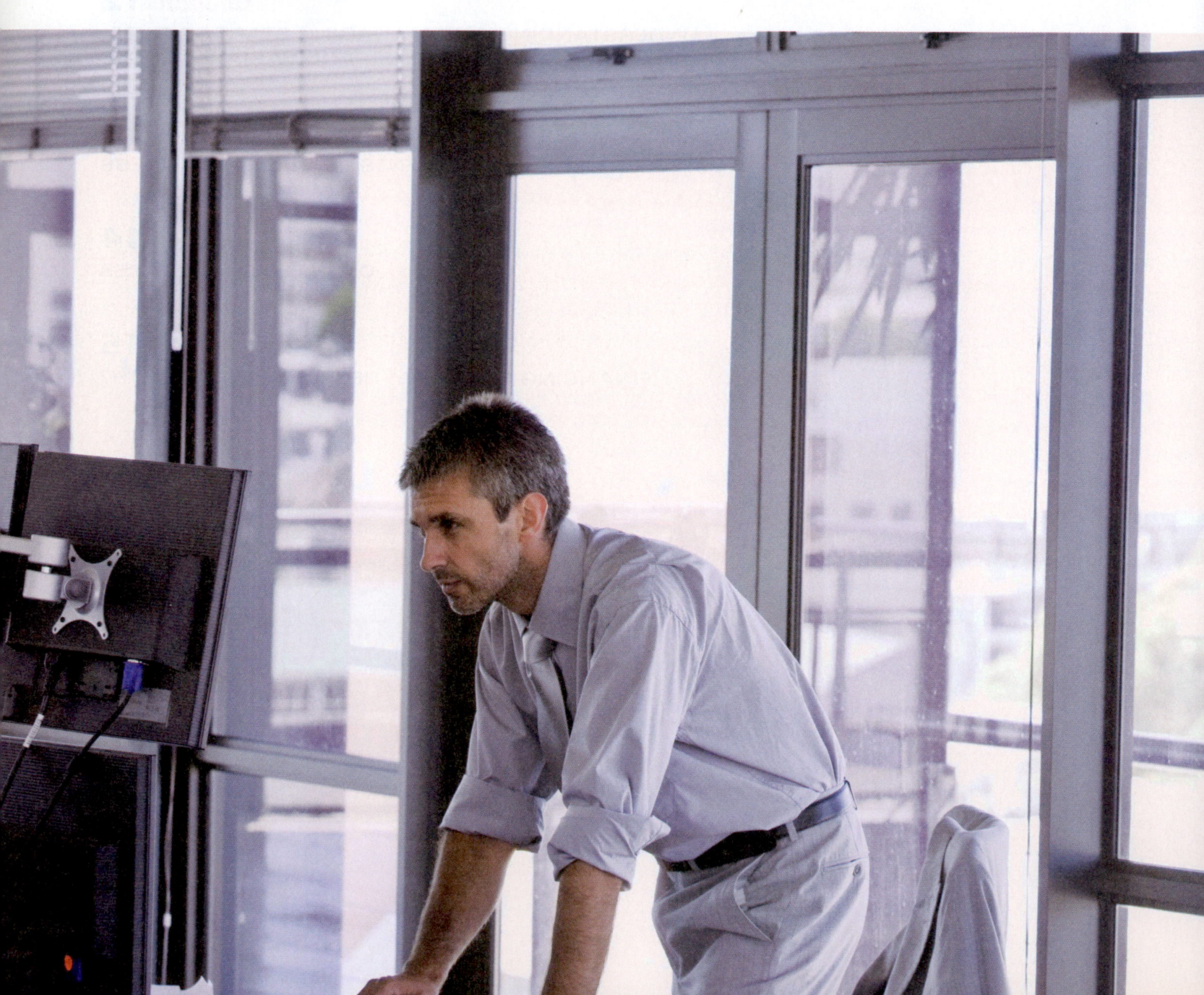

> **"All our records had to be hits because we couldn't afford any flops."**
>
> —Berry Gordy, founder, Motown Record Company

Almost anyone could spend unlimited amounts of money and create a viable product, but the entrepreneur's goal is to create one that costs less to make than customers are willing to pay for it. An entrepreneur's ability to find ways to manage costs can often mean the difference between a struggling business and a thriving one.

Entrepreneurs searching for ways to control their costs have resulted in spectacular breakthroughs. When Henry Ford was trying to make his vision of an automobile in front of every home in America a reality, it was the *cost* of building a horseless carriage that stood in his way. The motorcar was considered a novelty for rich people, but Ford was determined to build one that almost anyone could afford.

In those days, cars were put together one at a time. This was a slow, expensive process that involved a good deal of labor. To cut manufacturing costs, Ford had his cars assembled as they moved on a conveyer belt past the workers, with each being responsible for attaching one item. This moving assembly line produced cars quickly with a much lower labor cost per unit. The assembly-line concept revolutionized manufacturing and was adopted by many companies to make products that were previously too expensive for the average consumer. Industrial production exploded in America, as the moving assembly line made it possible for companies to lower their costs enough to mass-produce items, such as washing machines and refrigerators, that previously only the well-to-do could afford. Henry Ford revolutionized industry by introducing the concept of mass production on a grand scale.

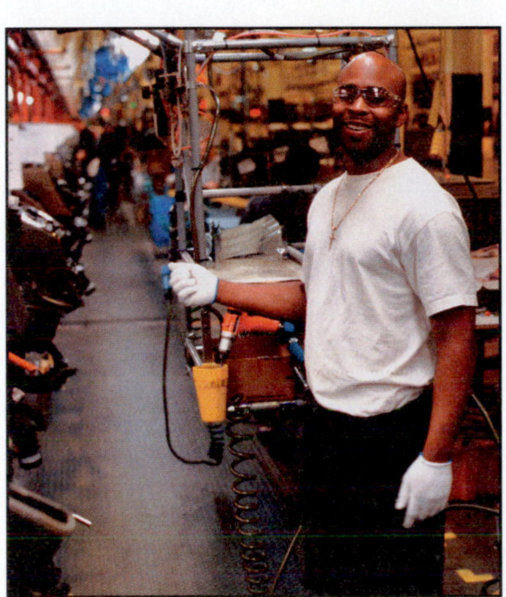

Performance Objectives

1. Identify the investment required for business startup.
2. Describe the variable costs of starting a business.
3. Analyze your fixed operating costs and calculate gross profit.
4. Set up financial record keeping for your business.

What Does It Cost to Operate a Business?

To run a successful business, you will need to keep track of your costs and have more cash coming in than going out. The bedrock principle of business is that it earns a profit by selling products or services for more than they cost.

Because everything sold has related costs, a business can make a profit only if the selling price per unit is greater than the cost per unit. A litmus test for profitability is the *economics of one unit* (EOU), as discussed in prior chapters. It tells an entrepreneur if the business is earning a profit on each individual unit. Knowing your EOU will be helpful as you determine your venture's viability.

Many costs are associated with the establishment and growth of a small business. These include start-up purchases, fixed and variable costs, and cash reserves. Each will be discussed in turn. All are components of your accounting records, the documents that are used to classify, analyze, and interpret the financial transactions of an organization.

Start-Up Investment

Performance Objective 1

Identify the investment required for business startup.

seed capital (start-up investment) the one-time expense of opening a business.

There is another critical cost to discuss before you can establish good accounting records for your business. We have talked about the costs of producing one unit and the costs of operating a business, but what about the money required to *start* the business? Start-up investment, or **seed capital**, is the one-time expense of opening a business. In a restaurant, for example, start-up expenses would include stoves, food processors, tables, chairs, silverware, and other items that would not be replaced very often. Also included might be the one-time cost of buying land and constructing a building. Some entrepreneurs also choose to consider the time they put into getting their businesses off the ground as part of the start-up investment. To do so, place a value on your time per hour and multiply by the number of hours you think you will need to put in to get your business going. You might be shocked at how big that number is.

For a hot dog stand, the start-up investment list might look like this:

Hot dog cart	$2500
Business licenses (city and state)	200
Business cards and flyers	150
Beginning inventory (hot dogs, mustard, buns, etc.)	50
Cash box and other	100
Total start-up investment without contingency	$3000
Contingency @ 10% of start-up investment	300
Total start-up investment with contingency	$3300

prototype a model or pattern that serves as an example of how a product would look and operate if it were produced.

A fitness center is an example of a complex business.

For a more complex business, like a 24-hour franchise fitness center being opened in an existing, leased space, the summary start-up sheet could be as shown in **Exhibit 12-1**. The items would be broken down into greater detail in order to secure quotations. For example, each piece of equipment would be identified and a quote secured, assuming the franchisor does not have a specific package of equipment for purchase.

For a manufacturing business, developing a prototype for the item being manufactured may be a major start-up cost, sometimes totaling in the millions. A **prototype** is a model or pattern that serves as an example of how a product would look and operate if it were manufactured. Companies that specialize in creating prototypes can be found in the *Thomas Register of American Manufacturers*.

Brainstorm to Avoid Start-Up Surprises

Before starting your business, try to anticipate every possible cost by thinking of all components of the investment. Talk to other business owners in your industry and ask them what start-up costs they failed to anticipate. Use **Exhibit 12-2** to estimate your start-up investment.

Once you have brainstormed a list, take it to your advisors or mentors and have them look it over. They will probably find start-up costs you have overlooked. You might not have realized that the electric company may require a $1000 deposit to

Exhibit 12-1 *Seed capital estimate for a 24-hour fitness center.*

Item/Category	Cost	Estimate or Quote?
Equipment, furniture, and fixtures	$105,000	Quote
Leasehold improvements	$3,200	Quote
Installation of equipment and fixtures	$2,800	Quote
Computers and other technology	$5,000	Quote
Employee wages, salaries, and benefits	$3,100	Estimate
Owner time (valued at $25 per hour)*	$5,000	Estimate
Professional services (attorney, accountant, architect, engineers, and the like)	$3,000	Estimate
Promotions and advertising	$1,800	Mixed
Licenses and permits	$300	Quote
Deposits on rent and utilities	$5,600	Quote
Rent on location identified	$2,000	Quote
Utilities	$400	Estimate
Insurance	$1,000	Quote
Debt service (interest on $130,000 at 10%)	$2,167	Estimate
Taxes (wage and other)	$500	Estimate
Memberships (trade associations, chambers of commerce, and the like)	$900	Mixed
Training, conventions, and seminars	$1,000	Quote
Franchise fees	$40,000	Quote
Financing costs and fees (2% of $130,000)	$2,600	Estimate
Supplies	$400	Estimate
Inventory	$200	Estimate
Petty cash	$300	Quote
Total pre-opening investment	$186,267	
Allowance for contingencies/ emergencies (10%)	$18,626	
Initial Investment**	**$204,893**	

*If no wage or salary is being paid to the owners, this is a "soft" cost and can be considered an optional item on the list. However, including it makes the list more comprehensive and more reflective of the total cost.

**This figure does not include cash reserves, or cash requirements for initial cash shortfall during operations. Both should be added to reflect total financing needed.

turn on service, for example. Or you may need licenses and insurance you did not expect. Tack on an additional 10 percent to your estimates for contingencies and emergencies.

Research the Costs

In addition to brainstorming and consulting with your advisors, you can do some research to accurately assess your start-up costs. Look at business plan models in your industry, if possible. Adapt the cost data to fit your business and obtain quotations on pricing from potential suppliers.

Exhibit 12-2 *Start-up investment checklist.*

Item/Category	Cost	Estimate or Quote?
Land and building (if constructing or purchasing)		
Equipment and machinery		
Furniture and fixtures		
Leasehold improvements (if renting)		
Installation of equipment and fixtures		
Computers and other technology		
Employee wages, salaries, and benefits		
Owner time (valued at $ _______ per hour)*		
Professional services (attorney, accountant, architect, engineers, and the like)		
Promotions and advertising		
Licenses and permits		
Deposits on rent and utilities		
Rent		
Utilities		
Insurance		
Debt service (normally interest only)		
Taxes (wage and other)		
Memberships (trade associations, chambers of commerce, and the like)		
Registration fees		
Training, conventions, and seminars		
Licensing or franchising fees		
Financing costs and fees		
Supplies		
Inventory		
Petty cash		
Total pre-opening investment		
Allowance for contingencies/emergencies (10%)		
Initial Investment**		

*If no wage or salary is paid to the owners, this is a "soft" cost and can be considered an optional item on the list. However, including it is more comprehensive and more reflective of total costs.
**This figure does not include cash reserves, or cash requirements for initial cash shortfall during operations. Both should be added to reflect total financing needed.

Look at available industry data. Do not be caught by surprise on costs that you could have predicted.

Keep a Reserve Equal to One-Half of Start-Up Investment

cash reserve emergency funds and a pool of cash resources.

Start-up investment should include one more thing: a **cash reserve**, or emergency funds and a pool of cash resources, which should equal at least half your start-up costs. For the previously mentioned hot dog cart example, therefore, the reserve would be half of $3300, or $1650, making the total required $4950.

Entrepreneurs must be prepared for the unexpected; the only good surprise is no surprise. The reserve will provide a moderate cushion of protection when you need it. When your computer goes down or your biggest supplier raises prices, you will be glad you had this money on hand.

Having a cash reserve will also allow you to take advantage of opportunities. Say you own a vintage clothing store, and you hear from a friend whose great-aunt died and left him a great deal of authentic vintage clothing and jewelry. He is willing to sell you the whole lot for $500, which you figure you can resell in your shop for at least $2000. If you did not have the extra cash on hand, you might have lost this profitable opportunity.

Predict the Payback Period

When compiling and analyzing start-up costs, one consideration will be how long it will take for you to earn back your start-up investment. The **payback period** is an estimate for you and your investors of how long it will take your business to bring in enough cash to cover the start-up investment. It is measured in months.

payback period estimated time required to earn sufficient net cash flow to cover the start-up investment.

$$\text{Payback} = \frac{\text{Start-Up Investment}}{\text{Net Cash Flow per Month}}$$

Example: Ashley's business requires a start-up investment of $1000. The business is projecting a net cash flow per month of $400. How many months will it take to make back her start-up investment?

$$\text{Payback} = \frac{\$1000}{\$400} = 2.5 \text{ Months}$$

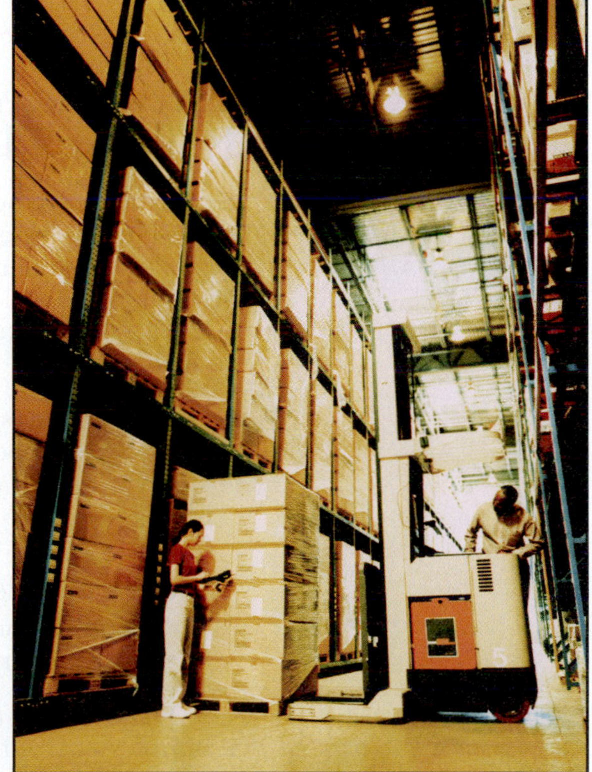

Knowing the payback period is important for a start-up, or an existing firm, so that the time horizon is known and timing of funds availability is clear. However, the payback period does not take into consideration the future earnings, opportunities for alternative investments, or the overall value of the company. It is based upon net cash and is a good indicator of the time needed to earn back initial funds.

Estimate Value

Financial managers use several tools to determine the current value of proposed investments, of which net present value (NPV) is widely accepted as the most theoretically sound. Entrepreneurs can use such a technique to consider the financial returns on their initial investment. If the NPV calculation yields a positive value, the investment will result in a positive return based upon the owner's (and investors') required rate of return.

There are multiple methods of calculating NPV, including using a formula, tables, a spreadsheet program, or a financial calculator. You can calculate NPV with the following information: required rate of return (%), annual net cash flows (see Chapter 14), initial investment, and number of years of cash flows. **Exhibit 12-3** shows an NPV calculation for a business with an initial investment of $1.5 million.

Exhibit 12-3 *Calculating net present value with Excel.*

Description	Data	Notes
Initial investment	$1,500,000	Seed capital needed to start the business
Required rate of return	0.12	Return required by investors (owners)
Net Cash Year 1	$—	First year of operations yielding no net cash
Net Cash Year 2	$100,000	Second year of operations with earnings
Net Cash Year 3	$200,000	Subsequent year
Net Cash Year 4	$500,000	Subsequent year
Net Cash Year 5	$850,000	Subsequent year
Net Cash Year 6	$1,200,000	Subsequent year
Net Cash Year 7	$600,000	Results show declining market
Net Cash Year 8	$400,000	Further decline
Net Cash Year 9	$—	Company closed
Calculated Present Val.	$2,063,067.47	Use formulas financial NPV
Net Present Value	**$563,067.47**	Value above initial investment
NPV > $0?	Yes	NPV is positive, so it is "a go"

Fixed and Variable Costs: Essential Building Blocks

variable costs expenses that vary directly with changes in the production or sales volume.

Small business owners divide their costs into two categories. **Variable costs** change based on the volume of units sold or produced. **Fixed costs** are expenses that must be paid regardless of whether or not sales are being generated.

Variable costs change with production and sales. They fall into two subcategories:

1. Cost of goods sold (COGS), or cost of services sold (COSS), which is associated specifically with each unit of sale, including
   - The cost of materials used to make the product (or deliver the service)
   - The cost of labor used to make the product (or deliver the service)
2. Other variable costs include:
   - Commissions or other compensation based on sales volume
   - Shipping and handling charges

Performance Objective 2

Describe the variable costs of starting a business.

Fixed costs stay constant whether you sell many units or very few. Examples of fixed costs include rent, salaries, insurance, equipment, and manufacturing plants.

Henry Ford spent money on efficient manufacturing equipment (a fixed cost) but saved a fortune on labor (COGS) by doing so. This reduced his total costs because labor was used in each of the millions of cars Ford produced, but he only had to pay for the plant and equipment once.

For any product, you can study its economics of one unit to figure out what it cost to make that sale. **Exhibit 12-4** shows an example from a business that sells hand-painted vintage T-shirts.

Exhibit 12-4 *Manufacturing business: Unit = 1 hand-painted T-shirt.*

Economics of One Unit (EOU) Analysis (Define the Unit of Sale)				
Selling Price (per Unit)				**$35.00**
COGS (Cost of Goods Sold)				
Materials per Unit		$7.00		
Labor per hour	$10.00			
# of Hours per Unit	0.75			
Total Labor per Unit	7.50	7.50		
Total COGS (per Unit)		$14.50	$14.50	14.50
Gross Profit (per Unit)				**$20.50**
Other Variable Costs				
Commission (10%)		3.50		
Packaging		0.50		
Total Other Variable Costs		$4.00	4.00	4.00
Total Variable Costs (per Unit)			**$18.50**	
Contribution Margin				**$16.50**

Calculating Critical Costs

To determine the most important factors with respect to costs in your business, you can calculate *critical* costs. This will help you to determine profitability and the factors that can and cannot be easily changed to impact your profits and cash flow.

Calculating Total Gross Profit (Contribution Margin)

You can use EOU to calculate whether and by how much you will come out ahead on your per-unit costs for each sale. By using the EOU, you can figure the gross profit per unit (**contribution margin** per unit sold, the selling price minus total variable costs plus other variable costs).

contribution margin gross profit per unit—the selling price minus total variable costs plus other variable costs.

Calculating EOU When You Sell Multiple Products

Most businesses sell more than a single product and they can also use EOU as a value measure of product profitability. A business selling a variety of products has to create a separate EOU for each item to determine whether each is profitable. When there are many similar products with comparable prices and cost structures, a typical EOU can be used.

Example: Jamaal sells four kinds of candy bars at school. He sells each bar for $1, but he pays a different wholesale price for each:

Snickers	36¢ each
Almond Joy	38¢ each
Butterfinger	42¢ each
Baby Ruth	44¢ each

Rather than make separate EOUs, Jamaal uses the average cost of his four candy bars (see **Exhibit 12-5**).

Exhibit 12-5 *Retail business: Unit = 1 candy bar.*

Economics of One Unit (EOU) Analysis		
One Unit of Sale = One Candy Bar		
Selling Price		**$1.00**
COGS (direct cost of the product or service)		
Average Cost of Candy Bars (COGS)	0.40	
Average Shipping Cost per Unit	0.06	
Total COGS	**0.46**	**0.46**
Gross Profit		**0.54**
Other Variable Costs (none)	–	–
Contribution Margin		**$0.54**

Costs of the four candy bars = (36¢ + 38¢ + 42¢ + 44¢) ÷ 4

Average cost of the four candy bars = $1.60 ÷ 4

Average cost of each bar = 40¢

Using an average works if the costs are close, and as long as Jamaal sells roughly the same number of each brand of bar. If he can no longer get Snickers and Almond Joy at some point, for example, he should then change his EOU to reflect the higher price of the other two bars.

What if each unit of sale is made up of a complex mix of materials and labor? The EOU can still help you figure the COGS, other variable costs, and gross profit for the product, although the process will be more complex.

Many small businesses have inventory costs.

inventory costs expenses associated with materials and direct labor for production until the product is sold.

Example: Denise sells sandwiches from her deli cart downtown on Saturdays. She sells each for $5. The materials and labor that go directly into making each sandwich are the COGS. The costs of the materials and direct labor for production are called **inventory costs** until the product is sold. There will also be some other variable costs such as napkins, a paper wrapping for each sandwich, and plastic bags.

First, make a list of the COGS and any other variable costs:

COGS

a. Turkey costs $2.60 per lb. Each sandwich uses 4 oz. of turkey meat (1/4 lb.).
b. Large rolls cost $1.92 per dozen. One roll is used per sandwich.
c. One ounce of mayonnaise is used per sandwich. A 32-ounce jar of mayo costs $1.60.
d. Lettuce costs 80 cents per lb. and 1/16 of a pound (1 ounce) is used on each sandwich.
e. Tomatoes cost $1.16 each. Each sandwich uses a fourth of a tomato.
f. Each sandwich comes with two pickles. Pickles cost 5 cents each.
g. Employees are paid $7 per hour and can make 10 sandwiches per hour (we are assuming no down time and no payroll costs).

Exhibit 12-6 *Retail business: Unit = 1 turkey sandwich.*

	Price	Units	Quantity Used	Cost Each	
Selling Price per Unit:					**$5.00**
Cost of Goods Sold					
Turkey (4 oz.):	$2.60	Per lb.	¼ lb.	$0.65	
Bread (roll):	$1.92	Per dozen	1/12 dozen	$0.16	
Mayonnaise (1 oz.):	$1.60	Per 32-oz. jar	1/32 jar	$0.05	
Lettuce (1 oz.):	$0.80	Per lb.	1/16 lb.	$0.05	
Tomato (¼ lb.)	$1.16	Each	¼ each	$0.29	
Pickles (2):	$0.05	Each	2 each	$0.10	
Direct Labor (6 min.):	$7.00	Per hr.	1/10 hr.	$0.70	
Total Cost of Goods Sold per Unit:				**$2.00**	2.00
Gross Profit					**$3.00**
Other Variable Costs					
Napkin:	$3.00	Per 100-pack	1/100 pack	$0.03	
Paper Wrapping:	$0.20	Per foot	2 feet	$0.40	
Plastic Bag:	$7.00	Per roll (100)	1/100 roll	$0.07	
Total Other Variable Costs per Unit:				**$0.50**	
Total Variable Costs per Unit:					0.50
Contribution Margin per Unit:					**$2.50**

Other Variable Costs

The following supplies are used every time a sandwich is sold, but are not strictly part of the sandwich's production:

a. Napkins cost $3 per pack of 100. One napkin is included with each sale.

b. Paper wrapping costs 20 cents per foot (on a roll). Each sandwich uses two feet of paper.

c. Plastic carryout bags cost $7 per roll of 100. Each sandwich sold uses one plastic carryout bag. (In reality, more than one sandwich might go into a bag.)

The EOU for the turkey sandwich is shown in **Exhibit 12-6**.

Fixed Operating Costs

Costs, such as rent or the Internet bill, which do not vary per unit of production or service, are called **fixed operating costs**. Fixed operating costs are not included in COGS (or COSS) because they are not directly related to the creation of the product (or service).[1] Fixed operating costs are not included in other variable costs because they do not vary directly with the number of sales made.

fixed operating costs expenses that do not vary with changes in the volume of production or sales.

Fixed operating costs do not change based on sales; therefore, they are not included in the EOU. A sandwich shop has to pay the same rent each month whether it sells one turkey sandwich or a hundred. However, the owner of the shop can change the cost of the rent by moving, or can increase or decrease the advertising budget, and the like. These changes are not calculated on a per-unit basis.

Performance Objective 3

Analyze your fixed operating costs and calculate gross profit.

[1]Cost of goods sold is used for businesses that sell products. Service businesses use the term cost of services sold.

An easy way to remember the seven common fixed operating costs is with the acronym USAIDIR:

Utilities (gas, electric, telephone, Internet service)
Salaries (indirect labor)
Advertising
Insurance
Depreciation
Interest
Rent

depreciation the percentage of value of an asset subtracted periodically to reflect the declining value.

Most of these categories are self-explanatory, but *depreciation* may need clarification. **Depreciation** is the percentage of value of an asset subtracted each year until the value becomes zero, to reflect wear and tear on the asset. It is a method used to expense (listed as an expense on the income statement) costly pieces of equipment. Fixed costs are expensed during the year the money is spent. When a company pays for advertising, it subtracts that cost from the gross profit for that year. Some items, however, such as a computer, are expected to last for a number of years. A business could choose to expense a computer during the year it was bought, but that would not be accurate. A computer that will be used for four years will have been only 25 percent "used up" during the year it was purchased. Expensing the entire cost of the computer during that year would make the accounting records and financial statements inaccurate. If more than 25 percent of the computer's cost is expensed in the first year, the income statement will show a lower profit than it should. Meanwhile, profits in subsequent years will appear to be higher than they should.

This problem is addressed by depreciation, which spreads the cost of an item purchased by a business over the period of time during which it will actually be in use. If the computer will not be replaced for four years, then the full price should be shown as an asset, and then expensed 25 percent each year. In this way, the cost of the computer and its value to the company will be reflected more accurately.

Fixed Operating Costs Do Change over Time

If you pay your restaurant manager $3600 per month in salary, you will have to pay that amount whether the restaurant sells one meal or a thousand. The cost is fixed.

Fixed operating costs do change over time; at some point you may give your restaurant manager a raise. Or, you might hire a new manager at a lower salary. The word *fixed* does not mean the cost *never* changes,

Global Impact . . .

Direct Foreign Investment

Global companies experience opportunities and challenges when determining initial investments in foreign countries. Opportunities arise from such sources as incentives for direct foreign investment (DFI) and lower facilities construction and fit-out costs. In addition, start-up inventory may be more economical. At the same time, there may be barriers to DFI, such as legal and permitting costs, standards, and requirements that increase initial investment. Clearly, having a full understanding of the initial start-up investment is crucial and is potentially more complex.

Exchange rates and the economic and political environment in a foreign country have a potentially significant impact on start-up investment. As is true with domestic startups, the estimate of the initial investment is a vital consideration in the investment decision.

just that it does not change in response to units of production or sales. For instance:

- ***Advertising.*** The cost of advertising will change based on decisions the entrepreneur makes about how much to spend to reach the consumer, not because of current sales (although low sales may provoke an increase in advertising).
- ***Heating and cooling costs.*** The price of heating and cooling goes up or down based on the weather and utility prices, not on the amount of revenue the business earns.

Allocate Fixed Operating Costs Where Possible

Business owners like to know, whenever they make a sale, how much of that revenue will have to be used to cover the cost of goods sold and other variable costs.

Whatever is left over after you pay the COGS and other variable costs is your *contribution margin* (gross profit). You will pay your fixed operating costs from the contribution margin. Whatever is left over after you pay your fixed operating costs (and taxes) is your **net profit**.

net profit the remainder of revenues minus fixed and variable costs and taxes.

Fixed operating costs can be dangerous because they have to be paid whether or not the business has a gross profit. The entrepreneur should be careful about taking on fixed costs, but does not have to worry so much about variable costs because, if sales are low, variable costs will be low as well. Wherever possible, the entrepreneur should seek to allocate or distribute as many costs as possible by making them variable.

Here is an example of how to fully allocate your costs, so that you know, each time you sell a unit, how much of your fixed and variable costs the sale is covering.

Example: If you sell 300 watches per month at $15 per watch (see **Exhibit 12-7**), your COGS is $2 per watch, and your other variable costs are commissions of $2 per watch and shipping charges of $1 per watch.

Gross profit per unit is $13 ($3900 in gross profit divided by 300 watches sold). Contribution margin per unit is $10 ($3,000 ÷ 300). Some of this gross profit will have to be used to cover the business's fixed operating costs. It is helpful to determine how much profit will be left over after paying the fixed operating costs, assuming your sales are stable. **Exhibit 12-8** shows the calculation of the total cost per unit.

Exhibit 12-7 *Retail business: Unit = 1 watch.*

Analysis—300 Watches Sold			
Sales (300 watches × $15 per watch):			**$4,500**
COGS ($2 per watch × 300 watches):		**$600**	**600**
Gross Profit (on 300 watches sold)			**3,900**
Other Variable Costs			
Commission ($2 per watch)	**$600**		
Shipping ($1 per watch)	**300**		
Total Other Variable Costs	**$900**	**900**	**900**
Total Variable Costs (per Unit)		**$1,500**	
Contribution Margin			**$3,000**

Exhibit 12-8 *Retail business: Total cost per unit.*

Total Variable Costs (COGS + Other Variable Costs):		$1,500
Fixed Operating Costs (per month):		
Utilities	$50	
Salaries	100	
Advertising	50	
Insurance	50	
Depreciation	50	
Interest	50	
Rent	100	
Total Fixed Operating Costs:	$450	450
Total Costs (Fixed + Variable) =		$1,950
Total Cost per Unit ($1,950 ÷ 300 watches) =		$6.50 per watch

For every watch you sell, your total cost, fixed and variable, is $6.50. If you receive $15 for each watch, therefore, your profit before tax is the following:

$15.00 Selling Price – $6.50 Total Cost per Unit = $8.50 Profit before Tax

The Dangers of Fixed Costs

If a business does not have enough sales to cover its fixed costs, it will lose money. If losses continue, the business will have to close. As we have discussed, fixed costs are dangerous because they must be paid whether or not the business is making enough sales to cover them. Variable costs, on the other hand, do not threaten a business's survival because they are proportional to sales.

Bob Kaufman of Bob's Discount Furniture.

Step into the Shoes . . .

Bob's Discount Furniture[2]

Bob Kaufman owns 32 furniture stores in New England and New York.[3] Bob's Discount Furniture, the 2008 Furniture Retailer of the Year, is one of the largest TV advertisers in Connecticut. When Bob was starting out in the furniture business in 1982, though, he needed to find creative ways to cut his costs.

Bob found a store to rent for his furniture business, but the landlord wanted him to sign a one-year lease. Bob knew that rent was a fixed cost. This meant he would have to pay rent every month, whether he could afford to or not, for a full 12 months. He realized that if sales were low he would get into trouble quickly because he would not have cash in reserve.

What Bob needed was to change his rent from a fixed to a variable cost. He negotiated with the landlord to pay the rent as a percentage of the monthly sales. That way, if sales were low, Bob's rent would also be low. If sales were high, his rent would go up, but he would be able to pay it. Rent was Bob's largest fixed cost. By changing it into a variable cost, he cut a lot of the risk out of his new business venture.

Bob's Discount Furniture became extremely successful. That arrangement helped Bob out when his business was small. Today, the company owns many of its locations and pays fixed rent on the rest.

[2]Thanks to John Harris for the original case.
[3]Bob's Discount Furniture Web site, http://www.mybobs.com (accessed on July 28, 2009).

How Inflation Can Hurt Small Business Owners

Inflation is the gradual, continuous increase in the prices of products and services, usually resulting from an increase in the amount of money in circulation in an economy. It can be the enemy of the small business owner. If you save $600 per year to buy new tables and chairs (which cost $3000 the last time you bought them) for your restaurant, but you find at the end of five years that the cost of replacing them has risen to $5000 because of inflation, your business could be in trouble if you cannot get the additional $2000. Savvy entrepreneurs keep up with economic trends by reading the financial section in the newspapers, as well as financial magazines and Web sites. By staying up to date on what is happening, you can invest wisely and plan effectively for the future.

inflation the gradual, continuous increase in the prices of products.

Using Accounting Records to Track Fixed and Variable Costs

Now you are ready to set up your financial records. Nothing that you learn as an entrepreneur will be more important than keeping accurate records of the money flowing in and out of your business. The systematic recording, reporting, and analysis of the financial transactions of a business (keeping statistical records of inflows and outflows) is called *accounting*. It is the primary language businesspeople use to communicate. When you talk to an investor or a supplier about your business, you will need to use accounting terms. He or she will want to see the financial statements for your business that describe its performance at a glance.

Performance Objective 4

Set up financial record keeping for your business.

Before you can create financial statements, however, you must be able to keep track of your daily business transactions. If you develop record keeping into a habit, you will be well ahead of the many businesspeople that tend to get careless when it comes to keeping good records consistently.

Three Reasons to Keep Good Records Every Day

1. ***Keeping good records will show you how to make your business more profitable.*** Perhaps your profits are down this month over last. Did your expenses go up? Maybe you need to try lowering your costs. Did your sales drop? Maybe you are not spending enough on advertising. Use accurate records as a base to constantly improve your business.
2. ***Keeping good records will document your business profitability and cash position.*** If you want people to invest in your business, show them that it is profitable. Keep accurate records to create financial statements and ratios that prove your business is doing well. Remember, you will *always* need to maintain your business's financial statements so that you will be up to date on your company's performance.
3. ***Keeping good records proves that payments have been made.*** Accurate, up-to-date records help prevent arguments, because they prove you have paid a bill or that a customer has paid you. Records can also prove that you have paid your taxes—the fee charged (*levied*) by a government on an income, product, or activity that is imposed on an individual or legal entity (corporation). Sometimes the Internal Revenue Service, the federal agency that collects taxes, will visit a business and check its financial records in a process called an **audit**. If you keep good records and pay your taxes in a timely fashion, you will have nothing to fear from audits.

audit a review of financial and business records to ascertain integrity and compliance with standards and laws, particularly by the U.S. Internal Revenue Service.

U.S. tax law allows business owners to deduct many expenses from their taxes. These deductions, or write-offs, are reductions in the gross amount on which taxes are calculated, and they will save you money. But you must keep receipts and record check payments to show that you actually had the expenses. A good practice is to write the purpose of an expense on the receipt.

Accounting Software

There are many excellent computer software programs on the market to help the small business owner keep good records and generate financial statements and analytical reports. These include Intuit QuickBooks, Microsoft Office Accounting, and Peachtree Accounting. In addition, companies such as Net Suite offer Web-based accounting for a monthly access fee. There are also programs to help you manage your money. You can use them to write checks, balance your bank account, and track your income. Some software creates project quotes and invoices. There is specialized software for particular types of businesses and for nonprofit organizations. It may save you time and money to purchase industry-specific software from the start.

The URLs for some of the accounting software companies are:

Microsoft, *http://www.microsoft.com*
QuickBooks, *http://www.quickbooks.com*
Peachtree Software, *http://www.peachtree.com*

Many software companies offer free products that you can try for a limited period of time, or that are free but do not have as many features as the versions for sale. This is a great way for you to try out different accounting and other business software before you buy. The costs of these packages have dropped considerably over time, making them a better value for even the smallest companies. For example, if your business provides services, and potential customers expect estimates, they can be generated and tracked by professional-services software. Take the time to find the software best suited to your needs.

Receipts and Invoices

For a very small business, it is possible to work with a manual system, including a journal and files for storing records of your transactions. As your business grows, you can add organizational tools. However, if you are intending to grow the business beyond a handful of transactions per week, you should use a good computer-based system from the start. Whatever system you elect to use, there are certain records that should be kept.

John D. Rockefeller.

Step into the Shoes . . .

Rockefeller's Record Keeping

John D. Rockefeller, who founded Standard Oil (now ExxonMobil) and built one of the most famous family fortunes in history, reportedly kept track of every penny he spent from age 16 until his death, in 1937, at the age of 98. His children said that he never paid a bill without examining it, and being certain that he understood it.

Being up to date with your financial records will give you control over your business and a sense of security.

- A *receipt* is a slip of paper with the date and amount of the purchase on it. *Always get a receipt for every purchase you make.* Issue a receipt for all sales if you have a retail business, whether you create it manually or from your point-of-sales system.
- An *invoice*, or bill, shows the product or service sold and the amount the customer is to pay. Your invoice becomes the customer's receipt. Keep a copy of each invoice in an organized fashion (i.e., numerically, alphabetically, or in order by date), and record all payments promptly.

Keep at Least Two Copies of Your Records

Always keep a copy of your financial records in a location away from your business, preferably in a fire-retardant safe or concrete-lined file cabinet. If you are using software, back up your data and keep the media (CD, jump drive, etc.) in a different location. At the end of each day, week, or month, move your new receipts and invoices to this location. How often you do this will depend upon your transaction volume and how much data you are willing to risk losing. By having regular off-site backups if anything happens to your journal or your business site, you will still have your financial records. Follow federal records-retention rules with these documents.

Use Business Checks for Business Expenses

Get a checking account to use only for your business. It is inadvisable to comingle your personal and business funds, regardless of your business type. Financial institutions routinely require business checks to be deposited into business accounts rather than personal ones, so any customer check payments made out to your business name will have to be deposited into a business account.

Avoid using cash for business. If you must pay in cash, get an itemized receipt, record the expenditure, and file the receipt promptly. It is easy to lose track of cash receipts and miss out on tax deductions for business expenses.

Deposit money from sales right away. When you make a sale, the transaction will not be complete until the cash is deposited, or until the check has cleared if the payment was made by check. Again, recording every sale is critical to documenting profitability and cash flow. It will also ensure that business receipts and sales match in transaction records.

Cash versus Accrual Accounting Methods

Financial accounting for companies is divided between the cash and accrual methods, and companies elect which method they will use. Small businesses use either method, whereas large firms almost invariably use accrual accounting. It is best to seek professional advice on this issue when starting your business. With the **cash accounting method**, the only time an accounting entry is made is when cash is paid or received. With the **accrual method**, entries are made according to the occurrence of the transaction, without regard to the date of payment (i.e., for a manufacturer, purchases would be billed when the product is shipped).

cash accounting method the method wherein transactions are recorded as cash is paid out or received.

accrual method accounting method wherein transactions are recorded at the time of occurrence, regardless of the transfer of cash.

Recognizing Categories of Costs

Even if you are using accounting software to record your business transactions, it will be helpful to understand the key categories of accounting data. These are briefly described below. A more detailed list appears in the Appendices, and will be particularly useful if you elect to use a manual record-keeping system.

- ***Variable costs (VC).*** Any cost that changes based on the number of units sold. Includes cost of goods sold (COGS). Multiply COGS by the number of units sold to get total COGS.
- ***Fixed costs (FC).*** Business expenses that must be paid whether or not sales are made. Remember USAIIRD: utilities, salaries, advertising, insurance, interest, rent, and depreciation.
- ***Capital Equipment.*** Money spent on business equipment that is expected to last a year or more.
- ***Investment.*** Start-up capital plus any money you or others have invested in the business, but not loans. This is only for money invested in exchange for part ownership (equity).
- ***Loans.*** Any funds you have borrowed to start or operate the business.
- ***Revenue.*** Money received from sales.
- ***Inventory.*** Anything purchased for resale is *inventory.* Includes shipping costs from the supplier.
- ***Other Costs.*** Anything that does not fit into the other expense categories.

Chapter Summary

Now that you have studied this chapter, you can do the following:

1. Identify the investment required for business startup.
   - Brainstorming, consulting advisors, and research can be combined to create a comprehensive set of investment requirements.
   - Contingency funds and cash reserves should be added to minimize the impact of unanticipated costs and to permit flexibility to take advantage of opportunities.
   - Payback period is estimation of time required to bring in enough cash to cover the seed funding.
   - Net present value addresses the viability of an investment opportunity that considers investment-return criteria.
2. Describe the variable costs of starting a business.
   - Start-up investment is the one-time expense of starting a business.
   - Cost of goods sold is the direct cost of producing the product or service.
   - Operating costs comprise the funds necessary to run the business, not including the cost of goods sold. Operating costs can almost always be divided into seven categories. An easy way to remember these is through the acronym USAIDIR:
     - Utilities (gas, electric, telephone, Internet)
     - Salaries
     - Advertising
     - Insurance
     - Depreciation
     - Interest
     - Rent
3. Divide your costs into two categories: variable and fixed.
   - Variable costs change (*vary*) with sales. They are divided into two subcategories:
     a. Cost of goods sold, which are the costs associated specifically with each unit of sale, including
        - the cost of materials used to make the product (or deliver the service) and
        - the cost of labor used to make the product (or deliver the service).

b. Other variable costs, including
   - commissions and
   - shipping and handling charges, etc.

- Fixed costs stay constant whether you sell many units or very few. Examples of fixed costs include rent, salaries, and insurance.
- Set up a financial record-keeping system for your business.
- Recognize the importance of keeping complete, accurate, and timely records.
- Determine whether to use the cash or accrual accounting method.
- Categorize the accounting entries properly, whether using a manual or computer-based accounting system.

Key Terms

accrual method
audit
cash accounting method
cash reserve
contribution margin
depreciation
fixed operating costs
inflation
inventory costs
net profit
payback period
prototype
seed capital
variable costs

Entrepreneurship Portfolio

Critical Thinking Exercises

1. Give an example of a business that you have observed lowering the price of a product. How do you think the business was able to reduce the price?
2. Describe the record-keeping system you intend to set up for your business.
3. What bank accounts do you intend to open for your business? Which bank will you use? Why?
4. Imagine that you have invented a guitar strap that goes over both shoulders, thereby reducing shoulder strain for the guitarist. This item could be a big seller, but, before you can apply for a patent or convince investors to back your producing it, you will need a prototype. Find at least three manufacturers that could create such a prototype for you.
5. For a business you would like to start, estimate what you think the fixed and variable costs would be. Choose a category for each cost from USAIDIR: Utilities, Salaries, Advertising, Insurance, Depreciation, Interest, and Rent.

Key Concept Questions

1. What is the reason to calculate the payback period and the net present value for a business investment? What distinguishes the two?

2. Calculate Total Revenue for the items below.

Units Sold	Selling Price	Total Revenue
a. 25	$4.64	$116.00
b. 30	$10.99	________
c. 12	$1,233.00	________
d. 75	$545.75	________
e. 20	$45.03	________

3. Calculate Total Variable Costs for the same items.

Units Sold	Total Variable Costs per Unit	Total Variable Costs
a. 25	$2.00	$50.00
b. 30	$5.50	________
c. 12	$620.00	________
d. 75	$280.00	________
e. 20	$20.00	________

4. Calculate Total Contribution Margin for the same items.

Total Revenue	Total Variable Costs	Total Contribution Margin
a. $116.00	$50.00	$66.00
b. ________	________	________
c. ________	________	________
d. ________	________	________
e. ________	________	________

5. Calculate Total Profit for the same items.

Total Contribution Margin	Total Fixed Operating Costs	Total Profit
a. $66.00	$25.00	$41.00
b. ________	$60.00	________
c. ________	$425.00	________
d. ________	$12,000.00	________
e. ________	$200.00	________

6. Calculate Profit per Unit for the same items.

Units Sold	Total Profit	Profit per Unit
a. 25	$41.00	$1.64
b. 30	________	________
c. 12	________	________
d. 75	________	________
e. 20	________	________

7. The business concepts below have been developed by your colleagues and they have asked you to provide feedback on each as a potential investment. Using the data provided, calculate the payback period and NPV of each.

Project	Seed Capital	Rate of Return (%)	Net Cash Flow Year 1	Net Cash Flow Year 2	Net Cash Flow Year 3	Net Cash Flow Year 4	Net Cash Flow Year 5	Other Net Cash Flow	Payback Period	NPV
A	$1,000	5%	$200	$300	$400	$500	$0	$0		
B	$250,000	8%	$2,000	$25,000	$25,000	$1,000,000	$148,000	$200,000 per year for 5 years		
C	$8,000,000	17%	$0	$0	$0	$1,000,000	$5,000,000	$6,000,000 for 3 years		
D	$50,000	25%	$0	$1,000	$29,000	$35,0000	$70,000	$0		
E	$120 million	6%	$0	$0	$20 million	$80 million	$40 million	$20 million in Year 6, $5 million in Year 7		

Application Exercise

Sue, of Sue's Sandwich Shoppe, sells sandwiches and soda from a sidewalk cart in a popular park near her home. She sets up her rented cart in the summers to raise money for college. Last month, she sold $3,000 worth of product (sandwiches and sodas) to 300 customers. She spent $600 on the sandwich ingredients and buying the sodas wholesale. Her monthly costs are the following: Utilities = $60, Salary = $1500, Advertising = $0, Insurance = $50, Interest = $0, Rent = $300, Depreciation = $0.

a. What are Sue's variable costs? Explain.
b. What is Sue's COGS? Explain.
c. What are her other variable costs? Explain.
d. What are her fixed costs? Explain.
e. What is Sue's EOU?
f. How much cash reserve should she keep in the bank?

Exploring Your Community

Ask an entrepreneur in your neighborhood to discuss his or her accounting system. Write a one-page essay about the pros and cons of the system and use it to make an oral report to the class.

Exploring Online

Research different accounting software programs online. Choose a program (or programs) for your business and explain your choice in a brief essay.

In Your Opinion

Would you rather keep your financial records in an accounting ledger or on your computer? Why? In each case, how would you protect your records from being lost in a disaster, such as a fire, or, in the case of the computer, a hard-drive crash?

Case Study | The Importance of Cash

Jack Wilson has had a 30-year career in the building and managing of Web pages with two very well-known Web-based marketing companies. During his career, Jack has been in contact with hundreds of individuals and companies through projects and industry gatherings. For the past four years, and on his own time, Jack has been developing new ways of making it easier for users to maintain and upgrade Web-page information. Jack is entering the final stages of writing the software that will provide these benefits, and he wants to leave his present position and devote all his time to the project. Jack's employment contract calls for him to honor a noncompete clause for 12 months, and he will receive a severance payment of $80,000, which is equal to the total of his approximate annual earnings for the previous two years.

The new Web-page software will cost about $75,000 in programming fees, and $30,000 in legal fees will be necessary to ready the product for testing and sale. Jack is not experienced in marketing, but a consultant that he has met with has predicted that it will take about $30,000 for product packaging and early promotional expenses. The product will probably sell for $2500 per copy, based on similar software. The market for this type of software will be mainly small-to-medium-sized businesses that maintain their own Web sites. Jack is aware of a handful of existing software companies whose product line would be a good fit for what he is developing. (Some software developers have sold their concepts to larger companies, rather than try to handle the details and expense of launching a product themselves.)

Jack has liquid savings of $18,000 and another $90,000 in an IRA account. He owns a home without a mortgage, that is worth about $150,000. Jack is a conservative person and does not lead a lavish lifestyle. He has worked long and hard on his new product idea and feels as though this is his opportunity to make a contribution to his field and be in charge of his own company. Jack also has the opportunity to provide consulting services to other programming organizations on a project-by-project basis. This work could bring in fees of $40,000, probably from six months to a year after completion of the software.

Case Study Analysis

1. Does Jack have enough money to start this business? What strategy would you recommend he pursue over the next year?
2. What strategies would you suggest that this entrepreneur adopt with respect to his use of cash?
3. Is there enough information given for you to make some early suggestions to Jack about pursuing the product on his own, versus selling his idea to an established company?
4. What amount of cash reserve for the business should Jack include in his plan?

Case Study | Futrell Party Promotions[4]

The Problem

The telephone rang. Richard Futrell put on his headset and answered, "Good evening, Boston Teen Hotline. My name is Richard. How can I help you?" The year was 1999. Richard had been working as a hotline counselor at the mayor's youth committee for three years. Every night, from 6 to 11 p.m., he took calls from teenagers in the Boston area, advising them on many different issues: relationships, family problems, school, and more. Richard had a natural talent for being a good listener. In fact, he listened so well that over time he started noticing similarities in the types of problems that young people were discussing on the hotline. Specifically, Richard observed that younger teens in the Dorchester and Roxbury communities did not feel safe going out on the weekends in their own neighborhoods. Parents were also worried about the safety of their children, and sometimes called to ask whether the Youth Committee ever sponsored teen parties or other gatherings. Richard always felt bad telling parents that the committee did not have the funds to organize these types of events. Richard liked helping people, but this was the kind of problem he did not feel he could solve.

Problems Can Lead to Opportunities

But then, one day in October, Richard came up with an idea:

> *Everybody was asking, "Is there going to be a Halloween party?" But there was not anyone who was throwing a party, so I said, I'll throw my own party. I did not know how to DJ, but I had friends who worked as professional DJs. I just contacted everyone I knew who could help out and then made it happen.*

Richard decided to use all $700 of his own personal savings to purchase services and supplies for the party. His intention was to earn this money back and also generate a profit, by charging a $10 admission fee. He thought that $10 was a reasonable price, because it was about the same amount that teens would typically spend on a weekend night to go out to a movie or play video games at the arcade. Richard knew that he

had to be careful about how he allocated his resources, because a $700 start-up investment was not going to get him very far.

Getting Organized

Richard's first step in planning his party was to brainstorm a list of all the things he would need to purchase and arrange. The list he created was as follows:

Item	Cost
Space Rental	________
DJ	________
Security	________
Insurance	________
Flyers	________
Food	________
Party Decorations	________

He thought this was a pretty good list; the only problem was that he did not know how much each item would cost. Could he pay for these goods and services with his limited funds? He was not certain. First, he needed to do some research.

Richard Investigates His Costs

Richard called his friend James, who worked as a professional DJ, to find out how much he

[4]This case is based on a real-life example, but selected details have been fictionalized. Thanks to Stephen Spinelli and Alex Hardy, of Babson College, for granting permission to adapt this case from its original version.

would charge to spin records at the party. James normally got $200 as a DJ at Boston's hottest clubs, but he agreed to reduce his fee to $100, because he saw that Richard was trying to do something positive for the community.

Richard then spoke with another friend, who worked as a security guard, to ask if he could organize a security squad for the event. The friend agreed to find four coworkers who could staff the party for $50 each.

Richard needed a large, centrally located venue where he could host the party. He remembered that his friend Janelle had once rented a dance studio in an old, converted factory. The studio would be perfect because it was located in the heart of downtown Boston, near the highway and directly across the street from a subway station. He contacted the studio's owner and negotiated a deal to rent the space for $200 for four hours. This rental fee included insurance, in case there was an accident.

Throughout the planning process, Richard leveraged his personal network to assemble the necessary components for the party. He explained:

> *If I had to go out and hire professionals, I wouldn't know them. And the fact that I did not have the money right then to pay full market prices for people's services—but these people trusted me and said, "We believe in what you're doing, so we'll provide our services at a discount."*

Richard's final step was to get the word out about the party to teens and parents. He called his friend Zeke, who freelanced as a graphic designer, and offered to pay him $50 to design and print 300 flyers. By this point, Richard had already committed $600 of his savings towards entertainment, space rental, security, and promotional costs. With his remaining $100, he decided to purchase chips, soda, cups, and napkins. He figured that he could recoup his investment by selling these snacks at a modest profit.

After making these arrangements Richard filled in the actual cost of each item on the list.

Item	Cost
Space Rental and Insurance	$200
DJ	$100
Security	$250
Graphic Design and Flyer Production	$50
Food, Decorations, and Misc. Supplies	$100
TOTAL	$700

Richard felt satisfied that he had managed his limited resources effectively. He was finally ready for the party. All he had left to do was decide on what costume to wear.

The Party

On the night of the party, Richard arrived early to set up. Despite weeks of planning, he still felt nervous. He had never done anything like this before. What if no one showed up and he lost all his money? The doors opened at 9 p.m., and by 10 only 20 people had arrived. Richard realized that, at $10 apiece, that was only $200. The room looked empty, no one was on the dance floor, and Richard's nerves were on overdrive. Suddenly, at 10:30, the party filled up quickly and, by 11, Richard was amazed to see that a line of kids had formed outside the door. The studio had a fire-hazard limit of 300, and by 11:30 the party was filled to capacity.

Keeping Good Records

In the end, Richard's party was a great success, personal and financial. When he sat down to calculate his revenue, he discovered that the party had generated $3750. Richard tabulated his receipts and created the chart below, so that he could see how he had accomplished this.

Item	Selling Price per Unit	Number of Units Sold	Revenue Generated
Admission Tickets	$10.00	300	$3000.00
Chips	$0.50	300	$150.00
Soda	$1.00	600	$600.00
TOTAL SALES REVENUE			$3750.00

It had taken Richard three long years of careful saving to put away $700 from his part-time job at the hotline, so he was amazed that so much money could be generated in a single evening. As he reflected on the experience, Richard realized:

> *Even if not many people had come to the Halloween party, it would have been a success because I put something together, and I profited from it. Not only profited financially, but profited as an individual. It was something deeper than just the money. You've got to go into business because it is something you love to do and you want to create that independence. If you do something that you love, you always do your best.*

Future Possibilities

As he drove home after the party, Richard's mind was reeling. He was thinking about the future and what he wanted to accomplish. Maybe he would use some of the profit he earned to throw an even bigger party, or perhaps start a party-planning business. He was not sure. After all, organizing the party had caused him a lot of stress. Or maybe he would put the money in his bank account so that he could save up for graduate school. He had several possibilities to consider. Richard parked his car, got ready for bed, and resolved to think further about his future plans in the morning.

Case Study Analysis

1. Assume that Richard decides to start a party-planning business:
   a. Identify two ways he could assess the cost of goods or services sold for this business.
   b. Which costs, described in the case, would become part of Richard's operating-cost structure?
   c. Make a list of additional items Richard will need to purchase to get his business off the ground. Research the cost of these items.
2. One of the reasons why Richard earned a substantial profit is because he convinced his personal contacts to provide their services at a discounted rate. If Richard decides to grow his party-planning business, do you think that he can continue to use this strategy? Why or why not?
3. Brainstorm three things Richard might have done differently in planning his party to increase his sales revenue.
4. At the end of the case, Richard describes how he profited as an individual from the experience of throwing the Halloween party. What do you think he meant by this? Is it possible to profit from something on a personal level, even if you do not necessarily earn a financial profit? Can you think of an example from your own life where this happened? Explain.

Chapter 13

USING FINANCIAL STATEMENTS TO GUIDE A BUSINESS

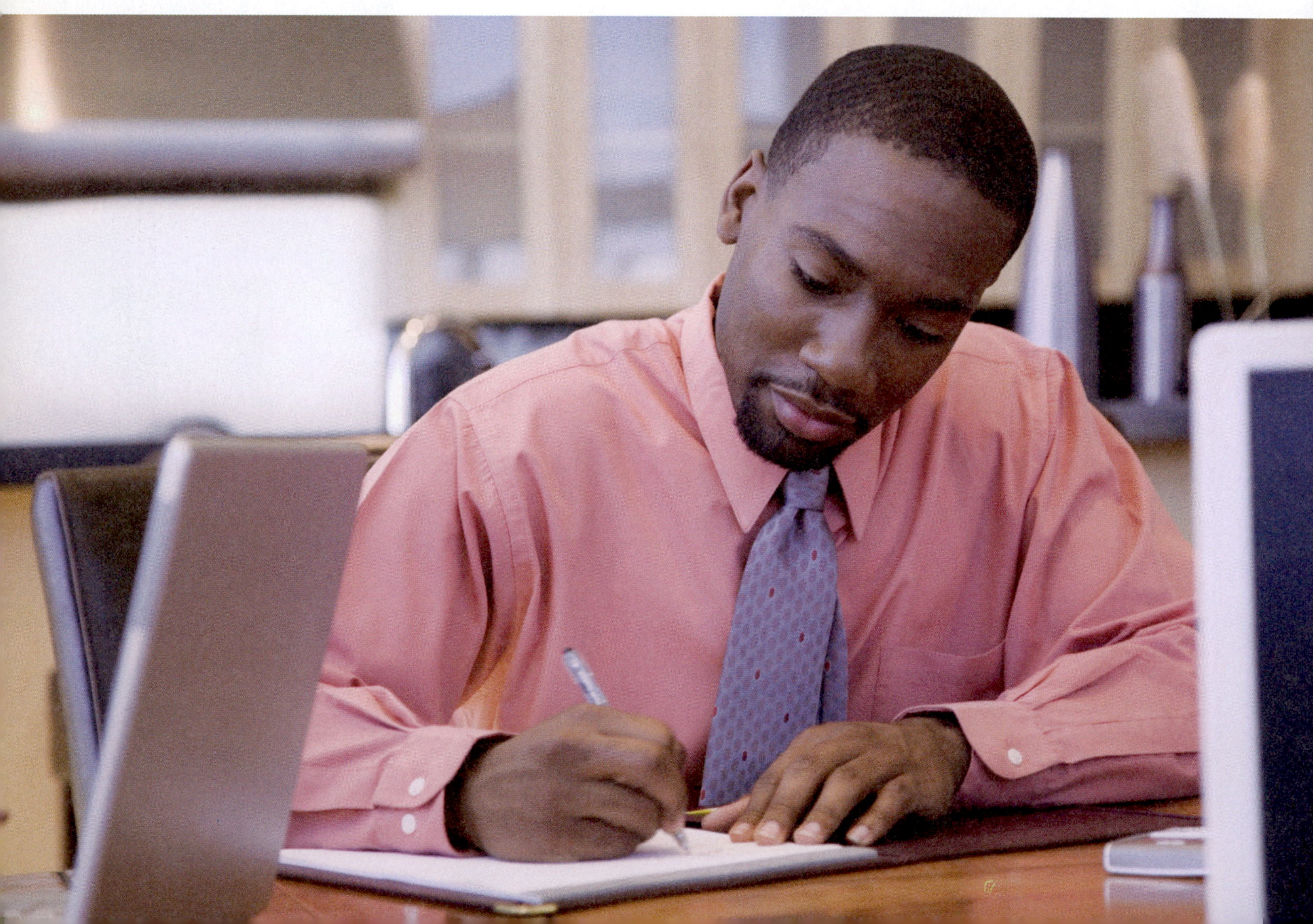

"The propensity to truck, barter, and exchange one thing for another is common to all men."

—Adam Smith, Scottish economist

Partners Gary and Steve decided to start an Internet café in Hoboken, New Jersey, when the concept was relatively new. Hoboken had a large community of freelance workers, artists, and other types of people who Gary and Steve thought would patronize their business.

The partners used extensive start-up funds to install super-fast equipment, and make the café look up to date. The furniture was custom-designed for the space, as were the metallic ceiling and wall panels. The partners decided to serve gourmet coffees, cakes, and simple sandwiches.

Because so much money was spent on start-up, Steve and Gary tried to cut costs by hiring as staff local kids who would work at minimum wage. It soon became apparent to frustrated customers, however, that the staff could not solve technical problems. Customers who were having trouble printing or accessing documents were often told, "Wait until Gary or Steve comes in," which often was not until late in the afternoon.

Internet café interior.

Neither Gary nor Steve had had previous entrepreneurial experience and most of the financing had come from their respective families. Because neither knew how to prepare an income statement, there was no effective way of keeping track of the money coming in and going out of the business. Within 14 months, the partners had to close their venture because they were not covering their operating costs. If they had been preparing monthly income statements, they could have seen the problems developing and taken action to solve them.

Performance Objectives

1. Understand an income statement.
2. Examine a balance sheet to determine a business's financing strategy.
3. Use the balance sheet equation for analysis.
4. Perform a financial ratio analysis of an income statement.
5. Calculate return on investment.
6. Perform same-size (common-size) analysis of an income statement.
7. Use quick, current, and debt ratios to analyze a balance sheet.

Scorecards for the Entrepreneur: What Do Financial Statements Show?

In this chapter you will learn how to prepare and use the income statement and balance sheet to guide your business and keep it strong. Entrepreneurs use three basic financial statements to track their businesses:

- an income statement,
- a balance sheet, and
- a cash flow statement.

Together, these three documents show the health of a business at a glance.

Best practice for entrepreneurs is to use their financial records to prepare monthly income statements and balance sheets, and then finalize these at the end of the fiscal year. Cash flow statements (as will be discussed in Chapter 14) should be prepared at least monthly. These statements will provide concise, easily read and understood company financial pictures. Whereas transaction records such as a journal or check register will provide the cash balance on hand, the income statement and balance sheet give a comprehensive overview of the organization. By performing financial-statement analysis, you can gain a comprehensive understanding of any enterprise.

Income Statements: Showing Profit and Loss over Time

The income statement shows whether the difference between revenue (sales) and expenses (costs) is a profit or a loss over a given time period. If revenues are greater than expenses, the income-statement balance will be positive, showing that the business is profitable. If costs are greater than sales, the income statement balance will show that the business has incurred losses (is unprofitable).

The income statement is a scorecard for the entrepreneur. If the business is not making a profit, examining the statement can reveal what may be causing the problem. Steps can then be taken to correct it and prevent insolvency. *Profit* is a reward for making the right business choices. The income statement will enable you to determine whether your decisions have kept you on the right track.

Parts of an Income Statement

Performance Objective 1 ➤
Understand an income statement.

The income statement is composed of the following:

1. ***Revenue.*** Income from sales of the company's products or services. For companies using the cash method of accounting, sales are recorded when payment is received.
2. ***COGS (Cost of goods sold)/COSS (Cost of services sold).*** These are the costs of materials used to make the product (or deliver the service) plus the costs of the direct labor used to make the product (or deliver the service). An income statement reports total COGS for a period.
3. ***Gross profit.*** Equals revenues minus COGS.
4. ***Other variable costs (VC).*** Costs that vary with sales.
5. ***Contribution margin.*** Equals revenues minus COGS and other variable costs, or gross profit minus other variable costs.
6. ***Fixed operating costs.*** Costs of operating a business that do not vary with sales. The most common fixed operating costs are utilities, salaries, advertising, insurance, depreciation, interest, and rent, (USAIDIR).
7. ***Earnings before interest and taxes (EBIT).*** Equals gross profit minus other variable costs minus fixed costs, except interest and taxes.
8. ***Pre-tax profit.*** EBIT minus interest costs. This is a business's profit after all costs have been deducted, but before taxes have been paid. Pre-tax profit is used to calculate how much tax the business owes.
9. ***Taxes.*** A business must pay taxes on the income it earns as a separate entity from the owners' personal taxes, depending upon its legal form (e.g. a corporation). It may have to make monthly or quarterly estimated tax payments.
10. ***Net profit/(loss).*** This is the business's profit or loss after taxes have been paid.

Entrepreneurial Wisdom...

Whenever a number in a financial statement is enclosed in parentheses, it is negative. If you see ($142,938) at the bottom of an income statement, it means the business had a net loss of $142,938.

A Basic Income Statement

The power of the income statement is that it will tell you whether you are fulfilling the formula of buying low, selling high, and meeting customer needs. See **Exhibit 13-1** for an example of an income statement for a relatively simple business. It illustrates how the income statement functions.

Exhibit 13-1 *Basic income statement.*

A Basic Company, Inc.
Income Statement
for the Month Ended June 30, 2011

Sales/Revenue			$ 24,681
COGS (Cost of Goods Sold)			
Total Materials	$ 2,468		
Total Labor	3,579		
Total COGS	$ 6,047	$ 6,047	$ 6,047
Gross Profit			$ 18,634
Other Variable Costs			
Commissions	$ 1,234		
Packaging	236		
Total Other Variable Costs	$ 1,470	$ 1,470	1,470
Contribution Margin			$ 17,164
Fixed Operating Costs (USAIIRD)			
Utilities	$ 200		
Salaries	3,000		
Advertising	600		
Insurance	300		
Interest	300		
Rent	1,000		
Depreciation	50		
Other	50		
Total Fixed Operating Costs:	$ 5,500		$ 5,500
Pre-Tax Profit			$ 11,164
Taxes (0.34%)			3,796
Net Profit			$ 7,368

Total Sales/Revenue = Units Sold × Unit Selling Price

Total Cost of Goods or Services Sold = Units Sold × Cost of Goods or Services Sold per Unit

Gross Profit = Sales − COGS

Total Other Variable Costs = Units Sold × Other Variable Costs per Unit

Total Variable Costs = Total Cost of Goods or Services Sold + Total Other Variable Costs

Contribution Margin = Total Sales − Total Variable Costs

Total Fixed Costs = Total of USAIDIRO

Pre-Tax Profit/(Loss) = Contribution Margin −Total Fixed Costs

Taxes = Profit × .34 (Estimated)

Net Profit = Pre-Tax Profit − Taxes

Exhibit 13-2 *Handbag store income statement.*

David's Income Statement

Handbag sales at flea market (one time) – for one month

Sales:	100 handbags × $25/bag		$2,500
Less COGS	100 handbags × $10/bag	$1,000	1,000
Gross Profit			$1,500
Other Variable Costs	100 charms × $0.50/charm	50	50
Total Variable Costs		$1,050	
Contribution Margin			$1,450
Fixed Costs			
Rent ($500 to rent booth)		$500	
Advertising ($25 for flyers)		25	
Total Fixed Costs		$525	525
Pre-Tax Profit			$925
Taxes (25%)			231
Net Profit			$694

Let's say that David buys 100 handbags at $10 each and sells them all at $25 each at a flea market, for revenue of $2500. He gives each customer a little charm (at a cost of 50 cents) to attach to the handbag. He also spends $25 on flyers to advertise that he will be selling on Saturday at the flea market, and $500 to rent the booth. The income statement in **Exhibit 13-2** quickly shows whether or not he made a profit.

The income statement not only shows that David's business is profitable but also illustrates exactly *how* profitable.

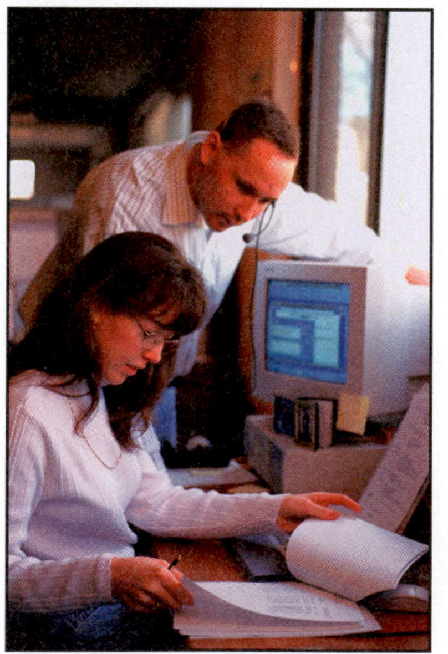

Working on an income statement with a colleague.
(Frank Sileman, Omni-Photo Communications, Inc.)

The Double Bottom Line

You have certainly heard the expression, "What's the bottom line?" It refers to the last line on an income statement, which shows whether a business has made a profit or not.

Another bottom line can be considered, though, aside from whether the organization (either for-profit or not-for-profit) is making money. Is your business achieving its mission? If your dream was to have your venture fill a need in the community, is this goal being realized? Are you able to make a profit and operate the business in a way that makes you feel satisfied and fulfilled? Goals that go beyond profit might include:

- being a good citizen by doing business in a way that respects the environment: recycling, minimizing waste, looking for energy sources that do not pollute;
- encouraging local people to invest in the business and become equity owners;
- always dealing honestly with customers and suppliers, and treating everyone you do business with the way you would like to be treated; and
- treating employees with respect regarding their health and safety; setting up profit-sharing plans, especially so that they will share in the success they help create.

Ideally, you want to have a positive *double* bottom line; you are making a profit so you can stay in business *and* achieve your mission. Not-for-profit

Exhibit 13-3 *Income statement for Lola's Custom Draperies, Inc. for the month of March 2011.*

Sales:		$85,456
Cost of Goods Sold:		
Materials	$11,550	
Labor	17,810	
Total COGS:		29,360
Gross Profit:		$56,096
Other Variable Costs:		
Sales Commissions	8,000	8,000
Contribution Margin:		$48,096
Fixed Operating Costs:		
Factory Rent and Utilities	$8,000	
Salaries and Administrative	12,000	
Depreciation	2,000	
Total Fixed Operating Costs:		22,000
Profit Before Taxes:		$26,096
Taxes (25%):		6,524
Net Profit/(Loss):		$19,572

organizations all have a double bottom line to measure. They must achieve successful financial results in order to continue operations and work toward their mission. Not-for-profits explicitly strive to attain successful double bottom lines.

An Income Statement for a More Complex Business

The income statement in **Exhibit 13-3** follows the same format as the previous one and its goal is still the same—to show how profitable the business is. However, this statement includes the category of depreciation.

Publicly traded companies have the same essential format as shown here. Their statements are available to shareholders and other members of the public through their quarterly and annual filings with the U.S. Securities and Exchange Commission (10Q and 10K reports) and annual reports to shareholders. If you are not familiar with financial statements, it may help to look at the annual report of a large public company in a peer industry. The reports are generally available in the investor- or shareholder-relations section of company Web sites.

Balance Sheets: Snapshots of Assets, Liabilities, and Equity at a Point in Time

You can quickly see a company's financing strategy by looking at its *balance sheet* (see **Exhibits 13-4** and **13-5**). A balance sheet is a financial statement that shows the assets (what the business owns), liabilities (debts), and the **net worth** of a business. The net worth is the difference between assets and liabilities and is also called **owner's equity**.

net worth (owner's equity) the difference between assets and liabilities.

owner's equity (net worth) the difference between assets and liabilities.

Exhibit 13-4 *Balance sheet (horizontal).*

A Basic Company, Inc.
Balance Sheet
As of December 31, 2011

Assets			**Liabilities**	
Current Assets			**Current Liabilities**	
Cash		$75,000	Accounts payable	$475,000
Accounts receivable		250,000	Notes payable	175,000
Inventory		500,000	Accrued wages payable	75,000
Supplies		80,000	Accrued taxes payable	20,000
Prepaid expenses		15,000	Accrued interest payable	25,000
Total Current Assets		**$920,000**	**Total Current Liabilities**	**$770,000**
Long-Term (Fixed) Assets			**Long-Term Liabilities**	
Land		$500,000	Mortgage	$900,000
Buildings	$700,000		Notes payable	500,000
Less accum. depreciation	70,000	630,000	**Total Long-Term Liabilities**	**$1,400,000**
Vehicles	$200,000			
Less accum. depreciation	60,000	140,000	**Owner's Equity**	
Equipment	$250,000		Prime Owner, paid in capital	$197,500
Less accum. depreciation	12,500	237,500	Common stock	100,000
Furniture and fixtures	$50,000		**Total Owner's Equity**	**$297,500**
Less accum. depreciation	10,000	40,000		
Total Fixed Assets		$1,547,500	**Total Liabilities and Owner's Equity**	**$2,467,500**
Intangibles (goodwill)		$0		
Total Assets		$2,467,500		

Performance Objective 2

Examine a balance sheet to determine a business's financing strategy.

1. ***Assets.*** Things a company owns that are worth money.
2. ***Liabilities.*** Debts a company has that must be paid, including unpaid bills.
3. ***Owner's Equity (OE).*** Also called net worth; this is the difference between assets and liabilities. It shows the amount of capital in the business. It consists of common equity, preferred equity, paid-in capital, and retained earnings.

fiscal year the financial reporting year for a company.

The balance sheet for a large business is typically prepared quarterly and at the end of the fiscal year, unlike cash flow and income statements, which are prepared monthly. The **fiscal year** is the 12-month accounting period chosen by the business. A fiscal year may differ from the calendar year (January 1 through December 31). A business that uses the calendar year as its fiscal year would prepare its balance sheet for the period ending December 31.

Many entrepreneurs, however, also prepare a balance sheet monthly. To keep the business on track, business owners use these three financial tools: an income statement, a cash flow statement (to be discussed in Chapter 14), and a balance sheet.

Short- and Long-Term Assets

Assets are all items of worth owned by the business, such as cash, inventory, buildings, vehicles, furniture, machinery, and the like. Assets are divided into short-term (current) and long-term (fixed).

current assets cash or items that can be quickly converted to cash or will be used within one year.

- **Current assets** are cash itself or items that could be quickly turned into cash *(liquidated)*, or will be used by the business within one year. Current assets include accounts receivable, inventory, and supplies.

Exhibit 13-5 *Balance sheet (vertical).*

A Basic Company, Inc. Balance Sheet As of December 31, 2011		
Assets		
Current Assets		
Cash		$75,000
Accounts receivable		250,000
Inventory		500,000
Supplies		80,000
Prepaid expenses		15,000
Total Current Assets		**$920,000**
Long-Term (Fixed) Assets		
Land		500,000
Buildings	$700,000	
Less accum. depreciation	70,000	630,000
Vehicles	$200,000	
Less accum. depreciation	60,000	140,000
Equipment	$250,000	
Less accum. depreciation	12,500	237,500
Furniture and fixtures	$50,000	
Less accum. depreciation	10,000	40,000
Total Fixed Assets		**$1,547,500**
Intangibles (goodwill)		**$0**
Total Assets		**$2,467,500**
Liabilities		
Current Liabilities		
Accounts payable		$475,000
Notes payable		175,000
Accrued wages payable		75,000
Accrued taxes payable		20,000
Accrued interest payable		25,000
Total Current Liabilities		**$770,000**
Long-Term Liabilities		
Mortgage		$900,000
Notes payable		500,000
Total Long-Term Liabilities		**$1,400,000**
Owner's Equity		
Prime Owner, paid in capital		$197,500
Common stock		100,000
Total Owner's Equity		**$297,500**
Total Liabilities and Owner's Equity		**$2,467,500**

- **Long-term assets** are those that would take more than one year for the business to use. Equipment, furniture, machinery, and real estate are examples of long-term assets.

long-term assets those that will take more than one year to use.

Current and Long-Term Liabilities

Liabilities are all debts owed by the business, such as bank loans, mortgages, lines of credit, and loans from family or friends.

- **Current liabilities** are debts that are scheduled for payment within one year. These include the portion of long-term debt due within that year.
- **Long-term liabilities** are debts to be paid over a period of more than one year.

current liabilities debts that are scheduled for payment within one year.

long-term liabilities debts that are due in over one year.

The Balance Sheet Equation

Performance Objective 3

Use the balance sheet equation for analysis.

The terms *owner's equity, capital,* and *net worth* all mean the same thing, what's left over after liabilities are subtracted from assets. Owner's equity is the value of the business on the balance sheet to the owner. The equation for calculating owner's equity is the *balance sheet equation*. As the name suggests, the balance sheet must always be in balance, with assets equal to the sum of liabilities plus equity. A sure sign of a calculation or record-keeping error is to have an imbalance.

Assets − Liabilities = Net Worth (or Owner's Equity or Capital) or

Assets = Liabilities + Owner's Equity or

Liabilities = Assets − Owner's Equity

- If assets are greater than liabilities, net worth is positive.
- If liabilities are greater than assets, net worth is negative.

For example, if Dos Compadres Restaurant has $10,000 in cash on hand, owns $8000 in equipment, and owes $5000 in long-term liabilities, what is the restaurant's net worth?

$18,000 (Assets) − $5000 (Liabilities) = $13,000 (Net Worth)

The Balance Sheet Shows Assets and Liabilities Obtained through Financing

Every item a business owns was obtained through either debt or equity. That is why the total of all assets must equal the total of all liabilities and owner's equity.

- If an item was financed with *debt,* the loan is a liability.
- If an item was purchased with the owner's own money (including that of shareholders), it was financed with *equity.*

If a restaurant owns its tables and chairs (worth $3000), its stoves (worth $5000), has $10,000 in cash, and $4000 in inventory, the business has a total capital equipment investment of $3000 + $5000 = $8000, and $4000 in inventory plus the $10,000 in cash. The restaurant also has a $5000 long-term loan, which was used to buy the stove. Its total assets are $22,000. It has $5000 in liabilities (the loan for the stove), which leaves $17,000 of owner's equity (OE).

Assuming the restaurant has no other assets and liabilities, **Exhibit 13-6** shows how its balance sheet would look.

Again, on a balance sheet, assets must equal the total of liabilities and owner's equity.

Total Assets = Total Liabilities + Owner's Equity (OE)

The OE is $17,000. It is equal to the total of the cash ($10,000), the stove, tables, and chairs ($8000), plus $4000 in inventory, minus the $5000 in liabilities.

The stove is financed with a ($5000) loan (debt financing). This is a long-term liability. Together, the liabilities and the owner's equity, have paid for the assets of the business. When reviewing a side-by-side balance sheet, remember that the assets (what you own) on the left are funded by the liabilities (what you owe), plus equity (the owners' stake), on the right.

Exhibit 13-6 *Balance sheet.*

Restaurant Balance Sheet as of Dec. 31, 2008			
Assets		**Liabilities**	
Cash	$10,000	Short-Term Liabilities	$ 0
Inventory	4,000	Long-Term Liabilities	5,000
Capital Equipment	8,000		
Other Assets	—	Owner's Equity	17,000
Total Assets	**$22,000**	**Total Liabilities + OE**	**$22,000**

The Balance Sheet Shows How a Business Is Financed

The balance sheet is an especially good tool for looking at how a business is financed. It clearly shows the relationship between debt and equity financing. Sometimes businesses make the mistake of relying too heavily on either debt or equity. The appropriate mix depends upon the industry and the individual firm.

- An entrepreneur that relies too much on equity financing from outside owners can lose control of the company. If the other owners control enough of the business, they may insist on making the decisions, or may impede decision-making and create inefficiency.
- An entrepreneur who takes on too much debt and is unable to make loan payments can lose the business, and possibly personal assets, to banks or other creditors.

All the information you need to analyze a company's financing strategy—total debt, equity, and assets—is in its balance sheet. People who invest in businesses use *ratios* to grasp a company's financial situation quickly. As an entrepreneur, you will want to understand these ratios so you will be able to talk intelligently with investors, and to analyze costs (your vendors) and sales (your customers).

Unorganized financial records can lead to chaos in a business.
(A. Chedderros/Getty)

Analyzing a Balance Sheet

Comparing balance sheets from two different points in time is an excellent way to see whether or not a business has been financially successful. If it is, the owner's equity (OE) will have increased. For example, the ending balance sheets for two years may be compared to analyze annual progress.

Let's look at the restaurant example again. This time, several other assets and liabilities have been included (see **Exhibit 13-7**).

The first balance sheet was prepared as of December 31, 2010. The ending balance sheet was compiled a year later, on December 31, 2011. Compare the two balance sheets (Exhibit 13-7) to see how the numbers have changed over the course of a year.

Assets

- *Cash* has decreased from $10,000 to $8000. Businesses have cash coming in and going out all the time, so this is not necessarily a bad thing as long as the bills are being paid, but it should be monitored carefully.
- *Inventory* has increased from $4000 to $5000. If more inventory will help the restaurant put more items on the menu, it could help increase business. If inventory is accumulating without adding value, it can be problematic, because it is effectively cash sitting on the shelf. In any case, inventory is an asset because it has monetary value.
- *Capital equipment* has increased from $8000 to $9000. The restaurant must have bought more equipment during the year. This is another increase in assets.
- *Other assets* have remained constant.
- *Total assets* have not changed. The business is keeping less cash but now has more inventory and capital equipment with which to operate.

There are no more assets at the end of the year than there were at the beginning. Does this mean it did not have a successful year? (The rest of this analysis will help you figure that out.)

Liabilities

- *Short-term liabilities* have increased from $0 to $1000. On the surface, this seems to be a negative because it means the restaurant

Exhibit 13-7 *Comparative balance sheet.*

Restaurant Balance Sheet

	As of Dec. 31, 2011	As of Dec. 31, 2010
Assets		
Current Assets		
Cash	$8,000	$10,000
Inventory	5,000	4,000
Less accum. depreciation	9,000	8,000
Total Assets	**$22,000**	**$22,000**
Liabilities		
Total Current Liabilities	$1,000	$0
Long-Term Liabilities	4,000	5,000
Owner's Equity	17,000	17,000
Total Liabilities and Owner's Equity	**$22,000**	**$22,000**

owes more money than it did before. However, it may mean that suppliers have extended trade credit to the company, so that it can add inventory without tying up as much cash.

- *Long-term liabilities* have declined from $5000 to $4000 because the restaurant paid off 20 percent of the loan principal. When you make monthly payments on a loan, it is usual for part of the payment to go for interest and the rest to paying off the principal. So, part of the payment is an expense and part is reducing a liability.
- *Owner's equity* has stayed the same. The restaurant has no more value it had at the beginning of the year, even though its assets and liabilities are distributed differently.

The restaurant does not have more total assets than it had at the beginning of the year, however, and it has less cash. On the other hand, the business has less debt than it did. The balance sheet equation shows that the owner's equity in the business has not changed because, although the owner paid down some long-term debt, short-term debt was added.

Exhibit 13-8 shows another look at the balance sheet, with a percentage-change column added. This represents how much change took place over the year. (Note that any value set in parentheses is negative.)

Total assets are unchanged, and the restaurant's liabilities (debts) are the same, which is an unusual set of circumstances. Short-term liabilities are $1000 greater, and long-term liabilities are less than they had been at the start of the year. Owner's equity is the same.

The restaurant used its cash to increase its inventory and capital equipment, keeping its debt and equity the same. Reallocating your asset mix in such a way can be a smart strategy.

The growth of owner's equity is one good way to measure company success. **Exhibit 13-9** shows how investors might view different rates of owner's-equity growth.

Depreciation

As we have learned, depreciation is a certain portion of an asset that is subtracted each year until the asset's value reaches zero. Depreciation reflects the wear and tear on an asset over time, or other loss of value,

Exhibit 13-8 *Balance sheet variance analysis.*

Restaurant Balance Sheet

	As of Dec. 31, 2011	As of Dec. 31, 2010	% Change
Assets			
Current Assets			
Cash	$8,000	$10,000	(20)%
Inventory	5,000	4,000	25%
Capital Equipment	9,000	8,000	13%
Total Assets	**$22,000**	**$22,000**	**0%**
Liabilities			
Short-Term Liabilities	$1,000	$0	N.A.
Long-Term Liabilities	4,000	5,000	(20)%
Owner's Equity	17,000	17,000	0%
Total Liabilities and Owner's Equity	**$22,000**	**$22,000**	**0%**

Exhibit 13-9 *Annual rates of growth in owner's equity of major U.S. corporations.*

Annual Growth	Assessment of Annual Growth Rate
3%	Very slow, and unsatisfactory in most cases
6%	Slow, but acceptable in some cases
10–11%	Average growth rate
16%	High growth rate
24%	Extremely high growth—not many companies can achieve this, much less keep it up

through obsolescence. Depreciation reflects this reduction in the asset's value. A used car or computer, for instance, is almost always worth less money than a new one.

Balance sheets with significant long-term assets show depreciation as a subtraction from those assets. Because different types of assets depreciate at different rates, and because assets are purchased at various times, businesses keep depreciation schedules to track the valuation of each asset that is being depreciated. There are multiple methods of depreciation, and it is best to consult with an accounting/tax professional on this topic.

Financial Ratio Analysis: What Is It and What Does It Mean to You?

So far, we have only looked at how an income statement and balance sheet can tell you whether or not your business is making a profit, and whether owner's equity is increasing or decreasing. This is only the tip of the iceberg with respect to what you can learn about a business through financial statement analysis. You can also create financial ratios from your income statement and balance sheet that will help you analyze your business in greater depth. By making comparisons of your company's performance from period to period and against industry norms, you can adapt your operations and strategies to improve results.

Income Statement Ratios

To create income statement ratios, analysts simply divide sales into each line item and multiply by a hundred. In this way, line items are expressed as a percentage of sales. Expressing an item on the income statement as a percentage of sales makes it easier to see the relationship between items than when dollar values are used. In the example shown in **Exhibit 13-10**, for every dollar of sales, 40 cents went to the cost of goods sold. The contribution margin per dollar was 60 cents. The net profit was 20 cents, after 30 cents was spent on operating costs and 10 cents on taxes.

Performance Objective 4

Perform a financial ratio analysis of an income statement.

Analyzing the common-sized (or "same size") income statement makes clear how each item is affecting the business's profit. Examining the income statement makes it easy to experiment with ways to improve your business, by changing values to test different financial scenarios.

To increase contribution margin, you could try cutting the cost of goods sold by 10 percent. The next time you analyze your monthly income statement, you will be able to see if this cost-cutting increased the contribution margin and by how much.

Exhibit 13-10 *Common-sized income statement.*

Excellence, Inc.
Income Statement for the Month Ending June 30, 2011

	Amount (in millions)	Calculation	% of Sales
Sales	$10	$10/$10 × 100	100%
Less Total COGS	$ 4	$4/$10 × 100	40%
Less Other Variable Costs	$ 0		
Contribution Margin	$ 6	$6/$10 × 100	60%
Less Fixed Operating Costs	$ 3	$3/$10 × 100	30%
Profit	$ 3	$3/$10 × 100	30%
Taxes	$ 1	$1/$10 × 100	10%
Net Profit/(Loss)	$ 2	$2/$10 × 100	20%

Return on Investment

An **investment** is something you put time, energy, or money into because you expect to gain profit or satisfaction in return. When you start your own business, you are investing time and energy into the venture, as well as money. You do this because you believe that someday your business will return more than the value of the time, energy, and money you put into it. One way to express this idea mathematically is to calculate a **return on investment (ROI)**, the net profit of a business divided by the start-up investment, expressed as a percentage of that investment.

Investors think in terms of **wealth**—the value of assets owned minus the value of liabilities owed at a particular point in time, rather than money, per se, because a business may own assets (such as equipment or real estate) that have value but are not actual cash. Return on investment measures how wealth changes over time. To measure ROI, you have to know these three things:

1. *Net profit.* The amount the business has earned beyond what it has spent to cover its costs.

Performance Objective 5

Calculate return on investment.

investment something that a person or entity devotes resources to in hopes of future profits or satisfaction.

return on investment (ROI) the net profit of a business divided by its start-up investment (percentage).

wealth the value of assets owned versus the value of liabilities owed.

Global Impact...

Accounting Differences between Countries

Businesses in different countries prepare and present the income statement differently, and even have different names for it. In the United Kingdom, for example, the income statement is called a "group profit and loss account." Topics where global practices can differ widely include inventory measurement methods and ways in which property and equipment are valued. Countries also have varying laws regarding when a sale can be recognized as income and included on an income statement.

In the United States, United Kingdom, Denmark, Norway, Belgium, Brazil, and Japan, for instance, income from a long-term contract can only be included on the income statement as each percentage of the contract is completed. If you have done 10 percent of the work, you can show 10 percent of the income on your statement. In Germany, on the other hand, you cannot include any of the income on your statement until the contract has been 100 percent completed.

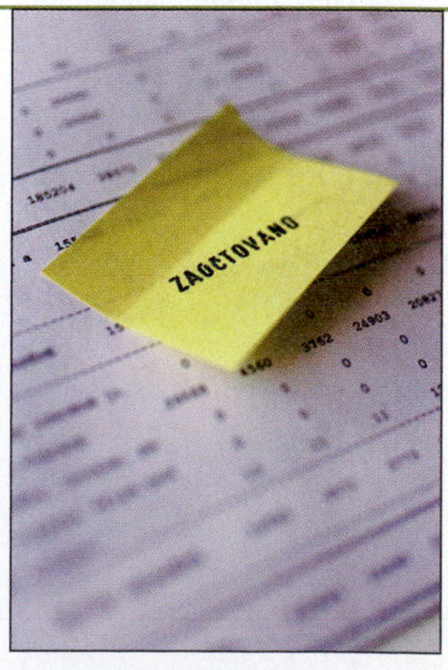

Accounting rules differ among countries.

2. *Total investment in the business.* This includes start-up investment (the amount of money that was required to open the business plus all later additional funding).
3. *The period of time for which you are calculating ROI.* This is typically one month or one year.

$$\text{ROI Formula} = \frac{\text{Net Profit}}{\text{Investment}} \times 100 = \text{ROI}$$

There is an easy way to remember the ROI formula: *What you made over what you paid, times one hundred.* Normally, ROI is calculated on an annual basis, although it can be calculated for shorter time increments, such as days, months, or quarters.

If David wants to figure out what his ROI was for the day at the flea market, he must know the following:

1. ***Net profit.*** His income statement shows this to be $694.
2. ***Investment.*** David invested $1000 in handbags, $25 in flyers, $50 for charms, plus $500 to rent a booth at the flea market, for a total of $1575.
3. ***Time period.*** In this case David is calculating his ROI for one day.

He divides his investment into the net profit.

$$\frac{\text{Net Profit (\$694)}}{\text{Investment (\$1000 + 25 + 50 + \$500)}} \times 100 = \frac{\$694}{\$1{,}575} \times 100$$

$$= .4406 \times 100 = 44\%$$

David's ROI was 44 percent for the day. ROI will tell you what the rate of return was on your investment.

Return on Sales

return on sales (ROS) net income divided by sales for a particular time period (percentage).

Return on sales (ROS) is the percentage created when sales are divided into net income. This is an important measure of the profitability of a business.

$$\text{Return on Sales (ROS)} = \frac{\text{Net Income}}{\text{Sales}}$$

profit margin (return on sales) net income divided by sales (percentage).

ROS is also called **profit margin**. To express this ratio as a percentage, multiply it by 100 (as you would to express any ratio as a percentage).

A high ROS ratio can help a company make money more easily; however, the amount of revenue makes a difference. The size of the sale will also make a difference. Hardware stores sell inexpensive items, so they have to have a higher profit margin on each to make a profit. Auto dealers sell expensive items, so they can afford a smaller ROS on each car they sell. **Exhibit 13-11** provides a visual description of this concept.

Exhibit 13-11 *ROS (profit margin) table.*

ROS	Margin Range	Typical Product
Very low	2–5%	Very high volume or very high price
Low	6–10%	High volume or high price
Moderate	11–20%	Moderate volume and moderate price
High	20–30%	Low volume or low price
Very high	30% and up	Very low volume or very low price

Common-Sized Statement Analysis

Financial ratio analysis will also allow you to compare the income statements from different months or years more easily, even if the sales are different amounts. The percentages let you compare statements as if they were the same size. For this reason, financial ratio analysis is sometimes called same-size analysis, as well as common-sized analysis.

Performance Objective 6

Perform same-size (common-size) analysis of an income statement.

When the ratio of expenses/sales is used to express expenses as a percentage of sales, it is called an **operating ratio**. The operating ratio expresses what percentage of sales dollars the expense is using up. You can use operating ratios to compare your expenses with those incurred by other businesses in your industry, or for your own company at different times. If your rent is $2000 per month, and your sales in a given month are $10,000, your operating ratio for rent is 20 percent. Is that high or low for your industry? Check trade association data or statement studies to find comparative values. If it is high, you might want to consider moving to another location. Remember that industry norms may not be industry ideals; the whole industry may be operating inefficiently, and you can bring efficiency to it. Also, look at whether a ratio is higher or lower than it was a year earlier. This is particularly helpful for analyzing variable costs within a company, as company performance versus industry performance.

operating ratio an expression of a value versus sales.

Relating each element of the income statement to sales in this fashion will help you notice changes in your costs from month to month or year to year.

Balance-Sheet Analysis

Taking the time to perform a similar analysis on the balance sheet can also yield valuable historic information, and provide perspectives on opportunities for improvement.

Quick and Current Ratios

In addition to what you can learn from an income statement, a balance sheet will tell you about a business's **liquidity**, that is, its ability to convert assets into cash. Business people use quick ratios and **current ratios** to immediately understand what is going on with a business's liquidity. Many entrepreneurs prepare a balance sheet monthly and at the end of the fiscal year, to keep an eye on liquidity.

liquidity the ability to convert assets into cash.

current ratio liquidity ratio consisting of the total sum of cash plus marketable securities divided by current liabilities.

$$\text{Quick Ratio: } \frac{\text{Cash + Marketable Securities}}{\text{Current Liabilities}}$$

Some entrepreneurs create fortunes by establishing successful businesses, selling them, and using the resulting wealth to create new enterprises and more wealth. Entrepreneurs also use their wealth to support political, environmental, and social causes. The major philanthropic thrust of the Estée Lauder Company is providing support to the Breast Cancer Research Foundation, which addresses a major health concern of its customer base. What will you do with *your* entrepreneurial wealth?

Performance Objective 7

Use quick, current, and debt ratios to analyze a balance sheet.

Example

Compare the common-sized income statements shown in **Exhibit 13-12**. Rocket Rollerskate did not have as much revenue and did not make as much profit in February as it did in January. The company was able to lower both its COGS and its other variable costs in February, though. Which month was better for Rocket? Can you explain your thinking?

marketable securities investments that can be converted into cash within 24 hours.

quick ratio indicates adequacy of cash to cover current debt.

Marketable securities are investments, such as certificates of deposit or Treasury bills, which can be converted to cash within 24 hours. The **quick ratio** tells you whether you have enough cash to cover your current debt. The quick ratio should always be greater than 1. This means that you would have enough cash at your disposal to cover all current short-term debt. In other words, if you had to pay all your bills tomorrow (not loans, just bills), you would have enough cash to do so.

$$\text{Quick Ratio: } \frac{\text{Current Liabilities} - (\text{Inventory} + \text{Prepayments})}{\text{Current Liabilities}}$$

Exhibit 13-12 *Common-sized income statements.*

Rocket Rollerskate Co. Income Statement				For the Month of January 2008
Revenue		*100%*		**$250,000**
COGS		*24%*	$60,000	60,000
Gross Profit		*76%*		**$190,000**
Other Variable Costs		*14%*	35,000	35,000
Total Variable Costs		*38%*	$95,000	
Contribution Margin		*62%*		**$155,000**
Fixed Costs		*34%*		85,000
Pre-Tax Profit		*28%*		**$70,000**
Taxes	(20%)	*5.6%*		14,000
Net Profit		*22.4%*		**$56,000**

Rocket Rollerskate Co. Income Statement				For the Month of February 2008
Revenue		*100%*		**$225,000**
COGS		*20%*	$45,000	45,000
Gross Profit		*80%*		**$180,000**
Other Variable Costs		*12%*	27,000	27,000
Total Variable Costs		*32%*	$72,000	
Contribution Margin		*68%*		**$153,000**
Fixed Costs		*38%*		85,000
Pre-Tax Profit		*30%*		**$68,000**
Taxes	(20%)	*6.0%*		13,600
Net Profit		*24.2%*		**$54,400**

Estee Lauder.

Step into the Shoes...

Estée Lauder Delivers Beauty

Estée Lauder, born Josephine Esther Mentzer in 1906, parlayed a skin-cream formula developed by her uncle into a company selling products in over 100 countries. Lauder started selling the cream in 1946, and introduced Youth-Dew fragrance in 1953. The company that she built with her husband found a niche for women's beauty care and evolved from the single beauty cream into multiple complete lines of skin care, makeup, fragrances, and hair-care products. Today, the company bearing her name includes numerous brands, such as Clinique, Prescriptives, MAC Cosmetics, Coach, and Aveda. The Lauder family continues to control 70 percent of the company.

Named one of *Time* magazine's 20 most influential business geniuses of the twentieth century, Estée Lauder's name is synonymous with beauty and wealth.

It is also a good idea to maintain a current ratio greater than 1. This indicates that, if you had to, you could sell some assets to pay off all your debts.

$$\text{Current Ratio: } \frac{\text{Current Assets}}{\text{Current Liabilities}}$$

Debt Ratios: Showing the Relationship between Debt and Equity

Most companies are financed by both debt and equity. The financial strategy of a company will be apparent from certain simple financial ratios. If a company has a **debt-to-equity ratio** of one-to-one (expressed as 1:1), for example, it means that for every one dollar of debt the company has one dollar of assets.

debt-to-equity ratio compares total debt to total equity.

$$\frac{\text{Debt}}{\text{Equity}} = \text{Debt-to-Equity Ratio}$$

All the information you need to analyze a company's financing strategy is in its balance sheet. It is used to create the following ratio.

$$\text{Debt Ratio: } \frac{\text{Total Debt}}{\text{Total Assets}}$$

The **debt ratio** describes how many of the total dollars in the business have been provided by creditors. A debt ratio of 55 percent means you are in debt for 55 percent of your assets. You will not actually own those assets outright until you pay off the debt. On the other hand, if you need to go to a bank to borrow money, or to a supplier to establish credit, these creditors will want you to have a moderate debt ratio, so you will have to manage your debt based on your objectives, industry norms, and creditor requirements.

debt ratio measures total debt versus total assets.

A debt-to-equity ratio of 100 percent would mean that for every dollar of debt the company has a dollar of equity. As noted previously, equity is ownership, which is either kept by the entrepreneur or sold in pieces to investors. If the investors hold a significant enough portion of the equity in a business, they could take over control from the entrepreneur; and this sometimes happens.

Operating-Efficiency Ratios

Once the income statement and balance sheet have been prepared, you can analyze your business's operating efficiency using the following ratios:

1. Collection-period ratio.

$$\frac{\text{Average Accounts Receivable (Balance Sheet)}}{\text{Average Daily Sales (Income Statement)}} = \text{\# of days}$$

Exercise

Using the balance sheet for the restaurant in **Exhibit 13-7**, calculate the quick, debt, and debt-to-equity ratios. Write your answers on a separate sheet of paper. What do the ratios tell you about how the restaurant is doing?

This ratio measures the average number of days that sales are going uncollected. If you extend credit, it is critical to minimize this number to keep cash flowing. It can be compared to industry norms for additional information.

2. Receivable turnover ratio.

$$\frac{\text{Total Sales (Income Statement)}}{\text{Average Accounts Receivable (Balance Sheet)}} = \text{\# of times}$$

This also measures the efficiency of your company's efforts to collect receivables.

3. Inventory turnover ratio.

$$\frac{\text{Cost of Goods Sold (Income Statement)}}{\text{Average Inventory (Balance Sheet)}} = \text{\# of times}$$

This is a measure of how quickly inventory is moving (is sold). The higher the turnover, the more effectively you are investing in inventory. Inventory that is held too long often becomes obsolete or, in the case of food and other perishable goods, literally spoils. Inventory that is not turning is tying up cash flow. At the same time, the amount of inventory in stock has to be balanced with customer needs and wants.

By using all of these ratios, you can create an internal scorecard for your business, perhaps on a consolidated key-performance-indicators report. You will be able to tell at a glance whether you are attaining your goals, where you stand from period to period, and how you compare with your industry. The Appendices in this book include a set of useful formulas and equations to use for such a scorecard.

Chapter Summary

Now that you have studied this chapter, you can do the following:

1. Understand an income statement.
   - An income statement shows whether the difference between revenue (sales) and expenses (costs) is a profit or a loss.
   - If sales are greater than costs, the income-statement balance will be positive, showing that the business earned a profit. If costs are greater than sales, the balance will be negative, showing a loss.
   - The elements of an income statement are:
     a. ***Revenue.*** Money a business makes for selling its products or services.
     b. ***Cost of goods sold.*** The cost of goods sold for one unit times the number of units sold. Never disclose your cost of goods sold. You want to keep your profit margin private.
     c. ***Gross profit.*** Revenue less the cost of the product or service.
     d. ***Other variable costs.*** Costs that vary with sales.
     e. ***Contribution margin.*** Sales minus variable costs (cost of goods sold + other variable costs).
     f. ***Fixed operating costs.*** Items that must be paid to operate a business. These items include utilities, salaries, advertising, insurance, interest, rent, and depreciation (referred to as USAIIRD).
     g. ***Profit before taxes.*** A business's profit after all costs have been deducted but before taxes have been paid.

   h. ***Taxes.*** A business must pay income tax on its profit. (Sales, property, and other taxes are business expenses and are not included on this line.)
   i. ***Net Profit/(Loss).*** A business's profit or loss after taxes.
2. Examine a balance sheet to determine a business's financing strategy.
   - A balance sheet is a financial statement showing the assets (items the business owns), liabilities (debts), and net worth of a business.
   - Every item a business owns was obtained through either debt (bonds, loans) or equity (selling ownership); therefore, the total of all assets must equal the total of all liabilities and owner's equity.
3. Use the balance sheet equation for analysis.

$$\text{Assets} - \text{Liabilities} = \text{Net Worth (or Owner's Equity or Capital)}$$

   - The balance sheet shows the use of debt and equity to support the business.
   - Comparing balance sheets from two points in time can provide insights into the business operations and reveal opportunities for improvement.
   - Depreciation affects the values of assets by reducing them to reflect wear and tear and obsolescence.
4. Perform a financial ratio analysis of an income statement.
   - Expressing each item on the income statement as a percentage of sales makes it easy to see the relationship between items.
   - Financial ratio analysis will also allow you to compare the income statements from different months or years more easily, even if the sales are for varying amounts.
   - The percentages let you compare statements as if they were the same size. For this reason, financial ratio analysis is also sometimes called same-size, or common-sized, analysis.

$$\frac{\text{Net Income}}{\text{Sales}} = \text{Return on Sales (ROS)}$$

5. Calculate return on investment (ROI).
   - ROI is the net profit of a business divided by the start-up costs, which are the original investment in the business.

$$\frac{\text{Net Profit}}{\text{Investment}} \times 100 = \text{Return on Investment (\% ROI)}$$

6. Perform same-size analysis of an income statement.
   - Represent expenses as a percentage of sales or operating ratios.
   - Compare with others in the industry.
7. Use quick, current, and debt ratios to analyze a balance sheet.

$$\text{Quick Ratio} = \frac{\text{Current Liabilities} - (\text{Inventory} + \text{Prepayments})}{\text{Current Liabilities}}$$

$$\text{Current Ratio} = \frac{\text{Current Assets}}{\text{Current Liabilities}}$$

$$\text{Debt Ratio} = \frac{\text{Total Debt}}{\text{Total Assets}}$$

$$\text{Debt-to-Equity Ratio} = \frac{\text{Total Debt}}{\text{Equity}}$$

Key Terms

- current assets
- current liabilities
- current ratio
- debt ratio
- debt-to-equity ratio
- fiscal year
- investment
- liquidity
- long-term assets
- long-term liabilities
- marketable securities
- net worth
- operating ratio
- owner's equity
- profit margin
- quick ratio
- return on investment (ROI)
- return on sales (ROS)
- wealth

Entrepreneurship Portfolio

Critical Thinking Exercises

1. Repeat the exercise from Key Concept Questions using accounting software. Then run the following what-if scenarios and create graphs or other visuals showing how each would affect the business's monthly and yearly financial picture:
   a. What if the restaurant finds a supplier that is willing to provide paper for only $8000 in June and $96,000 for the year?
   b. What if sales for June were $250,000 and sales for the year were $2,000,000? (Do not forget the tax rate assumed at 25 percent.)
   c. What if the owner of this franchise faced start-up costs of $400,000 instead of $300,000? How would that affect the ROI?
2. If you were to open a clothing store, what do you think would be a reasonable operating ratio for the rent, and why?
3. Which items in your business would you depreciate, and why?
4. Using **Exhibit 13-13**, the balance sheet of Angelina's Jewelry Company at the end of July shown below, calculate all four financial ratios (quick, current, debt, and debt-to-equity) for the business.
5. Write a memo analyzing the financial strengths and weaknesses of Angelina's venture. Use the same-size analysis shown below. Would you invest in her business? Why or why not?

Exhibit 13-13 *Balance sheet for Angelina's Jewelry Company.*

Angelina's Jewelry Company Balance Sheet as of July 30, 2009

Assets		**Liabilities**	
Current Assets		**Short-Term Liabilities**	
Cash	$ 1,000	Accounts Payable	$ 1,000
Inventory	1,000	Short-Term Loans	500
Securities	1,000	**Total Short-Term Liabilities**	**$ 1,500**
Total Current Assets	**$ 3,000**	**Total Long-Term Liabilities**	**1,500**
Long-Term Assets	**7,000**	**Owner's Equity**	**$ 7,000**
Total Assets	**$10,000**	**Total Liabilities +OE**	**$10,000**

Exhibit 13-14 *Comparative balance sheet for Angelina's Jewelry Company.*

Angelina's Jewelry Company Balance Sheet	As of July 30, 2009	As of Aug. 30, 2009	% Change
Assets			
Current Assets			
Cash	$ 1,000	$ 500	(50)%
Inventory	1,000	2,000	100%
Securities	1,000	1,500	50%
Total Current Assets	**$ 3,000**	**$ 4,000**	**33%**
Long-Term Assets	**7,000**	**7,000**	**0%**
Total Assets	**$10,000**	**$11,000**	**10%**
Liabilities			
Short-Term Liabilities			
Accounts Payable	$ 1,000	$ 1,500	50%
Short-Term Loans	500	—	(100)%
Total Short-Term Liabilities	**$ 1,500**	**$ 1,500**	**0%**
Total Long-Term Liabilities	**1,500**	**500**	**(67)%**
Owner's Equity	**$ 7,000**	**$ 9,000**	**29%**
Total Liabilities + Owners' Equity	**$10,000**	**$11,000**	**10%**

6. Using the restaurant balance sheet in **Exhibits 13-7** and **13-8**, answer the following:
   a. What are the debt-to-equity ratios at the beginning and end of the 2011 fiscal (business) year? Has it improved? If so, by how much?
   b. The restaurant has less cash at the end of the year than it had at the beginning. Is this a bad thing or not? Explain.
   c. Do you think the restaurant has enough cash to pay its expenses going into 2012?
   d. The restaurant grew its owner's equity by 31 percent during the 2011 fiscal year. At that rate, how much will the business have in owner's equity after one more year (on December 31, 2012)?
   e. The restaurant added some capital equipment during the year. Do you think it took out another loan for that equipment, or did it pay cash? Explain your thinking.
7. On a separate sheet of paper, or using a spreadsheet, create a balance sheet for Tropical Aquaculture, a farm for shrimp, using the information below. Calculate and analyze the quick, debt, and debt-to-equity ratios.

Cash	$45,000
Accounts receivable	$12,000
Shrimp feed	$8,400
Accounts payable	$9,700
Equipment	$75,000
Bank loan	$20,000
Property and ponds	$124,000

8. Use the following balance sheet to answer the questions:

Jean M's Florida-Style Subs, Inc.: Balance Sheet Ending December 31		
	2011	**2010**
ASSETS		
Current Assets		
Cash and cash equivalents	$10,000	$10,000
Accounts receivable	2,000	7,000
Inventory	20,000	25,000
Total Current Assets	**$32,000**	**$42,000**
Fixed Assets		
Plant and machinery	$5,000	$9,000
Land	9,000	8,000
TOTAL ASSETS	**$46,000**	**$59,000**
Liabilities		
Accounts payable	$10,000	$15,000
Taxes payable	6,000	5,000
Total Liabilities	**$16,000**	**$20,000**
OWNER'S EQUITY	**$30,000**	**$39,000**
LIABILITIES and OWNER'S EQUITY	**$46,000**	**$59,000**

As you can see, total liabilities and owner's equity equal the total assets.

a. What is the year-to-year percentage change in the value of the following:
   - inventory,
   - accounts payable,
   - land,
   - taxes payable, and
   - liabilities and owner's equity.

b. What is the ratio of the following:
   - Cash equivalent to inventory in 2011? How has it changed from 2010?
   - Owner's equity to total assets in 2011? How has it changed from 2010?

c. Investors and buyers like to put their money into companies that have a low ratio of liabilities to assets. Has that ratio become more or less appealing from 2010 to 2011?

9. Create a projected balance sheet for your business for one year.

a. Create a pie chart showing your current assets, long-term assets, current liabilities, and long-term liabilities.

b. What is your debt ratio?

c. What is your debt-to-equity ratio?

Key Concept Questions

1. Given the following data, on a separate sheet of paper create monthly and yearly income statements for this fast-food restaurant in New York City.

a. Sales for the month of June were $300,000. Sales for the year were $2,600,000.
b. The sum of $66,000 was spent on food in June (it was $792,000 for the year). The store spent $9000 on paper to wrap food items in June and $108,000 for the year.
c. Taxes for June were $15,000. For the year, they were $233,000.
d. Fixed operating costs for June were $175,000. For the year, they were $1,000,000.
e. Use Excel or other software to create a graph showing the monthly and yearly income statements for this business.

2. If the owner of this fast-food restaurant invested $300,000 in start-up costs, what was his ROI for the year? (Assume June as average.)
3. Calculate the financial ratios (ROI and ROS) for the monthly and the yearly income statement. What do the financial ratios tell you about this business?
4. What would the profit before taxes be if the owner found a paper supplier who only charged $100,000 for the year?
5. What would the profit margin for the year be in that case?
6. Suppose you wanted to raise profits by $5000 a month. What would you do, and why?
7. State the financial equation for the balance sheet in three different ways.
8. How is depreciation treated on the balance sheet and what is the logic behind this treatment?

Application Exercise

Below is Donald Trump's balance sheet (in millions) as of December 31, 1988.[1] All the businesses in his real estate empire were separately incorporated for liability reasons, and many of them were heavily *leveraged*—debt-financed. Eventually, Trump was unable to make certain loan payments, and his bank creditors took some of his properties. Through perseverance and determination, however, Trump rebuilt his holdings and cleaned up his debt problems.

Calculate the debt ratios for each of Trump's properties, then answer the questions.

Asset	Estimated Worth	Debt	Net Worth	Debt Ratio*
Taj Mahal	$834	$834	$0	1
West Side Yards	480	172	28	________
Trump Plaza Casino	637	273	343	________
Trump Casino	606	410	6	________
Trump Shuttle	400	400	0	________
Trump Tower	200	100	0	________
Cash	130	157	–27	________
Trump Condos	111	6	46	________
Marketable Securities	88	75	14	________

(*continued*)

[1]*Fortune*, 1988.

Asset	Estimated Worth	Debt	Net Worth	Debt Ratio*
Trump Palace	77	77	0	________
Trump Plaza	70	48	2	________
Grand Hyatt (50%)	70	30	40	________
Trump Regency	63	85	–22	________
Trump Plaza Coops	46	0	25	________
Trump Air	41	0	31	________
Personal Transportation	37	0	31	________
Personal Housing	30	39	–9	________
Total (in millions)	$___	$___	$___	________

*$Debt\ Ratio = \frac{Debt}{Assets}$

"Donald Trump's Balance Sheet as of December 31, 1988" from "Will Donald Trump Own the World?" from *Fortune* ©, November 21, 1988, Time Inc.

1. What was Trump's highest-priced asset? ________
2. What was Trump's net worth for the Trump Shuttle? Why? ________
3. On which asset was Trump's net worth the greatest? ________
4. Which asset carried the most debt? ________
5. Which properties did Trump own free of debt? ________
6. On which properties did Trump owe one dollar of debt for each dollar of the asset? ________

Exploring Online

Use the Internet to find the balance sheets of two companies with which you are familiar. Use percentages to analyze these balance sheets, and compare how well each is doing compared to the restaurant example from this chapter. Then compare them to each other. Consider choosing either two similar companies, such as Target and Wal-Mart, or two different industries, such as an airline and a car manufacturer.

1. How do the companies compare in growing owner's equity?
2. How do the companies compare in reducing debt?
3. Describe how you think market conditions (such as gas prices, for example) are affecting each company's growth.

Case Study

Cactus & Tropicals: Using Financials to Build Employee Performance

***Small Business School* video clips are available**

Lorraine Miller decided that she would rather be her own boss than work for someone who made her feel insignificant. That's why she started her own business in 1975. She had a secure job as a lab technician, working in her field of study, but the owner of that company refused to answer her inquiries about how things worked, and made her feel undervalued and disrespected. She quit the secure position and, with just $2,000 of her own money, she started selling plants.

Today, the company that Lorraine founded, Cactus & Tropicals, provides indoor and outdoor landscaping for over 500 customers, and the retail stores and greenhouses are full of exotic plants and gifts. Not only has Miller grown the business to one of the largest of its kind in Salt Lake City, she was named Utah's Small Business Person of the Year in 1994, and received a national award from the U.S. Small Business Administration. Lorraine was named by Ernst & Young as one of Salt Lake's outstanding entrepreneurs in 1997.

Lorraine has said, "I start from the premise that I can grow my business to a certain point, and then after that, I'm stuck, because I can only juggle so many bottles at once. If I don't teach employees everything I know, I simply cannot grow the company." This is the reason that teaching is Lorraine's top priority. She has to grow her own talent.

Lorraine's philosophy has always been that work should not be grueling. It should be pleasant, and even fun. She believes in treating employees with great respect, as if the company were one big family. One of Lorraine's employees said, "I worked in the corporate world for about 11 years, and there you're just a number. And you come here, and each one of us is asked to express our opinion."

Part of being a member of a company of family members is that self-determination and goal setting is expected from everyone, and at Cactus & Tropics employees set goals for their own departments. This goal setting includes reviewing the financial statements of the company, and setting financial and other performance

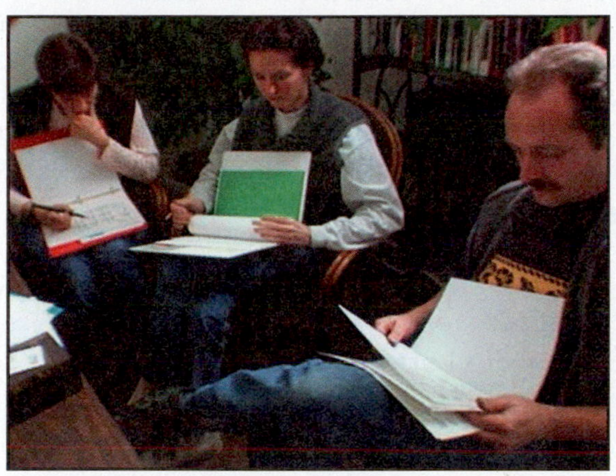

goals. They are privy to the costs of doing business, in addition to knowing the revenue values. It is very common for employees to know what the sales are, but most don't know what it costs to run a business.

As often happens when a company owner is brave enough to open its books to employees, Lorraine's were surprised, and had greater respect for her once they saw how much it really costs to run a business. In fact, they encouraged her to take more personal salary and benefits from the business, once they learned to interpret the financial statements and reports. They realized that employees cost far more than their salaries or wages, because of the additional 25 to 30 percent, or more, that employers pay for taxes and benefits. Employees are often shocked to see the cost of a lease, insurance, utilities, advertising, computing, telephones, and the like.

Lorraine argues against the notion that owners do not have time to teach employees to understand, or to share information with them. She says the benefits derived from sharing information far outweigh the cost of taking the time to do so. To learn how to run her company with open-book management techniques, Lorraine took a course taught by Jack Stack, author of *The Great Game of Business*.

Lorraine's goal at Cactus & Tropicals has always been to deliver to customers more than they paid for, and to do that by finding people who want to work in a place where they are given guidelines—not rules. The staff at Cactus & Tropicals is expected to ask questions, create, improvise, and serve customers with little or no supervision. Lorraine cut her schedule to only a few days a week and invested her time in teaching everyone how to read a balance sheet, how to do sales forecasting, how to measure individual and team productivity, and how to earn performance-based bonuses. Lorraine learned to value her employees and give them the opportunity to succeed through their own knowledge, skills, and abilities.

Case Study Analysis

1. How can a person's life experience affect the way they manage people? Use Lorraine Miller's story to illustrate one example.
2. How did Lorraine finance the startup of her business?
3. How do we know what others think of Lorraine and her business?
4. Why did Lorraine decide to involve her employees in the financial aspects of her business?
5. What is the risk in teaching employees how to read the company financial statements?
6. What do you think about the word *boss*? Would you rather be supervised by a person who is more of a teacher or mentor or coach than one who simply tells you what to do?

Case Sources

Case prepared by Hattie Bryant, creator of *Small Business School*, the television series made for PBS and Voice of America, http://SmallBusinessSchool.org.

Case Study | Portland Freelancers' Café: Amy and Steve's Business Idea*

In 2003, Amy Chan and Steve Lee formed a partnership to start an Internet café in Portland, Oregon. For many years, Amy and Steve had worked as freelance writers. They enjoyed bringing their laptops to local coffeehouses to complete their writing projects. Having an endless supply of good strong coffee at their disposal helped them to stay focused on their work.

Over time, they began to daydream about owning their own café. Although Portland already had many great coffee shops, Amy and Steve felt that none of them catered well to freelancers like themselves. More and more, people in Portland seemed to be doing their work in informal settings. Everywhere they turned, twenty- and thirty-somethings were sipping lattes while conducting business deals on cell phones. Amy and Steve sometimes wondered if anyone worked in a traditional office anymore.

We Can Do Better

As much as they enjoyed Portland's café culture, they felt that a fatal flaw compromised each of their favorite coffee spots. One was too loud. Another had uncomfortable chairs, and tables that weren't well suited for laptop users. Their particular favorite, The Magic Bean, only had three outlets, which meant that only a few laptops could be plugged in at one time. Just a handful of the coffee shops in downtown Portland offered high-speed Internet access at that time.

Amy and Steve felt that they could do a better job of running a café that catered to the needs of freelancers. They made a list of everything they would want in a café, and then asked their freelance friends for additional feedback. The two partners resolved that, in their café, customers would be able to enjoy high-speed Internet access; laser printers; a soundproof, quiet room; and comfortable, up-to-date work stations. To attract their target market, Amy and Steve decided to name their business the Portland Freelancers' Café.

Deluxe Purchases

They spent $10,000 up front installing super-fast T1 Internet lines. They imported a $7000, top-of-the-line espresso machine from Italy. To make the café

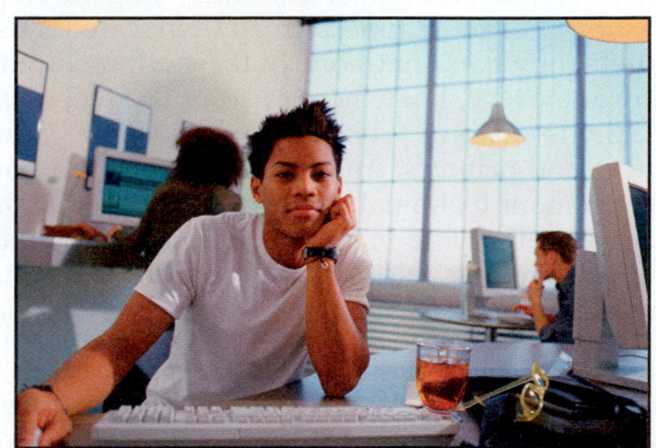

look sleek and modern, all of the furniture was custom-designed for the space, as were the curved metallic ceiling, and wall panels. Installing the soundproof interior room was more costly than they had anticipated. Their equipment costs totaled $25,000. At $500 per month, they had negotiated a good deal on their rent, so they figured that they could afford to splurge on these other features.

Financing

The café's start-up investment totaled $100,000. This included a $10,000 cash reserve. Amy and Steve contributed a combined $20,000 of their personal savings. Steve's brother invested another $20,000, in exchange for a 20-percent equity stake. Amy's mother wrote a check for $10,000, which she gave to the partners as a gift. Also, Amy and Steve received a $50,000 loan from Amy's uncle. The partners agreed to pay back the loan with interest at an annual rate of 12 percent.

Funding Source	Equity	Debt	Gift
Personal Savings	$20,000 (80% equity)		
Steve's Brother	$20,000 (20% equity)		
Amy's Uncle		$50,000 (@ 12% interest rate)	
Amy's Mother			$10,000
Subtotal	$40,000	$50,000	$10,000
Total Start-Up Investment	$100,000		

*Note: This is a fictional case.

Computer Glitch

Because so much money was needed for start-up, Amy and Steve tried to cut costs by hiring a local high school student, who agreed to work 100 hours per month for an hourly wage of $10. It soon became apparent to frustrated customers, however, that none of the staff, including Amy and Steve, knew how to solve the technical problems customers encountered with the computers and printers. Amy and Steve tried to find a permanent technical support person, but computer experts were in high demand at the time, and the partners felt that they couldn't afford to pay a competitive salary.

Business Troubles Brew

Before starting their business, Amy and Steve assumed that revenue would come from two primary sources, food and beverage sales and computer/Internet services. Together they had calculated two economics-of-one-unit analyses, one for each of the two sources.

Amy and Steve's EOU

The partners originally assumed that the average customer would spend $6 at the café and that $2 of this revenue would be generated by food and beverage sales. The remaining $4 would come from the sale of computer and Internet services. They believed that the business could be very successful if they did well selling computer services. After all, they could charge customers $4 for an hour of service that would only cost them 45 cents to provide. In comparison, food and beverage sales would not be nearly as profitable. For every $2 of lattes and muffins sold, they would pay $1 in direct costs.

Amy and Steve built a 5 percent manager's commission into their EOU, even though they did not yet have the funds to hire a manager. They wanted to account for this cost because they did plan to hire a manager at some point in the future and the commission would be a real cost of doing business.

Here is what the café's EOU looked like when Amy and Steve examined both revenue streams together:

EOU for Food and Beverage Sales	
Average Sale per Customer	
• Food/Beverage Sales	$2.00
Variable Costs per Unit	
COGS per Unit	
• Food/Beverage Costs	$1.00
TOTAL COGS per Unit	$1.00
EOU for Food and Beverage Sales	
Other Variable Costs per Unit	
Manager's Commission @ 5%	$0.10
Total Variable Cost per Unit	$1.10
Contribution Margin per Unit	$0.90
EOU for Computer/Internet Services	
Average Sale per Customer	
• Computer Services	$4.00
Variable Costs per Unit	
COGS per Unit	
• Paper, Toner	$0.25
TOTAL COGS per Unit	$0.25
Other Variable Costs per Unit	
Manager's Commission @ 5%	$0.20
Total Variable Cost per Unit	$0.45
Contribution Margin per Unit	$3.55

In Hot Water

When the Portland Freelancers' Café first opened, Amy and Steve were encouraged by how busy things seemed. The café was buzzing with customers and they received some positive reviews in the local papers. They expected to lose money at first, but figured that, in a few months' time, the business would become profitable. After three months, they had a major shock when they realized that this was not happening. What went wrong?

Changes in the Environment

Initially, Amy and Steve's customers willingly paid $4 an hour to use the computers and high-speed Internet connection. However, soon after the grand opening, wireless Internet service became available throughout the Portland area. Within two months, the café's customers no longer wanted to pay to go online. They put pressure on Amy and Steve to become a wireless hot spot. This meant that Amy and Steve would have to foot the bill of providing free Internet service.

The partners carried out some research and learned that it would cost $300 to purchase the basic equipment for wireless Internet connectivity, plus an additional $30 per month in service fees. They had counted on charging their customers for Internet access and now it looked like *they* would have to pick up the tab. They wondered how they could pay for this unexpected cost

EOU: Average Sale per Customer	
Average Sale per Customer	
• Computer Services	$4.00
• Food and Beverage Sales	$2.00
Variable Costs per Unit	
COGS per Unit	
• Paper, Toner	$0.25
• Food/Beverage Costs	$1.00
TOTAL COGS per Unit	$1.25
Other Variable Costs per Unit	
Manager's Commission—Computer Services @ 5%	$0.20
Manager's Commission—Food and Beverage @ 5%	$0.10
TOTAL Commission Costs	$0.30
Total Variable Cost per Unit	$1.55
Contribution Margin per Unit	$3.20

and also make up the lost revenue they *weren't* selling. On the other hand, they feared that the Portland Freelancers' Café would not be able to compete unless they adapted to changes in the market.

Amy and Steve's EOU Revisited

Three months after they opened the café, Amy and Steve discovered that their monthly unit sales of computer services had been cut by more than half. In their first month, they had sold 1,500 units, but by month three they were only averaging 600. They worried that this number would only continue to decline.

The café was holding steady with its food and beverage sales—in fact, the monthly units sold had climbed steadily from 4,500 units in month one to 5,000 in month three. Customers were enjoying the café's free wireless service. This feature created a situation where people would stay longer and order more coffee. But even with increased sales of cappuccino, the overall finances of the operation were not improving. In looking at their economics-of-one-unit analysis of food and beverage sales, the partners could see that their gross profit per unit for food and beverage sales was only 90 cents. Even if they sold 5,000 food and beverage units per month, they would still only be earning $4,500 in gross profit. In the scheme of things, this was not very much money—not nearly enough to cover the monthly fixed costs of $8,332.

An Uncertain Future

One year into their venture, Amy and Steve began to seriously doubt their decision to start the Portland Freelancers' Café. In hindsight, they realized that they knew a lot about being customers but running a state-of-the-art coffee shop was a lot harder than they had imagined. By the end of the year, the Portland Freelancers' Café was on the verge of going out of business. Take a look at the café's financial statements in **Exhibits 13-15** through **13-18** and then analyze why this happened.

Case Study Analysis

1. Evaluate the economics-of-one-unit analysis that Amy and Steve conducted and then answer the following:
   a. Amy and Steve assumed that, for every $6 in sales, $4 would come from selling computer-related services. Calculate what percentage of their total sales revenue per unit this $4 represents.
   b. For every $2 in food and beverage sales, Amy and Steve assumed that their COGS per unit would be $1. Calculate the markup percentage.
   c. For every $4 in computer services sales, Amy and Steve assumed that their COGS per unit would be 25 cents. Calculate the markup percentage.
2. List three things that Amy and Steve should have considered doing to adapt to the changes in the environment now that their customers no longer wanted to pay for Internet services, and expected the café to provide free wireless connections.
3. Evaluate Amy and Steve's income statement for their first month of operations:
   a. Is the café operating at a profit or a loss?
   b. How many units above or below breakeven were sold?
4. Amy and Steve decided to take on a $50,000 loan to finance their start-up investment. Each month they are paying $1469 in interest charges. Look at their total monthly fixed costs. What percentage of their total monthly fixed costs does this $1469 represent?
5. What is the debt-to-equity ratio of the Portland Freelancers' Café?

Exhibit 13-15 *Start-up investment and economics of one unit.*

Start-Up Investment	
Start-up Costs	
Soundproof Room	$15,000
Espresso Machine	7,000
High-Speed Internet Access Setup	10,000
Workstations	20,000
Supplies/Equipment	25,000
Furniture	8,000
Fixtures	5,000
Cash Reserves	10,000
Total Start-up Investments	**$100,000**

Economics of One Unit (EOU)
Unit of Sale: Computer/Internet Services (Average per Customer)

Average Sale Total (Revenue)				**$4.00**
Less COGS				
Computer time		–		
Printer materials		0.25		
Total COGS		0.25	0.25	0.25
Gross Profit				**$3.75**
Less Other Variable Costs				
Commission	5% to manager	0.20		
Total Other Variable Costs		0.20	0.20	0.20
Total Variable Costs (COGS + Other VC)			0.45	
Contribution Margin				**$3.55**

Economics of One Unit (EOU)
Unit of Sale: Food and Beverage Sales (Average per Customer)

Average Sale Total (Revenue)				**$2.00**
Less COGS				
Food		0.80		
Beverage		0.20		
Total COGS		1.00	1.00	1.00
Gross Profit				**$1.00**
Less Other Variable Costs				
Commission	5% to manager	0.10		
Total Other Variable Costs		0.10	0.10	0.10
Total Variable Costs (COGS + Other VC)			1.10	
Contribution Margin				**$0.90**

Exhibit 13-16 *Income statement.*

The Portland Freelancers' Café
INCOME STATEMENT
for the Year Ending 12/31/2011

		Jan	Feb	Mar	Apr	May	Jun	Jul	Aug	Sep	Oct	Nov	Dec	Year
No. Units sold—Computer Services		1,500	1,000	600	550	550	500	500	450	450	450	400	400	7,350
No. Units sold—Food and Beverage		4,500	4,750	5,000	5,100	5,200	5,300	5,400	5,500	5,600	5,700	5,800	6,000	63,850
Revenue														
Computer Service Fees		$ 6,000	$ 4,000	$ 2,400	$ 2,200	$ 2,200	$ 2,000	$ 2,000	$ 1,800	$ 1,800	$ 1,800	$ 1,600	$ 1,600	$ 29,400
Food and Beverage Sales		9,000	9,500	10,000	10,200	10,400	10,600	10,800	11,000	11,200	11,400	11,600	12,000	127,700
Total Revenue		**$15,000**	**$13,500**	**$12,400**	**$12,400**	**$12,600**	**$12,600**	**$12,800**	**$12,800**	**$13,000**	**$13,200**	**$13,200**	**$13,600**	**$157,100**
Less COGS														
Printer Mat'ls (paper, ink)		375	250	150	138	138	125	125	113	113	113	100	100	1,838
Food		3,600	3,800	4,000	4,080	4,160	4,240	4,320	4,400	4,480	4,560	4,640	4,800	51,080
Beverages		900	950	1,000	1,020	1,040	1,060	1,080	1,100	1,120	1,140	1,160	1,200	12,770
Total COGS		$ 4,875	$ 5,000	$ 5,150	$ 5,238	$ 5,338	$ 5,425	$ 5,525	$ 5,613	$ 5,713	$ 5,813	$ 5,900	$ 6,100	$ 65,688
Gross Profit		**$10,125**	**$ 8,500**	**$ 7,250**	**$ 7,163**	**$ 7,263**	**$ 7,175**	**$ 7,275**	**$ 7,188**	**$ 7,288**	**$ 7,388**	**$ 7,300**	**$ 7,500**	**$ 91,413**
Less Other Variable Costs														
Commission, Computer	(5%)	300	200	120	110	110	100	100	90	90	90	80	80	1,470
Commission, Food/Bev.	(5%)	450	475	500	510	520	530	540	550	560	570	580	600	6,385
Total Other Variable Costs		$ 750	$ 675	$ 620	$ 620	$ 630	$ 630	$ 640	$ 640	$ 650	$ 660	$ 660	$ 680	$ 7,855
Total Var. Costs (COGS + Other VC)		5,625	5,675	5,770	5,858	5,968	6,055	6,165	6,253	6,363	6,473	6,560	6,780	73,543
Contribution Margin*		**$ 9,375**	**$ 7,825**	**$ 6,630**	**$ 6,543**	**$ 6,633**	**$ 6,545**	**$ 6,635**	**$ 6,548**	**$ 6,638**	**$ 6,728**	**$ 6,640**	**$ 6,820**	**$ 83,558**

* Remember: Revenue – COGS = Gross Profit – Other Variable Costs = Contribution Margin.

(*continued*)

Exhibit 13-16 *(Continued)*

The Portland Freelancers' Café
INCOME STATEMENT
for the Year Ending 12/31/2011

		Jan	Feb	Mar	Apr	May	Jun	Jul	Aug	Sep	Oct	Nov	Dec	Year
Less Fixed Costs (USAIIRD)														
Utilities														
Electricity		150	150	150	150	150	150	150	150	150	150	150	150	1,800
Gas		250	250	250	250	250	250	250	250	250	250	250	250	3,000
Water		100	100	100	100	100	100	100	100	100	100	100	100	1,200
Telephone		75	75	75	75	75	75	75	75	75	75	75	75	900
High-Speed Internet		425	425	425	425	425	425	425	425	425	425	425	425	5,100
Wireless Internet Service		30	30	30	30	30	30	30	30	30	30	30	30	360
Total Utilities		$1,030	$1,030	$ 1,030	$ 1,030	$ 1,030	$ 1,030	$ 1,030	$ 1,030	$ 1,030	$ 1,030	$ 1,030	$ 1,030	$ 12,360
Salaries														
Amy & Steve Salary		1,000	1,000	1,000	1,000	1,000	1,000	1,000	1,000	1,000	1,000	1,000	1,000	12,000
Tech Support (Part time)		1,000	1,000	1,000	1,000	1,000	1,000	1,000	1,000	1,000	1,000	1,000	1,000	12,000
Total Salaries		$2,000	$2,000	$ 2,000	$ 2,000	$ 2,000	$ 2,000	$ 2,000	$ 2,000	$ 2,000	$ 2,000	$ 2,000	$ 2,000	$ 24,000
Advertising		1,000	1,000	1,000	1,000	1,000	1,000	1,000	1,000	1,000	1,000	1,000	1,000	12,000
Insurance		500	500	500	500	500	500	500	500	500	500	500	500	6,000
Interest		1,469	1,469	1,469	1,469	1,469	1,469	1,469	1,469	1,469	1,469	1,469	1,469	17,628
Rent		1,000	1,000	1,000	1,000	1,000	1,000	1,000	1,000	1,000	1,000	1,000	1,000	12,000
Depreciation		1,333	1,333	1,333	1,333	1,333	1,333	1,333	1,333	1,333	1,333	1,333	1,333	15,996
Total Fixed Costs		$8,332	$8,332	$ 8,332	$ 8,332	$ 8,332	$ 8,332	$ 8,332	$ 8,332	$ 8,332	$ 8,332	$ 8,332	$ 8,332	$ 99,984
Pre-Tax Profit		**$1,043**	**($507)**	**($1,702)**	**($1,790)**	**($1,700)**	**($1,787)**	**($1,697)**	**($1,785)**	**($1,695)**	**($1,605)**	**($1,692)**	**($1,512)**	**($16,427)**
Taxes	(20%)	209	—	—	—	—	—	—	—	—	—	—	—	—
Net Profit		**$ 834**	**($507)**	**($1,702)**	**($1,790)**	**($1,700)**	**($1,787)**	**($1,697)**	**($1,785)**	**($1,695)**	**($1,605)**	**($1,692)**	**($1,512)**	**($16,427)**

Exhibit 13-17 *Cash flow statement.*

The Portland Freelancers' Café
CASH FLOW STATEMENT
for the Year Ending 12/31/2011

	Jan	Feb	Mar	Apr	May	Jun	Jul	Aug	Sep	Oct	Nov	Dec	Year
Number of Units—Computer Services	1,500	1,000	600	550	550	500	500	450	450	450	400	400	7,350
Number of Units—Food & Beverage Sales	4,500	4,750	5,000	5,100	5,200	5,300	5,400	5,500	5,600	5,700	5,800	6,000	63,850
Cash Flow from Operating:													
Cash Inflows:													
Computer Usage Fees	$ 6,000	$ 4,000	$ 2,400	$ 2,200	$ 2,200	$ 2,000	$ 2,000	$ 1,800	$ 1,800	$ 1,800	$ 1,600	$ 1,600	$ 29,400
Food and Beverage Sales	9,000	9,500	10,000	10,200	10,400	10,600	10,800	11,000	11,200	11,400	11,600	12,000	127,700
Total Cash Inflows	**$15,000**	**$13,500**	**$ 12,400**	**$12,400**	**$12,600**	**$12,600**	**$12,800**	**$12,800**	**$13,000**	**$13,200**	**$13,200**	**$13,600**	**$157,100**
Cash Outflows:													
Variable Costs													
COGS	$ 4,875	$ 5,000	$ 5,150	$ 5,238	$ 5,338	$ 5,425	$ 5,525	$ 5,613	$ 5,713	$ 5,813	$ 5,900	$ 6,100	$ 65,688
Other Variable Costs	$ 750	$ 675	$ 620	$ 620	$ 630	$ 630	$ 640	$ 640	$ 650	$ 660	$ 660	$ 680	$ 7,855
Utilities													
Electricity, Gas, Water, Telephone	$ 500	$ 500	$ 500	$ 500	$ 500	$ 500	$ 500	$ 500	$ 500	$ 500	$ 500	$ 500	$ 6,000
High-Speed Internet Access	425	425	425	425	425	425	425	425	425	425	425	425	5,100
Wireless Internet	30	30	30	30	30	30	30	30	30	30	30	30	360
Salaries													
Part-Time Tech Support Salary	$ 1,000	$ 1,000	$ 1,000	$ 1,000	$ 1,000	$ 1,000	$ 1,000	$ 1,000	$ 1,000	$ 1,000	$ 1,000	$ 1,000	$ 12,000
Amy and Steve's Salary	$ 1,000	$ 1,000	$ 1,000	$ 1,000	$ 1,000	$ 1,000	$ 1,000	$ 1,000	$ 1,000	$ 1,000	$ 1,000	$ 1,000	$ 12,000
Advertising	$ 1,000	$ 1,000	$ 1,000	$ 1,000	$ 1,000	$ 1,000	$ 1,000	$ 1,000	$ 1,000	$ 1,000	$ 1,000	$ 1,000	$ 12,000
Insurance	$ 500	$ 500	$ 500	$ 500	$ 500	$ 500	$ 500	$ 500	$ 500	$ 500	$ 500	$ 500	$ 6,000
Interest Expense	$ 1,469	$ 1,469	$ 1,469	$ 1,469	$ 1,469	$ 1,469	$ 1,469	$ 1,469	$ 1,469	$ 1,469	$ 1,469	$ 1,469	$ 17,623
Rent	$ 1,000	$ 1,001	$ 1,002	$ 1,003	$ 1,004	$ 1,005	$ 1,006	$ 1,007	$ 1,008	$ 1,009	$ 1,010	$ 1,011	$ 12,000
Total Cash Used in Operating Activities	**$ 12,549**	**$ 12,600**	**$ 12,696**	**$ 12,784**	**$ 12,895**	**$12,983**	**$13,095**	**$13,183**	**$13,294**	**$13,405**	**$13,494**	**$13,715**	**$156,626**
Net Cash Flow from Operating	**$ 2,451**	**$ 900**	**($ 296)**	**($ 384)**	**($ 295)**	**($ 384)**	**($ 295)**	**($ 383)**	**($ 294)**	**($ 205)**	**($ 294)**	**($ 115)**	**($ 474)**

(*continued*)

Exhibit 13-17 *(Continued)*

The Portland Freelancers' Café
CASH FLOW STATEMENT
for the Year Ending 12/31/2011

	Jan	Feb	Mar	Apr	May	Jun	Jul	Aug	Sep	Oct	Nov	Dec	Year
Cash Flow Out from Investing:													
Soundproof Room	$ 15,000	$ 0	$ 0	$ 0	$ 0	$ 0	$ 0	$ 0	$ 0	$ 0	$ 0	$ 0	$ 15,000
Espresso Machine	7,000	0	0	0	0	0	0	0	0	0	0	0	7,000
High-Speed Internet Access Setup	10,000	0	0	0	0	0	0	0	0	0	0	0	10,000
Workstations	20,000	0	0	0	0	0	0	0	0	0	0	0	20,000
Supplies/Equipment	25,000	0	0	0	0	0	0	0	0	0	0	0	25,000
Furniture	8,000	0	0	0	0	0	0	0	0	0	0	0	8,000
Fixtures	5,000	0	0	0	0	0	0	0	0	0	0	0	5,000
Net Cash Flow Out from Investing	**$ 90,000**	$ 0	**$ 0**	**$ 0**	**$ 0**	**$ 0**	**$ 0**	**$ 0**	**$ 0**	**$ 0**	**$ 0**	**$ 0**	**$ 90,000**
Financing:													
Cash Received from Uncle (12% APR)	$ 50,000	$ 0	$ 0	$ 0	$ 0	$ 0	$ 0	$ 0	$ 0	$ 0	$ 0	$ 0	$ 50,000
Cash Received from Brother	20,000	0	0	0	0	0	0	0	0	0	0	0	20,000
Cash Received from Mother	10,000	0	0	0	0	0	0	0	0	0	0	0	10,000
Cash Received from Personal Savings	20,000	0	0	0	0	0	0	0	0	0	0	0	20,000
Net Cash Flow In from Financing	**$100,000**	**$ 0**	**$ 0**	**$ 0**	**$ 0**	**$ 0**	**$ 0**	**$ 0**	**$ 0**	**$ 0**	**$ 0**	**$ 0**	**$100,000**
Net Increase (Decrease) in Cash	$ 12,451	$ 900	($ 296)	($ 384)	($ 295)	($ 384)	($ 295)	($ 383)	($ 294)	($ 205)	($ 294)	($ 115)	$ 10,474
Cash, Beginning:	**$ 10,000**	**$22,451**	**$23,351**	**$22,055**	**$22,671**	**$22,376**	**$21,992**	**$21,697**	**$20,314**	**$20,020**	**$20,815**	**$20,521**	**$ 10,000**
Cash, End:	**$ 22,451**	**$23,351**	**$22,055**	**$22,671**	**$22,376**	**$21,992**	**$21,697**	**$20,314**	**$20,020**	**$20,815**	**$20,521**	**$20,406**	**$ 20,474**

Exhibit 13-18 *Balance sheet.*

Portland Freelancers' Café
BALANCE SHEET
for the Year Ending 12/31/2003

	Opening	Closing
ASSETS		
Current Assets:		
Cash	$110,000	$20,474
Accounts Receivable	0	0
Total Current Assets	**$110,000**	**$20,474**
Fixed Assets (Property and Equipment):		
Soundproof Room	$ 15,000	$15,000
Espresso Machine	2,000	2,000
Workstations	30,000	30,000
Supplies/Equipment	25,000	25,000
Furniture	3,000	3,000
Fixtures	5,000	5,000
Total Property and Equipment	**$ 80,000**	**$80,000**
Less Accumulated Depreciation	**$ 0**	**$15,996**
Total Property and Equipment (Net)	**$ 80,000**	**$64,004**
Total Assets	**$190,000**	**$84,478**
LIABILITIES AND OWNER'S EQUITY		
Current Liabilities:		
Accounts Payable	$ 0	$ 0
Total Current Liabilities	**$ 0**	**$ 0**
Long-Term Liability (Uncle's Loan)	**$ 50,000**	**$32,377**
Total Liabilities	**$ 50,000**	**$32,377**
Owner's Equity	**$140,000**	**$52,101**
Amy	40%	40%
Steve	40%	40%
Steve's Brother	20%	20%
Total Liabilities and Owner's Equity	**$190,000**	**$84,478**

6. Look at each section of the café's cash flow statement. Write a memo highlighting three insights you have about why this business is not succeeding, based on what you see in its cash flow statement.

7. Review the café's balance sheet. Explain why the net value of the café's property and equipment has decreased from $80,000 in month one to $64,000 at year's end.

Chapter 14

CASH FLOW AND TAXES

"If you do your job well, the last thing you have to worry about is money, just as if you live right, you will be happy."

—Edwin Land, founder of Polaroid Corporation

At age 28, David Kendricks started his own recording label, Kickin' Records. He began by searching for and producing hip-hop artists from his hometown of Newark, New Jersey.

David invested $25,000 in his new business. He saved the money by working two jobs for five years. He set up a Web site to sell his CDs. He bought a business telephone number with voicemail, and created and printed his own stationery and business cards. He regularly invests time from eight in the evening until three in the morning looking for groups to sign to his recording label.

David has been spending about $100 a night on cover charges and drinks at nightclubs, and tickets for concerts, including transportation. He has found, however, that the groups at the better clubs and concerts are already signed and have producers. David has had no sales, because he has not yet produced a CD. After six months, he is almost $20,000 in debt. David hasn't kept a close watch on his cash flow, and this has threatened the existence of his business.

Performance Objectives

1. Understand the importance of cash flow management.
2. Know the difference between cash and profits.
3. Read a cash flow statement.
4. Create a cash budget.
5. File appropriate tax returns for your business.

Cash Flow: The Lifeblood of a Business

Cash is the energy that keeps your business flowing, the way electricity powers a lamp. Run out of cash, and your business will soon go out like a light. Without cash on hand, you will not be able to pay essentials, even while the income statement says you are earning a profit. If your phone is cut off, it will not matter what the income statement says. The success of your business will depend upon cash, from start-up through its entire existence. Cash is essential for the initial investment, ongoing operations, and growth. Managing cash is more critical than managing sales, because sales without cash receipts are a recipe for disaster. Cash truly is the lifeblood of a business.

Performance Objective 1
Understand the importance of cash flow management.

The income statement shows you what the situation is with sales and profits over a period of time. It tells you how much revenue has come in and how it relates to the cost of goods sold and operating costs. The balance sheet is a snapshot of your business. It shows your assets and liabilities and net worth at one moment in time. Each of these statements and the associated ratios is important, but without a firm handle on the cash situation, business success will be elusive.

The Income Statement Does Not Show Available Cash

Once you start a business and are using the accrual method of accounting, however, you will notice that, sometimes, even when the income statement says you are making a profit, you have no money. There is

BizFacts

You can calculate your ongoing cash balance by subtracting cash disbursements from cash receipts. You should never have a negative cash balance.

often a time lag between making a sale and getting paid. If you make a sale, and the customer promises to pay you in a week, the sale is recognized on the income statement immediately, but you will not have the cash until the check is received, deposited, and available at the bank. Also, there may be a lag between paying for labor and/or materials and receiving payment for the finished goods. If a company is using the accrual method of accounting, it records sales when goods are shipped/delivered, even though payment has not been received. Thus, a company may show a profit and have a negative cash flow. Cash and profit are not the same.

For all the good information and guidance a monthly income statement can provide, you cannot base your business's daily operations on using the income statement alone. You will also need a **cash flow statement** that summarizes the cash coming into and going out of the business over a specified time frame.

cash flow statement financial report that shows the money coming into and going out of an organization.

Performance Objective 2

Know the difference between cash and profits.

You can calculate your cash balance by subtracting cash disbursements from cash receipts, as you do when balancing your checkbook. Your goal is never to have a negative cash balance. A negative balance means that you are overdrawn in one or more of your bank accounts. This will reflect poorly on your banking relationships, can trigger the accumulation of fees and penalties, and result in bounced checks to critical vendors and the like. More basically, a negative cash balance means that there are problems in your cash flow.

Author William Stolze calls the cash flow statement "By far the most important financial control in a start-up venture."[1] The cash flow statement records inflows and outflows of money as they occur. If a sale is made in June, but the customer does not pay until August, the cash flow statement will not show the revenue until August, when the cash "flows" into the business. If you are keeping your accounting records on a cash basis, you would not show the sale on the income statement until you received payment. If you use the accrual method, the sale will appear on the income statement in June, but not in the cash flow statement until August.

Step into the Shoes...

King C. Gillette Faces a Cash Crunch

King Gillette was a traveling salesman for 28 years. In his spare time, he tried to invent a successful consumer product. He invented all kinds of gadgets that did not pan out, but in 1885, when he cut himself shaving with his dull, straight razor, inspiration hit. Gillette thought of a disposable safety razor.

Gillette and a partner eventually got financing together and launched their business. The future seemed bright, but soon the company was $12,500 in debt. By 1901, even though people were excited about the product, "We were backed up to the wall with our creditors lined up in front waiting for the signal to fire," Gillette wrote later.[2]

Gillette convinced a Boston investor to put money in the company, and by the end of 1904, his company was producing a quarter million razor sets per year. This is an example of how crucial an infusion of money can be to a business. A temporary cash crunch nearly destroyed a company that is now more than a century old.

[1]William Stolze, *Start Up: An Entrepreneur's Guide to Launching and Managing a New Business* (Franklin Lakes, N.J.: Career Press, 1994), p. 96.
[2]Russell B. Adams, *King C. Gillette: The Man and His Wonderful Shaving Device* (New York: Little, Brown, 1978).

Exercise

Name three kinds of businesses that bring in a lot of cash during part of the year and not much the rest of the time.

Rules to Keep Cash Flowing

Cash flow is primarily a factor of accounts receivable, accounts payable, and inventory. By controlling these factors, a company can control its cash flow. In order to avoid getting caught without enough cash to pay your bills, follow these rules:

1. ***Collect cash as soon as possible.*** When you make a sale, try to get paid immediately. If you must extend credit, make sure you collect the cash as scheduled.
2. ***Pay your bills by the due date, not earlier.*** You do not have to pay a bill the day it arrives in your mailbox. Look for the due date, and send your payment so it arrives by that date. This will conserve precious cash.
3. ***Check on your available cash every day.*** Always know how much cash you have on hand. Your cash flow will be reflected in your up-to-date accounting journal. Remember, your true balance takes into account any checks or bank debits outstanding.
4. ***Lease or finance instead of buying equipment, where practical.*** Leasing distributes costs over time. Better yet, acquire functional used equipment rather than new equipment, if it makes sense.
5. ***Avoid buying inventory that you do not need.*** Find the point where you stock the minimal inventory necessary to satisfy customer demand. Inventory ties up cash: the cash you use to purchase inventory and the cash you spend storing it.

Noncash Expenses Can Distort the Financial Picture

The income statement is not an accurate reflection of your cash position when it includes **noncash expenses**, or expenses recorded as adjustments to asset values such as depreciation. When you depreciate an asset, you are deducting a portion of its cost from your income statement. But you aren't actually spending that cash; you are reducing the value of the asset. You do not pay out money when you record a depreciation expense on your income statement.

noncash expenses adjustments to asset values not involving cash, such as depreciation.

Depreciation is a noncash expense because no money is actually disbursed. When depreciation is deducted from an income statement, therefore, the statement no longer accurately reflects how much cash the business is really holding. By the same token, the cash flow statement does not include depreciation, because no actual cash leaves the business.

The Working Capital Cycle

Once a business is operational, an entrepreneur must keep an eye on the **working capital**, the formula for which is current assets minus current liabilities:

working capital the value of current assets minus current liabilities.

$$\text{Current Assets} - \text{Current Liabilities} = \text{Working Capital}$$

Working capital tells you how much cash the company would have if it paid all its short-term debt with the cash it had on hand. What's left over is cash the company can use to build the business, fund its growth, and produce value for the shareholders.

All other things being equal, a company with positive working capital will always outperform a company with negative working capital. The latter cannot spend the money to bring a new product to market. If a company runs out of working capital, it will still have bills to pay and products to develop; it may not be able to stay afloat. When determining cash requirements for your business, remember working capital.

The Cyclical and Seasonal Nature of Cash Flows

The entrepreneur needs a cash flow statement to depict the cash position of the business at specified points in time. The cash flow statement records inflows and outflows when they occur. There are cash flow cycles that occur for every business that are important to understand because they can make the difference between success and failure. **Figures 14-1** and **14-2** show cash flow cycles for a manufacturer and a residential cleaning company, respectively.

The length of the cycle, amount of cash involved, and upfront cash outlays will differ substantially for these businesses. For example, a manufacturer may have to pay its suppliers and employees before getting paid by a customer. A residential cleaning service, on the other hand, may collect customer payments on the same day as the cleaning is provided, so that payment of wages falls after the cash is received. Thus, their planning and budgeting should also differ significantly.

In addition to having cash flow cycles relative to specific transactions, cash flow can be seasonal for many businesses, meaning that the amount of cash flowing into a business may depend on where the business is in its fiscal year. A flower store will have a lot of cash coming in around Mother's Day and Valentine's Day, for example, but may have very little during the fall. A college campus bookstore will have to stock up on books before each semester starts, and will have a lot of cash coming in when students arrive to buy books for their classes.

This is why keeping an eye on cash flow at all times will be crucial to the survival of your business. Utility companies, vendors, and lenders will not care that you won't have money coming in over the next three months; they will want their regular monthly payments, unless you negotiate special payment schedules in advance. When you create your business plan, describe your expectations for seasonal changes in your cash flow, and how you will manage your cash to cope with this. Remember, you can ask lenders to create payment schedules based upon the seasonal nature of your business. It is often in their best interest to do so, and they may appreciate you planning ahead.

Reading a Cash Flow Statement

Knowing how to read a cash flow statement is a valuable skill for any businessperson. Whereas income statements and balance sheets provide considerable insight into a company, the cash flow statement gives a clear picture of its cash position. A simple cash flow statement for a business provides information about the cash that comes into and goes out of the organization. The first section records all sources of income. These are cash inflows, or *cash receipts* (not to be confused with receipts for purchases). The next section reports cash outflows, or necessary *disbursements* for that month: insurance and interest payments, cost of goods sold, salaries, and so forth. Some cash flow statements break down inflows and outflows according to whether they are related to operations, investing, or financing.

Figure 14-1 *Cash flow cycle for a manufacturer.*

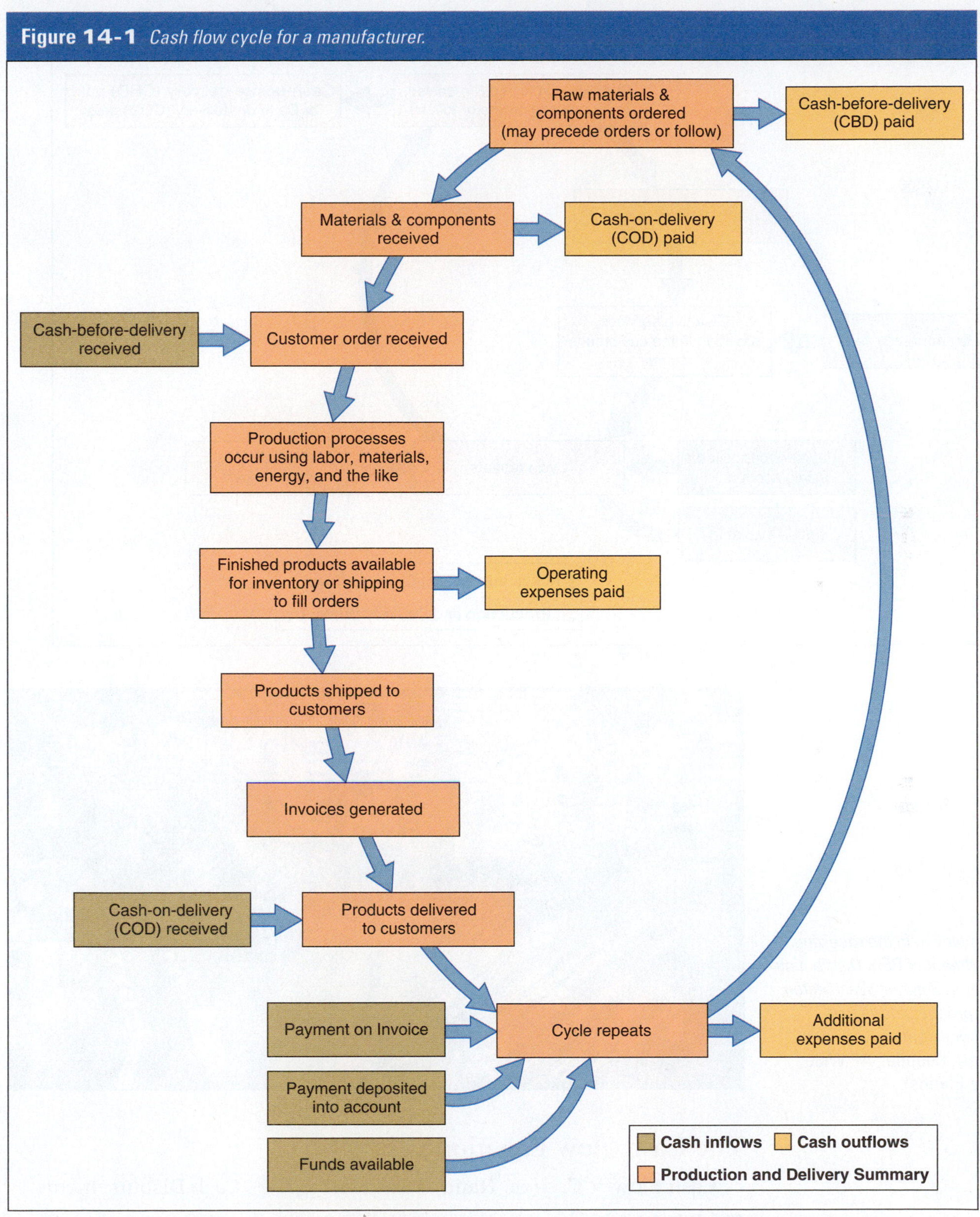

The last section shows the net change in cash flow. This tells the entrepreneur whether the business had a positive or negative cash flow that month. You can have all the sales in the world and still go out of business if you do not have enough cash flowing in to cover your monthly cash outflows.

Performance Objective 3

Read a cash flow statement.

Figure 14-2 *Cash flow cycle for a residential cleaning company.*

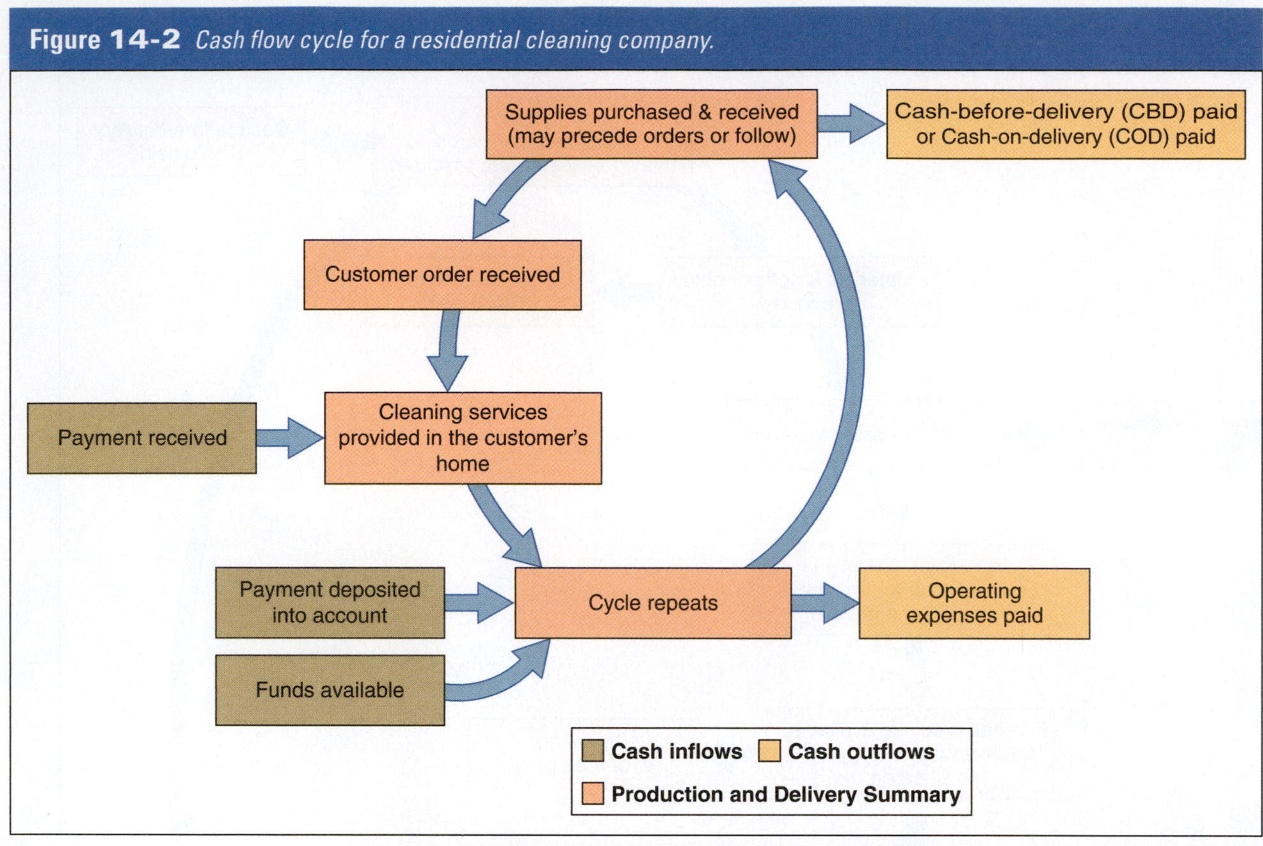

An employee in the receiving department of REI's Distribution Center in Sumner, Washington, sorts products during an October inventory. (Dean J. Koepfler, AP Wide World Photos)

The Cash Flow Equation

Cash Flow = Cash on Hand + Cash Receipts − Cash Disbursements

Exhibit 14-1 is an example of a cash flow statement. Inflows and outflows of cash are divided into three categories:

1. ***Operations.*** Money used to run the business.
2. ***Investment.*** Money going into and out of investments in the business, such as equipment, vehicles, or real estate.
3. ***Financing.*** Money used to finance the business (debt and equity).

Exhibit 14-1 *Sample cash flow statement.*

Cash Flow Statement for Lola's Custom Draperies, Inc. for the Month of March 2011		
Cash Flow from Operations		
Cash Inflows		
Sales (net of returns)	$65,400	
Total Cash Inflows	**$65,400**	
Cash Outflows:		
Variable Costs		
COGS	$29,360	
Other VC (Sales Commissions)	6,540	
Fixed Costs		
Factory Rent & Utilities	$8,000	
Sales & Administrative	12,000	
Part-Time Tech-Support Salary	1,000	
Taxes	2,875	($11,500 × 0.25)
Total Cash Used in Operating Activities	**$59,775**	
Net Cash Flow from Operations	**$5,625**	($65,400 − $59,775)
Cash Outflow from Investing		
Purchase of Building	0	
Purchase of Equipment	(6,000)	
Net Cash Flow from Investing	**($6,000)**	
Cash Flow from Financing:		
Loans	$25,000	
Gifts	0	
Equity Investment	0	
Net Cash Flow from Financing	**$25,000**	
Net Increase/(Decrease) in Cash	**$24,625**	($5,625 − $6,000 + $25,000)
Cash, Beginning	**$500**	
Cash, Ending	**$25,125**	($500 + $24,625)

Forecasting Cash Flow: The Cash Budget

Performance Objective 4
Create a cash budget.

As you get your business off the ground, and even after it has operated for many years, you should prepare cash flow projections to make sure there is enough money to pay the bills. In the beginning, monthly, or even weekly, cash flows are in order.

There are two steps to forecasting cash flow receipts:

1. Project cash receipts from all possible sources. Remember, orders are not cash receipts, because they may not become cash. Some may be canceled and some customers may not pay. Cash receipts are checks that have cleared, or credit card payments, or cash itself. Plus, note the assumptions you are making to arrive at these figures, so that others can understand the logic behind the statements.
2. Subtract expenditures that would need to be deducted to meet this level of cash receipts. Cash expenditures are only those expenses you will actually have to pay during the projected time period.

Exhibit 14-2 *Cash flow budget for three months ending June 30, 2011.*

	April	May	June
Monthly Sales Net of Returns	$20,000	$22,000	$25,000
Inventory Purchased ($10,000 in March)	11,000	12,500	14,000
Cash Flow from Operations			
Cash Inflows			
In Month of Sales	$10,000	$11,000	$12,500
One Month Later	0	6,000	6,600
Two Months Later	0	0	4,000
Total Cash Receipts from Operations	$10,000	$17,000	$23,100
Cash Outflows			
Inventory Payments			
One Month after Purchase	$8,000	$8,800	$10,000
Two Months after Purchase	0	2,000	2,200
Total Cash for Inventory	$8,000	$10,800	$12,200
Payments for Other Operational Expenses	8,600	8,000	8,000
Interest on Loans	0	100	100
Taxes	0	0	0
Total Cash Payments for Operations	$16,600	$18,900	$20,300
Total Cash Flow from Operations	**($6,600)**	**($1,900)**	**$2,800**
Cash Flows from Investments			
Purchase of Equipment	**($20,000)**		
Cash Flows from Financing			
Commercial Loan for Equipment	$20,000		
Line of Credit Draw			$10,000
Owner's Personal Investment	35,000		
Total Cash Flows from Financing	**$55,000**	**$0**	**$10,000**
Total Net Cash Flow	**$28,400**	**($1,900)**	**$12,800**
Beginning Cash Balance	$0	$28,400	$26,500
Ending Cash Balance	$28,400	$26,500	$39,300

Exhibit 14-2 is a sample company budget and **Exhibit 14-3** shows the assumptions underlying a sample budget.

You know that any projections will not be completely accurate, but you should create them to the best of your ability and review and update them routinely. They will be useful to anticipate any shortfalls, so that you can make adjustments to costs, push for increased sales, and/or arrange short-term financing as needed.

Exhibit 14-3 *Cash flow assumptions.*

Category	Assumption
Accounts Receivable	50% in month of sale
	30% one month later
	20% two months later
Inventory (Payable)	0% in month of purchase
	80% one month later
	20% two months later
Utilities	$500 per month
Salaries and Benefits	$6,000 per month
Advertising	$1,000 in April, and $600 per month thereafter
Insurance	$100 per month
Rent	2,000 square feet of space at $6 per square foot per year = $1,000 per month
Depreciation	$0 (Depreciation is not a cash expenditure)
Taxes	Paid quarterly–none in this period
Interest	Interest only on line of credit and commercial loan for three months
Commercial Loan 1	$20,000 for seven years at 6% for equipment purchase = $100 per month interest only for three months
Line of Credit	$50,000 revolving line of credit, interest only at 12% per year, and no funds drawn until June

Creating a Healthy Cash Flow

Healthy cash flow management means keeping sufficient cash on hand and available to pay your bills in a timely fashion and have financial resources available to you when you need them. Most entrepreneurs struggle at various times to have sufficient cash to pay for materials, rent, and other expenses. As a business becomes more stable and successful, deciding when and where to invest excess cash to maximize earnings at the appropriate risk level becomes an important part of managing the company.

Cash inflows and outflows can be managed to control overall cash flow. **Figure 14-3** shows categories of cash flows and the way they affect a company.

Global Impact...

Cash Flow Statements Are Not Required in Every Country

In the United States, public corporations are required by law to present cash flow statements as part of their compliance reporting. In some countries, however, businesses are not required to present either a statement of cash flow or statement of fund flow. This is the case in Germany, Italy, and Denmark. In Germany, many large companies voluntarily provide either a cash flow or fund flow statement. The United Kingdom does require cash flow statements but only for very large companies. The international trend, however, is moving toward the U.S. practice of requiring cash flow statements from public corporations, as governments recognize that income statements do not reveal a company's true cash position and can be misleading to investors. In light of recent corporate scandals, the trend is toward greater transparency and more disclosure.

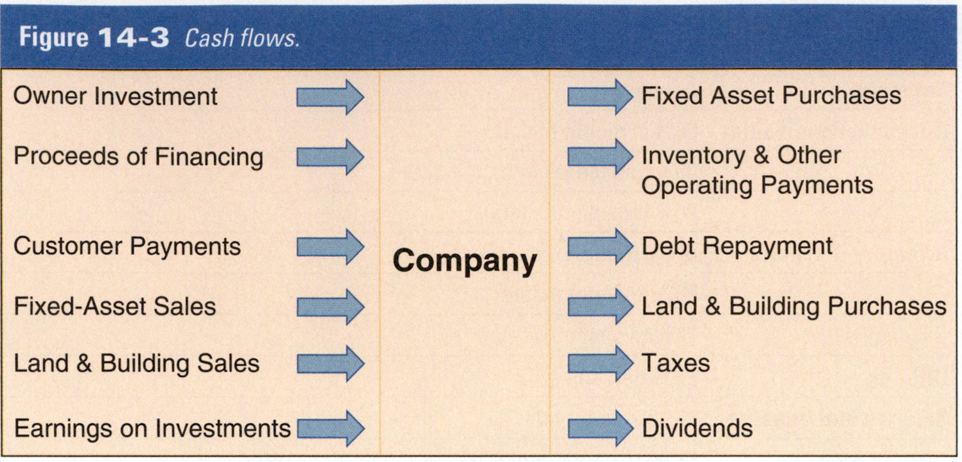

Figure 14-3 *Cash flows.*

Managing Inventory to Manage Cash

Inventory is often one of the largest components of a company's assets, and controlling it is a critical step in managing company cash flow. An entrepreneur takes a risk every time he or she spends cash. If you buy inventory, for example, you run the risk that no one will buy it at a price that will give you a profit, or even buy it at all. When you invest in inventory, cash is tied up and cannot be used for other purposes, such as rent, payroll, and debt service. By managing the level of inventory on hand, you will be dealing with one of the three primary controllable factors in cash availability.

pilferage theft of inventory.

There are two other risks involved with inventory—storage costs and **pilferage**, which is theft of inventory. You will have to be sure you can sell the inventory at a price that will include the cost of storing it, and cover pilfering. Barneys, the famous New York clothing store, eventually had a 7-percent pilferage rate, which helped drive the company out of business (although it made a comeback later). Remember to account for these inventory-related costs in your projections.

You should also be cautious about adding inventory based on the expectation of receiving cash from the customers who owe you money. Because a percentage of the receivables owed to you may never be collected, counting on getting all of the cash could cause liquidity problems. You must keep track of your cash flow, or you can get caught in a squeeze between your suppliers, who want you to pay for inventory you have purchased, and customers who have not yet paid for what they bought. If you cannot pay your creditors, you could lose ownership of your business. That's what happened to Donald Trump and the Taj Mahal, in Atlantic City some years ago. He couldn't pay his loans, so he had to turn over 80 percent ownership in the casino to the banks.

Freeing Up Cash by Reducing Inventory

Conceptually, it is clear that reducing inventory releases cash. However, reducing inventory once accumulated is generally easier said than done. If it is finished-goods inventory, it has to be liquidated—sold—if it is to be converted into cash. This often means discounting products in ways that are not in alignment with your overall pricing strategy. If inventory is in the form of work-in-process or semi-finished goods, additional materials and labor costs may have to be invested to make it ready to sell. Thus, freeing up cash by reducing inventory is a valid option that can work, but should be well considered and realistically projected.

Tracking Inventory

Keeping timely and accurate inventory records is vital to controlling inventory costs. Regardless of the methods you select to control your inventory levels and determine your order point(s), the process will only work effectively if you keep accurate records of what inventory you have on hand and on order. Depending on the type of business you operate, you might use a computer-based tracking system, perhaps with bar codes or other scanning or automated techniques. More sophisticated methods can tell you where products are located at any given time, and what quantity is available for sale. For a less complex business, you can keep a simple manual system or basic spreadsheet tabulation. You will also need to keep accurate track of the lead times on materials for production and inventory supplies, so that you can avoid stock outs and overages.

Controlling Inventory Levels

By using one of the many available inventory control methods (see Chapter 17), you can minimize the amount of cash tied up in inventory. Tight inventory controls reduce waste, obsolescence, and spoilage. By managing inventory to control costs, you are also overseeing your cash flow.

Managing Receivables to Manage Cash

Managing your accounts receivable to generate prompt payment is another way to conserve cash. In retail trade, payments generally are made immediately (cash) or with a slight delay (debit or credit card or check). Once you are in a business that extends credit terms to its customers, you will need to manage the timing of payments. The sooner you collect on receivables the better, from a cash flow perspective.

The Cash Effects of Accounts Receivable

Receivables affect cash availability. If you are not actively billing and collecting the monies owed, you can rapidly find yourself with too little cash to operate your business. You will be, in effect, lending your precious cash to your customers while they have the use of your products and/or services.

The Life Cycle of Accounts Receivable

An accounts receivable has a life cycle and this cycle will vary according to your type of business. For most retail businesses, there is no extension of credit and receivables effectively do not exist. Wholesale and manufacturing companies routinely have receivables that depend upon their credit policies and collection efforts. One tool that companies employ to manage their receivables is an aging schedule for accounts receivable. **Exhibit 14-4** is an example of such a schedule.

By creating and updating an aging schedule on a routine basis, you can keep track of your collections and anticipate your cash flow. You can easily identify problem customers and attempt to work with them to improve payment promptness. Also, using "aging" information can help to establish a forecast of cash flow.

Exhibit 14-4 *Aging schedule for accounts receivable—as of June 30, 2012.*

Name	#	Not Due (in disc.)	Not Due (no disc.)	15 Days Past Due	30 Days Past Due	60 Days Past Due	90 Days Past Due	120 Days Past Due
Adams	0123	$120		$240				
Bourdon	0246						$190	$300
Chevaux	3579		$480	$960	$720			
Young	0579					$560	$240	
Zaninga	5811	$480	$1200					
Total		**$600**	**$1680**	**$1200**	**$720**	**$560**	**$430**	**$300**
%		**10.9%**	**30.6%**	**21.9%**	**13.1%**	**10.2%**	**7.8%**	**5.5%**

Of course, aging reports are only part of the cash-flow management process. Timely billing and effective collection are critical. If you are extending credit to your customers, a fundamental rule is: If you don't ask, you won't get. You have to invoice promptly and collect regularly. Whereas this may seem obvious, one of the most common cash-flow issues for companies is their failure to bill and collect effectively.

One challenge that entrepreneurs face is segregating the collection process from sales and customer relations. A legitimate concern is the potential for losing a customer by asking for, or demanding, payment for previous purchases. A failure to collect on a timely basis can lead to financial disaster for an entrepreneurial venture. Overly aggressive collection attempts can also lead to financial disaster, through the loss of key customers. However, there are a few guidelines to keep in mind that will help to keep a balance:

- establish clear credit arrangements with customers that reflect acceptable terms for both of you;
- create comprehensive written credit and collection policies, share them with your team, and implement them;
- use collection techniques appropriate to the level of delinquency;
- avoid using salespeople as collectors on their assigned accounts;
- comply with the Fair Debt Collection Practices Act and do not use intimidation or deception in collections; and
- recognize that some customers are worth "firing" as credit customers.

The Financing of Accounts Receivable

Accounts receivable can provide a ready source of cash for your company if you are in a bind. Receivables financing, or **factoring**, provides cash to companies in exchange for the rights to the cash that will be collected from their customers. When you *factor* your receivables, you provide a list of the outstanding amounts and their status in an aging chart to the finance company, and they will offer you a percentage of each category of receivable in exchange for the right to those proceeds when collected. Fresh accounts are worth significantly more than aged ones. Sometimes, you can be charged for accounts that do not pay within a specified length of time. Factoring is common in some industries and highly unusual in others. You will need to understand your industry to determine the applicability. The key thing to remember is that you will forgo the opportunity to control the collection process, and give up potential profits, in exchange for immediate cash. As a general rule, factoring is not the ideal option because it can become the proverbial slippery slope.

Managing Accounts Payable to Manage Cash

Credit is the ability to borrow money. It enables you to buy something without spending cash at the time of purchase. Once you have established a relationship with a supplier, he or she may be willing to extend credit. If you own a store, you might be able to buy Christmas ornaments from a supplier in October and pay for them in 60 days, after your Christmas sales.

credit the ability to borrow money.

If you aren't managing your cash carefully, however, you could get caught in the squeeze discussed above, between your suppliers and your customers. Your suppliers might not extend credit to you in the future. If you get into a position where you cannot pay your suppliers, you will have no further inventory and, thus, no business.

Negotiating Payment

You will have multiple opportunities to negotiate vendor payments and you should be prepared to take advantage of them when they arise. When you establish a customer-vendor relationship, payment terms will be part of the price negotiation. The leverage that you have to negotiate will depend upon the balance of power in the relationship. Often, new accounts have less favorable terms with vendors until they establish a solid track record. Other times, a company may offer extended payment terms as part of a new-customer incentive, or other promotional program. Once you have been a customer for a while, and have demonstrated that you are a desirable customer in terms of purchase volume and timely payment, you can revisit your payment terms to secure additional time. As you become an increasingly significant customer for your vendor, you can renegotiate prices, including payment terms.

You also may be able to negotiate payment terms when you are experiencing difficulty with cash flow. This is not something that you should do routinely. However, if you can see that your cash flow will not permit you to pay part or all of the balance due on time, you should notify your supplier/vendor/creditor and negotiate realistic payment terms. This should be handled deftly, so that they understand you genuinely need their cooperation, but they should not be alarmed and retrench on future supplies or credit terms. This can be a delicate transaction.

Timing Payables

Just as you should establish an accounts receivable aging schedule, you should also create an accounts *payable* aging schedule (see **Exhibit 14-5**). In addition to noting where you are in terms of days outstanding, be certain to indicate terms received, and variances. Recognize that you may have to

Exhibit 14-5 *Aging schedule for accounts payable as of June 30, 2012.*

Name	Vendor Number	Not Due (in discount)	Not Due (no disc.)	15 Days Past Due	30 Days Past Due	60 Days Past Due
Ace Supply	51-09238		$5,000			
Big Guys	62-78749				$1,000	
Champions	10-83297			$4,000		$2,000
Youth Style	23-83940	$7,500				
Zoo Pals	51-10239	$1,000			$2,000	
Total		**$8,500**	**$5,000**	**$4,000**	**$3,000**	**$2,000**
%		**37.8%**	**22.2%**	**17.8%**	**13.3%**	**8.9%**

start out with prepayment or payment upon delivery, which will be difficult for cash flow because you will have to disburse money before you sell anything. Depending upon the business you are in, this could be a long interval.

The aging schedule for accounts payable makes your cash requirements clear. You can see what is coming due, where you can benefit from discounts, and where there are problems. This simple approach can be invaluable to your cash management.

Capital Budgeting and Cash Flow

Cash management is not only for operating cash and financing. It also includes the planning for *capital assets* (fixed assets, or earning assets). The purchase of machinery, equipment and its installation, and the like, requires initial cash outflows for assets and incremental working capital for new projects, the inflow of cash from operations as a result of purchases, and terminal cash flows from liquidation of old, outdated, or replaced equipment.

Capital budgeting will help you understand the cash flow required for investments, and the expected impact on operating cash flows. Budgeting will lead you to calculate the depreciation associated with capital investment, so that you can anticipate the tax effects. (Remember, increased depreciation means decreased taxes.) Finally, as you budget for the terminal values, you will see cash flow effects from disposal of assets and the related tax consequences. Making a capital budget can shed considerable light on cash flow expectations. **Exhibit 14-6** shows a capital budget for

Exhibit 14-6 *NRG Savers, Inc. capital budget 2012.*

	Year 1	Year 2	Year 3	Year 4	Year 5
Initial Investment					
Machinery and Equipment	$82,000				
Installation	18,000				
Working Capital	10,000				
Total Initial Investment	**$110,000**				
Operating Cash Flows					
Operating Cash Inflow	$200,000	$300,000	$400,000	$500,000	$550,000
Depreciation	20,000	32,000	19,000	12,000	12,000
Net Change in Income	$180,000	$268,000	$381,000	$488,000	$538,000
Tax Effect (@ 30%)	48,000	80,400	114,300	146,400	161,400
Net Operating Cash Flow	**$132,000**	**$187,600**	**$266,700**	**$341,600**	**$376,600**
Terminal Cash Flow					
Sale of Equipment					$40,000
Tax on Income (sale)					10,500
Net on Sale of Equipment					$29,500
Recover—Working Capital					10,000
Total Terminal Cash Flow					**$39,500**
Project Cash Flow	**$22,000**	**$187,600**	**$266,700**	**$341,600**	**$416,100**

NRG Savers, Inc., as they consider the purchase and installation of equipment for a new line of environmentally friendly products.

We can see that the components of the capital budget fit into the full cash-flow budget of a company once the project is accepted or rejected. By creating and analyzing each capital project separately, you can apply your decision criteria and determine which to accept and which to reject. You can plan for your financing needs well in advance and be prepared to justify your repayment plans.

The Burn Rate

When you start your business, it is normal to have a negative cash flow from operations for at least the first few months. You are likely to spend more than you earn in the beginning stages. Some businesses, such as biotechnology companies, that spend a great deal on research and development (R&D), can have a negative cash flow of as much as $1 million per month. You will need to build these initial cash deficits into your business plan so that they can be covered in start-up costs.

Because a new company will probably spend more money than it earns while it is getting off the ground, the question will be: how long can you afford to lose cash? The answer will depend on the amount of capital invested and the amount of revenue being earned.

The pace at which your company will need to spend capital to cover overhead costs before generating a positive cash flow is called the **burn rate**. The burn rate is typically expressed in terms of cash spent per month. A burn rate of $10,000 per month means that the company is spending that amount monthly to cover rent and other operating expenses. If the company has $20,000 in cash and is making $2,000 a month in sales, how long could it hold out?

burn rate the pace at which a company spends capital before generating positive cash flow.

$$\frac{(\text{Cash Available} + \text{Revenue})}{\text{Negative Cash Outflow per Month}} = \text{Number of Months before Cash Runs Out}$$

The Value of Money Changes over Time

When considering cash and cash flow, it is also important to evaluate the changing value of money over time. A dollar today, available for investment, is worth more than a dollar tomorrow. Cash goes up or down in terms of buying power depending upon several factors. For example, the value of a dollar changes depending upon inflation rates and variations in exchange-rate strength relative to foreign currencies. Finally, it can grow as the interest earned previously continues earning additional interest.

The Future Value of Money

Interest-earning funds grow fastest in investments that offer a *compound* rate of return, that is, those that are calculated on interest that has already accumulated. The younger you are when you start saving for a goal, such as retirement, the more compounding will help your money grow. Suppose you put $100 into an investment that pays 10 percent compounded annually. At the end of a year, you will have $110 ($100, plus $10 interest). At the end of the next year, you will have $121 ($110 plus $11 interest). Your money will grow faster each year because you are earning interest on the interest. The formula for this is

$$\text{FV} = \text{PV}(1 + i)^n$$

Where **FV** is the future value of the investment; **PV** is the present value, or amount invested today; $\boldsymbol{i}$ equals the interest rate per compounding period,

Figure 14-4 *Effect of compound interest.*

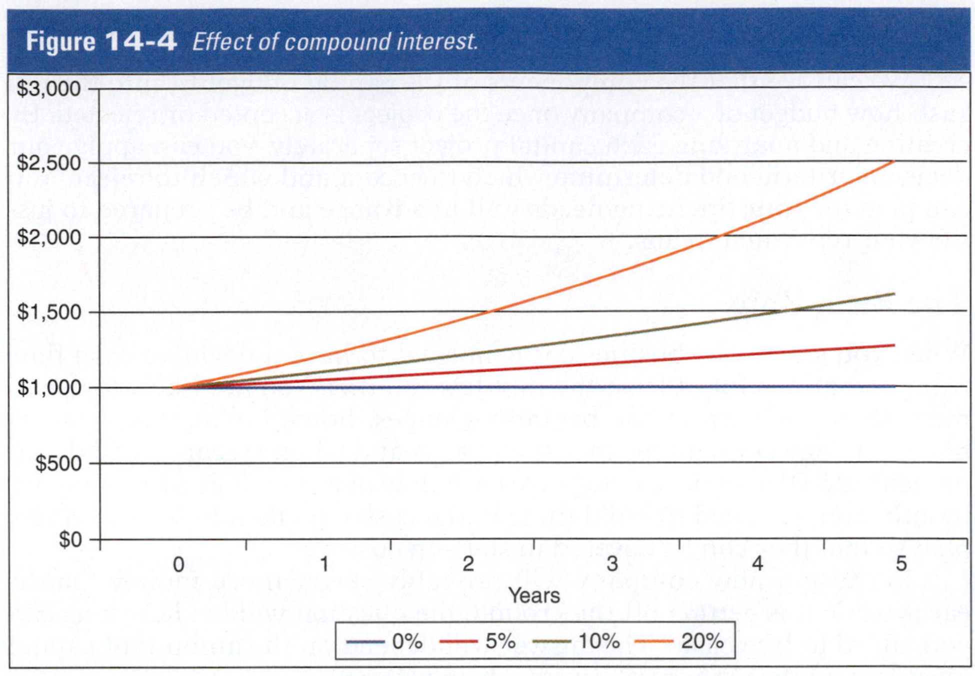

and n equals the number of compounding periods. For example, $1200 invested at 5% per year for 10 years will total

$$FV = \$1200(1 + 0.05)^{10} = \$1954.67$$

Figure 14-4 shows the effect of compounding $1,000 at 0%, 5%, 10%, and 20% for five years.

future value the amount an asset will gain over time.

The **future value** of money is the amount it will *accrue* (gain) over time through investment. For a single investment at a constant interest rate, you can use the formula provided, or you can determine this easily using a future value chart such as the one in **Exhibit 14-7**. Look up 10 periods at 10 percent on the chart, and you will find that $100 invested at 10 percent will grow to $259 in 10 years. Note that these values can also be figured on

Exhibit 14-7 *Future value of $1 in n periods.*

Periods	1%	3%	5%	8%	10%
1	1.0100	1.0300	1.0500	1.0800	1.1000
2	1.0201	1.0609	1.1025	1.1664	1.2100
3	1.0303	1.0927	1.1576	1.2597	1.3310
4	1.0406	1.1255	1.2155	1.3605	1.4641
5	1.0510	1.1593	1.2763	1.4693	1.6105
6	1.0615	1.1941	1.3401	1.5869	1.7716
7	1.0721	1.2299	1.4071	1.7138	1.9487
8	1.0829	1.2668	1.4775	1.8509	2.1436
9	1.0937	1.3048	1.5513	1.9990	2.3580
10	1.1046	1.3439	1.6209	2.1589	2.5937
15	1.1610	1.5580	2.0789	3.1722	4.1773

a financial calculator and via spreadsheet software, such as Excel. If there are multiple amounts, variable interest rates, and the like, you can consult a basic financial management book or the Internet for appropriate calculation methods. Remember, **compound interest**, money making money, is the essence of investment.

compound interest used with interest or rate of return and applied when earning also accumulate interest or other returns in addition to earnings on principal.

The Present Value of Money

Another way to look at investing is summed up by the old saying, "A bird in the hand is worth two in the bush." You always prefer to have your money *now*. If you cannot have it immediately, you want to be compensated with a return.

Your money is worth more to you when it is in your hand for three reasons.

1. ***Inflation.*** When prices rise, a dollar tomorrow will buy less than a dollar does today.
2. ***Risk.*** When you put money into an investment, there is always some risk of losing it.
3. ***Opportunity.*** When you put money into an investment, you are giving up the opportunity to use it for what might be a better investment.

Say a customer promises to pay you $10,000 three years from now for designing a Web site. Your next-best opportunity for investment has an ROI of 10 percent.

Present value is the amount an investment is worth discounted back to the present. Look at the present value chart (see **Exhibit 14-8**) under period three (for three years) and 10 percent. The present value of $1 at three years and 10 percent is $0.751. The present value of the promise of $10,000 in three years, therefore, is $7510 ($10,000 × 0.751 = $7510). Your client's promise is worth only $7510 in the present. If you accept this arrangement, you should charge interest because you are essentially providing a $10,000 loan for three years. Anytime you are asked to wait for payment, you should be compensated, because money in your hand now is worth significantly more than money promised for the future. If you

present value what the future amount of an asset or other investment is worth at face value discounted back to the present.

Exhibit 14-8 *Present value of $1 to be received* n *periods in the future.*

Periods	1%	3%	5%	8%	10%
1	0.990	0.971	0.952	0.926	0.909
2	0.980	0.943	0.907	0.857	0.826
3	0.971	0.915	0.864	0.794	0.751
4	0.961	0.886	0.823	0.735	0.683
5	0.951	0.863	0.784	0.681	0.621
6	0.942	0.837	0.746	0.630	0.584
7	0.933	0.813	0.711	0.583	0.513
8	0.923	0.789	0.677	0.540	0.467
9	0.914	0.766	0.645	0.500	0.424
10	0.905	0.744	0.614	0.463	0.386
15	0.861	0.642	0.481	0.315	0.239

BizFacts

When you sell a business, the price reflects more than the nuts and bolts of the operation. You are also selling the future stream of income that the business will be expected to generate. This income is reflected in the price of the business, which is its *present value*. This is why businesses typically sell for several times their annual net income.

want to calculate this using a mathematical formula, you can use the inverse of the future value formula.

$$PV = FV(1/(1 + i)^n)$$

So, the prior example would be $PV = \$10{,}000(1/(1 + 0.10)^3) = \$7510$.

Understanding the time value of money permits managers to compare investment options and other opportunities based upon their real values, so that they can better manage cash flows.

self-employment tax federal tax that business owners pay on wages paid to themselves.

sales tax tax levied by governments on purchases and collected by merchants.

Taxes

Another factor that affects cash flow for a business is taxes. Like other creditors, tax-levying bodies expect payment in a timely fashion. More importantly, tax payments must be kept current, because some delinquencies can result in business closure and substantial personal penalties.

Performance Objective 5

File appropriate tax returns for your business.

Cash and Taxes

Once your business begins making a profit, you will have to pay taxes on those profits, whether or not you have a positive cash flow—and that will also have an impact on it. Regardless of whether they make a profit, self-employed people, such as consultants or sole proprietors, must pay their own **self-employment tax** on any payroll wages paid to themselves. This is the Social Security tax obligation for those who are self-employed, and is the equivalent of the combination of the employee and employer taxes paid for employees. These taxes must be paid quarterly, so you will need to be putting aside cash in order to make the payments on the due dates.

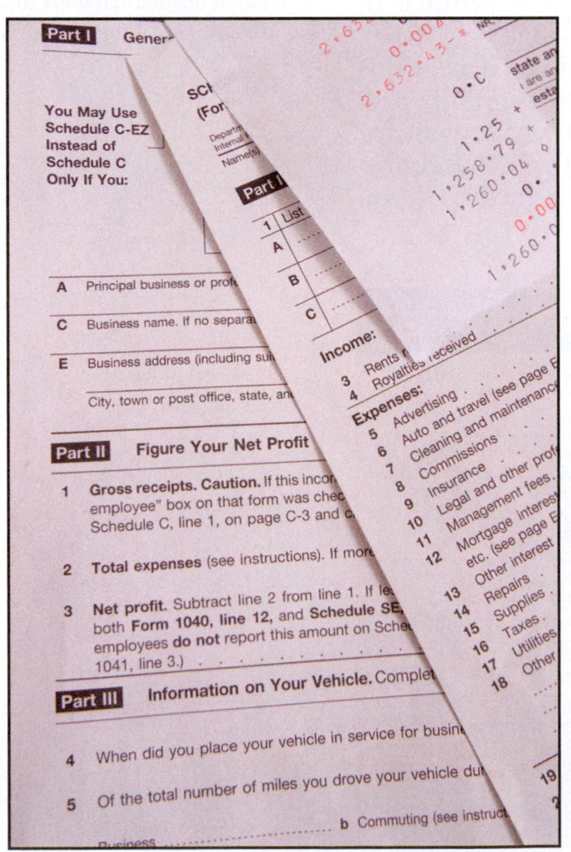

As an employer, you will collect and pay all employment taxes to the appropriate government entities. These taxes are particularly important to report accurately and pay on time. Federal penalties for tax code violations with respect to wage taxes are especially harsh. The government may "sweep" your company bank accounts (take out any available funds), assess significant fines, and secure your personal assets. Using withheld wage taxes as a source of cash flow and/or failing to pay these taxes would be a disastrous choice.

The federal government is financed primarily by personal and corporate income taxes. States usually raise money from **sales taxes** on goods (not services). Most states also levy an income tax. City and other local governments are supported primarily by taxes on property.

Filing Tax Returns

Corporate, partnership, and individual income tax and self-employment tax returns must be filed (mailed or submitted online) to the U.S. Internal Revenue Service (IRS) by specific dates each year. Corporate returns are due on a different schedule (earlier) from the traditional April 15 deadline for individual returns. If you file late, you may have to pay penalties and interest. You can check the IRS Web site at http://www.irs.gov for deadlines, instructions, and forms.

The tax code is very complex. Check the aforementioned IRS Web site for information, but if you are still not certain which tax forms to file and when to do so, the IRS also offers booklets and telephone service to help answer questions. Help with the 1040, the most common individual return form, is available at 1-800-424-1040. You can also go to your local IRS office and meet with an agent who will guide you through the forms for free. It can be worth investing the time and money to ensure your own correct tax filings (rates and forms can change from year to year). As soon as your business starts earning income, you will probably want to seek the services of a tax professional (an accountant, or CPA). Remember, in addition to federal taxes, businesses are subject to state and local taxes. Check with state and local revenue departments.

Collecting Sales Tax

If you sell products or services to the public, you will have to charge state sales tax in most states, and then turn over the collected money monthly or quarterly to the state. Apply to your state's department of taxation for the necessary forms. In New York State, for example, entrepreneurs use the New York State and Local Sales and Use tax return to report quarterly sales tax. Some states only charge tax on products; some charge tax on products and services, whereas a very few do not have a sales tax.

Tax Issues for Different Legal Structures

The legal structure best suited to a business depends upon a number of variables, which will be discussed later in this text. Each legal structure has tax advantages and disadvantages.

- ***Sole proprietorship.*** All profit earned by a sole proprietorship belongs to the owner, and affects his/her tax liability. The business does not pay taxes on profits separately.
- ***Partnership.*** The tax issues are basically the same as for the sole proprietorship, except that profits and losses are shared among the partners, who report them on their respective personal income tax returns.
- ***Limited partnership.*** This is treated in the same way as a partnership, except that a limited partner can use losses as a tax shelter without being exposed to personal liability. This can be an incentive for potential investors.
- ***Corporation (subchapter C).*** A corporation's profits are taxed whether or not a share of the profits is distributed to the owners. Owners must also pay personal income tax on any profit distribution they receive. This "double taxation" is considered a disadvantage of C corporations.

- ***S corporation.*** Small companies can use this structure to avoid the double taxation mentioned above. The S corporation does not pay tax on profits. Profit is taxed only once, as owner income on personal tax returns. This structure requires all partners to take profits and losses in proportion to their ownership (thus it does not offer the tax-shelter advantages of the limited partnership).
- ***Limited liability company (LLC).*** This structure separates the owner/partners from personal liability and provides a more flexible allocation of profits and losses.

Finally, note that dividends paid by a business to stockholders are not tax deductible, but interest payments made to creditors are. This can be an incentive to raise capital via borrowing, depending on the tax issues your business faces.

Make Tax Time Easier by Keeping Good Records

You and your tax preparer will have an easier time if you have been keeping accurate records throughout the year. You will have to determine your net income. If you have kept accurate and timely accounting records, this should not be difficult.

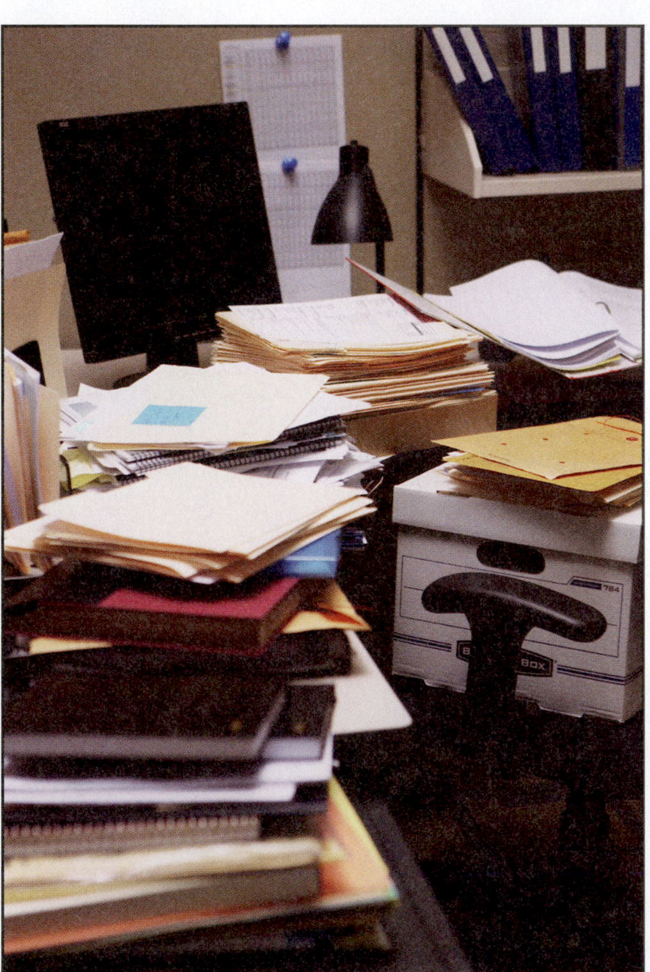

Mistakes on your tax return, or just the luck of the draw, could cause the IRS to *audit* you. The IRS will send an agent (auditor) to your business to examine your ledgers and receipts and invoices to make sure your taxes were filed correctly. An audit can be a time-consuming and stressful process. This is another excellent reason to keep good records and file all invoices and receipts, whether or not you use an accountant for tax preparation.

Do not confuse accounting with taxation. Your accounting software generates financial records, but you will still need tax-preparation assistance, and/or tax software, to prepare your returns. Some accounting software, will allow you to export your financial information into your tax program.

If you do prepare your own tax returns on a computer, it is still a good idea to have a tax professional review them. An accountant will be familiar with changes to the tax code and can offer valuable advice. Accountants often will not charge for questions asked throughout the year, if they have been hired to prepare your annual tax return.

One of the best business investments you can make is to hire a top-notch small-business tax accountant or attorney as a consultant. Maximize the amount of professional advice and you will minimize the chances of problems with the IRS.

Chapter Summary

Now that you have studied this chapter, you can do the following:

1. Understand the importance of cash flow management.
   - Cash flow is the difference between the money you take in and the money you disburse.
   - Without cash on hand, you can find yourself unable to pay crucial bills, even while the income statement says you are earning a profit.
2. Know the difference between cash and profits.
   - Profits are based upon accrued revenues and expenses for most businesses.
   - It is possible to be profitable and to be out of cash.
3. Read a cash flow statement.
   - The first section of the cash flow statement records all sources of cash income that come into the business.
   - The next section reports cash outflows (disbursements) that must be made that month.
   - The last section shows the net change in cash flow.
4. Create a cash budget.
   - Project your cash receipts from all possible sources.
   - Subtract the expenses you expect to have from these projected cash receipts.
   - Understand the future value of money.
   - Calculate the present value of money.
5. File appropriate tax returns for your business.
   - Both income tax and self-employment tax returns must be filed by specific dates (corporate returns are due earlier than individual returns).
   - Tax returns must be filed on time and accurately.
   - Collect sales tax. If you sell products or services to the public, in most states, you will have to charge your customers applicable sales tax and then turn it in to the state periodically.
   - Apply to your state's department of taxation for the necessary forms.
6. Calculate working capital.
   - The formula for working capital is: current assets minus current liabilities.
   - It tells you how much cash is left over after paying all your short-term debt.
   - Working capital should be considered when creating cash flow projections.

Key Terms

burn rate
cash flow statement
compound interest
credit
noncash expenses
pilferage
present value
sales tax
self-employment tax
working capital

Entrepreneurship Portfolio

Critical Thinking Exercises

1. Describe what you think the seasonality scenario would be for one year for a business you can imagine starting. Explain how you think the cash flow will be affected over the course of the year.
2. Imagine you are the owner of an upscale clothing store, like Barneys in Manhattan, which was driven out of business by a 7-percent pilferage rate. What creative solutions could you identify to reduce pilferage?
3. Give three rules for managing your cash.
4. Calculate the projected burn rate for your planned business.
5. Figure out how much income tax each of the following individuals owes. The marginal tax rates are structured as follows:
   - income up to $42,350 is taxed at 15 percent;
   - income between $42,350 and $61,400 is taxed at 28 percent; and
   - income between $61,401 and $128,100 is taxed at 31 percent.

   The different rates apply to different portions of one's income.

Taxable Income	Tax Due
Jim: $42,000	______
Michael: $98,750	______
Susan: $24,000	______
Kate: $100,520	______

Key Concept Questions

1. Create a cumulative cash flow graph for a business with the following monthly cash balances:

January	$40,000
February	$25,000
March	$13,000
April	$5,000
May	$12,000
June	$2,000
July	0
August	0
September	$1,500
October	$8,500
November	$12,000
December	$21,000

2. Fill in the following table, using the future value chart in this chapter, to show the amounts of one invested dollar's growth at the interest rates and time periods given.

Periods	Interest Rate (%)	Future Value of $10
2	5	$11.0250
5	8	______
10	10	______
1	1	______
7	3	______

3. Fill in the following table, using the present value chart, to show the amounts of the net present value of $100 at the interest rates and time periods given.

Periods	Interest Rate (%)	Present Value of $100
2	5	$90.793
5	8	______
10	10	______
1	1	______
7	3	______

4. Calculate working capital for Angelina's company. Describe how her level of working capital might affect her business decisions.

Angelina's Jewelry Company 7/30/11		
ASSETS		
Current Assets		
Cash	$10,000	
Inventory	10,000	
Other Current Assets (Securities)	10,000	
	$30,000	
Total Current Assets		30,000
Long-Term Assets		70,000
TOTAL ASSETS		100,000
LIABILITIES		
Short-Term Liabilities		
Accounts Payable (AP)	$10,000	
Short-Term Loans	5,000	
Total Short-Term Liabilities		$15,000
Total Long-Term Liabilities		15,000
OWNER'S EQUITY		70,000
TOTAL LIABILITIES + OE		$100,000

Application Exercise

Create a projected cash flow statement for your business for one year.

Exploring Online

1. Print the tax documents list available at http://www.ideacafe.com/bizforms/tax.html and highlight the forms you think you will need.
2. Visit Business Owners Idea Café online and use the tool at http://www.businessownersideacafe.com/financing/index.htm to figure out how much capital you will need to get your business off the ground.

Case Study | Ed's Auto Parts

Ed Hernandez worked in auto parts stores for most of his life. After working with a large corporation for more than 10 years, he decided to open his own business to serve both auto repair shops and the general public. Because of his experience in the industry, he was well known by many of the owners of local auto repair shops and also by the residents of his community. In the first year of business, the company grossed $290,000 and had a net profit before taxes of $8,000.

Although his retail customers paid with cash or by credit card, Ed offered the auto repair shops 30-day credit terms. This was necessary in order to be competitive with other parts stores in the area. The increasing level of accounts receivable placed a great strain on the company cash flow, and because of the lack of cash, Ed found it difficult to replace the inventory as quickly as it sold. When the business first opened, the inventory level was $65,000 and the accounts receivable was zero; however, by the end of the first year, accounts receivable were $25,000, and the inventory had dropped to $50,000. Ed's Auto Parts did not have a problem with bad debts; in fact, almost all his customers paid within the 30 days, and only a few took 45 to 60 days. However, the normal 30-day credit was enough delay to cause cash problems.

Ed was concerned that the drop in inventory could result in lost sales if the customers could not get the parts they needed. He might also lose the repair shops as customers if the inventory shortages occurred frequently. Ed decided to ask his bank for a loan of $25,000. He planned to use $15,000 to restock inventory to its original level; the remaining $10,000 would be used as working capital.

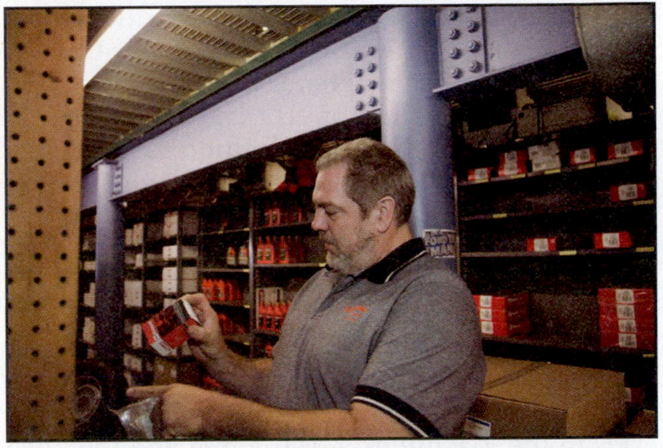

Case Study Analysis

1. In addition to the bank loan, what could Ed do to try to collect his receivables faster?
2. Consider the request for $25,000. Is this the optimum amount? Why or why not?
3. Does the cash flow problem indicate that Ed is a poor manager? What could he have done differently, if anything?

Case Study | Managing Cash: CakeLove and Love Café

How does a lawyer with a Master's degree in public health from George Washington University become a cake magnate? Warren Brown was a 28-year-old Washington, D.C., attorney who, in 1999, made a New Year's resolution to learn how to bake. He practiced health care law in the Inspector General's Office for the U.S. Department of Health and Social Services from 1998 until he left to become a baker, in 2000. Warren opened his first CakeLove bakery on U Street, N.W., in Washington in March of 2002, and the Love Café 17 months later.

Today, he is the owner of six CakeLove bakeries in the Washington, D.C., area and the Love Café, also in Washington. CakeLove pound cakes, brownies, scones, and cookies are available via the Internet for delivery nationwide (http://www.cakelove.com). Warren's first cookbook, *CakeLove,* arrived on bookstore shelves in the spring of 2008, and his second book, *United Cakes of America,* highlights his favorite recipes from every state. To top it off, he hosted the Food Network's *Sugar Rush*. Warren was named U.S. Small Business Administration Entrepreneur of the Year in 2006, and CakeLove was selected top bakery in Washington, D.C., in the *Washington Post Best Bets* readers' poll in 2005 and 2006, and the *Washington Post Express* in 2009.

This meteoric rise in business required a number of essential ingredients. In addition to the all-natural components used in CakeLove's products, the business aspects had to be properly balanced and mixed. Such rapid change demanded a lot of hard work, passion, determination, and cash flow. When Warren stepped away from his full-time job into full-time entrepreneurship, he began with $10,000 of personal resources, including his credit card. In order to open his first storefront, Warren needed $125,000. Fortunately, he was able to secure a commercial loan from his community bank, CityFirst Bank of D.C., that he used for expansion and continues to do business with. Commercial lenders at larger, mainstream financial institutions were not convinced that a self-taught baker who had abandoned a promising legal career was a particularly good credit risk. Warren maintained 100 percent ownership of CakeLove through the acquisition of start-up capital, and he continues as the sole owner after significant growth.

Within a couple of months of opening CakeLove, Warren decided to open Love Café directly across the street from the bakery. The space popped up as an opportunity, and he wanted to take advantage of it. This required an additional infusion of capital for leasehold improvements, equipment, furnishings, and other start-up costs. There were few expenses from CakeLove that Love Café could leverage for this start-up, to attain economies of scale. Aside from being able to sell bakery-direct, he had little obvious financial advantage. However, the bakery is strictly a take-out facility, housing the production and sales areas, whereas Love Café is a full-service establishment serving a menu of baked goods, sandwiches, and coffee in what Warren describes as a "laid back, relaxed atmosphere incorporating natural elements and including WiFi, sofas, large windows." Because CakeLove was new and had little positive cash flow, Warren could not finance the second location with the cash flow of the first. So, he turned again to CityFirst Bank.

Warren Brown of CakeLove and Love Café.

Between September 2007 and July 2008, CakeLove opened three additional retail bakeries. Each successive expansion created a need for additional cash. Warren managed to avoid selling shares of the company by leveraging resources and partnering with community lenders. His banking partner, CityFirst, financed each location to supplement earnings generated from existing operations.

Growth in the number of retail bakery storefronts has taken the business to new heights. Warren continues to serve as the primary manager of cash flow and human resources for his organization. Whereas inventory theft has not been a significant issue because of the store layouts and procedures, CakeLove has established cash-handling policies (cash-counting systems) to prevent pilferage from the cash drawers. Because CakeLove sells baked goods and other perishable items, spoilage and unsold product can become significant contributors to cash flow problems. Warren and his team have instituted a waste-tracking system and have been able to keep a "pretty good eye on the way inventory is moving."

The growth of the organization has not been the greatest challenge to cash flow for CakeLove. Warren notes that diets have been more of a detriment to the business than expansion or an abysmal economy. CakeLove experienced its most significant cash-tightness at the height of popularity for the Atkins Diet, when counting carbohydrates led dieters to cutting out sweets and bakery treats. During times of reduced cash inflow, Warren and his team have to look to cut costs, particularly by monitoring labor costs more closely than usual. When Warren opened his first CakeLove bakery, he had three employees, including himself. As of July 2008, he had 105. This means meeting the cash flow requirements of a payroll and associated expenses for the six locations, including supporting numerous families.

Warren Brown has the following advice for aspiring entrepreneurs, "Do the homework. Know the industry you want to enter cold, so that you absolutely know how to make or do whatever it is that you want to make or do. Don't rush in. See it well and don't be afraid to get messy and to keep an open mind. There is always a way to improve. Know the product very well and have good confidence in what you are selling. People will always have unsolicited advice for you. If you don't have that confidence, you will get little chinks in your armor that can make your business less enjoyable and even miserable. Confidence is critical." Warren's recipe for growth has produced sweet rewards.

Case Study Analysis

1. How has Warren Brown been able to finance the growth of his company?
2. What methods has CakeLove used to manage cash flow? What others might it adopt?
3. What types of cash flow management issues would you expect CakeLove to encounter if it continues to grow at a rate of three bakeries per year or more?
4. How do Warren Brown's recommendations to aspiring entrepreneurs pertain to cash flow?

Case Sources

CakeLove Web site at http://www.cakelove.com.

"Lawyer Turned Entrepreneur of the Year, Warren Brown of CakeLove," *The AfricanaConnect*, http://www.theculturalconnect.com/new/2007/11/23/warren-brown-africana (accessed January 12, 2008).

Warren Brown, *CakeLove: How to Bake Cakes from Scratch* (New York: Stewart, Tabori and Chang, 2008).

Chapter 15

FINANCING STRATEGY: DEBT, EQUITY, OR BOTH?

"You do not get what you deserve, you get what you negotiate."

—Chester L. Karrass, pioneer of negotiation theory

Anita Roddick, founder of The Body Shop, opened her first store in England in 1976. Within a few months, she was eager to open a second store because the first one was doing so well, but no bank would lend her money. Because borrowing was not an option, Roddick turned to investor financing. Her friend Ian McGlinn offered to give her the equivalent of $7500 in exchange for half the business. Roddick accepted and used the money to open her second store.

McGlinn's share of The Body Shop came to be worth over $240 million, a dramatic return on investment. Roddick later said that she did not regret exchanging half her company for $7500 because without McGlinn's infusion of equity, she would not have been able to expand her business.

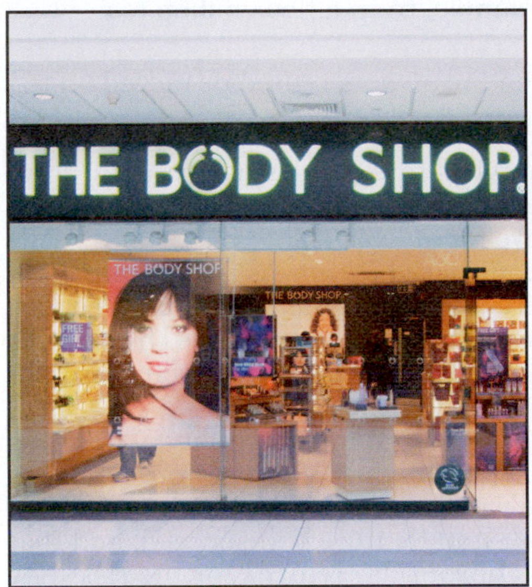

Performance Objectives

1. Explore your financing preferences.
2. Identify the types of business financing.
3. Compare the pros and cons of debt and equity financing.
4. Identify sources of capital for your business.
5. Understand stocks and bonds as investment alternatives.

Going It Alone versus Securing Financing

To start or expand a business, you will need to have money, either on hand or through **financing**, which is the act of providing or raising funds (capital) for a purpose. For entrepreneurs, that means obtaining the money to start and operate a successful business.

financing the act of providing or raising funds (capital) for a purpose.

There are three ways to finance a business, assuming you do not have enough funds in your savings:

1. obtain gifts and grants,
2. borrow money (debt), and
3. exchange a share of the business for money (equity).

For many (or even most) people who want to start a business, there is a need for financing. Whether that need is for $500 or $5 million, the entrepreneur will have to bridge the gap between what he or she has and what the business cash flows and prudent reserves require. Sometimes an entrepreneur can use home equity, credit cards, or funds from friends or family to make up this shortfall. In other cases, these resources are not available, are not sufficient, or would not make sense for the business. In those situations, debt or equity financing becomes a necessity.

How Often Do Small Businesses Really Fail?

Before you search for financing, you may want to know more about success and failure rates for startups. It is a popular misperception that four out of five small firms fail in the first five years of operation. You are likely to hear this from well-meaning friends, family, and potential investors. According to *The Portable MBA in Entrepreneurship,* however, "This claim has no basis in fact. Actually, there is good evidence that more than half—rather than one-fifth—of new small firms survive for eight or more years."[1]

creditor person or organization that is owed money.

Business failure is defined by Dun & Bradstreet (D&B), which operates the largest and oldest commercial credit-rating service in the United States, as "business termination with losses to creditors." A **creditor** is an organization or individual that you have borrowed from and must repay. D&B, which followed 814,000 small firms formed in 1977–1978 for eight years, reported that only 20 to 25 percent actually closed because of bankruptcy—of those small ventures that were recorded as terminated during their first eight years of operation. The other 75 to 80 percent were reported as terminations, but they were:

- businesses that were sold to new owners;
- businesses that changed—for example, from a flower shop to a general nursery; and
- businesses that were closed when the owners retired or moved on to other businesses.

The article concludes that the survival rate of the small firm, far from being one out of five, is closer to one out of two. More than half of all new small companies can expect to survive for at least eight years.[2]

For many, a small business is considered a high-risk, high-return investment, although in truth entrepreneurs are generally calculated risk takers, and only pursue opportunities after they have weighed the chances of success. For the investor willing to accept the risk, a small business can be a great opportunity. The return on investment (ROI) of a successful small business can be thousands of percent, but the possibility of business failure is also relatively high. If your business fails, you and your investors will lose money. Your task, when you write your business plan and do your research, will be to demonstrate how your venture will succeed, and that your investors can look forward to appropriate returns for the risk they are assuming.

What Is the Best Type of Financing for You and Your Business?

Performance Objective 1

Explore your financing preferences.

Financing is not a one-size-fits-all proposition. Each business and business owner has unique personal requirements and circumstances, along with the structure and challenges of the selected industry. For some businesses, such as restaurants, standard commercial loans may not be an option because commercial lenders will not be willing to make them. For others, such as research-based technology firms, equity will be needed. Regardless of your preferences and the types of financing available, you will invariably have to be the first investor in your business. Lenders and investors alike will insist that entrepreneurs have their personal resources involved, before they will risk additional funding. It is easier to persist and work hard when you have a personal financial stake in success. If putting your personal assets at risk is not something you (or your family) are willing to do, expect to be rejected by investors and lenders.

risk tolerance the amount of risk or threat of loss that an individual is willing to sustain.

Your **risk tolerance**, meaning the amount of risk (threat of loss) that you are willing to sustain, will also help to define possible financing

[1]William D. Bygrave and Andrew Zacharkis, eds., *The Portable MBA in Entrepreneurship* (New York: John Wiley & Sons, 1997), p. 199.

[2]E. Lewis Bryan, "Financial Management and Capital Formation in Small Business," *Journal of Small Business Management,* July 1, 1984.

options. For example, if you own a home and are seeking a commercial loan, you will likely have to put it up as security, in case you cannot repay the debt. Or, if you are giving up ownership through equity, you may be giving up control of the company you founded to obtain needed financial resources. Be prepared to face these types of decisions, as you seek financing that works.

There are three ways for a business to raise the capital it needs to grow.

1. ***Finance with Earnings.*** If a company is profitable and has positive cash flow, it can use some of its profits to finance expansion. This will help ensure that the company does not take on too much debt, or grow more quickly than its finances can handle.
2. ***Finance with Equity.*** If a company is incorporated, it can sell stock privately, or on the stock market, to raise capital. People who purchase shares of stock are receiving equity. Other types of businesses may also have equity investors.
3. ***Finance with Debt.*** Any type of business, depending upon its *creditworthiness,* and that of its owner(s), can borrow money. An incorporated company can also sell *bonds,* although it is difficult and cost-prohibitive for small businesses to do so. People who purchase bonds will receive interest on the loan they are making to the company, with repayment of principal in a lump sum at maturity.

Both stocks and bonds are heavily regulated by the federal government. Issuing either requires considerable technical guidance and cost. This is not a do-it-yourself process. Rather, the counsel of investment bankers, accountants, and attorneys is needed.

Performance Objective 2

Identify the types of business financing.

Gifts and Grants

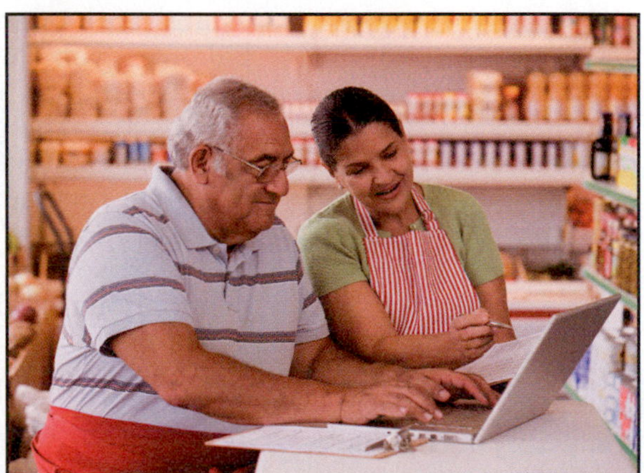

The opportunities for gifts and grants to businesses do exist. However, both must be pursued with caution because gifts may come with strings attached, and grants may have specific requirements. Gifts include such items as cash, free use of facilities and equipment, unpaid labor by friends and family, and forgiveness or deferral of debts. Other forms of gifts, given primarily by the federal government, are for specific types of investments, geographic areas, or to support particular populations, such as **tax abatements** (legal reductions in taxes), and **tax credits** (direct reduction of taxes). Business grants are primarily for research and commercialization efforts and are difficult for start-up, low-technology companies to acquire. Because gifts and grants do not require repayment or incur financing costs, they are often at the top of the entrepreneur's list of desired resources. They are also among the hardest to obtain.

tax abatement legal reduction in taxes.

tax credit direct reduction of taxes.

Debt Financing

Many businesses have some combination of debt and equity financing. The variety of loans and investments is quite large and growing. One challenge that you may face is determining what type of debt financing to

Exhibit 15-1 *Percentage of small firms using credit, by credit type.*

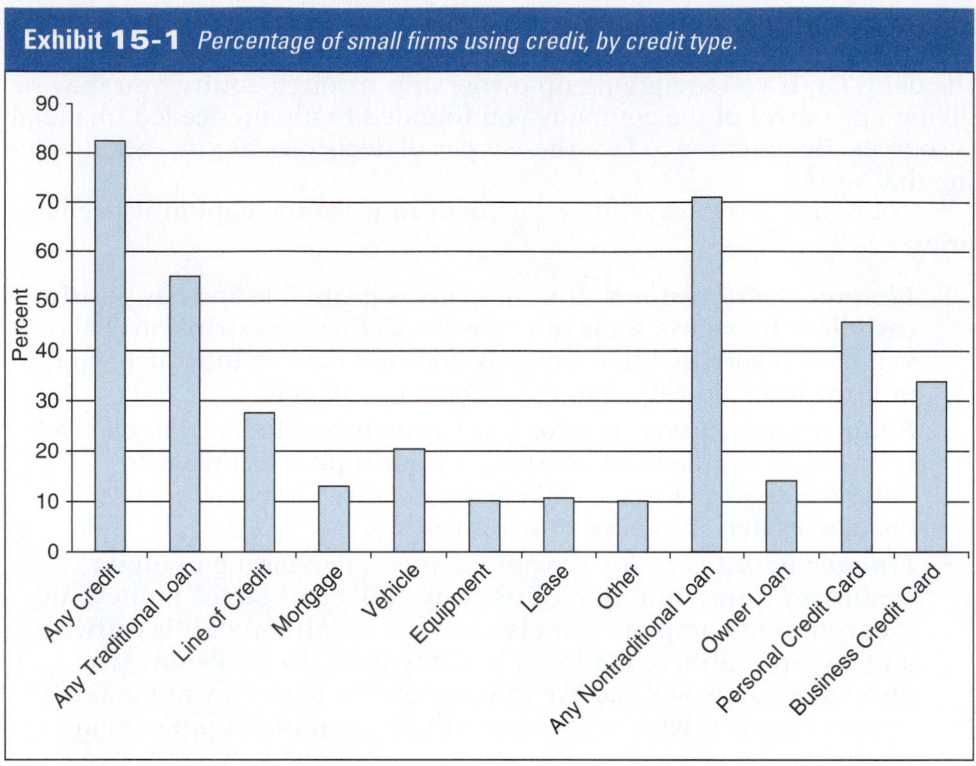

Note: Owner loans for corporations and partnerships only.
Source: U.S. Small Business Administration, Office of Advocacy, "Financing Patterns of Small Firms: Finding from the 1998 Survey of Small Business Finance," September 2003.

pursue, based upon your business type and life-cycle stage, your personal finances, wealth and preferences, and the options available to you. Before pursuing debt for your business, calculate your personal *net worth* by tallying your assets (i.e., cash, investment accounts, personal property, real estate, and intangibles) and subtracting your debts (i.e., credit card balances, vehicle loans, mortgages, and other loans). Your lenders will want to know what you own, what you owe, and what your business finances are. The percentage of small firms using credit by credit type is shown in **Exhibit 15-1**.

Debt financing comes in many forms, with widely varying repayment and qualification terms. Different types of lenders will have various rates and fees, so it is worthwhile to compare the total package costs. Some debt options are discussed below.

Debt Financing: Pros and Cons

promissory note a loan document that is a written promise to pay a specific sum of money on or before a particular date.

principal the amount of debt or loan before interest and fees are added.

Performance Objective 3

Compare the pros and cons of debt and equity financing.

To finance through debt, the entrepreneur applies to and contracts with a person or an institution that has money, and borrows it, signing a **promissory note**, a document agreeing to repay a certain sum of money (with interest) by a specified date.

Interest is determined as a percentage (interest rate) of the loan principal. The **principal** is the amount of the loan or outstanding balance on the loan amount, not including interest. If $1200 is borrowed at 10 percent to be paid back over one year, the interest on the loan is $120 ($1200 × 0.10). Typically the borrower makes monthly payments until the loan is fully paid. The term, or length, of the loan generally depends on what is being financed, with working capital having the shortest term and real estate the longest.

Debt Category	Description	Common Types	Terms
Commercial Loans	Business loans typically provided by a bank or other financial institution.	• Real estate • Equipment and improvements • Working capital • Asset based • Accounts receivable factoring	Up to 20 years Up to 7 years 1 year or less Depends on the type of asset pledged Often 30 days
Personal Loans	Loans taken out on your personal credit and used for the business. May have a fixed term (length) or a "revolving" one.	• *Credit cards* • *Home equity loans* • *Title loan* • *Payday loan*	Revolving Variable terms; some are lines of credit Short-term fixed repayment Short-term fixed repayment
Leases	Debts incurred for the rights to use specific property, such as automobiles, trucks, or equipment.	• *Vehicle lease* • *Equipment leases*	Often for 2 or 3 years with a purchase option at the end of the term Varies widely depending on the nature of equipment leased
Bonds	Long-term debt instruments used by corporations to raise large sums of money.	See Bonds section later in the chapter	

The lender essentially has no say in the operations of the business, as long as the loan payments are made on time and loan terms are met. They will have a say in how the funds are initially disbursed (according to a schedule that you provide) and may set restrictions (protective covenants). The payments are predictable, although they may vary with changes in key interest-rate measures, if the interest rate is variable rather than fixed. If the loan payments are not made in a timely way, the lender can force the business into liquidation or bankruptcy, even if that loan balance is only a fraction of what the business is worth. Also the lender can take the home and personal possessions of the owner, depending on the agreement.

Debt should be carefully considered by the beginning entrepreneur, because it often takes time for a new business to generate cash for repayment. One risk of debt is that failure to make loan payments can destroy the business before it can generate positive cash flow.

Debt Advantages

- The lender has no say in the management or direction of the business, as long as the loan payments are made and contracts are not violated.
- Loan payments are predictable; they do not change with the fortunes of the business.
- Loan payments can be set up so that they are matched with the seasonal sales of the business.
- Lenders do not share in the business's profits.

Debt Disadvantages

- If loan payments are not made, the lender can force the business into bankruptcy.
- The lender can take the home and possessions of the owner(s) to settle a debt in case of **default**—when the borrower fails to meet the repayment agreement.

default the results of a borrower failing to meet the repayment agreement on a debt.

Step into the Shoes...

Donald Trump and Overreliance on Debt

Companies that rely heavily on debt financing are described as highly ***leveraged***, meaning financed with debt. This strategy works well when business is good. When business is slow, debt payments can be difficult to meet.

Real estate tycoon Donald Trump made the mistake of relying too heavily on debt in the early 1980s. Trump did not want to give up managerial control by selling stock when he needed financing. Because of his reputation and wealth, banks were willing to lend him a great deal of money. When the economy took a downturn in the late 1980s, however, Trump could not make his loan payments. The banks took possession of several of his most valuable properties. By reducing his real estate holdings and paying off some debt, Trump was able to recover, and go on to expand his empire.

leveraged financed by debt, as opposed to equity.

- Debt payments increase a business's fixed costs, thereby lowering profits.
- Repayment reduces available cash.
- Lenders expect regular financial reporting and compliance with the loan contracts.

Equity Financing

Equity means that, in return for money, an investor will receive a percentage of ownership in a company. For the $1200 investment discussed earlier, an equity investor might want 10 percent ownership of the company, which would mean 10 percent of the business's profits. (This would indicate that the business was valued at $12,000.) The investor is hoping that 10 percent of the profits will provide a high rate of return, over time, on the initial investment of $1200.

Equity Financing: Pros and Cons

The equity investor assumes greater risk than the debt lender. If the business does not make a profit, neither does the investor. The equity investor cannot force the business into bankruptcy to get back the investment. If creditors force a business into bankruptcy, equity investors have a claim on whatever is left over after the debt lenders have been paid. The potential for return is also higher. The equity investor should make an investment back many times over if the business prospers.

Money raised via equity does not have to be paid back unless the business is successful. Equity investors may offer helpful advice and provide valuable contacts. However, if the entrepreneur gives up more than 50 percent ownership, control of the business may be taken over by the equity holders. Even with less than half the ownership, investors may attempt to assert managerial influence.

Equity Advantages

- If the business does not make a profit, the investor does not get paid.
- There are no required regular payments in the form of principal or interest, and dividends for common stockholders are at the discretion of the board of directors.

Step into the Shoes...

Apple's Steve Jobs

Relying too heavily on equity can also be the downfall of a founding entrepreneur, as the story of Steve Jobs, cofounder of Apple Computer, illustrates. Because Jobs and his partner, Stephen Wozniak, were young men with very little money, debt financing was not an option. To raise money, they sold pieces of the company.

By the late 1980s, Apple had become so successful that Jobs hired a prominent PepsiCo executive, John Sculley, as Apple's chief executive officer. Sculley gradually convinced Apple's board of directors that Jobs was a disruptive influence in the company. Eventually a vote was taken of Apple shareholders, and Jobs did not own enough equity to fend off Sculley's effort to fire him. He was voted out of the highly successful company he started.

Jobs was invited back to lead Apple as interim CEO in 1997, however, and was elected permanent CEO by the shareholders in 2000.

- The equity investor cannot force the business into bankruptcy in order to recoup the investment.
- The equity investor has an interest in seeing the business succeed and may, therefore, offer helpful advice and provide valuable contacts.

Equity Disadvantages

- Through giving up too much ownership, the entrepreneur could lose control of the business to the equity holders.
- Even with small amounts of equity, investors may interfere with the business via unsolicited advice and/or continuous inquiries.
- Equity financing is riskier for the investor, so the investor frequently wants both to be able to influence how the company is run and to receive a higher rate of return than a lender.
- The entrepreneur must share profits with other equity investors.

Where and How to Find Capital That Works for You

The decision of where to seek capital is complex, and the options that are available will depend upon both personal and business factors. Your preferences should weigh heavily in the decision. However, it is a rare business owner that wants to pledge all family assets, pay high interest rates and fees, or give up majority ownership. Yet, many start-up and experienced entrepreneurs must do just that in order to secure the funds that they need. Identifying and securing financing often involves exploring multiple potential options, and creating a complex, multilayered financing mix. The optimal resources for a business may not be the obvious ones. Therefore, it is valuable to understand the range of sources.

There are many potential sources of capital and it may take you numerous attempts to find what works. Some sources of capital are identified in **Exhibit 15-2**.

Performance Objective 4

Identify sources of capital for your business.

Exhibit 15-2 *Selected sources of business financing.*

Financing Source	Category of Financing	Type(s) of Financing	Uses of Funds	Notes
Entrepreneur/Self	Debt or Equity	Loan or Owner's Equity	Any	Debt terms to be established at borrowing. Earnings through dividends and/or sale of company.
Friends or Family	Debt or Equity	Loan or Stock	Any	Negotiable on debt. Earnings through dividends and/or sale of stock.
Small Business Investment Companies (SBICs), Minority Enterprise SBICs (MESBICs), Rural Business Investment Companies (RBICs), New Markets Venture Capital funds (NMVC) *http://www.sba.gov/inv/index.html*	Debt or Equity	Loan or Stock	Varies according to licenses with the SBA and the types of entities served. Funds are to be used as requested by the businesses.	Generally installment loans for debt. Earnings through dividends and/or sale of stock.
Small Business Innovation Research (SBIR) or Small Business Technology Transfer (STTR) *http://www.sba.gov/aboutsba/sbaprograms*	Grant	Research Grant	Specific research as defined in grant application.	Must complete requirements of grant funding.
Community Development Corporations *http://www.opportunityfinance.net*	Linked Deposits and Savings	Gift	According to program guidelines.	Savings and financial literacy requirements.
Venture Capitalists	Equity	Stock	Start-up or growth	IPO, buy-out, dividends, royalties
Community Development Venture Capital Funds *http://www.cdvca.org*	Equity	Stock	Start-up or growth	IPO, buy-out, dividends, royalties
Angel Investors	Equity	Stock	Start-up or growth	IPO, buy-out, dividends, royalties
Investment Banks	Equity	Stock	Private or public placements (IPOs)	Paid in fee income.
Economic Development Agencies *http://www.eda.gov*	Debt	Varies	Varies	Varies broadly from state to state and other localities.
Leasing Companies	Debt	Vehicles or Equipment	To acquire use of vehicles and/or equipment.	Monthly payments of fees. Purchase option generally available at end of term.
Banks/Financial Institutions	Debt	Real Estate Loans	Real estate	Mortgage—long term with installment payments.

Financing Source	Category of Financing	Type(s) of Financing	Uses of Funds	Notes
		Equipment, Vehicle, or Other	Equipment and other capital as specified in the loan request.	Promissory note—medium term with installment payments.
		Working Capital	Supplies, materials, cash flow.	Lines of credit usually with a maximum of 1-year term. Must be paid to $0 annually.
		Home Equity	Personal loan for any purpose secured against a home.	Many variations; often a monthly payment.
		Credit Card	Unsecured loan for business or consumer use.	Revolving credit with minimum monthly payments.
Mortgage Companies	Debt	Real Estate Loans Home Equity	Real estate Personal loan for any purpose secured against a home.	Mortgage—long term with installment payments. Many variations; often a monthly payment.
Insurance Companies	Debt	Policy Loan	Any	Reduces cash surrender value. Varies.
Community Development Banks *http://www.opportunityfinance.net*	Debt	Similar to Banks	Capital to rebuild communities through targeted lending.	Terms vary according to mission and community need.
Community Development Credit Unions *http://www.natfed.org*	Debt	Loans to Members	Per community ownership	Varies depending on type of loan.
Community Development Loan Funds *http://www.opportunityfinance.net*	Debt	Equipment, Leasehold, or Other Working Capital	Purchase of essential equipment and improvement for start-up and growth operation.	Primarily term loans. Some lines of credit. Typically for nontraditional credit. May include microloans, lending to not-for-profits, and to developers of affordable housing.
Microenterprise Development Loan Funds *http://www.microenterpriseworks.org* *http://www.opportunityfinance.net*	Debt	Primarily Working Capital and Start-Up	Relatively small loans ($35,000 maximum) for purpose detailed in applications and/or business plans.	Installment loans. Designed for nontraditional customers.
Receivable Factors	Debt	Accounts Receivable	Any	Factor is repaid by entrepreneur's customers. Receivables discounted and funds held back until they are paid.
Title Lenders	Debt	Title Loans	Any	Short terms with high interest rates.
Pay Day Lenders	Debt	Pay Day Loans	Any	Short terms with high interest rates.
Vendors	Debt	Trade Credit	Any	Entrepreneur delays payment of invoices.

Having an Excellent Business Plan Goes a Long Way

When you seek financing for your business, the quality of your business plan could make the difference between success and failure. Lenders and investors alike will need to recover their principal plus interest, or investment plus a rate of return. If your business plan realistically, clearly, and convincingly demonstrates that you can and will achieve your goals, your chances of obtaining financing will greatly increase.

How Capital Sources Read Your Business Plan

People read business plans in different ways, but rarely are they read through from front to back as written. For example, a lender may look at the cash flow projections first. But one thing is for certain; you will need to capture the reader's attention in the executive summary or the plan is unlikely to be read.

Family and Friends

Family and friends are obvious sources for loans. But what about offering them equity instead? Explain that if they *loan* you money, they will only earn back the amount of the loan plus interest. If they invest capital in exchange for *equity*, on the other hand, they could get back much more than the original amount. Acknowledge that equity is more risky than debt but explain that the potential for reward is much higher. Be careful not to take money from friends and family members who could not afford to lose it if the business failed.

Also, be sure that any financial agreements are properly documented and signed, so that there is no misunderstanding later. There are services such as VirginMoneyUS.com (formerly CircleLending.com) that create formal business agreements between family members. Nothing ruins a good relationship more quickly than a dispute over money. As Polonius states in Shakespeare's *Hamlet*, "Neither a borrower nor a lender be; for loan oft loses itself and friends." Whereas borrowing may be unavoidable, the cautionary note on borrowing from friends is well-directed.

Financial Institutions and Dimensions of Credit

It can be difficult for new entrepreneurs to get loans from banks and other financial institutions partially because bankers tend to be conservative lenders and startups are riskier than established businesses; their performance information is based upon projections rather than historic data. Banks are in the business of lending money they are confident will be repaid. Bankers operate on the principles of the Five Cs of credit:

1. ***Collateral.*** Property or other assets pledged against the loan that the lender can take and sell if the loan is not repaid. Examples of such assets are business real estate, equipment, inventory, an owner's home, certificates of deposit, money market accounts, stock certificates, and bonds. Commercial lenders never want to have to take such assets, but they need collateral so that they can be confident of some level of repayment.
2. ***Character.*** Typically analyzed in the form of the owner's personal credit (ability to borrow money) for a small business. Before a financial services company will lend you money, it will want to know your **credit history**, which is the record of how reliably and punctually you or your company has paid past debts. The lender will obtain

credit history a record of credit extended and the repayment thereof.

your credit report from a **credit reporting agency (CRA)**. These companies, primarily TransUnion, Equifax, and Experian, collect and analyze information supplied by financial institutions, and others, who extend credit.

3. ***Capacity.*** The business cash flow must be sufficient to cover the monthly loan payments and expenses. You will have to report your projected cash flow so the lender can determine whether you will be able to repay the loan. Your **debt service** is the amount you will have to pay over a given period of time, until the loan is repaid.
4. ***Capital.*** How much of your own money have you invested in your business? Have you gotten friends or family to invest? As we have noted, a banker wants to see that you are risking your own resources, as well.
5. ***Conditions.*** This is the state of the industry and economic climate at the time the loan is made, and during its anticipated term. If inflation is on the rise, for example, the bank may be concerned that your earnings will not keep pace with it, thus reducing your capacity to repay the loan.

credit reporting agency (CRA) an organization that collects and analyzes information supplied by financial institutions and others who extend credit, and then resells it.

debt service the amount a borrower is obligated to pay in a given period until a loan is repaid.

Lenders will expect you to sign a **personal guarantee**, which states that you will be responsible for paying off the loan in the event that the business cannot do so. In other words, in the case of default, the lender will have the right to take both business and personal assets.

personal guarantee the promise to pay issued by an individual.

What constitutes good credit is not intuitively obvious. It is not merely the absence of bad credit. You may think that you have good credit because you have never borrowed money or used a credit card. You are wrong. What you have is *no* credit. To establish credit, you must prove that you are capable of making regular payments on debts. Typically, most banks will not lend to anyone without a credit history, but many stores will, through revolving **charge accounts**, which are credit accounts that have a single borrowing limit and may be used and repaid on a repeated cycle. One way to begin a good credit history is to open one of these store accounts, charge a few small purchases, and never miss a payment, or pay later than the due date. This record of on-time payment will become a part of your credit report.

charge account credit extended by a company allowing qualified customers to make purchases up to a specified limit, without paying cash at the time of purchase.

Figure 15-1 *The Five Cs of credit.*

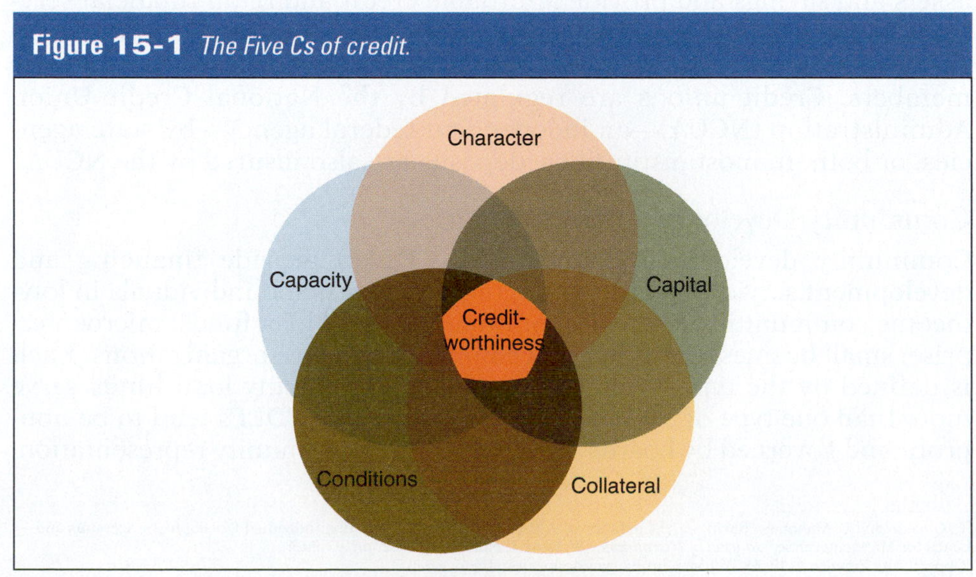

There have been efforts to encourage the acceptance of regular savings and/or timely payments of rent and utilities in lieu of a traditional credit history.[3] However, when credit markets contract, these flexible credit options are easily discarded.

It will be wise to check your credit reports with the major credit reporting agencies at least once a year, to ensure accuracy. Under the Fair Credit Report Act, federal law gives you the right to see and challenge your credit reports from TransUnion, Equifax, and Experian. You can visit http://www.annualcreditreport.com to obtain your reports. Rather than getting the reports all at once, it is better to space them four months apart so that you can better check for errors. For your business credit reports, you can establish a history at Dun & Bradstreet by self-reporting. Further information about this option is available at http://www.smallbusiness.dnb.com/manage-business-credit/get-duns-details.asp.

Community Development Financial Institutions[4]

There are a number of alternate lending institutions that can serve a broad range of needs in emerging domestic markets. Although they share the common vision of expanding economic opportunity, and improving the quality of life for low-income people and communities, the four CDFI sectors—banks, credit unions, loan funds, and venture capital (VC) funds—are characterized by different business models and legal structures:

Community Development Banks

Community development banks (CDBs) provide capital to rebuild economically distressed communities through targeted lending and investing. They are for-profit corporations with community representation on their boards of directors. Depending on the individual charter, such banks are regulated by some combination of the Federal Deposit Insurance Corporation (FDIC), the Federal Reserve, the Office of the Comptroller of the Currency, the Office of Thrift Supervision, and state banking agencies. Their deposits are insured by the FDIC.

Community Development Credit Unions

Community development credit unions (CDCUs) promote ownership of assets and savings and provide affordable credit and retail financial services to low-income individuals, often with special outreach to minority communities. They are nonprofit financial cooperatives owned by their members. Credit unions are regulated by the National Credit Union Administration (NCUA)—an independent federal agency—by state agencies, or both. In most institutions, deposits are also insured by the NCUA.

Community Development Loan Funds

Community development loan funds (CDLFs) provide financing and development services to businesses, organizations, and individuals in low-income communities. There are four main types of loan funds: microenterprise, small business, housing, and community service organizations. Each is defined by the type of client served, although many loan funds serve more than one type of client in a single institution. CDLFs tend to be nonprofit and governed by boards of directors with community representation.

[3] C. Glackin and E. Mahoney, "Savings and Credit for U.S. Microenterprises: Integrating Individual Development Accounts and Loans for Microenterprise," *Journal of Microfinance*, Volume 4, Number 2, 2002, pp. 93–125.
[4] Opportunity Finance Network Web site, http://www.opportunityfinance.net.

Community Development Venture Capital Funds

Community development venture capital funds (CDVCs) provide equity and debt-with-equity features for small- and medium-sized businesses in distressed communities. They can be either for-profit or nonprofit and include community representation.

Community Development Financial Institution Resources

Opportunity Finance Network	*http://www.opportunityfinance.net*
Association for Enterprise Opportunity	*http://www.microenterpriseworks.org*
Aspen Institute	*http://www.aspeninstitute.org*
Calvert Foundation	*http://www.calvertfoundation.org*
Corporation for Enterprise Development	*http://www.cfed.org*
Coalition of Community Development Financial Institutions (CDFI Coalition)	*http://www.cdfi.org*
Community Development Venture Capital Alliance	*http://www.cdvca.org*
First Nations Oweesta Corporation	*http://www.oweesta.org*
National Community Investment Fund	*http://www.ncif.org*
National Federation of Community Development Credit Unions	*http://www.natfed.org*
Our Native Circle	*http://www.ournativecircle.org*

Venture Capitalists

There are also investors and investment companies whose specialty is financing new, high-potential entrepreneurial companies, and second-stage companies. Because they often provide the initial equity investment, or venture capital, to start a business venture, they are called **venture capitalists**.

venture capitalist an investor or investment company whose specialty is financing new, high-potential entrepreneurial companies and second-stage companies.

Global Impact...

Kiva—Person-to-Person Lending

A relatively new player in the field of socially responsible lending is Kiva. This not-for-profit venture has served as a connector between businesses in need of small amounts of credit and individuals that want to support them. Kiva's mission is "to connect people through lending for the sake of alleviating poverty."[5]

The organization serves as an intermediary between individuals willing to invest at least $25 to a particular microbusiness and the microfinance institutions that will provide direct loans. What makes Kiva noteworthy is the ability to provide person-to-person lending and to have individuals lend without expectation of financial return (no interest is paid to them).

Kiva's microlending partners made $80,956,410 in loans from October 12, 2005 through July 16, 2009, using the person-to-person lending model. The delinquency rate (late payment) was only 3.82 percent, and the default rate (failure to pay) was 1.39 percent. Until June of 2009, these loans have been made outside of the United States.

[5]Kiva Web site, http://www.kiva.org (accessed July 16, 2009).

Venture capitalists seek high rates of return. They typically expect to earn six times their money back over a five-year period, or a 45 percent return on investment. Professional venture capitalists will not usually invest in a company unless its business plan shows it is likely to generate sales of at least $25 million within five years. The ideal candidates for venture capital are businesses with financial projections that support revenue expectations of over $50 million within five years, growing at 30 to 50 percent per year, with pretax profit margins over 20 percent.

If your business plan supports those kinds of numbers, you may be able to interest venture capitalists in your idea. Venture capitalists want equity in return for their capital. They are willing to take the higher risk for higher returns. Venture capitalists sometimes seek a majority interest in a business so that they will have the final word in management decisions. They can structure deals in a variety of ways.

To finance the Ford Motor Company, Henry Ford gave up 75 percent of the business for $28,000 in badly needed capital. It took Ford many years to regain control of his company. Still, many small business owners turn to venture capital when they want to grow the business and commercial banks are not a good fit.

Venture capitalists typically reap the return on their equity investments in one of two ways:

1. by selling their percentage share of the business to another investor through a private transaction; or
2. by waiting until the company goes public (starts selling stock on the open market) and trading their ownership shares for cash by selling them. The shares can now be traded in the stock market.

Angels

angel investor a wealthy individual who invests in businesses.

If your business does not meet the high-flying profit picture that would attract venture capitalists, or does not require so much financing, it might still be of interest to **angel investors**, wealthy private individuals who are interested in investing in entrepreneurial ventures for a variety of reasons, from friendship to a desire to support entrepreneurship in a given field. Bill Gates, for example, has invested in several biotechnology startups because of such an interest. Often, successful entrepreneurs want to invest some of their earnings in other ventures that interest them, and they become angel investors to do so. The University of New Hampshire Center for Venture Research reports that, in 2008, angel investors numbered 260,500, and they invested in 55,480 companies, for a total of $19.2 billion.[6]

If your business has good management in place and a solid business plan, you might be able to raise angel financing. This type of investment is typically in the $100,000 to $500,000 range. Angels tend to seek a return of 10 times their investment at the end of five years, but their requirements vary widely. Angels may require fees for application and for presentations; their national association recommends that they be limited to a few hundred dollars for applications and $500 for presentations.[7]

The idea is to get one angel in place and to recruit that individual to find co-investors. Angels can be hard to find. However, there are a number of national and regional venture capital networks, which often connect entrepreneurs and angels. The regional networks can be helpful because

[6]Jeffrey Sohl, "The Angel Investor Market in 2009: A Down Year in Investment Dollars but Not in Deals," Center for Venture Research, March 26, 2009.
[7]Angel Capital Association Web Site, http://www.angelcapitalassociation.org (accessed October 31, 2009).

angels tend to invest in businesses they can visit frequently. The U.S. Small Business Administration developed ACE-Net (now Active Capital), which is a national network of angels. There is an annual fee, and certain restrictions apply. However, the network provides investments of up to $5 million, with most being under $1 million. The Angel Capital Association (http://www.angelcapitalassociation.org) and *Inc.* magazine (http://www.inc.com) compile directories of angel investors, with the Association's list being global. If you search for angel investors, look for people who are interested in or familiar with your markets and field. Angels prefer manufacturing, energy, technology, and some service businesses. They tend to avoid retail ventures.

Insurance Companies

Business owners may obtain a **policy loan**, which is made to a business using a whole-life, variable-life, or universal-life insurance policy based on the policy's cash surrender value. In essence, the owner is borrowing against personal savings.

policy loan a loan made against an insurance policy with cash value.

Vendor Financing

Entrepreneurs frequently benefit from the establishment of trade credit from vendors. By eliminating the need for cash in advance, or at the time of purchase, businesses can hold onto the money for a longer period, or will have more time to generate cash for payment. In essence, the vendor is providing financing for the business. The **float** is the term for the time between a payment transaction and when the cash is actually in the seller's account. If you receive your phone bill on March 1 and pay it on March 20, you have *floated* the bill for 19 days.

float the time between a payment transaction and when the cash is actually in the payee's account.

Accounts payable is money a business owes its suppliers. You should negotiate the best possible payment terms with your suppliers in advance, so that your business can use float to have as much cash on hand as possible. This is a form of short-term financing from your own company. As you grow and/or establish a record of timely payment, you can ask for better payment terms. If you are not able to pay on time, always call the creditor and discuss the late payment. Never just skip a payment.

Federally Supported Investment Companies

The U.S. government has supported the establishment of a number of privately owned and managed investment funds, primarily licensed and regulated by the SBA, that use their own capital, plus money borrowed with federal guarantees, to make equity and debt investments in qualifying small businesses.[8] They may provide debt or equity for early-stage companies that otherwise could not obtain financing.

The general name for these is Small Business Investment Companies (SBICs). If you are African American, Hispanic, Asian, or belong to another minority group, also look into Minority Enterprise Small Business Investment Companies (MESBICs). Also, the SBA and USDA have partnered to create Rural Business Investment Companies (RBICs) to support profit-oriented rural enterprises. In addition, New Markets Venture Capital Companies (NMVCCs) serve smaller enterprises located in low-income geographic areas. All are described, and those in your locality can be found, on the SBA Web site at http://www.sba.gov.

[8]SBA Web site, http://www.sba.gov/aboutsba/sbaprograms/inv/esf/inv_sbic_financing.html.

Financing for Rural/Agricultural Businesses

Whereas business owners often think of the SBA in terms of financial support and assistance, the U.S. Department of Agriculture (USDA) also has a long tradition of providing financial and technical assistance to rural/agricultural businesses, through a variety of programs. In addition to the RBICs noted above, there are programs of grants, guarantees, and loans described on the USDA Web site at http://www.usda.gov. Some of these programs include: the Farm Service Agency's farm ownership and operating loans, Rural Development's Business and Industry Guaranteed Loan Program (B&I), and the Rural Energy for America Program (REAP) grants and loans. Each program has specific options and limits, and can prove invaluable if your business is located in an area served by these USDA grants or loans.

Youth Financing

If you are a young entrepreneur (generally defined as under age 25), you may qualify for grants, scholarships, or awards designed to promote youth entrepreneurship. Such sources of start-up capital and/or scholarships for young entrepreneurs include

Name	Web Address
Ernst & Young Entrepreneur of the Year Award	*http://www.ey.com/global/content.nsf*
Guardian Life Insurance, Girls Going Places Entrepreneurship Award Program	*http://www.guardianlife.com/womens.channel*
National Association for the Self-Employed, Scholarship Program	*http://benefits.nase.org*
NFTE Young Entrepreneur of the Year	*http://www.nfte.com*
SBA Young Entrepreneur of the Year Award	*http://www.sba.gov*

Self-Funding: Bootstrap Financing

bootstrap financing financing a business by creatively stretching existing capital as far as possible, including extensive use of the entrepreneur's time.

Last but not least, there is always **bootstrap financing**, which is finding creative ways to stretch existing capital resources as far as they can go. If you cannot secure bank, venture, or angel financing, it does not mean that your business model/idea is not good. It may be that it simply does not fit their criteria. It is important to listen to constructive criticism, and recommendations from the financing sources that do not fund you. They may provide you with valuable nuggets of information that will help you find ways to bootstrap more successfully. Many hugely successful businesses have been started for under $10,000 by entrepreneurs who used a variety of techniques to stay afloat, including

- hiring as few employees as possible by using temporary service agencies for staffing needs, to help cut down on insurance and tax expenditures;
- leasing rather than buying equipment;
- getting suppliers to extend your credit terms so you can take longer to pay bills;
- using personal savings, taking a second mortgage, arranging low-interest loans from friends and relatives;
- floating accounts payable;

- working from home, or borrowing office space, to save on fixed costs;
- starting on a smaller scale or with more used equipment to establish a track record for traditional financing in the future; and
- putting profits back into the business to keep it going.

Accessing Sources through Online Networking

The more people who are aware of your product or service and its benefits, the more likely they are to buy it or refer you to someone who will do so. It is also true that the more you explore possibilities in financing options, the more likely you are to find what you need. Networking is the exchange of valuable information and contacts among businesspeople. The Internet is an important extension to your options for networking. You can search for angels and connect with other entrepreneurs online. Use search engines such as Google, Bing, Excite, and Yahoo! to find such Web sites as the Entrepreneurs' Organization, at http://www.eonetwork.org. Other sites that might be of value:

ACCION USA	*http://www.accionusa.org*
Active Capital (formerly ACE-Net)	*http://www.activecapital.org*
Angel Capital Association	*http://angelcapitalassociation.org*
Association for Enterprise Opportunity	*http://www.microenterpriseworks.org*
ICR Angel Financing	*http://www.icrnet.com*
Opportunity Finance Network	*http://www.opportunityfinance.net*

Be wary of any service that requires upfront payment, will not provide complete references, or in any other way raises a red flag. If a financing source seems to be too good to be true, it often is. That does not mean you should ignore or reject all online options. On the contrary, explore them, but use good judgment.

Global Impact...

The United States Encourages Other Nations to Become More Entrepreneurial

Entrepreneurship educators encourage you to think globally when it comes to finding customers, researching the competition, and looking for capital. If you live in the United States, you are probably in the best place to find capital for your business. According to a PricewaterhouseCoopers/National Venture Capital Association Money Tree Report, venture capitalists made 3980 deals totaling nearly $28 billion in the United States during 2008.[9] U.S. venture capital investment totaled $5.27 billion with 595 deals, whereas Europe had 272 deals for $831 million, of the $1.46 billion invested outside of the United States during the second quarter of 2009.[10] Europe's share of the venture capital market for that period was only 20 percent.

European countries are trying to change that, however. The members of the European Union have set forth an agenda for creating a dynamic, entrepreneurial, knowledge-based economy. Venture capital (called risk capital in Europe) was identified as a key factor in achieving this. Other countries and regions are undertaking similar efforts to become more entrepreneurial, which means more investors in these countries will be looking to finance small businesses.

[9]National Venture Capital Association Web site, http://www.NVCA.org (accessed October 31, 2009).
[10]"International Venture Capital Investment Continues Decline, Down 63% in Q2," Dow Jones Venture Source, July 23, 2009 http://www.reuters.com (accessed October 31, 2009).

Investors Want Their Money to Grow: Can You Make It Happen?

When you ask a banker or friend for money for your business, you are asking for an investment. You should know, therefore, about some of the other options available to your potential investors. After all, they are only going to put money in your venture if you can convince them that it is a more attractive investment than their other options. As your company grows and prospers, you also may become more interested in financial investments. Or, you may already have one and need to decide whether your business idea is the best one. The following sections are a primer on investment.

Performance Objective 5

Understand stocks and bonds as investment alternatives.

There are three categories of financial investments that can provide funds:

1. ***Stocks.*** Shares of company ownership (equity)
2. ***Bonds.*** Loans (debt) to companies or government entities for more than one year
3. ***Cash.*** Savings accounts, Treasury bills, and other investments that can be *liquidated* (turned into cash) within 24 hours

Real estate, land, or buildings, is another important investment. All investments involve some risk, which is the possibility that the money could be lost. There is a definite relationship between risk and reward:

The greater the potential reward of an investment, the more risky it probably is.

High Risk = High Reward

And so, if an investment has little risk, the reward will probably not be great.

Low Risk = Low Reward

How Stocks Work

share a single unit of corporate stock.

A corporation, whether privately held or publicly traded, is owned by its stockholders. Each **share** of stock represents a percentage of ownership. A stock certificate indicates how many shares were purchased and how big a piece of the company is owned.

If Street Scooters, Inc., has sold 10 shares of stock, each share to a different individual, it would mean there were 10 stockholders, each would own 1/10th of the company. If Street Scooters sold 100 shares of stock, each share to a different individual, there would be 100 stockholders. Each would own 1/100th of the company.

The "stock market" is in more than one location. It is made up of a collection of *exchanges* around the world where stocks are traded. The New York Stock Exchange (http://www.nyse.com) is the most well known in the United States. In recent years it has expanded to become NYSE Euronext, having added a number of European exchanges, and the American Stock Exchange (Amex). The electronic exchange that is home to many new and high-technology stocks is the NASDAQ (http://www.nasdaq.com), and it is joined by regional exchanges. Internationally, the London, Tokyo, and Hong Kong exchanges are the most recognized. Stocks may be traded on multiple exchanges, but the companies must meet the criteria for each.

Public corporations sell their stock to the general public to raise *capital*. They use the capital to expand the company or pay off debts. Typically, a corporation sells its stock to an investment banker, who pays an agreed-upon price and then handles the marketing and sales to get the stock into the public market. A public corporation receives the proceeds from the sale before the offering. Once the stock is sold, however, the corporation no longer has control over it. It is traded in the secondary market. The stock can be bought and sold by anyone. Such trading activity occurs continually on the stock market between brokers. A *stockbroker* has a license that confers the right to make trades for customers.

Stocks may be either *preferred* or *common,* with preferred stock having aspects of debt and common stocks being true equity. Preferred stock typically has a fixed dividend that is paid quarterly, and takes precedence over common stock in the case of liquidation. Many companies do not issue preferred stock. Common stock represents the true ownership of a company. It is the type of stock that is most often held, and can be made available in different classes that define whether it comes with voting rights or not. In case the business is liquidated, common stockholders get repaid after all debt holders and preferred stockholders.

The price of a stock at any given moment reflects investors' opinions about how well that business is going to perform. If the company does well, or its investors expect it to do well, the price of the stock is likely to rise. Investors make their returns by selling stock at a higher price than the one at which they bought it. They also may earn *dividends*, which are the portion of a corporation's earnings distributed to shareholders, typically on a quarterly basis. Dividends are paid at the discretion of a company's board of directors.

The daily record of trading activity appears in tables published in *The Wall Street Journal* and in the business sections of many other newspapers. They are also available online from numerous services. These tables allow investors to track the changing value of their investments. Information about stocks is available through brokerage firms and services, such as ValueLine and Morningstar.

A trader checks stock prices on his computer.
(© John Stuart, Creative Eye/ MIRA.com)

Let's say you own 10 shares of a stock you bought at $10 per share (for a total of $100). You see in the stock table that the price per share has declined to $8.50 that day. Your $100 investment is now worth only $85 (10 shares × $8.50/share = $85). You have three choices:

1. sell the shares before their value declines further;
2. keep them, hoping the decline is temporary and that the price will go back up; or
3. buy more shares at the lower price to increase your profit when the price does go back up.

How Bonds Work

Corporations may also use the financial markets to borrow money by issuing *bonds*. Bonds are interest-bearing certificates that corporations offer in order to raise capital. In addition, the federal government, state governments, and even city and town governments use bonds to finance roads, bridges, schools, and other public projects.

Bonds are loans; the original amount borrowed, plus interest, must be paid by the borrower. If you purchase a corporate or government bond, you are loaning your money to the company or government.

Owners of common stock are not certain whether they are going to receive dividends, or if the value of a stock is going to increase. They may make or lose money on the investment. The risks, and therefore the rewards, can be high. Bondholders, on the other hand, are promised a specific return (the coupon interest rate on the bond) and will get the investment back after a given time period. Bonds are rated by several organizations to reflect the levels of respective risk. Bonds and stocks together are referred to as **securities**.

Bonds are different from other loans, because the corporation that issues a bond does not have to pay regular monthly payments on the principal (the amount of a debt before the interest is added). A bond usually pays its yearly interest rate semiannually to the bondholders until **maturity**, when it is redeemed, meaning that the investor gets the face value back on that date.

By financing with bonds instead of a bank loan, a company does not have to make payments on the principal; it only has to make payments on the interest. On the other hand, the company must manage its money carefully, so that it will have the cash available when the bond matures.

If a corporation stops paying interest on a bond, the bondholders can sue the company. A court may force the company to sell assets to pay not only the interest, but the full amount of the bond.

Until maturity, bonds may be traded publicly, with their price going above or below their **face value**. The face value of a single bond, also referred to as **par**, is usually $1000 (with bonds being sold in lots of $10,000). This is the amount to be repaid by the corporation or government at the maturity date of the bond.

When the bond's market value rises above par, it means it is being traded for more than $1000; perhaps someone purchased it at $1,020. A bond trading above par is trading at a **premium**; in this case, the premium is $20. A bond trading below par is trading at a **discount**. If the above bond were trading at $940, the discount would be $60. Prices are quoted with the coupon rate (interest rate) and the price at maturity. For example, a five-year, 12-percent bond might be selling for $899.40 with a par value of $1000. This means that coupon interest payments will be $120 per year and the investment will yield a 15-percent return based on

security an investment instrument representing ownership in an entity (stock) or debt (bond) held by an investor.

maturity the date at which a loan must be repaid, including when a bond must be redeemed by the issuer.

face value the amount of a bond, also known as par, to be repaid by the corporation or government at its maturity date.

par the face value of a bond (typically $1,000) and the stated value of a stock.

premium (regarding bonds) the amount above par for which a bond is trading in the market.

discount (referring to bonds) the difference between a bond's trading price and its par value when the trading price is below par.

annual interest payments. Another five-year, 12-percent bond might be selling for $1,116.70, for a yield of 9 percent. The price an investor is willing to pay will depend upon the return that he or she needs to earn on the investment.

When you are buying or selling a bond, the critical determinant of price is the combination of the coupon rate, maturity date, risk, and required return. As an issuer of bonds, you will need to obtain enough financing at a cost that works for you. As an investor, you will have to meet or exceed your required return at a risk level that you can tolerate and on a time horizon that suits your needs.

Chapter Summary

Now that you have studied this chapter, you can do the following:

1. Explore your financing preferences.
   - Understand how much risk you are willing to take when financing your business.
   - Know the success rate in your industry.
   - Determine realistic financing options.
2. Identify the types of business financing.
   - Gifts and grants. Money or in-kind gifts given to support the business without a return required.
   - Debt. You borrow the money and promise to pay it back over a set period of time at a set rate of interest. Corporations sell debt in the form of bonds. You could borrow money from family or friends to finance your business.
   - Equity. You give up a percentage of ownership in your business for money. The investor receives a percentage of future profits from the business based on the percentage of ownership. Corporations sell equity in the form of stock. You cannot sell stock unless your business is incorporated, but you *can* sell equity. You could offer ownership and a share of your future profits in exchange for financing.
3. Compare the pros and cons of debt and equity financing.

   Debt Advantages
   - The lender has no say in the management or direction of the business as long as the loan payments are made.
   - Loan payments are predictable; they do not change with the fortunes of the business.

   Debt Disadvantages
   - Debt can be an expensive way to finance a business if interest rates are high.
   - If loan payments are not made, the lender can force the business into bankruptcy.
   - The lender may be able to take the home and possessions of the owner of a sole proprietorship or of the partners in a partnership to settle a debt.
   - Loan payments increase fixed costs and decrease profits.

   Equity Advantages
   - If the business does not make a profit, investors do not get paid. The equity investor cannot force the business into bankruptcy in order to retrieve the investment.

- The equity investor has an interest in seeing the business succeed, and may offer helpful advice and obtain valuable contacts.

Equity Disadvantages

- Through giving up ownership, the entrepreneur can lose control of the business to the equity holders.
- Equity financing is risky, so the investor frequently wants both to receive a higher rate of return than a lender, and to be able to influence how the company is operated.
- The entrepreneur will share profits with other equity investors.

4. Identify sources of capital for your business:
   - entrepreneurs, friends, and family;
   - financial institutions;
   - community development financial institutions;
   - venture capitalists;
   - angels;
   - vendors; and
   - federally supported investment companies.
5. Understand stocks and bonds as investing alternatives:
   - public corporations sell their stock to the general public to raise capital; and
   - bonds are interest-bearing certificates that corporations (and governments) issue to raise capital.

Key Terms

angel investor
bootstrap financing
charge account
credit
credit history
credit reporting agency (CRA)
creditor
debt service
default
discount
face value
float
leveraged
maturity
par
personal guarantee
policy loan
premium
principal
promissory note
risk tolerance
security
share
tax abatement
tax credit
venture capitalist

Entrepreneurship Portfolio

Critical Thinking Exercises

1. What type of financing will you seek as start-up capital, and why?
2. What steps could you take to improve your creditworthiness?
3. How would you counter the argument from a potential investor that most small businesses fail?
4. What challenges do start-up businesses face? Explain.

Key Concept Questions

1. Calculate the annual amount of interest (assuming no principal repayment) for each of the following:
   Term loan of $122,000 over 15 years at 6.5% ________
   Line of credit for $50,000 drawn 50% all year at 10% ________
   15 shares of stock purchased at $12.50 per share ________
   Bonds trading at par for $2000 with a 7% rate ________
2. If the owner of Bright Rays Tanning Salon, Inc. invested $200,000 and had an investor pay in $45,000 for 15% of the corporation, what is the valuation of the business?

Application Exercises

1. If you currently subscribe to or use an online service, BBS, or ISP (Internet Service Provider), discuss what you like and dislike about the service and why you chose it.
2. How could accepting an equity investment change your business plans?

Exploring Online

1. Visit http://www.privacyrights.org/fs/fs6-crdt.htm to learn about your rights to financial privacy; then answer the following:
   a. Who has access to your credit reports?
   b. What information cannot be legally included in your credit reports?
   c. After how many years is unpaid debt erased from your credit reports?
2. Visit the SBA Web site at http://www.sba.gov. Find four possible funding sources for a computer rental and repair company. Describe the pros and cons of each and create a proposed financing mix, assuming a need for $58,000 in start-up funds divided as follows:

Equipment	$27,000
Software	$10,000
Supplies	$ 1,000
Marketing	$ 6,000
Utilities/services	$ 4,000
Working capital	$10,000

Exploring Your Community

1. Find and list three networking opportunities in your community. Describe how you could take advantage of them for your business.
2. Visit a local bank and ask about its commercial lines of credit. Have the banker explain the terms to you and what a small start-up business would have to show to qualify for a line of credit. Report back to the class.
3. Are there any angel investors that might be interested in your business? Who are they and how did you find them?

Case Study | Digging Up Financing to Remove Trees and Stumps—Oscar Dolorier

Oscar Dolorier studied law and business administration in Peru but, when he came to the United States, he took jobs doing anything that would pay the bills. After working as a cook and handyman, Oscar started his own business removing trees and stumps, in 2003. "I didn't have any money," he remembers. "I had only my will and my belief in myself."

Oscar had the classic bootstrap financing for his start-up, using his own resources to purchase basic equipment for his Miami, Florida-based business. This work would result in about \$100 of cash flow by month's end. He was the only employee and fondly remembers, "I would think, I've got two helpers . . . this arm and this arm."

Today, Oscar has a crew of four and \$130,000 in assets, including machinery, tools, and trucks. His business grosses about \$15,000 a month. It was working capital that finally put success in reach. Oscar knew about microlenders from ACCION International's Peruvian partner, Mibanco, and when he read about ACCION USA, he immediately went to apply for a loan.

Unfortunately, like many small business owners, Oscar had none of the paperwork he needed to qualify. "He had no bank account, no receipts from his business, no corporation registered, nothing in his name at all," remembers loan officer William Mateo. At the time, Oscar was driving around in a two-door Toyota Tercel, weighed down with landscaping equipment. When William saw it, he decided to take a chance on him. "I thought: 'If this guy's willing to do landscaping like this, he's got to be serious.'"

William told Oscar to open a bank account, even if it had a very low balance, just so he would have an official financial record. He also told him to get receipts from his customers and for any equipment he purchased, and to make sure he got a utility bill in his name. Oscar came back three months later with everything William had asked for, and was approved, for a loan of \$7000. Later he refinanced the loan to \$10,000 to buy a professional stump-grinding machine.

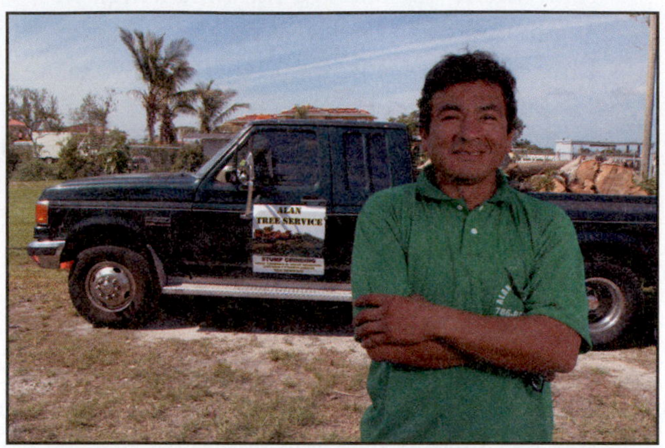

"I am very grateful to ACCION USA," Oscar says. "If they hadn't given me a hand, I wouldn't have been able to build this business."

Case Analysis

1. Why did Oscar Dolorier turn to microlending as a source of capital for his business?
2. Did ACCION USA provide 100 percent of the financing?
3. How was Oscar able to combine financial resources to reach his goal?
4. What factors made Oscar's company a business that did not qualify for mainstream financing (specifically discuss the Cs of credit)?
5. When, if ever, would you advise Oscar to approach mainstream lenders?

Case Sources

ACCION USA Web site, http://www.accionusa.org (accessed June 14, 2010).

Case Study | Lee's Ice Cream

As the bell rang and the clock struck three, South High School social studies teacher Jimmie Lee raced to the parking lot. It was a sunny afternoon in May, a perfect day to sell ice cream. Four years before, Jimmie had begun selling frozen treats in the spring and summer to children on Cleveland's east side. He had always wanted to be his own boss, and driving an ice cream truck seemed like a great idea because he could operate his business in the afternoons and during the summer months, when school was not in session. It helped that he was one of the most popular teachers at South High. All of Jimmie's students and their parents bypassed the other ice cream trucks and waited for Mr. Lee to drive down the block.

Getting Started: Jimmie Does His Research

To get Lee's Ice Cream off the ground, Jimmie had to learn to be creative, resourceful, and patient. When he first decided to bring his idea to reality, Jimmie called his friend Joy Greaves, who had worked in the ice cream business for over 15 years. He wanted to know how much Joy thought it would cost to start his business. Joy estimated that Jimmie would need about $25,000 dollars to purchase the necessary supplies and equipment, which would include the list below.

Joy's Start-Up Investment Estimates	
Item	**Estimated Cost**
Ice cream truck	$18,000
Freezer	3,000
Soft-serve ice cream machine	2,200
300 portions of soft-serve ice cream, napkins, toppings, and ice cream cones	200
Insurance, first quarterly payment	500
Commercial vendor's permit	100
Electric generator	1,000
Total estimated start-up investment	**$25,000**

Can Jimmie Reduce His Start-Up Investment?

As a public school teacher, Jimmie did not earn a large salary. He had $7000 in savings but, based on Joy's projections, this was not going to go very far. Initially, Jimmie was discouraged, but then he started to brainstorm. Perhaps he could lower his start-up investment by purchasing used equipment. He wondered whether or not this would pay off in the long run, if this equipment would need costly repairs or replacement parts that were no longer being manufactured. He scoured the local classifieds for used trucks, generators, and freezers, to see how much he could save. Based on this research, Jimmie calculated a revised start-up investment budget:

Jimmie's Start-Up Investment Estimates	
Item	**Estimated Cost**
Used ice cream truck (including freezer)	$10,000
Used soft-serve ice cream machine	1,500
300 servings of soft-serve ice cream, napkins, toppings, and ice cream cones	200
Insurance, first quarterly payment	500
Commercial vendor's permit	100
Service fees for refurbishing used equipment	1,000
Used electric generator	700
Total estimated start-up investment	**$14,000**
Difference between Joy's total start-up investment estimate and Jimmie's estimate	$11,000

If Jimmie purchased the equipment he researched, he would save $11,000. This was a lot of money. He decided it was worth the risk. He hoped that, if he ever did have to pay for repairs, it would cost less than $11,000, in which case he would still come out ahead.

Financing Strategy

Jimmie felt better knowing that he would only need $14,000 to get his business off the ground. He already had $7000, which covered half of the projected costs. He wondered how he could raise the rest of the money. A friend suggested that he apply for a bank loan, but when he inquired at his bank, he was told that the chances of obtaining a loan were slim. Jimmie had never run a business before and the loan was small, so the bank was hesitant to invest in him. What other options did he have?

Jimmie decided to pitch his idea for Lee's Ice Cream to his friends and family. Perhaps they would be willing to loan him money if he agreed to pay them back with interest. He asked his brothers and sisters, but they turned him down. They did not think Jimmie was truly serious about his business. Then he called his best friend, Greg Allen, who worked as an auto shop teacher at South High, to see if he had any ideas. Greg said that he had an old electric generator he would be willing to repair and donate. He even agreed to install it free of charge. Jimmie had planned to pay $700 for a used generator, so this was a great savings. Jimmie was one step closer to achieving his dream.

After hanging up the phone with Greg, Jimmie decided to visit his mother, to see if she would be willing to give him a loan. At first Jimmie's mother was resistant, but he took the time to walk her through the business plan he had created. His mother was not totally convinced, but she liked the fact that Jimmie had thoroughly researched what he would need. She decided to loan him $3000. Jimmie promised that he would pay her back, at 8 percent interest, within a year.

Where Is the Money Coming From?

At this point, Jimmie was close to having his funding in place. He made a chart to get a clearer picture of his start-up progress.

Jimmie was so close to having all his start-up investment capital in place, he could practically taste it. He only needed $3300. That evening, Greg called to say that he had finished repairing the electric generator and could install it as soon as Jimmie was ready. Jimmie explained that he did not feel comfortable purchasing a truck until he had secured his total start-up investment. "How much do you still have left to raise?" Greg asked. "Only $3300," Jimmie replied. "Well, if you will sell me an equity stake in your company," Greg said, "I'll write you a check for $3300."

To Sell or Not to Sell?

Jimmie was not sure how he felt about this. He really liked the idea of owning his business outright. Did he want to share ownership with someone else, even if it was Greg, his best friend? Also, Jimmie was not sure what percentage of his total equity he should offer Greg in exchange for $3300. How could he figure out what Lee's Ice Cream was worth if his business had not yet earned a dime? Jimmie thanked Greg for his offer and explained that he needed to think about it overnight. He promised to call him back first thing in the morning.

Funding Source	Equity	Debt	Gift
Personal Savings	$7000		
Relatives		$3000 loan from his mother (to be paid back at 8% interest within one year)	
Friends			
Grants or Gifts			Electric generator ($700 value)
Other			
Subtotal	$7000	$3000	$700
Total Equity + Total Debt + Total Gift = Total Financing: $10,700			
Difference between Total Start-Up Investment and Total Financing = $14,000 − $10,700 = $3,300			

Case Study Analysis

1. If you were in Jimmie's shoes, would you sell Greg an equity stake in Lee's Ice Cream? Explain. If Jimmie does sell equity to Greg for $3300, what percentage of the business should he offer?
2. Assume that Jimmie rejects Greg's offer. Brainstorm three other financing strategies for Jimmie to investigate.
3. Jimmie's mother agreed to loan him $3000 at 8 percent interest. Calculate the total amount Jimmie will owe to his mother.
4. Jimmie will sell his ice cream cones for $2 each. Assume the following about Jimmie's cost of goods sold for one ice cream cone:

Soft-serve ice cream:	$0.20
Ice cream cone:	$0.05
Napkin:	$0.02
Topping:	$0.03

   - What is the total COGS for one ice cream cone?
   - What is Jimmie's gross profit per unit?
5. Jimmie believes that he can sell an average of 150 ice cream cones per day at $2 per cone. Jimmie operates his business 7 days per week between May and August, for a total of 123 days. Calculate the following:
   - How many ice cream cones would Jimmie sell in total?
   - What would Jimmie's total revenue be?
   - What is Jimmie's total COGS?
   - Calculate Jimmie's gross profit.
   - Assume that Jimmie's total monthly operating costs are $1500. His business operates for four months of the year. Calculate his total net profit for one year of business operations.
   - Create a projected income statement for the period from May 1 until August 31, 2012. Remember to include the interest to his mother for the four months and taxes at 25%. Assume that there is no depreciation or operating costs other than those described above.
6. Examine Jimmie's projected income statement that you developed for the previous question. Assume that Jimmie does decide to sell Greg partial ownership in Lee's Ice Cream. Using the projected income statement as a guide, determine what percentage of his total equity Jimmie should offer Greg in exchange for $3300. Is this a different percentage from the answer you gave in question 1? Explain.

Bridgecreek Development: Creativity and Persistence

Small Business School **video clip titles are in red**

Frank Jao worked as a translator for the American military during the war in Vietnam, so when Saigon fell, in 1975, he and his wife, Kathy, were flown out of the war zone to Camp Pendleton, California. Together they had the clothes on their backs and about 20 U.S. dollars. They were told not to worry, because they would be assigned to an American family that would help them settle in their new country.

WORK TO MAKE YOUR DREAMS COME TRUE

The couple's sponsoring family told them to relax and not even think about working for a few months. The Americans knew that Frank and Kathy had gone through a terrible ordeal, and they needed to take their time trying to figure out how to build a new life thousands of miles away from everyone and everything they had known.

Frank did not take their advice. He got a job selling vacuum cleaners door to door within 48 hours of arriving in California. While continuing to work, he met with a community college counselor who discovered that Frank had sold heavy equipment before he started working for the military. The counselor suggested that, because such equipment was a big-ticket item with a long sales cycle, perhaps Frank should try real estate—which also is a big-ticket item with a long sales cycle.

It didn't take Frank long to complete a real estate course and pass the exam to get his license. He said, "I was very lucky. I came into the real estate market when the economy was booming. The real estate was selling fast—house prices in 1976 and 1977 would go up on a daily basis. So it doesn't take much skill—under that environment—to get the job done. Education is a main thing. I continued to take as many real estate classes and seminars as there were available in those days. And I bought as many books in that area as possible so that I would be able to get the knowledge I needed to succeed."

DON'T SPEND, INVEST

Frank joined a firm that had commercial and residential divisions, and he was assigned to work in residential sales. He noticed that the agents working on the commercial side were doing bigger deals and making more money than those in his group, so he set a goal to earn the right to move to the commercial side. In 1979, he made a sale so large that his commission was $350,000. Rather than buy something like a house for himself and Kathy, or a new car, he used the earnings to purchase a parcel of raw land in Westminster, California.

Frank said, "In Asia only money makes money. In America you might have a skill or a specific education that might get you a job with a paycheck but I learned as a child that I needed my money to make money."

LEARN TO SEE WHAT'S NOT THERE

The reason Frank bought the raw land is that he had an idea of how to develop it into what is his core business today. He dreamed of building and running a shopping area that provided a place for the Vietnamese community to sell and buy the types of products and services they enjoyed in their native land. This dream was realized as Asian Garden. It is a modern indoor mall that stands at the center of what is known in Orange County as Little Saigon. Frank has done so much for this community that the city leaders gave him his own exit off of the busy 405 freeway.

LEARN THE LANGUAGE OF BANKING

Was it easy to parlay the $350,000 into the Asian Garden Mall? No. Remember that Frank put all of his cash into the raw land. Next, he had to convince a banker to loan him the $3 million he needed to build on the land.

Meeting with the banker was an education. The banker told Frank that to get a loan he must bring back a feasibility study and a loan package. In 1979, he couldn't access the Internet to find free business-plan templates and read the feasibility studies created by the best consultants in the world. Frank was able to hire an expert to do the feasibility study, but he didn't have enough money to pay for a professionally prepared loan package with a business plan.

The night Frank met with his loan officer, after the bank closed and when the parking lot was dark, he climbed into the bank dumpster, in which he found a few loan packages (privacy rules were different in 1979). He figured that, because they were in the trash, no one would miss them. Using these as guides, he was able to write, and Kathy was able to type up, the loan package that might win over the banker. Three weeks after his first meeting with a commercial lender, Frank was back with a complete loan package, and that banker made the $3-million loan.

Because of Frank and Kathy's creativity, courage, and persistence over the years, Bridgecreek has developed more than 2 million square feet of retail, condo, and apartment space. It owns and manages 1.5 million square feet of space in Southern California and has 18 employees.

COMBINE TANGIBLES WITH INTANGIBLES

Frank said, in an interview with Wells Fargo Bank, that he charges 300 percent more for rent at Asian Garden than others charge in his area.[1] At the same time, whereas others have vacancies, Asian Garden has a waiting list. This is proof that you can charge more for space if your space is cleaner, safer, and more attractive to the shoppers, and can generate higher sales per square foot. Frank had a target audience in mind and built for that specific audience. Bridgecreek doesn't just provide a place for its tenants to operate businesses; it provides what Frank calls a cultural center for the Vietnamese community.

Just four years after Frank and Kathy Jao arrived from Vietnam, they launched the real-estate-development effort that made them

[1]Formichelli, Linda. "Sharpen Your Competitive Edge: Successful Companies Focus on Being Competitive Today and in the Future," *Wells Fargo Business Advisory Magazine*, Vol. 5, Issue 3.

wealthy—from a 900-square-foot apartment. They have not only created millions in annual revenue for their own company, they have provided a place for hundreds of retailers to thrive, while serving hundreds of thousands of happy customers.

While taping this episode of *Small Business School*, I met many of the employees at Bridgecreek, and interviewed Kathy. I asked her what her role in the company is now, and she said, "My job is to make sure everyone is happy." On the surface, this answer might sound flippant or glib, but it is one of the most difficult objectives any leader can set. This is not a goal that can be measured easily, like sales, cost of goods sold, or fixed overhead. This aim is measured by evaluating things like employee turnover, customer complaints, customer compliments, new ideas presented by employees, employees who take initiative, etc. With just 18 employees, Kathy is able to know each individual's likes, dislikes, and his or her family situation; and she can read body language.

Kathy told me that all of her efforts translate to the bottom line because, after three decades of working to build a business, she knows that happy people get more done in less time that do people who are unhappy. She also knows that attitudes are contagious, and that one grouch can spoil the atmosphere.

Anyone can imagine a better world, a better community, or a better neighborhood. Even as a child, Frank imagined a better life for himself. At the age of 11, he told his mother that, because the house was so crowded and there wasn't enough food to go around, he would go off on his own. He was one of eight children. By the time he was 16 years old, he spoke Vietnamese, Chinese, French, and English; and he had six boys working for him delivering newspapers in the city of Da Nang.

But Frank hasn't just dreamed. He starts with a dream; then he decides what he really wants. The novelist Willa Cather has written, "Desire is the talent." So you can't just dream about what you want.Your desire must be so deep that you are willing to do the work to make your dreams a reality. Most people walk through the world assuming it must stay as it is, and that they must adapt. Entrepreneurs like Frank and Kathy Jao walk through the world dreaming about how to make it better, and then, fueled by desire, they work to create a new reality.

Case Analysis

1. What opportunities did Frank identify?
2. How did Frank finance his dream of being a developer?
3. Why is Bridgecreek so profitable?
4. What question would you ask Frank and Kathy if you had the opportunity?

Case prepared by Hattie Bryant, creator of *Small Business School*, a television series made for PBS and Voice of America, http://SmallBusinessSchool.org.

UNIT 5

OPERATING A SMALL BUSINESS EFFECTIVELY

Chapter **16**

ADDRESSING LEGAL ISSUES AND MANAGING RISK

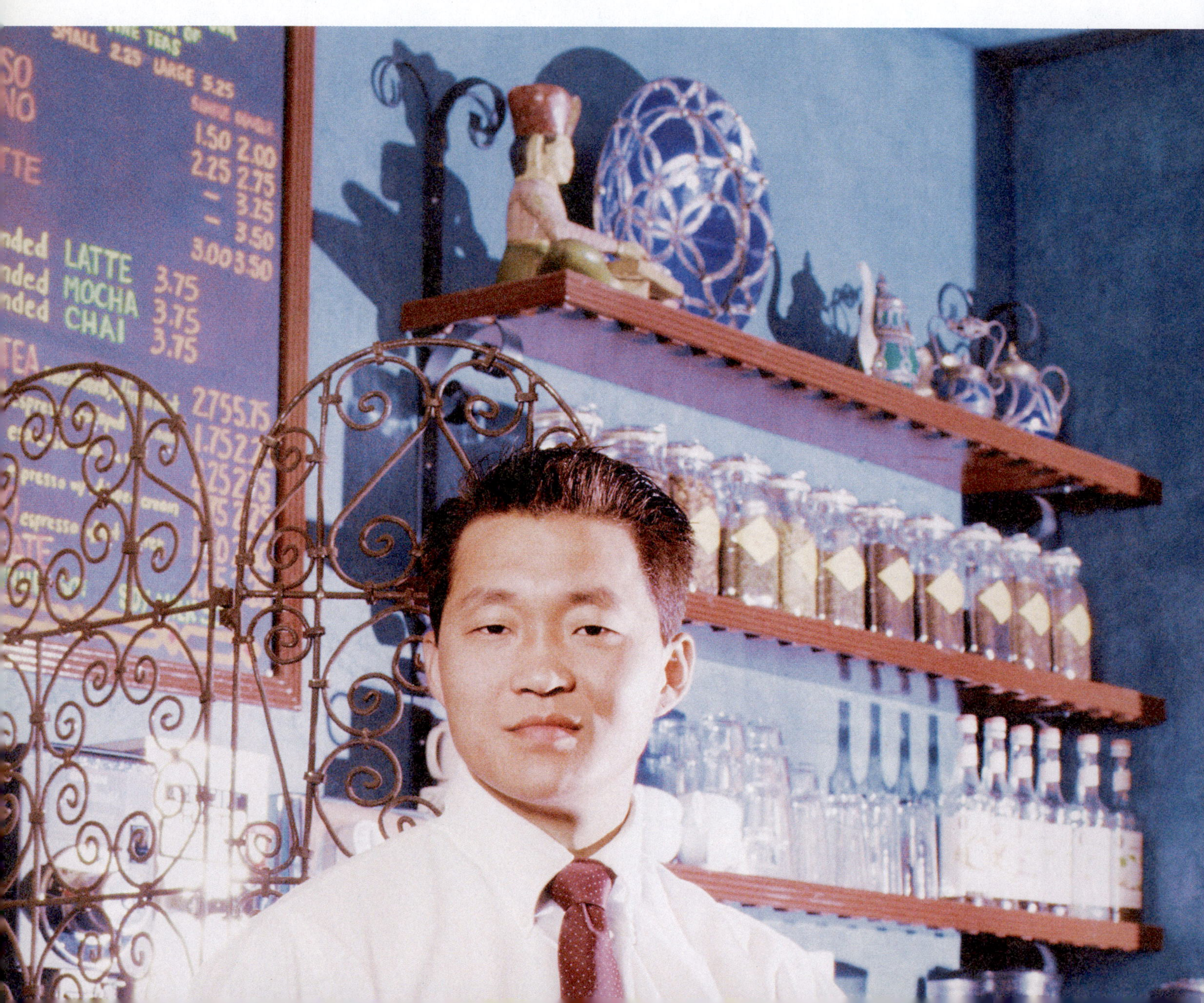

"Remember that time is money."

—Benjamin Franklin, American statesman, inventor, and writer

On May 8, 1886, Dr. John Stith Pemberton, an Atlanta pharmacist, produced the syrup for Coca-Cola and brought a jug of it to Jacobs' Pharmacy, where it was mixed and sold as a soda fountain drink. The beverage was proclaimed to be "delicious and refreshing," a theme that Coca-Cola reinforces today.

Dr. Pemberton's partner and bookkeeper, Frank Robinson, thought that "two C's would look well in advertising," and recommended the name *Coca-Cola,* and created the famous trademark in his own script.

Dr. John Stith Pemberton.

Over time, businessman Asa Candler bought into the company and eventually acquired complete control of it. According to the Web site, in May of 1889, Candler published a full-page advertisement in *The Atlanta Journal* that proclaimed his wholesale and retail drug business as "sole proprietors of Coca-Cola. . . . Delicious. Refreshing. Exhilarating. Invigorating." By 1892, Candler's flair for merchandising had boosted sales of Coca-Cola syrup nearly tenfold. With his brother John, Frank Robinson, and two other associates, Candler formed the Coca-Cola Company as a corporation. The trademark *Coca-Cola,* which had been used since 1886, was registered in the United States Patent Office in 1893, and has been renewed periodically.[1]

Performance Objectives

1. Choose a legal structure for your business.
2. Understand the importance of contracts.
3. Recognize key components of commercial law.
4. Protect your intellectual property.
5. Protect your tangible assets and manage risk.

Business Legal Structures

Most businesses, no matter how humble their beginnings, have the potential to grow into much larger ventures, so it is important that founders think through every step of the company's development. How the entrepreneur organizes the company, such as the legal structure chosen, the relationships developed with suppliers, the managers hired, will all have vital impact on the ability to grow.

Performance Objective 1

Choose a legal structure for your business.

After you pick the kind of business and industry you want to be in, you will know where you fit in the production-distribution chain; you will be able to research markups, markdowns, and discounts in your industry in order to be competitive. You will also have to choose one of the three basic legal structures:

1. sole proprietorship,
2. partnership, or
3. corporation.

Sole Proprietorship

sole proprietorship a business owned by one person who has unlimited liability and unlimited rights to profits.

A **sole proprietorship** is a business owned by one individual, who often is the only employee. This owner receives all the profits from the business and is also responsible for all losses. Most U.S. businesses are sole proprietorships.

[1]Information from Coca-Cola Web site, http://www.Coke.com.

The sole proprietor is personally *liable*, or responsible, for any lawsuits that arise from accidents, faulty merchandise, unpaid bills, or other business problems. This means a sole proprietor could lose not only business assets in a lawsuit, but could be forced to sell private possessions, to satisfy a court judgment. He or she could lose a house or a car, for example.

Advantages of a Sole Proprietorship

- It is relatively easy to start. A person becomes a sole proprietor—albeit not a registered, legal one—simply by selling something to someone else.
- Proper registration does not require much paperwork, and registration is relatively inexpensive.
- There are fewer government regulations than for the other forms of business.
- Sole proprietors can make quick decisions and act without interference from others.
- A sole proprietor is entitled to all the profits from the business.

Disadvantages of a Sole Proprietorship

- It can be difficult to raise enough money by oneself to start or expand a business.
- A sole proprietor must often put in long hours, working six or even seven days a week, with no one to share the responsibilities.
- There is no way to limit personal legal liability from lawsuits related to the business.
- There is often no one to offer encouragement or feedback.
- All profits earned are taxed personally, whether or not the funds are withdrawn from the business, or cash is left in it.

How to Register a Sole Proprietorship

In most states and localities, it is easy and relatively inexpensive to register a sole proprietorship. When you do, you will have a legal business.

- If you operate a business without registering it, you may be liable to civil or even criminal penalties.
- Registered sole proprietorships can use the court system and bring lawsuits.
- Banks like to see legal business ownership the way employers like to see that employees have had previous work experience. If your business is not registered, banks will not even *consider* loaning you money, although some alternative lenders might do so. The time that you operated without registration will be discounted. Lack of registration can be perceived as a lack of integrity.

Steps to Registering

The registration process varies from state to state and by municipality, but there will be a few common steps:

- Choose a name for your business.
- Fill out a registration form, which sometimes requires a *doing business as* (DBA) form that will show the name of the business and your name, so the state will know who will be responsible for tax payments.

- An official may then conduct a name search, to make sure the name you have chosen is not already being used in that jurisdiction. You may even be asked to help research the records yourself.
- Once your registration is completed satisfactorily, you will pay the required fee. This fee can range from under $100 to several hundred, depending upon the type of business and state and municipal laws and regulations. Professional firm registrations, in particular, can become quite expensive.
- You may be asked to take the form to a **notary**, a person who has been given the authority by the state to witness the signing of documents, to have it *notarized* and then brought back to the registration office. You will have to show the notary valid identification to prove who is signing the form. A notary usually charges a modest fee.

notary a person who has been authorized by the state to witness the signing of documents.

Partnership

A **partnership** consists of two or more owners, who make the decisions for the business together and share the profits, losses, assets, and liabilities. As in a sole proprietorship, partners face unlimited liability in any lawsuits. This means that *each* partner can be held responsible for paying debts or judgments, even those incurred by other partners without their knowledge or agreement.

partnership a business with two or more owners that make decisions for the business together and share the profits, losses, assets, and liabilities.

The exception to this is the **limited partnership**. The limited partners have no official say in the daily operation of the business and have, as a result, liability limited to the amount of their investments. One or more *general* partners manage the company and assume legal liability. There must be at least one general partner in a limited partnership, who is liable for all partnership debts.

limited partnership business partnership wherein there is a general partner with unlimited liability, and one or more limited partners with no official input in daily operations and limited liability.

Ideally, partners bring different strengths and skills to a business. This can help the venture grow and succeed. In addition, partners can support and advise each other. On the other hand, partnership disagreements can become intolerable and destroy the partnership, the friendship, and the business.

Despite the advantages of partnerships, caution is the watchword. You should be extremely careful and thorough about entering into a partnership, particularly with a good friend or relative. A lawyer should be consulted, and a partnership agreement drawn up, that carefully defines the roles and responsibilities of each partner. A partnership agreement is absolutely critical, regardless of how well or poorly the company ultimately performs.

Corporation

corporation a legal entity composed of stockholders under a common name.

There are several types of **corporations**, but each is considered a legal person, or *entity,* composed of stockholders under a common name. A corporation has rights and responsibilities under the law and it can buy and sell property, enter into leases and contracts, and be prosecuted. Corporations issue stock that is divided among the founders and sold to investors. These *shareholders* then elect a board of directors that is responsible for representing their interests in the management of the company. The shareholders who own the stock own the corporation, in proportion to the number of their shares.

The corporate legal structure offers three key advantages:

1. Corporations may issue stock to raise money. Essentially, the company sells pieces of itself in the form of equity to stockholders.
2. The corporation offers limited personal liability to its owners. Unlike sole proprietorships and partnerships, the owners of a corporation are protected from having their personal assets taken to pay business lawsuit settlements or debts. Only the assets of the corporation can be used to pay corporate debts. However, most lenders will not loan money to a small, closely held corporation unless the owners personally guarantee the debt, in which case the owners do become personally liable and can have their personal property confiscated to pay it. In addition, it is possible to pierce the corporate veil if the business affairs of the corporation and its shareholders are tightly entwined, so that shareholders may be held personally liable in a lawsuit. This is a strong argument for keeping business and personal finances separate.
3. Corporations can exist indefinitely, so they do not cease when an owner dies or leaves.

A disadvantage of corporations is that corporate income is taxed twice. A corporation must pay corporate income tax on its earnings because it is a legal entity. Then, the corporation may distribute earnings as dividends to stockholders. The stockholders must include those dividends as personal income on their tax returns. For example, a corporation with taxable income of $100,000 that distributed $10,000 in dividends would have a tax bill of $34,000 (34-percent corporate tax rate), and its shareholders would owe $2800 (28-percent personal tax rate) more, for a total tax of $36,800. The total tax on $100,000 for a sole proprietor could be $28,000 (28-percent personal tax rate), reflecting no dividends—for an $8800 difference.

If corporate stock is privately held, the shares are typically owned by only a few investors and are not *traded* (bought and sold) publicly, such as on the New York Stock Exchange, or that of London or Tokyo. In a public corporation, such as Ford or IBM, the company's stock is offered for sale to the general public; anyone with sufficient resources may purchase it at the market price. Stockholders may be paid dividends when the company's management considers they are warranted, by profits or other considerations. Dividends are part of the stockholders' return on their investment in the company.

There are several types of corporations:

- ***C corporation.*** Most large companies and many smaller ones are C corporations. They sell ownership as shares of stock. Stockholders have the right to vote on important company decisions at the annual meeting, or to vote by proxy. To raise capital, the C corporation can sell more stock, issue bonds, or secure other types of loans.
- ***Subchapter S corporation.*** This type of corporation has a limit of 75 stockholders. It offers most of the limited-liability protection of the C corporation, but Subchapter S corporate income is only taxed once, as the personal income of the owners. It is a pass-through entity for tax purposes. Often, a company will start as an S corporation and change to a C type when it begins to earn profits, through a formal process with the Internal Revenue Service. The net profits of an S corporation are taxed at the personal income-tax rates of the individual shareholders, whether or not the profits are distributed.

BizFacts

Advantages of Corporations

- Limited personal legal liability for shareholders.
- Funds can be raised through the issuance of stock.
- Ownership can be transferred easily.
- The legal entity survives beyond the life span or participation of individuals.

Disadvantages of Corporations

- Corporations are often more heavily taxed than sole proprietorships or partnerships. Their profits are taxed twice: first, as the income of the corporation (except S corporations), and again as personal income, when dividends are distributed to stockholders.
- The founder of a corporation may lose control to the stockholders if he or she no longer owns more than half the stock. (This happened to Steve Jobs, cofounder of Apple Computer, who at one point was fired by his own company—although eventually rehired.)
- It is more expensive to start a corporation than a sole proprietorship.
- Corporations are subject to many government regulations.

- ***Professional corporation (PC).*** Medical practices, engineering firms, law firms, accounting firms, and certain other professions can form professional corporations. The initials PC after a doctor or lawyer's name means that that individual has incorporated the practice or belongs to a group of practitioners that has incorporated. Each state designates which professions can form such corporations. Professional corporations are subject to special rules, such as meeting the licensing requirements of bar associations or medical societies. Professional corporations cannot protect individual members from malpractice liability, but the other members of a PC are protected from liability arising from the negligence of one of the group.
- ***Nonprofit corporation.*** A nonprofit corporation is not set up for the purposes of shareholder financial gain, but rather with a specific mission to improve society. Churches, museums, charitable foundations, and trade associations are examples of nonprofit corporations (also called not-for-profits). Nonprofits are *tax-exempt*. Nonprofits may not sell stock or pay dividends. There are no individual shareholders for a not-for-profit corporation, and any net profits that are earned must go toward the advancement of the mission, so there are no dividends issued and income taxes are not paid. Not-for-profits may have members rather than shareholders. Such organizations must be careful to follow applicable laws, rules, and regulations in order to maintain their tax-exempt status.
- ***Limited liability company (LLC).*** The LLC combines the best features of partnerships and corporations, and can be an excellent choice for small businesses with a limited number of owners. In an LLC, profits are taxed only as the personal income of the members, whose personal assets are protected from lawsuits as in a C corporation. In addition, many of the restrictions regarding the number and type of shareholders that apply to the Subchapter S corporation do not apply to LLCs, making them even more attractive. An LLC has a variety of options that make it a flexible type of legal entity. The advice of legal counsel is vital in establishing an LLC, because each state has different laws, and the creation and maintenance of LLC status requires continued compliance.

To compare these legal structures, see **Exhibit 16-1**.

Tips for Entrepreneurs Who Want to Start a Nonprofit Organization

There are huge needs in society for food, shelter, education, and more; and there are many people who cannot access these fundamental conditions and requirements. In the United States, there is the 501(c)(3) nonprofit (not-for-profit) corporation to help address this situation. A 501(c)(3) is a tax-exempt legal structure (as discussed above) that can receive charitable donations from individuals, businesses, the government, and philanthropic foundations. Examples of well-known nonprofit corporations include the Boys and Girls Clubs, the YMCA, and the Sierra Club. People who donate money to not-for-profits benefit from their generosity by knowing that they are making a gift to a cause in which they believe. Also, they are able to deduct these contributions from their taxable income.

In the United States, close to 1 million organizations were registered with the IRS as public charities in 2007, compared with 600,000 in 1993.[2]

[2]The Urban Institute, National Center for Charitable Statistics, Business Master File 12/08, http://nccs.urban.org/statistics (accessed November 12, 2009).

Exhibit 16-1 *Comparison of legal structures.*

COMPARISON OF LEGAL STRUCTURES						
	Sole Proprietorship	**General or Limited Partnership**	**C Corporation**	**Subchapter S Corporation**	**Nonprofit Corporation**	**Limited Liability Company**
Ownership	The proprietor	The partners	The stockholders	The stockholders	No one	The members
Liability	Unlimited	Limited in most cases	Limited	Limited	Limited	Limited
Taxation Issues	Individual* (lowest rate)	Individual* (lowest rate)	Corporate rate; "double taxation"	Individual* (lowest rate)	None	Individual* (lowest rate)
How profits are distributed	Proprietor receives all	Partners receive profits according to partnership agreement	Earnings paid to stockholders as dividends in proportion to the number of shares owned	Earnings attributed to stockholders as in proportion to the number of shares owned	Surplus cannot be distributed	Same as partnership
Voting on policy	Not necessary	The partners	Common voting stockholders	Common voting stockholders	The board of directors/trustees	Per agreed-on operating procedure
Life of legal structure	Terminates on death of owner	Terminates on death of partner	Unlimited	Unlimited	Unlimited	Variable
Capitalization	Difficult	Easier than sole proprietorship	Excellent—ownership is sold as shares of stock	Good—same as partnership	Difficult because there is no ownership to sell as stock	Same as partnership

*When the double taxation of corporations is taken into account.

Charitable donations rose from $148 billion to $308 billion in the same period, accounting for about 22 percent of total revenues in 2007.[3] Whereas competition for financial resources has increased, more technical and educational resources are now available to support the management and growth of organizations that choose to incorporate as not-for-profits.

Like any business, a not-for-profit will need to generate revenue to cover its expenses. Failure to meet cash requirements will mean a failure to survive. A not-for-profit needs to identify a target market (constituency) and determine how it will deliver its products and services. Some key differences and considerations exist, however, and you should be aware of them before you apply to the IRS for approval:

- ***No individual can own a not-for-profit organization.*** A nonprofit cannot be bought and sold like other businesses. You would not be able to dissolve and sell it for financial gain. Nor could you issue stock to raise money. These organizations are meant to improve society, not create wealth for the founder, shareholders, or employees.
- ***Nonprofits are mission-driven.*** Before you can operate as a nonprofit, you will need to be crystal clear about your organization's mission. What problem(s) are you trying to solve? The IRS will not grant tax-exempt status without such a mission and considerable additional information. Also, ask yourself if there is another organization that is working toward the same goal. Could you work together rather than creating a new entity and duplicating services and costs? Is there a large enough donor base and grant supply to combine with fee income for sustainability? Also, do you expect the organization to accomplish its mission and cease to need resources in the foreseeable future?
- ***Define your unit of change.*** In a for-profit business, the return on investment is calculated by looking at the corporation's financial records. Not-for-profit entrepreneurs need to think about their ROI a little differently. Not-for-profits do not exist to make money, so the ultimate measure of success will not be financial, although financial goals and measures are part of the equation. Your ROI will be based on how much it will cost you to provide your services as compared with the level of change that was brought about as a result of this investment.
- ***Determine how you will evaluate your success.*** As a not-for-profit entrepreneur, you will need to set goals regarding the changes you wish to effect. How many homeless people will you feed? How many students will graduate as a result of your dropout-prevention program? What changes in knowledge, skills, or attitudes will result from the efforts of your organization? The output and outcome goals that you establish must tie back into your financial and human-resource inputs. How much does it cost to provide these services? Given the costs, how many units of change did your organization achieve? How can you document that your organization brought about these changes?
- ***Analyze your financing strategy.*** Nonprofit corporations can borrow money, as well as earn it. They also have access to a revenue stream that other business structures cannot tap. Not-for-profits generate revenue through grants and gifts (donations) from individuals and organizations, but they cannot sell stock to raise equity.

---

[3]The Urban Institute, National Center for Charitable Statistics, Business Master File 12/08, http://nccs.urban.org/statistics (accessed November 12, 2009) and Jessica Stannard-Friel, *MBAs at the Crossroads of Corporate and Nonprofit America*, from "On Philanthropy" Web site, http://www.onphilanthropy.com (accessed December 3, 2004).

Contracts: The Building Blocks of Business

Regardless of the type of legal entity you elect to form, you will need to enter into a variety of legal covenants. A **contract** is a formal agreement between two or more parties to perform or refrain from performing particular actions. When you sign up for mobile telephone service with a provider, such as Verizon or AT&T, you are signing a contract. You agree to pay for the service at a specified price per month, and in return the company agrees to provide you with access to telephone service, voice mail, data services, text messaging, and the like. Remember that rental leases, any promissory notes or mortgages, advertising or partnership agreements, are all contracts. How they are written (their terms and conditions) can often make or break your business.

contract an agreement between two or more parties that is enforceable by law.

Contracts are the building blocks of business. The relationships between the links in a production-distribution chain are defined by contracts. For example, if a department store wants to sell your hammered-silver necklaces, you might create a six-month contract specifying how many necklaces you will supply at what price and how and when the store will pay you.

Performance Objective 2

Understand the importance of contracts.

With that contract in hand, you can call your wholesaler. Because you have a large order, you will want to get your supplies in bulk. With the contract as written proof of your relationship with the store, wholesalers may give you credit. You can arrange to buy the silver you need now to fill the order, and pay for it after you sell the necklaces to the store. You can also plan ahead with your advertisers, or work out an advertising plan with the store as part of the contract. Or, you may be able to secure bank financing for the contract production.

The power of a contract is that, once the individuals or other entities involved have signed it, they are obligated to comply with its terms and conditions or risk being sued and penalized according to the contract terms, or in a court of law. If the store fails to buy your necklaces as agreed, you can go to court to force payment. Because of the contract, you will be able to honor your contract with your supplier. At the same time, the contract obligates you to produce what you have promised and deliver it when you said you would.

Working with an Attorney

There are certain times in the life of an organization when investing in the cost of professional services is essential, even though the out-of-pocket cost may seem high at the time. Contract drafting and review is one of them.

- Never sign a contract without having an attorney examine it for you.
- Never sign a contract that you have not read completely and carefully, even if your lawyer tells you it is all right. Ultimately, you are responsible for what you sign.

If you are ever taken to court and argue, "I didn't understand that part of the contract," it will not satisfy the judge. Your signature at the bottom tells the court that you read, understood, and agreed to every word.

Attorneys typically charge by the hour, so be as prepared and organized as possible before visiting one. Many issues can be resolved efficiently and effectively through e-mail and telephone calls, so that billable hours are minimized. Always read the contract ahead of time and make a copy of it. Mark sections that you do not agree to or understand, preferably using features of the word-processing software. Indicate your suggestions for changes. This will help your attorney advise you effectively.

Drafting a Contract

boilerplate language a standard format for a specific type of legal agreement.

Consult an attorney if you need to *draft,* or write, a first version of a contract or agreement, with the understanding that it will probably need to be developed and rewritten. Be certain that you identify and make a list of the key points in advance. Attorneys often have standard formats for specific types of legal agreements, sometimes called **boilerplate language**, which can make the process quicker and less costly.

A Successful Contract Should Achieve the Four As:

1. **Avoid** misunderstanding,
2. **Assure** work,
3. **Assure** payment, and
4. **Avoid** liability.

Avoid Misunderstanding

When putting together a contract, clearly state everything that will be done by all parties, even what is obvious. Go into full detail (not just how many shirts you will supply to the store and when, but which types, colors, and sizes). If you do not cover all the details, the person with whom you are contracting may add provisions or find loopholes you will not like. At the same time, leave enough flexibility to accomplish what needs to be done successfully.

Assure Work

For a contract to be legally binding, all parties will be required to do one of the following:

- perform an action or exchange something of value, or
- agree *not* to do something the party was legally entitled to do.

Sometimes one dollar is exchanged, as a token payment to legalize a contract. The contract should assure that each party fulfills some kind of obligation. The exact nature of the obligation, and the time frame for accomplishing it, should be specified fully.

Assure Payment

A good contract specifies how payment will be made, and when and for what. It should leave no room for misinterpretation.

Avoid Liability

contingency a condition that must be met in order for something else to occur.

Because this world is full of surprises, your contract should spell out **contingencies**, unpredictable events beyond your control that could cause delay or failure to fulfill contractual responsibilities. The contract should list contingencies for which you would not be liable. Common contingencies are "acts of God" (earthquake, hurricane, etc.) or illness.

When you share the draft or a list of key topics of your contract with an attorney, ask these two basic questions:

1. Will this agreement fully protect my interests?
2. What would you add, drop, or change?

Letter of Agreement

Sometimes you will not need a full, formal contract, because the relationship is going to be brief or the work and money involved are relatively minor. In such cases, a **letter of agreement** that puts an oral understanding in writing, in the form of a business letter, may be enough. The other party must respond to it in writing, either approving it or suggesting changes, until an agreement is reached. However, use this option with care and with legal advice.

letter of agreement a document that puts an oral understanding in writing, in the form of a business letter.

Breach of Contract

A contract is broken, or *breached*, when a **signatory**, an individual that signed the contract, fails to fulfill it. The person injured by the signatory's failure to comply with the contract may then sue for **breach of contract**.

For a contract to be breached, it must first be legally binding. Most states require that all signatories be at least 18 years of age and that the contract represent an exchange of value. If a contract is breached, legal action must be brought by the injured party within the state's **statute of limitations**, the time period within which legal action may be taken.

A lawsuit is an attempt to recover a right or claim through legal action. Because attorney's fees are expensive and court cases time-consuming, lawsuits should be avoided whenever possible. Other options are **small claims court** and **arbitration**.

signatory a person who signs a contract.

breach of contract the failure of a signatory to perform as agreed.

statute of limitations the time period in which legal action may be taken.

small claims court a legal option for solving conflicts involving less than a certain sum of money.

arbitration a method of dispute resolution using an arbitrator to act as the decision maker rather than going to court.

Small Claims Court

Conflicts involving less than a certain sum of money, which varies by state law, can usually be resolved in a small claims court. In Delaware, for example, claims for $15,000 or less can be settled through civil action in the justice of the peace court. In small claims court, each person is allowed to represent him- or herself before a court official. The official hears each side's arguments and makes a decision that is legally binding.

Arbitration

Sometimes contracts specify that conflicts may be settled through *arbitration* instead of in court. An *arbitrator*, someone both sides trust, is chosen to act as the decision maker to resolve the conflict. The parties agree to abide by the arbitrator's decision.

A Contract Is No Substitute for Trust

A contract is not a substitute for understanding and communication. If you do not like or trust someone, having a contract will not improve the relationship, but it will address your concerns in writing. However, entering into a business contract with someone you do not trust could lead, instead, to a lawsuit. Avoid signing a contract with someone you do not trust.

A good reason never to sign a contract with such a person is that you might need to renegotiate the terms at some point, and you may have an even harder time coming to terms then. Running a small business is challenging and unpredictable. In the jewelry example mentioned previously, how would you pay back the silver supplier if the store decided not to buy the necklaces after all? If you have a friendly relationship, you may be able to discuss your situation and renegotiate or cancel the contract.

The Uniform Commercial Code (UCC)

Performance Objective 3 

Recognize key components of commercial law.

Contract law varies from state to state, with a common set of standardized practices. The Uniform Commercial Code (UCC) is a collection of business laws adopted by most states that directs a broad spectrum of transactions, such as loans, contracts, and the like. The UCC is a joint project of the American Law Institute and the National Conference of Commissioners on Uniform State Laws, and was first issued in 1952. It is not law, rather, it is a recommendation for laws that states can adopt as written or with modification (or not at all). Because so many commercial transactions involve parties in more than one state, consistency becomes important. For example, if you buy a forklift that is manufactured in Michigan, warehoused in Georgia, sold to you by a company in New Jersey, and delivered to your warehouse in South Carolina, it is simpler to have uniform laws governing these transactions than four distinct sets of statutes. Note that the UCC is focused on movable property rather than "real" (immovable) property.

The UCC consists of a series of Articles that covers the range of commercial transactions:

ARTICLE	TITLE
1	General Provisions
2	Sales
2A	Leases
3	Negotiable Instruments
4	Bank Deposits
4A	Funds Transfers
5	Letters of Credit
6	Bulk Transfers and Bulk Sales
7	Warehouse Receipts, Bills of Lading and Other Documents of Title
8	Investment Securities
9	Secured Transactions

Source: Copyright © by the American Law Institute and the National Conference of Commissioners on Uniform State Laws. Reproduced with the permission of the Permanent Editorial Board for the Uniform Commercial Code. All rights reserved.

The Law of Agency

The subject of agency law (principal–agent) is a vital area of commercial contract law. An agent (third party) is authorized to act on behalf of a principal (primary party) to create a legal relationship with another individual or business. Common agency relationships include

- employment (employer, employees);
- real estate (real estate agents);
- financial services (stock brokers, insurance agents); and
- promotion (modeling, acting, music, publishing, and sports agents).

Agency law is the branch of legal activity that addresses relationships between each party in a situation where one individual or company is authorized to work on behalf of another.

Businesses commonly rely upon agents to conduct their affairs, although they are not always perceived as such. Employees are agents of their employers. All individuals carrying out the work of a corporation are agents, because a corporation is a legal entity (person). The principal in an agency relationship (company or person) is contractually bound by any agreement entered into by the agent, as long as the agent is operating within his or her authority.

This is particularly important for you to understand as an entrepreneur. When you authorize others to act for you, you can be legally bound by their actions, for better or worse. Authority can be granted, or perceived to have been granted, by several means:

- contractually, through a written contract;
- words or conduct, if the principals' actions or words would make it so that a reasonable person would assume authority (you say or do something that implies it);
- ostensible authority, if the principal makes it appear to the third party that the agent is authorized, such as putting the agent in a position of authority (think manager, supervisor, or sales representative); and
- implied—the level of authority, is considered necessary to fulfill the agent's job, such as a partner or senior executive in a business (responsibility and authority are the norm in certain positions).

The area of agency law is quite complex, and significant to the entrepreneur. If you are in a partnership, any partner is presumed to have the authority to enter into agreements that bind the other partners (agency power). This could lead to financial disaster. Or, consider a salesperson attempting to close a sale. This individual could commit to giving discounts without your knowledge or approval. As far as the customer is concerned, your company has made the offer. If the offer is not satisfactory to you, as the owner, you are in the awkward position of either doing as promised to keep the customer happy, or attempting to renege and alienating the customer, with perhaps further consequences to follow. The law of agency sets parameters for the liability of each party.

Bankruptcy

Although entrepreneurs are an optimistic lot, business sometimes does not progress as planned, and **bankruptcy** becomes the best option. Bankruptcy is the legal process in which an individual or business declares the inability or impaired ability to pay debts as they come due. This may be a voluntary petition by the debtor, or it may be forced by creditors (involuntary bankruptcy). Bankruptcy is often used as a way to reorganize finances and secure some breathing room for businesses that are insolvent. The process is meant to ensure fair treatment of creditors as well as the debtor.

bankruptcy the legal process in which an individual or business declares the inability or impaired ability to pay debts as they come due.

Many companies, large and small, have filed for and emerged from bankruptcy. For example, General Motors, Macy's, and Delta Airlines have all done it. **Figure 16-1** shows the number of business bankruptcy filings from 1985 through 2008. As a business owner, you will not want to file for bankruptcy unless it is your best remaining strategy. As a creditor, you do not want your customers to file for bankruptcy protection because you will have to wait for payment and may lose the money altogether.

The Bankruptcy Reform Acts of 1978 and 2005 govern the eight "chapters" under which bankruptcy may be filed. Chapters 7, 11, and 13 generally apply to small businesses, with Chapters 7 and 11 the most common. Entrepreneurs often have the choice of *liquidation* (conversion of assets to cash with business closure) or *reorganization* (creating a plan and continuing operations).

Figure 16-1 *Business bankruptcy filings from 1985–2008.*

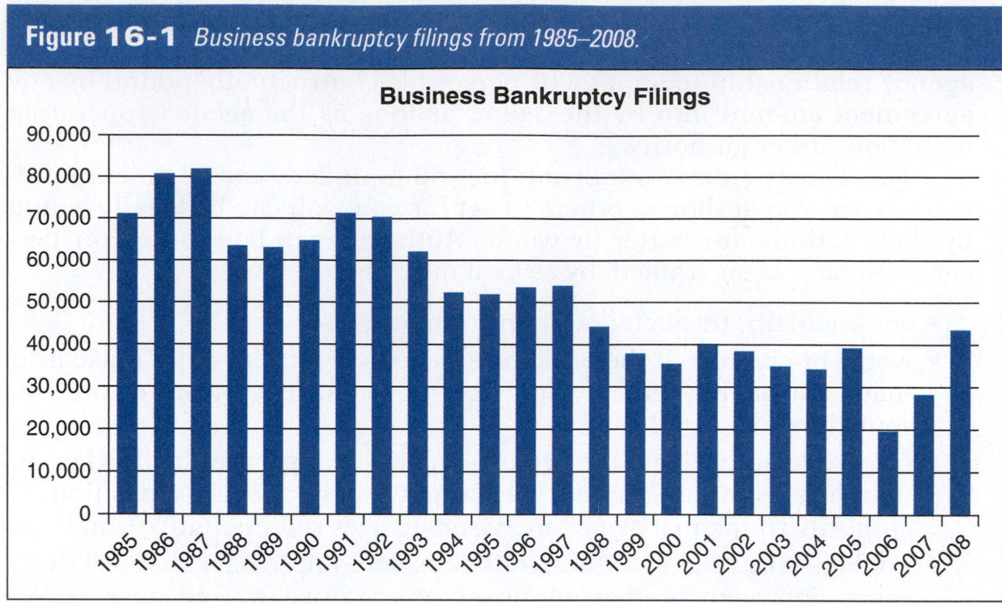

Courtesy of bankruptcydata.com (accessed July 16, 2009).

Chapter 11: Reorganization

This is the form of bankruptcy that can prove to be a lifeline for a company. Businesses can pay off some or all of their debts under court supervision, while continuing to operate. Creditors cannot file legal claims against the company while it creates a reorganization plan and schedules debt repayment, or negotiates settlements on the amounts owed. The bankrupt party, known as the *debtor in possession,* gets 120 days to file a reorganization plan with the bankruptcy court. This plan must detail all debts, all categories or classes of creditors (i.e., secured, provisional, and unsecured), how much each will be paid, and the timing and method of compensation. If the debtor fails to file on time, creditors or any other parties involved may submit a plan. They then must approve or reject the plan.

Chapter 7: Liquidation

When this form of bankruptcy protection is sought by individuals or corporations, they must identify all assets and liabilities, turn the assets over to a trustee (court-appointed or elected by creditors), and allow them to be sold. Creditors receive funds from the proceeds ranging from 0 to 100 percent of their debt claims. Once the funds are paid out, any remaining debts are *discharged* (no longer owed); and the business, if a corporation, is officially dissolved.

It is important to note that debtors cannot avoid the liquidation of assets by transferring ownership to others just ahead of filing for protection. In fact, any transfers of property within the two years prior to filing may be ignored and the assets made a part of the bankruptcy case. Deliberate transfer of assets to avoid debt repayment is a form of fraud, and the entire Chapter 7 bankruptcy petition can be thrown out by the judge, if he or she feels that this has occurred.

On the other side, not all assets are subject to liquidation in a Chapter 7 bankruptcy. The items that are exempt vary by state. Regardless of the asset exemptions, a Chapter 7 bankruptcy filing is financially and emotionally painful, and has long-term impacts on credit.

Chapter 13: Individual Debt Reorganization

This is the consumer version of Chapter 11, which is available to individual debtors with secured debts less than $922,975, or unsecured debts below the sum of $307,675. Chapter 13 must be a voluntary filing and the repayment plan can only be filed by the debtor. The plan may include full or partial payment of debts through installments, taking into consideration the debtor's income expectations, and must be approved by a bankruptcy judge. Repayment typically occurs over a three- to five-year period, and the filer can retain individual property. Because a sole proprietorship is essentially an individual, Chapter 13 is of significance to small business.

The bankruptcy of business partnerships, or of major stockholders for privately held corporations, can have other effects upon businesses and individuals that are beyond the scope of this text. For additional information, consult with appropriate advisory resources.

Protecting Intangible Assets: Intellectual Property

A critical practice for any entrepreneur is to protect his/her ideas, products, inventions, and designs. Federal and state laws are designed to help individuals and organizations protect these kind of assets from abuse, reputational damage, or theft.

Performance Objective 4

Protect your intellectual property.

Trademarks and Service Marks

Whether you are advertising your business with flyers at the local laundromat or through a storefront on the Internet, you will need an easily recognizable logo for your product or business (such as McDonald's "golden arches"). A logo is printed on the business's stationery, business cards, and flyers, and virtually any other company document or product.

As discussed previously, a trademark is any word, phrase, symbol, or design, or combination of words, phrases, symbols, or designs, that identifies and distinguishes the source of the goods (products) of one party from those of others.[4] A **service mark** is the equivalent of a trademark, except that it identifies and distinguishes the source of a service rather than a product.

service mark a design that identifies and distinguishes the source of a service rather than a product.

A company uses a trademark so that people will recognize its product instantly, without having to read the company name or even having to think about it. NutraSweet's red swirl and the Nike swoosh are examples of trademarks most people recognize. Rights to a trademark are reserved exclusively for its owner. To infringe on a trademark is illegal.

Exercise

Perform each of the tasks identified below and record your information on a separate piece of paper.

Carry out a search online for the name you intend to use for your business. What did you find?

Will you still use this name? Why or why not?

How do you plan to protect the name of your business?

[4]U.S. Patent and Trademark Office, at http://www.uspto.gov/go/tac/doc/basic/trade_defin.htm.

Global Impact . . .

Protecting Your Trademark Worldwide

If you plan to do business outside the United States, you will need to make sure your trademark is properly registered and protected. The International Trademark Association (http://www.inta.org) is an excellent resource. It can help you apply for a Community Trade Mark (CTM), which provides trademark protection in the 27 members of the European Union (Austria, Belgium, Bulgaria, the Czech Republic, Cyprus, Denmark, Estonia, Finland, France, Germany, Greece, Hungary, Ireland, Italy, Latvia, Lithuania, Luxembourg, Malta, the Netherlands, Poland, Portugal, Romania, Slovakia, Slovenia, Spain, Sweden, and the United Kingdom). The Office for Harmonization in the Internal Market, based in Spain, administers the CTM.

A trademark or service mark does not have to appear on the U.S. Patent and Trademark Office's Principal Register to be legitimate, but there are advantages to being listed on it:

- a notice to the public of your ownership claim;
- legal presumption of your exclusive right to use the mark as registered;

Figure 16-2 *Map of the EU members.*

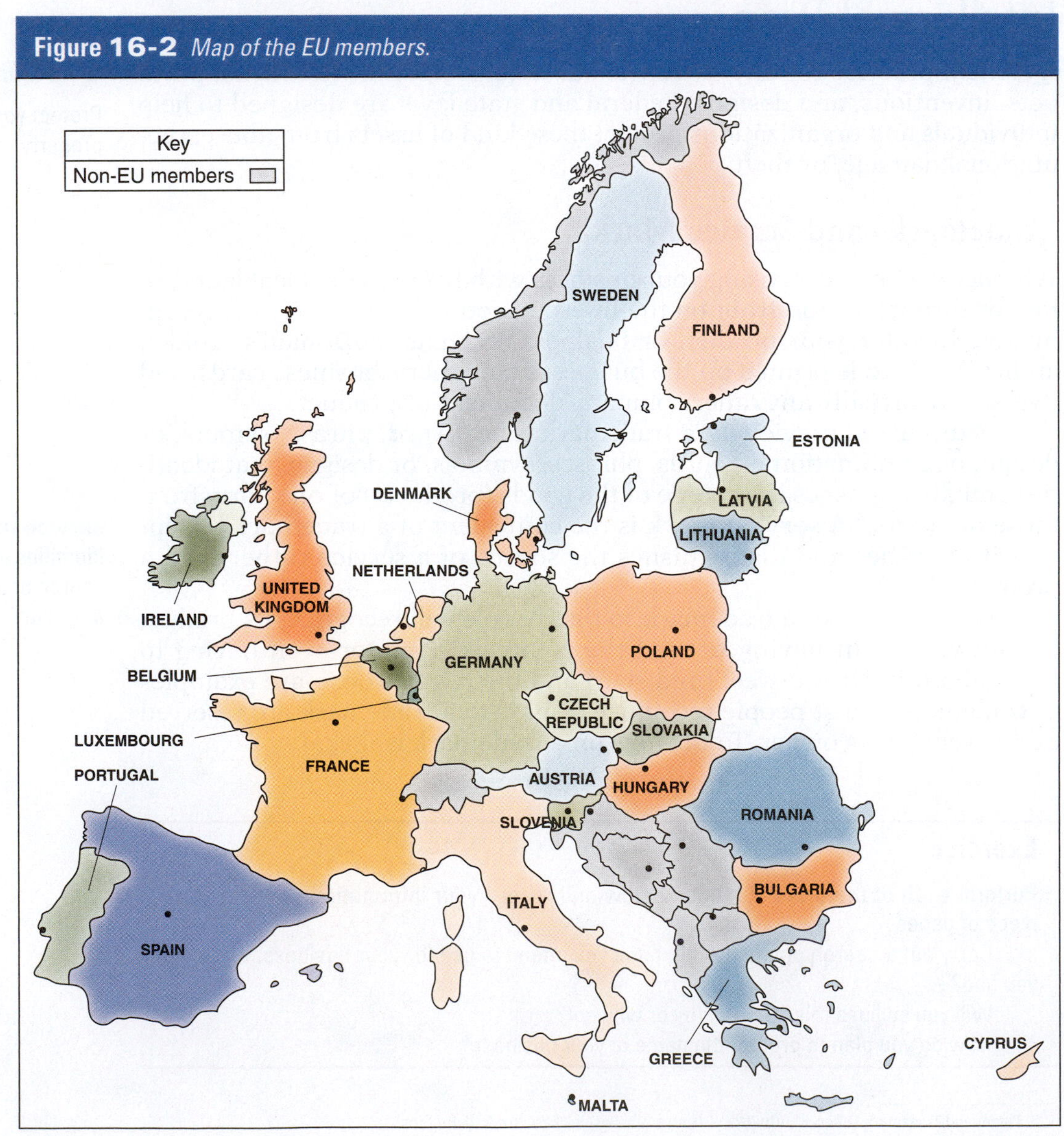

- the ability to bring an action concerning the mark in federal court;
- the use of the U.S. registration to obtain registration of your mark in other countries; and
- the ability to file this mark with the U.S. Customs Service, so that others cannot import foreign goods with your mark on them.[5]

You do not need to file an application with the USPTO to use ™ (trademark) or ℠ (service mark). However, you cannot use ® until it has been officially registered, and then it can only be used for what is listed in the federal registration. To obtain application information, visit the USPTO Web site at http://www.uspto.gov.

Copyright

If you are a songwriter, author, or visual artist, you will be creating works that you might sell. If you do not protect your work, however, someone else can appropriate it. A copyright is the form of legal protection offered under U.S. law to the authors of "original works of authorship," including literary, dramatic, musical, and artistic works.[6] Copyright protection is offered for both unpublished and published works. The owner of a copyright has the sole right to print, reprint, sell and distribute, revise, record, and perform the work under copyright. The copyright protects a work for the life of the author/artist plus 70 years. Only the author or someone assigned rights by the author can claim a copyright.

When a work is created, its copyright is automatically secured. According to the Copyright Office, "A work is 'created' when it is fixed in a copy or phonorecord for the first time." The use of a notice of copyright is not required, but is recommended, and official registration of the copyright has certain advantages. The elements of notice for visually perceptible copies requires:

- the symbol © (the letter c in a circle) and/or the word "copyright," or the abbreviation "copr." and the current year, and
- the name of the owner of the copyright, or an abbreviation by which the name can be recognized, or a generally known alternative designation of the owner.[7]

  Example: *Copyright © 2008 by Janina Joyce*

There are variations for sound recordings. Legal counsel should be sought for any issues that are unclear. To learn how to register a work, visit the U.S. Copyright Office Web site at http://www.copyright.gov.

Electronic Rights

Now that writing, photographs, art, and music can be posted on the Web, entrepreneurs must protect their intellectual property online, as well. The right to reproduce someone's work online are called **electronic rights**.

electronic rights the right to reproduce someone's work online.

Using artwork without permission, even if it is a song or photo or poem posted online, is Internet piracy. President Bill Clinton dealt a blow to Internet piracy in 1998 when he signed the Digital Millennium Copyright Act into law. The act protects copyrighted software, music, and text on the Internet by outlawing the technology used to break copyright-protection devices.

[5]U.S. Patent and Trademark Office.
[6]U.S. Copyright Office, http://www.copyright.gov.
[7]U.S. Copyright Office.

There are certain steps that you should take to protect your electronic rights. Beware of contracts that include the following:

- ***Work-made-for-hire:*** This means you are giving up the rights to your work. Now the buyer can use it anywhere without paying anything beyond the original negotiated fee.
- ***All rights:*** This means you are handing over all rights to your work to the buyer.

Here are some strategies for protecting your electronic rights.[8]

- Get the buyer to define exactly what is included in electronic rights. Does it include online publication, CD-ROMs, or anything else?
- Put a limit on how long the buyer can have the electronic rights—one year, for instance.
- Ask for an additional fee for each additional set of rights. A good rule of thumb would be to ask for 15 percent of the original fee every time your work is used somewhere electronically. If you sell a drawing to a newspaper for $1000, you could ask for $150 if the paper wants to use it on its Web site.

Patents

patent an exclusive right, granted by the government, to produce, use, and sell an invention or process.

If you have invented a product or process that you want to turn into a business, or to license, you may want to obtain a **patent**, which is an exclusive right granted by the government to produce, use, and sell an invention or process. The term of a patent is generally 20 years from its date of filing. A patent grants "the right to exclude others from making, using, offering for sale or selling" the invention in the United States or bringing it into the country via import.[9] Patents come in three forms: *utility* (process or improvement), *design*, and *plant* (varieties of vegetation). A patent cannot be granted unless it is for something that is "useful, novel, and nonobvious."

[8]Adapted from the *National Writers Union Guide to Negotiating Electronic Rights.* For more information, see http://www.nwu.org.
[9]U.S. Patent and Trademark Office, http://www.uspto.gov.

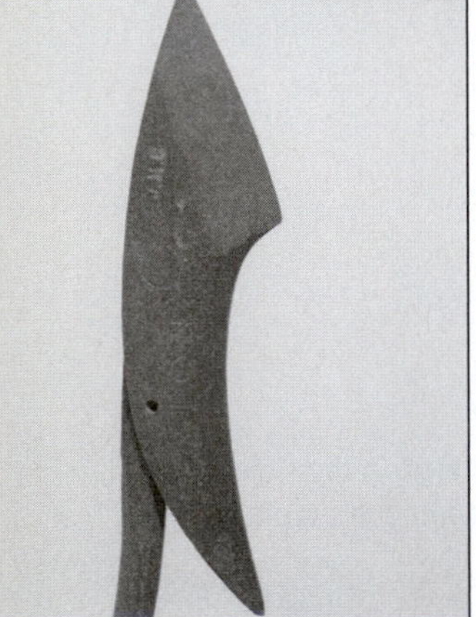

Step into the Shoes...

Louis Temple Invents the Toggle Harpoon and Dies Poor

Obtaining a patent can mean the difference between earning millions and living in poverty, as the case of Louis Temple illustrates. Temple was an African American living in New Bedford, Massachusetts, in the first half of the nineteenth century. In those days, whales were hunted for the rich oil derived from their blubber (fat). The oil was used for lighting lamps and making candles. New Bedford was the capital of the whaling industry.

Whales were hunted with spears called *harpoons.* Temple, a blacksmith, invented a "toggle" harpoon, which had a moveable head that prevented the whale from slipping free. Temple gave prototypes of the harpoon to several New Bedford ship captains to try on their whale-hunting voyages.

Whaling voyages took about two years. By the time the ships returned and reported the harpoon's great success, Temple's invention had become "public domain." He had made no attempt to secure a patent during this time, and other blacksmiths in the town were making their own versions of the harpoon. Although he made some money and opened a larger shop, it was nothing like the fortune he would have earned if he had patented his invention. Temple was injured in a fall at the age of 54 and died soon afterward. His family had to sell everything they owned to pay his debts. If his toggle harpoon had been patented, Temple and his family might have become extremely wealthy. How will you protect *your* intellectual property so you can profit from it?

A patent cannot be obtained for a mere idea or suggestion. An invention should be fully developed and actually viable before you can seek patent protection. You will have to prepare detailed drawings showing exactly how it works. If an invention is put into use by the inventor, or discussed publicly for more than one year without obtaining a patent, the invention is considered to be in the **public domain**, which means that a patent will no longer be granted; anyone may use or make it without payment. It is important that you not divulge a proprietary invention or concept in meetings or at events without seeking at least preliminary protection.

public domain property rights available to the public rather than held by an individual.

You do not need to obtain a patent unless you:

- have invented a product that you intend to market yourself or sell to a manufacturer, or
- believe that someone else could successfully sell your invention by copying it.

The average patent takes at least two years to obtain. A patent search has to be undertaken to ensure that the idea is new. Getting a patent is a complex legal process. Before starting it, consult with a registered patent agent or an attorney.

The process of obtaining a patent is lengthy, time-consuming, and costly. There are many legitimate sources of assistance, including inventors' groups sponsored by state economic development offices, small business development centers, and community development venture capital groups. There are also unscrupulous companies and individuals that promise phenomenal success in commercializing ideas at prices that are inappropriate. Be careful to select reputable advisors, including patent attorneys. To learn more about patents, visit the U.S. Patent and Trademark Office Web site at http://www.uspto.gov.

Protecting Tangible Assets: Risk Management

Performance Objective 5

Protect your tangible assets and manage risk.

In addition to protecting your intellectual property, you should manage risk by protecting your physical property. Imagine if you lost your business to a fire or flood, and did not have the insurance to rebuild and restock. Or, think about an employee being injured and having no insurance for medical care. Risk management goes far beyond insurance. However, understanding business insurance is a good start.

Insurance Protects Your Business from Disaster

Insurance is a system of protection for payment provided by insurance companies to reimburse people or businesses whose property or wealth has been damaged or destroyed. There are many kinds of insurance and almost anything can be insured.

insurance a system of protection for payment provided by insurance companies to protect individuals and organizations from having property or wealth damaged or destroyed.

If you owned a restaurant, for example, one type of insurance you would need would be fire insurance. Your insurance agent would help you calculate how much money it would take to rebuild the restaurant in case of fire, and replace everything in it. If you borrowed money from a bank to buy equipment for the restaurant, the bank would require you to carry insurance (with the bank as the named insured) to cover the loan in case the equipment was destroyed.

Assume that rebuilding your restaurant would cost \$150,000. You would need an insurance policy that would guarantee you \$150,000 in

premium the cost of insurance.

case of fire. You might pay $100 per month for this insurance. This monthly cost of insurance coverage is called a **premium**.

As long as you pay the premiums on your fire insurance policy, you will not have to worry about losing your restaurant to a fire. If it does burn down, your insurance company will pay you to rebuild and restart the business. If you carry business interruption insurance, you may get compensation for lost revenue. Insurance helps to prevent random events from destroying you financially.

Basic Coverage for Small Business

You will not necessarily need insurance if you are selling ties on the street or candy at school, but the moment you move your business into a building, or have concerns about people being injured while buying or using your product, you will need it.

deductible the amount of loss or damage a policyholder covers before the insurer pays on a claim.

A **deductible** is the amount of loss or damage you agree to cover before the insurance pays on a claim. In the restaurant example, the owner might feel confident that he or she could pay $5000 for damages from a fire. The insurance company would then pay the remaining $145,000. With this higher deductible, the premium would be lower, perhaps $90 per month. The policyholder pays a lower premium in exchange for a higher deductible. When buying insurance, choose the policy with the highest deductible you can afford to cover. This will give you the lowest possible premium.

Lower deductible = *Higher premium*

Higher deductible = *Lower premium*

Although state laws vary, most require business owners who have people working for them to carry:

- ***Workers' Compensation Insurance.*** Compensates employees for loss of income and medical expenses due to job-related injuries.
- ***Disability Insurance.*** Compensates employees for loss of income due to a disabling injury or illness.

Insurance protects your business from disasters like this fire, being fought by firefighters in Virginia. (Joe Sohm/Chromosohm, The Stock Connection)

If you have an automobile or truck that is owned or leased by the business, you must carry the following:

- ***Commercial Fleet Insurance*** covers your liability for personal injuries in an accident, damages to any vehicle involved, and injuries to others.

Other useful types of insurance are:

- ***Property Insurance*** provides protection against risks to property, such as theft, fire, or weather damage, as specified in the policy. There are certain types of "disaster" insurance, such as flood and earthquake, that also fall under this category.
- ***Liability Insurance*** covers the cost of injuries to a customer or damage to property on a business's premises—for example, a customer slipping and falling in your store.
- ***Product Liability Insurance*** covers the risk of your product harming someone. It is a subset of liability insurance. For example, a caterer may need to be concerned about food-poisoning claims.
- ***Business Income Insurance.*** This is also known as "business interruption" insurance and is the equivalent of disability insurance for your business. It provides coverage if you have a temporary shut-down or a significant limitation on your business. Property insurance may replace your facilities and equipment, but it will not compensate for lost business revenue the way this form of insurance does.
- ***Errors and Omissions Insurance.*** This is designed to cover you in the event that you have overlooked something and a customer is harmed. It is particularly valuable for service businesses.
- ***Key Person Life Insurance*** covers the life of the owner(s) or other top employees, to assist in the transition and costs of recruitment in the case of death.

Still other types of insurance are available that can be tailored to the needs and resources of your business. When you are ready to take this step, ask other businesspeople to refer you to a good insurance agent. Be certain to shop for the best overall value.

How Insurance Companies Make Money

By now you may be wondering, "How can an insurance company afford to pay $150,000 to a restaurant owner whose business has burned down, if that individual has only been paying the insurance company $100 a month?

Entrepreneurial Wisdom . . .

Lying about the Risks of Your Product Is Fraud

Failure to inform a customer of potential danger from your product or service, or misrepresenting it in any way for commercial benefit, is a type of fraud. If a customer proves that you knew your product or service was dangerous, but you sold it anyway, you could be directed by a court to pay damages. Your insurance company will not be expected to pay for costs in the case of fraud.

The entrepreneur has a moral duty to inform customers of possible danger. It is best not to sell a product or service that could cause harm when in normal use. Even if you are selling something as "safe" as neckties, make sure they are not made of highly flammable material!

Before you decide to sell a product or offer a service, try to imagine how it might possibly cause injury to someone. If you think it might harm a customer when used according to directions, do not sell it.

The answer is that insurance companies employ experts, known as actuaries, who calculate the odds of a particular event actually happening. A company that specializes in fire insurance will have information about fires in restaurants going back many years. Analysts at the company study this information and determine how often fires tend to occur, and the value of what is destroyed. Even if some fires do take place, the cost of insurance paid out to one policyholder has been covered by the premiums paid by many others.

Protect Your Computer and Data

Data are critical to any business. Important business information on your computer might include mailing lists, invoices, letters, and financial records. The risk of the loss of this information is a very real one that you will need to address proactively. Because your computer is an electronic device, you should protect it from the three primary occurrences that can easily wipe out your data:

1. ***Power Surges or Outages:*** A power blackout can destroy data. You can purchase an "uninterruptible power supply" (UPS) that will keep your computer running for a certain amount of time when the power goes out. A power surge can damage your computer as well as destroy the data stored on it. Plug all your computer equipment into a multi-outlet surge protector, which can be bought at any hardware store. Or, better yet, invest in a surge protector UPS unit for each computer.
2. ***Computer Viruses:*** Viruses are malicious computer software that can attach themselves to your software or files and ruin them. Protect your computer with virus-protection software like Norton, or McAfee. Remember to set the software to automatically scan your computer frequently.
3. ***Disk Failure:*** Hard drives can crash (fail), destroying valuable data. To prevent this, save everything you do to back-up media, such as external drives, CDs, or jump drives. Periodically back up your entire drive and store it in another location.

Disaster Recovery Plans

What will you do in case of fire, or other catastrophe, that will make carrying on your business difficult or impossible? Insurance policies may cover many things, but they do not ensure smooth business operations in times of disaster. Whether you operate a small, home-based business or a large, multinational enterprise, you should have a disaster-recovery plan appropriate to the scale and complexity of your organization. Be sure to write it down and share it with your employees. Practice it once or twice a year with the whole team; the investment of time and money is worthwhile. Include critical information that team members keep securely off-site. Some issues to address are:

- ***Communications:*** Who will contact each person in the company, and critical vendors and customers? How will they reach them? Include names, titles, telephone numbers, e-mail addresses, and street addresses. Update the contact information regularly. Also, know what the message will be.
- ***Base of Operations:*** Where will people go if the normal place of business is inaccessible? This could be someone's home, another company site, or another location entirely.
- ***Priority Activities:*** Which business activities are most essential/time-sensitive? Which activities could be postponed? What is the time frame for reactivation?
- ***Return to Facilities:*** Define a process for regrouping and planning, and designate a leader.

The above is a partial and hypothetical list for a disaster recovery plan. Whereas it may seem to be more than is needed, a straightforward plan put in place before disaster strikes can make the difference between business failure and survival.

Licenses, Permits, and Certificates

There is more to creating a legal business than naming and registering it. Once registered, you will need to comply with any federal, state, and local regulations that apply to your business. You should research these regulations before deciding to start your business because they may affect what you can do, how you can do it, where you can operate, and when. Such regulations can completely change your potential business operations.

Zoning regulations often prohibit certain types of businesses from operating in specified areas. There may be other regulations, too, such as restrictions on obtaining a liquor license for a bar or restaurant. If your business involves food, you will need to comply with safety and health regulations, conduct food safety training, and obtain certain permissions and certificates.

Contact local, county, and state government offices, or your chamber of commerce, to find out which licenses and permits are necessary.

- **Permit** An official document that gives you the right to engage in a specific activity, such as holding an outdoor concert.
- **License** An official document that gives you the right to engage in an activity for as long as the license is valid. A driver's license, until it expires, gives you the right to operate a motor vehicle. A child-care license permits you to operate a particular size and type of child-care facility.
- **Certificate** Official document that verifies something. A certificate of occupancy proves that a building is safe and ready for use.

permit an official document that gives a party the right to put on a specific event.

license an official document that grants the right to engage in an activity for a specified period of time.

certificate an official document that verifies something.

If you hire people to work for you, there will be federal, state, and local regulations regarding employees that will come into effect.

Chapter Summary

Now that you have studied this chapter, you can do the following:

1. Choose a legal structure for your business.
   - A sole proprietorship is owned by one person who also may be the sole employee.
   - A partnership consists of two or more owners who make the decisions for the business together and share the profits and losses.
   - A corporation is a legal entity composed of stockholders under a common name.
   - A Subchapter S corporation limits the number of stockholders to 75. It offers most of the limited liability protection of the C corporation, but Subchapter S corporate income is only taxed once—as the personal income of the owners.
   - A nonprofit (or not-for-profit) corporation is set up with a specific mission to improve society. Churches, museums, charitable foundations, and trade associations are examples of nonprofit corporations. Nonprofit corporations are tax-exempt.
   - A limited liability company (LLC) combines the best features of partnerships and corporations and is an excellent choice for many small businesses.
2. Understand the importance of contracts.
   - A contract is a formal agreement between two or more parties.
   - The relationships between the links in a production-distribution chain are defined by contracts.
   - Never sign a contract without having an attorney examine it.
   - Never sign a contract that you have not read yourself from top to bottom.
   - A successful contract should:
     - Avoid misunderstanding
     - Assure work
     - Assure payment
     - Avoid liability
3. Recognize key components of commercial law.
   - The Uniform Commercial Code is a collection of business laws adopted by most states that covers a broad spectrum of transactions.
   - The law of agency addresses principal-agent relationships.
   - The bankruptcy code concerns the inability or impaired ability to pay debts as they come due.
4. Protect your intellectual property.
   - Your ideas and creations are your intellectual property.
   - Trademarks and service marks protect your brand identity.
   - Copyrights protect works of authorship.
   - Patents protect invented products and processes.
5. Protect your tangible assets and manage risk.
   - Insurance protects people and businesses from the risk of having property or wealth stolen, lost, or destroyed.

- When buying insurance, choose the policy with the highest deductible you can afford. This will give you the lowest possible premium.
- Consider the normal and customary types of business insurance:
  - workers' compensation,
  - disability,
  - commercial fleet,
  - property,
  - liability,
  - business income,
  - errors and omissions, and
  - life.
- Create and practice a disaster recovery plan.

Key Terms

arbitration
bankruptcy
boilerplate language
breach of contract
certificate
contingency
contract
corporation
deductible
electronic rights
insurance
letter of agreement
license
limited partnership
notary
partnership
patent
permit
premium
public domain
service mark
signatory
small claims court
sole proprietorship
statute of limitations

Entrepreneurship Portfolio

Critical Thinking Exercises

1. What can happen to an entrepreneur who is personally liable for the business? How can an entrepreneur protect herself from personal liability? Say your friend wants to start a business making custom skateboards. Write a memo to your friend, explaining the risks involved and suggestions for limiting liability.
2. With a partner, make a list of the technological tools each of you could personally access. Brainstorm how you might combine your resources to create a successful business. Describe in detail how the partnership would work. For example, would the partner contributing more technology have a larger share of the business, or would profits and expenses be split equally? Draw up a partnership agreement that specifies each partner's duties and how much money and time each will invest.
3. Which legal structure will you choose for your business?
   Sole proprietorship ______________
   Partnership ______________

Limited partnership ______________
C corporation ______________
Subchapter S corporation ______________
Limited liability company (LLC) ______________
Nonprofit corporation ______________

a. Why did you choose this structure?
b. Who will the partners or stockholders for your company be?
c. Describe the steps you will take to register your business.

4. If your business is incorporated, what percentage of your company is owned by one share of stock? Is your corporation's stock publicly or privately held?
5. Use computer software to create a logo for your business. Do you intend to trademark your logo? Explain.
6. Describe any intellectual property you are developing (without improperly disclosing a potential patent).
7. How do you plan to protect your intellectual property? Explain why it would qualify for protection.
8. Give an example of a business in your community that you think may be infringing on someone else's intellectual property.
9. What types of insurance will your business need and why? What is the highest deductible you feel you can afford? Pick one type of insurance you want to have for your business and find a company online that sells it. List the premium, deductible, and payout.

Key Concept Questions

1. What is the most important contract you will need to run your business? Describe any additional contracts you have or plan to secure.
2. Negotiate and write a letter of agreement between you and a fellow student. You could agree to become business partners, for example, or to supply a product or service for the other student's business.
3. Find a lawyer who might be willing to help you with your business. Ask your parents/guardians who are in business, or store owners in your community for referrals. The Small Business Administration or Community Legal Aid Society sometimes offers free or low-cost legal services to entrepreneurs.
4. What is the purpose of having a form notarized?
5. What does your signature at the bottom of a contract mean in a court of law? What two things should you do before signing a contract?
6. Suki is buying an old van from her brother to start her flower-basket delivery service. She planned to buy auto insurance that would pay all her expenses in case she ever got into an accident. She finds that such insurance will cost $3000 per year, which, according to her business-plan projections, is more than she can afford. What do you think Suki should do?
7. Some businesses do sell products and services that can injure customers. List three examples and explain how these companies probably use insurance.

Application Exercise

Assume you and a friend have decided to produce and sell recordings of your original songs. What legal structure do you think would work best? Explain. What type of intellectual property protection should you seek?

What sort of contracts would you need? What types of insurance would be important?

Exploring Your Community

1. For the business you plan to start, research licensing regulations in your area and describe how they will affect your operation.
   a. Have you applied for a sales tax ID number?
   b. What are the zoning laws in your location? Does your business comply?
2. What nonprofit business could you start in your community? Answer the following questions to describe it:
   a. What is the name of your nonprofit?
   b. What problem(s) are you trying to solve?
   c. Describe the mission of your organization.
   d. Describe the programs and services you plan to create.
   e. How will your organization achieve the changes you intend to bring about?
   f. What is the unit of change (per person, animal, house, etc.)?
   g. How will you measure these changes?
   h. Who are your competitors?
   i. How much will it cost to deliver one unit of service?
   j. What sources of funding will you seek?
3. Interview an entrepreneur about insurance policies. Ask how he or she decided what kind of insurance to carry and whether to have high or low deductibles. Present a report on your entrepreneur's insurance plan to the class.

Case Study | How to Organize

Sam Jones, Mary Adams, and Larry Brown have been talking about starting their own business for several years. Sam is an electronics repairman, Mary is a partner in a large law firm, and Larry is an excellent salesperson. It will cost $100,000 to start this business. Sam has no money, Mary has $60,000, and Larry has $40,000. Sam has contacts with three organizations that appear willing to buy services from the new company for a minimum of two years, each at about $50,000 annually. The service to be provided is new to the waste disposal field and was developed by Larry and Sam over the previous three years. Mary has been their advisor on legal and design-protection issues, and she has not charged any fees with respect to the development of the concept or the business. Because the service is new, there is some concern about the amount of liability insurance that would be necessary. One of the primary tasks of the new company will be to build a service center, which will require financing a building, probably through a bank loan. Sam and Mary have excellent credit ratings, but Larry has accumulated some credit problems relating to a failed housing-development venture four years earlier. Several of Sam and Larry's colleagues have been following the plans for the new waste disposal service and have expressed an interest in investing some money.

Case Study Analysis

1. What information about forms of organization does the group need?
2. What form of organization would you recommend to the group and why?

Case Study | Magnetic Poetry

Dave Kapell's Magnetic Poetry, Inc., is a successful Minnesota-based business that designs and markets theme-based poetry kits, each containing 470 words on magnetic strips that people typically affix to their refrigerators and rearrange creatively—plus a multitude of related products. From 1993 through 2009, Magnetic Poetry sold over 3 million kits. But, almost 20 years ago, Kapell was a struggling songwriter who tried to overcome writer's block by cutting out words from newspapers and magazines and arranging them in random order for inspiration. Dave had allergies and would often sneeze, which sent the words of the lyrics flying. Then he had the idea of gluing the words on magnets and using a cookie tray as a sheet of paper.

When Dave's friends came over, they would play with the word magnets, which were on the refrigerator by this time. In 1993, a friend suggested that he try to sell his magnets as word sets at a local crafts fair. Kapell got to work and laboriously produced a hundred magnetic word kits, using a typewriter, a magnet sheet, laminate coating, and scissors. Much to his surprise, all the kits sold within three hours. He knew that he was on to something.

Kapell realized that he couldn't tackle the manufacturing of the word kits on his own and decided to hire friends to help him. For $10 an hour, along with free pizza and beer, they created several hundred new kits. According to Kapell, "That was the start of about 3 years of absolute cranking, keeping up with demand."[10]

As word continued to spread about his product, he realized that he needed to upgrade his manufacturing process. He and his friends were losing sleep by staying up all night fulfilling orders. Kapell decided to invest $5000 in sales revenue to hire a local graphic-design firm to produce 1000 prototype kits. He continued to use this same supplier, but became increasingly frustrated when his orders were placed at the end of the list whenever bigger clients wanted their products made.

Kapell realized that he needed to have more control over his manufacturing. He decided to start a second business, separate from Magnetic Poetry, called U.S. Magnetix, which was solely dedicated to printing and producing flexible magnetic products. Kapell put up $100,000 from his cash flow to cover the basic equipment costs for launching U.S. Magnetix. This initial investment bought him a 40-percent stake in the business. He now had the means of production in place to turn around orders for magnetic word kits in three days. Magnetic Poetry was ready to go to the next level.

During the start-up phase of his business, Dave chose to operate Magnetic Poetry as a sole proprietorship. Initially, this structure worked well. All he had to do to make his business official was go down to the local county courthouse and file a DBA form and he was up and running. Yet, as his company grew, Dave's lawyer advised him to register his business as a Subchapter S corporation. Under this legal structure, Dave would not be personally liable in the event that Magnetic Poetry was sued or went bankrupt.

The next problem Kapell needed to solve was how best to distribute his product. He had developed an ingenious, one-of-a-kind idea and had been successful in selling it locally. But how

[10]Alyson Ward, "Still Drawn to the Tiles: Magnetic Poetry Strong after 10 Years on Market," *Contra Costa Times*, September 22, 2003.

could he increase his distribution network? He began to investigate how he could sell Magnetic Poetry kits wholesale. Kapell approached Pam Jones, who managed a museum gift shop in Minneapolis. She liked Kapell's poetry kits but was unimpressed with his no-frills cardboard packaging. So Kapell got to work and repackaged the kits in clear-plastic boxes. Jones liked what she saw and bought several dozen kits at a wholesale price of $9.50 each. Within a day, she had sold a dozen kits at $20 retail.

In 1996, Magnetic Poetry took a major leap forward with its distribution when it made a deal with Barnes & Noble, the national book retailer. In celebration of National Poetry Month, Barnes & Noble announced that it would sell Magnetic Poetry kits at all of its retail outlets in the United States. Up until this point, Kapell had primarily been distributing his product to independent bookstores and specialty gift shops. The Barnes & Noble deal connected Kapell's company to a nationwide distribution channel. Soon customers in such locations as Texas and New Mexico were snapping up Magnetic Poetry kits. Then Kapell started producing kits in foreign languages. His distribution network now includes international retailers in France, Spain, Germany, and Italy.

Over the last 15 years, Magnetic Poetry has grown from a local business that was essentially started by accident into a multimillion-dollar enterprise with worldwide reach. Kapell's company has been credited with inspiring scores of people to find their inner poet or overcome writer's block.

In 2001, Kapell decided to sell the 40-percent stake in his second company, U.S. Magnetix, so that he could fully focus his energies on developing new products and marketing ideas for Magnetic Poetry. Whereas he no longer owns the manufacturing arm of his business, he still serves as one of U.S. Magnetix's biggest customers, responsible for 15 percent of its annual revenue. Kapell believes that Magnetic Poetry is poised for continued growth. Whereas his youthful dream was to become the next David Bowie, Kapell found his niche as an entrepreneur.

Case Study Analysis

1. Magnetic Poetry kits are currently sold in bookstores, specialty gift shops, and online. Brainstorm three additional distribution outlets for this product.
2. Do you think it was a good idea for Kapell to sell his 40-percent ownership of U.S. Magnetix? What are some things he will need to consider now that he no longer has an ownership stake in the manufacturing aspect of his business?
3. As Magnetic Poetry evolved from a startup into a thriving business, Dave made the decision to change his legal structure from a sole proprietorship into a Subchapter S corporation. What are the advantages and disadvantages of each of these forms? Why do you think that Dave's advisors encouraged him to change his legal structure?
4. Go online and visit Magnetic Poetry's Web site at http://www.magneticpoetry.com. What other products has this company developed? How do these products connect to Kapell's original concept?
5. Assume the following about Magnetic Poetry's cost structure: The wholesale price for one Original Magnetic Poetry Kit is $9.50. The retail price is $20. It costs the company as follows:

   $2.50 to manufacture one Original Magnetic Poetry Kit,

   $0.50 to package it,

   $0.50 for shipping and handling, and

   $1.00 of variable costs per kit

   a. Calculate the contribution margin.

   b. Assume that Magnetic Poetry has monthly fixed costs of $20,000. How many kits would the company need to sell in order to break even?

   c. Calculate the markup percentage for the following:
      - Manufacturer ➔ Retailer
      - Retailer ➔ Consumer

Case Sources

Magnetic Poetry Web site, http://www.magneticpoetry.com. Paul Levy, "Magnetic Poetry Proves Attractive," *Minneapolis–St. Paul Star Tribune*, December 28, 2001.

Tim Gihring (Associated Press), "Poetry to the People: Mantra of Magnetic Poetry Kit Maker," *South Coast Today.com* (*The Standard Times*), http://www.southcoasttoday.com (accessed May 20, 1996).

Monte Hanson, "A Magnetic Partnership," *Finance and Commerce,* at http://www.finance-commerce.com/recent_articles/011229.htm (accessed December 29, 2001).

Alyson Ward, "Still Drawn to the Tiles: Magnetic Poetry Strong after 10 Years on Market." Posted on September 22, 2003: Knight Ridder Newspapers (http://www.contracostatimes.com/mld/cctimes/6831510.htm?1c).

Chapter 17

OPERATING FOR SUCCESS

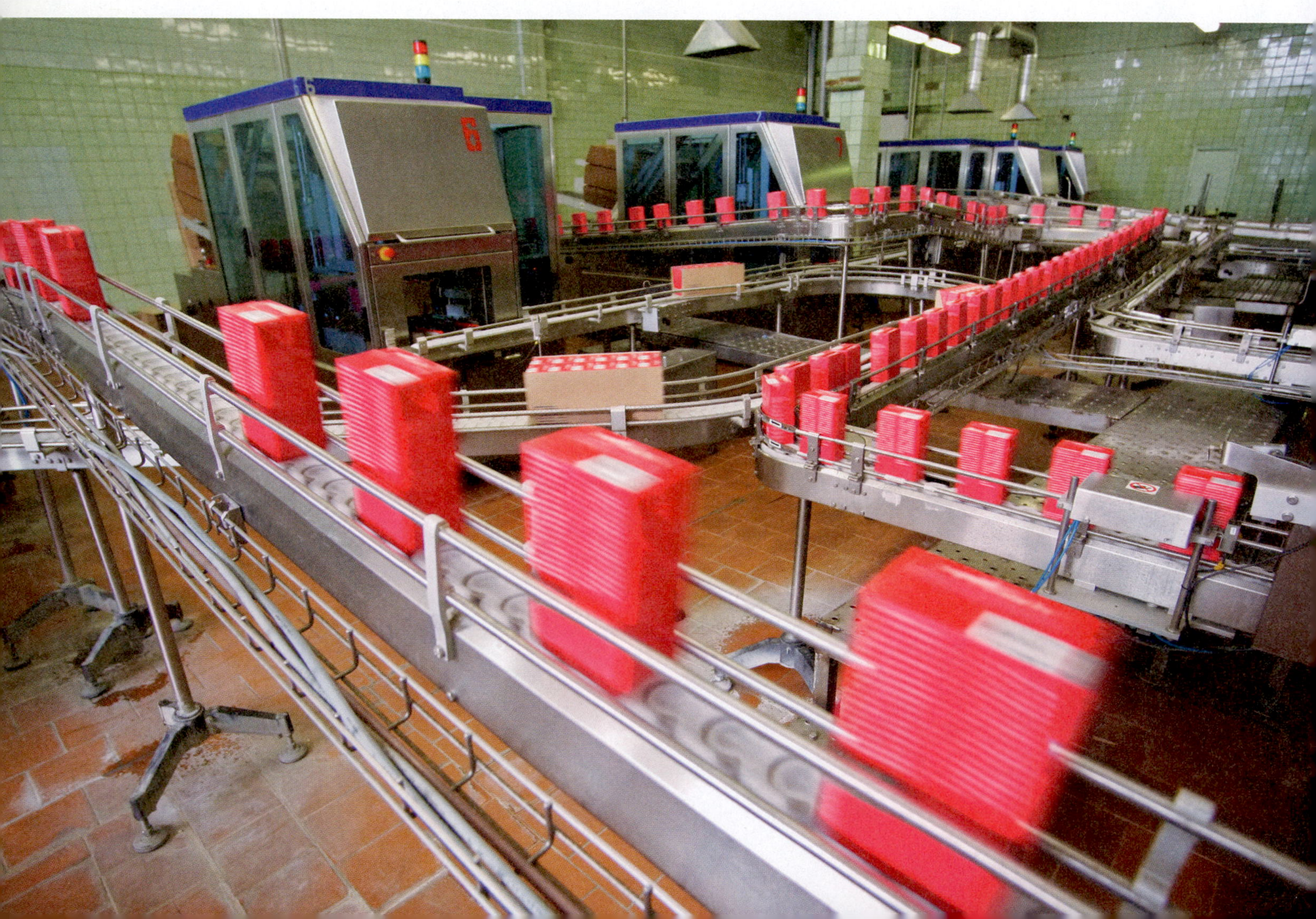

"Excellent firms don't believe in excellence—only in constant improvement and constant change."

—Tom Peters, author and management consultant

Cramer Products, Inc., was founded in Kansas in 1918 by Charles Cramer, a pharmacist. Cramer had created a liniment to treat his own sprained ankle several years earlier. The company was the first devoted to helping athletes prevent injuries and return to action more quickly if hurt.[1] Cramer Products sold primarily to interscholastic sports teams and was an industry leader for over a half a century. That changed in the early 1980s, when athletic programs were disappearing, new products appearing, and competition growing.

Cramer decided on a retail strategy to replace its lost revenues. In 1990, management signed super athlete Bo Jackson to a joint venture for a new brand, called Bo Med, and targeted it to people who engaged in recreational athletics. The line debuted in October. In January, after having been chosen for both the Major League Baseball All-Star Team and the National Football League's Pro Bowl, Jackson suffered an injury that ended his football career. Although he continued playing baseball, his star power suffered.

The Bo Med venture was a failure, and Cramer Products was left deeply in debt with a great deal of unsaleable inventory. The company's position in its primary market was under assault, its viability as a retailer was damaged, and its management team was demoralized.

Cramer Products' president resigned and was replaced by Thomas Rogge. The new president introduced a style that encouraged a free exchange of ideas. He reorganized the management team and gave individual managers more authority. Cramer liquidated the Bo Med line, salvaging as much of the product as possible for repackaging under the Cramer label, and selling the rest to a distressed-inventory merchant.

To rebuild the core business, Rogge broadened the audience from coaches and trainers to include school nurses and physical therapists, and he set up a team to develop new products. He put out a new retail line, using the Cramer name. Packaging of both the retail and interscholastic products was consolidated into one format, creating a single inventory.

More than 60 new products were added. In 1994, new products accounted for 12 percent of sales. Rogge reexamined all operational departments; cut the workforce by 25 percent, to 65; and assigned tasks to underused employees, improving productivity.

After two years of decline, sales increased 8 percent in 1993 and 12 percent in 1994. Profits set records. Retail growth has improved steadily ever since: four major sporting goods retailers with more than 200 outlets added the Cramer line in 1994 alone.[2] Cramer Products, like so many of the athletes it has helped, recovered from its injuries. Many years later, Cramer is still going strong.

Performance Objectives

1. Understand the significance of *operations* in a business.
2. Develop a production-distribution chain for your business.
3. Manage suppliers and inventory.
4. Explore the idea-to-product process.
5. Ensure product quality.
6. Use technology to benefit your business.

[1]Excerpted from Cramer Products: Treating an Injured Company. *Insights and Inspiration: How Businesses Succeed: the 1995 Blue Chip Enterprise Initiative*. Published by *Nation's Business* magazine on behalf of Connecticut Mutual Life Insurance Company and the U.S. Chamber of Commerce, in association with the Blue Chip Enterprise Initiative, 1995, p. 47.
[2]Available at http://www.cramersportsmed.com.

Operations Permit Businesses to Deliver on Their Promises

Performance Objective 1
Understand the significance of *operations* in business.

operations a set of actions that produce goods and services.

In order for a company to be successful, it must deliver on its promises to customers. Marketing sets the expectations and makes the promises. Finance and accounting ensure that the financial resources are available to produce the promised products and services. Legal structures and staff are in place to support success. Ultimately, the company must deliver the product or service to the customer as expected, or better. **Operations** is the set of actions that produce goods and services, and operational efficiency is critical to business success.

What constitutes operations and the precise steps involved in carrying them out will depend on the nature of your industry and the specific business. As discussed previously, a manufacturing business is one that makes a tangible product and, generally, does not sell goods directly to consumers. It typically sells large quantities of product to wholesalers. A wholesale business sells smaller quantities to retailers, from warehouses. A retail business typically sells single items directly to consumers; they operate stores (physical and virtual) that are open to the public. The fourth type of business is service. A service business provides intangible benefits such as time, skills, or expertise in exchange for a fee. Your business may fit neatly into this construct or it may be a combination. For example, if you produce jewelry and sell it online and at fairs, you are both manufacturer and retailer. In any case, there is the process of converting inputs to outputs. See **Figure 17-1** for an illustration of this process.

Regardless of what route your business takes, it is important to understand the process of operations. The details of operating all the various kinds of businesses are far too extensive to include here, and are described in publications that pertain to operating a retail store, creating an online business, becoming a wholesale distributor, and so forth. In this chapter, you will learn about operations from the manufacturing perspective: securing suppliers, assuring quality, and delivering the product.

The Production-Distribution Chain

The consumer is the final link in a chain that extends from the manufacturer through the wholesaler and retailer. When a consumer buys a pair of athletic shoes in a sporting goods store, for example, the chain would be

1. the manufacturer produces a great quantity of a style of athletic shoe,
2. the wholesaler buys a large number of these shoes from the manufacturer,

Figure 17-1 *Converting inputs to outputs.*

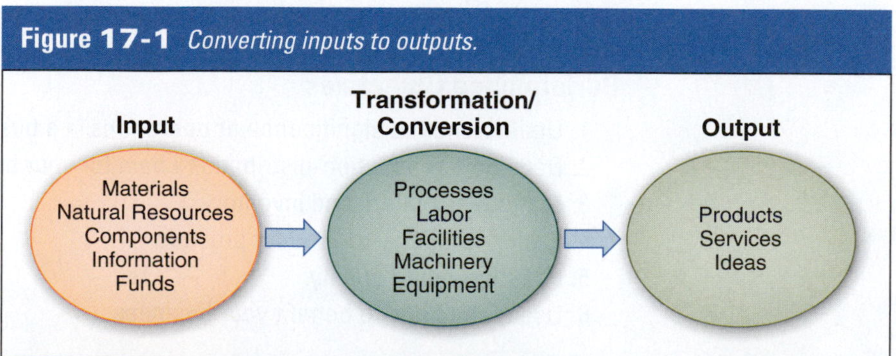

Source: Adapted from Jae K. Shim and Joel G. Siegel, *Operations Management* (Hauppauge, N.Y.: Barron's Educational Series, Inc., 1999), p. 2.

Figure 17-2 *Production-distribution chain variations.*

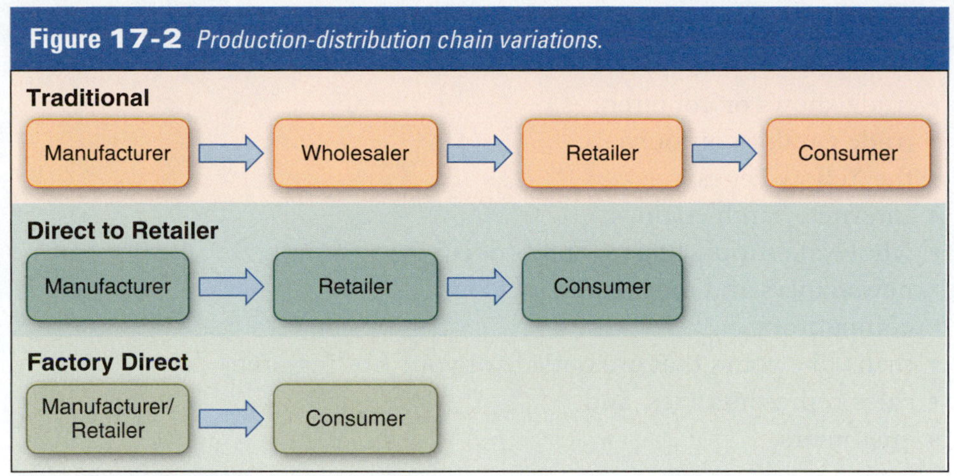

3. the retailer buys a much smaller number of these shoes to stock a store, and
4. the consumer walks into the retailer's store and buys one pair of shoes.

At every link in the chain, there are suppliers and customers. For the manufacturer, the suppliers are those who sell the components and raw materials that are needed for production, and the customers are the wholesalers. For the wholesaler, the suppliers are the manufacturers and the customers are the retailers or, as in the case of a plumbing wholesaler, the contractors that provide a service using the wholesaler's goods. For the retailer, the suppliers are the wholesalers and the customers are the public—consumers. Consumers are the final customers. Some variations on this chain appear in **Figure 17-2**.

Performance Objective 2

Develop a production-distribution chain for your business.

Supply Chain Management

The management of sourcing, procuring, production, and logistics to go from raw materials to end consumers across multiple intermediate steps constitutes **supply chain management** (SCM). In order to create and maintain efficient material (supply) flows between supply points, SCM addresses models and relations. Various partners must work together to use tools and techniques for increased efficiency and to apply their knowledge in making decisions. As you find a place for your company in a supply chain, or multiple chains, you can also develop relationships up and down the line to enhance your efficiency and that of your supply-chain partners. Critical components of this process will be identifying and securing suppliers and managing inventory.

supply chain management (SCM) the management of sourcing, procuring, production, and logistics to go from raw materials to end customers across multiple intermediate steps.

Finding Suppliers

The world is literally your market for suppliers. Raw materials, component parts, subassemblies, and completed products may be available to you from around the world. You may be growing and packaging your own fruits and vegetables and have seed, fertilizer, packaging, and machinery and equipment suppliers. Or, you may be creating Web sites where your suppliers are software companies, hardware companies, and Internet service providers. Or, you may own a retail gift store with hundreds of suppliers who themselves each have dozens of suppliers. Regardless of the

Performance Objective 3

Manage suppliers and inventory.

simplicity or complexity of your supply partners, you will have to find them and work with them. Some places to look:

- trade shows or conferences,
- trade catalogs or journals,
- the Yellow Pages,
- Internet search engines,
- wholesale supply houses and brokers,
- newspapers and magazines,
- competitors,
- firms like yours that are outside of your trading area,
- sales representatives, and
- customers

Your suppliers will become partners in your business. Your success will depend upon their capacity to deliver what you need, when you need it, and at a price you are willing to pay. Their success depends on you delivering your product or service and getting paid for it, preferably on a repeat basis, so they can get paid and be successful, too.

Managing Inventory

Managing inventory is vital to marketing success and to cash flow and there will be an ongoing tension between them. If inventory is kept at a maximum, customer satisfaction may be satisfied, but costs can become prohibitive. If inventory is maintained at very low levels, customers may become dissatisfied (even leaving entirely), but cash tied up in inventory is minimized. In order to balance service and cost management, factors such as demand, cost, sales price, carrying costs, order and setup costs, and lead times must be known values. In reality, demand projections, lead times, and other variables are generally estimated—with varying degrees of accuracy. Business owners can use the best information, as well as established techniques and tools, to make inventory management decisions.

Visual Control

visual control inventory-management method in which an individual assesses the stock level on hand by visual inspection and reorders when the supply appears low.

A common approach to inventory management in small companies is **visual control**, which simply means that you look at the inventory on hand, and when the stock level of an item appears to be low, you reorder. This decidedly unscientific method of choosing when to order will be dependent on you knowing the product-selling rate and delivery time. It is most effective when you sell relatively few items and are actively involved in the business.

Safety Stock and Reorder Points

safety stock the amounts of inventory or raw materials or work-in-progress that are kept to guarantee service levels.

reorder point (ROP) the level at which materials need to be ordered again.

To avoid running out of materials, businesses frequently establish **safety stock** levels, which are the amounts of inventory or raw materials and work-in-progress that are kept to insure satisfying customer demand. The inventory **reorder point (ROP)** is the level at which materials need to be ordered again. A challenge for any business is to find the optimal safety stock levels and reorder points for all items and supplies that are stocked. If too much inventory is on hand, the costs of storage and tying up money may be too great. If too little inventory is available, the costs associated with lost sales and loss of goodwill may be significant. In addition to the holding and stock-out costs, the expenses associated with last-minute (rush) ordering may be substantial.

There are a variety of methods for calculating safety stock and reorder points. The calculation of the ROP requires a knowledge or projection of demand, lead time, and safety stock level, and is calculated as

$$\text{ROP} = (\text{Average Demand per Unit of Lead Time} \times \text{Lead Time}) + \text{Safety Stock}$$

For example, if the lead time for showerheads is two weeks, and you sell 25 showerheads per week, so that you always want at least 10 showerheads in stock, the calculation is

$$\text{ROP} = (25 \times 2) + 10 = 60$$

So, whenever inventory falls to 60 showerheads, it is time to reorder. **Figure 17-3** shows this in graph form.

Economic Order Quantity

The **economic order quantity (EOQ)** is the amount of inventory that will equal the minimum total ordering and holding costs, and is calculated as

economic order quantity (EOQ) the amount of inventory to order that will equal the minimum total ordering and holding costs.

$$\text{EOQ} = \sqrt{\frac{2DO}{C}}$$

in which D equals annual demand for the item in units (not dollars), O equals ordering cost per order in dollars or other currency (not units), and C equals the carrying cost per unit in dollars or other currency. For example, Dominique's Bridal Shop buys bridal veils at \$80 per unit from its supplier. Dominique's sells 640 veils annually, distributed evenly over the months. The holding cost (also known as carrying cost) is 5 percent of the total, or \$4 per veil per year. The ordering cost is \$20 per order. So,

$$\text{EOQ} = \sqrt{\frac{2(640)(\$20)}{\$4}} = \sqrt{6400} = \textbf{80 veils}$$

The total number of orders to place per year = D/EOQ = 640/80 = **8 orders.**

$$\begin{aligned}\text{Total Inventory Costs} &= \text{Carrying Cost} + \text{Ordering Cost}\\ &= (C \times EOQ/2) + (O \times D/EOQ)\\ &= (\$4)(80/2) + (\$20)(500/80) = \textbf{\$285 per year}\end{aligned}$$

From this example, Dominique's Bridal Shop should have an inventory policy of ordering 80 veils at a time and should place eight orders per year. This inventory will cost the store \$285 per year. **Figure 17-4** illustrates the calculation of economic order quantity in a graph.

If the company manufactured products and wanted to calculate the most economical size for a production run, it would use the same calculation methodology, but *O = setup costs* rather than *order costs*.

Creating a Purchasing Plan

One essential aspect of an inventory management system is the purchasing plan, so that the items needed are in stock when they are needed. Plans should be developed early enough that there are no last-minute panic purchases.

Figure 17-3 *Inventory cycles.*

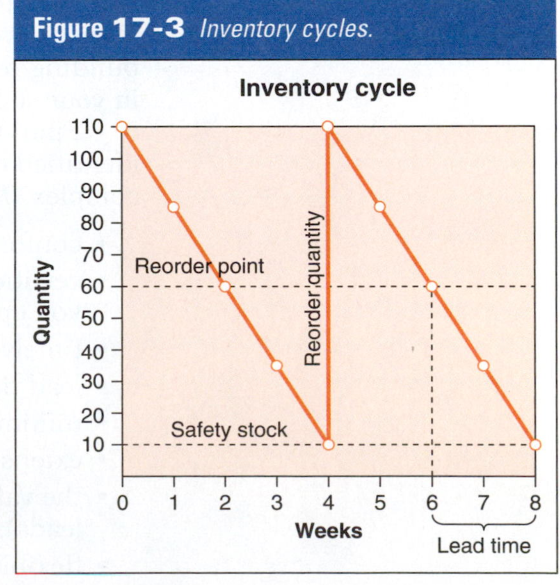

Figure 17-4 *Economic order quantity.*

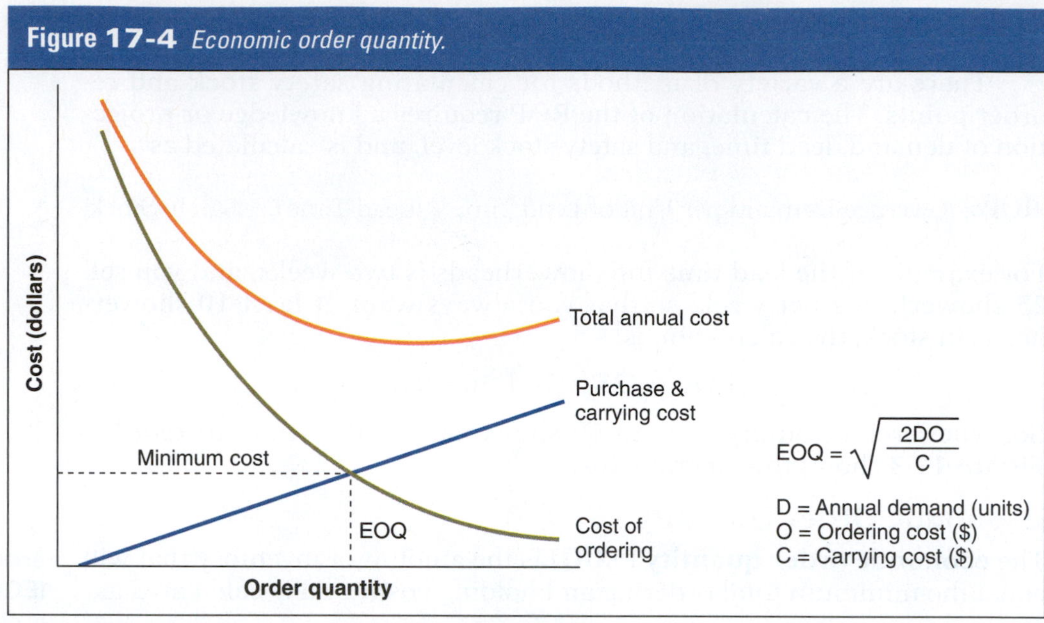

The purchasing plan will include

- when orders should be placed to have products as promised,
- an estimate of when the product will reach its peak to know when replacement orders need to be in place,
- understanding when to stop ordering a product and drop it from production, and
- the end date for stocking particular inventory.

Managing the Chain: Analyzing and Selecting Vendors

The process of analyzing and selecting vendors should be strategic rather than purely tactical, and be driven by your purchasing plan. As you develop your business and have sufficient volumes of revenue, vendors will seek you out to present their goods and services. The issue often is not the lack of potential suppliers, it is identifying the best suppliers for your company. As you work to construct a solid supply chain for your business, building relationships with vendors that will be complementary partners in your success will be critical.

Finding suppliers can be accomplished by using the various resources identified earlier in this chapter. Determining which ones are best is more complex. There are many factors to consider when selecting suppliers:

- conformance of products to your quality standards;
- certification, either from an official organization or via a process that you employ;
- timely delivery;
- lead times;
- minimum-order quantities;
- extension of trade credit;
- the value added to your business (e.g., training, promotion, customer leads); and
- flexibility and responsiveness.

You can find numerous vendor-selection checklists and guidelines on the Internet that can serve as a foundation for creating your own methodology. Of particular value may be articles in trade publications for your industry, because they are tailored more to the requirements of businesses like yours. Regardless of your starting point, you may want to create minimum criteria for potential supplier consideration, and a set of rank-ordered or scaled criteria such as the above, but in greater detail, depending upon the item to be purchased. More sophisticated selection models and criteria have been created, including multivariate analysis and decision models; and these may apply to your company, depending upon its nature and complexity.[3] Among the challenges involved is determining how to evaluate the trade-offs between different and sometimes conflicting goals simultaneously, to arrive at the best decisions.

Legal Considerations

The creation of a supply chain should be undertaken with due consideration of legal issues and concerns. Specifically, honesty, integrity, and staying within the law are not only right, but they are also best. Be careful of becoming a "lying buyer"who provides false information to potential suppliers regarding competitive products and sales terms. Make sure you have proper legal agreements where needed, and do not accept any terms that are not aboveboard.

The Idea-to-Product Process

Performance Objective 4

Explore the idea-to-product process.

Taking an idea and turning it into a product can range from a simple to a highly complex process. Some entrepreneurs are excellent idea people but have no interest in the nuts and bolts of bringing the concepts to reality. For these individuals, securing intellectual property rights and licensing can often be the best option. Other entrepreneurs like to take an idea, whether it is their own or licensed, from the idea stage through production to marketing and sales. If your concept is for a product (rather than a service), understanding the idea-to-product process is critical.

Why Manufacturing Is Unique

Although entrepreneurs have successfully started all types of businesses, manufacturing companies offer some unique advantages as startups. Manufacturers can

- make products that do not exist yet,
- fine-tune the design and features of a product in ways that resale businesses cannot, and
- get a patent on product designs to discourage competitors and provide legal protection.

There are disadvantages to starting a manufacturing business, however, including these caveats:

- It can cost a lot to set up and maintain a manufacturing company. Manufacturing equipment can be expensive and so can the costs of purchasing (or leasing) a suitable manufacturing plant.

[3]Rainer Lascha and Christian Janker, "Supplier Selection and Controlling Using Multivariate Analysis," *International Journal of Physical Distribution*, 2005, Volume 35, Issue 6, pp. 409–425. José Gerardo, Martínez-Martínez, "The Use of Alternative Decision Support Systems in Vendor Selection Decisions," *Inter Metro Business Journal*, Fall 2007, Volume 3, Issue 2.

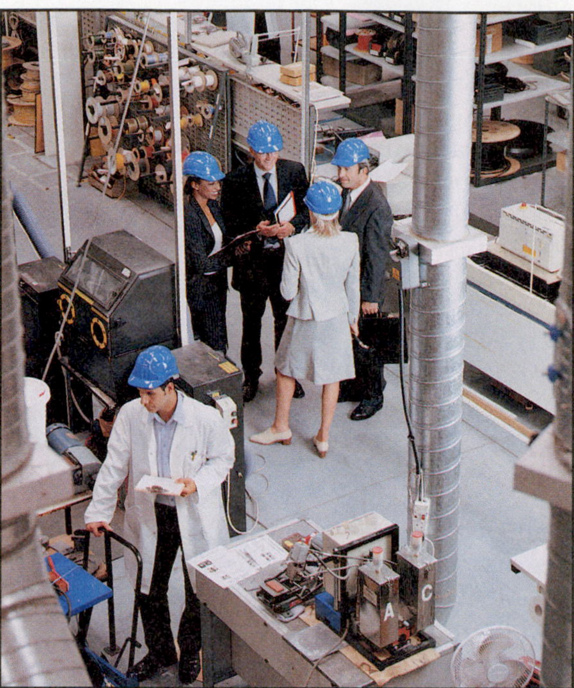

- It can be costly to hire and train workers.
- Manufacturers have to pay to make the product first, but must then wait for it to sell before getting their money back. The more processes that are needed, the more costly it can be. Thus, the cash requirements can be quite substantial.

A manufacturer can make every piece of its own product, or have parts or subassemblies made by suppliers. Many companies make the most important or complex parts of their products, but purchase minor ones. Manufacturers like Ford and General Motors rely on other companies for parts that go into their cars. Many companies do the final assembly, regardless of who makes the parts.

Job Shops

Some manufacturing companies do not actually make a final product, for consumers or end-customers. Instead, **job shops**, or jobbers, are suppliers or subcontractors for other manufacturers. They use their manufacturing plant and equipment to make parts, or even entire products, for other companies, usually working with drawings and specifications provided by their customers. They commonly get work by submitting and winning a bid. Job shops are useful to manufacturers because they are often able to

job shop a subcontractor for a manufacturer.

- produce parts of consistent quality;
- make a part less expensively;
- deliver a part more quickly;
- maintain and provide specialized equipment, so the major manufacturers do not have to purchase or maintain it themselves; and
- provide manufacturing facilities to companies that do not have their own.

Whether a company makes its own product, or has parts or all of it made by suppliers, what counts is that it controls the design, formula, or specifications of how the product is to be made.

The manufacturer controls the design of the product and also provides the following:

tolerance the range of acceptable size variation.

prototype a model or pattern that serves as an example of how a product would look and operate if it were manufactured.

value-engineer to reduce the cost in a product while maintaining quality standards.

tooling cost the expense of creating the specialized equipment for manufacturing.

setup cost the expense of establishing a production run.

- ***Drawings and Specifications.*** Diagrams and renderings tell others how to make the product and its parts. This includes written information about the materials, dimensions, **tolerances** (ranges of acceptable size variation), and parts to be used.
- ***Parts and Materials List.*** This list includes all the materials and separate parts needed to make the product.
- ***Prototype.*** A **prototype** is a model or pattern that serves as an example of how a product would look and operate if it were manufactured. A prototype gives you the opportunity to determine whether it will work correctly. You may also find ways to improve the product or to **value-engineer** it (reduce the cost), while constructing and testing the prototype. Because you are only making one (or a few), prototypes normally cost a lot more than the actual product will per unit when it is produced in large quantities.

In addition, manufacturing involves **tooling costs** and **setup costs**, which are the expenses of creating the specialized equipment and establishing a production run, respectively. Manufacturers calculate these costs before starting to make the product.

- Tooling costs are required to make or adapt the equipment for a product. These are one-time expenses because there are no additional tooling costs for additional orders. Manufacturers usually do not include these expenses in their per-unit costs of the product, but they do need to recover their investment in a timely manner. Some products have significant tooling costs, whereas others have none.
- Setup costs have to be paid each time you make a production run, or a "lot," of the product. This covers the time and effort of getting ready to make the product for each run. For example, a pattern-cutting machine must be reset for each style and size of a suit jacket. The larger the quantity produced, the smaller the setup costs will be per item manufactured, because the cost is distributed across more units. Almost all products have setup costs.

Manufacturing Tips

If you plan to operate a small-scale, home-based manufacturing business, you will have extra factors to consider:

- You may be able to make part of, or your entire product, in your home; however, most cities and towns have zoning laws that limit what you can do in a residential area. Check the zoning limitations *before* basing your business plan on a home business. If your business involves large trucks making deliveries, you will probably have to find a location in a commercial area.
- If manufacturing your product requires expensive equipment, consider working with a job shop that can make it for you, at least initially. You can use one job shop or many, depending on the item. Even if your product is complicated, you may be able to buy the parts and do the final assembly yourself.
- People who work in job shops know how to make things efficiently. They are seldom asked for design advice because "that's engineer's work." But see if you can get your jobber to help you improve your design and make it affordable.
- Look at all aspects of your operation to find ways to maximize your efficiency and minimize waste.

BizFacts

To find a company to make your prototype, look online at ThomasNet.com. The Thomas Register of American Manufacturers published its 100th and final print edition in 2006, and went to an online-only version consisting of more than 650,000 manufacturers and distributors. This online database is searchable in various ways, and includes drawings of parts and components as well as resource listings. The global version of the Thomas Register includes international suppliers and product information, and is available in English, German, French, Spanish, Italian, Dutch, Portuguese, Chinese, and Japanese. You can access Thomas online at

http://www.ThomasNet.com (national catalog)
http://www.thomasglobal.com (international catalog)

Exercise

A small, youth-owned company in New York makes skateboards. It has six styles, each of which uses a different wooden body. These bodies must be glued to waterproof plywood, then steamed and bent to form the correct shape. The outside contour of the body is cut out with a band saw. The owners do this after school in their high school's Tech Ed room. They can make the bodies themselves or pay other students to do it. Every skateboard style uses the same wheel assemblies and fasteners, obtained from an online wholesaler.

The teenagers have signed a contract with a Madison Avenue marketing firm to create designs using the names of players from the NBA. They have to agree to pay a royalty of $2 for every skateboard they manufacture, whether they sell it or not.

On a separate piece of paper, note four ways you could apply JIT concepts to this business.

Just-in-Time Manufacturing

just-in-time manufacturing (JIT) manufacturing methodology focusing on making the smallest amount of product needed, quickly and efficiently.

Although it is often less costly to manufacture products overseas, many American companies are taking advantage of updated manufacturing methods to stay competitive. **Just-in-time manufacturing (JIT)** was developed in Japanese factories, but it can be very effective for an entrepreneur anywhere.

JIT manufacturers eschew traditional concepts, such as increasing the size of lots to take advantage of mass production methods. Instead, JIT focuses on making the smallest amount of product possible, while doing it quickly and efficiently. Goals of JIT manufacturing include

- running the smallest lots (batches) feasible,
- reducing setup time and cost to the bare minimum,
- scheduling production so that products are finished "just in time" to be shipped, and
- staying flexible, to make the widest range of products with the smallest setup and changeover costs.

Companies frequently have large sums of money invested in inventory so, if those items go out of style, or are made obsolete by new technology or fashion, they cannot be sold. This excess inventory creates losses that cost manufacturing businesses many millions of dollars each year. JIT can be efficient because it does not waste raw materials, labor, shipping, or warehousing on products that might never be sold. If you decide to implement JIT, be careful not to fall into the production trap of just *a little too late* and failing to deliver on time.

Product Design and Costs

Another aspect of production that is of vital importance is the physical product design and the costs associated with it. When products are developed to fill market needs or demands, they have built-in price ranges that are viable for the consumer. In order for the product to be successful, it has to be designed so that it can be produced at a profit when manufactured in moderate volume. So you cannot design a luxury product using expensive components and expect to sell it at an economy price.

Cost factors will arise in all aspects of a product, from design and patenting costs (if applicable) to tooling, prototypes, equipment, and facilities, to raw materials, components, production, assembly, quality assurance, packaging, and delivery. The primary delineation of costs lies between the *functional* design (the product itself) and the *production*

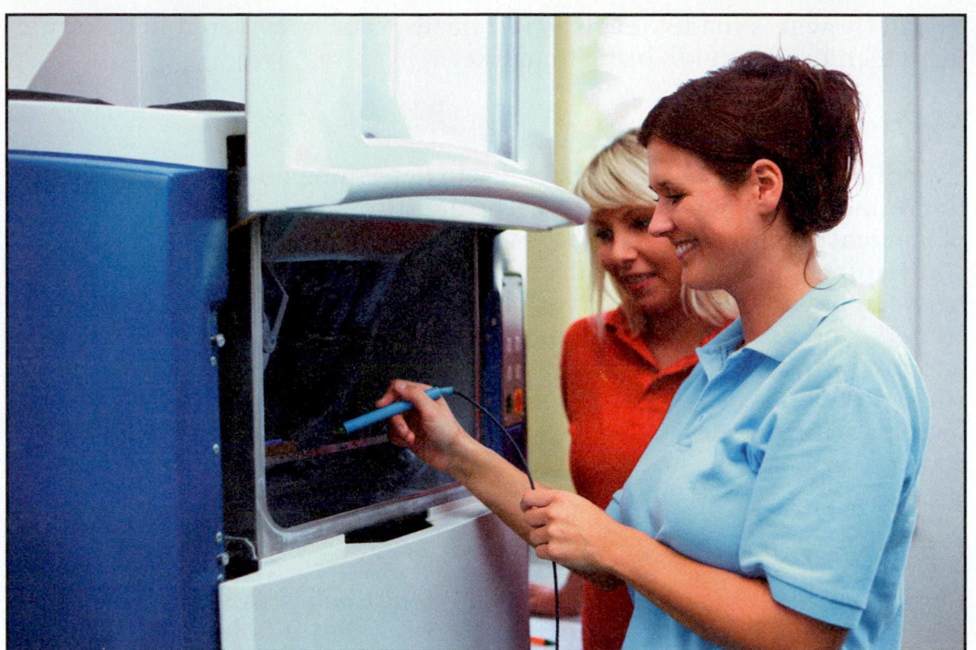

Global Impact . . .

Paper Wealth

Zhang Yin of Nine Dragons Paper.

Zhang Yin (Cheung Yan) of Nine Dragons Paper (Holdings) Limited, in China, is the richest self-made woman in the world. Her personal wealth is estimated at $4.7 billion.[4] Her company recycles scrap paper, often from the United States, and produces cardboard. The cardboard is used to make boxes for Chinese goods, many of which find their way to the United States.

Zhang Yin, originally an accountant from Guangdong Province, has moved between China and the United States, first opening a paper company in Hong Kong (1985) with $3800 in cash and then a paper-export company in the United States (1990). American Chung Namp, Inc., became the largest exporter of waste paper from U.S. sources. Working with her Taiwan-born and Brazil-raised husband, and her brother, Zhang Yin, she cofounded Nine Dragons in Hong Kong in 1995. The company raised almost $500 million through its initial public offering on the Hong Kong Stock Exchange in 2006.

American Chung Namp and Nine Dragons are able to maintain low overhead by hauling away unwanted scrap and by creatively exploiting shipping opportunities.[5] Rates to China are particularly attractive because of excess capacity on ships returning to China from the United States.

As of 2007, Nine Dragons had 5300 employees, 11 huge papermaking machines, and reported profits of $175 million on $1 billion in annual revenues.[6] It expanded into a third manufacturing plant located near Shanghai in August of 2008, and a fourth facility opened in Tianjin in September 2009.[7] By using the latest in machinery, and less costly labor and fuel, the company has significant production advantages. Nine Dragons obtained ISO Quality and Environmental Standards and Occupational Health and Safety Management System Certification to assist in continuous improvement. In addition to paper production, according to its Web site, the company has facilities to provide, "power, steam, water treatment and excellent logistical support. The integration of these facilities provides and increases the Group's operational flexibility and control, while enabling the Group to facilitate best practices in terms of environmental protection."

The Nine Dragons Web site clearly states the company's goal, "The Group aims to become the world's leading containerboard product manufacturer in capacity, profitability and efficiency."

---

[4]Allen Cheng, "Cardboard Puts Woman at Top of China's Rich List," *The Standard,* January 17, 2007, http://www.thestandard.com.hk/ (accessed November 14, 2009).

[5]Ibid.

[6]David Barboza, "Blazing a Paper Trail in China," *New York Times*, January 16, 2007, http://nytimes.com/2007/01/16/business/ (accessed on November 13, 2009).

[7]Nine Dragons Paper (Holdings) Limited Web site, http://www.ndpaper.com (accessed on November 13, 2009).

design (how it is made). Each aspect needs to be considered in determining which product(s) to bring to market.

Making versus Buying

vertical integration the process of going forward or backward on the idea-to-market continuum.

Every business that sells a product has to determine how much of it, if any, to produce and how much to buy. The question may be one of the degrees of **vertical integration**—going forward or backward on the idea-to-market continuum—that it wants to incorporate. This is similar to the difference between having bread delivered to your retail store and selling it to consumers, and growing and milling the grain and other ingredients, mixing and preparing the dough, baking it, packaging it, and then selling the finished product. What you will choose in your business will depend on many factors. Critical issues include: capacity for production at each phase of the process, cost effectiveness, and customer requirements and preferences.

Facilities Location and Design

Regarding retail business, you have no doubt heard the cliché about the importance of "location, location, location"—but it is true. For all businesses, location and layout are critical. Where you locate your business will have considerable impact on your access to supplies and customers. For example, you may want to be near critical suppliers, or customers, or somewhere with ready access to a major highway, rail service, or airport. You may want to be in a retail location, an office building, or an industrial park. Your business must be located where zoning laws permit its operation. In fact, you may have a *virtual* business with no physical store front, manufacturing facility, or warehouse. More information regarding site selection is included in Chapter 18.

Defining Quality: It Is a Matter of Market Positioning

quality degrees of excellence; conformance to specifications or standards.

Performance Objective 5
Ensure product quality.

The concept of **quality** is used broadly, and has multiple definitions, including how to determine degrees of excellence and conformance to specifications or standards. As a business owner, quality products or services will be largely defined by your market-positioning strategy. For example, a meal at a five-star restaurant will be vastly different from one at a local diner. In either case, excellence is a matter of consistently performing (producing) to the standards that have been established to meet or exceed customer expectations. However you position your organization, your quality and the viability of the business will depend on the match between the expectations that you create through market positioning and the experience of your customers.

Profits Follow Quality

For many years, American companies had focused less on quality than on short-term profits. In the early 1950s, however, American economist W. Edwards Deming argued that business should focus on making quality products instead of on maximizing profits, and that profit would follow from that focus. His revolutionary concept was ignored by American corporations, so he went to Japan, which was rebuilding after the devastation of World War II.

Step into the Shoes...

Positioning Stone Hill Winery through Quality

Stone Hill Winery.

Jim and Betty Held took over the Stone Hill Winery in 1965, with four young children and a vision of restoring the historic Hermann, Missouri, winery to its pre-Prohibition glory days.[8] They succeeded until the 1970s, when high interest rates combined with escalating costs. The winery grew slowly during the 1980s and into the 1990s and more rapidly from the later 1990s.

Sweet and semi-sweet wines have always been the most popular items that Stone Hill Winery produced. Jon Held states, "We have provided a wide spectrum of wine styles to satisfy all consumers rather than only the tastes of a select few wine elite. Most importantly, we have listened to our customers rather than to the wine pundits." The Helds analyzed consumer loyalty to wine brands, and discovered that one significant factor was first-time consumption of the product, specifically the atmosphere in which it was consumed. They differentiated their advertising message, proclaiming, "Come out to the winery and have a great time."

The Helds knew that if they could invest in new vineyards and equipment they could attain economies of scale.[9] As recently as 2008, the winery expanded through the addition of new fermentation and storage capacity totaling 99,000 gallons. They needed to apply the latest grape-and-wine production technology so that the winery could consistently produce a range of wine styles of high quality and value. To raise money for this technology, they had to grow significantly. The marketing approach and the application of technology worked.

Stone Hill Winery is a three-location tourist destination. It now produces over 260,000 gallons annually with gross revenues of over $9 million per year while employing the Helds, two of their adult children, and more than 100 others. Stone Hill has 170 acres of vineyards under cultivation and uses grapes from other Missouri vineyards to supplement production.

Jim and Betty Held and their family combined market research, determination, state-of-the-art production equipment and techniques, and quality assurance to create an award-winning enterprise.

In those days, Japan was notorious for the poor quality of its manufactured goods. The phrase "Made in Japan" was jokingly used to refer to anything poorly fabricated. Deming gave a series of lectures in Japan, though, that the Japanese took to heart. They began focusing on quality and soon proved that Deming's theory: Profits follow quality—was correct. The subsequent quality of Japanese cars and stereos became famous and won customers world wide.

American entrepreneurs and corporate executives traveled to Japan to study why the Japanese had become so successful. They brought Deming's ideas back home, where they finally began to be adopted.

As you develop your business, it will be the consistent quality of your product or service that will lead to profits. If you can develop a way to deliver quality consistently, you will have a business concept that can be profitable, with the potential for generating even greater revenues in the future.

Organization-Wide Quality Initiatives

It is clear that quality management and quality assurance is not solely the job of the production team. As organizations have evolved in our rapidly changing technology- and service-driven environment, quality has come to mean the active involvement of the entire company. A number of initiatives and methods have been formed to help businesses ensure quality. Among these are Lean Manufacturing, Benchmarking, ISO 9000, Six Sigma, Total Quality Management, and the Malcolm Baldrige Award. Each of these can assist your company in providing the quality that your customers should expect.

[8] Portions of this profile are available at http://www.stonehillwinery.com/ourWinery/ (accessed November 15, 2009).

[9] "Stone Hill Winery: New Tastes, New Approach," *Insights and Inspiration: How Businesses Succeed, The 1995 Blue Chip Enterprise Initiative®*. Published by *Nation's Business* magazine on behalf of Connecticut Mutual Life Insurance Company and the U.S. Chamber of Commerce, in association with the Blue Chip Enterprise Initiative, 1995, p. 27. Courtesy of Stone Hill Winery.

Benchmarking

benchmarking the comparison of a company's performance against that of companies in the same industry, or against best practices, standards, or certification criteria.

One the most basic organization-wide approaches that you can pursue is the use of **benchmarking**, which is the comparison of your company's performance against that of other companies in your industry, or against best practices, standards, or certification criteria. Benchmarking is what you are doing when you create a competitive comparison for marketing purposes, or when you compare your projected or actual financial ratios to industry levels. In addition to standard performance measures, such as return on investment, profitability, market share, and the like, individual industries have benchmarks. For example, retail stores measure sales per square foot and restaurants evaluate by customers per labor hour. By using benchmarking, you can identify opportunities for improvement.

A simple method of benchmarking is to create a list of measures that are important to your customers (using primary market research) or to customers in your industry (using secondary research, such as trade-journal reports), and comparing outcomes. You can then compare other statistics, if it is helpful. **Exhibit 17-1** illustrates a portion of such a table for a restaurant.

ISO 9000

The family of standards for quality management systems established by the International Organization for Standardization (ISO) is ISO 9000. These standards are certified by independent companies to document that consistent business procedures are being used, and that the organization has been independently audited for compliance. Initially, ISO standards were applied solely to manufacturing. However, service firms have become the predominant recipients of certificates. Organizations will sometimes market their ISO certification as a mark of excellence, although it is, rather, a guarantee of compliance with standards.

process management the measurement, monitoring, and optimization of tasks.

There have been numerous standards employed under varying numbers. Beginning with the ISO 9001:2000 version, **process management** (measuring, monitoring, and optimizing tasks), upper management involvement, continuous improvement, recording customer satisfaction, and utilizing numeric measures of effectiveness all became critical to the

Exhibit 17-1 *Quality measures for the country diner.*

Measure of Quality	Rating (1 Is Poor, 5 Is Excellent—Based on Industry and Customer Data)				
Customers per labor hour	1	2	3	(4)	5
Average customer wait time for seating	1	2	3	4	(5)
Satisfactory inspection ratings	1	(2)	3	4	5
Number of meals returned to the kitchen	1	2	(3)	4	5
Customer satisfaction ratings	1	2	3	(4)	5
Amount of food wasted	(1)	2	3	4	5
Return on sales	1	2	3	(4)	5

process. There are industry-specific variations that may apply to your business. There are eight quality-management principles for organizational improvement:

1. customer focus,
2. leadership,
3. involvement of people,
4. process approach,
5. system approach to management,
6. continual improvement,
7. factual approach to decision making, and
8. mutually beneficial supplier relationships.

Regardless of the size of your firm, you can find considerable information on the ISO standards and can build them into your organization from the start. Assistance is available through the American Society for Quality (ASQ) at http://www.asq.org, the American National Standards Institute, at http://www.ansi.org, and ISO at http://www.iso.ch.

Six Sigma

Six Sigma is a measurement of quality that was originated in the 1980s by Motorola engineers. It is the use of statistical methods to eliminate defects to a failure rate of 3.4 defects per one million opportunities, or a 99.9997-percent success rate. This is a rigorous process-improvement program that aims to achieve near perfection. The two submethodologies employed are DMAIC and DMADV.[10] The DMAIC (define, measure, analyze, improve, and control) system is intended to enhance existing production. The DMADV (define, measure, analyze, design, and verify) process is meant to support new procedures and products.

For most enterprises, this is a very intense program, and maybe more so than is practical in the early stages of a business. However, it may be worthwhile to learn about it and consider whether you can include such methods to build in high standards from the start. Further information is available at:

SSA & Company	*http://ssaandco.com*
The Quality Portal	*http://www.thequalityportal.com*
iSixSigma LLC	*http://www.isixsigma.com*
Motorola	*http://www.motorola.com/motorolauniversity.jsp*

Total Quality Management

The quality-assurance methodology of striving for strategic advantage through quality concepts inspired by Deming is called **total quality management (TQM)**. Although developed in the 1950s, many of the principles of TQM are still valid and valued. The central notion of **continuous improvement**, or always identifying and implementing changes throughout the organization, to focus on requirements of internal and external customers, is valid for any business. TQM involves constant improvement of processes, typically using specific measures of quality, such as compliance with product specifications and operating standards, volume of production, on-time delivery, and repeat rates.

total quality management (TQM) the quality-assurance methodology of striving for strategic advantage through quality.

continuous improvement always identifying and implementing changes throughout the organization to focus on the requirements of internal and external customers.

[10] Available at http://www.isixsigma.com.

TQM's success is dependent upon the commitment of all employees toward treating one another as customers, and working together to ensure that standards are met at all stages. Each employee accepts responsibility for a role in the production of the products and services.

Malcolm Baldrige Award

Whereas the previous concepts have focused on quality-management methodologies, the Malcolm Baldrige Award (MBA) is a competitive process established by the United States Congress in 1987 that recognizes quality management. The Baldrige Award is given to businesses and educational and nonprofit organizations by the president of the United States, and is administered by the National Institute of Standards and Technology (NIST).[11] Organizations apply for the award and are judged in the areas of:

- leadership: organizational leadership and social responsibility;
- strategic planning: strategy development and deployment;
- customer and market focus: market and customer knowledge and customer relationships and satisfaction;
- measurement, analysis, knowledge management: measurement and analysis of organizational performance and management of information and knowledge;
- human resources focus: work systems, employee learning and motivation, and employee well-being and satisfaction;
- process management: value-creation and support processes; and
- business results, including customer-focus, product and service, financial and market, human resources, organizational effectiveness, governance, and social responsibility.

Thousands of organizations use the Baldrige criteria for self-assessment, training, and the creation of business processes. You can obtain these Baldrige standards and incorporate them into your business at any time. They are more comprehensive than many of the specific production and process measures identified above.

Using Technology to Your Advantage

Performance Objective 6

Use technology to benefit your business.

Regardless of the size or nature of your business, technology can work to your advantage if you use it effectively. Even if your business is not technological, you can apply technology to make your operations more efficient and effective. The technology could be as simple and common as a telephone or as complex as a specialized piece of medical equipment. What *is* important is that you are aware of the technology available to you and how it might benefit your business. At the same time, you should be wary of adopting technology just for the "wow" factor. A cost/benefit analysis for technology implementation is as important as for any other substantial investment.

Computer Access Is Essential

Advances in technology that ordinary people can use have been an important part of the entrepreneurial wave of at least the last decade. With this in mind:

- every entrepreneur should have access to a computer;
- every business should have a Web site and electronic mail access;

[11]Available at http://www.nist.gov/public_affairs/factsheet/.

- every business should hire employees who are conversant and comfortable with technology, and
- every entrepreneur should be aware of the specialized computer software and equipment that is designed for his/her industry.

The Internet came into being in 1989, when an Englishman named Tim Berners-Lee invented **hyperlinks,** words that, when clicked on, transferred the reader to a new document page anywhere on the Internet. Today, pictures, or even video, can be links as well. Every Web page has an address, called a **URL (uniform resource locator)**, and you can surf from one URL to another using hyperlinks. Web pages are **hypertext** documents, meaning they combine text with graphics, video, or sound.

One of the best early investments you can make for your business is a computer. You do not need to have the latest model, or even a new one; refurbished computers can be purchased quite inexpensively. Even the most basic model can be used to:

hyperlink word(s) that, when clicked on, transfer the computer user to a new Web page.

uniform resource locator (URL) a Web page address.

hypertext Web-based documents that combine text and graphics.

- access the Internet;
- create stationery and business cards (although professional designs are preferable);
- produce professional letters and check spelling, grammar, and syntax;
- keep financial records, and
- maintain an updated mailing list of customers and printed mailing labels.

If you do not own a computer, consider making arrangements to borrow or use one part time until you can buy one. You can also rent computer time or get it for free at Internet cafés, or some office supply stores. Most public libraries and colleges even offer free Internet access. However, it is best to have your own computer, so you can keep your company's books, records, and other proprietary information private.

Capture the Potential of the Telephone

Do not forget, however, that technology does not have to be new to be useful. The telephone is still one of the businessperson's most important technological tools. You can turn your phone into an answering service for your business by using a voice-mail system, or you can hire an answering service to provide a more personal touch. Either approach is acceptable until you have staff to answer customer inquiries; although today some companies use automated telephone-answering systems, even if they have hundreds, or even thousands, of employees.

Whether you use voice mail or an answering service, make sure the message that callers hear represents your desired business image and is clear and professional. Change your message periodically to advertise specials and sales and to keep customers listening. Use mobile phones to stay in touch with customers, employees, and suppliers.

A separate telephone line for your business will provide a number of advantages. Business telephones can be listed under your business name in the telephone book, and you will know to always answer with your business name when that phone rings. Also, if you have a home-based business and children, it will be easier to have them resist answering the phone when it is clearly the office line. With text messaging and e-mail sent over mobile phones, the versatility and importance of telephones to today's businesses cannot be overstated.

Identify Market-Specific Software and Technology

In order to increase efficiency and effectiveness in operations, businesses use software and technology designed for their industry or type of business. For example, retail stores often use point-of-sales (POS) systems that are tailored to their products, and restaurants use ordering systems customized to their menus. Not-for-profits have specialized fund-raising and accounting software. Sports stadiums, concert venues, and movie theaters have ticketing systems. Manufacturing plants have materials-planning and inventory systems.

Typically, trade journals feature advertisements for software specific to an industry. The software companies commonly exhibit at trade shows and conferences. Evaluations and comparisons of hardware and software solutions are listed in trade publications and on the Internet.

The investment in industry-specific technology is often many times greater than in generic business equipment and software. However, the upfront investment may lead to both considerable efficiency and savings over the short and/or long term.

Electronic Storefront (Web Site)

electronic storefront an online site that customers can visit to view a company's catalog, price lists, and documentation.

No matter what type of business you have, opening an **electronic storefront** will make it more accessible to local customers and can introduce it to potential customers all over the world. An electronic storefront is an online site that customers can visit to view your catalog, price lists, and other information. Today, it is relatively easy to add the option of purchasing your products online, either directly, through a credit-card merchant account, or through a service such as PayPal.

You will need to decide if you want to put your store up with an online service or by yourself. An online service would typically build your storefront for you, and include promotion and advertisements as part of the deal to help make its subscribers aware of your store. On the other hand, if you put a site up yourself, you would have more control over what it looked like and where it was located; and your potential customers would not be limited to the subscribers to a particular online service. One of the most cost-efficient ways to set up an electronic storefront is to hire a competent consultant to help you design it and choose which server to use.

Chapter Summary

Now that you have studied this chapter, you can do the following:

1. Understand the significance of operations in a business.
   - Operations is the delivery on promises.
   - What is required depends on the specific industry and business.
   - Inputs are transformed or converted into outputs through operations.
2. Develop a production-distribution chain for your business.
   - Manufacturers make products in large quantities.
   - Wholesalers buy smaller quantities in bulk from manufacturers.

- Retailers buy from wholesalers (and sometimes manufacturers).
- Consumers buy from retailers.

3. Manage suppliers and inventory.
   - Supply chain management is used to create and maintain efficient flow of materials between supply partners.
   - Suppliers may be found in a variety of ways and may be located worldwide.
   - Inventory can be managed to minimize cost and maximize customer satisfaction.
4. Explore the idea-to-product process.
   - Different people are interested in and skilled at fulfilling specific stages of a business.
   - Ideas may evolve into patentable product designs with drawings and specifications.
   - Product designs can be made to test and improve prototypes.
   - Parts and materials lists are needed for sourcing and production.
   - Manufacturing can be done directly, with part and/or subassembly suppliers, and through job shops.
   - Manufacturing methodologies, location, and purchasing all have important roles.
5. Ensure product quality.
   - Quality is determined by meeting and exceeding standards, including customer satisfaction.
   - Profits follow quality.
   - Organization-wide approaches to quality include
     - ISO 9000 certification,
     - Six Sigma certification,
     - total quality management (TQM), and
     - Malcolm Baldrige Awards.
6. Use technology to benefit your business.
   - Technology can provide competitive advantage.
   - Computers are a necessity in today's business world.
   - The telephone continues to be a major asset.
   - Industry-specific software and equipment is frequently beneficial.
   - Electronic storefronts provide additional distribution opportunities.

Key Terms

benchmarking
continuous improvement
economic order quantity (EOQ)
electronic storefront
hyperlink
hypertext
job shop
just-in-time manufacturing (JIT)
operations
process management
prototype
quality
reorder point (ROP)
safety stock
setup cost
supply chain management (SCM)
tolerance
tooling cost
total quality management (TQM)
uniform resource locator (URL)
value-engineer
vertical integration
visual control

Entrepreneurship Portfolio

Critical Thinking Exercises

1. Production-distribution chain
   a. How do you plan to distribute your product to your target market?
   b. What is the estimated delivery time between when you place an order with your supplier and when the product will be available for your customers?
2. A manufacturer makes a line of women's handbags. This company offers 6000 different styles of handbags in its catalog. It sells almost 25,000 handbags per year, but it is not known which style is going to sell from one week to the next.

   The company has both a JIT system and a mass-production system to make the same line of handbags. Both manufacturing systems work well, and both cost about the same to operate. The JIT system can make up to 100 handbags a day; however, it is very flexible. If necessary, it can produce 100 different styles in a single day of operation.

   The mass production system takes half a day to set up and can make 1000 handbags—all the same style—in the second half of the day. It is 10 times as fast as the JIT system.

   Raw materials cost $4 per handbag and are the same whichever system is used to do the work. The company likes to order enough materials to make 2000 handbags, which is usually enough to cover a month of orders.

   The company has discovered a trick to run more than one style of handbag with the mass-production system. If it sets up in the morning and runs just one handbag until noon, it can use the afternoon to change over to a different style and still have time to run another handbag before closing at 5:00. This gives it two handbags produced in one day, if necessary.

The Average Day: 100 Handbags, Each of a Different Style, Are Ordered	Mass-Production System, Using the Regular Method	Mass-Production System, Using the Two Setups Trick	JIT System
Units shipped	1	2	100
Percentage of orders for the day filled	1%	2%	100%
Amount of unsold inventory created	999	0	0
Raw materials available for future work	1000 units / $4000 value	1998 units / $7992 value	1900 units / $7600 value

   a. Which system is more efficient? Why?
   b. If the company could only keep one of these manufacturing systems, which do you think it should keep? Explain.
3. Give an example of a business that is known internationally for the quality of its products; what defines quality for this company?
4. How does the design of a facility affect product quality and production efficiency?
5. Choose a partner in class and make a list of the technology each of you can personally access. Brainstorm how you might combine your technological resources to create a successful business. Describe in detail how the partnership would work. For example, would the

person contributing more technology have a larger share of the business, or would profits and expenses be split equally? Draw up a partnership agreement that specifies each partner's duties and how much money and time each will invest in the business.

6. Examine the labels on the shoes and clothing you are wearing today. Which items were made in foreign countries? How many dollars per hour do you think the people earned who made these articles of clothing? Why do you think the company that manufactured these items had them made abroad?

Key Concept Questions

1. Use your local telephone company's business-to-business directory or *The American Wholesalers and Distributors Directory* to locate wholesalers you could visit, or from whom you could order products for resale.
2. Choose one of the quality-assurance methodologies described in this chapter and explain how it might apply to your educational institution.

Application Exercises

1. What might the supply chain look like for one of the following:
   a. manufacturer of custom rims for automobiles
   b. car dealership
   c. building materials wholesaler
2. Suggest at least three quality-assurance measures for the following businesses:
   a. bank
   b. residential cleaning service
   c. commercial HVAC (heating, ventilation, and air conditioning) contractor
   d. computer manufacturer

Exploring Your Community

Identify two businesses in your community with which you are familiar. Suggest four measures of quality for each. Rate each business on these quality dimensions. Then, answer the following questions.

Measure of Quality	Rating (1 Is Poor, 5 Is Excellent)				
	Company Number 1				
Measure 1	1	2	3	4	5
Measure 2	1	2	3	4	5
Measure 3	1	2	3	4	5
Measure 4	1	2	3	4	5
	Company Number 2				
Measure 1	1	2	3	4	5
Measure 2	1	2	3	4	5
Measure 3	1	2	3	4	5
Measure 4	1	2	3	4	5

1. What do these measures tell you about the respective businesses?
2. How might they improve on one of the indicators?
3. Does each business have a customer feedback mechanism? If so, what is it? If not, what would you recommend?

Case Study | Producing Quality Parts: Small Parts Manufacturing

Small Parts Manufacturing Company Inc. (SPM) is a custom-fabricated metal parts manufacturing company founded in 1946 by Merton Rockney in Portland, Oregon. This specialty machine shop continues to be operated by his son, Merton Rockney, Jr., and by 2007 it had 48 employees and sales of approximately $6.5 million. Steady growth over the decades has been the result of numerous factors, in particular, an emphasis on quality.

SPM is a contract manufacturer, a job shop that makes metal, machined parts for companies that either use them as components for larger assemblies or resell them. They have a state-of-the-art facility to create the parts, and a group of certified subcontractors that provide additional processing to meet individual orders, such as plating, painting, and bending. Customers provide SPM with their specifications and request price quotes—a service available through SPM's Web site. Team members work with prospective customers to provide innovative solutions that meet the quality and delivery requirements.

As a job shop, SPM has a variety of equipment for the machining of parts and a staff of skilled tool makers, machinists, and computer technicians. They start with extruded bar stock in round, hexagonal, or square shapes from which the parts are made. Materials include low-carbon, alloy, or stainless steel, brass, aluminum, plastics, and exotic metals. The company uses traditional machinery such as screw machines, bench grinders, drill presses, and turret lathes. SPM also employs computer-controlled (CNC) machines and computer-aided design and manufacturing (CAD/CAM), which they house in a climate-controlled room.

Quality assurance is critical to SPM's success. Machining parts to very tight (exact) tolerances is a requirement for their customers. One example of the company's quality-assurance process is its use of Statistical Process Control (SPC), with seven networked data-collection stations providing in-process measurements throughout the facility. SPM also uses a machine—a Gage-Master optical comparator with digital readout—to check features that would otherwise be difficult to measure. SPM is ISO 9001:2000-registered and promotes this on its Web site.

SPM has been delivering on its promise to provide high-quality parts to its customers for over 60 years.

Case Study Analysis

1. How has SPM brought modern technology to the traditional processes of machining custom parts?
2. What is the source of production inputs for SPM?
3. How does SPM assure quality? Do you agree that they chose the right type of quality assurance? Why or why not?
4. What types of regulations are particularly important to SPM and its employees, given the nature of the business?

Case Source

Small Parts Manufacturing Web site, http://www.machiningcompany.com, and http://www.Hoovers.com/small-parts-manufacturing, accessed November 15, 2009.

Case Study | Sewing Up Business in New Ways—Sew What? Inc.

Question: What do Maroon 5, Slip Knot, Green Day, Rod Stewart, Elton John, Madonna, and schools near you have in common?

Answer: They are customers of Sew What? Inc., a manufacturer of custom draperies and curtains for theaters, concert tours, exhibitions, and special events.

Megan Duckett, founder of Sew What?, has been passionate about theater and concert production since high school. She started her career as a part-time employee at the Arts Centre in Melbourne, Australia, before she graduated from a Church of England girls' grammar school (high school). The Arts Centre, the heart of theater in Melbourne, provided an opportunity to apprentice as a lighting technician with master theatre electrician Jim Paine. There, Megan was exposed to the businesses that serve the theater industry and she discovered that working in this industry was what she was born to do.

Not long after that, 18-year-old Megan moved into the rock and roll marketplace and continued to work as a lighting technician, and on other backstage aspects of the business. A critical turning point in her life came unexpectedly one year later. She was assigned to driving Billy Joel's band around while they were in Melbourne. They had an instant rapport, and the crew invited her to visit the United States. Much to their surprise, Megan showed up on their doorstep shortly thereafter and soon got a job at a staging company for rock concerts. Megan knew that she needed to find her niche and stand out from everyone else. As she has noted, "I needed to be invaluable and irreplaceable." Little did she know that sewing would be her ticket to success.

The opportunity to make her mark through sewing essentially came out of nowhere. However, Megan quickly realized that it was the opportunity she sought. Her first sewing job was to reupholster 10 coffins for a Haunted Halloween show. She had neither the equipment nor the materials to do the job when she accepted it. Undeterred, Megan rented a sewing machine and went to a local fabric store, where she bought the necessary supplies (at full retail price) and did the work at her kitchen table. The customer could see that it was wonderfully done and called

Megan Duckett.

two weeks later with more work. That customer referred others and the business took off. That was in 1992. For five years, Megan says, "The phone kept ringing with orders."

As Megan was preparing her taxes in 1997, she realized that her earnings from the custom projects sewn at her kitchen table matched the pay from her 40-hour-a-week job. She and her husband, Adam, had just purchased a home and had transformed the garage into a sewing room. After considerable discussion, Megan left her steady, full-time employment, incorporated Sew What? a few weeks later, and rented an 800-square-foot space a few miles from her house. She had no formal advisors and no written plan, but she did have a strong customer base, determination, and an understanding of the business. Just six weeks later, Megan landed a contract big enough so that she had to hire her first employee, a stitcher named Maria, who continues as part of the Sew What? family to this day. In 2002, Adam quit his own job and joined Sew What?

Megan relates, "The soft-goods industry is traditionally very much a cottage industry and is not known for embracing technology. We didn't like the way that felt." From the beginning, the

Ducketts incorporated technology into the business. The company team recognized that, as the quality of the clientele and the size of the contracts increased, customers would expect excellence. Sew What? began deliberately streamlining and fine-tuning both the product and service aspects of the business.

Advances in technology were instituted throughout the operation. The office equipment was upgraded to include a network setup, faster computers, and multiple servers to increase speed, in order to function in real time with customers. Sew What? is currently on its third inventory-management system. The first was an Excel-based configuration that they developed themselves. The second method was part of the automated accounting program. The most recent arrangement is a sophisticated manufacturing system called VISTA, from Epicor. Sew What? has moved into lean manufacturing procedures and every function is timed, scanned, and measured to reduce waste and maximize use of resources. In addition, some patterns are cut using computer-guided tools, although many are still cut by hand—because runs of fabric can be so long and the tolerances so tight, that hand cutting makes the most sense.

The company's Web site is a particularly important sales tool. Megan lost a substantial job early on because, without one, her business lacked credibility with that prospective customer. Whereas Megan resisted the idea of putting up a Web site, she came to realize that she needed it, so she built one over a weekend using clip art, a far cry from the professional site Sew What? has today. Megan notes, "Generation Y will be the purchasing agents of the future. They expect a Web site. They need the visual communication." A Web site is particularly helpful for Sew What?, which has clients across the country and around the world (the company is headquartered in Rancho Dominguez, California). The site includes e-swatches, so that visitors can look at fabric samples online.

The sales force and production team also benefit from the use of technology, through a custom software program. By means of a series of drop-down menus, they can select such variables as fabric, color, and production method. To that they add dimensions and other specifications. The system calculates a "bid window" of the high and low price that can be offered. It determines the minutes of labor and the yards of materials. Once the job is sold and a contract secured, the file is digitally editable and the Sew What? team can make final adjustments. It is then sent to a report generator (Crystal Reports), and automatically translated into Spanish for the team of stitchers. This system permits Sew What? to sell more effectively, quote more accurately, replicate the work more easily, and make fewer mistakes. Sew What? has used its technological infrastructure to maximize productivity.

The company won the Dell/NFIB (National Federation of Independent Business) 2006 Small Business Excellence Award, and was featured on

the Dell Web site for the Integration of Technology into a Business. With a 15,000-square-foot building, and a staff of more than 30, finding ways to maximize technology was essential.

The sales and order cycles for Sew What? are largely dependent on the type of customer. For example, rock and roll touring curtains might take anywhere from three days to four weeks, from inquiry to order. These customers may also recycle or replace their curtains after a tour. They may even donate them to charity. Often, quick delivery is important for the touring customers, and because Sew What? generally uses only U.S.-milled products, the production cycle can be relatively quick after the order is placed.

For a school or church group buying or replacing stage curtains, the cycle is often three to six months. The process generally includes multiple steps, such as: a group realizes the drapes don't open/close properly or it needs new ones. A student or PTA parent researches available vendors, so they call Sew What? The sales team educates them by focusing first on making sure they know what they need and what they are getting. The customer is directed to samples and possible solutions, often through the Web site. Sew What? submits a price; the gatherer compares prices; and the school or church group fundraises. With money in hand, they finalize the order, and Megan's team speaks with the person who will install the drapes. Sew What? makes and ships the drapes, the customer receives and installs them, and Megan reaches out to see that they are satisfied.

Megan was thrilled to have her products on the cover of the 1000th issue of *Rolling Stone*. She won a 2007 Stevie Award for Most Innovative Company of the Year (up to 100 employees), was a finalist for the 2008 Enterprising Woman of the Year, and Sew What? was named to DiversityBusiness.com's list of the top 500 small businesses in the United States (2008). In her feature as a young millionaire in *Entrepreneur* magazine, Megan stated, "The secret [to success] is hard work, dedication, and being able to take a blow and get up and move forward again. Be willing to accept criticism and comments, find mentors and learn from others. Try to be inspired by other people's success." With sales of about $5 million annually, the answer to *Sew What?* is "sewing up business." Or, as the company's Web site states, "Sew What? Inc. It's not a question, it's the answer."

Case Study Analysis

1. How does technology sustain Megan Duckett's business?
2. Why does Megan credit computer technology and the Web for a significant portion of her company's growth?
3. What have been some critical steps in the growth of the company?
4. What is (are) the sales cycle(s) for Sew What?
5. What channels of distribution would you expect the company to use?

Case Sources

Dell Case Studies, at http://www.dell.com/html/us/segments/bsd/case_studies/sew/index.html.

Sew What? Inc. Web site, http://www.sewwhatinc.com (accessed November 15, 2009). Courtesy of Sew What? Inc.

"Young Millionaires Say More," http://www.entrepreneur.com/slideshow/184476.html.

Chapter 18

LOCATION, FACILITIES, AND LAYOUT

"We succeed in enterprises which demand the positive qualities we possess, but we excel in those which can also make use of our defects."

—Alexis de Tocqueville, author of *Democracy in America*

Frederick W. Smith wrote a paper about air-freight shipping in the coming computer age while an undergraduate at Yale in 1965.[1] Just a few years later (1971), after four years in the Marine Corps, Smith purchased controlling interest in an Arkansas-based aviation company. As he evolved the ideas from his term paper, Smith explored locations for his venture. Though incorporated as Federal Express in 1971, Smith's company began actual operations in Memphis, Tennessee (rather than Arkansas), in 1973.

Smith selected Memphis for a number of reasons. It was centrally located for the original target market. The weather in Memphis is such that airport closures are rare. And the Memphis International Airport had hangar space for the 14 Federal Express Dassault Falcon jets, and was willing to adapt its facilities to accommodate this start-up venture.

Since then, FedEx has continued to expand its operation globally and is the largest airline in the world, based upon number of aircraft and tons of freight flown. The 658 planes in today's FedEx fleet fly to over 375 destinations. FedEx continues to have its headquarters and "super hub" at Memphis. However, there are now seven other domestic hubs: Anchorage, Forth Worth, Indianapolis, Miami (Florida), Newark (New Jersey), and Oakland.

The most recently added hub, in Greensboro, North Carolina, began operations in 2009. International hubs are located in Paris, Toronto, and Gaungzhou Baiyun International Airport in Southern China. An additional hub, at Cologne-Bonn Airport in Germany, is under development.

FedEx has expertise in identifying locations that will support the logistical requirements of the business with appropriate facilities.

Performance Objectives

1. Understand the importance of the physical location of a business.
2. Know the key factors to consider in the location decision.
3. Learn how location needs differ by business type.
4. Determine locations via multiple methods.
5. Explore the design of facilities and their layouts.
6. Recognize the special considerations for home-based businesses.
7. Describe location factors for Web-based businesses.

The Importance of Physical Location

The choice of location for your business can make the difference between success and failure. The oft-quoted business mantra, "location, location, location" is broadly accepted as critical for retail stores. However, the choice of site is a critical strategic decision for manufacturing, wholesale, and Web-based businesses as well, albeit for different reasons. The location decision may be a one-time process, although as the FedEx example illustrates, it may occur multiple times during the life of a business. Location strategy has critical impacts on revenues, customer satisfaction, fixed and variable costs, and the overall levels of risk and profitability.

[1]FedEx Website at http://about.fedex.com/our_company/ (accessed November 19, 2009).

Performance Objective 1

Understand the importance of the physical location of a business.

Whether your business needs are to generate customer floor traffic; provide conveniently located services; have ready access to highways, a port, a railroad line, or an airport; or can operate virtually anywhere, the location decision will determine your access to markets and affect essential portions of your cost structure. For a traditional brick-and-mortar retailer, the amount of marketing expense required to generate floor traffic in a low-traffic location will probably be significantly higher than in an area where there is already high traffic. For businesses in which transportation costs are high, operating expenses can become prohibitive. On the other hand, distribution-cost efficiencies can save money and be a competitive advantage.

Key Factors in Deciding upon a Location

Performance Objective 2

Know the key factors to consider in the location decision.

The key factors in deciding upon a location are dependent upon the nature of the business and its customers. Considerations include

- access for customers;
- access to suppliers;
- climate and geography;
- convenience;
- cost of facilities (rent, construction, and the like);
- demographics;
- economic conditions and business incentives;
- governmental regulations and laws, including environmental impact;
- labor pool;
- proximity to competitors, and
- visibility.

Figure 18-1 shows the factors affecting location decisions at the country, regional/community, and site levels.

Different Types of Business Have Different Location Needs

Performance Objective 3

Learn how location needs differ by business type.

Each business has a unique set of location criteria and priorities. Each industry and business type provides some insight into location issues through trade publications and industry information. What's important to a specialty retailer at a brick-and-mortar location might be meaningless for a service business. The challenge is to identify the critical success factors for your business, tempered by the realities of budgetary and other constraints, to find your best available option.

Options and Criteria for Manufacturing Facilities

Manufacturing facilities have multiple location-criteria considerations that are primarily centered on customer service and costs. Manufacturers need to meet and exceed customer delivery and quality goals. That means being located within ready access for distribution (perhaps near warehousing and/or transportation routes), and having a labor pool of sufficient size and skill to produce to quality standards. Also, labor wage rates and productivity should be considered. For example, a producer of organic fertilizer may locate close to its plant-growing customers. A machine shop may be best served by locating in a community with trained CAD/CAM operators and machinists. In addition, some manufactured goods cannot be moved over long distances without transportation costs becoming prohibitive

Figure 18-1 *Some considerations and factors that affect location decisions.*

	Critical Success Factors
Country Decision	1. Political risks, governmental regulations, national attitudes, and incentives 2. Cultural and economic issues 3. Location of markets 4. Labor talent, attitude of labor pool, productivity, costs 5. Availability of supplies, communications, energy 6. Exchange rates and currency risk
Regional/Community Decision	1. Corporate desires 2. Attractiveness of region (culture, taxes, climate, etc.) 3. Labor availability, costs, attitudes toward unions 4. Cost and availability of utilities 5. Environmental regulations 6. Government incentives and fiscal policies 7. Proximity to raw materials and customers 8. Land/construction costs
Site Decision	1. Site size and cost 2. Air, rail, highway, waterway systems 3. Zoning restrictions 4. Proximity of services/supplies needed 5. Environmental-impact issues

Source: Jay Heizer and Barry Render, *Operations Management*, 8th ed., (Upper Saddle River, N.J.: Pearson Prentice Hall, 2007), p. 249.

Step into the Shoes...

Finding the Location that Fits

When José Echeverri left Merrill Lynch to start his own financial planning firm, he chose a location in a small city near his home on a well traveled road and furnished it like an executive office at a major brokerage house. He invested precious start-up funds in leasehold improvements and in quality furniture and décor. A couple of years later, José determined that he could find opportunities in a small but rapidly growing community 20 miles away. He opened a second office in that town and hired a colleague to operate it.

After a year, José found that the majority of his business was coming from the second office, which had been chosen based on demographics rather than proximity. He moved his primary location to that town, expanded the office slightly, and closed his initial location. As it turned out, he needed a modest office in a community with stronger demographics more than a fancy space in a less-well-chosen location. José now says, "One of my biggest mistakes in starting this business was trying to create a mini-Merrill rather than finding my own niche from the beginning. Now that we are in the right place and doing the right things, the business is stronger than ever."

Courtesy of José Echeverri.

(mattresses, for example), such that they effectively have only local markets and must locate in relatively close proximity to potential customers. For others, global options are available.

Other factors for manufacturers to consider include access to suppliers, cost of facilities, and laws and regulations. When product freshness or speed of delivery of supplies is essential to business success, manufacturers need to consider their proximity to suppliers. This is also true for heavy, bulky, fragile, or expensive finished goods and their delivery. Bakeries and bottlers often locate near customers for this reason. If delivery can be made on a timely basis without nearby suppliers, this factor loses its significance.

The cost of facilities, whether leased or purchased, will be a significant expense among the fixed costs of a manufacturer, with considerable impact on its operating breakeven point, operating leverage, and overall business viability. The cost of manufacturing facilities varies widely. It is important to consider current and future needs and to carefully assess them to select a location that balances these factors with costs. The costs will probably include rent or mortgage payments; leasehold improvements, renovation, or construction; maintenance; energy and utility charges; and property taxes.

Finally, laws and regulations with respect to manufacturing can make a difference between operating efficiently and being fined, temporarily shut down, or permanently closed. In particular, compliance with zoning regulations at the proposed location is critical. Zoning laws define the types of businesses that can be located in particular places. For example, a heavy manufacturing plant cannot be operating in an area zoned for light manufacturing. Zoning laws may prohibit specific types of manufacturing, or all manufacturing, in residential neighborhoods. State and local environmental regulations vary from place to place, and must be taken into consideration in making a location decision for a manufacturing business. There could be a financial incentive to support selection of one site over another. For example, there might be low-cost financing or tax breaks associated with a particular location.

Options and Criteria for Wholesale Businesses

Wholesale businesses face many of the same options and criteria as manufacturers, although with fewer constraints on their operations. For

wholesalers, the ability to efficiently distribute goods to customers is the primary consideration. Proximity to customers and/or suppliers is important, as is the availability of a well-developed transportation network. Tangible costs such as rent or mortgage, utilities, taxes, labor, and transportation are paramount. As with manufacturers, government regulations and incentives contribute to the decision-making process.

Options and Criteria for Retail Businesses

Retail businesses with brick-and-mortar sites focus heavily upon the revenue-generating aspects of locations, as opposed to the cost focus of manufacturers and wholesalers. As a retailer, you will have to concentrate on the drawing power of your location, the match between your target market and the demographics of the customer-drawing area and the competitive environment. The ability to attract paying customers in sufficient volume and adequate frequency is essential to success. Demographic data from the U.S. Census (http://www.census.gov), the U.S. Economic Development Administration (http://www.eda.gov), state and local economic development offices, and chambers of commerce can provide considerable insight into local demographics.

Customer convenience and company image is vital. Also, the proximity to **traffic generators**, which are complementary businesses that attract customer traffic to the retailer's area, can significantly increase revenue generation. For example, a nearby child-care center and a toy store will almost certainly assist in drawing business to a children's clothing boutique. Be sure that the value gained from traffic generators will be greater than the incremental cost. For example, a mall location next to a supermarket may be, because of the random traffic created, worth higher rental fees. Sometimes, proximity to direct competitors as traffic generators, **clustering**, may be a viable strategy. In commercial areas there might be, respectively, clusters of antique dealers, jewelers, or automobile dealerships.

traffic generators complementary businesses that attract customer traffic to the retailers' area.

clustering locating near direct competitors as a strategy.

Researching the average sales per square foot in your industry can help you determine a good location by permitting comparison of your anticipated performance to others in the vicinity. If there is a great variation, you may need to reconsider your site selection. The sources of such statistics include trade associations for your industry and the International Council of Shopping Centers (ICSC, at http://www.icsc.org); the public library reference area; annual reports of publicly traded companies; the U.S. Census Bureau (http://www.census.gov); and businesses like yours outside of your geographic area. You may find that the results vary because of particularly good or poor locations, or because of any number of market, marketing, or operating factors. But, calculating your anticipated average sales per square foot can assist in site selection.

Another reason to research sales per square foot is to determine the amount of space you will need for your retail location. Until you know how much **selling space**—actual retail floor space excluding storage and warehousing, administrative, and utility areas—you need, it will be impossible to determine which sites will be appropriate for your business. In order to calculate the selling space, you will need the industry data on sales per square foot and the estimate of your annual sales volume. That formula is

selling space actual retail floor space excluding storage and warehousing, administrative, and utility areas.

Selling Space = Sales Volume/Sales per Square Foot

If you expect your New Age boutique to generate $300,000 in annual sales, with average sales per square foot of $200, you would need about 1500 square feet of selling space. Then, add sufficient area for storage, offices, and restrooms—but be wary of being either overly optimistic in your estimates for current and future needs, or of acquiring too little space.

Cost factors, as always, are important, but will be relatively stable once a location is selected. Generally, retail stores incur rental costs and salaries and wages as major factors. Rent will be determined by the location of the property, and should be weighed against the revenue-generating potential.

Options and Criteria for Service and Professional Businesses

Service and professional businesses face divergent requirements. The choice of location for service and professional firms will depend upon many of the factors discussed above. Such companies differ considerably with respect to customer convenience, depending upon the type of service and how it is delivered. Some businesses, such as cleaning companies, temporary staffing firms, home health care, and delivery services go to their customers on-site to provide the service, and need to have efficient access to their customer base. Physicians, dentists, and other health-care providers often locate in areas where the population fits the service's target demographics and frequently near other health-care providers or close to hospitals. Attorneys frequently locate where there is convenient access to the local court house and other legal practices, often in central business districts. With the advent of the electronic filing of court documents, this need for geographic proximity is diminishing. Accountants have multiple location options, depending upon their clientele.

Another factor to be considered in the location decision for service and professional firms is image, or positioning. A firm wishing to convey an upscale, high-end image will be better served by locating in an elegant suite in a prestigious office building than in a down-scale strip mall outside of town. By the same token, a firm providing telemarketing services could be located anywhere where the technology and labor force meets its requirements. That explains why such businesses are often located outside of metropolitan areas where facility and labor costs are lower. The success of call centers in Bangalore, India, for U.S.-based companies is one example of this phenomenon. For health care professionals, accessibility for their patients and proximity to other providers is more important than top-of-the-line space (with a few exceptions), but patients also expect a certain level of cleanliness and quality. The recent emergence of medical travel to other parts of the globe (such as to Brazil, Mexico, and India from the United States) for treatment has redefined the meaning of accessibility in some areas of health care. In all cases where customers travel to a service or professional firm, access from highways/street and/or public transportation, as well as safety and security, matter.

Evaluating Location Alternatives

Performance Objective 4

Determine locations via multiple methods.

The selection of a location is a critical business success factor, is often a one-time event, and is generally an expensive one to change; familiarizing yourself with some of the methods for evaluating location alternatives is good practice. These methods range from simple and inexpensive to highly sophisticated and costly. The expense of selecting the profit-maximizing location for your business is an important investment in its future success.

Global Impact...

Aravind Eye Care System

Location of medical services has become global with advances in technology, ease of travel, and variety of cost structures. Aravind Eye Care System (AECS), a social enterprise, is based in Maduri, India, and claims it is "the largest and most productive eye care facility in the world." Aravind provides eye surgery and outpatient care at each of its five[2] hospitals. AECS was founded in 1976 by Dr. Govindappa Venkataswamy with the goal of eliminating blindness. In 2008, Dr. P. Namperumalsamy, Chairman of AECS, was awarded the Ernst & Young Entrepreneur of the Year for Health Care in Mumbai.

In addition to the facilities at its five hospitals, AECS provides award-winning telemedicine services in rural areas of the country. It has become an international training center (Lions Aravind Institute of Community Ophthalmology), and AECS treats patients from around the globe. The program has focused on creating cost efficiencies in the delivery of care to enable outreach to a broader base of patients. In addition, AECS manufactures optical products (specifically, intraocular lenses for cataract patients) through its Aurolab division for use in their hospitals, and for outside sale to raise funds to serve more patients in poverty. Funding for AECS comes from organizations around the world, and among the ophthalmology interns are many from the United States.

The efficiencies achieved by AECS allow it to provide well over half of its surgical care at no cost or reduced fees. By creating what is essentially an assembly-line process and layout for cataract surgeries, and working in small, specialized teams, the time necessary for each surgery is minimized; and the surgeons complete a maximal number of operations per day. Also, because Indian laws differ from those in the United States, more than one patient can be in an operating room at a time, so that surgeons can rapidly move from one patient to the next with minimal down time.

Between April 2008 and March 2009, in excess of 300,000 people underwent surgeries at one of the Aravind Eye Hospitals, and more than 2.7 million obtained care on an outpatient basis. More than half of the surgeries were under its free-care programs for the poor.

Source: Aravind Eye Care System Web site, http://www.aravind.org (accessed February 16, 2009).

The simplest method of selecting a location is that commonly employed by small business owners. Go with the one you know. Although this is a more intuitive method than the others, it can be effective. For a lifestyle business, one that draws from a limited local area, or one where physical location is less critical, such an approach may produce the best results. When you live and/or work in an area, you become familiar with the demographics, traffic patterns, and existing businesses through daily observation. However, it is risky to assume that your perceptions are entirely correct. This method is best used as a preliminary filter, to be followed up with research.

Another common technique for location analysis is the **factor-rating method**, whereby decision criteria are prioritized and weighted to eliminate subjective factors. This method will incorporate quantitative and qualitative considerations into your decision. The factor-rating method can be employed for any type of business, and you can include as many or as few factors as you wish to rate in its six basic steps:

factor-rating method location decision approach whereby decision criteria are prioritized and weighted to eliminate subjective decisions.

1. develop a list of critical success factors,
2. determine the weight of each factor according to its relative importance,
3. create a measurement scale for the factors,
4. score each proposed location for each factor (best if done by a team) according to the scale,
5. multiply the factor weight times the factor score for each factor in each location, and
6. use the sum of these weighted factors for the locations, to compare them and make a location recommendation/decision.[3]

[2]As of January 2010.
[3]Heizer and Render, p. 253.

Exhibit 18-1 *Factor-ratings for a hybrid automobile manufacturing plant.*

Critical Success Factors	Weight	Scores (out of 10)		Weighted Scores	
		Michigan	Delaware	Michigan	Delaware
Labor (United Auto Workers Union)/ Management Relations	0.25	5	10	1.25	2.50
Readiness of Facility	0.20	7	9	1.40	1.80
Proximity to Customers	0.20	7	7	1.40	1.40
Tax and Financial Incentives	0.20	10	6	2.00	1.20
Proximity to an Atlantic Port	0.15	3	10	0.45	1.50
Total	1.00	XXX	XXX	6.50	**8.40**

Exhibit 18-1 shows factor-rating for a proposed electric car manufacturing plant. In 2009, an innovative, federally funded, and venture-backed company faced a location decision that literally included the entire United States (limited to a U.S. location because of the federal funding). After management decided to consider only locations where automotive plants had recently closed, the decision alternatives rapidly narrowed.

Although the factor-rating decision is highly speculative, the firm did, in fact, make a commitment to a location in Delaware rather than in the heart of car country.

One tool that is available to entrepreneurs at all stages is geographic information systems (GIS). These structures include demographic data; extensive maps; topographic data; and major transportation routes, health care facilities, and the like. When you identify the factors that are important to your business, you can use a GIS system to discover potential profit-maximizing locations.

Larger businesses often develop customized GIS systems tailored to their particular location requirements. For example, franchisors such as Dunkin' Donuts can use GIS to target areas for new franchises. For entrepreneurs with fewer resources, Microsoft MapPoint 2010 software may be well suited. MapPoint includes demographics and maps that can be combined with firm-specific or industry data. **Figure 18-2** shows a GIS map for Prince William County, Virginia.

A decidedly more low-tech approach to assessing location is to gather demographic, psychographic, and geographic data and competitive information to create location options for consideration. The U.S. Census Bureau (http://www.census.gov) provides an abundance of data to inform your decision. Maps and traffic data can be added to the mix, as can information from trade associations. For example, if your trade association reports that customers will travel two miles to purchase jewelry, your target customer is a 45- to 55-year-old married woman who lives in a household that has an income of over $85,000, and you need a population of 50,000 of these women within a two-mile radius, you can identify possible locations. Then, you can narrow your choice by assessing the competitive environment (both clustering in jewelers' row and stand-alone should be considered), weighing personal preferences, site availability in the potential locations, traffic counts, and other success factors.

Figure 18-3 shows a drawing of the population of the United States. If you want a business location within 10 miles of a population area of 200,000 or greater, this drawing will provide an excellent visual guide. **Figure 18-4** shows a census map of Santa Fe, New Mexico, with concentric circles drawn from the heart of its highest-income census tract to

Figure 18-2 *GIS map for commuter lots in Prince William County, Virginia.*

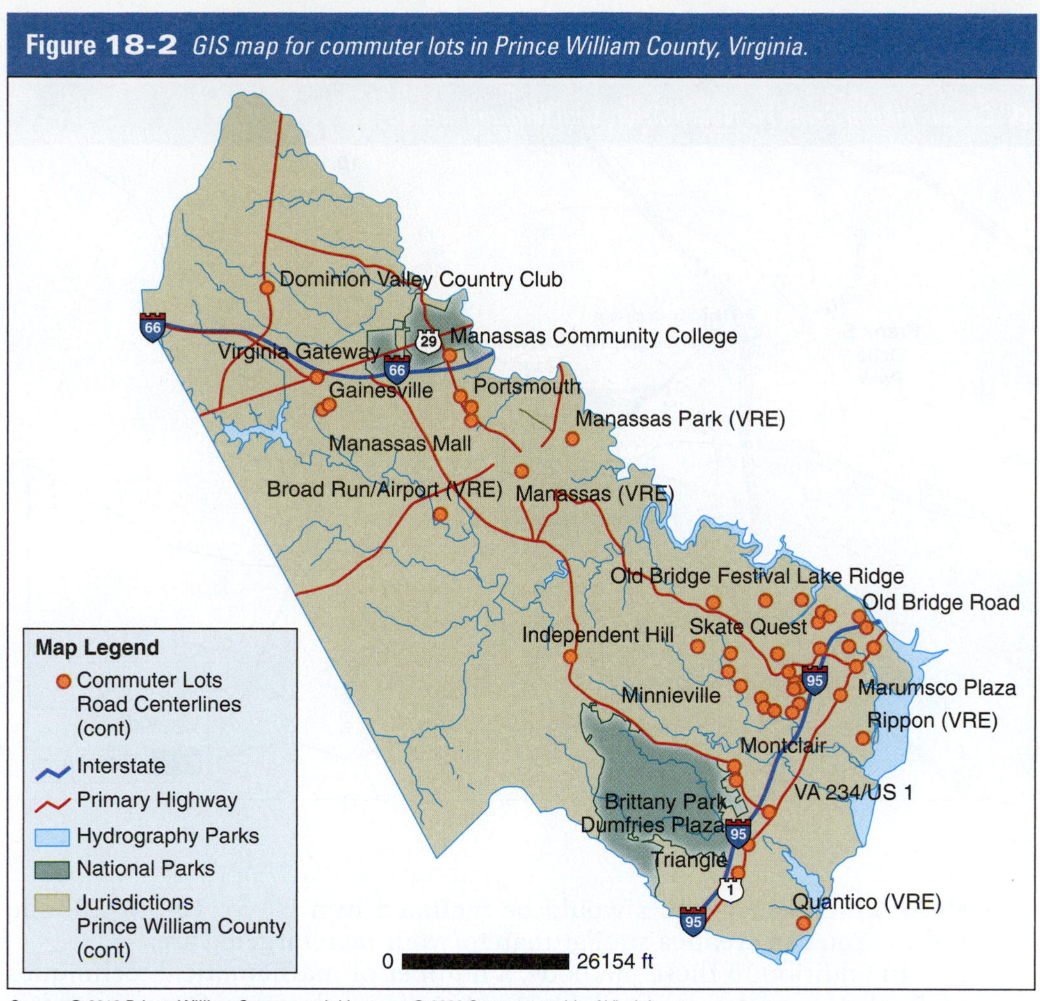

Source: © 2010 Prince William County; aerial imagery © 2009 Commonwealth of Virginia

Figure 18-3 *Population of the United States.*

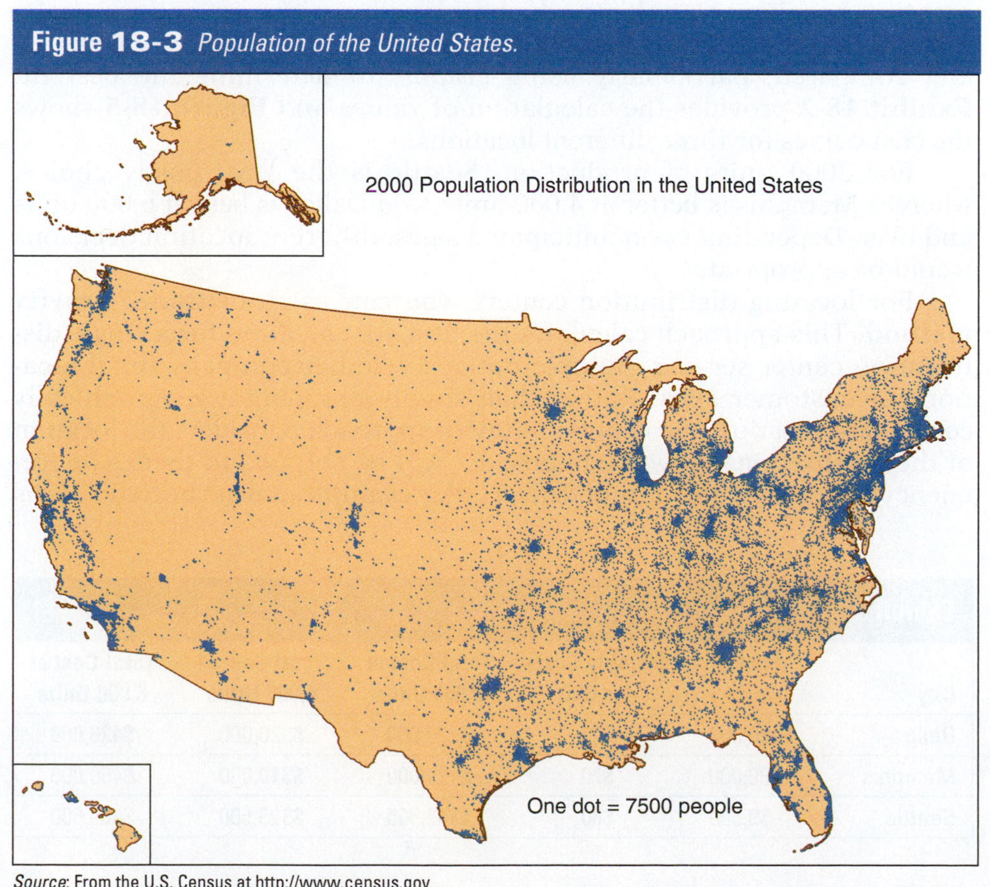

Source: From the U.S. Census at http://www.census.gov

Figure 18-4 *Census map of Santa Fe, New Mexico, with targeted areas.*

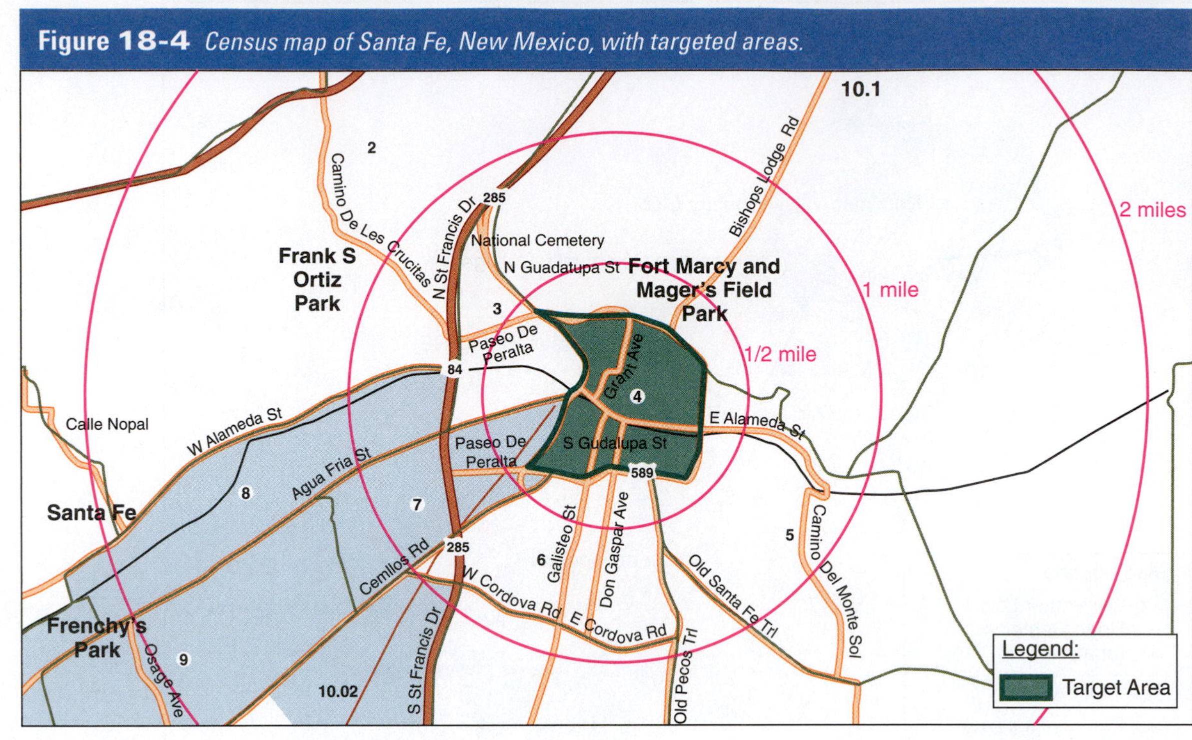

show which other tracts would be included in a 2-, 5-, 10-, or 20-mile radius. You can create a similar map for your own targeted area.

location breakeven analysis a location selection method using cost-volume analysis.

In addition to these methods, a number of mathematical techniques and other models are available for location selection. One method is **location breakeven analysis**, which is done by using cost-volume analysis. The fixed and variable costs for different locations can be calculated and compared, particularly using graphs, to determine the best fit. **Exhibit 18-2** provides the calculation of values and **Figure 18-5** shows the cost curves for three different locations.

For 2000 units of production, Seattle is the least costly choice, whereas Memphis is better at 4,000 units, and Dallas is best at 6,000 units and over. Depending upon anticipated sales, different location decisions would be appropriate.

center-of-gravity method location decision approach that calculates the best cost location for a distribution center serving multiple sites.

For locating distribution centers, you can use a **center-of-gravity method**. This approach calculates the best cost location for a single distribution center serving multiple outlets, whether company retail locations or customer sites. Rather than simply mapping a geographically centralized location, the center-of-gravity approach considers the location of the destinations, how much product will be shipped to them, the frequency of delivery, and cost of delivery. For example, a distributor in Texas

Exhibit 18-2 *Location breakeven analysis.*

City	Fixed Costs	Variable Costs per Unit	Total Cost at 2,000 Units	Total Cost at 4,000 Units	Total Cost at 6,000 Units
Dallas	$120,000	$50	$220,000	$320,000	**$420,000**
Memphis	$30,000	$70	$170,000	**$310,000**	$450,000
Seattle	$9,500	$80	**$169,500**	$329,500	$489,500

selling to customers in Dallas, Houston, San Antonio, and El Paso would be located in or near San Angelo, based solely upon its central location. However, if they shipped five times as much product to Dallas as to any other place, and very low volumes at infrequent intervals to El Paso, they should be located nearer to Dallas, using a center-of-gravity approach (see **Figure 18-6**). You can access computer models to calculate center-of-gravity, should this method be appropriate to your business.

Figure 18-5 *Location breakeven graph.*

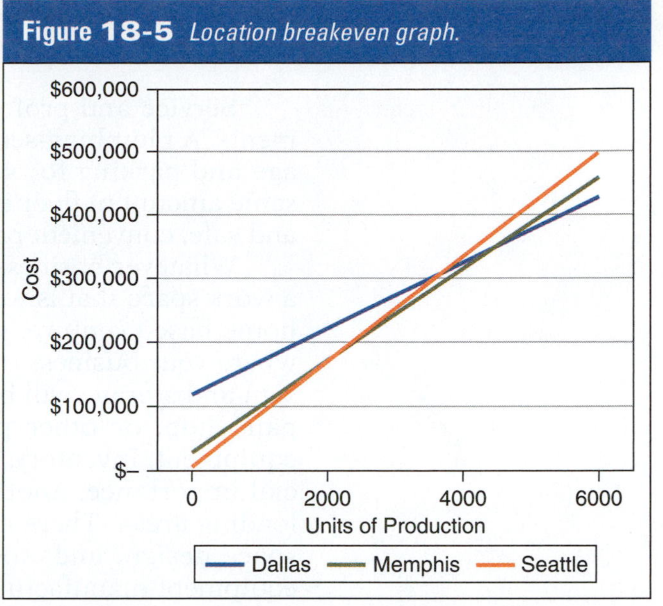

Facilities Design and Layout

Facilities are important for the geographic location and for suitability of use. You may have seen signs from real estate companies stating, "Will build to suit." This means that they will build a facility appropriate for your business. A purpose-built structure will always be necessary for certain businesses, such as restaurants or hotels. Other buildings may be put up in a more generic manner and outfitted for a specific business through additional construction. If a building is leased, these changes to adapt an existing structure for a particular business are called **leasehold improvements**.

leasehold improvements changes to adapt a rented property for a particular business.

Performance Objective 5

Explore the design of facilities and their layouts.

The type and size of facility, as well as other physical requirements, depend upon the type of business you are operating. For manufacturing, warehousing, and distribution firms, key considerations include

- capacity for efficient movement of materials, equipment, and people (floor space and ceiling height will matter);
- flexibility to adapt to changing business requirements;
- loading docks and vehicle access for deliveries and outbound shipments;
- environment conducive to work requirements (natural light, appearance, and the like);
- ability to include requisite controls, such as regulation of temperature and humidity, and cleaning rooms;
- parking for commercial and employee vehicles, as well as spaces for visitors and the handicapped;
- adequate utility services to the building—including power, water, and telecommunications, and
- security and safety.

Retail facilities must meet such business requirements as

- appropriate selling area and configuration of that space;
- permission to complete necessary leasehold improvements, or improvements to be done by landlord;
- space for offices, storage, restrooms, deliveries, and other special needs;
- signage for rules/regulations;

Figure 18-6 *Center of gravity versus central location.*

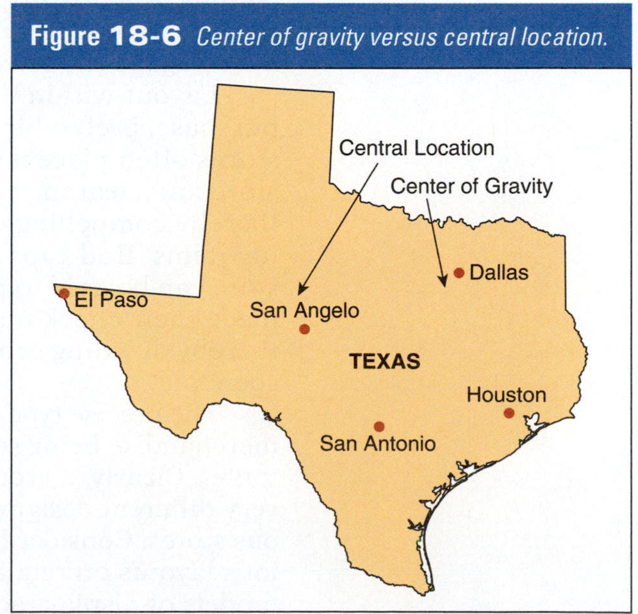

- parking that is adequate for the anticipated customer volume, and
- lighting and security.

Service and professional businesses have unique facilities requirements. A plumbing-service company may need space for basic parts storage and parking for service vehicles. A physician's office may need the same amount of floor space but require waiting areas, examination rooms, and safe, convenient patient parking.

Whatever business and facility you decide on, you will need to create a work space that is well suited to the business's operations. If you have a home-based venture, you will have to create an area in your living space where your business operations can operate. With a retail store, floor design and storage will be critical to successful operation. For a factory, repair shop, or other production facility, the layout of the machinery, equipment, inventory, raw material, and component areas will be of crucial importance. Another consideration is the access to loading and unloading areas. There are professionals who specialize in floor planning, space design, and work flow. Some of these may be employed by the equipment manufacturers and landlords who want you as a customer. Do not hesitate to ask for free services in these areas. **Figure 18-7** shows the layout of a mattress factory.

product layouts mass production layouts appropriate for continuous production processes.

process layouts functional layouts that work well where there are common processes.

fixed-position layouts used for the production of large objects where materials and teams are brought to a single location, as in manufactured housing.

Manufacturing layouts can be categorized as **product layouts**, **process layouts**, and **fixed-position layouts**. If a product is made through a continuous process, a mass-production or product layout is likely to be best. For example, an automobile assembly line is a product layout. When there are common processes used on varied products, a *process* or functional layout may work well. For example, a layout with departments or shops, such as a faucet-manufacturing plant, with casting, grinding, polishing, plating, packaging, and other departments, is a process layout. A fixed-position layout is appropriate for the production of very large items that are either difficult to move or are designed to stay in place. In this case, the materials and production teams are brought to a single location. Commercial and residential construction and yacht building are examples of fixed-position layouts.

Store layout is a particularly important part of a retail business's marketing and revenue-generation operations. The exterior of the store, including window displays and signage, can attract customers or cause them to walk on by. Even the cleanliness of the windows themselves sends a message to the consumer.

Layout within the store should be designed to entice customers to purchase, preferably into buying more than they initially sought. Retail stores often place new items, or signature products, at the front of the store and clearance or sale goods toward the rear, or against the walls, thereby compelling customers to pass by a variety of potentially enticing items. End-caps and other prominent display areas throughout the store can be used to push certain items. Also, well-designed stores rarely place their check-out registers directly in front of the entrance doors, thereby avoiding reminders to the customers of the money they will be spending.

The precise type of layout that is best for a retail store depends on the merchandise being sold and the shopping experience desired for the customer. Clearly, a grocery store, bridal salon, and car showroom warrant very different designs. Pay attention to the layouts you encounter in various stores. Consider hiring a specialist in your industry, and/or try out various layouts on retail-design software. You may even want to build scale models of display racks and tables out of cardboard to get a better sense

Figure 18-7 *Factory layout, mattress factory.*

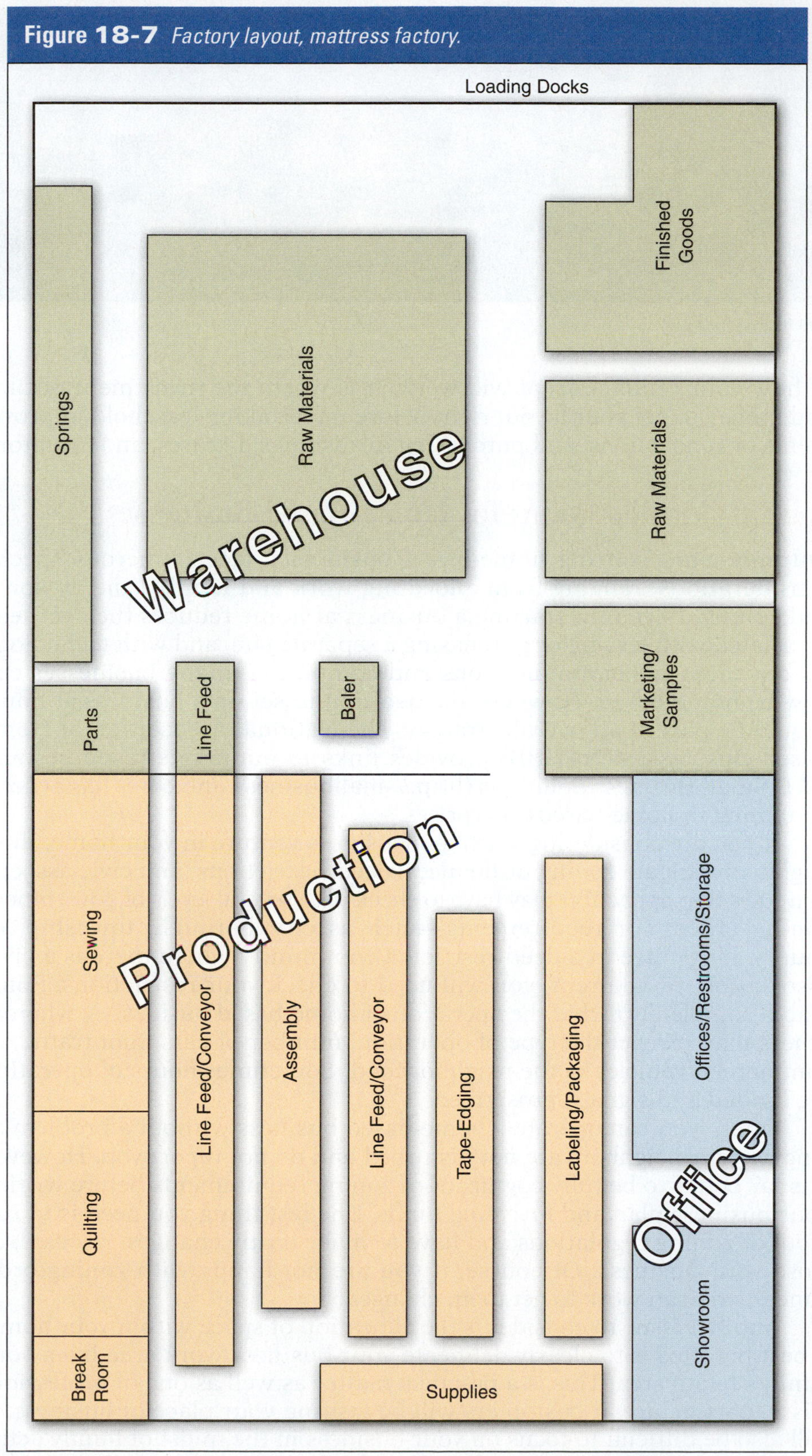

© JG Photography/Alamy

of how your retail concept will work. It is worth the investment of time and money to get your layout right before undertaking leasehold improvements or renovations, and purchasing furnishings, fixtures, and inventory.

Special Considerations for Home-Based Businesses

Entrepreneurs starting home-based businesses face numerous special considerations, ranging from allocating work and family time, to space and zoning. Certainly, starting a business at home reduces the overhead associated with leasing or purchasing a separate site, and with technological advances in communications and computing, many businesses can now be home-based. However, the decision to set up a business at home should be part of an overall strategy. The National Association of Home Based Businesses (NAHBB) provides links to numerous resources and D&B Small Business Solutions (http://smallbusiness.dnb.com) has articles pertaining to home-based enterprises.

If you are considering starting a business venture in your home, thoroughly investigate zoning ordinances, deed restrictions, and civic association rules that apply. You may have to check with several levels of government zoning offices for requirements—such as city, borough, township, or county. If you live in a deed-restricted community where there is a civic association, or you rent, you will need to check your restrictions. Some places completely forbid the operation of home-based businesses; whereas others may restrict the type of operation, number of cars, foot traffic, or commercial vehicles in the neighborhood. Sometimes hours of operation are limited and signage proscribed.

Performance Objective 6

Recognize the special considerations for home-based businesses.

Often, you can operate a home-based business without a problem as long as your neighbors are not disturbed and do not report you. However, it is far better to be fully cognizant of zoning requirements before writing your business plan and investing funds. The last thing you need is to run afoul of zoning regulations and have to make costly changes, relocate, or close your business. Of course, if you are not happy with zoning ordinances, you can work to get them changed.

Another issue to consider is the allocation of space within your home. A best practice is to clearly delineate your business/work area from your family's living area. This is a practical matter as well as one of professionalism, particularly if customers will be visiting your place of business. It will also be difficult to focus on your business in the midst of family activities. Crying children and barking dogs will detract from your customer interactions and make it appear that you are not seriously in business. Establish family ground rules with respect to the way you will interact while you are working, so that there aren't conflicts caused by differing expectations. Also, if you elect to have a home-based business, furnish it appropriately, and get a separate telephone line. A separate entrance for customers is also desirable.

One consideration is your **space percentage**, the portion of your home used for business, versus your living area. This can affect the type of zoning that you require. In addition, you may find out quickly that your home simply is not suitable for operating a business or that the space is inadequate. It is better to be realistic about these issues up front.

A home-based business may be viable from a zoning and space perspective but still not be the best choice. This is particularly true for businesses such as retail, service, and professional firms that have walk-in customers. Customers will need the location to be safe, convenient, and appealing. They may simply prefer to visit an office building, or a store that is not in someone's home.

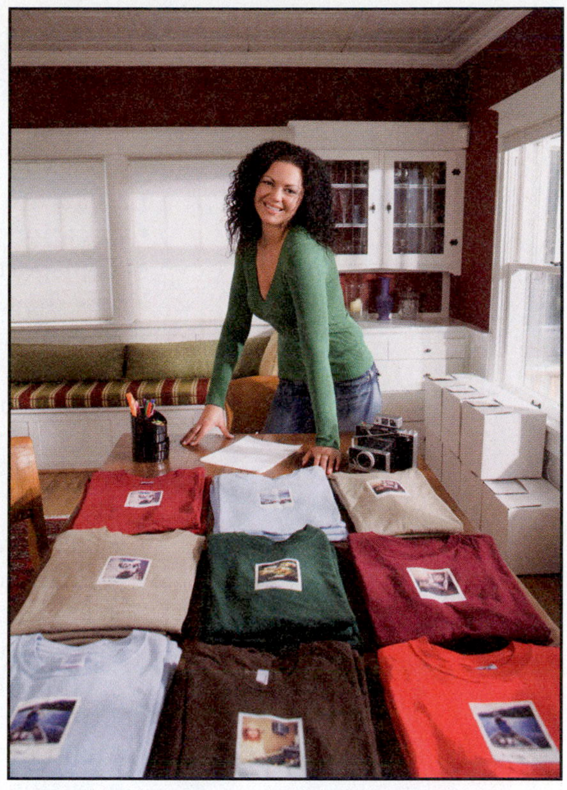

© Blend Images/Alamy

Special Considerations for Web-Based Businesses

Web-based businesses face many of the same location, facilities, and layout decisions as other types of enterprises but encounter unique opportunities and challenges, as well. Because they conduct business on the Internet, such companies can literally be located anyplace in the world, with staff that may work remotely from anywhere. The physical space needed for operations could be as small as a one-room office, if you take orders only online and drop ship directly from suppliers, provide online delivery of goods or services, or offer a service performed in the customer or client's home or office. For completely online businesses, and those using drop shipments, location is more a function of personal preference, cost, or proximity of vendors.

space percentage the portion of the home used for business versus living space.

Performance Objective 7

Describe location factors for Web-based businesses.

Location, facility, and layout decisions for many Web-based businesses should minimize distribution costs (and time). Amazon.com can have its call centers, computer processing, and the like, almost anywhere; but its distribution centers require considerable location analysis.

Many technology-based companies have preferred to cluster with similar firms, and ended up in the area called Silicon Valley, in California, or on the Route 128 corridor, outside of Boston. There may be synergies involved in such proximity, particularly in regard to the availability of a skilled labor force and venture capitalists. In this field, the systems analysts, programmers, and managers are the personnel of most interest. A selected group of Web-based businesses and their headquarters locations are listed in **Exhibit 18-3**. Note the number of California-based companies, including Facebook, which originated in Cambridge, Massachusetts.

For a Web-based business, finding the location that best balances customer needs, owner interests, and labor-pool requirements is essential.

Exhibit 18-3 *Headquarters locations of selected Web-based businesses.*

Business	Location
Amazon.com, Inc.	Seattle, WA
Ancestry.Com Inc.	Provo, UT
eBay, Inc.	San Jose, CA
Facebook, Inc.	Palo Alto, CA
Google Inc.	Mountain View, CA
Hungry Girl	Encino, CA
ING Bank, fsb	Wilmington, DE
MySpace.com	Santa Monica, CA
Shutterfly, Inc.	Redwood City, CA
Yahoo! Inc.	Sunnyvale, CA
YouTube, LLC	San Bruno, CA
Zappos	Henderson, NV
Zynga Game Network, Inc.	San Francisco, CA

Chapter Summary

Now that you have studied this chapter, you can do the following:

1. Understand the importance of the physical location of a business.
   - Location determines access to markets.
   - Costs are often largely dependent upon location.
   - Location is an essential part of marketing for many businesses.
   - Transportation and distribution costs are a function of location.
2. Know the key factors to consider in the location decision.
   - The most important factors will be governed by the nature of the business.
   - Key factors for most firms include
     - access for customers and to suppliers,
     - climate and geography,
     - cost of facilities,
     - demographics,
     - economic conditions and business incentives,
     - laws and regulations,
     - workforce readiness, and
     - competitive environment.
3. Learn how location needs differ by business type.
   - Manufacturing.
     - customer service
     - cost of facilities and distribution
     - labor pool
     - laws and regulations
   - Wholesalers/distributors.
     - economical distribution costs
     - tangible costs of facilities
     - incentives
     - workforce
   - Retail businesses.
     - revenue-generation potential
     - drawing power
     - traffic generators
     - competitor locations
     - rental costs
     - safety/security
   - Service and professional businesses.
     - vary considerably according to the service or profession
     - customer access
     - proximity to complementary or competitive businesses
     - image/positioning
     - safety/security
4. Determine locations via multiple methods.
   - Select a location you know.
   - Use factor-rating methods to prioritize decision criteria and weigh them to reduce subjectivity.
   - Access geographic information systems (GIS) to pinpoint prospective locations using maps, demographics, and other data.
   - Research markets using geographic, psychographic, and demographic information.
   - Opt for cost-volume analysis using location breakeven analysis.

- Find the best cost location for a distributor using the center-of-gravity approach.

5. Explore the design of facilities and their layouts.
   - Manufacturing, warehousing, and distribution facilities must provide the space to operate cost effectively.
   - Retail facilities must draw maximum revenue from design and layout.
6. Recognize the special considerations for home-based businesses.
   - Zoning may regulate what kind of businesses may exist in a given area, and establish parameters for their operations.
   - It is important to balance work and living space.
   - Determine whether a home-based business is best for you.
7. Describe location factors for Web-based businesses.
   - It may be possible to locate, literally, anywhere in the world that has the infrastructure to support the business.
   - Fully online businesses and those that drop ship have ultimate flexibility.
   - Where distribution centers are used, their location may be more crucial than that of the home office.
   - Technology-based companies frequently like to cluster where there is an abundant labor pool.

Key Terms

center-of-gravity method
clustering
factor-rating method
fixed-position layouts
leasehold improvements
location breakeven analysis
process layouts
product layouts
selling space
space percentage
traffic generators

Entrepreneurship Portfolio

Critical Thinking Exercises

1. Identify two sets of business clusters in your area. Explain why they may have been formed.
2. Where would you locate your business, and why?
3. If you were to start a home-based business, what would it be? Why? What key factors would you consider before startup?
4. Why is physical location critical for a distribution business?
5. What is the role of demographic information in the selection of a retail-location option?

Key Concept Questions

1. What is a traffic generator and why might it be important to a retail store?
2. What factors are most critical to the location decision for a manufacturer?
3. How can zoning affect location for a home-based business?
4. What is a fixed-position layout? What types of businesses use this type of layout?

Application Exercises

1. Jessica Martin is establishing a company that would be well suited to three areas, New Orleans, Los Angeles, and New York. The respective fixed and variable costs for one year are as follows:

City	Fixed Costs	Variable Costs per Unit	Total Cost at 1,000,000 Units	Total Cost at 2,000,000 Units	Total Cost at 3,000,000 Units
New Orleans	$500,000	$100	$1,500,000	$2,500,000	$3,500,000
Los Angeles	$800,000	$80	$1,600,000	$2,400,000	$3,200,000
New York	$950,000	$60	$1,550,000	$2,150,000	$2,750,000

   Using the location breakeven method, determine the best cost location for 1,000,000, 2,000,000, and 3,000,000 units. Plot the options on a graph and indicate the areas of lowest cost.

2. Xavier Zumsteg is selecting a location for his upscale urban fashion boutique. He has selected three cities to consider and needs to make a choice. Using the factor-rating method, identify the five key factors to consider and their weights. Then, rate each of the cities on a scale of 0 to 100. Calculate the most preferable option.

Factor	Factor Weight	Detroit Rating	Atlanta Rating	Boston Rating	Detroit Weight	Atlanta Weight	Boston Weight
Total	1.00	xxxxxx	xxxxxx	xxxxxx			

Exploring Online

1. Visit the Web site of a business that you know has at least three locations in your area (preferably not a franchise or chain).
   a. Obtain the addresses of the locations nearest to your home (up to 10).
   b. Map these locations on an ordinary street map.
   c. Map them on a census map.
   d. What geographic pattern, if any, emerges?
   e. Is there a common set of demographic data? If so, what?
   f. Name a couple of competitors and map up to 10 of their locations.
   g. Does the pattern that emerges show clustering?
2. Visit the U.S. Census Bureau Web site at http://www.census.gov. Pull up the census tract data both for your home address and for your campus address. If the tracts are the same, pick another college or university. Compare and contrast the two locations as potential sites for each of the following. Use a street map, too, if it will help.
   a. A bookstore
   b. A store specializing in golfing-related goods
   c. A children's day-care center
   d. A distribution center for cleaning supplies

Case Study | Virtual IT Training in a Classroom

ONLC Training Centers has used their many locations to drive significant sales growth and become one of the leaders in the IT training industry, an industry that was in rapid decline from 2000 through 2009. Today, ONLC has over 250 locations from coast to coast; but as recently as 2004 they only had offices in Philadelphia; Wilmington, Delaware; and Princeton. In 2009, ONLC Training Centers was named the eighth-fastest-growing education company on *Inc.* magazine's list of fastest growing companies. How have they achieved such remarkable growth in a declining industry during the worst economic downturn in 70 years?

Bucking the industry and economic trends, ONLC was able to realize multiple new revenue streams by rapidly expanding their geographic distribution of classroom training. In 2009, approximately 50 percent of ONLC's revenues came from sites that were not open a year earlier. Two of the key drivers to their success were the strategic use of locations, to accelerate sales, and the redefinition of classroom training.

Andy Williamson and Jim Palic formed the company in 1983, and they were at the leading edge of the PC revolution when they began offering classroom training to individuals using personal computers in the workplace. Throughout the 1980s and 1990s, their original facilities were traditional IT classrooms designed for face-to-face instruction. However, as corporate training and travel funds dried up after 2000, the demand for such services dropped precipitously and the industry consolidated rapidly. Many companies with large computer training facilities closed or switched to other lines of business, such as IT consulting.

Andy and Jim recognized that, although the demand for training had significantly declined, it had not disappeared. To serve the smaller market demand for public IT training, they needed to transform their business model. They considered offering virtual training, where people would join ONLC's classes from their homes or offices. That would certainly lower their costs. However, their years of industry experience taught them that people preferred classroom training for many good reasons. A formal classroom provides an interruption-free environment in which to learn. There are fewer technical issues when training is conducted in a classroom. And last, but not the least important, going to an offsite location elevates the importance of the event and helps people focus on the job of learning.

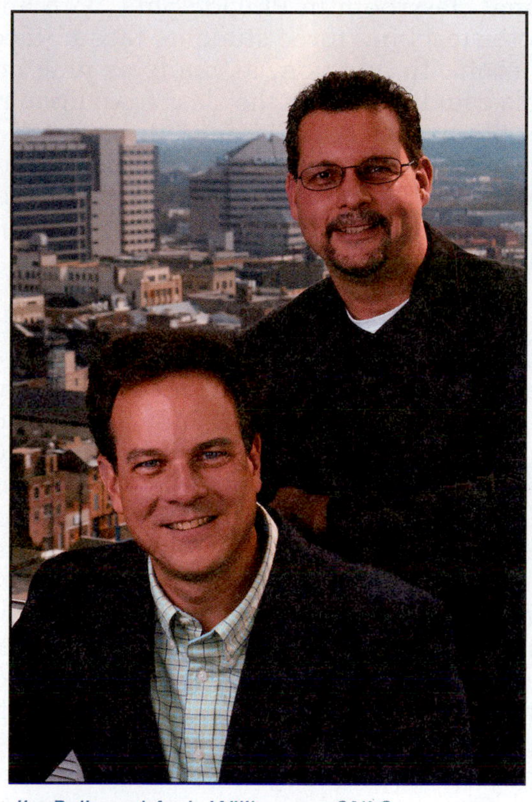

Jim Palic and Andy Williamson, ONLC.

They thought that maybe they could design a training offering that would include the classroom as an important part of the mix. Adding the classroom to a virtual training offering would significantly increase their costs, but provide a better learning experience. In addition, they saw that their competitors were beginning to offer virtual training. If hundreds of other companies started to offer training virtually, how would ONLC be able to differentiate itself?

So, instead of abandoning bricks-and-mortar classroom-based training, they decided to go deeper into that strategy. They designed a virtual training solution that keeps the classroom as part of the solution and called it "remote classroom instruction" (RCI). This provides their clients with a higher-quality learning solution and gives ONLC a more defensible position in the market.

Their solution works like this. A single national training schedule is promoted on the ONLC Web site. If people see a class that they want to take that is running on January 15, for example, they can register for that class in any one of over 250 locations around the country.

These locations contain small classrooms that can seat two to four people at a time. The class running on January 15 might be taught in a traditional classroom in Philadelphia, with an instructor teaching three students face-to-face in that room. In addition, as many as nine other people could be joining the class from up to nine other physical locations around the country.

"It is our ability to easily aggregate low demand for public training that makes our model successful," said Andy. By combining the enrollments from hundreds of locations, they are able to have fewer classes cancelled because of low enrollments. In any given city, there might only be one or two people interested in an event. Whereas competitors who needed a large number of students in a room with an instructor would have had to cancel the event, ONLC is able to run it with one attendee.

ONLC management has carefully studied potential opportunities, and identified strategic roll-out priorities, by looking at U.S. Census data by Metropolitan Statistical Areas (MSAs). Unlike its old business model, in which leases were secured for multiple years and each site had to be staffed, the new model relies on a network of executive suite locations. The company can sign short-term, six-month leases for only the needed space. They can start by renting a single classroom in any city. If demand becomes strong enough, they can rent additional rooms; if demand is low, they can cancel the lease at the end of the term and redeploy their computer hardware to a new, more productive location.

Training sites in areas with greater population densities have survived because there were more people. However, some rural areas are also successful. While those areas have lower demand, there are typically no competitors. So whereas the total demand in the area might be relatively low, the demand facing the firm is higher, because ONLC is able to capture a larger share of the market. In addition, their small-site strategy helps them be more cost effective.

By creating hundreds of very small, efficient training facilities, and aggregating the demand for training across the country through their remote-classroom-instruction model, they are able to cost-effectively capture the demand for public IT classes.

ONLC estimates that over 80 percent of the U.S. population is within an hour's drive from one of their training sites. Andy explains how ONLC has overcome the tyranny of geography that author Chris Anderson defines as an audience being spread so thinly that it is the same as no audience at all.[4] Andy observes, "People wanting training in remote locations have been suffering from the tyranny of geography where no classroom training is available to them because demand is so low. When demand for a particular class drops below a certain point, a traditional face-to-face class is taken off the schedule of the local training company. When demand for IT training in general drops below a certain point, the traditional training company closes its doors."

By rapidly expanding the number of training facilities to give them nationwide coverage and by redefining classroom training with their RCI model, ONLC can cost-effectively deliver classroom training where its competitors can't. As Andy says, "Lowering the cost of delivery has radically changed the economics of providing training, and has democratized distribution. It has also positioned ONLC for a successful future delivering virtual training in a classroom."

Case Study Analysis

1. What does ONLC do to determine where to offer training? What are the critical location factors?
2. How does this business model democratize distribution?
3. How can ONLC have over 200 locations and maintain an efficient cost structure at low volumes in each?
4. What is the level of importance of the location of the ONLC headquarters? Why?
5. What were the main differentiating characteristics of ONLC's remote-classroom-instruction offering, compared to its competitors who were also offering virtual training?

[4]Chris Anderson, *The Long Tail: Why the Future of Business is Selling Less of More* (New York: Hyperion, 2006).

Case Study | The Nightmare—Mike the Mechanic[5]

Mike Jones worked as a mechanic for 15 years at a large automobile dealership in a small southern town. The owner liked Mike and entrusted him with considerable authority. Everyone in town knew Mike. His work was of high quality. He was fast. He always gave a quick diagnosis of the problem and made practical, reasonably priced repairs. He had a reputation for being able to figure out tough problems that other mechanics couldn't solve.

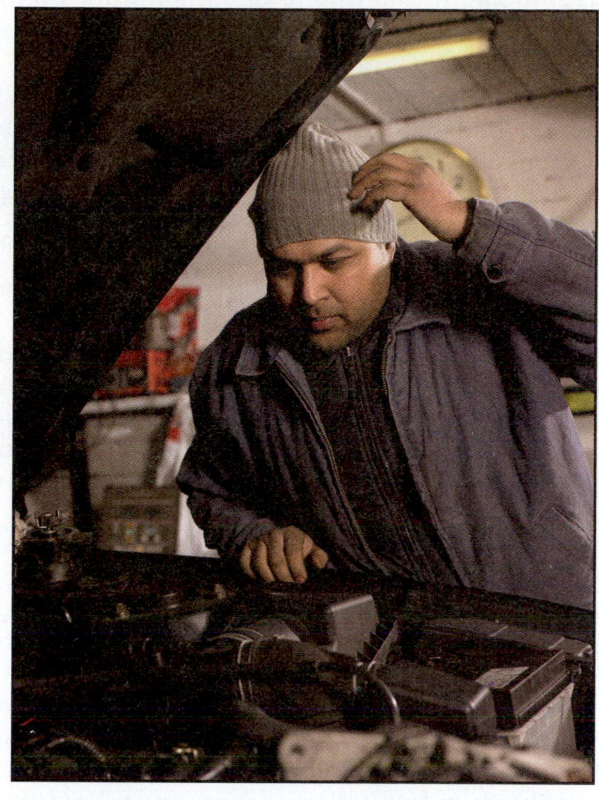

The owner retired and sold the dealership to his son-in-law and nephew. The new owners were people that Mike couldn't stand. They were bossy and ordered him around. They tried to force him to comply with repair standards and schedules and wanted him to perform and sell more services than customers needed.

After listening to Mike complain about his job, many of his customers told him, "You should start your own business. You would have more work than you could handle." After about six months of gnashing his teeth, Mike decided it was time to cut loose. He started his own automotive service garage.

Mike had some acreage out in the country, about 11 miles from town. He quit his job. He built a large pole building, using some savings and taking out a second mortgage on his property. He purchased new equipment and tools. He painted a sign on a piece of plywood and hung it from his mailbox at the end of his gravel driveway. He placed a small ad in the local newspaper.

Prior to leaving his job, Mike told a number of his customers how unhappy he was with the new owners and that he was starting his own business. He gave them his home phone number.

Some weeks later, Nancy Wagner, a longtime customer of Mike's, noticed her car wasn't running properly. She had heard that Mike had started his own business. She didn't know Mike's last name. When she called the dealership to find Mike, they were rude and told her they didn't know anything about where he had gone. Nancy asked some of her neighbors and co-workers about Mike, and finally found someone who knew his phone number.

Nancy called Mike's number. A child answered the phone. When Nancy asked if Mike was available, the child yelled *"Daaaaad,"* without putting down the telephone. Nancy heard a "clunk," some dogs barking, a baby crying, and the noise from a television or radio. Some minutes later, a man's gruff voice said, "Yeah?"

"Mike?" asked Nancy. "Yeah," he responded. Nancy told him who she was and explained that her car was making a noise. She asked if Mike could work on her car. Mike said, "We got one up on the hoist now, waiting for parts. Got another out in the yard waiting for the hoist." Nancy, unsure of what this meant, asked again, "Can you work on my car and, if so, when?" Mike mumbled to himself, then finally told Nancy to bring it out on Thursday morning.

Nancy asked for directions, which were go west on the main highway for seven miles, then south on the gravel county road for two miles, then west on another gravel county road for two miles to the first driveway on the left. "You'll see the sign," Mike said.

Nancy made arrangements with a friend to follow her out to Mike's. On a rainy April Thursday, she and her friend began the trip. She found

[5]Adaptation of a case study from the Northeast Entrepreneur Fund's *Core Four*® Business Planning Course, 2003. © Northeast Entrepreneur Fund. Courtesy of Northeast Entrepreneur Fund. Used with permission.

the first gravel road, missed the second because there was no sign, backtracked three miles, guessed at which road to take, drove two miles and saw no sign for Mike's repair shop. Backtracking again, she finally saw the mailbox with a small wooden sign on it. Pulling up to the sign, she saw, Mike's Garage.

She pulled into the driveway. After heavy rains, it had turned into two muddy ruts. The driveway was about half a mile long. Her friend in the car behind her was skidding and swerving, trying to stay on the road.

They finally pulled into a yard. There was a white house on the right, badly in need of paint. There were several large outbuildings as well: a barn, what appeared to be a machinery shed, and another building. Two large dogs came running from the porch of the house, barking and growling. They leaped at Nancy's driver-side window. They ran back and forth between the two cars, growling and leaping.

Terrified, Nancy drove right up to the house and honked her horn. A woman came out the front door. Nancy cracked her window and yelled, "Where's Mike?" The woman pointed to the machinery shed.

Nancy backed up and drove over to the machinery shed, where there was a large overhead door that was shut, and a smaller door that was ajar. The dogs had followed her car and ran into the shed. Nancy waited a minute or two. No one came out of the shed. She honked her horn. After another minute Mike peered out the door. Nancy rolled her window down slightly and said, "I'm afraid of your dogs."

By now the two dogs were leaping at Mike. He kicked one, hollered something, pushed them into the shed and disappeared. Moments later, he returned and said he had locked up the dogs.

Nancy got out of her car and explained to Mike that her car was making a clanking sound and that it squealed horribly when she turned left. Mike stared at Nancy. Then he began explaining that he still had one car on the hoist and was waiting for parts. He complained that he had to pay C.O.D. for the parts and that they were going to be expensive. He said to Nancy that if she needed parts, she would have to pay up front so that he could get them faster. Nancy asked what parts Mike thought he would need and how much they would cost. Mike explained that he didn't know and wouldn't know until he could get the car up on the hoist.

Mike also said that, although his parts prices were high, he had reduced his labor rate to half of what the competition was charging. He muttered that it was unfair that his vendors were "jerking him around."

Nancy asked when Mike would be able to get her car up on the hoist. Mike didn't know; he was waiting for parts. They were supposed to be there later that day. If they didn't come that day, they should be there the next, Friday. Nancy asked how long he would have to work on the other car after he got the parts. Mike wasn't sure. Nancy asked if she could reschedule for another day. Mike wasn't sure.

Nancy thanked Mike for his time and signaled to her friend that they were leaving. Nancy got into her car and left. When she got back to town, she drove directly to the auto dealership and met with the service manager, who scheduled her repairs for later that day. Her car would be ready by 4:00 p.m., and the manager asked her if she needed a "loaner." Nancy said no, and got a ride to work from her friend. The ordeal with Mike had taken two hours; scheduling the repairs with the dealership had taken 10 minutes.

A few months later, Mike sold his fishing boat so he could make a mortgage payment and pay some vendors. A month later he sold his canoe and his four-wheeler to make another mortgage payment. A few weeks after that, Mike sold his interest in a hunting shack to one of his neighbors so that he could make another mortgage payment and buy more parts.

Mike finally cashed in the retirement fund he had from working at the dealership. He paid some bills and bought a new piece of equipment.

Mike's banker called him several months later, explaining that Mike's mortgage payments were now two months overdue. Mike's vendors refused to sell him any more parts. Mike's phone had been disconnected twice, and he not only had to pay the past bills but a reconnect fee (he used the money in his son's savings account). Mike's customers were refusing to pay their bills. One of them was suing Mike.

After about eight months, Mike Jones filed for bankruptcy and closed his business. His wife had taken their two children and moved in with her parents. The homestead was foreclosed on and eventually sold. Mike moved into a small trailer on a friend's farm. Mike started drinking and going to the casinos. He told everyone he met that starting your own business was a horrible idea, that bankers were all jerks, that people just wanted to rip you off, and that his customers were a bunch of cheap, whiny idiots that he never should have done business with.

Case Study Analysis

1. List 10 mistakes that Mike made with respect to customer relations and management of his business.
2. For each business error, identify why it was a mistake. For example, poor customer relations, lack of planning, and poor cash-flow management are some identifiable errors.
3. If you could turn back the clock and work with Mike from the start, what would you suggest he use as his one-minute sales pitch?
4. If you were a consultant, what advice would you have given Mike and why? Identify at least three short recommendations. Make the recommendation and explain why you made it.

Chapter 19

HUMAN RESOURCES AND MANAGEMENT

"Give a man a fish and you feed him for a day. Teach a man to fish and you feed him for a lifetime."

—Lao Tzu, founder of Taoism

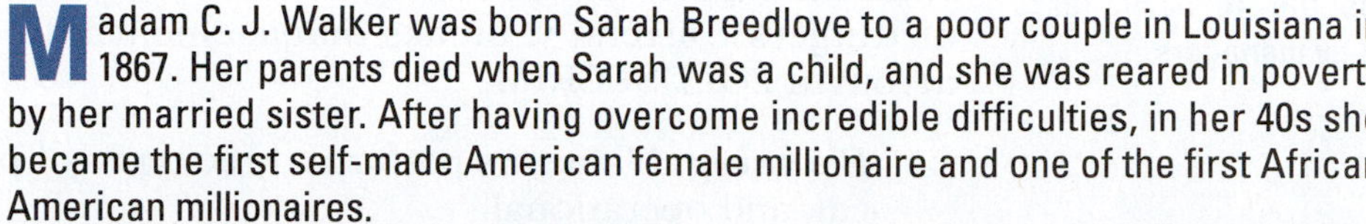

Madam C. J. Walker was born Sarah Breedlove to a poor couple in Louisiana in 1867. Her parents died when Sarah was a child, and she was reared in poverty by her married sister. After having overcome incredible difficulties, in her 40s she became the first self-made American female millionaire and one of the first African American millionaires.

Breedlove worked for many years in the cotton fields and as a laundress, moving to St. Louis, Denver, and Indianapolis, before inventing and marketing hair-care products for African American women. Madam Walker (her married name) quickly became successful enough to build a factory to manufacture her line of products. At first she had sold her shampoos and hair-growth merchandise door to door, but soon organized and trained a group of agent-operators.

At the peak of her career, Walker employed 2000 agents. One of her successful marketing strategies was to organize the agents into clubs that promoted social and charitable causes in their respective African American communities. She offered cash prizes to the clubs that accomplished the most. She also encouraged her agents to open beauty salons and other corollary businesses. Not only did Madam Walker's methods foreshadow the emphasis we see on socially responsible entrepreneurship, she also created a rich legacy of black female entrepreneurial leadership.

Madam C. J. Walker.

Performance Objectives

1. Describe the 10 basic tasks handled by managers.
2. Recruit your employees.
3. Know where and how to find qualified job candidates.
4. Develop your organizational culture.
5. Determine your organizational structure.
6. Understand the functions of human resources management.

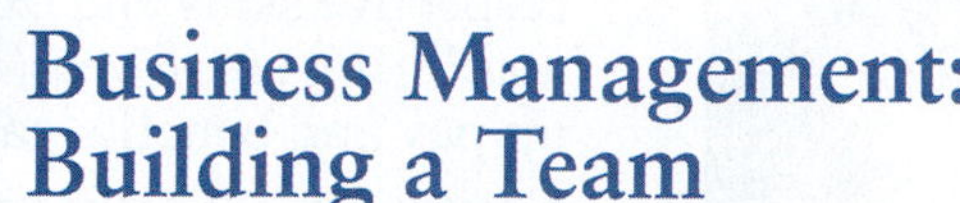

Business Management: Building a Team

As a small business grows, it will reach a point where the entrepreneur and a few employees cannot handle operations efficiently. At that stage, the company will probably need professional management to meet its goals efficiently.

Many successful entrepreneurs are creative individuals who tend to get bored with the everyday details of running a business, until suddenly there is a crisis in management. Or, they simply dislike managing employees or recognize that their strengths lie elsewhere. Wise entrepreneurs recognize these characteristics if they have them and hire managers to run the business.

An entrepreneur with a growing corporation can raise capital by selling stock. Some of this capital can be used to hire managers to organize the business. This will free the entrepreneur to spend less time managing and more time thinking up new ideas, pitching product, or doing whatever he or she does best.

What Do Managers Do?

Performance Objective 1

Describe the 10 basic tasks handled by managers.

There are numerous descriptions, conceptions, and misconceptions about what managers do and do not do with their time. Nathan Himmelstein, of Rutgers University, breaks management into 10 functions, using the acronym POLDSCCRIM.

strategic plan typically a three- to five-year overall design to achieve long-term growth, sales, and positioning goals for a business.

tactical plan a short-term (one year or less) implementation that has limited, specific objectives.

operational plan the stated short-term methods for achieving tactical goals.

1. ***Planning.*** Managers perform three types of planning: strategic, tactical, and operational.
   - ***Strategic plans*** are typically three- to five-year overall strategies for achieving a business's long-term growth, sales, and positioning goals.
   - ***Tactical plans*** provide the short-term implementation to accomplish strategic goals. Tactical plans are for one year or less and have limited, specific objectives.
   - ***Operational plans*** are short-term procedures for achieving tactical goals. These include budgets, regulations, and schedules for day-to-day operation of the business.
2. ***Organizing.*** This function includes everything from finding resources to hiring employees to buying/leasing equipment. It includes setting up an organizational chart and defining each person's responsibilities.
3. ***Leading.*** This function is about the style in which you and your managers direct the company. Achievement-oriented managers encourage employee input, share authority and responsibility, and focus on achieving long-term goals. This style is the most appropriate for a small business, although sometimes managers will have to temporarily adopt another style to deal with a crisis or to stabilize operations.
4. ***Directing.*** After you and your managers have made your plans and organized your employees and resources, it is time to direct and motivate employees to perform the work that will move the company toward its strategic goals.
5. ***Staffing.*** This function involves managing the people in the company by making sure they are in the positions that best use their respective skills and experience. It includes screening, recruiting, and hiring employees, training and developing them, and setting up pay and benefits packages.
6. ***Controlling.*** This step involves measuring the business's performance and determining how to improve it. Is the business adhering to its budget? Are products achieving the level of sales and quality goals that were set? How about customer service? If there are variances between what was planned and what the company actually achieved, controlling will require corrective action to align plans and actions.
7. ***Coordinating.*** This is the task of combining all management efforts into a unified system. Coordinating includes creating in-house communications and teaching everyone to use them, scheduling regular meetings and updates, and generally making sure all managers are using appropriate styles and are working toward the same goals.
8. ***Representing.*** Managers represent a company to its people and its people to the company; they also represent the company to the outside world. Managers need to appear and behave in a way that accurately reflects the company culture.

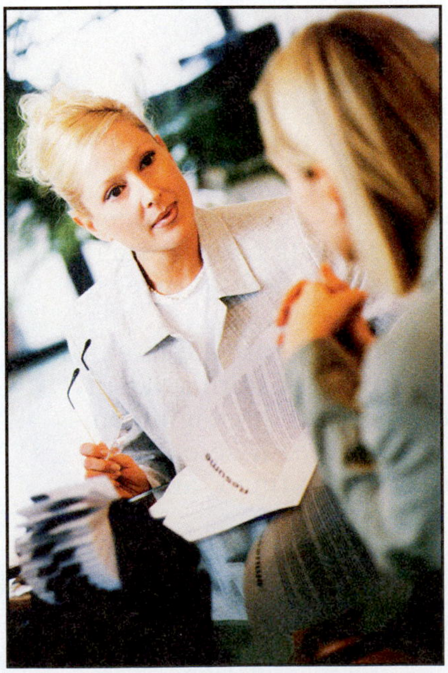

Businesswomen conferring.
(Color Day Production/Getty Images)

9. ***Innovating.*** Managers should always be developing new ways to meet strategic, tactical, and operational goals. The entrepreneur may be the guiding creative force behind the company, but managers should also be innovative problem solvers.
10. ***Motivating.*** Managers need to understand their employees' skills, knowledge, and work styles to be effective. It is important that managers understand that employees are not all the same and will need to be handled individually. Effective managers can adapt to the employee or situation. Decisions managers make may affect employee motivation and morale—positively or negatively. A manager's assumptions about the employees may have an effect. If a manager assumes that people need to be pushed in order to work, for example, and treats them that way, he/she may incur resentment. A manager who assumes that employees want to do their best and embrace responsibility will likely be more successful. Some ways managers can motivate include involving employees in decisions, providing meaningful work, recognizing contributions, giving consistent, meaningful feedback, regularly evaluating performance, and rewarding achievement.[1]

Adding Employees to Your Business

One of the most important things you can do as a business owner is to bring in capable, motivated people. It is a major decision to become responsible for the wages and salaries of others. For many entrepreneurs, the decision to hire is an agonizing one because they fear having to let the individual go at a later date, or may fear giving up some control of the business. Businesses may bring in employees too soon and not be able to afford them, or too late, and face overwhelming challenges. If you have a carefully developed operational plan for your business, and keep it updated, you should know when to add employees to the mix. This process of finding and hiring employees is sometimes called **recruitment**.

recruitment the act of finding and hiring employees.

Performance Objective 2

Recruit your employees.

In *Good to Great,* management expert Jim Collins says that great leaders "get the right people on the bus—sometimes even before a company decides exactly what business it will be in."[2] Louise Hay, founder of Hay House, Inc., a publisher, once said, "In the early days, I didn't have the money to pay decent salaries, so I didn't get good people. I got nice people, but I didn't get good employees." Be certain to get the best employees you can!

Some possible ways to bring good employees into your business are

- Bring them in as partners. Partners share the risks and rewards of the venture and will co-own the business with you. They will have the incentive to work diligently for the company's success.
- Hire experts to accomplish specific tasks on a contractual or hourly basis. You may not need full-time, or even part-time, employees for professional staff positions, but some expertise will be needed on a limited basis. For example, you might hire a professional accountant to work one day per month to review your record keeping.
- Hire someone as a part-time or full-time regular employee. Be prepared to invest the time and money required to recruit and hire the best-qualified person that you can afford. Remember that taxes and benefits add to employee costs, beyond basic salaries or wages.

[1]Kathleen R. Allen and Earl C. Meyer, *Entrepreneurship and Small Business Management*, 3rd ed. (Blacklick, Ohio: Glencoe/McGraw-Hill, 2005).

[2]Jim Collins, *Good to Great: Why Some Companies Make the Leap . . . and Some Don't* (New York: HarperCollins Publishers, 2001), p. 13.

There are specific steps in the recruiting process:

job profile identifies the knowledge, skills, and abilities required to perform the specific tasks of a job.

position description includes the knowledge, skills, and abilities from the job profile, as well as the reporting and working relationships, plus the goals and objectives.

1. ***Defining the job.*** First, think about what you need this employee to do and what kinds of skills are needed, to create a job profile and then to develop a position description. The **job profile** identifies the knowledge, skills, and abilities required to perform the specific tasks of the job. The **position description** includes the knowledge, skills, and abilities from the job profile, as well as the reporting and working relationships, and the goals and objectives of the position. It should also contain a description of the physical requirements and special working conditions of the job (for example, lifting, bending, walking, etc.). Prioritize the list of key requirements that you will develop with those who will work with the new hire. Be certain to designate specific experience, qualifications, characteristics, and traits that will be required. Also, decide on the wage or salary range that fits your budget before beginning to recruit.
2. ***Posting and advertising the job.*** Determine how people will find out about the position. Are there potential internal candidates? Will you place an ad in a newspaper, run online ads, or solicit employee referrals? Finding good employees has become much easier with the advent of online job-listing services such as Career Builder (*http://www.careerbuilder.com*) and Monster.com (*http://www.monster.com*), as well as industry-specific sites, which are often managed by trade and professional associations.
3. ***Screening resumes and/or applications.*** A resume is a concise summary of an individual's education and work experience. When you post the opportunity, ask interested parties to send their resumes. Some online services permit you to screen resumes using keywords that will be important to your search. Other times, you might have an individual, team, or committee review all applicants against basic requirements. You then may want to have a secondary review to narrow the search to the top three to five candidates, whom you will then interview.
4. ***Assessing skills.*** Identify pertinent skills and determine ways to assess them. For example, if a new employee is supposed to write grants,

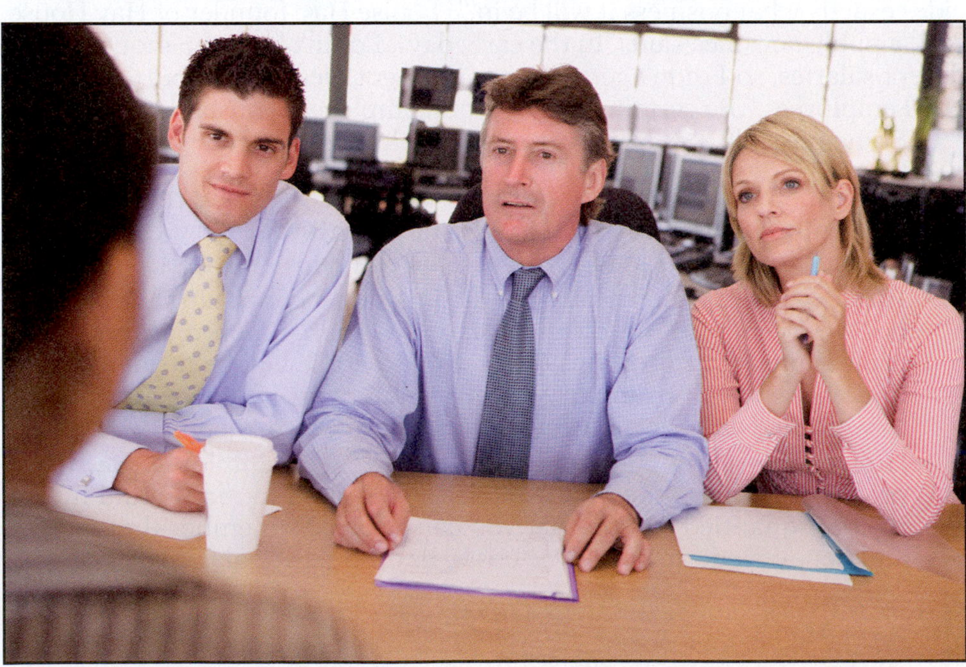

create a brief scenario and ask the applicant to create a document according to your specifications. For an administrative staff member, typing skills, as well as written communications and editing skills, may be required and can be tested using well-developed instruments. If a job requires measurement and math skills, both can be evaluated easily. It is far better to eliminate unqualified applicants early in the process rather than waste their time and yours. The time to find out if a candidate is capable is before the hiring rather than after.

It is critical to use the same process (such as a typing test) at the same stage in the interview for all applicants, to guard against the appearance of discrimination, especially vis-à-vis "protected classes." For example, if a typing test is given to administrative job applicants, it should be given to all applicants at the same time (usually prior to the job interview). It is also important to ensure that the assessment-instrument design could not be perceived as discriminatory. It is best to use instruments that have already been validated. Instruments that are not scientifically validated are potentially dangerous because a protected-class applicant that is not hired because of a test score might have a valid case for legal action.

5. ***Interviewing candidates.*** Based on the resumes you receive, select several individuals to interview. Prepare before any hiring an **interview guide**, a document to assist you or your interviewer in developing questions regarding an applicant's knowledge, skills, abilities, and interests. You will need to determine who will interview the candidates and whether the interviews will be performed one on one or by a panel with several interviewers together. There are many books, articles, and online resources that can guide you in creating a **behavioral interview**, which is designed to determine the fit of a prospective employee with the requirements of the position, using prior-experience examples. Remember, the candidate should be provided with the interview schedule in advance. **Exhibit 19-1** suggests the topics to cover in an interview. **Exhibit 19-2** provides some sample interview questions.

interview guide a document to assist in question development regarding an individual's knowledge, skills, abilities, and interests.

behavioral interview an interview designed to determine the fit of a prospective employee with the requirements of the position, using prior-experience examples.

6. ***Checking references.*** Ask the candidates that interest you to provide at least three references from previous employers, or others who could tell you about their character and work performance. Check them. Create a few questions that are pertinent to the job being filled and the related career paths. Include questions about how the candidate and his/her reference know each other. One question that often provides critical insight (used only with former co-workers, managers/supervisors, and others with direct experience) is, "Would you rehire this person?" Remember, some former employers will only provide confirmation of former employees' dates of employment, so you might need to request additional references. Reference-check forms should be consistent, and ask the same questions for each candidate being considered for a particular position.

Exhibit 19-1 *Examples of competencies that may be included in job interviews.*

- General questions on skills and interests
- Teamwork
- Problem solving
- Communications
- Productivity/time management
- Customer service (internal or external customers)
- Interpersonal

Exhibit 19-2 *Sample interview questions.*

General

- Could you share with us a recent accomplishment of which you are proud?
- What are your qualifications in this area of expertise; i.e., what skills do you have that make you the best candidate for this position? Discuss any special training you have had (on-the-job, at college, continuing education, seminars, reading, etc.) and related work experience.
- Tell us about a personal or career goal that you have accomplished and why it was important to you.
- Why should we hire *you*?
- If you were offered this position, when would you be available to start?
- Tell us anything else you would like us to know about you that will aid us in making our decision.
- What questions would you like to ask us?

Teamwork

- How do you think the people you work with would describe you?
- Tell us about the most effective contribution you have made as part of a task group or special project team.
- When groups work together, conflicts often emerge. Tell us about a time that conflict occurred in one of your work groups and what you did about it.

Problem Solving

- What was one of the toughest problems you ever solved? What steps did you take to solve it?
- How do you analyze the different options to determine which is the best alternative? Give an example of when you have done this.

Communications

- Describe a time when you were able to overcome a communication barrier.
- Give an example of how you consider your audience prior to communicating. What factors influence your communication style?

Productivity/Time Management

- When you have a lot of work to do, how do you get it all done? Give us an example.
- Describe a time you identified a barrier to your (and/or others') productivity and what you did about it.
- How do you determine what amount of time is reasonable to complete a task? Please give an example.

Customer Service

- We all have customers or clients. Who are your clients and how do you identify them?
- Tell us about a time when you went out of your way to give great service to a customer.
- Tell us about a time when you had trouble dealing with a difficult or demanding customer. How did you handle this?

Interpersonal

- Describe what you see as your strengths related to this job/position. Describe what you see as your weaknesses related to this job/position.
- Describe how you prefer to be managed, and the best relationship you've had with a previous boss/supervisor.
- What kind of people do you find most difficult to work with? Give an example of a situation where you had difficulties dealing with someone different from yourself. How did you handle it?
- What do you do when you know you are right and your manager disagrees with you? Give an example of this happening in your career.
- Describe a difficult time you have had dealing with an employee, customer, client, or co-worker. Why was it difficult? How did you handle it? What was the outcome?
- Describe a situation you wish that you had handled differently, based on the outcome. What would you change when faced with a similar situation?

Adapted from the Society for Human Resource Management, http://www.shrm.org (accessed January 2, 2010).

Some search firms and other potential employers will request an extensive list of references. For example, Diversified Search, a top headhunting firm in Philadelphia, routinely requests 10 references and completes 30-minute or longer interviews with each of them. By the time the recruiter has completed the reference-checking process, a comprehensive picture of the candidate has emerged. Such an extensive process is reserved for the finalists in executive-level searches, but could be applied at whatever level you might deem helpful. The exercise of requesting so many references offers information in and of itself. Some candidates can send the complete list virtually immediately, whereas others simply vanish at that point. One human resources professional tells the story of calling several references provided by a candidate, who looked excellent on paper and interviewed like a dream. Each and every reference directly told her to avoid hiring him at all costs. This reinforces the reasons to check references.

You also may want to call previous employers and interview each supervisor (be sure to have a release signed by the applicant). By the time this process is complete, you will have a better picture of the candidate. This vetting process is time-consuming, but it can prevent considerable damage down the line. Consider the case of a small business that had found an ideal marketing manager, until it made reference checks and was repeatedly told to stay away from that individual for both legal and ethical reasons.

Whether you request a few or many references, be sure to contact them and ask sound, well-thought-out questions.

7. ***Negotiating compensation.*** You and the candidate you choose will have to negotiate how much you will pay, as well as any benefits the job includes, such as paid vacation, sick leave, and health insurance. You should have a clearly defined pay range for each position, and stay within it. Don't fall in love with a candidate you just cannot afford. However, you also should be realistic about the compensation package you are offering. Benchmark your total package against that of other potential employers.

   Recently, one top manager found himself in an untenable position. He had begun a search to fill a critical leadership position, formed a search committee, advertised in professional journals and at conferences, had extensive two-day interview schedules for five finalists, received two recommendations from the committee, and threw out the search. He decided he needed a more experienced candidate and insisted on a second search. Committee members were outraged. They had found three fully qualified candidates based upon the position description and the charge given to them and the salary available. Some of the committee members participated in a second-round search, eventually making an offer to a candidate satisfactory to their manager. The candidate declined the offer. Again, the committee members conducted a search, with particular weight placed on meeting individuals at an annual professional conference. Round three also fell flat because the salary to be offered was $25,000 to $35,000, too low to attract ideal candidates. The position has remained unfilled for almost two years while the search has dragged on; the compensation issue stands in the way, not to mention the frustration level of the search committee and the unfilled responsibilities of the job.

8. ***Hiring.*** After negotiating compensation, you will have additional work to complete before the new employee's start date. Some of

job offer letter a formal written invitation extended by an employer to a candidate selected for hiring that states basic employment terms—such as the starting date, the position offered, the salary, and so forth.

these tasks include background checks, drug testing, offer letters, and physicals. The **job offer letter** is a formal, written invitation extended by an employer to a candidate selected for hiring that states basic employment terms such as the start date, the position being offered, the salary, the benefits start date, and other pertinent information. Employers typically have the candidate sign and return the letter to indicate acceptance and an understanding of what is being offered. A physical examination may be required, depending upon the physical demands of the job, and this must be performed after the offer has been accepted but prior to the start date.

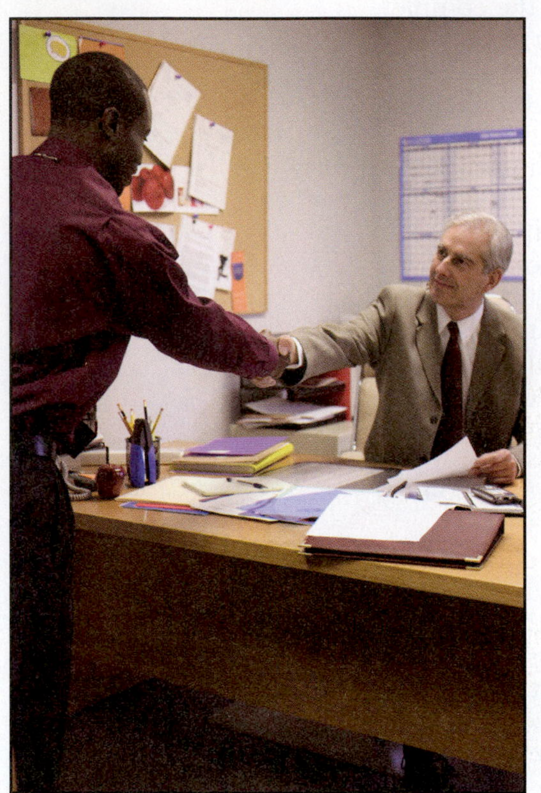

The nature and extent of a background check (including reference checking) will depend upon the specific position. It is good practice to have a basic background check, a criminal background check, and drug testing. The $50 or so investment in a criminal background check could save literally thousands of dollars. You do not want to be guilty of negligent hiring because you have ignored this precaution. A small, rural taxi service recently closed after the bad publicity generated by the arrest of one of its drivers on charges of assaulting an elderly passenger. The driver had a history of assaulting older women, and the company was held liable for putting him in a position in which he had the opportunity to commit another crime. In addition to criminal background checks, you may also want to examine official copies of college transcripts, or a high school diploma, and check previous employment history, such as positions held and dates of employment. If the job requires driving, a check with the Department of Motor Vehicles is also appropriate.

Be certain to comply with all employment laws in carrying out these checks and investigations, and that you get signed release forms as required. Drug-test authorization and background-check release forms are typically provided as part of the employment application package, and should be completed prior to interviewing the candidate. Once you decide to hire someone, you will also have to complete an I-9, and tax and payroll forms. The I-9 form must be completed on the first day of hire, to ensure that the employee is legally authorized to work in the United States.

9. ***Orientation.*** This is the process of introducing the employee into the company, including its mission and its culture, and teaching him or her about the position. It can save you a great deal of money to have a printed employee manual that has passed legal review before you begin hiring. Orientation should be more than a brief talk about employee benefits and how to complete necessary forms, and more than reviewing the employee handbook. Ideally, orientation is an extensive process of helping a new employee understand the structure of the organization and its mission, getting to know other employees, and even circulating through various departments. Some companies, such as the innovative online financial institution ING Direct, require all new hires, regardless of position, to work in customer service as part of orientation. Retail organizations may have all employees work on the floor or as a cashier or point-of-sales employee, to experience customer contact. What would you do to orient your employees?

More on Interviews

Interviews should be carefully planned so that they provide the data needed to accurately assess the quality of fit between the company's needs and the candidate's qualifications and suitability. A poorly planned interview can easily result in a bad fit, and unhappiness for both the employer and employee. Interviews should consist of several parts, which may be adapted according to the company culture. Some aspects include

- welcome and icebreaker,
- formal interview, and
- informal interview.

Welcome and Icebreaker. Candidates are often nervous and self-conscious when they arrive for an in-person interview. Companies can create a welcoming environment by greeting the candidate warmly and professionally, offering to validate parking and/or reimburse expenses as appropriate, asking whether the candidate would like refreshment, and asking whether he or she might need to freshen up before the interview. If the candidate is early, offering a seat and some company information for reading is appropriate. The interviewer should not start the interview late. It is inconsiderate and may give the candidate an unfavorable impression of the company.

Once in the interview room, preferably a quiet conference room that is free of distractions rather than an individual office, the interviewer can help start the process by making small talk to put the candidate at ease, and then briefly provides an overview of the company and position.

Formal Interview. The interview itself should be thoughtfully prepared to elicit the best information to assess a candidate. The inclusion of consistent, core questions that address experiences and behaviors will help to increase objectivity and compare candidates. This question bank should include formulations that

- Assess capacity for and interest in the requirements of the position.
- Ask behavioral interview questions—meaning they include job-related situations and open-ended questions to better understand the candidate's prior performance; these can be an excellent indicator of future performance. The questions should elicit the situation, the action taken, and the results achieved, through each inquiry.
- Bring out valuable information about the candidate's character and traits by using questions such as, "How do you . . . ?" or "What would you . . . ?"or "How do you feel when . . . ?"
- Encourage candidates to discuss their successes and failures. You will frequently learn more from the answers to how they acted in difficult situations than those where they easily succeeded.
- Give an opportunity for the candidate to express reasons for interest in the company and position.
- Discuss geographic fit in terms of relocation, commuting distance, and the like.
- Leave an opening for questions from the candidate.

During an interview, what a candidate doesn't say can be as important as what is said. As you take notes, pay attention to when the candidate avoids answering a question directly; these are clues to probe further.

Informal Interview. Whereas the formal interview (or series of interviews) is generally conducted in an office or conference room, and may include executives, managers, and peers, individually or on a panel, informal interviews are typically peer-to-peer and conducted in a less "official" setting. For example, a casual lunch or coffee break with a few team members could reveal a lot about a candidate. Paying attention to the personal interaction, manners, and interest of a candidate can be illuminating. For example, the candidate may not show any interest in what his/her prospective peers have to say, or may be casually rude to wait staff in a restaurant.

On a cautionary note, you and your team must avoid asking questions that are overly personal or may be discriminatory. The easiest way to avoid problems with the Equal Employment Opportunity Commission (EEOC)—or equivalent departments in state governments—with respect to hiring practices is to focus on the knowledge, skills, abilities, and traits pertinent to the job. By concentrating on such questions, you will likely avoid peripheral ones that could land you in trouble. **Exhibit 19-3** provides some examples of questions to avoid and a brief explanation of why.

As you proceed through the interview and conclude it, remember that an interview is somewhat like a date; both parties are trying to be attractive while deciding whether they want to see each other again. As an entrepreneur, you want a candidate to be interested in pursuing the employment opportunity, and he or she wants you to make a job offer. Deciding to move forward should be a mutual decision based upon a realistic assessment of fit and potential.

You should conclude the interview process with a brief wrap-up that includes discussing the candidate's final questions and shoring up interest.

Exhibit 19-3 *Interview questions to avoid.*

Question(s)	Reason It Is Inappropriate
Where were you born? Are you a U.S. citizen?	Immigration Reform and Control Act prohibits discrimination on the basis of national origin.
How old are you?	Age Discrimination in Employment Act (ADEA) prohibits discrimination on the basis of age. If there is a minimum age, it is okay to ask whether the candidate is above it.
How much alcohol do you drink each day? Week? Month?	Okay to ask whether drugs or alcohol are used but not what sort or how often.
Have you ever been arrested?	Asking about convictions is legal, but an arrest is not a conviction and this question is not acceptable.
Are you married?	Implied discrimination against a particular group (married or single people) is inappropriate.
Do you presently have children or plan to have them?	This is discrimination against women (sex discrimination) and violates Title VII.
Have you ever filed a lawsuit against an employer?	Multiple federal laws protect workers who file claims against their employers.
Do you have any physical disabilities or chronic illnesses that would prevent you from doing any part of your job?	Violates the Americans with Disabilities Act. You are, however, able to ask, "Are you able to fulfill the physical requirements of this position with or without accommodation?"
Do you have mental health issues?	Violates the Americans with Disabilities Act (ADA).
What is your religion?	Violates Title VII of the Civil Rights Act of 1964.

In addition, you should thank the candidate and apprise him or her of the time line and path forward. Once the candidate has departed, interviewers should compare notes (if more than one interviewer). After all candidates have been seen, the interview team should convene and make a selection.

Growing Your Team

Performance Objective 3

Know where and how to find qualified job candidates.

Once you decide to add employees to your company, it could take considerable time and effort to identify and hire the right talent. Even in times when the economy is weak and unemployment is high, qualified candidate pools may be thin. You may have to find individuals to bring into your organization, rather than waiting for them to come to you. The less known your company is or the more remote its location, the more likely it is that you will have to actively recruit candidates.

Companies plan and hire according to staffing requirements and budgets and typically use a combination of internal recruiters (employees), outside recruiters (retained search firms or contingency search firms), and Internet job-board postings. Certainly, advertising and online postings may uncover a strong candidate pool and eliminate the need for internal or external recruiters. However, from time to time, you may need to use either or both of them. If you are growing rapidly and are looking for a skilled, educated work force, or are hiring executives, recruitment may be the key to successful hiring. Some ways to find the employees that fit your company include

- ***Campus Recruiting.*** Established companies from all industries visit college campuses every year to meet and scout students who are about to graduate. Firms in banking, consulting, accounting, consumer products, technology, health care, and other segments of the economy are all major recruiters on college campuses. Smaller employers also may participate in job fairs and other recruitment events. Contact the career service offices of the colleges and universities of interest to find out about recruitment and internship possibilities.
- ***Executive or Retained Searches.*** When companies need to hire a senior executive, they engage in an executive, or retained, search. These top job openings are often not advertised, and the process is frequently managed by a retained search firm. Executive search firms perform a full range of recruitment, screening, interviewing, and reference services. They will work with you to develop a detailed job profile and position description, and create a profile of the ideal candidate. In the end, though, you will decide which candidate to hire. Retained search firms are paid for searches regardless of whether they fill the position or not. Contingency searches are much like retained searches, but compensation is based upon finding a successful applicant.

Linda Resnick, founder and president of CEO Resources, has built her firm on comprehensive, retained executive-search services, from the initial assessment of hiring needs to the integration of qualified executive talent into the new company. CEO Resources primarily fills a broad range of executive, general management, and top technological/scientific positions, at an annual compensation level of more than $150,000. However, the firm also offers a la carte services such as creating hiring and recruiting strategies, defining executive positions, assessing team capabilities and candidate qualifications, completing candidate due-diligence and 360° reference checks, and succession planning.

Creating and Managing Organizational Culture

Performance Objective 4
Develop your organizational culture.

A primary role of the founding entrepreneur is to carry and convey the vision for the company and to foster its culture. The *culture* of an organization is the shared beliefs, values, and attitudes among employees—also referred to as "how things are done around here." The culture of an entrepreneurial firm can be its competitive advantage. As a company grows and adds employees, one challenge for an entrepreneur is to maintain the culture, or to guide its evolution strategically. When culture is explicit and strategic, it is more readily conveyed through orientation and storytelling. Hewlett-Packard was famously recognized for stories told about its founder that conveyed and reinforced the Hewlett-Packard way.

The culture that you create for your business should be a strategically developed translation of your vision and mission into norms, values, and behaviors. It should combine the best practices in business with the type of work environment you want the company to have. Your business will reflect the messages you send. Consciously or not, employees take their cues from their managers. For better or worse, what you say and do (or don't do) telegraphs messages to your team.

Culture is not an isolated aspect of your business, rather a combination of its parts. Company culture incorporates qualities of integrity; diversity; concern for society, community, employees, and customers; quality of products and/or services; and mission. For many companies today, this includes a focus on the balance between work and family life and the need for a positive, enjoyable environment.

Organizational culture is sometimes located in the continuum between the entrepreneurial and the administrative. Firms of most any size can be placed somewhere within these parameters, although it becomes increasingly difficult to operate effectively in an informal, entrepreneurial style as a firm adds employees. A company's culture is made clear through a multitude of words and actions. The type of culture you create is a strategic choice that you make, reinforce, and revise on a continuous basis. **Exhibit 19-4** identifies cultural clues, large and small. Consider the messages they send and which ones you would want to incorporate into your business culture.

Determining Organizational Structure

As you create and grow your company, you will change its organizational structure to meet your evolving requirements. Initially, you may be a one-person band, handling all responsibilities by yourself. Or, you may start out with a founding team that serves as a centralized locus of control, with team members serving in multiple roles. With growth comes a need for specialization, delegation, supervision, and management. Whereas a relatively "flat" organization may work with few employees and ready communications, as the number of employees changes, so must the organizational structure. One of the most difficult transitions for founding entrepreneurs is often that from entrepreneur to entrepreneurial manager—a critical success factor for growth.

Exhibit 19-4 *Selected aspects of organizational culture communications.*

Structure and Hierarchy	
Positive, upbeat, affirming	Doom-and-gloom, mean-spirited, sarcastic, teasing, cursing
Information-sharing, including financial performance	Information held closely, with sharing on a need-to-know basis
Employees contribute ideas and input, which is valued	Employees may be heard but not listened to
Employees address one another as peers	Hierarchy reinforced through the use of formal titles and forms of address (i.e., Mr., Mrs., Dr.), or formal address for managers and informal address for others
Customers spoken about with respect and value	Customers ridiculed or spoken about as an inconvenience
Storytelling used as a way to share history and culture	History and culture communicated through orientation and indoctrination
Telephones answered promptly and in a polite and friendly manner	Telephones answered slowly or not at all and in a grudging or unfriendly manner
Face-to-face communication valued highly	Formal written communications valued and face-to-face communications avoided or discounted
Structure and Hierarchy	
Flat organization with few levels of supervision	Hierarchical organization with multiple layers and clear distinctions between them (i.e., everyone communicates with only those one level above or below, and their peers)
Individual and communal	Paternalistic
Quick discussion and task-focused decisions	Meetings, meetings, meetings
Empowerment	Single locus of control
Flexible work schedules	Punching a time clock or closely observed comings and goings
Telecommuting	Anchored to the office/plant
No offices or little distinction in work environments	Office or workspace laid out by rank
Common eating area/cafeteria	Executive dining room
Shared parking area—first come, first served	Reserved parking for select individuals
All employees initially trained in a common customer-contact role, such as customer service or point of sales	No common training experience
Employee input in performance review and goal setting	Manager or supervisor prepares performance reviews and sets goals
Shared dress code, as appropriate to work conditions	Executives, the "suits," dress distinctly differently from others
Other	
Egalitarian	Elitist
Equal treatment	Preferential treatment with respect to such things as punctuality, extended meals, family

(*continued*)

Exhibit 19-4 *(Continued)*

Individual and team recognition	Individual performance valued most highly
Environmental concerns practiced (e.g. reducing carbon footprint, recycling, energy efficiency)	Lack of environmental concern, or active damage to the environment
Community involvement encouraged (e.g. paid volunteer time, United Way corporate campaign, charitable contributions, or product tie-ins)	Community involvement discouraged (i.e., charitable contributions and work-time volunteerism avoided)
Ethics, or the focus on doing the right things	Focus on profitability over ethics
Quality, or the focus on doing things right; meeting and exceeding standards	Focus on profitability over quality
Personal space, if any, reflects the employee	Sterile personal space
Fun, playful, positive work environment	Dour, dull, negative environment
Opportunities to fail as a positive	Failure is not an option
Trust	Distrust
Shared glory	Blame game
Clean, well-maintained physical environment	Poor maintenance and dirty physical environment
Family friendly—such as photos in offices, child care on site, maternity and parental leave, referral services for child and/or eldercare, children welcome at work in emergencies, telecommuting, sick days available for child illness	Unfriendly to families; parents act as if their families didn't exist during working hours

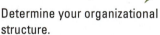

Performance Objective 5 

Determine your organizational structure.

A number of organizational structures may be viable for emerging companies. The evolutionary process for a business involves moving from one stage of maturity and structure to another. This process is not defined by time. A five-year-old company could be a nascent business. It is not strictly defined by the number of employees, either. However, communications, control, and coordination are primary drivers. With emerging structural changes, companies often evolve from simple **line organizations**, in which each person reports to one supervisor, to **line and staff organizations** that also include specialists, such as attorneys, who assist in the management. Managerial **spans of control**, or the number of direct reports, become more defined, and the **chain-of-command**, or hierarchy of reporting and communications, is more distinct. A management organizational chart for a typical small business might look like **Figure 19-1**.

line organization a structure where each person reports to a single supervisor.

line-and-staff organization an organizational structure that includes the line organization, plus staff specialists (such as legal) who assist management.

span of control the number of direct reports for a manager or supervisor.

chain-of-command hierarchy of reporting and communications.

Whatever organizational structure you choose for your company at each stage of growth, it should be a strategic design based upon the needs of the business. Be careful not to create a hodgepodge of positions in a convoluted structure in order to keep people who do not fit.

Getting the Best Out of Your Employees

When you do hire people, treat them fairly and with respect. As noted in a previous section, a culture of respect for individuals, diversity, and a balance of work and family create a culture that affirms the value of employees. Employees who are valued are likely to want to go the extra mile for their employers. In addition to creating a strong, positive culture, many

Figure 19-1 *Management organizational chart.*

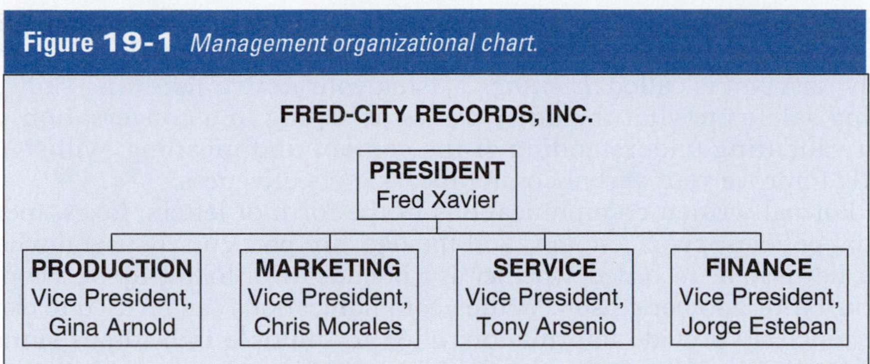

companies make their employees owners by giving them shares of corporate stock, thereby entitling them to a portion of the company profits, or offering various incentives for positive performance.

Follow these basic guidelines to be a good to excellent employer:

- Get the right people. Taking the time and effort to get the right people in the right jobs is at least half the battle. This means getting to know each employee's knowledge, skills, abilities, interests, and character traits.
- Provide a competitive salary and superior working conditions.
- Share your vision for the company and create an environment that encourages buy-in.
- Give employees incentives to work effectively. Ensure that the incentives match the company's goals and objectives and do not skew results.
- Empower employees by giving them control over their work.
- Provide career opportunities and training and development.
- Communicate expectations and goals clearly and provide ongoing feedback and recognition.

Communicating Effectively

Much of the success or failure of a manager depends upon his or her communications effectiveness. The same message may be interpreted in many ways, if not delivered clearly and understood as intended. As a manager, you will communicate in writing, verbally, and nonverbally. Which form of communication is best will depend upon the circumstances.

Face-to-face communication is often best for individual discussion. The addition of the nonverbal communication that comes with a face-to-face meeting will add meaning to what is being said. As a manager, your verbal communication skills, including your ability to speak clearly and to listen effectively, will be one of your most important weapons in the arsenal of managerial skills. What you say and how you say it are crucial. Knowing your audience, and speaking with them in terms that are meaningful, is vital. The words you use to describe research findings and their implications at a professional conference are likely to differ from those you would use with your employees at a company-wide meeting.

More importantly, managers need to listen effectively, rather than just hear what they are told. They should not discount communications through the **grapevine**, informal channels of communication for both information and rumors. Effective verbal communications require the speaker and recipient to be active participants. "It can be stated, with practically no qualification, that people in general do not know how to

grapevine an informational communication channel that transmits information and rumors.

active listening act of focusing solely on what the other person is saying in a conversation, and then validating understanding of the message content and meaning.

listen. They have ears that hear very well, but seldom have they acquired the necessary aural skills which would allow those ears to be used effectively for what is called *listening*."[3] Using your **active listening** skills, focusing solely on what the other person is saying in a conversation, and then validating understanding of the content and meaning, will significantly improve your verbal-communication effectiveness.

Formal written communications in the form of letters, faxes, memoranda, policies, plans, e-mails, and the like, are particularly useful when a topic needs to be recorded, whether as a prelude to, or follow-up of, a conversation, or for another reason. Written communications can be used to clearly and concisely provide information, often to multiple individuals simultaneously. With respect to human resources, written communications can be used to extend job offers, provide performance and disciplinary data, commend superior performance, or terminate employment—among many other subjects.

Anything put into writing, including electronic communications, should be something you would be willing to have examined in a court of law, so be careful what you write. Also, recognize that lack of clarity can cause problems in employee relations, including legal costs, depending upon the situation. More significant on a day-to-day basis is the fact that, with written communications, nonverbal signals are missing, so that the emotional import and underlying message may be open to interpretation.

With respect to what might be called informal written communications, such as quick e-mails to relay an anecdote or bit of information, electronic invitations, and tweets on Twitter.com, it is important to note that no communication is truly informal. Be careful to consider clarity and potential secondary audiences. Don't write anything that you would not want the world to see—because it just might.

Human Resources Fundamentals

human resources the segment of a business that hires, trains, and develops a company's employees.

Human resources is the department of a company that is responsible for staffing, training and development, compensation and benefits, employee relations, and organizational development. Human resources is commonly referred to as HR, human capital, casting (Disney term), or personnel.

Step into the Shoes...

Growing the Team: Metal Recycling Services Inc.[4]

Jeremy and Josh Rozsak and Will Simmons founded Metal Recycling Services Inc. (MRS) in 1999, while in college. A fourth partner, Jason Horner, joined the company in 2003. MRS collected scrap metal, processed it, and sold it to industrial customers. By 2008, the company had grown to over 150 employees, processing 220,000 tons of scrap, and generating revenues of $70 million annually. The MRS team was named the Small Business Administration's Young Entrepreneurs of the Year in 2005. It was also the Ernst and Young Entrepreneur of the Year 2007 for the Carolinas, and ranked 77th in *Entrepreneur*'s Hot 500 in that same year.

The MRS team invested over $7 million in creating a brand-new facility in 2005. They installed a state-of-the-art automobile shredder, one of only 230 in the United States. At this point, they were operating two facilities and the number of customers and staff was growing quickly.

Such remarkable growth and success caught the attention of industry leaders. In the spring of 2008, MRS was acquired by Nucor Corporation. In less than 10 years, MRS grew from 3 partners to 150 employees, and from a closely held company into a subsidiary of a large, publicly traded corporation. These four entrepreneurs turned scrap into big profits and personal wealth.

[3]Ralph G. Nichols and Leonard A. Stevens, "Listening to People," *Harvard Business Review*, September–October 1957.
[4]"Hot 500: The Fastest-Growing Businesses in America—#77 Metal Recycling Services Inc.," *Entrepreneur*, August 2007. And Metal Recycling Services' former Web site, http://www.metalrecyclingservices.com (accessed September 2007).

For a business just starting out, it may not be practical to have a director of human resources, as the entrepreneur will handle these tasks. A business will probably not need a full-time human resources professional until it has 20 or more employees.

Regardless of how many, once you have employees, there will be human resources functions to be managed. For companies of sufficient size, each of the following areas might represent one or more full-time jobs in the HR department.

Performance Objective 6

Understand the functions of human resources management.

Compensation and Payroll

The compensation and payroll area of HR addresses such issues as the level of wages and base salary, bonuses, sales commissions, stock grants, stock options, other forms of compensation, and the issuance of payroll and associated taxes (although the payroll is often a finance function). Along with the entrepreneur and top management, it addresses which employees receive stock in the company, in what amounts, and under what terms. It analyzes how compensation ties into the overall strategy and finances of the business and how the company's compensation program compares to that of competing companies. Human resources executives work closely with finance managers to answer questions about compensation and to set company policy accordingly.

Benefits

Full-time employees expect to be provided an array of paid benefits and opportunities to purchase discounted benefits as part of their compensation package. Basics may include health insurance (including the employee's family), life and AD&D insurance, paid holidays, vacation and sick time, and retirement savings plans. Other options may include tuition reimbursement, disability, and insurance discounts such as automobile, long-term care, and pet health insurance. HR usually leads the process of selecting the benefits programs that the company makes available. It is common practice to provide employees with benefit options and to have them share in the cost of their benefits, particularly for medical, dental, and vision care insurance.

Organizational Development

The HR team plays a pivotal role in organizational development. The key components are

- ***Organizational Structure.*** The HR department will help the founder, CEO, management team, and board of directors identify and analyze the pros and cons of different options, establish the appropriate organizational structure, and help manage transitions from one framework to another.
- ***Employee Retention.*** Sometimes compensation alone is not sufficient to prevent an individual from being lured away to work for a competitor. Human resources develops employee-retention programs that help build morale, create mentoring opportunities, and provide professional development and other benefits to keep employees excited about staying. The cost of losing a skilled, valued employee is high in terms of impact on the company and co-workers, and in terms of the cost of recruiting, hiring, and training a new employee.

BizFact

Many companies staff their human resources units using a ratio of one HR executive per 50 to 200 employees.

- ***Succession Planning.*** As employees are promoted, retire, or resign, it will be important to have plans in place to fill their positions. This is particularly true in key leadership roles that are not easily replaced. When you promote your sales manager to vice president of sales, who will fill the vacancy? The HR department will work with managers to find the best successor and will make succession plans for key executives while they are in place, so that sudden changes are not devastating.

Education and Development

Even senior executives require ongoing professional-development education from time to time. Human resources managers develop employee training in-house, and may also use outside training providers for specific situations. There are businesses that help companies train their sales teams. Leading institutions, such as the Wharton School and Harvard Business School, offer executive-education curriculum.

Labor Law and HR Compliance

The United States has well-developed laws to protect the rights of workers and employees. Everyone involved in hiring, firing, and managing people needs to be aware of both the letter and the spirit of these laws, which are typically translated into policies by the HR, and legal teams at a company. For example, laws forbid companies from not hiring or promoting on the basis of age or race. It is illegal for employers to ask candidates how old they are, whether they are married and/or have children, or where they are from, during the interview process. Companies can expose themselves to significant liability if they do not properly manage the process of hiring, rewarding, and terminating employees.

As the business grows and you hire employees, you will have to become familiar with the laws and tax issues affecting employment. There are attorneys that specialize in labor law whom you may contact regarding the legality of your hiring process, including the job application and interview questions; your employee manual; your performance-appraisal process; compliance with antidiscrimination, fair labor, and other such laws; and firing and termination procedures. Some of the laws and tax issues of concern include

payroll tax employers must deduct this tax from their employees' pay and forward it to the designated governmental entity.

- **Payroll tax** is a series of wage taxes based on earnings that will be deducted from your employees' pay. Your accountant can advise you in more detail when you get to this point, and you can find information on the IRS Web site (http://www.irs.gov) and those of state and local revenue departments. For now, it is important that you know you will be responsible for contributing to Social Security, unemployment compensation, and other programs on their behalf. Of particular importance are the withholding taxes that must be paid in a timely fashion, because the penalties for not doing so can be devastating.
- The **Equal Pay Act of 1963** requires employers to pay men and women the same amount for substantially equal work.

- The **Fair Labor Standards Act** was passed in 1938 and requires that employees receive at least the federally mandated minimum wage. It also prohibits hiring anyone under the age of 16 full time. Also, minimum-wage information must be posted where it is visible.
- **Title VII of the Civil Rights Act of 1964** prohibits discrimination against applicants and employees on the basis of race or color, religion, sex, pregnancy, or national origin, including membership in a Native American tribe. It also prohibits harassment based on any protected characteristics, such as those listed here, and prohibits employer retaliation against those who assert their rights under the Act. This Act is enforced by the U.S. Equal Employment Opportunity Commission (EEOC).
- The **Age Discrimination in Employment Act (ADEA)** prohibits discrimination against and harassment of employees aged 40 or older. Employers may not retaliate against those who assert their rights under the Act. This Act is also enforced by the EEOC.
- The **Americans with Disabilities Act (ADA)** prohibits employers from discriminating against a person who has a disability, or who is perceived to have a disability, in any aspect of employment. It also prohibits refusal to hire or discrimination against someone related to or an associate of someone with a disability. ADA prohibits harassment and retaliation in the cases above. This Act is enforced by the EEOC and the U.S. Department of Justice.
- The **Immigration Reform and Control Act of 1986 (IRCA)** prohibits employers from discriminating against applicants or employees on the basis of their citizenship or national origin. In addition, it affirms that it is illegal for employers to knowingly hire or retain in employment individuals who are not authorized to work in the United States. Employers must keep records that verify that all employees are authorized to work here.

Performance Management

Just as you want to take the time to develop job specifications and position descriptions and follow best practices in hiring, you can maintain and build your team through appraisal and thorough follow-up. Although it has a tradition of being dreaded, a **performance appraisal**, the formal process used to evaluate and support employee performance, is valuable for both employees and employers when done well. It is an opportunity to set goals, assess progress, identify opportunities for improvement, plan for individual growth and development, and provide performance feedback. Done poorly, the process is a waste of time and energy at best, and counterproductive at worst.

performance appraisal the formal process used to evaluate and support employees' performance.

The key to valuable performance appraisal is planning and consistency. Be clear about the purpose of appraisal and create a system for it. Clearly, nothing in the appraisal process should come as a surprise for anyone involved, if performance feedback is discussed routinely and course corrections are made throughout the year. Good channels of communication make the performance-appraisal process work more fluidly.

Performance appraisal is an opportunity to communicate goals, establish training and development needs, and provide feedback to increase productivity and employee retention. An effective process will also link performance to pay, which will help create a high-accomplishment culture in which superior performers earn higher pay increases than lower ones.

It also can help to protect a company against lawsuits by employees that have been fired, demoted, or not given a pay raise. They provide formal documentation for specific discussions on performance that can be used for any of these purposes.

There are multiple methods of implementing performance appraisal, and these often vary according to the size and culture of an organization. Some companies have managers and supervisors review direct reports and provide feedback. Others have employees complete a self-appraisal and then have managers and supervisors put together reviews for discussion. Still others use feedback, including impressions from the entire spectrum of staff that interact with a particular employee—such as peers, direct reports, customers, and others.

For some organizations, performance is broken down into key aspects of the job, typically based upon the position description, as well as annual goals, and rated on a scale. A subset of these organizations provides descriptions of the meaning of each numeric value to create greater consistency in ratings. Generally, a brief statement of examples to support the rating is required. A condensed version of the supervisor/manager portion of a performance review form appears in **Exhibit 19-5**. If the employee does a self-appraisal, it will be similar. There are numerous variations on the forms used and the style of presentation. Consulting any of the many books on human resources, or visiting the Society for Human Resource Management (http://www.shrm.org), should provide ample information.

The performance-review meeting should be structured to create an environment for discussion and support rather than debate and contention. It should be scheduled in advance and held in neutral territory, rather than in the office or workspace of either participant. The environment should be free of distractions and interruptions. The manager can begin with a brief overview of the purpose of the appraisal and its objectives. Then, the employee should provide a statement of his or her own performance, not a step-by-step reading of the self-appraisal, but a verbal update. The next portion will be the planned performance appraisal from the manager. It should stay focused on the performance and avoid being diluted or personalized. It should provide feedback, and not be an item-by-item review of the form. An item-by-item review tends to lead to negotiation and/or confrontation. If there are performance problems, they should be discussed in terms of the gap between the actual performance and the goal. Remember, be careful to measure as per the agreed-upon goal, not some other standard. Once performance has been reviewed, a new action plan with goals and development objectives can be created. You can wrap up with a summary of the positives, remarks on the next steps, and a thank-you.

development plan a document stating how an employee will attain specific performance.

If there are issues to be worked on to specifically improve performance because of deficiencies during the review period, an additional plan may be needed. The manager and employee can create a **development plan**, which is a document stating how the employee will attain specific performance outcomes. The development plan includes action steps, such as any education and professional development, milestones with dates, and any feedback that is required. This document is meant to be agreed upon by both parties and should be signed.

Once the performance-appraisal process is complete, the manager or supervisor will continue to monitor employee progress. In addition, managers should evaluate their approach and methods of performance appraisal, identifying opportunities for improvement.

Exhibit 19-5 *Sample performance review form—supervisor/manager portion.*

Name: ______________________ Date of Review: ______________________
Period Under Review: ___________ Department: ______________________

Part A. Success Factors

Factors	Rating					Comments
I. KEY RESPONSIBILITIES FOR THIS POSITION						
Performs key responsibilities as articulated in the job description. *(insert each essential function from the position description)*	1	2	3	4	5	
II. CORE COMPETENCIES						
1. Inclusiveness (defined in greater detail)	1	2	3	4	5	
2. Problem solving / decision making	1	2	3	4	5	
3. Planning and organizing	1	2	3	4	5	
4. Communication	1	2	3	4	5	
5. Quality focus	1	2	3	4	5	
6. Leadership	1	2	3	4	5	
7. Teamwork	1	2	3	4	5	
8. Department-specific competency	1	2	3	4	5	

Part B. Last Period's Goals

Rate the progress made on each of the goals established at the beginning of the period and any new goals. Note any modifications to the original goals.

Goal	Rating					Comments
1. (specify as many goals as are appropriate for the employee)	1	2	3	4	5	
2.	1	2	3	4	5	
3.	1	2	3	4	5	

OVERALL RATING (based on Parts A and B)	1	2	3	4	5	

Part C. Next Period's Goals

Enter the performance goals for the next period to be evaluated.

1. Measure of success:
2. Measure of success:
3. Measure of success:

Progress toward meeting these goals will be reviewed at the time of the next evaluation.

Part D. Professional Development Plan

Signatures:
Employee: ______________________ Date: ______________________
My signature indicates that I have received a copy of this evaluation.
_______ I would like to include comments from my self-assessment.

Manager/Supervisor Name: ______________________

Signature: ______________________ Date: ______________________

Department Manager Name: ______________________

Signature: ______________________ Date: ______________________

Human Resources Strategy

Strategic human resources departments will also dedicate effort to identifying ways to maximize the productivity and effectiveness of the overall organization through its HR practices.

- ***Diversity.*** Many leading companies—for example, Avon Products—have found that they better represent and understand their customer base by creating a more diverse workforce in terms of gender and ethnicity. This translates into increased sales and greater customer loyalty. Avon is known for having a diverse workforce, from the CEO to the sales-representative level, and uses the tagline, "The Company for Women."
- ***Benchmarking.*** For companies to be competitive, they must understand their own employee base, but they must also understand the skills and motivations of the employees of the companies with which they compete. Benchmarking is a process that lets companies compare themselves with their competitors. As an entrepreneur, you will want to ensure that your employees' skills keep pace with or are ahead of those of your competitors.
- ***Retention.*** As noted earlier, it is paramount for companies to keep the employees who drive the business. HR strategy puts focus on programs and benefits that keep employees engaged and motivated, to fulfill the company's mission.

Firing and Laying Off Employees

Sometimes you hire someone and it just does not work out, even after repeated attempts to fix the problems. If you have to let someone go, you should document the reasons as they occur. You can be sued for wrongful termination, or breach of contract, if an employee believes he/she was fired for no good reason. The rules for termination vary from state to state, so it is essential to know your state's law.

- Protect your company from wrongful-termination claims by conducting regular employee-performance reviews. Use performance-improvement or development plans to give the employee an opportunity to fix those aspects of performance that are subpar.
- If an employee is violating rules, give notification in writing (and keep a copy for your records) and work on corrections as the problems arise, rather than waiting for a performance review. If performance

Global Impact...

Human Resources Service Firms

Many companies, large and small, are dedicated to providing human resources services to corporate clients around the globe. Here is how some leading firms got started: Adecco was founded in 1957, when Henri-Ferdinand Lavanchy, an accountant at the time, was asked by a client to help him fill a position. Today, Adecco provides staffing services to 250,000 clients around the world. In 1969, Lester Korn and Richard Ferry started a recruitment firm with a $10,000 investment. Today, with over $650 million in revenue, Korn/Ferry International specializes in helping clients hire top executives, including CEOs. When companies have thousands of employees, the task of getting paychecks out twice a month can be daunting. Payroll provider Automatic Data Processing Inc. (ADP) cuts checks for over 50 million people on behalf of its clients. ADP was started by Henry Taub in 1949, when he was 22. The company had eight clients and $2000 in revenue in its first year.

continues to be unsatisfactory, and you have to let the employee go, you will have documentation that there were problems with his/her performance. Be very careful to document the problem, not to editorialize or speculate about the employee.

Sometimes you might have to lay off employees. They may have performed their jobs well, but you either no longer need their skills or cannot afford to continue employing them. To minimize complications, if you can do so, offer employees **severance**, pay that is continued for a limited time as compensation for being let go, and make serious efforts to help them find new employment.

severance pay that is continued income for a limited time upon separation from a company.

Chapter Summary

Now that you have studied this chapter, you can do the following:

1. Describe the 10 basic tasks handled by managers.
   - Planning: strategic, tactical, and operational
   - Organizing
   - Leading
   - Directing
   - Staffing
   - Controlling
   - Coordinating
   - Representing
   - Innovating
   - Motivating
2. Recruit your employees.
   - Define the job.
   - Post the job.
   - Screen resumes and/or applications.
   - Assess required skills.
   - Interview candidates.
   - Check references and other background information.
   - Negotiate compensation.
   - Hire a candidate.
   - Orient the new employee.
3. Know where and how to find qualified job candidates.
   - Advertising (internal and external)
   - Online postings
   - Campus recruiting
   - Executive search firms
4. Develop your organizational culture.
   - The culture of a company is the shared beliefs, values, and attitudes among employees.
   - The entrepreneur can strategically determine the culture.
   - Cultures vary, from entrepreneurial to administrative.
   - There are a multitude of cultural components that are conveyed through words, actions, and structures.

5. Determine your organizational structure.
   - Structure evolves as the company grows and changes.
   - The transition from entrepreneur to entrepreneurial manager is often difficult.
   - There are different organizational stages related to the maturation of the company.
6. Understand the functions of human resources management.
   - Compensation and payroll
   - Benefits administration
   - Organizational development
   - Education and development
   - Labor law and HR compliance
   - Performance of appraisal and review
   - Human resources strategy
   - Firing and laying off employees

Key Terms

active listening
behavioral interview
chain-of-command
development plan
grapevine
human resources
interview guide
job offer letter
job profile
line organization
line-and-staff organization
operational plan
payroll tax
performance appraisal
position description
recruitment
severance
span of control
strategic plan
tactical plan

Entrepreneurship Portfolio

Critical Thinking Exercises

1. Will you be hiring employees during your first year of operations? If so, name their positions and describe the required qualifications, anticipated compensation, and how they will help your business.
2. Provide contact information for your accountant, attorney, banker, and insurance agent.
3. What are your policies toward employees? How do you plan to make your business a positive and rewarding place to work?
4. Provide information for each of your mentors or advisors. If there is a board of advisors, list each and describe his/her purpose on the board.
5. Why is establishing job profiles and position description before recruiting important?
6. What are the benefits of a well-executed performance-appraisal process?
7. Describe the components of an organizational culture that you would find appealing.
8. What are the characteristics of an organizational culture that you would find unappealing?

Key Concept Questions

1. How old does someone have to be before he or she can work full time in the United States?
2. What is one kind of tax employers have to pay for employees?
3. Can you legally fire an employee if you have an argument about religion?
4. What is nonverbal communication? How can it impact overall communications? How can the loss of nonverbal clues affect e-mail, instant messaging, and other written communications?
5. What is an interview guide? What are the critical components of an interview guide?
6. What are the 10 functions of management?
7. What are antidiscrimination laws? What protections do they include?

Application Exercises

1. What qualities and qualifications would you look for in employees for your business? List five and explain why they are the most important to you.
2. What would push you to fire an employee? List five reasons that you feel would justify termination. Describe how you would handle the firing.
3. Visit a local bricks-and-mortar business (not a Web site) where you buy products or services. Go through your shopping experience as you normally would. Once you have left the place of business, describe its culture. Use the information in **Exhibit 19-4** to assist you.

Exploring Online

1. Visit the Web site for a U.S. state, or use another reliable source, to identify the antidiscrimination laws in that state. What form(s) of discrimination do they prohibit? When were they enacted? To which organizations (type and size) do they apply?
2. Search the Internet for two position descriptions from different businesses. Make a chart identifying which of the following are included: job title; job summary; duties to be performed; nature of supervision, and the job's relation to others in the company. How might each description be improved?

In Your Opinion

Discuss with a group: Should an employer be able to fire an employee if the latter is often ill? Before the discussion, prepare by searching the Internet to determine what legal issues may be involved.

Case Study | If at First You Don't Succeed... Enablemart Learns a Valuable Lesson

Nick Tostenrude and Dennis Mouton founded Enablemart when they were freshmen at the University of Portland to bring rehabilitation software, developed by Dennis's father, to market. Founded in 1999, as Mindnautilus.com, and incorporated in 2000, Nick and Dennis soon discovered that their original business concept was not viable, and switched to making computers that were accessible to people with disabilities. This became a niche market to be served by Enablemart, which began marketing assistive technologies in 2001. Enablemart (enablemart.com) grew to become the world leader in assistive technology, with 14 employees and $9 million in annual sales in the United States and a subsidiary in the United Kingdom (TechReady.co.uk), at the time of its acquisition by Manufacturers Resource Network in 2007.

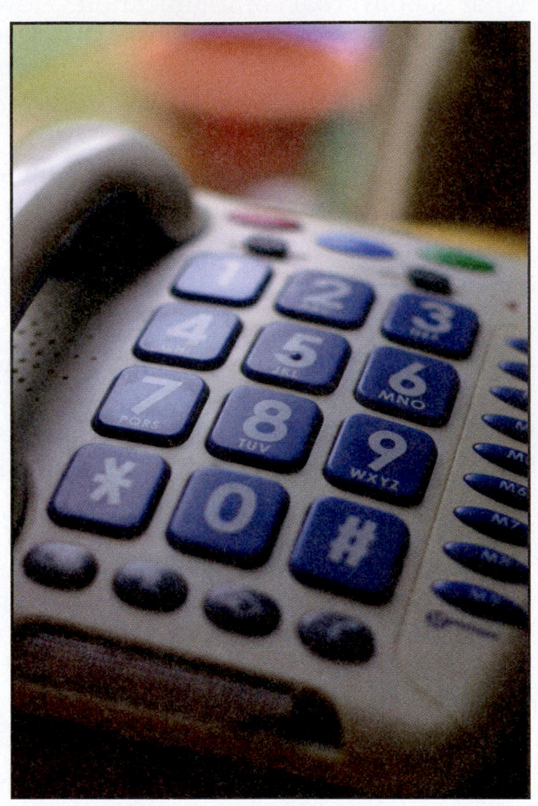

The path from the dorm room to the boardroom was not always smooth. Creating an advisory board with numerous industry pioneers went relatively well. However, Enablemart needed someone with credibility and access to capital. For Nick and Dennis, local entrepreneurial events provided networking opportunities and led to finding a candidate that Nick described: "We couldn't have asked for a better person to have in our corner." They found someone who was older, appeared to have experienced success as an entrepreneur, and had a passion for the work.

The next step was to secure an employment contract. The founders were pleased that the candidate offered to provide a contract that he had used previously. The contract was daunting, but Nick and Dennis trusted their new colleague. Nick later wrote, "We were a bit thrown back, but this individual seemed trustworthy because, after all, he believed in our idea. So we signed the contract and celebrated hiring our new chairperson."

This new chairperson was active for a couple of months, helping to find an excellent CFO, and then he gradually stopped working and communicating with Nick and Dennis. Lawyers reviewed the employment contract and, after they stopped laughing at how bad it was, they explained that the best thing to do was to avoid accomplishing the things that would trigger payouts to the chairman. The contract included giving him a portion of stock with a nondilution clause, and an option that permitted him to sell it to anyone he wanted at any time. Whenever they raised capital, he would receive substantial compensation. There was no way to hold the chairman accountable for poor performance because his job duties were so unclear. On top of all of these issues, rather than signing the agreement on behalf of the corporation, the founders had signed it personally.

Instead of continuing to pursue the high-growth strategy and raising significant capital as they had planned, Nick and Dennis again revised their game plan. They knew that investors would avoid them as long as the chairman's contract hung over them. After two years of a slow-growth strategy, fueled primarily with funds from friends and family, Enablemart bought out its chairman for $20,000 and terminated the contract, ending the protracted agony of their first executive hiring experience.

Case Study Analysis

1. Enablemart's founders created a board of advisors early in the life of the company. How might they have taken advantage of the advisors' counsel when hiring their chairman?
2. Name at least three steps that Nick and Dennis could have taken to avoid the dreadful experience they had with their first executive hire.
3. What are the implications of signing an employment contract personally, rather than as a representative of a corporation?
4. Nick and Dennis sought legal counsel when their chairman simply stopped working and they had to slow down their growth plans. Comment on how you think this affected them, and the company.

Case Sources

Nick Tostenrude, "Turning 25¢ into $1: The Unique Advantages and Disadvantages of Being Young Entrepreneurs," in *Student Entrepreneurs: 14 Undergraduate All-Stars Tell Their Stories*, compiled by Michael McMyne and edited by Nicole Amare (Nashville: Premium Press America 2003).

Profile of Nick Tostenrude on http://www.LinkedIn.com (accessed January 4, 2010).

Case Study | Casino Grande[5]

In the early afternoon of June 20, 1992, as Roger Parks, the reservation manager of Casino Grande was packing his briefcase to go out of town to a hospitality association conference, Randolph Jackson, the general manager, called him into his office and the following conversation ensued.

Jackson: Damn it, Roger, didn't I tell you to talk to those two girls about getting to work on time? All they do around here is drink coffee. I guess I'm going to have to install martial law around here. They both recently got raises, too; who do they think they are, anyhow? You tell them in no uncertain terms that if they don't shape up, we'll give them the sack. We can still hire people who follow the rules.

Parks: Whoa, back! What's going on? What in the heck are you talking about?

Jackson: Don't pretend with me. You know just what I'm talking about. It's those two girls, Kane and Palumbo. I saw them come into the employee cafeteria this morning at 8:00 and they were still there when I left at 8:20 to come upstairs. They couldn't have gotten to their desks until 8:30 or later! Then, at 10:30 they were back down there for coffee; I saw them with my own eyes! They're just going to have to shape up. Other people have noticed as well. Why, Cooperider (housekeeping assistant manager) mentioned it just the other day. Why on earth didn't you talk with them like I told you to do?

Parks: Cool it, Randy. I did talk the whole thing over with Marshall, and she talked with the two women. She told me later that she had, and said the women had agreed to do better from then on.

Jackson: Posh, they aren't doing it! We just gave them salary increases, too. We gave them increases, and that's how they're showing their appreciation. I say, if they don't shape up we fire their butts. That Kane's a pain. She says she wants more responsibility, we give it to her, and a raise; and then she comes in late every morning and drinks coffee all day long.

Parks: Simmer down, Randy. You'll have to admit we don't set much of an example. It seems there is always a gang of supervisors in the coffee line at all times, and your secretary and her friend stand around the cigarette machine way after 8:00 a.m.

Jackson: That's not relevant. You can't get cigarettes unless you stand in that line. Cripes, we can't go clear out to the lobby stand, can we? Oh, it's all right to grab a cup of coffee on occasion, but those two girls are always out together. They're abusing the privileges. They drive to work together every day; I've seen them, and then they go into the cafeteria at 8:00 and have breakfast. It's got to end.

Parks: Okay, okay. We'll have another chat with them. The offices and the whole back-of-the-house are pretty lax in regard to timeliness. I agree we don't want reservations standing out as the worst offenders. Part of it is that they go out together, and that makes it conspicuous alright. I'm leaving town this afternoon, but I'll talk with them personally today and let you know before I take off.

Jackson: Okay. Just make it good. We've got to stop abuses, or we'll just have to crack down on everyone. It's always a few who make it hard on everyone.

On the way back to his own office, Mr. Parks detoured into reservations and found Ms. Jean

[5]Craig C. Lundberg and Cheri A. Young, *The Hospitality Case Manual: Developing Competencies in Critical Thinking and Practical Action* (Upper Saddle River, N.J.: Pearson Education, Inc., 2009).

Marshall, talking on the telephone. When she hung up, Mr. Parks related his conversations with Mr. Jackson. This was the second time in two months that Mr. Jackson had called the behavior of Kane and Palumbo to his attention. After a brief discussion, they decided that the proper thing to do was to call the two women into the departmental conference room and talk with them. When Mr. Parks, Ms. Marshall, Mrs. Kane, and Mrs. Palumbo had assembled, the following conversation took place.

Parks: While I sure don't like to bring up a complaint a few hours before I go out of town, I've just come from Mr. Jackson's office. He has complained again about you two getting to work late and about you taking so much time away from your desks for coffee. He rather emphatically stated that he has seen you in the cafeteria after 8:00 several times and that you both seem to be there having coffee together every time he stops by. I believe Jean spoke with you about this several weeks ago. What do you think we ought to do about it?

Kane: Yes, Ms. Marshall talked to us before about it. We've been trying to watch it since then. I believe we've been doing a lot better. You know how hard it is to get to work winter mornings, and we do go down once in a while for a cup of coffee. The new cafeteria is so nice now. Everybody is using it more. Why shouldn't we?

Parks: Yes, you're right, of course. More people are using the cafeteria. You'll agree with me, I'm sure, that this property has a pretty relaxed attitude about getting to work on time occasionally and about getting out of the office for coffee or Coke or a smoke. But let's face it. Mr. Jackson is riled. If we abuse the privileges we have, it will be necessary for Jackson to create some rules that constrict us. We'll all suffer then. There must be some way you can work it out so you'll not be so conspicuous when you take a break once in a while? Isn't it possible for you two to get to work on time so when you take a break it won't be so objectionable?

Kane: All the other reservations women do it. All the office force does it. The smokers go out all the time. Most use the lavs, but it's always so crowded there we prefer to go down to the cafeteria.

Parks: Part of the problem, of course, is that you two are always seen together. That makes you stand out. Why can't you split up, or go some other place? Mrs. Kane, you've indicated more than once that you want more responsibility in reservations. Let's face it; we can't get it for you if the GM thinks you're abusing the situation.

Kane: Of course that makes sense. What do you want us to do? Stop taking breaks altogether?

Parks: Mrs. Palumbo, what do you think you should do?

Palumbo: Gee, I don't know. We don't do anything that the others don't do. But we don't want to get into trouble. The Casino has been generous enough.

Parks: The way things stand now, well, you can see how things are. Both Mr. Jackson and Cooperider have commented on you. Jackson's the GM, remember, he approves all job changes and all recommendations for raises. It's just not smart to have him on your case.

Kane: We want to do what's right, of course. I sure wouldn't want to do anything that would hinder my next promotion. I suppose we could go somewhere else and maybe not take so many breaks—at least not together. Suppose we lay low for a while until the top brass forgets about it?

Parks: And, get to work a little more promptly in the morning. Sure, all of us are a touch lax sometimes about getting in on time, but the finger is pointing at you, so how about doing a bit better than you've been doing of late?

Kane: Okay, but as you know, I've three kids to get off to school every day. What with car problems, the storms tying traffic up, it's awfully hard to get here on time.

Parks: I'll leave it up to you. I know you're both good workers, and I know you're both trying to get ahead here. You must realize that if old Jackson doesn't see an immediate turnaround, well, I'm not sure what he'll do. You've been talked to twice now. We wouldn't want our GM to do something that would hurt all of the staff, now, would we? (Pause) Jean, what do you think is the best thing to do?

Marshall: You've outlined the situation very well, Mr. Parks. I think these women are attracting undue attention by going out together all the time. The whole staff has been lax about starting promptly. I'll certainly work with reservations to see that we put a drive on to get us to work on time. I think they shouldn't take quite so many breaks, and not together. That way they won't cause so many negative comments.

Parks: Well, it's up to these women. I'm about to leave for a conference, tonight, in fact. I'll be away, so I won't hear anything. If Jackson gets in a twit, he'll no doubt call you down, Jean, and I know you'll do whatever he says. See if you two ladies can't stay out of trouble, please. I'll be back in five days. Good luck.

Roger Parks returned to his own office and telephoned Mr. Jackson. He told Jackson that he and Ms. Marshall had talked to Kane and Palumbo and that he believed that Jackson would see an immediate improvement. Parks asked Jackson to call Ms. Marshall if there are any further complaints. Jackson replied, "You're darn right I will."

About Casino Grande

Casino Grande was an older, mid-sized casino hotel, employing approximately 2000 people, on the boardwalk section of a mid-Atlantic city. Mr. Randolph Jackson was the general manager of Casino Grande and, as such, had the ultimate authority over all departments and functions at the property. He took unusual interest in the human resource activities of the casino/hotel, establishing both personnel policies and office procedure personally. The ordinary interpretation of these policies and procedures, however, was handled by the department managers and section supervisors with consultation available from the employee relations department.

Roger Parks was the manager of Casino Grande's reservations department. He had begun his employment with the casino in 1982 as a night programmer in the accounting department, while he was finishing his B.S. in hotel administration from a prominent eastern university. After graduation, Roger continued to work in accounting for two years, then he requested a transfer to the newly established computer system group, where he worked for another two years before he replaced a section head and, thus, acquired his first truly supervisory experience. In late 1987, Roger obtained an interview for a section manager's position in the front desk department, and for which he was hired. In 1990, Casino Grande significantly upgraded its computer facilities, including a sophisticated reservations system. Roger was transferred to the reservations unit to take charge of it. When he began to organize this function, he hired Ms. Marshall and two clerks. About a year later, when an opening occurred, Mrs. Kane was hired. In Mr. Parks's opinion, Ms. Marshall was a technical whiz who got along fairly well with her people. She had a reputation within the reservations group of sometimes being impatient; she kidded her workers a lot and usually got a lot of high-quality work from them, but was considered somewhat lax in enforcing discipline.

Mrs. Kane, about 39 years old, had three children of ages 11, 8, and 6. Her husband was a sales trainer with a major manufacturing company and was away from home for extended periods. Mrs. Kane's mother lived with them, taking care of the children so that Mrs. Kane could work. She was made senior reservations clerk on January 1, 1992, receiving a substantial raise. At that time, Mrs. Kane was told she was doing excellent work but had a quick temper that sometimes disturbed her fellow employees. She was also told that she often disrupted the office by talking too loudly and too often. The position of senior reservationist provided a wage differential over the others and required her co-workers to bring their questions about procedures and assignments to her. All other matters, such as salary and training questions as well as performance appraisals, were handled by Ms. Marshall. Mrs. Kane took her work seriously and expressed resentment toward the indifferent attitude of the younger reservation clerks. She was trying to get ahead financially. She did not like housekeeping or childcare and planned to continue working as long as her mother could look after her children.

Mrs. Palumbo was about 28 years old and a college graduate. Her husband was in the Army and had been in the Middle East for two tours after Operation Desert Storm. Mrs. Palumbo lived alone in a small apartment and planned on working only until her husband was posted in the United States. Mrs. Palumbo did a good job as a reservation clerk and got along well with everyone in the department. She also got a raise on January 1, 1992.

The office rules at Casino Grande did not permit smoking on the job but allowed personnel to leave the office to do so, although there were no designated smoking spaces.

On Monday, August 15, 1992, the following notice was posted on the bulletin board just inside the employees' entrance to the property:

> TO: All Casino Grande Office Personnel
>
> Some employees have been taking advantage of our company's coffee break privilege. In order to be fair to those who are being reasonable about going to the cafeteria for coffee, we do not wish to rescind this privilege altogether. We do expect all office employees to start work at 8:00 in the morning, meaning come ready to work, already having had breakfast. There is no excuse for having coffee, therefore, after 8:00 a.m.
>
> From now on the following rules will apply to coffee breaks:
>
> 1. No one should visit the cafeteria for coffee before 9:30 a.m.
> 2. Groups from the same department should not take breaks together, since this would disrupt the service provided.
> 3. No one should stay away from his/her workstation for longer than 15 minutes.
> 4. It is unnecessary to leave one's office for coffee or any other beverage more than once a day.
>
> These simple rules should be clear to everyone. If, in the future, these rules are ignored, the coffee break privilege will be canceled altogether. Your wholehearted cooperation is expected.
>
> R. L. Jackson
> General Manager

Case Study Analysis

1. List the pros and cons of Mr. Jackson's decision to post the coffee break notice. Was it a good management decision? Why or why not?
2. Imagine a scenario where you are Mr. Parks. What do you think you would have done after the conversation with Mr. Jackson? Write a paragraph describing your action plan.
3. Write a paragraph describing Mr. Jackson's philosophy of human-resources management.
4. List some examples of why the ladies might see the reprimands as unfair or unjust.
5. What is Jackson's leadership style?

UNIT 5 Operating a Small Business Effectively

Mo's Chowder: Sharpening the Pencil to Operate Effectively

Small Business School video clip titles are in red

BE THE AFFORDABLE HANG OUT

Cindy McEntee is owner of Mo's Restaurants, a place famous for serving hot clam chowder since 1951. There are three locations on the Oregon coast, and a chowder-base factory. The home office is in Newport, and the operation employs up to 200 people during peak season and generates $3.5 million in annual sales. Cindy owns an additional three locations with a group of partners. We met in the White House in June of 2001, when she was named Oregon's Small Business Person of the Year and first runner-up for the National Small Business Person of the Year award.

Cindy says, "Mo's is just a plain and simple restaurant with simple seafood dishes that aren't complex—it's for the everyday person. A Seattle food critic called us a dive and that's okay. I'm laughing all the way to the bank."

When her grandmother—Mo—opened for business, the town of Newport had a lively fishing industry, with hundreds of fisherman and a fish-processing plant across the street. Back then, Mo's was a fisherman's hangout, but today it is the foundation for Newport's tourism. This transition had to happen in order for Mo's to survive. In this case, the evolution demonstrates both the need to adapt to a changing market and the business acumen of its owner.

IMPLEMENT COST ACCOUNTING

Mo's is a landmark institution. Some would call it a national treasure, like a national park or a historic site. People come from miles away to eat there. Some even told us they had *flown* in to eat at Mo's. Of course, it's the food. Every restaurant owner will tell you that their staying power rests on the quality of the food. Good service cannot make up for poor ingredients, stale bread, or wilted lettuce.

But, it is more than chowder.

Mo's has a story to tell. Cindy loved her grandmother and what she stood for and considers herself to be the caretaker of a legacy. Cindy herself has been part of this story for 40 of the 50 years. And she knows that these stories about her grandmother capture a bigger truth.

Turn a Hobby Into a Business

When Cindy was 21 years old and working at Mo's, she asked her grandmother whether she knew how much they were paying for clams. Mo said she didn't know. This did not seem to be good operating practice, so Cindy began installing cost accounting and food preparation systems.

Mo's never made much profit before Cindy started her sharp-pencil techniques. At the same time Cindy was working to improve the internal processes, she was also telling stories, creating legends about how Mo gave plenty of fishermen food even when they couldn't pay, and about the lady who drove her car right into the restaurant, then stayed to eat.

On the walls in the original location there are photos, drawings, and framed write-ups about what has happened at Mo's through the years. The storytelling builds the legacy. Storytelling makes Mo's bigger than life. But, without systems that produce the quality product day in and day out, and that nurture employees, the legends are of no value.

Mo was happy operating one restaurant, but Cindy was hungry for more. When there were frequent lines of customers waiting outside the door, Cindy knew she could add locations to serve more customers. She realized that she had to put infrastructure in place. She attended seminars and classes to learn more about expanding a business. As a leader in her local chamber of commerce, she knew many business owners to whom she could turn for advice.

Pass Ownership Formally

Mo was inspired and impressed by her granddaughter and decided to give Cindy the opportunity to become the owner, through the purchase of stock over time. To do that, Mo changed her legal form of business from a sole proprietorship to a corporation and, in 1975, Cindy started buying stock in the company through payroll deductions.

Change when the Market Changes

Newport is still a working port, with all the sights and smells that come with hauling in fish from the sea. However, as the fishing industry has changed, there is less processing taking place. At the same time, the city leaders (and that includes Cindy) have been working on making the waterfront attractive, so tourists will come and watch the fishermen and spend money in the town. Knowing that their waterfront has maintained its turn-of-the-twentieth-century charm, they pooled resources to make Newport an important West Coast tourist destination. Cindy has not only worked hard to promote tourism in Newport, she has completely reinvented Mo's image to fit the tourism trade. Plenty of fisherman still stop in for chowder and beer, but the Mo's Chowder restaurants today are light, bright, family-friendly places where children are treated with great respect. Cindy says, "We eat where our children want to eat."

One very visible result of Cindy's tireless efforts to promote her hometown is the art that tourists and locals enjoy. She recruited some of the world's most famous artists to paint murals on Newport's waterfront buildings. Cindy has commissioned an artist to do a bronze statue of her grandmother, Mo, and other business owners who are doing their part to make their storefronts attractive, and at the same time keep the spirit of the working port.

Help Employees Accumulate Wealth

Cindy has built a business based upon tried-and-true recipes, but she had to learn through experience to operate an expanding company. In addition to monitoring every detail of the business by the numbers, to keep the company financially healthy, Cindy is committed to making employment at Mo's good enough work so that morale remains healthy. Employees at Mo's have excellent medical benefits and a 401(k) plan. Cindy uses fixed and variable compensation plans to maintain a strong team of valued employees. Fixed compensation, fair salaries and benefit plans are benefits each employee can count on. Helping employees feel safe and secure keeps morale high and turnover, always costly to any business, low.

What's really special about Cindy's compensation plan for Mo's is the variable compensation.

For example, in a year when breakage was low and there were no accidents, Cindy demonstrated the direct connection between these by using some of the cost savings to take 47 employees on a vacation trip to Hawaii. By doing this, she acknowledged the fact that both the low breakage and excellent safety record were a result of the employees' efforts, and that they deserved a share of the benefits.

Engage the Team

In monthly meetings, everyone is encouraged to comment on how they think the business is going. Often, there is a 15-minute training session on service. Customer comment cards, which are time- and date-stamped, are discussed. When specific employees are praised by a customer, that person is praised in the meeting. When customer comments are negative—for example, "The food was cold" or "My fish was undercooked" or "My fish was overcooked" or "The chowder wasn't hot," the team works together to figure out what happened so the problem will not recur.

Key numbers from Mo's financial statements are shared, so that employees understand how their performance affects the bottom line. Because of this training, when a tray of dishes is dropped, or a meal is returned to the kitchen, everyone knows how much the restaurant just lost.

Start Children at the Bottom

The third generation has joined the business and it has brought fresh energy and technological know-how to the operation. Dylan started by peeling potatoes, and Gabrielle began as a dishwasher. By doing every job in the business, these two are becoming better and more compassionate managers, fully aware of the challenges faced by each employee. They will find ways of improving the business at each level of operations as they fully participate in it. And perhaps most importantly, the other employees will know that the next generation is qualified to lead, that they have survived the internship, and that they are well positioned to strengthen the organization.

Gabrielle has a B.A. in sociology and her brother, Dylan, has a B.A. in hospitality management with a minor in business, then another degree in finance. Dylan says that, when he finished the second degree, "I got a job at GE and after about a year I realized—there is a lot of corporate bureaucracy." There was no guarantee that Mo's would have a place for Cindy's children, but about one month after Dylan decided he wanted to leave GE, the manager of Mo's chowder factory left. This provided an opening for Dylan, so he accepted his mother's offer of a job in the family business.

Gabrielle and Dylan have helped grow the business, and the family knows that their college degrees and big-business experience will continue to be beneficial for Mo's. Cindy is optimistic and says, "My children have joined this company and they are determined to make lots of changes. I mean, I took my grandmother to the calculator and they are taking me to the Web. We are doing it right."

Case Analysis

1. How did Cindy McEntee turn a hobby into a business?
2. How has Cindy operated the business to change over time?
3. What methods does Mo's Chowder use to retain and recruit employees?
4. Do you think Mo's will still be in business 20 years from now?

Case prepared by Hattie Bryant, creator of *Small Business School*, the television series made for PBS and Voice of America, http://SmallBusinessSchool.org.

UNIT 6

LEADERSHIP, ETHICS, AND EXITS

Chapter 20

LEADERSHIP AND ETHICAL PRACTICES

Chapter 21

FRANCHISING, LICENSING, AND HARVESTING: CASHING IN YOUR BRAND

Chapter 20

LEADERSHIP AND ETHICAL PRACTICES

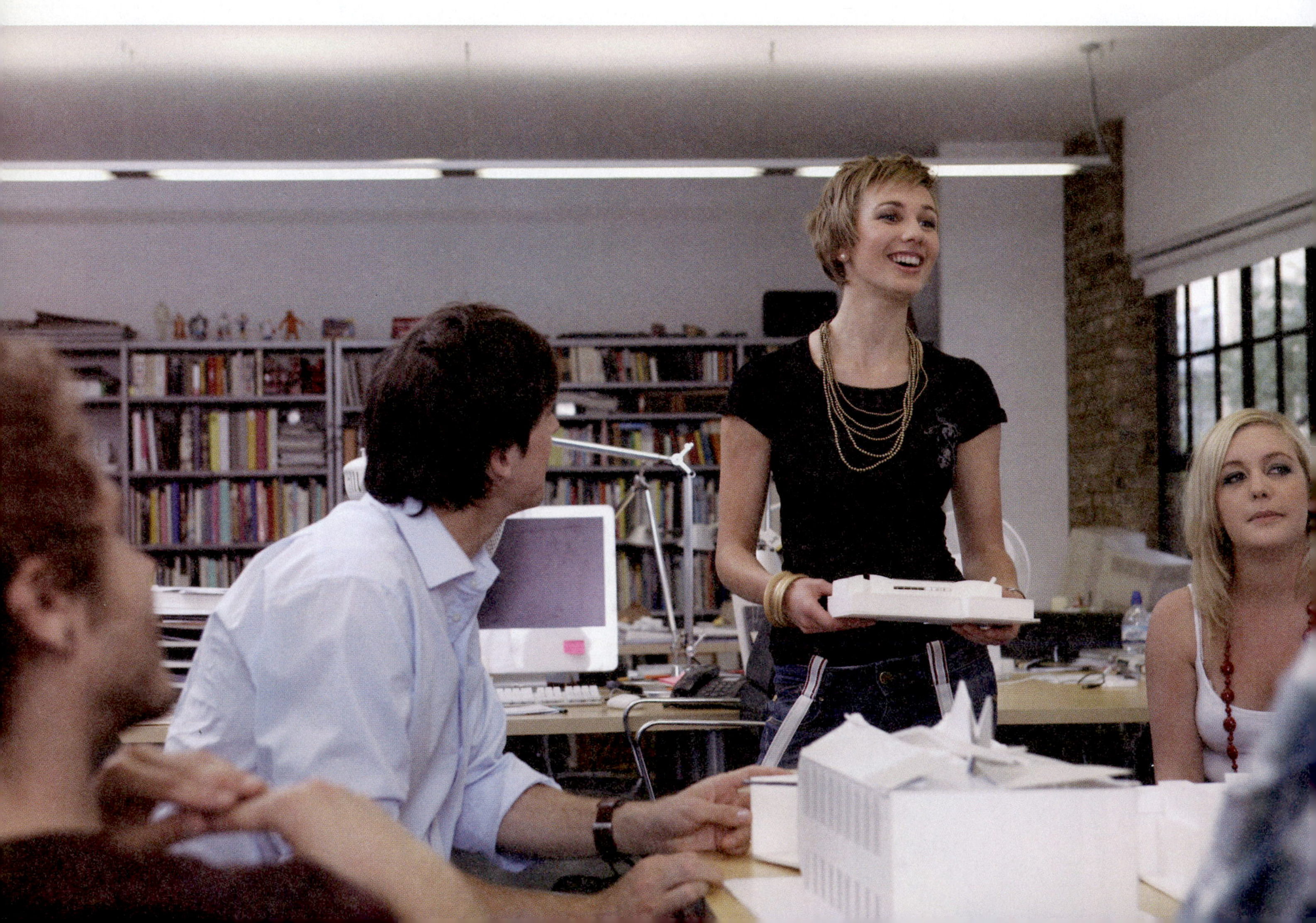

"Divorced from ethics, leadership is reduced to management and politics to mere technique."

—James MacGregor Burns, presidential scholar

In 1906, a Hungarian immigrant named Henry Feuerstein built a textile mill, Malden Mills Industries, Inc., outside of Boston. The business was passed down to Henry's grandson, Aaron. Malden Mills invented and marketed a unique fabric, called Polartec; it was a lightweight, warm, and durable fleece made from recycled plastics. Malden Mills used Polartec to manufacture jackets, vests, and other outerwear garments. In 1999, *Time* recognized Polartec as one of the top inventions of the century.

In the meantime, many manufacturing businesses had relocated overseas or to Mexico, where labor and production costs were lower. But Malden Mills kept its operations firmly planted in Massachusetts. Aaron Feuerstein had been raised by his father and grandfather to value his workers and to treat them with respect. As Feuerstein explained, "We have a mission of responsibility to both shareholders and our top asset: our employees. We're not prepared to skip town for cost savings."

Late in 1995, a devastating fire broke out at the Malden Mills plant, and most of the factory burned to the ground. The 3000 employees feared that their jobs had been destroyed. But, within a day, Feuerstein announced that "It was not the end" and that he would rebuild the factory buildings. He also vowed to use the insurance money to continue paying his employees with full benefits until the plant was back in business.

It took Feuerstein months to rebuild, and it cost millions of dollars to fulfill the promise he had made to his employees. Skeptics questioned Feuerstein's decision. It would have been cheaper to cash out of the business altogether, or to rebuild the plant in Asia. Feuerstein never second-guessed himself. "I consider our workers an asset, not an expense," he explained. "I have a responsibility to the workers, both blue-collar and white-collar. I have an equal responsibility to the community. It would have been unconscionable to put 3000 people on the streets and deliver a deathblow to the cities of Lawrence and Methuen. Maybe on paper our company is worth less to Wall Street, but I can tell you it is worth more."[1]

Performance Objectives

1. Identify leadership styles.
2. Organize for effective time management.
3. Pursue ethical leadership to build an ethical organization.
4. Make sure your business is run in an ethical manner.
5. Maintain your integrity.
6. Incorporate social responsibility into your company.

The Entrepreneur as Leader

No matter who you hire to manage your company, *you* will set the tone for how the business operates. Are you disorganized and chaotic? Chances are your company will be, too. Are you honest and straightforward? Your managers and employees are likely to behave similarly.

[1]Articles and press releases featured on the former Malden Mills Web site. See http://www.polartec.com/about/corporate.php.

Leadership Comes from Self-Esteem

leader a person who gets things done through influence, by guiding or inspiring others to voluntarily participate in a cause or project.

A **leader** is someone who gets things done through influence, by guiding or inspiring others to voluntarily participate in a cause or project. *Leadership* comes from self-esteem applied to knowledge, skills, and abilities. If you believe in yourself and know what you are doing, you can accomplish things confidently and inspire others. Develop a positive attitude, and you can become a leader. Great leaders are optimists; they have trained themselves to think positively. Running a successful business requires leadership.

Leadership Styles That Work

As your business grows, the type of leader that you are will be reflected throughout your company. Some leadership styles are more conducive to internal competition, whereas others foster teamwork and a collaborative environment. You may find that you have to blend leadership styles, or shift from one to another to some extent, as circumstances change.

Companies like Wal-Mart and Home Depot invest significant sums to create a work environment that inspires and motivates their employees. You may not have the sort of funds that they do, but you can model a positive leadership style. How you or your managers treat one another and the employees will determine the company culture. Adopt the best leadership style for your company, maintain it consistently, and learn to adapt it as needed. According to researcher Daniel Goleman, the principal styles and their advantages and drawbacks are[2]

Performance Objective 1
Identify leadership styles.

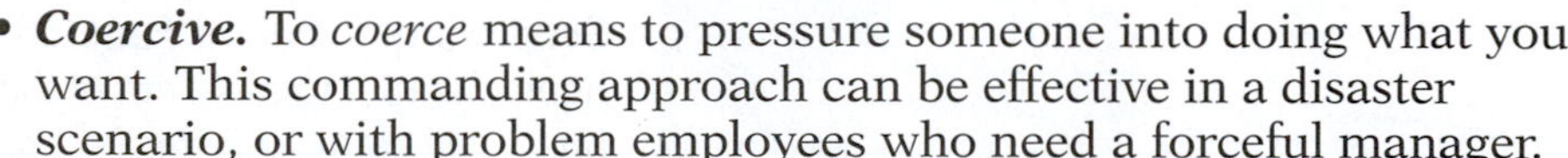

- ***Coercive.*** To *coerce* means to pressure someone into doing what you want. This commanding approach can be effective in a disaster scenario, or with problem employees who need a forceful manager. In most situations, however, a coercive leadership style damages employee morale and diminishes the flexibility and effectiveness of the company. Employees stop thinking and acting for themselves.

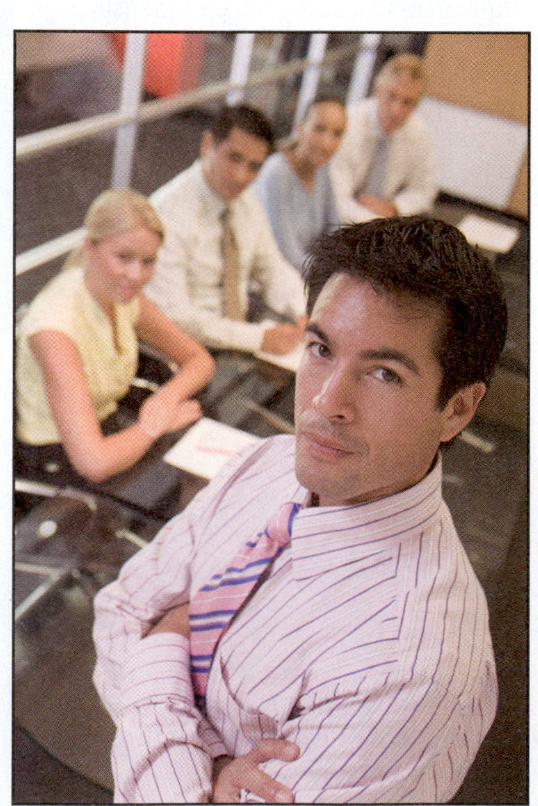

- ***Authoritative.*** An authoritative leader takes a "come with me" approach, stating the overall goal but giving employees freedom to figure out how best to achieve it. This can work well if the leader is an expert, but may not be so effective if the scenario is one of a nominal leader heading up a group of individuals who have more expertise in the field than he or she does (a team of scientists, for example).
- ***Affiliative.*** This is a "people come first" method that is effective when the business is in the team-building stage. It can fail when employees are lost and need direction.
- ***Democratic.*** This style gives employees a strong voice in how the company is run. It can build morale and work if employees are prepared to handle responsibility, but it could result in endless meetings and a sense of leaderlessness and drifting.
- ***Pacesetting.*** This type of leader sets very high personal performance standards and challenges employees to meet them, too. This can be very good when employees are also self-motivated and highly devoted, but can overwhelm those who are not so committed.

[2]Daniel Goleman, "Leadership That Gets Results," *Harvard Business Review*, March–April 2000.

- ***Coaching.*** This style focuses on helping each employee to grow, through training and support. This can be a good approach for starting and growing a business but may not work with employees who have been with the company for a while and may be resistant to change.

How Entrepreneurs Pay Themselves

Before you hire employees, figure out how to pay your first employee—yourself. Once your business is breaking even, decide how you will distribute the profit on a cash-available basis. The decision you make will affect your financial record keeping and your taxes, so think it through. But, remember, you can change it to fit circumstances, too. The choices are

- ***Commission.*** A set percentage of every sale. It is treated as a variable operating cost because it fluctuates with sales.
- ***Salary.*** A fixed amount of money paid at set intervals. You could choose to receive your salary once a week or once a month. A salary is a fixed operating cost because it is not intended to change with sales.
- ***Wages.*** If you have a service or manufacturing business, you could pay yourself an hourly wage. Wages are considered a cost of goods sold, because they are factored into the cost of the product or service.
- ***Dividend.*** A share of the company's profits issued to shareholders, based upon what remains after investments.

Entrepreneurs who do not pay themselves regularly tend to overstate their return on investment; they have not taken their compensation as a cost of business. Recognize that you can only pay yourself (or anyone else) when you have sufficient cash to do so.

Another reason to pay yourself is that it enables you to be honest about whether or not the business is really worth your time. Could you be making more money in a different business, or working for someone else? What are your opportunity costs? Is the best choice to keep working for yourself? Thinking entrepreneurially includes a realistic consideration of whether you would be happier *not* running a business, at least at the present time.

Manage Your Time Wisely

Performance Objective 2

Organize for effective time management.

Leaders learn how to manage their time, so they can accomplish more with less. One of the most important things you can do is to learn how to manage your time efficiently. Getting more done in less time can contribute to success.

Even if you do not have employees to manage, you could probably use your own time better. **Exhibit 20-1** is an example of a valuable tool called a PERT chart (Program Evaluation and Review Technique) that you can use to organize the many things you need to do. This one is related to business start-up tasks. As your venture grows, you can use the PERT concept to manage more complex operations. You can also create charts using software, such as Microsoft Project, and share them among team members. The best method to select is the one that you will actually use.

Leaders perpetually have more tasks to complete than there is time to complete them, even when project-management tools are in active use. It is easy to get sucked into unexpected meetings and conversations. For founders, this issue is compounded by the fact that they are often the locus of more company and product expertise than others, because of being

Exhibit 20-1 *Sample PERT chart.*

Task	Week 1	Week 2	Week 3	Week 4	Week 5	Week 6
Befriend banker	✓	✓	✓	✓	✓	✓
Order letterhead		✓				
Select location	✓					
Register business	✓					
Obtain bulk mail permit			✓			
Select ad agency	✓					
Meet with lawyer				✓		
Meet with accountant				✓		
Create vendor statement					✓	
Pay utility deposits					✓	
Order marketing material					✓	
Install phone system			✓	✓	✓	
Have Web site designed						✓
Set up database						✓
Network computers						✓

a "one-person band" or a large percentage of a small founding team. This means being called in as the fire-fighter or problem solver. The balancing act between being accessible and creating a positive environment, and being inaccessible, is a difficult situation that each individual addresses differently. Time management issues are also more difficult for leaders that cannot let go of decision making and involvement in every aspect of their company, by delegating responsibility.

There is a seemingly endless variety of books and articles available on time management, managerial effectiveness, and organizational effectiveness. Some tips that can assist in increasing effectiveness include

- Prioritize. Know what is important.
- Set realistic daily goals, allowing for customer contact, meetings, and some flexibility for other surprises.
- Check e-mail a limited number of times per day. It is easy to become distracted by checking too often. If you can check at the beginning, middle, and end of the day, you will be able to focus on other tasks as they need to be done.
- Avoid being distracted by portable electronic devices, such as Blackberries and iPhones. Whereas multitasking and constant availability may seem to increase efficiency, each interruption is a distraction from the work in progress, and may cause you to lose your train of thought. The interruptions may also distract your co-workers, decreasing productivity even more. If you are using your mobile phone as your customer-contact number, this suggestion will need to be adapted.
- Schedule sit-down meetings only when they will be more efficient than other, less time-consuming methods of communication. Try stand-up meetings. Also, consider going to other staff members' offices so that you can end the meetings easily.

- Only accept meeting invitations where your presence is required in order for progress to occur. As the firm grows, many of the operational meetings should disappear from your schedule. If you don't know why you have been invited to a meeting, don't attend it (try to find out why you should, first).
- Delegate responsibility and authority, and trust your team to do the right things and do them correctly. Hire the best people for the job and support them in their success. There is little that is more wasteful and counterproductive than a manager who does not delegate, or who nominally delegates and then undermines the team's work.
- Remember to allow yourself downtime, play time, and creative-thinking time. One of the reasons people become entrepreneurs is to gain control over their time. One of the most beneficial characteristics of entrepreneurs is creativity. By allowing time to think and relax, your company will benefit.

Ethical Leadership and Ethical Organizations

True leadership is more than the components described previously. It is all of the actions and attributes that have been noted, plus the personal values underlying them. **Ethics** are a system of principles that define a code of behavior to distinguish between good and bad or right and wrong. The Golden Rule, "Do unto others as you would have others do unto you," is a well-known and widely accepted ethic. A behavior may be legal and still not be ethical.

ethics a system of moral conduct and judgment that helps determine right and wrong.

Ethical business behavior is not only moral, but it also makes good business sense. Have you ever bought something from a store and felt you were cheated? How did you react? Did you want to go back? Probably not. You may have even told your friends about the experience. The store lost more than just one customer.

Performance Objective 3

Pursue ethical leadership to build an ethical organization.

Step into the Shoes...

Charles Schwab Does Well by Doing Good

Charles Schwab opened his own brokerage firm in the early 1970s when he was 34. Like Jacoby & Meyers with legal services, Schwab uncovered a market niche when he began offering discount pricing for informed investors who were tired of paying sizable commissions to stockbrokers. These investors did not need anyone else to do their research and make their decisions, and they flocked to take advantage of the lower rates. By 1981, Charles Schwab & Company's earnings were $5 million. In 1983, Bank of America bought the company for $55 million but left Schwab in place as CEO.[3] Just four years later, management repurchased the company and offered an initial public offering (IPO) as Charles Schwab Corporation. In the 1990s, Schwab became the leading online discount broker, and the fastest-growing American company of the decade.

Charles Schwab expressed his attitude toward employees as, "I have yet to find the man, however exalted his station, who did not do better work and put forth greater effort under a spirit of approval than criticism." As of the end of the second quarter of 2010, Schwab had 12,500 full-time employees, and client assets under management of $1.36 trillion, with 7.9 million brokerage accounts, 1.5 million corporate retirement plans, and 803,000 banking accounts. The Charles Schwab Foundation contributes to 2300 not-for-profits, with an average of $4 million in gifts annually.[4]

[3]Available at http://www.aboutschwab.com (accessed September 12, 2010).
[4]Ibid.

An Ethical Perspective

For a business, ethics are individual and organizational moral principles applied to actions and issues within the business context. In order to create an organization that is ethical, the values and standards of conduct must be clearly and broadly understood and accepted. Each substantive decision made has an ethical component, although sometimes the right thing to do is so evident to everyone that many choices are virtually automatic.

However, the right thing to do is not always easy to determine. Often the choice is not between right and wrong, rather between partially right and partially wrong, so that making a choice is difficult at best. There is sometimes a vast gray area between right and wrong that cannot be clarified by relying on individuals to simply know what's right.

Establishing Ethical Standards

One of the best ways to create an ethical business is to codify the fundamental rules of the game. Whereas the underlying values provide a basis for ethical behavior, clear, written guidelines can create a firmer foundation and more consistent implementation. Many companies create a code of ethics, a code of conduct, or a code of ethics and business conduct. A **code of ethics** is the statement of the values of a company. A **code of conduct** is a set of official standards of employee behavior. A **code of ethics and business conduct** combines the written statement of values with the official standards of employee behavior. By creating, disseminating, and establishing employee buy-in, a business will have more empowered employees, meaning they can make decisions and take action on their own, with a core set of ethical norms and rules for action.

code of ethics a statement of the values of a company.

code of conduct a set of official standards of employee behavior for a company.

code of ethics and business conduct a combination of a written statement of values with official standards of employee behavior.

ethical relativism situation where ethical standards are believed to be subject to interpretation.

ethical dilemma a circumstance when personal values conflict and thus muddy decision making.

A code of conduct can help to eliminate the problem of **ethical relativism**, which arises when ethical standards are believed to be subject to interpretation. It can also help to prevent or resolve **ethical dilemmas**, which are situations in which employees do not have a clear choice. By clarifying which actions should and should not be taken, many of the gray areas that invite confusion are eliminated. One recommendation is that organizations need to put into place a documented procedure for dealing with ethical challenges. This document will contain a basic method, with a multistep process of asking key questions, to get at the best answer with regard to ethical considerations. It should be customized for your company and the real scenarios that have arisen, or that could be expected to occur.

A comprehensive list of all potential ethical values would be quite long, but they are neatly summarized in the Six Pillars of Character as described in the following **Exhibit 20-2**.

Exhibit 20-2 *Six Pillars of Character: Ethical values.*

Value	Actualized Form
Trustworthiness	Honesty, integrity, reliability (promise-keeping), loyalty
Respect	Civility, courtesy, decency, dignity, autonomy, tolerance, acceptance
Responsibility	Accountability, pursuit of excellence, self-restraint
Caring	Concern for others, compassion, benevolence, altruism
Fairness	Process (open and impartial), impartiality, equity
Citizenship	Law abiding, volunteerism, environmental awareness, action

Six Pillars of Character® adapted from the Josephson Institute of Ethics, http://josephsoninstitute.org (accessed January 25, 2010). Six Pillars of Character is a registered trademark of the Josephson Institute. Used by permission.

By selecting six to ten of these actualized concepts, you can develop a core value set and create a code of conduct that specifies the actions that are in alignment with the values. For example, if impartiality is critical, the code of ethics might require that employees refrain from accepting personal gifts from stakeholders, such as vendors, considering the employee's role in the company. The example of PCI provided below shows how one company has developed a formal but clear and concise, code of ethics and business conduct.

As with any standards, a code of ethics and business conduct is only as good as its enactment. There have to be appropriate rewards for compliance, and consequences for breaches of ethics, in order to have a viable code of ethics. What happens to an employee who takes company funds? What if an employee takes extra-long lunches, comes in later than scheduled, or leaves early? What if he takes home pens and paper? What if she goes on Facebook or eHarmony during working hours?

At the same time, you should be wary of **ethical imperialism**, or believing that ethical standards are universal, and that those of your nation are held everywhere you will do business. For example, in some countries bribing public officials is considered a usual and customary part of securing contracts or otherwise doing business, whereas in others, this same behavior would be considered unethical and illegal.

ethical imperialism a belief that ethical standards are universal, and that those of your nation are held everywhere you will do business.

Step into the Shoes...

Publishing Concepts Inc. (PCI) Establishes Values

As a third-generation, family-owned business, PCI developed and defined its corporate culture and values. Advertising themselves as "notthebigcompany," PCI refers to its employees as "associates." PCI's Seven Driving Values are

1. Excellence. If it's worth doing, it's worth doing right.
2. People. We believe people have potential. We believe people have the capacity for greatness.
3. Integrity. We require complete honesty and integrity in everything we do. We are trustworthy. We keep our promises.
4. Service. We see each day as an opportunity to serve our clients and each other. We embrace the principles of servant leadership.
5. Fun. Work is an important part of life, and it should be fun.
6. Profitability. To meet our personal and professional goals, we must make money and generate cash.
7. Change. Like the samurai warrior, our motto is "Act Fearlessly."

The seven promises of PCI show how the values are actualized:

1. Be proactive; do it now.
2. Be accountable; own it.
3. Be professional; lead by example.
4. Be trustworthy; create lasting relationships.
5. Be smart; knowledge is power.
6. Be positive; "optimism is a force multiplier," according to Colin Powell.
7. Be passionate; love what you do.

For each of these promises, PCI lists examples of the value. Under "Be trustworthy" are found such details as

- Reputation is everything.
- Do not cut corners ethically.
- Listen first.
- Do whatever it takes to make the client happy.
- Search for the right way to resolve an issue, not the easiest way.
- Keep your promises. Always follow through.
- Act with integrity and openness. Be transparent. No hidden agendas.
- Work together. Care about and serve each other.
- We trust you to do the right thing. Now do it!

All of this information for associates was sent out to customers and prospects in lieu of a holiday greeting in December 2009. An enclosed note from Drew Clancy, president of PCI, states, "The booklet outlines the promises and commitments we make to ourselves, to each other, and to our clients—not only at this special time of year, but each and every day."

Source: PCI's Seven Driving Values and Seven Promises from PCI Holiday Mailing 2009. Courtesy of Publishing Concepts Inc.

Ethical Employer/Employee Relationships

It is important to treat your employees fairly and well. Aside from the fact that it is morally correct to treat people ethically, it is in your best interest to do so. As the entrepreneur, your values will set the ethical tone for your company. If you think it is okay to be rude or cheat a customer, your employees will not only copy your behavior, but they also will probably try to cheat you.

Employees who feel used by their employers will not do their best work. The most successful companies are those in which the employees' interests correspond with what is best for the company. Ethical employers have codes of conduct that apply to everyone in the company, including the executive management.

Report Ethical Concerns and/or
Violations at Ethos Company.
Calls are toll-free and confidential.
1-800-ETHICAL

What constitutes an ethical relationship can be defined in the code of ethics and business conduct. Some topics to be included could be: avoiding discrimination in any form, following instructions from managers, maintaining confidentiality, and not using company property for personal reasons. Employers may implement any number of methods to collect information and make changes that do not, in themselves, create ethical dilemmas—such as a "tip line" or "tip box" to identify ethical violations. **Whistle-blowers** are those who report illegal or unethical conduct to superiors or to the public, and generally are protected from retribution by federal law and company policies. If you want to ensure that violations are reported, you have to shield whistle-blowers.

whistle-blower a person that reports unethical or illegal conduct to a manager or to the public.

Employers that take the time to develop a code of ethics with employees across the organization set the tone for ethical employer/employee relationships. Employees that join the firm as time goes on have to be given the opportunity to learn, understand, and adopt the code of ethics as part of their formal training and orientation. Otherwise, the strength of the code will erode over time. For example, **embezzlement**, or the crime of stealing money from an employer, is clearly unethical and illegal, but is more explicitly understood as a violation where the environment supports strong corporate values. By the same token, situations in which personal considerations and professional obligations interfere with each other—**conflicts of interest**—can be largely avoided through open communications and widely shared codes of ethics and conduct.

embezzlement the crime of stealing money from an employer.

conflict of interest a circumstance in which personal benefits and professional obligations interfere with one another.

Corporate Ethical Scandals

The issue of business ethics exploded in 2002 when several large corporations were found to have published inaccurate financial statements. These false numbers made the companies look so good that they were some of the most highly recommended stock picks on Wall Street.

Top executives at Enron, WorldCom-MCI, Tyco, Global Crossing, and other well-known firms had inflated corporate earnings so that they would receive huge bonuses, while misleading shareholders and employees. When the truth came out, public confidence in the stock market plummeted along with stock prices. Investors lost millions.

One of the companies, the energy giant Enron, had strongly encouraged its own employees to invest most or all of their retirement savings in company stock, even while top executives knew the worth of that stock was based on false numbers. These employees had their life savings wiped out by the unethical behavior of the executives.

Enron collapsed, and thousands of employees lost their jobs and saw their pension funds reduced to nothing. Tyco was split into four different companies. Its CEO was forced to resign when it was learned that he had used company money to buy an $18 million apartment in Manhattan and furnish it with expensive artwork—among other egregious abuses.

Performance Objective 4

Make sure your business is run in an ethical manner.

The scandals of 2002 were a failure of **corporate governance**, meaning that these companies did not have rules and safeguards in place to ensure that executives behaved legally and ethically. Even at an early stage in developing your business, you must think about how you will guarantee that your company remains both ethical and legal as it grows.

corporate governance rules and safeguards to ensure that executives behave legally and ethically.

- ***Do not treat company profits as personal funds.*** Haphazardly taking business profits for your own use is a bad habit. Decide on a wage or salary you will pay yourself and always document this, as well as your business expenses. You should enjoy the rewards of a successful venture, but you need to be careful to do it ethically and legally. In particular, **tax evasion**, which is trying to avoid paying taxes through illegal or deceptive means, is to be avoided.

tax evasion the deliberate avoidance of an obligation to pay taxes; may lead to penalties or imprisonment.

- ***Keep accurate records.*** Have your business records checked once a year by a professional accountant. By the time your company becomes a multimillion-dollar corporation, you will have established a reputation for honest financial reporting.
- ***Use financial controls.*** This will help to eliminate the potential for embezzlement, which is the crime of stealing funds from a company. Once you have employees, use such simple financial controls as
  - Always have two people open the mail, so no one is tempted to take company checks.
  - Arrange for yourself and one other person to be required to sign all checks sent out by the business. Using a double signature will assure that no one can use the company money for personal expenses.
  - Implement a cash-counting and control system, if employees will be handling cash.
- ***Create an advisory board.*** Ask businesspeople and other community leaders you respect to be on your **advisory board** or **advisory council**. This group of people will provide you with sound, ethical business advice without being your board of directors. Choose them carefully, and listen to what they have to say.

advisory board or **council** a group that provides advice and counsel, but is not a board of directors.

Integrity and Entrepreneurial Opportunities

Stated company values are significant and will contribute to entrepreneurial opportunities—to the extent that they are implemented in day-to-day actions. The consistency and demonstrated commitment to the espoused values system can create further opportunities. For example, in the early 1980s, Johnson & Johnson earned the respect and acceptance of its many stakeholders when the company withdrew millions of bottles of potentially contaminated Tylenol from store shelves. Johnson & Johnson did not issue the recall because they were ordered to do so, rather, because it was the right thing to do. They put their money where their mouth was, acknowledged the problem, and took swift and decisive action. Although no longer a small entrepreneurial venture, Johnson & Johnson provided an excellent example of values in action.

What Is Integrity?

Integrity is upholding behavioral standards on the level of the ethical principles that an individual espouses. All codes of ethics and conduct are worthless without the integrity to put the words into action. That means acting ethically is not something to be done only when it is convenient, or when it will not be costly. It is a daily, decision-by-decision process.

Doing the Right Thing in Addition to Doing Things Right

Performance Objective 5
Maintain your integrity.

As a business, ethical practices involve doing the right things and doing them ethically. There is a potential tension between strategic priorities and ethical behavior. Profit maximization is one of the most common challenges to ethical behavior. By harming the environment, using substandard components, or cutting corners, a company can maximize its short-term profitability. A clearly defined and commonly shared code of ethics and business conduct can go a long way toward incorporating ethical decision making into strategic priorities. This will facilitate incorporating the right thing into strategy from the start, thereby avoiding ethical conflicts.

Balancing the Needs of Owners, Customers, and Employees

Although it may seem simple and straightforward to retain your integrity, it can become more complex as you add partners, customers, and employees to the equation. People's moral compasses do not always point in the same direction. What seems just, right, and fair to one person may seem unjust, unfair, and wrong to another. Often, this is caused by the conflicting needs of owners, customers, and employees.

Owners face multiple pressures, such as the need to have their businesses survive, the repayment of debts, and the welfare of employees. Customers need products and services that meet expectations. Employees need to earn a living wage and experience job satisfaction. On the surface, this should not pose ethical challenges.

However, as each constituency strives to meet its needs, ethical dilemmas may arise. As a business owner, for example, you may have to make a choice between paying a vendor in accordance with the credit terms, or as otherwise promised, and having sufficient cash to cover the employee payroll. Or, you might have to choose between paying a vendor for critical production materials or paying withholding taxes to the federal government. Making a choice between the two would certainly be an ethical dilemma. Who would you make wait for the money? Or, imagine yourself as an employee that has to make a choice between reporting illegal pollution by your employer, that could close down the company and result in your unemployment, or turning a blind eye to the situation to keep your family housed and fed. The short-term interest of both the company and the employee in the above examples would be to act unethically.

Or, envision the customer that benefits from a company's mistake and has to decide what to do. Have you ever been given too much change for a purchase or had an item left off a bill? You benefit and the company loses. On the flip side, a company may overcharge, double-bill, or somehow provide less than promised. Then you lose and the company benefits. The relationship between a company and its customers is fraught with potential ethical challenges.

Complying with the Law

One of the most difficult aspects of maintaining integrity for any entrepreneur is complying with the multitude of laws that apply to business. The number of laws and regulations from federal, state, local, and other authorities is seemingly endless and somewhat mind-boggling. In many cases, small firms (having fewer than 25 employees) are exempt from regulations that lawmakers consider unduly burdensome. However, for the most part, entrepreneurial firms must comply with the same laws as their larger brethren.

Ethics would dictate that companies avoid discrimination, harassment, and tax evasion. Providing a safe workplace and living wages also seem obvious. So do not polluting, or paying taxes on time. Problems arise when complying with the law is more costly and/or less convenient than not doing so. Many of the safeguards for employees, and the environment, add costs for employers. In some cases, businesses have to choose between compliance and profitability, or even continued existence. In a perfect world, entrepreneurs would never face a trade-off between doing what's legal and what is best for the business and themselves.

Because of the large number of laws and regulations, you may find it nearly impossible to know every one of these that applies to your business. Whether you are aware of them or not, you are responsible for compliance. The good news is that, if you act ethically, you *are* likely to be in compliance. If you have any questions regarding the law, check with your attorney or the statute or regulation. Don't rely upon hearsay or rumor. Also, make your best efforts to stay informed with respect to changes in laws. Often, state and local chambers of commerce are excellent sources of information and provide advocacy.

Remember, many activities are unethical but legal. For example, adjusting budget numbers, or telling your employee to do so, to get specific results, withholding vital decision-making information, and complaining about or bad-mouthing others, are not typically illegal behaviors but are unethical.

Social Responsibility and Ethics

Ethics, corporate social responsibility, and social entrepreneurship are three related topics that are often conflated. **Corporate social responsibility** is the ethical obligation of a company to its community. **Social entrepreneurship** is the sale of products and/or services on a for-profit

corporate social responsibility the ethical obligation of a company to its community.

social entrepreneurship the sale of products or services on a for-profit basis to benefit a social purpose.

Performance Objective 6 Incorporate social responsibility into your company.

basis to benefit society. Both have ethical components and can be of value to entrepreneurial firms.

in-kind donation a contribution of products or services that may include employee time, rather than cash.

Companies exhibit their commitment to the communities they serve through a variety of means and with varying motivations. Some examples of this are financial contributions to not-for-profit community organizations, supporting volunteerism, and in-kind donations. An **in-kind donation** is a contribution of products or services, including employee time, rather than cash. Companies can also show this commitment through the payment of livable wages and the provision of safe and sanitary working conditions. Another aspect of corporate social responsibility is to be sure to make any financial investment in only ethical and legal ventures in countries with human rights values in alignment with the company's ethics. Environmental friendliness is another way of demonstrating community care. For example, Peninsula Regional Medical Center, on the Eastern Shore of Maryland, is working toward becoming eco-friendly and energy efficient.

Leading with Integrity and Examples

Leading by example is the best way to command the attention and respect of others. If you refuse to accept inferior goods, your employees will, too. If you give voice and form to company values and demonstrate integrity, the workplace will become and remain a community of stakeholders that values integrity, honesty, and open communication. Modeling the behavior you desire is an excellent route to attaining the desired results.

Encourage Your Employees to Be Socially Responsible

Early in the twentieth century, Madam C. J. Walker motivated her employees by encouraging them to get involved in helping their communities, and in the process she became the first African American millionaire. There are many ways that entrepreneurs can use their businesses to contribute to

---

Global Impact...

Mohammad Yunus and Grameen Bank: Banker to the Poor

Mohammad Yunus, Nobel Peace Prize winner, social entrepreneur, and "banker to the poor," has used his entrepreneurial spirit to foster entrepreneurship and lift literally millions of people out of poverty. He describes his activities, "I did something that challenged the banking world. Conventional banks look for the rich; we look for the absolutely poor. All people are entrepreneurs, but many don't have the opportunity to find out."

Grameen Bank, founded in Bangladesh in 1976, became an official bank in 1983, and is largely owned by its borrowers. As of November 2009, Grameen Bank had disbursed $8.65 billion, and had $7.95 million in loans outstanding, from a population distributed across 83,453 villages, served by 2562 branches, with a staff of 23,311. Fully 97 percent of the borrowers are women. The stated mission of Grameen Bank is to assist borrowers' families in rising above the poverty line, and Grameen reports that 68 percent of them have done so.

The fundamental basis of Grameen Bank's relationship with its borrowers is a core set of values explicitly stated in its Sixteen Decisions. Grameen has found a way to flip conventional banking knowledge on its head. For Grameen Bank, credit is perceived as a human right, not a benefit for the wealthy. Its branches are distributed across rural areas, bringing the bank to the people.

In 2002, Grameen created its Struggling Members Programme, targeted at beggars. This initiative has encouraged people to give up begging and make a living as door-to-door salespeople. As of November 2009, nearly 20,000 of the 112,000 who joined the program had left begging. About 10 percent of the program members became members of mainstream Grameen groups, and 76 percent of the funds disbursed have been repaid.

Source: Grameen Bank Web site, http://www.grameen-info.org/ (accessed January 10, 2010).

society. By being an entrepreneur, you have already made an important contribution by providing goods and services to consumers in your area who need them. You can also use your business to support social issues that are important to you. By running your company in a way that is consistent with your ethics and core values, you will develop a socially responsible business.

Ways to make your business socially responsible include

- recycling paper, glass, and plastic;
- donating a portion of your profits to a charity;
- refusing to use animal testing on products;
- offering employees incentives to volunteer in the community; and
- establishing a safe and healthy workplace.

You can also emphasize being a **sustainable** business, as you ensure meeting the Earth's current needs while preserving resources for future generations.

sustainable situation in which current needs are met while preserving future resources.

Chapter Summary

Now that you have studied this chapter, you can do the following:

1. Identify leadership styles.
   - A leader is someone who has the confidence and energy to do things on his or her own.
   - Leadership comes from self-esteem. If you believe in yourself, you can do things with confidence and you will inspire confidence in others.
   - Leaders learn how to manage their time so they can get more done.
2. Organize for effective time management.
   - Use PERT charts or computer software to assist you.
   - Take advantage of the many methods of time management that are available.
3. Pursue ethical leadership to build an ethical organization.
   - View decisions through an ethical lens.
   - Establish ethical standards.
   - Build ethical employer/employee relationships.
4. Make sure your business is run in an ethical manner.
   - Do not take company funds to pay personal expenses.
   - Keep accurate records.
   - Use financial controls.
   - Create an advisory board.
5. Maintain your integrity.
   - Maintain your behavioral standards at the level of ethics you espouse.
   - Do the right thing, even when it is not the easy choice.
   - Recognize the importance of balancing the needs of various stakeholders.
   - Comply with the law.
6. Incorporate social responsibility into your company.
   - Encourage environmentalism.
   - Support charitable efforts.
   - Maintain a safe and healthy workplace.
   - Consider sustainability throughout the organization.

Key Terms

advisory board or council
code of conduct
code of ethics
code of ethics and business conduct
conflict of interest
corporate governance
corporate social responsibility
embezzlement
ethical dilemma
ethical imperialism
ethical relativism
ethics
in-kind donation
leader
social entrepreneurship
sustainable
tax evasion
whistle-blower

Entrepreneurship Portfolio

Critical Thinking Exercises

1. Describe three leaders you admire. What characteristics do you most admire about them and why?
2. Consider ways that you might find 10 additional hours in your weekly schedule to manage your business. Create a weekly time-management schedule for yourself reflecting this activity.
3. Fill out a PERT chart for your business or one that you can imagine, or use Microsoft Project or another software package to do the same thing.
4. Describe the corporate governance plan for your company. It should include five policies (rules) that will be the backbone of your company's ethics.
5. Thinnow Corporation, an entrepreneurial venture, has developed a weight-loss drug, Fatgo. After an intense FDA review and approval process, Thinnow has received permission to market Fatgo. Testing had shown that there may be serious (even deadly) side effects to consumers of Fatgo. A warning label is being provided. Identify the legal and ethical issues in this case.

Key Concept Questions

1. Compare and contrast two leadership styles as identified in this chapter.
2. What is a code of conduct? What are its potential benefits?
3. What is the relationship between social responsibility and ethics?
4. What is insider trading? Why is it unethical? If you owned a company and knew that it was about to report increased earnings and thus drive its stock price up, why would it be unethical for you to tell this to family members that own the stock?

Application Exercises

1. Identify a business leader, preferably an entrepreneur. Describe his or her leadership style based upon at least two public sources (excluding any wikis, such as Wikipedia) and give examples to support your conclusion.
2. Keep track of the direct opportunities to decide whether to act ethically/unethically and/or legally/illegally that arise during a 48-hour period. What, if anything, surprises you about the list?
3. Choose three things you would plan to do to run a socially responsible business, such as
   - recycling paper, glass, or plastic;
   - donating a portion of profits to a charity;
   - not testing on animals for product research;
   - offering employees incentives to volunteer in the community, and
   - establishing a safe and healthy workplace.

   Explain why you made the selections you did.

Exploring Online

1. Choose a corporation that has been involved in an ethical scandal and research it online. (Enter *corporate* and *scandal* into a search engine.) Present this story to the class. Describe the lessons you learned as an entrepreneur from researching this event.
2. Using an online search engine, find a company that practices corporate social responsibility and answer the following.
   a. Which values are important?
   b. How are these values translated into action?
   c. Are the values shared broadly within the company, or are they primarily those of the president/CEO?

Case Study | Crisis at Agritechno Hybrid

Agritechno geneticist, Dr. Lev Andropov, is working in his laboratory with his geneticist colleague, Dr. Tamika Brown, and his two lab assistants, André and Bonita. As the four are conducting their work, Donna Holbrook from Marketing, Stefan Girard from Accounting, and Jaylen Castillo from Product Development enter the lab with some discouraging news. They have been getting early reports from growers in the South that some of the caterpillar-resistant transgenic corn developed by Agritechno, and planted this year, is failing in areas with higher than normal rainfall. The group must decide what and how, if at all, they should report the information to growers and investors.

Dr. Andropov led the team that developed the caterpillar-resistant transgenic corn, in addition to having come up with numerous other strains of insect- and disease-resistant hybrids and varieties of this plant. Dr. Brown has worked alongside Dr. Andropov for many years, and is hoping to be promoted to heading up her own lab for the development of transgenic fruits. The success of the caterpillar-resistant corn would be essential to her being promoted this year. Doctors Andropov and Brown are disappointed to hear of the crop failures and would like to investigate the cause. They do not want to commit to time lines or solutions without proper scientific inquiry.

Stefan Girard is focused on shareholder value, and the potential damage to stock prices if these problems leak out to investors. He wants to send a letter to shareholders immediately, stating that the few incidents of crop failure are flukes. At the same time, Donna insists on sending a letter to the growers, alerting them to an overwatering problem. Donna, Stefan, and Jaylen all agree that the letters have to be sent right away because heavy rains are expected in Nebraska, where 40 percent of the seeds have been sold.

Dr. Andropov is frustrated, and nearing anger at these suggestions. He asks, "How can we do this? We don't even know that our product is flawed. We cannot send out conflicting messages." Also, he asked what they should tell people who are both growers *and* investors. Dr. Brown adds that they do not know that the problem is in the seeds, and they cannot say with certainty when an analysis will be completed and a solution found. She does not want to promise what the company cannot deliver.

Jaylen is more anxious about getting a letter out to investors immediately. She suggests telling them that Agritechno's scientists have figured out the problem and found a solution. The scientists bristle at the suggestion.

Donna then attempts to find a satisfactory approach for all participants by reframing the situation to focus on yields for the coming year. Dr. Andropov is not satisfied with this option, noting that Agritechno won't know how many bushels of the transgenic corn have been produced for another four or five months, and they won't be able to fully identify the problem until then. He suggests sending out a letter stating that a few crops have failed and Agritechno is investigating.

Stefan grumbles that he hates to report problems to investors because it scares them away.

Case Study Analysis

1. Why are Drs. Andropov and Brown frustrated and angry about the suggestions from Holbrook, Girard, and Castillo?
2. What are the arguments for and against notifying Agritechno's investors? What is the basis for each argument?
3. What are the arguments for and against notifying Agritechno's growers? What is the basis for each argument?
4. What method of communication, if any, would you recommend for investors? Growers?
5. What should Agritechno tell its investors and growers, if anything, about the crop failures and solutions?

Case Study | Albert Black: Leading by Example

Small Business School video clips are available

Albert Black founded On Target Supplies and Logistics in 1982 as a janitorial supply business. Over time, he perfected his delivery systems and changed the company's mission so that today the company is known for its supply-chain management. Companies including EDS, Texas Instruments, Southwestern Bell, Texas Utilities, American Airlines, and Verizon outsource their warehouse needs to On Target.

Albert is a role model for the employees of On Target. Even after his company was enjoying substantial success, Albert earned an MBA at Southern Methodist University. It took three years of attending classes on weekends and completing assignments, while spending at least 60 hours a week at On Target. He demonstrated his commitment to lifelong learning.

Albert believes that businesses ought to fund employee education. He points out, "We work with people on education. If you don't have a bachelor's degree, if you don't have a high school diploma, we'll send you back to school and we'll pay for it. Some employees have gone during working hours and we've paid them for that time. It's that important to us. I don't remember a situation where we've invested in education that I didn't feel like the company got more than a fair return." Albert also encourages financial-literacy education and financial success for his employees by teaching them to manage the money they are earning, and how to earn more money. Ninety-five percent of the employees are enrolled in the company's 401(k) plan. Albert's goal is for every employee to become part of the "affluent class."

At On Target, learning is continuous. Every Friday morning there is a hot breakfast and a training class on topics such as business operations, personal growth, and wealth accumulation. Albert suggests, "People are becoming members of the free enterprise system, they're saving, they're investing, they are building trust and for the first time in their lives are earning more money than they need."

Albert articulates a four-part leadership philosophy. He says leaders have to teach, preach, coach, and counsel. *Teach* means showing people the details of how a job should be done; *preach* means keeping them inspired by making sure they know the company's purpose; *coach* means controlling and directing the work; and *counsel* means demonstrating empathy when people encounter problems.

Albert Black, On Target Supplies and Logistics.

Noticeably absent from this philosophy is the need for Albert to tell people what to do or to be the "boss." There are many rules and cultural norms at On Target, and those rules and norms are made clear in employee orientation and practice. Thus, managers do not have to spend time repeating fundamentals. Albert believes his job is to encourage every individual on the payroll to reach his or her full potential, not to micromanaage the details of their work.

This company founder makes no apologies for being demanding. He said, "I get in the personal lives of the employees because they are in my personal life. I want them to push themselves to be better. Sometimes I have to do some arm-twisting to get people to make their 401(k) contribution, but I do it because I know down the road they will thank me."

Albert continued, "I build the people and the people build the business. That has been my mission from the beginning. I saw how not working had such a negative effect on the self-esteem of people that I determined to create jobs in a neighborhood where there were no jobs. To attract and keep good employees, On Target promises three kinds of income. It promises an educational income, a psychological income, and a financial income. It has open-book accounting so employees learn where the money in the business comes from and where it goes."

Further commenting on his style, Albert said, "We want you to feel good about what you're doing at On Target Supplies and Logistics. Just coming in with that esprit de corps, that attitude that says, 'Together we can climb mountains and win battles'—that's what we offer people, that psychological income of making a contribution every day that makes a difference."

On Target is proud to pay above the industry average because Albert does not want to lose a valued employee over compensation. He said, "If a person has a desire to leave it has to be based on our failure to provide the educational and psychological income."

Case Study Analysis

1. Why do you imagine Albert stopped selling janitorial supplies and started selling supply-chain management?
2. How does Albert encourage his employees to continue their education?
3. What happens every Friday morning at On Target?
4. What are the four parts of Albert's leadership strategy?
5. What types of compensation do On Target employees receive?
6. Why does Albert devote so much time to helping each employee learn and grow?
7. What type of leader do you think Albert is according to Goleman's typology?

By Hattie Bryant, creator of *Small Business School*, the television series made for PBS and Voice of America, http://SmallBusinessSchool.org

Chapter 21

FRANCHISING, LICENSING, AND HARVESTING: CASHING IN YOUR BRAND

> **"All businesses were launched by entrepreneurs and all were once small."**
>
> —Nat Shulman, family business owner and columnist

Liz Claiborne was a hugely successful entrepreneur who was born in Belgium to American parents in 1929. Women were not expected to work in those days, so when she fell in love with fashion and wanted to become a designer, her family was strongly against it.

Claiborne was determined, though, and at 21 she applied for a job on Seventh Avenue, in New York City's Garment District. She got employment as a sketcher, model, and pick-up-pins girl; and she got an opportunity to observe her market from the inside. Over the years, she observed that women had begun to join the workforce, but few designers were making clothes for them to wear to their jobs. Here was an opportunity to make clothes that women really needed. She founded Liz Claiborne, Inc., with her husband and two partners in 1976.[1] Today, it is a nearly $5 billion public company that provides quality affordable clothing for working women.

This is an example of how one entrepreneur can start a small business venture that grows from an idea to an international conglomerate. And, once the business has a name that stands for something attractive to consumers, the name itself becomes valuable. Liz Claiborne has a number of well-known brand names, such as Kate Spade, Lucky Brand Jeans, Juicy Couture, Liz & Co., and DKNY Jeans.

Liz Claiborne, Inc., sells clothes all over the world, and also *licenses* its name to other companies, "renting" the right to use the Claiborne name to sell products that reflect the Claiborne vision. In 2004, for example, Liz Claiborne announced that it would license its name to the Eastman Group (the licensee) to make men's shoes under the Claiborne label—and receive a fee for the license. "Licensing our brands is a key aspect of our growth strategy, enabling us to extend Claiborne's presence in the market," said Barbara Friedman, President of Licensing, in a press release. "We are pleased to be teaming with Eastman Group on our Claiborne footwear collection. Their innovative product design and expertise in manufacturing will help us offer superior product and value to the Claiborne customer. The addition of footwear to the Claiborne product mix furthers our goal of making a complete lifestyle statement."[2]

Max Mizrahi, president of Eastman Group, stated, "This is a great opportunity for us to partner with a classic American brand with a reputation for fashion and superb quality. We anticipate that our footwear expertise, coupled with Claiborne's reputation, will open many doors with retailers and make an impact immediately."[3]

Fashion designers and celebrities have made millions by licensing their famous names for perfume, athletic shoes, and other products. Licensing is also subject to fewer government regulations than franchising (which will be discussed later in the chapter).

Performance Objectives

1. Determine how you want to grow your business and eventually exit from it.
2. Describe how businesses use licensing to profit from their brands.
3. Explain how a business can be franchised.
4. Learn methods of valuing a business.
5. Discuss five ways to harvest a business.

[1]Available at http://www.lizclaiborneinc.com.
[2]"Liz Claiborne Inc. Announces Licensing Agreement with Eastman Group," *PR Newswire*, July 1, 2004.
[3]"Liz Claiborne," *PR Newswire*.

What Do You Want from Your Business?

Performance Objective 1

Determine how you want to grow your business and eventually exit from it.

Just as people start businesses for a wide variety of reasons and have very different goals and objectives, they have different reasons for continuing in business or departing from it, and different ways of doing so. Some entrepreneurs enjoy the stability and earnings associated with carrying on a successful business they have established. Others want to "grow and go." Still others are serial entrepreneurs, who create new ventures repeatedly. What do you want? **Exhibit 21-1** identifies some of the options available.

Regardless of which route you choose, your business plan should clearly state your intentions. If you are asking people to invest in your enterprise, you should tell them how they will realize the return on their investment. If it will take several years to grow the business, that should also be spelled out.

Continuing the Business for the Family

The multigenerational family-owned-and-operated business best exemplifies the company that provides continued employment and wealth to an entrepreneur and his/her relatives. Malden Mills in Chapter 20 is an example of a firm that was operated as a closely held private company for three generations, and had a clear interest in maintaining employment in its community. For this type of business, continued operations with sufficient cash flow for wages and operations is primary. If this kind of venture is your goal, create a growth plan that permits you to buy back any investments from outsiders, so that the business will be truly family-owned.

Exhibit 21-1 *Growth, harvesting, and exit strategies.*

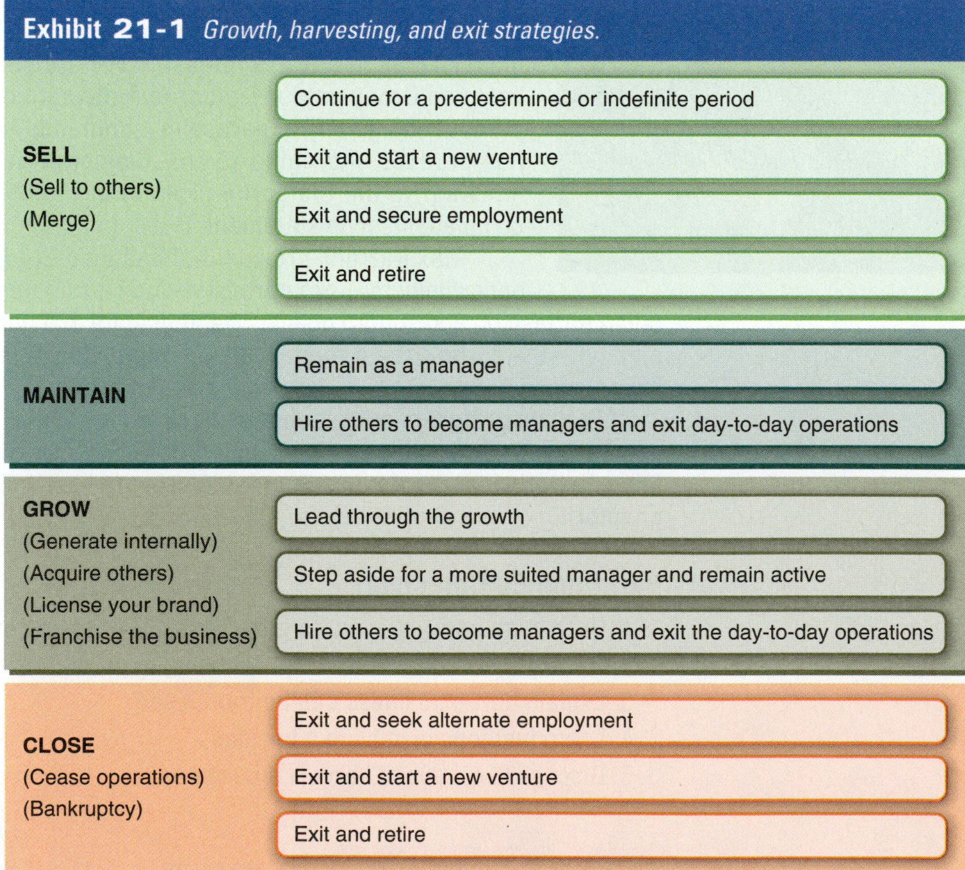

SELL
(Sell to others)
(Merge)
Continue for a predetermined or indefinite period
Exit and start a new venture
Exit and secure employment
Exit and retire
MAINTAIN
Remain as a manager
Hire others to become managers and exit day-to-day operations
GROW
(Generate internally)
(Acquire others)
(License your brand)
(Franchise the business)
Lead through the growth
Step aside for a more suited manager and remain active
Hire others to become managers and exit the day-to-day operations
CLOSE
(Cease operations)
(Bankruptcy)
Exit and seek alternate employment
Exit and start a new venture
Exit and retire

Growth through Diversification

One way to grow your business is to use **diversification**, which is the addition of product or service offerings beyond your core product or service. By diversifying your business, you are increasing the potential for sales. To a budding entrepreneur or a seasoned executive, diversification can appear to be the way to get more market share. On the flip side, author and marketing expert Al Ries argues that diversification comes with a price, "It unfocuses the company and leads to loss of power."[4] Focusing, in contrast, attracts exactly the right employees to a company and reinforces its strength in the marketplace.

diversification the addition of product or service offerings beyond a business's core product or service.

Growth through Licensing and Franchising

As mentioned at the beginning of the chapter, one way to grow without direct investment in considerable physical and human capital is through **licensing**, or renting your brand or other intellectual property to sell products. Another way to replicate a business formula is through franchising.

It is important that you are aware of the possibilities offered by franchising and licensing from the moment you start your business. Stay motivated to keep your business organized, and to try to develop a foolproof operational system. After all, someday hundreds, or even thousands, of entrepreneurs might be eager to buy or rent that system from you.

Franchising and licensing are called **replication strategies** because they are ways to obtain money from a business you created by letting others copy, or *replicate* it.

licensing renting your brand or other intellectual property to increase sales.

Performance Objective 2

Describe how businesses use licensing to profit from their brands.

replication strategy a way to obtain money from a business by letting others copy it for a fee.

line extension using an established brand to promote different kinds of products.

Focus Your Brand

As noted in Unit 3, a *brand* identifies the products or services of a company and differentiates them from those of competitors—representing the company's promise to consistently deliver a specific set of benefits to its customers. Customers who buy Liz Claiborne clothes, for example, expect classic styling suitable for the workplace. They have come to trust that brand to meet their needs.

Businesses do better when customers know what to expect from their brands, according to Ries.[5] He argues that, in industry after industry, the narrowly focused companies are the big winners. He contends that too many managers are hooked on growth for its own sake, and develop misguided expansion that dilutes the strength of a company's brand.

Many companies known for one type of merchandise, such as Adidas with its athletic shoes, have applied their brand with disastrous results, such as Adidas cologne. Sneakers and cologne were not a good association. Bic, known for its pens, branched into panty hose and had a similar failure.

Using an established brand to promote different kinds of products is called **line extension**. It can work if the brand is strong and the new product is not completely dissimilar to the original. For example, the Jell-O brand name was successfully applied to a line of puddings, after it had been established as the preeminent gelatin dessert.

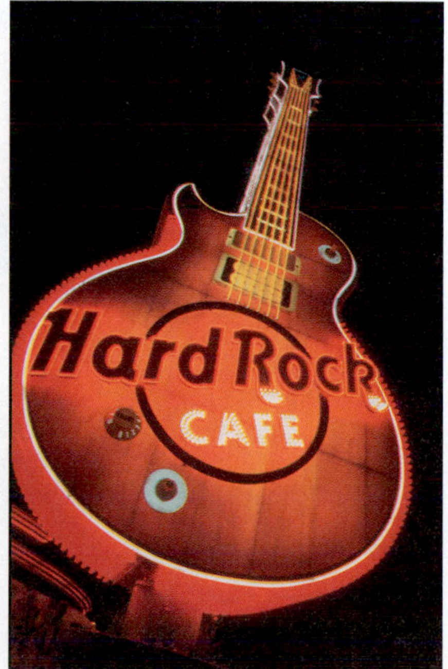

The Hard Rock Hotel and Casino, Las Vegas; a clearly focused brand can go a long way.
(© Wesley R. Hitt, Creative Eye/MIRA.com)

[4] Al Ries, *Focus: The Future of Your Company Depends on It* (New York: Harper Business, 1996), p. 273.
[5] Ries, *Focus*.

When Licensing Can Be Effective

A company can profitably license its brand when it has a core group of loyal customers. Licensing is effective when the licensor is confident that the company name will be enhanced by the licensee's use of it. If Coca-Cola licensed its name to a T-shirt manufacturer that wanted to print its logo on T-shirts, Coca-Cola would get free advertising as well as royalties.

However, licensing, if not handled carefully, can damage your brand. For example, if the T-shirt maker used the Coca-Cola logo on T-shirts that contained obscene messages, the company's reputation would be tarnished. Coca-Cola would not license its name to a soft-drink manufacturer, because a licensing agreement would not necessarily ensure standards or quality and, in any case, would become a direct competitor. Licensing your brand is one potential way to increase brand recognition and extend your product line, without investing in the costs of entry into additional markets, or investing in the expense of producing new product lines.

Franchising Revisited from the Franchisor Perspective

Performance Objective 3

Explain how a business can be franchised.

As discussed in Chapter 2, a franchise is a business that markets a product or service in the exact manner prescribed by the founder or successors of the parent business. Whereas one way for you to start a business would be to secure a franchise, you also could develop a concept and a business operation that could be reproduced and licensed to other entrepreneurs. They would buy the right to run the business in the way you prescribe, and pay you a franchise fee and a royalty.

A Pizza Hut franchise in Los Angeles.
(© Bill Aron, PhotoEdit)

There are numerous benefits and drawbacks to being a franchisor. The benefits include

- growth with minimal capital investment,
- lower marketing and promotional costs, and
- royalties.

The drawbacks of franchising to the franchisor include

- the franchisee may disregard the training and fail to operate the business properly, tarnishing the reputation of the entire franchise;
- it can be difficult to find qualified or trustworthy franchisees;
- franchisees that do not experience success may withhold payment and/or sue the franchisor, and
- there are many federal and state regulations regarding franchising, making it difficult and costly in some circumstances.

How a McDonald's Franchise Works

Let's look at how franchising can grow a business. McDonald's is an example of a franchise operation. McDonald's was developed by Ray Kroc, who had persuaded the McDonald brothers to let him become the franchising agent for their highly successful hamburger restaurant in San Bernardino, California, in 1955. Kroc's great insight was to realize that the people who bought McDonald's franchises would need extensive training and support in order to make the food taste like that of the original restaurant. Kroc timed and measured everything exactly. McDonald's franchisees are taught precisely how many minutes to fry potatoes and when to turn a burger, among a host of other details. They are even taught how to greet customers.

A McDonald's franchisee is an entrepreneur. The franchisee owns the restaurant, but agrees to market the food under the McDonald's name and trademark in the exact fashion developed by Kroc. This is spelled out in the franchise agreement. In return, the franchisee knows that he or she is investing in a proven, successful business concept. The franchisee also benefits from use of the McDonald's trademark, and from the management training, marketing, national advertising, and promotional assistance provided by the parent company. McDonald's, as franchisor, receives a franchise fee and royalties.

Although franchising has been around in the United States since the Singer Sewing Machine Company first used it in the 1850s, its popularity has exploded over the last couple of decades. The number of individual franchises has grown to approximately 750,000, with literally thousands of franchisors in the market space.

Do Your Research before You Franchise

Before you get involved in franchising your business, consult with a franchise attorney and carry out extensive research. The International Franchise Association (http://www.franchise.org) provides considerable information for current and prospective franchisors, including a prospective franchise forum. Use the resources available to you to understand what is expected of a franchisor, and how the relationship works, before speaking with an entrepreneur who is interested in a franchise. Recognize that your franchisees will expect significant support and attention for the fees that they pay you. To better understand the franchisee perspective, you can visit the American Association of Franchisees and Dealers at http://www.aafd.org. You must offer products or services that are sufficiently original and create unique marketing strategies, to justify the cost of the franchise.

Part of the process of franchising a business is to create a franchise agreement, which, as noted in Chapter 2, is the contract between the franchisor and franchisee. This contract establishes the standards that assure uniformity of product (or service) throughout the franchise chain.

Harvesting and Exiting Options

Licensing and franchising provide possible growth strategies for entrepreneurs that want to stay in one business. For those who do not wish to continue their businesses in perpetuity, harvesting and exiting are options.

When to Harvest Your Business

harvesting the act of selling, taking public, or merging a company to yield proceeds for the owner(s).

There will probably be times in the life of your business that you may want to close or leave it. **Harvesting** your business means you sell it, take it public, or merge with another company. This differs from replication in that the entrepreneur is usually no longer involved once the business is harvested, but walks away with a portion of the business's value as cash, stock, or a combination of the two. In the case of a merger, the founding entrepreneur may also work in the new organization for a specified time period.

In William Petty's article on harvesting,[6] he quotes Steven Covey, author of *The Seven Habits of Highly Effective People,* who says that a key to being effective in life is "beginning with the end in mind." To that, Petty adds, "If the entrepreneur's goal with the venture is only to provide a living, then the exit or harvest strategy is of no concern. But if the goal is to create value for the owners and the other stakeholders in the company, a harvest strategy is absolutely mandatory."

Although you want to be aware of all harvesting opportunities, it usually requires at least 10 years to build a company of sufficient value to harvest. You can make the timing of harvesting part of the plans for your business. The harvest strategy is important not only to the entrepreneur, but also to investors, because it lets them know up front how their investment should eventually be turned into cash or stock.

Not every business can be harvested. Some are loaded with debt or have not created a product or service of lasting value. The entrepreneur can only leave such a business via **liquidation** (selling all the assets), closure, or bankruptcy.

liquidation the sale of all assets of a business concurrent with its being closed.

[6] William Petty, "Harvesting," in *The Portable MBA in Entrepreneurship*, 2nd ed., William D. Bygrave, ed. (New York: Wiley, 1997).

Global Impact...

VISTA Staffing Solutions: Global Physician Staffing Founders Acquired

VISTA Staffing Solutions is a leading provider of permanent physician search services and *locum tenens*, or temporary physician staffing. The business was founded in 1990 as an employee-owned company with medical practices, hospitals, and governments as its primary clients. VISTA provides short- and long-term placements in the United States and internationally (Australia and New Zealand). The founders of VISTA are Mark Brouse, Katie Abby, and Clarke Shaw, who combined their industry and professional expertise to form the company.

On January 3, 2007, VISTA Staffing Solutions was acquired by On Assignment, Inc., a NASDAQ-traded leader in the professional staffing industry. The VISTA sale included $41 million in cash and an earn-out provision. VISTA shareholders and option holders could receive an additional $8 million, based upon its performance for the first two years after the sale. At the time of its acquisition by On Assignment, VISTA had a pool of more than 1300 physicians and had anticipated revenues in excess of $60 million.

Mark Brouse stated, "We are excited for our well-established physician staffing business to join an organization that shares our focus on providing highly skilled healthcare professionals. The two companies have remarkably similar cultures, putting people first and providing the best professional for each assignment. With the VISTA management team staying in place following the completion of the transaction, we believe the combined organization will be well positioned to maximize growth opportunities and achieve operating efficiencies." Two years after the acquisition, all three founders continued to manage VISTA Staffing Solutions.

Sources: On Assignment, Inc. Web site, http://www.onassignment.com, press release dated December 21, 2006, and VISTA Staffing Solutions Web site, http://www.vistastaff.com (accessed January 13, 2009).

How to Value a Business

Performance Objective 4

Learn methods of valuing a business.

Business valuation is both an art and a science. A business that is profitable and likely to be so in the future can be sold for a sum that represents its *net present value* today. This is net present value in action. (Most wealth is created by buying and selling assets that will have a future value.) Ultimately, a business is worth what others are willing to pay for it and that you will accept.

There are many ways to estimate the net present value of a business. Value, after all, is subjective, meaning it is subject to an individual's opinion or preferences. One person might be willing to pay a higher price for a particular business than another would. The first buyer feels more optimistic about the business's future (and may have some personal insight in that regard) or may simply want it more than the other potential buyer does.

Here are some methods entrepreneurs use to estimate the value of a business:

- Compare it with similar businesses. If you are looking to sell your dry-cleaning company, check out, if possible, how much other dry-cleaning stores in your area are bringing in when they are sold.
- In most industries, there are one or two key benchmarks used to help value a business. For gas stations, it might be barrels of gas sold per week; for a dry cleaner, it might be the number of shirts laundered per week.
- Look at a multiple of net earnings. One rule of thumb says a business can sell for around three to five times its annual net earnings. If the business earns $100,000 net profit per year, for example, it could be expected to sell for at least $300,000.

The ultimate goal of company valuation is to arrive at a **fair market value**, which, according to the IRS, is "The price at which property would change hands between a willing buyer and willing seller, neither under any compulsion to buy or sell and both having reasonable knowledge of the relevant facts."[7]

fair market value the price at which a property or business is valued by the market; the price it would fetch on the open market.

The Science of Valuation

There are three primary methods that buyers and sellers use: book value, future earnings, and market-based value. In practice, these three methods are often used concurrently, and all provide helpful perspectives on a company's value. Furthermore, there are many variations on each method. The SBA Web site provides assistance in valuation, and accountants and other professional business advisors can provide assistance as well.[8] Below is a more in-depth description of each.

- ***Book value (net worth = assets – liabilities).*** One of the most common methods for computing a company's valuation, the **book value** technique, looks at a company as assets minus liabilities. This way is the most common one used for valuing companies, and also the simplest.

book value valuation of a company as assets minus liabilities.

[7]Available at http://www.irs.gov.

[8]One source of information is SBA's Small Business Planner section, at http://www.sba.gov/smallbusinessplanner/exit/sellyourbusiness/index.htm.

- ***Future earnings.*** This method uses a company's estimated future earnings as the main determinant of its value. It is most useful for companies that are growing quickly. In these cases, past earnings are not accurate reflections of future performance. This method of valuation must take into account the time value of money, as well as the rate of return.
- ***Market-based (value = P/E ratio × estimated future net earnings).*** In the market-based approach, the value of the company is compiled from the price/earnings (P/E) ratio of comparable public companies. The P/E ratio is determined by dividing a company's stock price by its earnings per share. This method is effective because of its simplicity, but may be lacking when there are no similar public companies with which to compare the business.

Despite the sophistication of these three techniques, all of them are ultimately only estimates. Each business will have particular characteristics and special circumstances. In the end, it will be the entrepreneur's job to use negotiation to get the highest price possible.

Once you do decide to sell your business, or pursue some other exit strategy, use the Internet to maximize your prospects. If you decide to sell, you can list your business with databases such as http://www.BizBuySell.com or http://www.BizQuest.com, which send registered users who might want to buy your business e-mails alerting them to your offer.

Creating Wealth by Selling a Profitable Business

As noted above, a successful small business can usually be sold for between three and five times its yearly net profit, because the buyer expects the business to continue to keep generating income. If your net profit for one year is \$10,000, you should be able to get at least \$30,000 (3 × \$10,000).

Performance Objective 5

Discuss five ways to harvest a business.

From the buyer's perspective, this represents a 33 1/3 percent annual return on the investment required to buy the business (\$10,000/\$30,000 = 33 1/3%), which is a very attractive return.

If you are in business for three years, however, and increase your net profit each year, your business will be worth even more. If your company earns \$10,000 in year one, \$25,000 in year two, and \$60,000 in year three, it could be valued at \$180,000 by applying the three-times rule of thumb. How a business grows will affect its value. A business with increasing yearly net profit will be considered more valuable than a business with static earnings.

Entrepreneurs establish successful businesses, sell them, and use the resulting wealth to create new enterprises and more wealth. Entrepreneurs also use their wealth to support political, environmental, and social causes. What will you do with your wealth?

Harvesting Options

Harvesting options for exiting a business fall into five categories:

1. ***Increase the free cash flow.*** For the first 7 to 10 years of the business, you will want to reinvest as much profit as possible into the company in order to grow. Once you are ready to exit, however, you can begin reducing investment and taking cash out. This strategy will require investing only the amount of cash needed to keep the business effective in its current target markets, without attempting to move into new ones.

Step into the Shoes...

Flickr Turns Online Photo Sharing into Opportunities for Its Founders

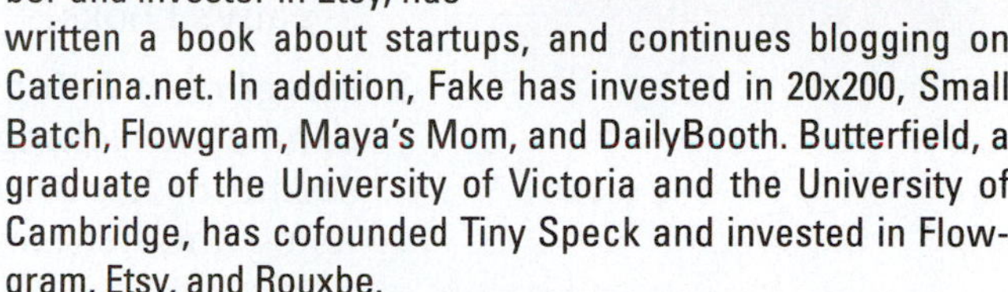

Stewart Butterfield and Caterina Fake launched Flickr in early 2004 and sold it just over one year later to Yahoo! The sale price was $35 million in cash. It would appear that the couple harvested their company very quickly, but the story begins several years earlier.

Flickr is an online site that hosts images and videos, is an online community, and provides Web services. It is most widely known and used for its photo-sharing capacity. However, Flickr was actually created by Vancouver-based Ludicorp (founded in 2002 by Butterfield and Fake) using tools for an online game, *Game Neverending*, that was never launched. Fake recognized that the photo-sharing technology was more marketable than the game, and Ludicorp pursued Flickr.

The couple remained at Yahoo! for the requisite three years after the sale but departed soon afterwards. Fake left Yahoo! in June of 2008, and her husband announced his resignation in the same month. Then Fake, a 1991 graduate of Vassar College, founded and became Chief Product Officer at Hunch, an Internet startup that provided recommendations on a multitude of user-generated topics. She is a board member and investor in Etsy, has written a book about startups, and continues blogging on Caterina.net. In addition, Fake has invested in 20x200, Small Batch, Flowgram, Maya's Mom, and DailyBooth. Butterfield, a graduate of the University of Victoria and the University of Cambridge, has cofounded Tiny Speck and invested in Flowgram, Etsy, and Rouxbe.

This couple found a way to translate a business idea into wealth and to use that wealth to found and invest in other startup companies.

Sources: Jefferson Graham, "Flickr of Idea on a Gaming Project Led to Photo Website," *USA Today*, February 27, 2007, http://www.usatoday.com. Crunchbase at http://www.crunchbase.com. Ludicorp Web site, http://www.ludicorp.com (accessed January 13, 2010).

Advantages

- You can retain ownership of the firm with this strategy.
- You do not have to seek a buyer.

Disadvantages

- You will need a good accountant to help avoid major taxes.
- It can take a long time to execute this exit strategy.

2. ***Management buyout (MBO)***. In this strategy, the entrepreneur sells the firm to its managers, who raise the money to buy it via personal savings and debt.

Advantages

- If the business has value, the managers often do want to buy it.
- The entrepreneur has the emotional satisfaction of selling to people he knows and has trained.

Disadvantages

- If the managers use primarily debt to buy the company, they may not be able to finish paying off the arrangement.
- If the final payment to the entrepreneur depends on the company's earnings during the last few quarters, the managers may have an incentive to attempt to lower the profits.

3. ***Employee stock ownership plan (ESOP)***. This strategy both provides an employee retirement plan and allows the entrepreneur and partners to sell their stock and exit the company. The firm establishes a plan that allows employees to buy company stock as part of their retirement; when the owners are ready to exit, the ESOP borrows money and uses the cash to buy their stock. As the loan is paid off, the stock is added to the employee benefit fund.

Advantages

- The ESOP has some special tax advantages; among them: the company can deduct both the principal and interest payments on the loan, and the dividends paid on any stock held in the ESOP are considered a tax-deductible expense.

Disadvantages

- This is not a good strategy if the entrepreneur does not want the employees to have control of the company. The ESOP must extend to all employees and requires the entrepreneur to open up the company's books.

4. ***Merging or being acquired.*** Selling the company to another company can be an exciting exit strategy for an entrepreneur who would like to see his or her creation have an opportunity to grow significantly by using another company's funds.

Advantages

- This strategy can finance growth that the company could not achieve on its own; the entrepreneur can either exit the company at the time of the **merger** or acquisition, or be part of the growth and exit later.

merger the joining of two companies to share their respective strengths.

Disadvantages

- This can be an emotionally draining strategy, with a lot of ups and downs during negotiations; a sale can take over a year to finalize.

5. ***Initial public offering (IPO).*** An initial public offering (IPO) or "going public" will mean selling shares of your company in the stock market. It requires choosing an investment banker to develop the IPO, making sales presentations ("the road show") to brokers and institutional investors nationally (and perhaps internationally) and, finally, offering your stock on the market and holding your breath as you watch its price go up—or not.

Advantages

- If your business is hot, this can be a very profitable way to harvest it. The market may place a large premium on your company's value.

Disadvantages

- An IPO is a very exciting, but stressful, all-consuming, and very expensive way to harvest a company, and it requires a lot of work from the entrepreneur; but ultimately it is the market that will determine the outcome. Very few entrepreneurial firms ever complete an IPO but, for many of them, it brings significant financial rewards.

This overview of harvesting strategies should help you plan the final stage of your relationship with the company you are starting to create now.

Exit Strategy Options

Simply claiming that your business will go public one day will probably get a skeptical reaction from potential investors. They understand that you cannot *guarantee* either how they will recoup their investment, or your exact exit strategy, but you can show you are aware that, for the vast majority of small businesses, going public is a fantasy. Demonstrate your understanding of exit strategies by thinking through the four basic possibilities below. Which one do you think best describes what you intend to make happen for your business?

1. ***Acquisition***. Do you believe you could create a business that someone would want to buy (*acquire*) one day? Your exit strategy could be creating a business that would be valuable for one of your suppliers, or a major competitor. The plan would be that the purchase price will pay you and your equity investors more money than you put into the business. A fair sale price, based on the business's annual net profit, should allow the original investors to realize a good return on their investment. As we have said, a common rule of thumb says that a small business is worth at least three times its annual net profit.
2. ***Earn out***. To use an earn-out strategy, you will need projected cash flow statements that show the business eventually generating a strong positive cash flow. At that point, you can start offering to buy out your investors' shares at a price greater than they paid for them. The purchase price usually rises over time.
3. ***Debt/equity exchange***. If your investors will be lending you money, eventually you can offer to trade equity for portions of the debt. This will slowly reduce the interest due over time (as the face value of the loan decreases). In this way, you can decide at what pace and at what price to reduce your debt.
4. ***Merge***. This strategy is similar to that of acquisition, but with a *merger*, two companies join together to share their strengths. One company might have an extensive customer base, whereas the other might possess a distribution channel the first company needs. Or perhaps each company is doing well in different geographical areas, and a merger would open up these respective markets to the other's products/services. Regardless, cash will change hands and the original investors can make their shares available for sale to complete the merger.

Investors Will Care about Your Exit Strategy, Too

As we have said, your exit strategy will be important to your investors. Your business plan should spell out in how many years you expect them to be able to cash out, and you will need to include financial data in your plan to forecast specifics. It will not be enough to mention that someday the company will go public and their share of the business will be worth a lot of money. Of the thousands of new ventures launched every year in the United States, only a small percentage will ever go public. Yet, according to David Newton, on Entrepreneur.com (January 15, 2001), over 70 percent of formal business plans presented to angel investors and venture capitalists cite going public as the primary exit strategy. Most estimate that going public will happen within just four years from the launch date. You will need to be more realistic.

Chapter Summary

Now that you have studied this chapter, you can do the following:

1. Determine how you want to grow your business and then exit from it.
   - Decide what your ultimate goals and objectives are.
   - Consider creating a business that will provide employment and wealth for your family.
   - Identify options to broaden product and service offerings through diversification.
   - Evaluate replication strategies.

2. Describe how businesses use licensing to profit from their brands.
   - A brand is a name, term, sign, logo, design, or combination of these that identifies the products or services of a company and differentiates them from those of competitors.
   - The licensee pays a fee for the license and may also pay a royalty (share of the profits) on sales to the licensor.
   - Licensing is only effective when the licensor is confident that his or her company name will not be tarnished by how the licensee uses it.
3. Explain how a business can be franchised.
   - A franchise is a business that markets a product or service in the exact manner prescribed by the founder or successors of the parent company.
   - As an entrepreneur, you could develop a concept and business operation that can be reproduced and sold to other entrepreneurs. They would pay you a fee for the right to run the business exactly the way that you direct, and pay you a royalty as well.
4. Learn methods of valuing a business.
   - Book value (net worth = assets – liabilities)
   - Future earnings
   - Market-based (value = P/E × estimated future net earnings)
5. Discuss five ways to harvest a business.
   - Increase the free cash flows. Once you are ready to exit, you can begin reducing reinvestment and collecting revenue as cash.
   - Management buyout (MBO). The entrepreneur sells the firm to the managers, who raise the money to buy it via personal savings and debt.
   - Employee stock ownership plan (ESOP). This provides an employee retirement plan and allows the entrepreneur and partners to sell their stock to the employees as they exit the company.
   - Merging or being acquired. Joining together with another company or being bought by one.
   - Initial public offering (IPO). Going public is getting your company listed on the stock exchange to be traded publicly.

Key Terms

book value
diversification
fair market value
harvesting
licensing
line extension
liquidation
merger
replication strategy

Entrepreneurship Portfolio

Critical Thinking Exercises

1. Describe the differences between a licensing and a franchising agreement.
2. Give an example of a business that could lead to licensing agreements and a business that could be franchised.

3. Do you plan to franchise your business or license any of your products? Explain.
4. Describe the exit strategy you plan to use to harvest your business. Why do you think this exit strategy will be attractive to potential investors?

Key Concept Questions

1. Identify two companies that merged during the past three years. Describe the structure of the merger and what has happened to the organizations since then.
2. Choose one of the harvesting strategies described in the chapter and research it in depth. Write a one-page report to present to the class.

Application Exercise

1. Look around your local community and select a popular business that is an independent company, not a franchise or part of a major corporation. Identify the possible harvesting strategies that the owners(s) could employ. What would you recommend and why?
2. For a business that you are planning, name your top two preferred exit strategies and explain the reasons for selecting them.

Exploring Online

The American Association of Franchisees and Dealers (AAFD) is a national trade association that represents the rights and interests or franchisees and independent dealers across the country. Visit this association online at http://www.aafd.org to learn more about franchises and the resources available. As a potential franchisor, you should know what your prospective customers are reading.

1. Search the site for the article, "AAFD Road Map to Selecting a Franchise." Read the section called "8 Things to Look for in a Franchise." For each of the eight tips in the article, write a one-sentence summary and note how it might apply to your business as the franchisor.
2. Find a franchise online like the one you might want to create. Answer the following:
   a. What is the franchise? What does it sell?
   b. Why are you interested in it?
   c. What is the franchise fee?
   d. What are the start-up costs?
   e. What is the royalty fee?
   f. Describe the training the franchisor offers to franchisees.
   g. Describe the marketing the franchisor provides for franchisees.
3. Find a company online that is similar to the type of business you would like to launch. Assume you would want to sell it. Describe how much you would expect from a buyer and explain your valuation method.

Case Study | Growth through Franchising: PODS Inc.

In the mid-1990s, Peter Warhurst, a former Largo (Florida) paramedic who had sold a company to Bell Atlantic for $10 million, started a second venture, which became PODS (Portable On Demand Storage). Initially, Warhurst and a partner built a mini-storage center in Clearwater to provide a source of revenue that required little time and few employees. They quickly encountered difficulty in finding a suitable location for a second center, and the idea of bringing storage to customers emerged. "I checked the Internet and nobody was doing it. I couldn't even find somebody to copy."[9] Peter, and two partners from the Largo Fire Department, developed a weather-proof storage unit and a patented hydraulic-lift system (Podzilla) to transport whatever customers put into their units.

Since the first storage-unit delivery in 1998, the business has grown swiftly. Initially, Peter thought he might be able to develop an 80-unit business.[10] He quickly learned that he had greatly underestimated the demand. Not only did customers want PODS for storing household and business items at a PODS facility, they wanted to use them for moving. Soon after start-up, PODS received numerous inquiries about investment and franchising.

PODS sold its first franchise that same year. "We want to get the nation populated with PODS," Peter stated.[11] As of April 2008, PODS was serving customers in the United States, Australia, and Canada, having made over 1 million reservations, completed some 150,000 long-distance relocations, and placed more than 130,000 containers in the market.[12] Franchise agreements were offered for markets of 200,000 to 400,000 with a required investment of about $1.5 million, an upfront fee of $75,000, and 10 percent of revenues (as of 2004) as a royalty. PODS maintains consistent product information and clear communications by centralizing and monitoring its functions. All phone calls are directed to PODS call centers, and billing, collections, and training are centrally controlled.

This franchise model has been a tremendous growth mechanism for PODS, providing much of the company's capital. In only 10 years, Peter Warhurst saw his business grow from an idea into a venture-backed company with franchises nationwide.

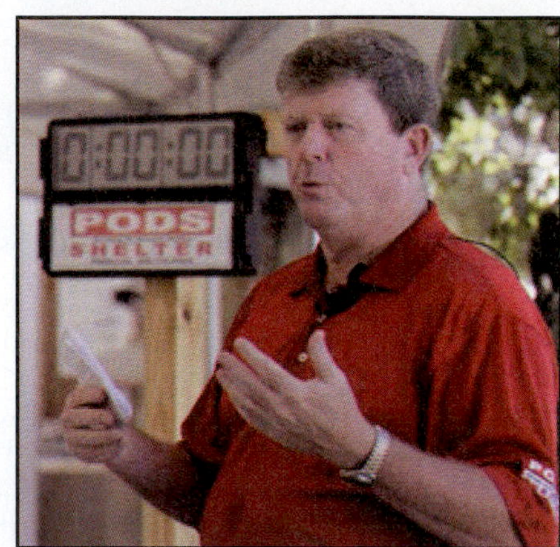

Following the sale of PODS, in late 2007, Warhurst stepped aside as president and CEO after having created a franchising phenomenon.

Case Study Analysis

1. What benefits did PODS gain from franchising?
2. PODS is the official moving and storage company of the PGA Tour, and prominently displays this information and the PGA logo on its Web site. Why would PODS and the PGA Tour be good partners?
3. What benefits do franchisees get from the PODS and Podzilla names?
4. Visit http://www.pods.com and find information about obtaining a PODS franchise.
   a. How much initial capital is currently required to secure a franchise? Where did you find this information?
   b. What is the current franchise fee structure?
   c. What are the competitive advantages that PODS identifies?
   d. How large of a non-compete territory is covered by one franchise license?

Case Sources

PODS Web site, http://www.pods.com.

Dee Gill, "The POD People," *Business Week*, December 17, 1999.

Kris Hundley, "Thinking in a Box," *St. Petersburg Times*, March 15, 2004.

Sun Coast Business Forum, interview with Peter S. Warhurst, May 31, 2007, http://www.wedu.org.

[9] Kris Hundley, "Thinking in a Box," *St. Petersburg Times*, March 15, 2004.
[10] Ibid.
[11] Ibid.
[12] PODS Web site, http://www.pods.com (accessed April 2008).

Case Study | Ben & Jerry's

In 1978, when Ben Cohen and Jerry Greenfield decided to sell homemade ice cream out of a converted gas station in Burlington, Vermont, they never imagined that Ben & Jerry's would eventually grow into an international premium brand. Twenty years later, the business had evolved from a homespun, Vermont-based scoop shop into a multimillion-dollar company with worldwide franchises in locations ranging from Boston to Tokyo to Paris. This upstart company became famous for putting out offbeat flavors, like Bovinity Divinity, Chubby Hubby, and Cherry Garcia, and for its colorful marketing campaigns. For instance, when Ben & Jerry's decided to hire a new CEO in 1994, it held a "Yo, I'm your CEO!" contest and invited customers to submit application essays for the job. In 1999, to commemorate its twenty-first anniversary, the company launched a "Coast-to-Coast Free Cone Day" and gave out 550,000 ice cream cones to happy customers.

A Commitment to Social Responsibility

Cohen and Greenfield rejected a profits-only, single-bottom-line approach to managing their business. Instead, they chose to invest in socially responsible causes and business practices that did not always earn maximum profits but, rather, gave something back to society and helped the environment. For example, they established a policy of contributing 7.5 percent of the company's pre-tax earnings to charity. In 1991, they paid out half a million dollars to help offset losses suffered by local Vermont milk suppliers during a time of intense price fluctuation in the dairy industry. They also spent many years perfecting the production of an ecopint ice cream container, made from unbleached paperboard and nontoxic color dyes. These kinds of corporate good works earned Ben & Jerry's a number one ranking for corporate social responsibility in a national poll conducted by Harris Interactive in 1999.

Unhappy Shareholders

By 2000, Ben & Jerry's was a publicly owned company traded on the NASDAQ and was generating over $200 million in annual sales with a net income of $3.3 million. But their shareholders were not happy. The stock price had been stagnant for many years, in 1997 slipping as low as $12 a share. By 2000, the stock had climbed to $20 but some shareholders wanted to earn a better return. A persistent challenge faced by the company was that it did not own its own distribution channels. As a result, it paid a high operating cost to get its products to market. Rumors began to circulate in the media that a large corporation might want to purchase this small, folksy company.

Takeover

By the end of the year, negotiations were underway between Ben & Jerry's corporate board and Unilever, a $52-billion European-based consumer goods firm. As word spread about the impending sale, grassroots "Save Ben & Jerry's" protest campaigns sprouted all over the United States. Loyal consumers who valued the company's commitment to social responsibility feared that a larger corporate entity would not continue to support causes like saving the rain forests or employing homeless people. Many opposed the sale, including Ben Cohen and Jerry Greenfield themselves, who unsuccessfully tried to execute a counterdeal with a venture capital firm that would have taken the company private. Vermont politicians weighed in and broadcast their view that the company should preserve its independence. After all, Ben & Jerry's had created many jobs in Vermont; and the company's policy of buying Vermont-only milk had been a major boon for local farmers. But, despite these collective protests, the company was bought by Unilever in 2000 for $326 million, or $43.60 per share.

How did this happen? According to corporate charter law, company boards are mandated to prioritize shareholders' interests when making decisions that impact the bottom line. In the

case of Ben & Jerry's, Unilever was offering to pay more than double the company's current $21-per-share stock price. The board felt that this was an offer it could not refuse.

An Uncertain Future

Under the terms of the deal, both Ben and Jerry remained employees of the company at annual salaries of $200,000 each. A new CEO was hired by Unilever to manage the company's operations. Unilever promised that it would continue Ben & Jerry's commitment to social responsibility, but many were skeptical about this. Several months after Unilever took the helm, Ben Cohen commented to the *New York Times* that "What Ben & Jerry's used to be is one of these smaller 'social values led' businesses. What Ben & Jerry's is in the process of becoming is an entity inside a larger business, trying to infuse those values into that business. We expect that it will be a long and winding road."[13]

Case Study Analysis

1. Why do you think Unilever was willing to purchase Ben & Jerry's for more than double the company's stock price? Why was Ben & Jerry's an attractive investment? (Remember: When Ben & Jerry's was sold, its stock price was $21/share. Unilever purchased the shares at $43.60.)
2. One of the ways that entrepreneurs earn money is by starting businesses and then selling them. When the sale went through, Jerry Greenfield sold his 900,000 shares in the company at $43.60 per share, and Ben Cohen got the same price for his 220,000.
   a. How much did Ben & Jerry earn respectively from the sale?
   b. When they started their company in 1978, Ben & Jerry each invested $6000. Calculate the return on investment for each.
3. Review the different harvesting strategies described in the chapter. Which strategy did Ben & Jerry's board use? What are the pros and cons of this strategy?
4. Go online and conduct research on Ben & Jerry's. Is the company more profitable now under Unilever? Does it still contribute a percentage of its profits to charity? Identify three ways the company has changed since it was sold.
5. Explain why the sale of Ben & Jerry's occurred, even though the company's founders did not want it to happen.

Case Sources

Ben & Jerry's Web site, http://www.benandjerrys.com.

Constance Hays, "Investment Group Makes Bid for Ben & Jerry's," *New York Times*, February 10, 2000.

Constance Hays, "Ben & Jerry's Deal Takes on Slightly New Flavor," *New York Times*, May 2, 2002.

[13]Constance Hays, "Ben and Jerry's Deal Takes on Slightly New Flavor," *New York Times*, May 2, 2002.

Avocent Corporation

http://www.avocent.com

Small Business School **video clip titles are in red**

FIND A BIG PROBLEM TO SOLVE . . . SOLVE IT AND GROW

Avocent Corporation is a company that provides IT operations and infrastructure management solutions, including software and hardware. Its KVM equipment remotely controls personal computers and servers from 25 feet away to 25,000 miles. In December 2009, Emerson Electronics, the St. Louis-based Fortune 100 company, acquired Huntsville, Alabama-based Avocent.

Avocent's story illustrates what can happen when a founder starts a business to solve a very big problem for customers that can afford to pay for a solution to that problem. In 1981, when he was 33 years old, Remigius Shatas started out with a big idea; and he did things right to incubate, nurture, grow, and ultimately sell his company for a profit of millions. His path to financial success, however, was not straight—it was full of twists and turns.

While working in a grommet factory on the night shift, Remigius observed that there was not enough room on desks for all of the requisite equipment, such as computers, keyboards, a mouse and a printer. That got him thinking about what would become his billion-dollar idea. But before he was able to build and sell that product, he experienced many false starts and delays. The company he launched with his cofounders was called Cybex Computer Product Corporation—Cybex being a contraction of cybernetic excellence—they originally intended to build robots. Remigius did consulting work to support himself while he developed his ideas and, in 1981, he recognized that the IBM Personal Computer would change the world of business computing.

Initially, Cybex generated sales by building mainframe-quality software for the PC focusing on vertical markets, including retail pharmacy, veterinary, and modular business systems. They were able to survive with these, but it was the company's eighth product that changed everything. That product today is called KVM.

Remigius invented KVM (keyboard, video, mouse) technology. According to Avocent's Web site, analog and digital KVM appliances, "consolidate access at the desk, at the rack or across the entire data center. Avocent has been at the forefront of KVM development from the start, saving space and improving staff efficiency in leading companies across the globe."[14] KVM not only keeps the desktop free of computers, it also keeps company-owned data safe in remote computers rather than on multiple desks.

Company president Steve Thornton said, in his *Small Business School* interview, "The bottom line is we make a very large problem manageable. Without our product, if you had 1000 computers you would need 1000 separate keyboards, monitors, and mice." The problem was so big that when we met Remigius and Steve, they were up to $228 million in annual sales. Cybex has gone public, with a $32.6 million IPO in 1995. They

[14]Avocent Web site, http://www.avocent.com (accessed May 3, 2010).

merged with Apex Inc. in 2000, their largest KVM competitor, to form Avocent Corporation. Avocent made a series of acquisitions prior to being acquired by Emerson Electric, as noted in the Table below.

Avocent Acquisitions	
Company Acquired	**Year**
Equinox Systems	2001
2CComputing	2002
Soronti, Inc.	2003
Crystal Link Technologies	2004
OSA Technologies, Inc.	2004
Sonic Mobility, Inc.	2004
Cyclades Corporation	2006
LANDesk Corporation	2006

PREPARE TO SUCCEED

Remigius explains in the interview why he was able to build a company that won the attention of the world. "I got the bug—I call it the bug of ambition—and I found out the bug of ambition is fatal. Once you've caught it, there's no cure except success. And it just drives your life. I didn't know at the time—in my early 30s—that what you have to do is look at markets. I was still looking at products. And the difference between a small company and a large company is the transition between the product mentality and the market mentality."

Going back to the origin of Cybex, we learned that Remigius liked his work at the grommet factory, but he was troubled by the work environment. He did not like the way people were treated, and he also did not like driving the 100-mile-round-trip commute. This unrest was a critical factor in Remigius's decision to start a business, much as it often is for entrepreneurs.

Remigius was thinking about other people, not only himself. Imagine being very tired from working nearly 24 hours, and facing a 50-mile drive so you could see your family and go to sleep in your own bed. One cold December morning, after spending the night at the office because he could not work on the computer systems during the day (employees needed them for their production work), Remigius decided to pursue his ideas and, start a business in which people could actually enjoy their jobs.

He did not say to himself that he wanted to make a lot of money or be the boss or change the world. Remigius was thinking about what work *could* be like. He had a vision of the type of business that he could create, and whereas he wanted to have financial security, it was the business culture and concepts that drove him, much like many other entrepreneurs. He wanted to solve a business problem and help others become financially secure while doing so.

In addition, Remigius reported that he had to stop thinking about what product to make and to start thinking about what problem to solve. And, of course, he knew that the bigger the problem he could solve, the bigger he could grow his business. An owner cannot expand a business for the long term, or sell it at a significant profit, if it is solely built on his personality, or a flimsy idea that very few people care about.

Remigius Shatas prepared to succeed, and that preparation included understanding his deep motivation and the market he wanted to enter.

HIRE YOUR OWN BOSS

In order to grow his firm, Remigius did what relatively few founders do voluntarily: he hired his own boss—when it became clear to him that the product he invented had huge market potential and that he was not equipped to manage the firm as it grew. He learned from his early experience at Cybex, with cofounders that quit within the first year of founding, that managing an entrepreneurial enterprise is neither easy nor natural. As he began to experience success, Remigius acted on his own insight that he needed to hire a CEO for the company. This was one of his most brilliant decisions. Making such a choice means that the stereotypical bull-headed founder has to reflect on his/her knowledge, skills, abilities, and interests honestly enough to recognize that someone else might be more capable of managing the growing company. Remigius had never been the CEO of anything; he had always been the "computer guy" focused on how to make things work. Making computers operate correctly is very different from making an organization work well and become successful.

Remigius did not have sufficient funds to hire the experienced leader he wanted. However, he figured out how to value the company and its potential and then asked Steve Thornton and Bob Asprey, managers he knew and respected, to bet on the future revenues. Rather than pay them the salaries they deserved, he offered them stock in the company. Remigius had to sell them on the bright future for KVM technology and the company. Both stepped up to the plate and, because they did, became very wealthy when the company went public.

When Remigius finally landed on the right product at the right time, he had to stop doing things on a small scale and look for ways to manage fast growth. While he worked on the markets, Bob worked on the product, and Steve worked on the processes.

There were continuous cash flow problems in the early days because it turned out they had the wrong business model. In many of the lean years, and when Steve, Bob, and Remigius could see that they would realize a profit, they did not write themselves paychecks; rather, they paid a year-end bonus.

As they grew, their bankers determined that the Shatas/Thornton formula was not quite right, and initially turned them down for a working line of credit. They had to stop building their new product in-house. This caused great disappointment among the team that had worked so hard over the years to get the products built. The leadership discovered that they literally did not have the skill to build the new products, so they had to find a factory to take over that work.

Remigius said, "Bob would keep me in check. I always had ideas, but it was Bob who could figure out if the idea could be manufactured and if it would make us money. He forced us to measure the cost of my wild ideas before we spent too much cash." Getting the balance right requires the business owner to continuously weigh ideas to decide if they are worth investing time, money, and attention to develop. The plague of too many ideas is that they can take a business "off path" so that it never completes or succeeds at anything. Fortunately for Remigius, with help from people like Bob, they stuck to their core winning products. Remigius Shatas's ownership was bought out in 2000 and, since then, he has spent his time investing in other entrepreneurs.

Case Analysis

1. What are some of the key decisions Remigius made that positioned his company for success?
2. Why was Remigius Shatas able to go public and then to leave the business with millions in his pocket?
3. Did Remigius launch the company with a winning product?
4. How did Avocent grow?

Prepared by Hattie Bryant, creator of *Small Business School*, the television series made for PBS and Voice of America, http://SmallBusinessSchool.org.

Appendix 1

The Daily Perc Appendices

The Daily Perc

Appendix 1-A

The Daily Perc—Sales Forecast

Unit Sales		Jun	Jul	Aug	Sep	Oct	Nov	Dec	Jan	Feb	Mar	Apr	May
Drive-thru #1	0%	0	0	0	17,500	23,047	24,199	22,989	23,047	24,199	22,989	23,047	21,895
Drive-thru #2	0%	0	0	0	0	0	0	0	0	17,500	23,047	21,895	23,047
Drive-thru #3	0%	0	0	0	0	0	0	0	0	0	0	0	0
Drive-thru #4	0%	0	0	0	0	0	0	0	0	0	0	0	0
Drive-thru #5	0%	0	0	0	0	0	0	0	0	0	0	0	0
Drive-thrus #6 & #7	0%	0	0	0	0	0	0	0	0	0	0	0	0
Drive-thrus #8, #9, & #10	0%	0	0	0	0	0	0	0	0	0	0	0	0
Drive-thrus #11, #12, & #13	0%	0	0	0	0	0	0	0	0	0	0	0	0
Mobile Café #1	0%	0	0	0	0	0	0	0	0	0	0	5,000	5,000
Mobile Café #2	0%	0	0	0	0	0	0	0	0	0	0	0	0
Mobile Café #3	0%	0	0	0	0	0	0	0	0	0	0	0	0
Mobile Café #4	0%	0	0	0	0	0	0	0	0	0	0	0	0
Website Sales/Premium Items	0%	0	0	0	0	0	0	0	0	0	0	0	0
Total Unit Sales		0	0	0	17,500	23,047	24,199	22,989	23,047	41,699	46,036	49,942	49,942

Unit Prices	Jun	Jul	Aug	Sep	Oct	Nov	Dec	Jan	Feb	Mar	Apr	May
Drive-thru #1	$1.85	$1.85	$1.85	$1.85	$1.85	$1.85	$1.85	$1.85	$1.85	$1.85	$1.85	$1.85
Drive-thru #2	$1.85	$1.85	$1.85	$1.85	$1.85	$1.85	$1.85	$1.85	$1.85	$1.85	$1.85	$1.85
Drive-thru #3	$1.85	$1.85	$1.85	$1.85	$1.85	$1.85	$1.85	$1.85	$1.85	$1.85	$1.85	$1.85
Drive-thru #4	$1.85	$1.85	$1.85	$1.85	$1.85	$1.85	$1.85	$1.85	$1.85	$1.85	$1.85	$1.85
Drive-thru #5	$1.85	$1.85	$1.85	$1.85	$1.85	$1.85	$1.85	$1.85	$1.85	$1.85	$1.85	$1.85
Drive-thrus #6 & #7	$1.85	$1.85	$1.85	$1.85	$1.85	$1.85	$1.85	$1.85	$1.85	$1.85	$1.85	$1.85
Drive-thrus #8, #9, & #10	$1.85	$1.85	$1.85	$1.85	$1.85	$1.85	$1.85	$1.85	$1.85	$1.85	$1.85	$1.85
Drive-thrus #11, #12, & #13	$1.85	$1.85	$1.85	$1.85	$1.85	$1.85	$1.85	$1.85	$1.85	$1.85	$1.85	$1.85
Mobile Café #1	$2.45	$2.45	$2.45	$2.45	$2.45	$2.45	$2.45	$2.45	$2.45	$2.45	$2.45	$2.45
Mobile Café #2	$2.45	$2.45	$2.45	$2.45	$2.45	$2.45	$2.45	$2.45	$2.45	$2.45	$2.45	$2.45
Mobile Café #3	$2.45	$2.45	$2.45	$2.45	$2.45	$2.45	$2.45	$2.45	$2.45	$2.45	$2.45	$2.45
Mobile Café #4	$2.45	$2.45	$2.45	$2.45	$2.45	$2.45	$2.45	$2.45	$2.45	$2.45	$2.45	$2.45
Website Sales/Premium Items	$10.00	$10.00	$10.00	$10.00	$10.00	$10.00	$10.00	$10.00	$10.00	$10.00	$10.00	$10.00

Sales	Jun	Jul	Aug	Sep	Oct	Nov	Dec	Jan	Feb	Mar	Apr	May
Drive-thru #1	$0	$0	$0	$32,375	$42,637	$44,769	$42,530	$42,637	$44,769	$42,530	$42,637	$40,505
Drive-thru #2	$0	$0	$0	$0	$0	$0	$0	$0	$32,375	$42,637	$40,505	$42,637
Drive-thru #3	$0	$0	$0	$0	$0	$0	$0	$0	$0	$0	$0	$0
Drive-thru #4	$0	$0	$0	$0	$0	$0	$0	$0	$0	$0	$0	$0
Drive-thru #5	$0	$0	$0	$0	$0	$0	$0	$0	$0	$0	$0	$0
Drive-thrus #6 & #7	$0	$0	$0	$0	$0	$0	$0	$0	$0	$0	$0	$0
Drive-thrus #8, #9, & #10	$0	$0	$0	$0	$0	$0	$0	$0	$0	$0	$0	$0
Drive-thrus #11, #12, & #13	$0	$0	$0	$0	$0	$0	$0	$0	$0	$0	$0	$0

The Daily Perc

Mobile Café #1		$0	$0	$0	$0	$0	$0	$0	$0	$0	$0	$12,250	$12,250
Mobile Café #2		$0	$0	$0	$0	$0	$0	$0	$0	$0	$0	$0	$0
Mobile Café #3		$0	$0	$0	$0	$0	$0	$0	$0	$0	$0	$0	$0
Mobile Café #4		$0	$0	$0	$0	$0	$0	$0	$0	$0	$0	$0	$0
Website Sales/Premium Items		$0	$0	$0	$0	$0	$0	$0	$0	$0	$0	$0	$0
Total Sales		$0	$0	$0	$32,375	$42,637	$44,769	$42,530	$42,637	$77,144	$85,167	$95,392	$95,392
		Jun	**Jul**	**Aug**	**Sep**	**Oct**	**Nov**	**Dec**	**Jan**	**Feb**	**Mar**	**Apr**	**May**
Direct Unit Costs													
Drive-thru #1	0.00%	$0.64	$0.64	$0.64	$0.64	$0.64	$0.64	$0.64	$0.64	$0.64	$0.64	$0.64	$0.64
Drive-thru #2	0.00%	$0.64	$0.64	$0.64	$0.64	$0.64	$0.64	$0.64	$0.64	$0.64	$0.64	$0.64	$0.64
Drive-thru #3	0.00%	$0.64	$0.64	$0.64	$0.64	$0.64	$0.64	$0.64	$0.64	$0.64	$0.64	$0.64	$0.64
Drive-thru #4	0.00%	$0.64	$0.64	$0.64	$0.64	$0.64	$0.64	$0.64	$0.64	$0.64	$0.64	$0.64	$0.64
Drive-thru #5	0.00%	$0.64	$0.64	$0.64	$0.64	$0.64	$0.64	$0.64	$0.64	$0.64	$0.64	$0.64	$0.64
Drive-thrus #6 & #7	0.00%	$0.64	$0.64	$0.64	$0.64	$0.64	$0.64	$0.64	$0.64	$0.64	$0.64	$0.64	$0.64
Drive-thrus #8, #9, & #10	0.00%	$0.64	$0.64	$0.64	$0.64	$0.64	$0.64	$0.64	$0.64	$0.64	$0.64	$0.64	$0.64
Drive-thrus #11, #12, & #13	0.00%	$0.64	$0.64	$0.64	$0.64	$0.64	$0.64	$0.64	$0.64	$0.64	$0.64	$0.64	$0.64
Mobile Café #1	0.00%	$0.64	$0.64	$0.64	$0.64	$0.64	$0.64	$0.64	$0.64	$0.64	$0.64	$0.64	$0.64
Mobile Café #2	0.00%	$0.64	$0.64	$0.64	$0.64	$0.64	$0.64	$0.64	$0.64	$0.64	$0.64	$0.64	$0.64
Mobile Café #3	0.00%	$0.64	$0.64	$0.64	$0.64	$0.64	$0.64	$0.64	$0.64	$0.64	$0.64	$0.64	$0.64
Mobile Café #4	0.00%	$0.64	$0.64	$0.64	$0.64	$0.64	$0.64	$0.64	$0.64	$0.64	$0.64	$0.64	$0.64
Website Sales/Premium Items	0.00%	$6.50	$6.50	$6.50	$6.50	$6.50	$6.50	$6.50	$6.50	$6.50	$6.50	$6.50	$6.50
Direct Cost of Sales													
Drive-thru #1		$0	$0	$0	$11,200	$14,750	$15,488	$14,713	$14,750	$15,488	$14,713	$14,750	$14,013
Drive-thru #2		$0	$0	$0	$0	$0	$0	$0	$0	$11,200	$14,750	$14,013	$14,750
Drive-thru #3		$0	$0	$0	$0	$0	$0	$0	$0	$0	$0	$0	$0
Drive-thru #4		$0	$0	$0	$0	$0	$0	$0	$0	$0	$0	$0	$0
Drive-thru #5		$0	$0	$0	$0	$0	$0	$0	$0	$0	$0	$0	$0
Drive-thrus #6 & #7		$0	$0	$0	$0	$0	$0	$0	$0	$0	$0	$0	$0
Drive-thrus #8, #9, & #10		$0	$0	$0	$0	$0	$0	$0	$0	$0	$0	$0	$0
Drive-thrus #11, #12, & #13		$0	$0	$0	$0	$0	$0	$0	$0	$0	$0	$0	$0
Mobile Café #1		$0	$0	$0	$0	$0	$0	$0	$0	$0	$0	$3,200	$3,200
Mobile Café #2		$0	$0	$0	$0	$0	$0	$0	$0	$0	$0	$0	$0
Mobile Café #3		$0	$0	$0	$0	$0	$0	$0	$0	$0	$0	$0	$0
Mobile Café #4		$0	$0	$0	$0	$0	$0	$0	$0	$0	$0	$0	$0
Website Sales/Premium Items		$0	$0	$0	$0	$0	$0	$0	$0	$0	$0	$0	$0
Subtotal Direct Cost of Sales		$0	$0	$0	$11,200	$14,750	$15,488	$14,713	$14,750	$26,688	$29,463	$31,963	$31,963

The Daily Perc

Appendix 1-B

The Daily Perc—Personnel Plan

		Jun	Jul	Aug	Sep	Oct	Nov	Dec	Jan	Feb	Mar	Apr	May
Drive-thru Team	0%	$0	$0	$0	$10,500	$10,850	$9,800	$9,800	$10,500	$19,624	$21,700	$21,000	$21,700
Mobile Café Team	0%	$0	$0	$0	$0	$0	$0	$0	$0	$0	$0	$4,700	$4,700
Equipment Care Specialist (Headquarters)	0%	$0	$0	$0	$0	$0	$0	$0	$0	$0	$0	$0	$0
Other	0%	$0	$0	$0	$0	$0	$0	$0	$0	$0	$0	$0	$0
District Manager (Four Drive-thrus)	0%	$0	$0	$0	$0	$0	$0	$0	$0	$0	$0	$0	$0
Corporate Events Sales Exec	0%	$0	$0	$0	$0	$0	$0	$0	$0	$0	$0	$0	$0
Director of Marketing	0%	$0	$0	$0	$0	$0	$0	$0	$0	$0	$0	$0	$0
Other	0%	$0	$0	$0	$0	$0	$0	$0	$0	$0	$0	$0	$0
Bookkeeper/Office Administrator	0%	$0	$0	$0	$0	$1,750	$1,750	$3,500	$3,500	$3,500	$3,500	$3,500	$3,500
Warehouse/Site Manager	0%	$0	$0	$0	$0	$0	$0	$0	$0	$0	$0	$3,500	$3,500
Inventory Clerk	0%	$0	$0	$0	$0	$0	$0	$0	$0	$0	$0	$0	$0
Other	0%	$0	$0	$0	$0	$0	$0	$0	$0	$0	$0	$0	$0
Chief Operating Officer	0%	$5,500	$5,500	$5,500	$5,500	$5,500	$5,500	$5,500	$5,500	$5,500	$5,500	$5,500	$5,500
Chief Financial Officer	0%	$0	$0	$0	$0	$0	$0	$0	$0	$0	$0	$0	$0
Chief Information Officer	0%	$0	$0	$0	$0	$0	$0	$0	$0	$0	$0	$0	$0
Other	0%	$0	$0	$0	$0	$0	$0	$0	$0	$0	$0	$0	$0
Total Staff		1	1	1	5	6	6	6	6	11	11	15	15
Total Payroll		$5,500	$5,500	$5,500	$16,000	$18,100	$17,050	$18,800	$19,500	$28,624	$30,700	$38,200	$38,900

The Daily Perc
Appendix 1-C

The Daily Perc—General Assumptions

	Jun	Jul	Aug	Sep	Oct	Nov	Dec	Jan	Feb	Mar	Apr	May
Plan Month	1	2	3	4	5	6	7	8	9	10	11	12
Current Interest Rate	10.00%	10.00%	10.00%	10.00%	10.00%	10.00%	10.00%	10.00%	10.00%	10.00%	10.00%	10.00%
Long-term Interest Rate	9.00%	9.00%	9.00%	9.00%	9.00%	9.00%	9.00%	9.00%	9.00%	9.00%	9.00%	9.00%
Tax Rate	0.00%	0.00%	0.00%	0.00%	0.00%	0.00%	0.00%	0.00%	0.00%	0.00%	0.00%	0.00%
Other	0	0	0	0	0	0	0	0	0	0	0	0

The Daily Perc
Appendix 1-D

The Daily Perc—Pro Forma Profit and Loss (Income Statement)

		Jun	Jul	Aug	Sep	Oct	Nov	Dec	Jan	Feb	Mar	Apr	May
Sales		$0	$0	$0	$32,375	$42,637	$44,769	$42,530	$42,637	$77,144	$85,167	$95,392	$95,392
Direct Costs of Goods		$0	$0	$0	$11,200	$14,750	$15,488	$14,713	$14,750	$26,688	$29,463	$31,963	$31,963
Sales Commissions		$0	$0	$0	$0	$0	$0	$0	$0	$0	$0	$708	$708
Cost of Goods Sold		$0	$0	$0	$11,200	$14,750	$15,488	$14,713	$14,750	$26,688	$29,463	$32,671	$32,671
Gross Margin		$0	$0	$0	$21,175	$27,887	$29,281	$27,817	$27,887	$50,456	$55,704	$62,721	$62,721
Gross Margin %		0.00%	0.00%	0.00%	65.41%	65.41%	65.41%	65.41%	65.41%	65.41%	65.41%	65.75%	65.75%
Expenses													
Payroll		$5,500	$5,500	$5,500	$16,000	$18,100	$17,050	$18,800	$19,500	$28,624	$30,700	$38,200	$38,900
Sales and Marketing and Other Expenses		$0	$0	$0	$0	$0	$0	$0	$0	$0	$0	$0	$0
Depreciation		$0	$310	$310	$1,565	$1,565	$1,565	$1,565	$1,565	$2,820	$2,820	$3,850	$3,850
Leased Offices and Equipment		$0	$0	$0	$0	$0	$0	$0	$0	$0	$0	$0	$0
Utilities		$0	$0	$700	$800	$920	$920	$1,050	$1,050	$1,050	$1,050	$1,050	$1,050
Insurance		$0	$0	$1,257	$1,257	$1,257	$1,257	$1,257	$1,257	$1,257	$1,257	$1,257	$1,257
Rent		$0	$0	$1,200	$1,200	$1,200	$1,200	$1,200	$1,200	$2,400	$2,400	$2,400	$2,400
Payroll Taxes	15%	$825	$825	$825	$2,400	$2,715	$2,558	$2,820	$2,925	$4,294	$4,605	$5,730	$5,835
Other General and Administrative Expenses		$0	$0	$0	$0	$0	$0	$0	$0	$0	$0	$0	$0
Total Operating Expenses		$6,325	$6,635	$9,792	$23,222	$25,757	$24,550	$26,692	$27,497	$40,445	$42,832	$52,487	$53,292
Profit Before Interest and Taxes		($6,325)	($6,635)	($9,792)	($2,047)	$2,130	$4,732	$1,125	$390	$10,012	$12,872	$10,234	$9,429
EBITDA		($6,325)	($6,325)	($9,482)	($482)	$3,695	$6,297	$2,690	$1,955	$12,832	$15,692	$14,084	$13,279
Interest Expense		$1,042	$1,018	$1,058	$1,019	$1,019	$1,019	$1,019	$1,019	$1,756	$1,702	$2,282	$2,210
Taxes Incurred		$0	$0	$0	$0	$0	$0	$0	$0	$0	$0	$0	$0
Net Profit		($7,367)	($7,653)	($10,850)	($3,066)	$1,110	$3,712	$106	($630)	$8,256	$11,170	$7,952	$7,219
Net Profit/Sales		0.00%	0.00%	0.00%	-9.47%	2.60%	8.29%	0.25%	-1.48%	10.70%	13.12%	8.34%	7.57%

The Daily Perc
Appendix 1-E

The Daily Perc—Pro Forma Cash Flow

		Jun	Jul	Aug	Sep	Oct	Nov	Dec	Jan	Feb	Mar	Apr	May
Cash Received													
Cash from Operations													
Cash Sales		$0	$0	$0	$32,375	$42,637	$44,769	$42,530	$42,637	$77,144	$85,167	$95,392	$95,392
Subtotal Cash from Operations		$0	$0	$0	$32,375	$42,637	$44,769	$42,530	$42,637	$77,144	$85,167	$95,392	$95,392
Additional Cash Received													
Sales Tax, VAT, HST/GST Received	0.00%	$0	$0	$0	$0	$0	$0	$0	$0	$0	$0	$0	$0
New Current Borrowing		$0	$0	$0	$0	$0	$0	$0	$0	$0	$0	$0	$0
New Other Liabilities (Interest-free)		$0	$0	$0	$0	$0	$0	$0	$0	$0	$0	$0	$0
New Long-term Liabilities		$0	$0	$5,300	$0	$0	$0	$0	$0	$98,184	$0	$77,979	$0
Sales of Other Current Assets		$0	$0	$0	$0	$0	$0	$0	$0	$0	$0	$0	$0
Sales of Long-term Assets		$0	$0	$0	$0	$0	$0	$0	$0	$0	$0	$0	$0
New Investment Received		$0	$0	$0	$0	$0	$0	$0	$0	$0	$0	$0	$0
Subtotal Cash Received		$0	$0	$5,300	$32,375	$42,637	$44,769	$42,530	$42,637	$175,328	$85,167	$173,371	$95,392

	Jun	Jul	Aug	Sep	Oct	Nov	Dec	Jan	Feb	Mar	Apr	May
Expenditures												
Expenditures from Operations												
Cash Spending	$5,500	$5,500	$5,500	$16,000	$18,100	$17,050	$18,800	$19,500	$28,624	$30,700	$38,200	$38,900
Bill Payments	$62	$1,866	$1,950	$5,095	$6,930	$14,585	$23,185	$21,242	$23,186	$50,340	$43,684	$48,049
Subtotal Spent on Operations	$5,562	$7,366	$7,450	$21,095	$25,030	$31,635	$41,985	$40,742	$51,810	$81,040	$81,884	$86,949
Additional Cash Spent												
Sales Tax, VAT, HST/GST Paid Out	$0	$0	$0	$0	$0	$0	$0	$0	$0	$0	$0	$0
Principal Repayment of Current Borrowing	$0	$0	$0	$0	$0	$0	$0	$0	$0	$0	$500	$1,000
Other Liabilities Principal Repayment	$0	$0	$0	$0	$0	$0	$0	$0	$0	$0	$0	$0
Long-term Liabilities Principal Repayment	$2,500	$3,116	$0	$5,166	$0	$0	$0	$0	$0	$7,216	$0	$8,471
Purchase Other Current Assets	$0	$0	$0	$0	$0	$0	$0	$0	$0	$0	$0	$0
Purchase Long-term Assets	$0	$0	$0	$0	$0	$0	$0	$0	$105,400	$0	$86,450	$0
Dividends	$0	$0	$0	$0	$0	$0	$0	$0	$0	$0	$0	$0
Subtotal Cash Spent	$8,062	$10,482	$7,450	$26,261	$25,030	$31,635	$41,985	$40,742	$157,210	$88,256	$168,834	$96,420
Net Cash Flow	($8,062)	($10,482)	($2,150)	$6,114	$17,607	$13,133	$546	$1,895	$18,117	($3,089)	$4,537	($1,028)
Cash Balance	$17,438	$6,956	$4,806	$10,920	$28,527	$41,660	$42,206	$44,101	$62,218	$59,129	$63,666	$62,639

The Daily Perc
Appendix 1-F

The Daily Perc—Pro Forma Balance Sheet

	Starting Balances	Jun	Jul	Aug	Sep	Oct	Nov	Dec	Jan	Feb	Mar	Apr	May
Assets													
Current Assets													
Cash	$25,500	$17,438	$6,956	$4,806	$10,920	$28,527	$41,660	$42,206	$44,101	$62,218	$59,129	$63,666	$62,639
Inventory	$35,000	$35,000	$35,000	$35,000	$23,800	$16,225	$17,036	$16,185	$16,225	$29,356	$32,410	$35,159	$35,159
Other Current Assets	$0	$0	$0	$0	$0	$0	$0	$0	$0	$0	$0	$0	$0
Total Current Assets	$60,500	$52,438	$41,956	$39,806	$34,720	$44,752	$58,697	$58,391	$60,326	$91,575	$91,539	$98,825	$97,798
Long-term Assets													
Long-term Assets	$131,400	$131,400	$131,400	$131,400	$131,400	$131,400	$131,400	$131,400	$131,400	$236,800	$236,800	$323,250	$323,250
Accumulated Depreciation	$0	$0	$310	$620	$2,185	$3,750	$5,315	$6,880	$8,445	$11,265	$14,085	$17,935	$21,785
Total Long-term Assets	$131,400	$131,400	$131,090	$130,780	$129,215	$127,650	$126,085	$124,520	$122,955	$225,535	$222,715	$305,315	$301,465
Total Assets	$191,900	$183,838	$173,046	$170,586	$163,935	$172,402	$184,782	$182,911	$183,281	$317,110	$314,254	$404,140	$399,263
		Jun	**Jul**	**Aug**	**Sep**	**Oct**	**Nov**	**Dec**	**Jan**	**Feb**	**Mar**	**Apr**	**May**
Liabilities and Capital													
Current Liabilities													
Accounts Payable	$0	$1,805	$1,782	$4,872	$6,454	$13,810	$22,478	$20,501	$21,501	$48,889	$42,079	$46,535	$43,909
Current Borrowing	$9,000	$9,000	$9,000	$9,000	$9,000	$9,000	$9,000	$9,000	$9,000	$9,000	$9,000	$8,500	$7,500
Other Current Liabilities	$0	$0	$0	$0	$0	$0	$0	$0	$0	$0	$0	$0	$0
Subtotal Current Liabilities	$9,000	$10,805	$10,782	$13,872	$15,454	$22,810	$31,478	$29,501	$30,501	$57,889	$51,079	$55,035	$51,409
Long-term Liabilities	$131,400	$128,900	$125,784	$131,084	$125,918	$125,918	$125,918	$125,918	$125,918	$224,102	$216,886	$294,865	$286,394
Total Liabilities	$140,400	$139,705	$136,566	$144,956	$141,372	$148,728	$157,396	$155,419	$156,419	$281,991	$267,965	$349,900	$337,803
Paid-in Capital	$225,270	$225,270	$225,270	$225,270	$225,270	$225,270	$225,270	$225,270	$225,270	$225,270	$225,270	$225,270	$225,270
Retained Earnings	($173,770)	($173,770)	($173,770)	($173,770)	($173,770)	($173,770)	($173,770)	($173,770)	($173,770)	($173,770)	($173,770)	($173,770)	($173,770)
Earnings	$0	($7,367)	($15,020)	($25,870)	($28,937)	($27,826)	($24,114)	($24,008)	($24,638)	($16,382)	($5,211)	$2,741	$9,960
Total Capital	$51,500	$44,133	$36,480	$25,630	$22,563	$23,674	$27,386	$27,492	$26,862	$35,118	$46,289	$54,241	$61,460
Total Liabilities and Capital	$191,900	$183,838	$173,046	$170,586	$163,935	$172,402	$184,782	$182,911	$183,281	$317,110	$314,254	$404,140	$399,263
Net Worth	$51,500	$44,133	$36,480	$25,630	$22,563	$23,674	$27,386	$27,492	$26,862	$35,118	$46,289	$54,241	$61,460

BARTHOLOMEW J. FISHER III
123 Money Lane
Seattle, Washington
bjfisheriii@dailyperc.com
(999) 999-9999

PROFILE

An experienced professional with strong interpersonal, managerial, and problem-solving skills. Resourceful, organized, analytical, and versatile.

EDUCATION

STANFORD UNIVERSITY — Master of Business Administration, 1988

Entrepreneurial Management major. Strategic Planning and Marketing concentrations.

UNIVERSITY OF SEATTLE — Bachelor of Science, 1983

Economics major. Marketing minor. Varsity lacrosse player.

PROFESSIONAL EXPERIENCE

WASHINGTON CENTER FOR ENTERPRISE DEVELOPMENT — Seattle, Washington

Director — 2000–Present

Direct this Small Business Development Center program that develops human capital among current and prospective entrepreneurs and enterprise managers for the support and growth of sustainable enterprises and wealth in the state of Washington.

FISHER INDUSTRIES, INC. — Seattle, Washington

General Manager — 1993–2000

Managed the Sales, Marketing, and Operations of this Krispy Kreme Doughnuts franchise.

FISHER, BAKER AND SCHNIDER — Berkeley, California

President — 1988–1993

Operated this advertising and marketing firm, which specialized in the design and implementation of marketing programs. Performed services including strategic and market analyses and advertising campaign creation. Conducted workshops, focus groups, and facilitation services. Wrote articles and press releases for client firms. Marketed FBS services to corporations and organizations.

STARBUCKS CORPORATION Seattle, Washington

Marketing Manager 1983–1986

Trainee in the Marketing Department. Performed strategic and tactical planning, forecasting, budgeting, financial analysis and modeling, and media and publicity planning.

AWARDS, AFFILIATIONS, & ACTIVITIES

Minority Business Advocate of the Year—Washington Office—U.S. Small Business Administration

Social Venture Partners Seattle—Partner

Urban League of Metropolitan Seattle—Economic Development Advisory Council Member

Rotary Club of Seattle—Member and member of scholarship committee

American Marketing Association—Puget Sound Chapter—Board of Directors

Greenpeace—Member

TERESA ANNE FISHER
123 Money Lane
Seattle, Washington
tafisher@dailyperc.com
(999) 888-8888

WORK EXPERIENCE

STARBUCKS CORPORATION

Senior Financial Analyst 1996–Present

- Lead the development of the business unit's annual operating budget and quarterly forecasts.
- Support the development of strategic and operating plans. Identify and communicate plans' risks and opportunities.
- Conduct decision analyses and communicate results. Build and maintain financial models.
- Perform due diligence for new initiatives.
- Build financial models and provide analytical support for business initiatives and contract negotiations. Identify, analyze, and communicate trends and issues affecting the business.
- Provide analysis and feedback on financial performance and key performance measures.
- Provide financial information and guidance to all levels of management. Ensure financial statements are complete, accurate, and timely.

Financial Analyst 1992–1996

- Supported the development of strategic and operating plans.
- Built financial models and provided analytical support for business initiatives and contract negotiations. Identified, analyzed, and communicated trends and issues affecting the business.
- Ensured financial statements were complete, accurate, and timely. Facilitated process development and improvement initiatives.

Store Manager	1990–1992
Assistant Store Manager	1988–1990
Barista	1986–1988

EDUCATION

UNIVERSITY OF SEATTLE BS, Accounting, 1988

ACTIVITIES

Seattle Area Chamber of Commerce—Retail Alliance member
Cascadia Loan Fund—Loan Review Committee
Rotary Club of Seattle—Member and Chair of Finance Committee
Junior League of Seattle—Life member
Northwest Sierra Club—Treasurer
Social Venture Partners Seattle—Partner

The Daily Perc Sample Business Plan

The Daily Perc sample business plan is one of over 500 business plans contained in the *Business Plan Pro*™ CD that accompanies this textbook. Copyright to this plan is owned by Palo Alto Software, Inc. Some explanatory information has been added and the order changed to conform to the format described in this text. For more information on Palo Alto Software's business planning products, go to: www.paloalto.com.

Attractive visual.

Prepared by:

Bartholomew & Teresa Fisher
The Daily Perc, Inc.
P.O. Box 888
Coffee City, WA 99999-0888
777-777-7777

Fisher@TheDailyPerc.com

Nondisclosure.

The information provided in this business plan is confidential; therefore, the reader agrees not to disclose it without express written permission. By accepting this document, the reader acknowledges that information furnished in this business plan is in all respects confidential in nature, other than information that is in the public domain through other means, and that any disclosure or use of same by reader may cause serious harm or damage to The Daily Perc. Upon request, this document is to be immediately returned. This business plan does not imply an offering of securities.

Table of Contents

Well-organized, neatly presented Table of Contents.

Page numbers included.

Appendices

1. Executive Summary

Introduced with a positive opening statement. *Use of innovative equipment to increase efficiency.* *Industry definition.* *The offer: the bundle of products and service to be provided.*

The Daily Perc, Inc. (TDP) is a specialty beverage retailer. TDP uses a system that is new to the beverage and food service industry to provide hot and cold beverages in a convenient and time-efficient way. TDP provides its customers the ability to drive up and order (from a trained barista) their choice of a custom-blended espresso drink, freshly brewed coffee, or other beverage. TDP is offering a high-quality option to the fast-food, gas station, or institutional coffee.

Innovation in product and service delivery. Use of trained staff to ensure product quality. Capacity to produce coffee on a custom basis. *Setting quality by comparison with other suppliers of coffee.* *Quality statement.* *More about offer.*

The Daily Perc offers its patrons the finest hot and cold beverages, specializing in specialty coffees, blended teas, and other custom drinks. In addition, TDP will offer soft drinks, fresh-baked pastries, and other confections. Seasonally, TDP will add beverages such as hot apple cider, hot chocolate, frozen coffees, and more.

Target markets that TDP will serve.

The Daily Perc will focus on two markets:

The Daily Commuter—someone traveling to/from work, out shopping, delivering goods or services, or just out for a drive.

The Captive Consumer—someone who is in a restricted environment that does not allow convenient departure and return while searching for refreshments, or where refreshments stands are an integral part of the environment.

Logic for selecting locations. *Facilities designed for the purpose of TDP. Design contributes to competitive advantage.* *Production and delivery capability.*

The Daily Perc will penetrate the commuter and captive consumer markets by deploying Drive-thru facilities and Mobile Cafés in the most logical and accessible locations. The Drive-thru facilities are designed to handle two-sided traffic and dispense customer-designed, specially ordered cups of premium coffees in less time than required for a visit to the locally owned café or one of the national chains.

The offer: adding philanthropy to the mix.

In addition to providing a quality product and an extensive menu of delicious items, to ensure customer awareness and loyalty, as well as good publicity coverage and media support, we will be donating up to 7.5% of revenue to local charities based upon customer choices.

Staffing as a component of quality. *Employees as a competitive advantage is using operations as an advantage.* *Inventory management plan.* *Critical financial and operational assumptions.*

The Daily Perc's financial picture is quite promising. Since TDP is operating a cash business, the initial cost is significantly less than many start-ups these days. The process is labor intensive and TDP recognizes that a higher level of talent is required. The financial investment in its employees will be one of the greatest differentiators between it and TDP's competition. For the purpose of this pro forma plan, the capital expenditures of facilities and equipment are financed. There will be minimum inventory on hand so as to keep the product fresh and to take advantage of price drops, when and if they should occur.

Definition of financing need.

The Daily Perc anticipates the initial combination of investments and long-term financing of \$515,000 to carry it without the need for any additional equity or debt investment, beyond the purchase of equipment or facilities. This will mean growing a bit more slowly than might be otherwise possible, but it will be a solid, financially sound growth based on customer request and product demand.

Proposing an IPO or private offering to generate cash. *Offering is not only for growth, but also the exit option the managers prefer.* *Growth strategy defined.*

The Daily Perc chooses to become the Drive-thru version of Starbucks between the mountains, obtaining several million dollars through an initial public or private offering that would allow the company to open 20 to 30 facilities per year in all metropolitan communities in the North, Midwest, and South with a population of over 150,000. This is the preferred Exit Strategy of the Management Team. The danger in this is that competitors would rise up and establish a foothold on a community before—or in the midst of—the arrival of The Daily Perc, causing a potential for a drain on revenues and a dramatic increase in advertising expenditures to maintain market share. Knowing these risks—and planning for them—gives TDP the edge needed to make this scenario work.

Showing net worth, cash, and earnings to value the company.

The balance sheet estimates a Net Worth of \$1,724,505 for the third year, cash balances of \$1,097,010, and earnings of \$1,294,371, based on thirteen Drive-thrus and four Mobile Cafés,

Providing current valuation standard. A citation for the source of this information would make it more credible.

it is not unrealistic to put a market value of between $4 million and $9 million on the company. At present, such companies are trading in multiples of 4 to 10 times earnings, and it is simple mathematics to multiply the success of TDP by the number of major and smaller metropolitan areas between the mountain ranges of the United States.

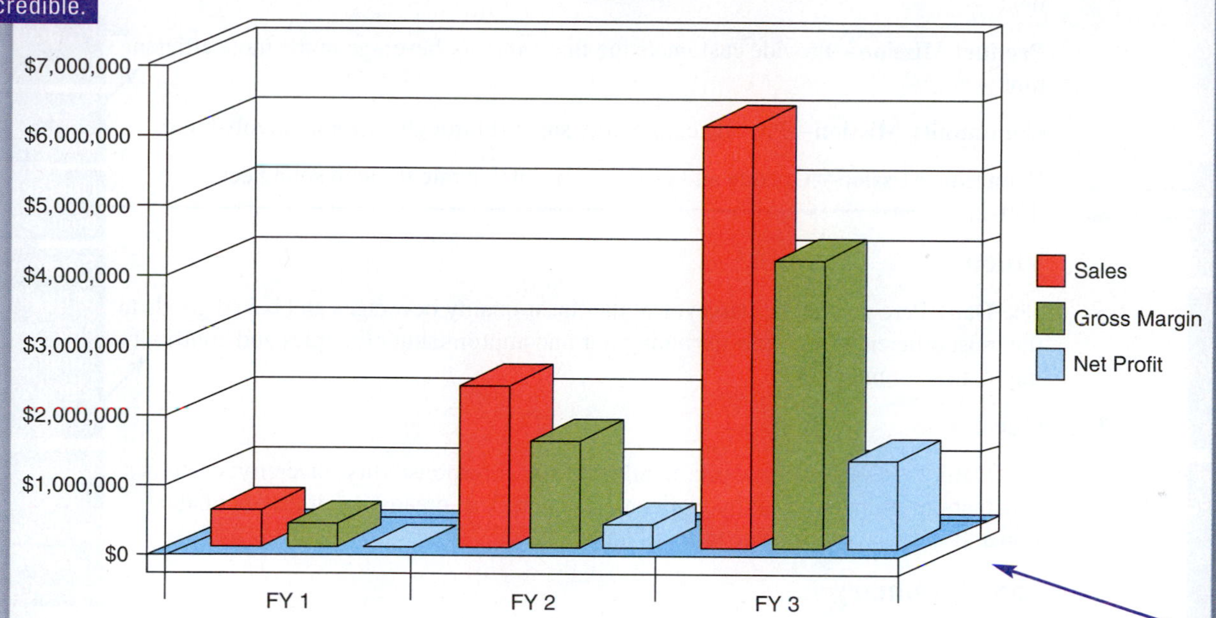

Clear visual representation.

1.1. Objectives

Statement of performance objectives over three years.

The Daily Perc has established three firm objectives it wishes to achieve in the next three years:

1. Thirteen Drive-thru locations and four fully booked Mobile Cafés by the end of the third year.
2. Gross Margin of 45% or more.
3. Net After-tax Profit above 15% of Sales.

1.2. Keys to Success

Physical location as a key to achieving objectives. Three factors identified. Need to attach clear measures.

Competitive advantage.

There are four keys to success in this business, three of which are virtually the same as any food service business. It is our fourth key—the Community Mission—that will give us that extra measure of respect in the public eye.

Location and delivery advantage.

Quality advantage.

Service advantage.

1. The greatest locations—visibility, high traffic pattern, convenient access.
2. The best products—freshest coffee beans, cleanest equipment, premium serving containers, consistent flavor.
3. The friendliest servers—cheerful, skilled, professional, articulate.
4. The finest reputation—word-of-mouth advertising, promotion of our community mission of charitable giving.

Product quality, as defined along four dimensions, to assist in achieving objectives. Need to attach clear measures.

Employees as a critical factor in achieving objectives. The four factors need clear measures.

Customer perception as defined by two measures. Clear measures needed.

BUSINESS PLAN

2. Mission, Vision, and Culture

The mission, vision, and culture of The Daily Perc are aligned for success. This is an organization that understands doing well by doing good and is designed to be profitable and an asset to the communities it serves.

2.1. Mission

The Daily Perc Mission is threefold, with each being as integral to our success as the next.

Product Mission—Provide customers the finest-quality beverage in the most efficient time.

Community Mission—Provide community support through customer involvement.

Economic Mission—Operate and grow at a profitable rate through sound economic decisions.

Product quality.

Service quality.

Operational goal.

Focus on growth.

Clear, concise, compelling.

2.2. Vision

The Daily Perc will be the purveyor of the finest-quality beverages and baked goods in the most efficient time while sustaining our uncompromising principles and contributing to our communities.

TDP vision is future-oriented, compelling, built upon core values, and energizes employees.

Summary of quality and operational goals along with ethics.

2.3. Culture

The Daily Perc values teamwork; family and social responsibility; diversity; customer satisfaction; and a fun, healthy work environment. This creates a culture of collaboration and of high performance in small units.

Orientation toward people.

Concern about the customer.

Concerns about people.

Focus on teams and outcomes.

TDP culture conveys core values.

Culture defined and underlying factors identified.

3. Company Summary

The Daily Perc is a specialty beverage retailer. TDP uses a system that is new to the beverage and food service industry to provide hot and cold beverages in a convenient and time-efficient way. TDP provides its customers the ability to drive up and order from a trained barista their choice of a custom blended espresso drink, freshly brewed coffee, or other beverage. TDP is offering a high-quality option to the fast-food, gas station, and institutional coffee.

Concise restatement of the Business Definition from the Executive Summary.

3.1. Company Ownership

The Daily Perc is a Limited Liability Corporation. All membership shares are currently owned by Bart and Teresa Fisher, with the intent of using a portion of the shares to raise capital.

Tells the reader the type of organization and ownership.

Legal structure defined.

Owners and their ownership intentions.

The plan calls for the sale of 100 membership units in the company to family members, friends, and Angel Investors. Each membership unit in the company is priced at $4,250, with a minimum of five units per membership certificate, or a minimum investment of $21,250 per investor.

Funding proposal that will need to be reflected in financials.

If all funds are raised, based on the pricing established in the financial section of this plan, Bart and Terri Fisher will maintain ownership of no less than 51% of the company.

Statement shows that owners intend to keep majority interest.

3.2. Start-Up Summary

The Daily Perc's start-up expenses total just $365,670. The majority of these funds—roughly $300,000—will be used to build the first facility, pay deposits, and provide capital for six months of operating expenses. Another $35,000 will be used for the initial inventory and other one-time expenses. The Daily Perc anticipates the need for roughly $25,500 in operating capital for the first few months of operation.

Uses of start-up funds summarized.

Table gives a more detailed perspective on the start-up costs by category. Specific detail can be provided in the appendices.

4. Market Analysis Summary

The Daily Perc—Start-Up

Requirements	
Start-Up Expenses	
Legal	$3,500
Office Equipment	$4,950
Drive-thru Labor (6 months)	$65,000
Drive-thru Finance Payment (6 months)	$12,300
Drive-thru Expenses (6 months)	$8,520
Land Lease (6 months)	$7,200
Vehicle Finance (6 months)	$3,700
Administration Labor (6 months)	$54,000
Web site Development & Hosting	$5,600
Identity/Logos/Stationary	$4,000
Other	$5,000
Total Start-Up Expenses	$173,770
Start-up Assets	
Cash Required	$25,500
Start-Up Inventory	$35,000
Other Current Assets	$0
Long-term Assets	$131,400
Total Assets	$191,900
Total Requirements	**$365,670**

Income statement items.

Balance sheet items.

Total amount of funding needed is clearly stated.

Start-Up

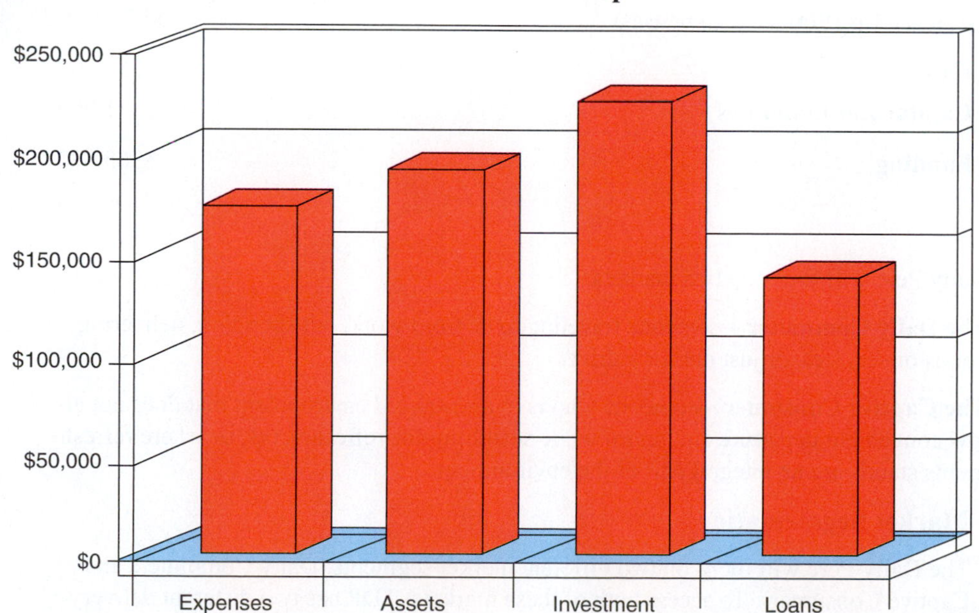

The Daily Perc Business Plan provided by Business Plan Pro® and used by permission of Palo Alto Software.

BUSINESS PLAN

The Daily Perc—Start-Up Funding

Start-Up Expenses to Fund	$173,770
Start-Up Assets to Fund	$191,900
Total Funding Required	**$365,670**
Assets	
Non-cash Assets from Start-Up	$166,400
Cash Requirements from Start-Up	$25,500
Additional Cash Raised	$0
Cash Balance on Starting Date	$25,500
Total Assets	**$191,900**
Liabilities and Capital	
Liabilities	
Current Borrowing	$9,000
Long-term Liabilities	$131,400
Accounts Payable (Outstanding Bills)	$0
Other Current Liabilities (Interest-free)	$0
Total Liabilities	**$140,400**
Capital	
Planned Investment	
Partner 1	$21,250
Partner 2	$21,250
Partner 3	$42,500
Partner 4	$25,500
Partner 5	$29,750
Other	$85,020
Additional Investment Requirement	$0
Total Planned Investment	**$225,270**
Loss at Start-Up (Start-Up Expenses)	($173,770)
Total Capital	$51,500
Total Capital and Liabilities	$191,900
Total Funding	$365,670

Carried over from previous table.

Inventory and long-term assets are included.

Debt for long-term assets.

Investors that purchase membership units priced at $4,250 in at least five-unit blocks.

This category should be explained.

Start-up loss is set to equal start-up expenses.

This total matches the total start-up requirements.

The Daily Perc will focus on two markets:

Target market # 1.

1. **The Daily Commuter**—someone traveling to or from work, out shopping, delivering goods or services, or just out for a drive.

Target market # 2.

2. **The Captive Consumer**—someone who is in a restricted environment that does not allow convenient departure and return while searching for refreshments, or where refreshments stands are an integral part of the environment.

4.1. Market Segmentation

Distinctive differentiation in approach to the segments.

The Daily Perc will focus on two different market segments: Daily Commuters and Captive Consumers. To access both of these markets, TDP has two different delivery systems. For the commuters, TDP has the Drive-thru coffeehouse. For the captive consumer, TDP has the Mobile Café.

Commuters are defined as any one or more individuals in a motorized vehicle traveling from point "A" to point "B." The Daily Perc's greatest concentration will be on commuters heading to or from work, or those out on their lunch break.

Definition of target market #1—no limit of distance or time stated.

Captive Consumers would include those who are tethered to a campus environment, or in a restricted entry environment that does not allow free movement to and from. Examples would include high school and college campuses, where there is limited time between classes, and corporate campuses where the same time constraints are involved, but regarding meetings and project deadlines, and special events—such as carnivals, fairs, or festivals—where there is an admission price to enter the gate, but exiting would mean another admission fee, or where refreshments are an integral part of the festivities.

Definition of target market #2—easily understood.

Good examples to clarify the definition.

The following chart and table reflect the potential numbers of venues available for the Mobile Cafés and what growth could be expected in those markets over the next five years. For a conservative estimate of the number of Captive Consumers this represents—multiply the total number of venues in the year by 1,000. As an example, in the first year, The Daily Perc is showing that there are a total of 2,582 venues at which we might position a Mobile Café. That would equate to a Captive Consumer potential of 2,582,000.

Explanation of a key assumption for volume.

Total market size clearly stated.

Similarly, there are well over 2,500,000 commuters in the metropolitan area, as well as visitors, vacationers, and others. It can also be assumed that these commuters do not make only one purchase in a day, but in many cases, two and even three beverage purchases.

Identification of another target.

Frequency of purchase estimate—critical for sales projections.

The chart reflects college and high school campuses, special events, hospital campuses, and various charitable organizations. A segment that is not reflected in the chart (since it would skew the chart so greatly) is the number of corporate campuses in the metropolitan area. There are over 1,700 corporate facilities that house more than 500 employees, giving us an additional 1,700,000 prospective customers, or total of 2,582 locations at which we could place a Mobile Café.

Explanation of another market opportunity and why it is not included in the chart.

Market Analysis

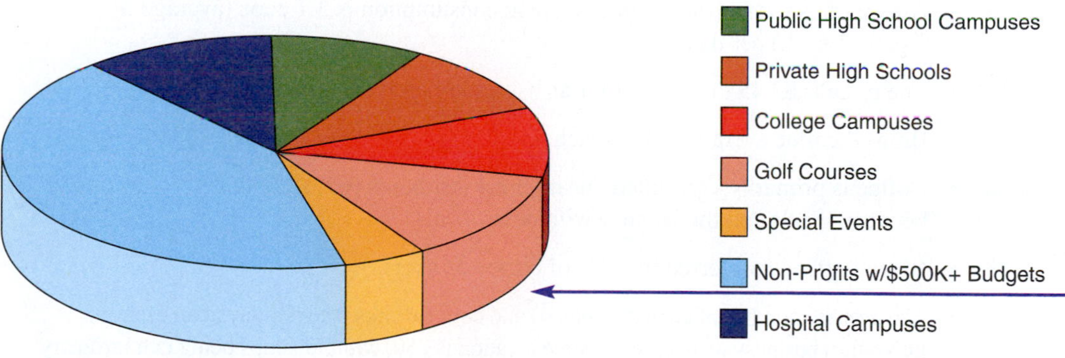

Visual representation of data. Helps to summarize and clarify potential locations.

Market Analysis

Visual representation of data. Helps to summarize and determine projected growth for potential locations.

Potential Customers	Growth	YR1	YR2	YR3	YR4	YR5	CAGR
Public High School Campuses	1%	80	81	82	83	84	1.23%
Private High Schools	0%	88	88	88	88	88	0.00%
College Campuses	0%	77	77	77	77	77	0.00%
Golf Courses	0%	99	99	99	99	99	0.00%
Special Events	3%	43	44	45	46	47	2.25%
Non-Profits w/$500K+ Budgets	2%	362	369	376	384	392	2.01%
Hospital Campuses	0%	100	100	100	100	100	0.00%
Total	1.10%	849	858	867	877	887	1.10%

Clear definition of TDP's target market by lifestyle.

Place defined. Location strategy explained.

Promotion strategy defined.

Promotion with social benefits.

4.2. Target Market Segment Strategy

TDP's target market is the mobile individual who has more money than time, and excellent taste in a choice of beverage, but no time to linger in a café. By locating the Drive-thrus in high traffic/high visibility areas, this unique—and abundant—consumer will seek The Daily Perc out and become a regular guest.

To penetrate the target market for the Mobile Cafés, these units will do what they were designed to do. The Daily Perc will take the café to the customer! By using the community support program TDP is instituting, arrangements will be made to visit a high school, college campus, or a corporate campus once or twice a month (even visit these facilities for special games, tournaments, recruiting events, or corporate open houses). And, for every cup or baked good sold, a portion is returned to the high school or college. It becomes a tremendous, painless way for the institution to gain a financial reward while providing a pleasant and fulfilling benefit to their students or employees.

Analysis of the overall industry, in this instance, the coffee industry, provides the broader context.

Industry growth.

4.3. Industry Analysis

The coffee industry has grown by tremendous amounts in the United States over the past five years. According to e-imports.com, "Specialty coffee sales are increasing by 20% per year and account for nearly 8% of the 18 billion dollar U.S. coffee market." Starbucks, the national leader, had revenues in fiscal 2000 of $2.2 billion. That is an increase of 32% over fiscal 1999. Starbucks plans to increase revenues to over $6.6 billion from 10,000 retail outlets by 2005.

Frequency of purchase data.

Volume per purchase.

Average price per purchase by product.

Timing of consumption.

Product preference measure.

Volume of sales by a particular business type.

Data that can be used in TDP sales and financial projections.

Even general coffee sales have increased, with international brands such as Folgers, Maxwell House, and Safari coffee reporting higher sales and greater profits. According to data gathered by the Specialty Coffee Association of America (SCAA), "Nearly 52% of Americans over 18 years of age drink coffee every day. They represent over 100 million daily drinkers. 30 million American adults drink specialty coffee beverages daily." Other interesting statistics are available from e-imports.com on coffee consumption:

- Among those who drink coffee, average consumption is 3.1 cups (average of 9 ounces each) per day.
- The price is $2.45 on average for an espresso-based drink.
- Brewed coffee averages $1.38 each.
- Coffee is primarily consumed during breakfast hours (65%), with 35% consumed between meals and the balance with other meals.
- Black coffee is preferred by 35% of coffee drinkers.
- The average number of cups of espresso and coffee drinks sold per day at an espresso Drive-thru business with a great visible location is 250, with 500 cups being extraordinary.
- 69% of the coffee sold by independent coffee shops is brewed coffee and 31% is espresso-based.

America is definitely a coffee country and the coffee industry is reaping the rewards.

Unique Selling Proposition.

4.3.1 Competition and Buying Patterns

There are four general competitors in The Daily Perc's Drive-thru market. They are the national specialty beverage chains, such as Starbucks and Panera, local coffeehouses—or cafés—with an established clientele and a quality product, fast-food restaurants, and convenience stores. There is a dramatic distinction among the patrons of each of these outlets.

Market positioning determined through the totality of experience. Quality factors described in subsequent sentences.

Patrons to a Starbucks, or to one of the local cafés, are looking for the "experience" of the coffeehouse. They want the ability to "design" their coffee, smell the fresh pastry, listen to the soothing Italian music, and read the local paper or visit with an acquaintance. It is a relaxing, slow-paced environment.

Emphasis on the difference in what defines a quality experience for a different customer segment.

Patrons of the fast-food restaurants or the convenience stores are just the opposite. They have no time for idle chatter and are willing to overpay for whatever beverage the machine can spit out, as long as it's quick. They pay for their gas and they are back on the road to work. Although they have the desire and good taste to know good from bad, time is more valuable to them.

Unique Selling Proposition for these patrons is speedy service, and concern for quality is not significant.

Important factors are speed of delivery and convenience.

Competitors to the Mobile Cafés on campuses would include fast-food restaurants—assuming they are close enough to the consumer that they can get there and back in the minimal allotted time—vending machines, and company or school cafeterias. The consumers in this environment are looking for quick, convenient, fairly priced, quality refreshment that will allow them to purchase the product and return to work, class, or other activity.

Excellent example of defining competitors. Important factors are speed of delivery, convenience, fair pricing, and quality of products.

Limited competition based upon geography. Less of a clear distinction.

Competitors to the Mobile Cafés at events such as festivals and fairs would include all the other vendors who are licensed to sell refreshments. Attendees to such events expect to pay a premium price for a quality product.

5. Strategy and Implementation Summary

Product quality as a positioning strategy. Some definition noted. Could enhance the description by identifying particular suppliers of high-end products. This is explained at the end of the section by the need to customize the product selection by location.

The Daily Perc will penetrate the commuter and captive consumer markets by deploying Drive-thru facilities and Mobile Cafés in the most logical and accessible locations. The Drive-thrus are designed to handle two-sided traffic and dispense customer-designed, specially ordered cups of specialty beverages in less time than required for a visit to the locally owned café or one of the national chains.

Place defined.

Product defined.

The Daily Perc has identified its market as busy, mobile people whose time is already at a premium, but desire a refreshing, high-quality beverage or baked item while commuting to or from work or school.

In addition to providing a quality product and an extensive menu of delicious items, to ensure customer awareness and loyalty, as well as positive public and media support, The Daily Perc could be donating up to 7.5% of revenue from each cup sold in individual Drive-thrus to the charities of the customers' choice.

Philanthropy defined for TDP.

5.1. Products

The Daily Perc provides its patrons the finest hot and cold beverages, specializing in specialty coffees and custom blended teas. In addition, TDP will offer select domestic soft drinks, Italian sodas, fresh-baked pastries, and other confections. Seasonally, TDP will add beverages such as hot apple cider, hot chocolate, frozen coffees, and more. The beverages come with a social mission, as up to 7.5% of revenues go to local charities selected by the customers. The precise list of products will be specific to the Drive-thru location selected.

5.2. Competitive Edge

Clear description of the competitive edge.

The Daily Perc's competitive edge is simple. TDP provides a high-quality product at a competitive price in a Drive-thru environment that saves time.

Competitive advantage based upon quality, value, and timeliness.

5.3. Marketing Strategy

First and foremost, The Daily Perc will be placing its Drive-thru facilities in locations of very high visibility and great ease of access. They will be located on high traffic commuter routes and close to shopping facilities in order to catch customers going to or from work, or while they are out for lunch, or on a shopping expedition. The Drive-thrus are very unique and eye-catching, which will be a branding feature of its own.

Description of the selection of locations and their design. Relationship between the location and the market.

Advertising plan limited to potential drive-time radio. This section could be expanded to include more information about the advertisements and the placement and costs.

The Daily Perc will be implementing a low-cost advertising/promotion campaign, which could involve drive-time radio, but not much more.

The Daily Perc Business Plan provided by Business Plan Pro® and used by permission of Palo Alto Software.

BUSINESS PLAN

Public relations strategy of providing community support.

Viral marketing as a marketing strategy.

The Daily Perc will rely on building relationships with schools, charities, and corporations to provide significant free publicity because of its community support program. By giving charitable contributions to these institutions, they will get the word out to their students/faculty/employees/partners about TDP. Word of mouth (or viral marketing) has always proven to be the greatest advertising program a company can instill. In addition, the media will be more than willing to promote the charitable aspects of TDP and provide the opportunity for more exposure every time TDP writes a check to another organization.

5.4. Sales Strategy

Using price reductions to generate sales.

Using design of the facilities to enhance sales.

Sales techniques with the baristas to encourage add-on sales.

There will be several sales strategies put into place, including posting specials on high-profit items at the Drive-thru window. The baristas will also hand out free drink coupons to those who have purchased a certain number of cups or something similar. TDP will also develop window sales techniques such as the baristas asking if the customer would like a fresh-baked item with their coffee.

5.4.1. Sales Forecast

Detailed sales projections translate concepts into product sales.

Using technology to support the business.

In the first year, The Daily Perc anticipates having two Drive-thru locations in operation. The first location will open in the third month of this plan and be fully operational beginning on the 1st day of September. The second Drive-thru will open six months later. TDP is building in a certain amount of ramp-up for each facility while commuters become familiar with its presence. The Drive-thrus will generate 288,000 tickets in the first year of operation, or approximately $558,000 in revenue. A detailed sales forecast for the first year appears in Appendix 1-A.

In the second year, The Daily Perc will add two more Drive-thrus and, in the third year, TDP will add an additional nine Drive-thru facilities. The addition of these facilities will increase the revenue from Drive-thrus to a total of over 1,000,000 tickets or $2.35 million in the second year and 2,675,000 tickets or just over $6 million in the third.

In addition to the Drive-thrus, The Daily Perc will deploy one mobile unit in the fourth quarter of the first fiscal year. TDP expects this mobile unit to generate 10,000 tickets each, at an average ticket price of $2.45, which will generate gross revenues of approximately $24,500.

In the second quarter of the second fiscal year, The Daily Perc will deploy a second and third mobile unit. TDP expects all three mobile units to generate

Visual representation of considerable data.

The Daily Perc—Sales Monthly

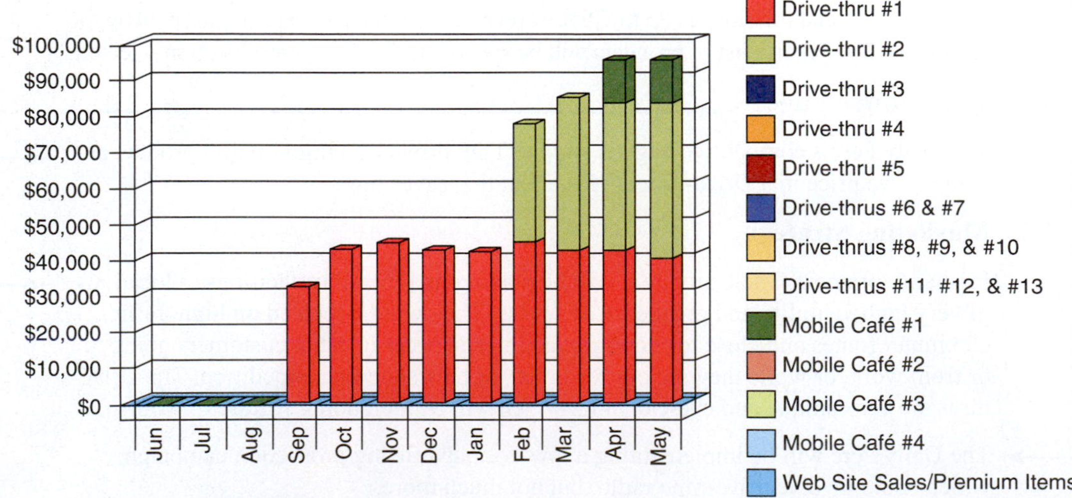

The Daily Perc Business Plan provided by Business Plan Pro® and used by permission of Palo Alto Software.

150,000 tickets, or gross revenue of $375,00 in the second year. In the third fiscal year, with an additional fourth mobile unit deployed, TDP expects to see 264,000 mobile unit tickets, or $673,200 in gross revenue.

The Daily Perc is also showing revenue from the commerce portion of our Web site, where it will sell "The Daily Perc" T-shirts, sweatshirts, insulated coffee mugs, pre-packaged coffee beans, and other premium items. TDP is not expecting this to be a significant profit center, but it is an integral part of the marketing plan—as a function of developing our brand and building product awareness. TDP expects revenues from this portion, to begin in the second fiscal year, to reach $26,000 initially, and $36,000 in the third fiscal year.

Place includes a Web site location.

Products to be sold on the site.

Total first year unit sales should reach 298,402, equating to revenues of $558,043. The second year will see unit sales increase to 1,177,400, or $2,348,900. The third year, with the addition of such a significant number of outlets, we will see unit sales increase to 2,992,000, equating to gross sales revenue of $6,022,950.

The Daily Perc—Sales Forecast

Detailed visual representation of the expected sales.

	FY 1	FY 2	FY 3
Unit Sales			
Drive-thru #1	202,913	300,000	325,000
Drive-thru #2	85,489	300,000	325,000
Drive-thru #3	0	275,000	325,000
Drive-thru #4	0	150,000	325,000
Drive-thru #5	0	0	300,000
Drive-thrus #6 & #7	0	0	450,000
Drive-thrus #8, #9, & #10	0	0	450,000
Drive-thrus #11, #12, & #13	0	0	225,000
Mobile Café #1	10,000	60,000	66,000
Mobile Café #2	0	45,000	66,000
Mobile Café #3	0	45,000	66,000
Mobile Café #4	0	0	66,000
Web Site Sales/Premium Items	0	2,400	3,000
Total Unit Sales	298,402	1,177,400	2,992,000

	FY 1	FY 2	FY 3
Unit Prices			
Drive-thru #1	$1.85	$1.90	$1.95
Drive-thru #2	$1.85	$1.90	$1.95
Drive-thru #3	$0.00	$1.90	$1.95
Drive-thru #4	$0.00	$1.90	$1.95
Drive-thru #5	$0.00	$1.90	$1.95
Drive-thrus #6 & #7	$0.00	$1.90	$1.95
Drive-thrus #8, #9, & #10	$0.00	$1.90	$1.95
Drive-thrus #11, #12, & #13	$0.00	$1.90	$1.95
Mobile Café #1	$2.45	$2.50	$2.55
Mobile Café #2	$0.00	$2.50	$2.55
Mobile Café #3	$0.00	$2.50	$2.55
Mobile Café #4	$0.00	$2.50	$2.55
Web Site Sales/Premium Items	$0.00	$11.00	$12.00

Note: The Daily Perc does not include a calculation of the economics of one unit. For TDP, one unit is likely to be a cup of coffee. With an average price of $2.00 per cup (calculated value from all varieties and cup sizes) and per unit Cost of Goods Sold of $0.70, the Gross Profit Margin is $1.30 per unit.

(continued)

The Daily Perc—Sales Forecast—continued

	FY 1	FY 2	FY 3
Sales			
Drive-thru #1	$375,389	$570,000	$633,750
Drive-thru #2	$158,154	$570,000	$633,750
Drive-thru #3	$0	$522,500	$633,750
Drive-thru #4	$0	$285,000	$633,750
Drive-thru #5	$0	$0	$585,000
Drive-thrus #6 & #7	$0	$0	$877,500
Drive-thrus #8, #9, & #10	$0	$0	$877,500
Drive-thrus #11, #12, & #13	$0	$0	$438,750
Mobile Café #1	$24,500	$150,000	$168,300
Mobile Café #2	$0	$112,500	$168,300
Mobile Café #3	$0	$112,500	$168,300
Mobile Café #4	$0	$0	$168,300
Web Site Sales/Premium Items	$0	$26,400	$36,000
Total Sales	$558,043	$2,348,900	$6,022,950

	FY 1	FY 2	FY 3
Direct Unit Costs			
Drive-thru #1	$0.64	$0.61	$0.59
Drive-thru #2	$0.64	$0.61	$0.59
Drive-thru #3	$0.00	$0.61	$0.59
Drive-thru #4	$0.00	$0.61	$0.59
Drive-thru #5	$0.00	$0.61	$0.59
Drive-thrus #6 & #7	$0.00	$0.61	$0.59
Drive-thrus #8, #9, & #10	$0.00	$0.61	$0.59
Drive-thrus #11, #12, & #13	$0.00	$0.61	$0.59
Mobile Café #1	$0.64	$0.61	$0.59
Mobile Café #2	$0.00	$0.61	$0.59
Mobile Café #3	$0.00	$0.61	$0.59
Mobile Café #4	$0.00	$0.61	$0.59
Web Site Sales/Premium Items	$0.00	$6.50	$6.50
Direct Cost of Sales			
Drive-thru #1	$129,864	$183,000	$191,750
Drive-thru #2	$54,713	$183,000	$191,750
Drive-thru #3	$0	$167,750	$191,750
Drive-thru #4	$0	$91,500	$191,750
Drive-thru #5	$0	$0	$177,000
Drive-thrus #6 & #7	$0	$0	$265,500
Drive-thrus #8, #9, & #10	$0	$0	$265,500
Drive-thrus #11, #12, & #13	$0	$0	$132,750
Mobile Café #1	$6,400	$36,600	$38,940
Mobile Café #2	$0	$27,450	$38,940
Mobile Café #3	$0	$27,450	$38,940
Mobile Café #4	$0	$0	$38,940
Web Site Sales/Premium Items	$0	$15,600	$19,500
Subtotal Direct Cost of Sales	**$190,977**	**$732,350**	**$1,783,010**

The Daily Perc Business Plan provided by Business Plan Pro® and used by permission of Palo Alto Software.

6. Management and Operations Summary

Management designed to create a culture of equality.

Presumption that decisions will be simplified and profitability enhanced.

The Daily Perc is a relatively flat organization. Overhead for management will be kept to a minimum and all senior managers will be "hands-on" workers. There is no intention of having a top-heavy organization that drains profits and complicates decisions.

Role of founders matched to the culture.

Background of founders identified. Pertinent details noted and readers referred to the appendices for resumes.

Division of responsibilities.

Owners Bart and Teresa Fisher will be actively involved in the management and operations of the sites. The founders of TDP bring a strong management and technical foundation to TDP. Terri Fisher has approximately 15 years of progressive experience at Starbucks Coffee Company, starting out as a barista and moving through the ranks to senior financial management (see Appendix 1-G for her resume). Bart Fisher brings talents and experience in retail sales and marketing, having owned and operated an advertising agency and several Krispy Kreme franchises (see Appendix 1-G for his resume). They will initially divide the overall management responsibilities, with Terri emphasizing accounting and finance and Bart leading marketing and sales. They also will be part of the staff at the Drive-thru sites.

Identification of executive positions.

Identification of mid-management roles and ratio of district managers to Drive-thrus.

At the zenith of this three-year plan, there will be four "Executive" positions: chief operating officer, chief financial officer, chief information officer, and director of marketing. There will be other mid-management positions, such as district managers for every four Drive-thrus, and a facilities manager to oversee the maintenance and stocking of the Mobile Cafés, as well as overseeing the maintenance and replacement of equipment in the Drive-thru facilities.

6.1. Personnel Plan

First-year plan, scaled to the startup with details included in the appendices.

The Daily Perc expects the first year to be rather lean, since there will only be two locations and one mobile unit—none of which will be deployed for the entire year. The total headcount for the first year, including management, administrative support, and customer service (production), will be 15, with a total payroll of $242,374, a payroll burden of $36,356, and a total expenditure of $278,730. The detailed first year personnel plan is in Appendix 1-B.

Plan for growth in the second year with specific positions, including initial mid-management, and payroll information.

The second year, with the addition of two Drive-thrus and two mobile units, The Daily Perc will add customer service personnel, as well as a district manager and some additional support staff at headquarters, including an inventory clerk, equipment technician, and administrative support.

The headcount will increase by nearly 100% in the second year to 29, with a payroll of $846,050 and a payroll burden of $126,908.

Creation of senior management team and significant growth in year 3.

The third year will see the most dramatic growth in headcount, due to the addition of nine Drive-thrus and another mobile unit. In the third year, there will also be an increase of 180% over the previous year. Total payroll for the third year will be $2,024,250, with a payroll burden of $303,638. There will be a significant increase in the senior management team, with the addition of a chief financial officer, a chief information officer, and a director of marketing. There will also be a second and third district manager, and a corporate events sales executive. Total personnel will reach 81.

Descriptions of the roles of the senior managers. Proposed position descriptions could be included in the appendices.

The chief financial officer will be brought on to oversee the increase in numbers of retail outlets and to manage a dramatically more detailed P&L statement and to manage the Balance Sheet. The chief information officer will be brought in to help us with the deployment of a point-of-sale computerized cash register system that will make tracking and managing receipts and charitable contributions more robust. Ideally, this individual will have a large amount of point-of-sale and Internet experience. Specifically, how to tie in POS systems to the Internet and inventory controls. Also, knowledge in establishing technology guidelines for the company and franchisees in the future. This individual will also be added in fiscal year three.

The director of marketing will be charged with managing the relationships with advertising agencies, public relations firms, the media, and our Web site.

Provides financial details and a schedule of positions.

The Daily Perc—Personnel Plan

	FY 1	FY 2	FY 3
Drive-thru Team	$135,474	$439,250	$1,098,650
Mobile Café Team	$9,400	$172,800	$225,600
Equipment Care Specialist (Headquarters)	$0	$22,000	$77,000
Other	$0	$12,000	$24,000
District Manager (Four Drive-thrus)	$0	$22,000	$77,000
Corporate Events Sales Exec	$0	$0	$36,000
Director of Marketing	$0	$0	$72,000
Other	$0	$0	$0
Bookkeeper/Office Administrator	$24,500	$46,000	$54,000
Warehouse/Site Manager	$7,000	$42,000	$48,000
Inventory Clerk	$0	$12,000	$42,000
Other	$0	$6,000	$12,000
Chief Operating Officer	$66,000	$72,000	$78,000
Chief Financial Officer	$0	$0	$96,000
Chief Information Officer	$0	$0	$84,000
Other	$0	$0	$0
Total People	15	29	81
Total Payroll	**$242,374**	**$846,050**	**$2,024,250**

Physical locations/facilities as a competitive advantage.

Factors that determine location.

Using design to support market positioning.

Number of prospective sites is significant, making TDP more attractive to investors.

6.2. Physical Locations/Facilities

One of the most exciting aspects of The Daily Perc is the flexibility in selecting locations. The Drive-thrus are relatively small and the Mobile Cafés are just that. Site selection is based upon population demographics and traffic patterns. With a focus on the Daily Commuter and the Captive Customers, locations are well-defined. Drive-thru espresso shops will be opened in metropolitan communities with a population greater than 150,000. These facilities will be located on accessible sites with high visibility, on high-traffic commuter routes and close to shopping facilities. Each Drive-thru will be double-sided and attractively decorated. According to the previously compiled market segmentation information, TDP has calculated 2,582 venues where Mobile Cafés might be positioned.

Using technology and inventory management for product quality.

Speed and consistent flavor are quality factors affected by the new equipment.

Using trained, more highly skilled labor improves quality.

Combination of factors yields a competitive advantage.

Using economic order quantity (EOQ).

6.3. Inventory, Production, and Quality Assurance

The Daily Perc uses innovative coffee brewing technology and tight inventory controls with excellence in quality assurance. TDP has adopted a new type of coffee equipment that produces espresso drinks very rapidly with consistently excellent flavor. By having trained baristas personally take customer orders and produce hot and cold beverages, quality is increased and production errors are decreased. Because of this delivery system, customers can buy high-quality, freshly prepared beverages in less time than is required for a visit to a locally owned café or chain.

Because of the technology used and the delivery system, inventory can be controlled through economic order quantities with a computer-based reorder system. The product line is sufficiently broad to satisfy customer requests, but sufficiently narrow as to

The Daily Perc Business Plan provided by Business Plan Pro® and used by permission of Palo Alto Software.

Should reduce lead times, increase product freshness, and permit lower inventory levels.

yield relatively straightforward inventory control. Coffees and teas served are all Fair Trade goods and the coffee beans are roasted locally. Bart Fisher manages the quality assurance with respect to the roasted beans. Each manager has a quality assurance manual and a test system for beverage production. Terri Fisher manages the quality assurance process for baked goods.

Product line considers customer satisfaction and inventory control.

Specific, written quality criteria and testing methodologies used to ensure customer expectations are met or exceeded.

7. Financial Plan

The Daily Perc's financial picture is quite promising. Since TDP is operating a cash business, the initial cost is significantly less than many start-ups these days. The process is labor intensive and TDP recognizes that a higher level of talent is required. The financial investment in its employees will be one of the greatest differentiators between it and TDP's competition. For the purpose of this pro forma plan, the facilities and equipment are financed. These items are capital expenditures and will be available for financing. There will be a minimum of inventory on hand so as to keep the product fresh and to take advantage of price drops, when and if they should occur.

The Daily Perc anticipates the initial combination of investments and long-term financing of $515,000 to carry it without the need for any additional equity or debt investment, beyond the purchase of equipment or facilities. This will mean growing a bit more slowly than might be otherwise possible, but it will be a solid, financially sound growth based on customer request and product demand.

Best to articulate more detailed financial assumptions in an appendix.

7.1. Important Assumptions

The financial plan depends on important assumptions, most of which are shown in the following table. The key underlying assumptions are:

- The Daily Perc assumes a slow-growth economy, without major recession.
- The Daily Perc assumes, of course, that there are no unforeseen changes in public health perceptions of its general products.
- The Daily Perc assumes access to equity capital and financing sufficient to maintain its financial plan as shown in the tables.
- Assumptions for the first year appear in Appendix 1-C.

Showing fundamental financial assumptions in a table.

The Daily Perc—General Assumptions

	FY 1	FY 2	FY 3
Plan Month	1	2	3
Current Interest Rate	10.00%	10.00%	10.00%
Long-term Interest Rate	9.00%	9.00%	9.00%
Tax Rate	0.00%	0.00%	0.00%
Other	0	0	0

Tax rate of 0% assumed because TDP is an LLC and taxes fall to the members.

Break-even equals the fixed cost of operations divided by the difference between the average price per unit and the average cost per unit.

7.2. Break-even Analysis

To arrive at the average monthly fixed costs, The Daily Perc calculated the fixed costs for the Drive-thru to be $28,294. Using the average price per unit, less the average cost per unit, divided into the fixed costs of operation, TDP concludes that we will need at least 23,001 units per month to reach break-even at $43,016 per month.

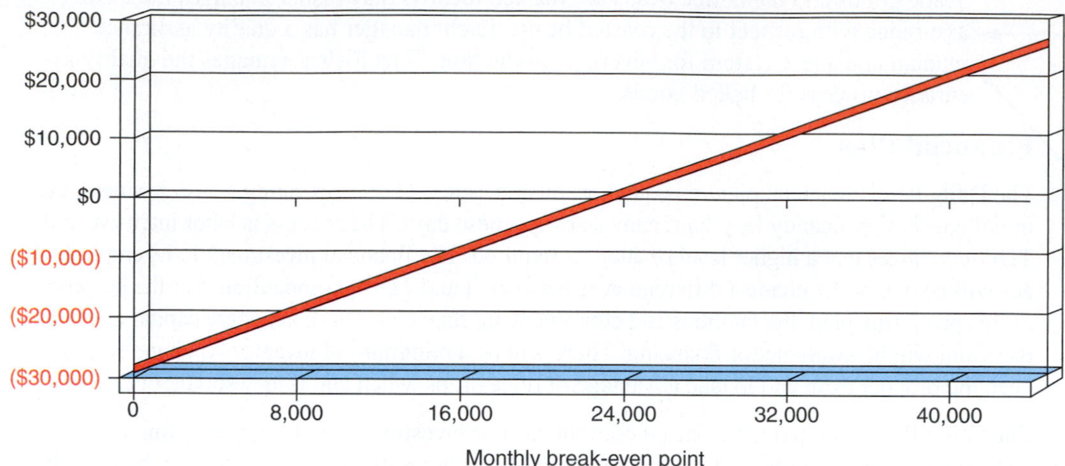

Simple chart that shows break-even information.

The Daily Perc—Break-even Analysis

Monthly Units Break-even	23,001
Monthly Revenue Break-even	$43,014
Assumptions:	
Average Per-Unit Revenue	$1.87
Average Per-Unit Variable Cost	$0.64
Estimated Monthly Fixed Cost	$28,294

Starting with a statement to generate interest and enthusiasm.

Describes the information contained in the income statement.

Summary data is clear and matches the figure that follows.

Refers to an appendix for in-depth data. Shortens the body of the plan and reduces confusion.

Explanation of the cost structure.

Steps to profitability.

Fulfilling the social promise (the fifth "P" of philanthropy).

Expansion plans. How TDP will grow significantly.

Increased expenses explained and positive impact still shown.

7.3. Projected Profit and Loss

The Daily Perc is expecting some dramatic growth in the next three years, reaching $558,043 in sales and a 65.5% Gross Profit Margin by the end of the first year. Expenses during the first year leave a Net After-tax profit of $9,960, or 1.8%. Detailed profit and loss information is included in Appendix 1-D.

Aside from production costs of 34.4%, which include actual production of product and commissions for sales efforts, the single largest expenditures in the first year are in the general and administrative (G&A) area, totaling 54.7% of sales. G&A includes expenses for rents, equipment leases, utilities, and the payroll burden for all employees.

Sales increase by nearly 400% in the second year, due to the addition of two more Drive-thrus and two more Mobile Cafés, reaching a total of $2,348,900. Although operating expenses double in the second year, The Daily Perc will be able to realize a Net After-tax profit of $368,675 or 15.7% of sales. In that same year, TDP will make charitable contributions of $70,000.

The third year is when The Daily Perc has the opportunity to break into markets outside the metropolitan area. TDP will see nine additional Drive-thru facilities open in the third year, which will drive sales to $6,022,950 and, even with a 200% increase in production costs, help reach a Gross Profit Margin of 68.9%. Several expenses take substantial jumps this year—advertising increasing from $36,000 to $72,000 and donations increasing from $72,000 to $180,000—and TDP will be adding several key management team members. These increases, as well as those for increased equipment leases and rents, raise our operating expenses to $2,772,993, leaving a Net After-tax profit of $1,294,371, or 21.5% of sales.

The Daily Perc—Profit Monthly

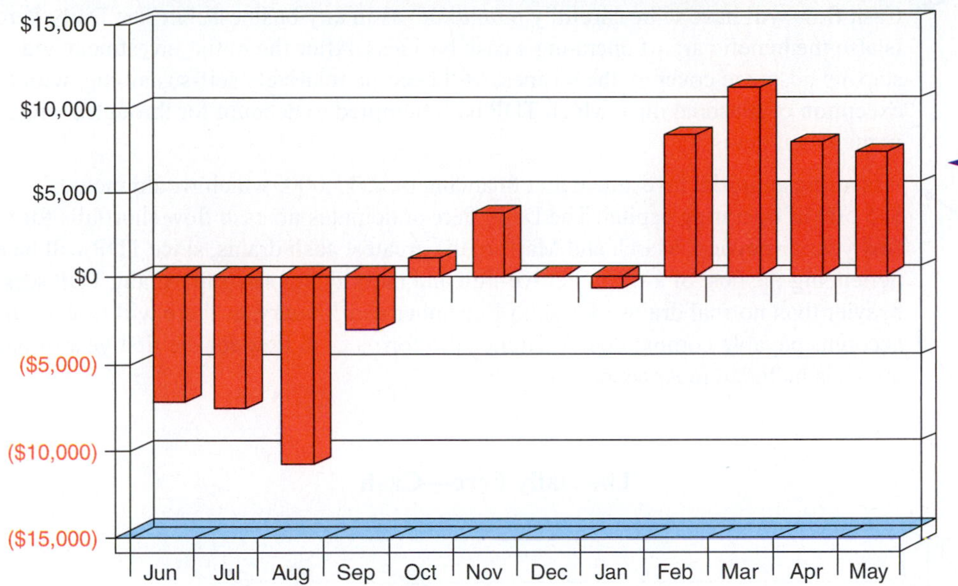

Visual of monthly projections that are included in the appendices. Could show quarterly or first three years to be more effective.

The Daily Perc—Pro Forma Profit and Loss

Summary of first three years. Could add quarterly values for the first year. Monthly and/or quarterly values can be in the appendices. Also called "Projected Income Statement."

	FY 1	FY 2	FY 3
Sales	$558,043	$2,348,900	$6,022,950
Direct Costs of Goods	$190,977	$732,350	$1,783,010
Sales Commissions	$1,416	$35,234	$90,344
Cost of Goods Sold	$192,393	$767,584	$1,873,354
Gross Margin	$365,650	$1,581,317	$4,149,596
Gross Margin %	65.52%	67.32%	68.90%
Expenses			
Payroll	$242,374	$846,050	$2,024,250
Sales and Marketing and Other Expenses	$0	$0	$0
Depreciation	$21,785	$92,910	$196,095
Leased Offices and Equipment	$0	$6,000	$18,000
Utilities	$9,640	$19,800	$41,100
Insurance	$12,570	$32,620	$63,910
Rent	$16,800	$50,400	$126,000
Payroll Taxes	$36,356	$126,908	$303,638
Other General and Administrative Expenses	$0	$0	$0
Total Operating Expenses	$339,525	$1,174,688	$2,772,993
Profit before Interest and Taxes	$26,125	$406,629	$1,376,603
EBITDA	$47,910	$499,539	$1,572,698
Interest Expense	$16,165	$37,954	$82,232
Taxes Incurred	$0	$0	$0
Net Profit	$9,960	$368,675	$1,294,371
Net Profit/Sales	1.78%	15.70%	21.49%

Clear statement of gross margin in the financial statement is helpful in the business plan.

TDP should show advertising and other marketing expenses explicitly. Charitable contributions also should be shown.

TDP is showing a small net profit in the first year. This is unusual among start-up businesses. Do not be alarmed if you suffer a loss in year 1.

Need for monitoring cash flow mentioned and that TDP is a "cash business" is highlighted. Unlike many companies, TDP does not offer credit to its customers.

A business should not project cash shortfalls in the business plan. Debt or equity should be sufficient to compensate for any operating deficits.

Explanation of anticipated variances due to startup.

Visual representation shows that cash flow is negative in certain months, but that the cash balance is always positive and on an upward trend after just a couple of months.

7.4. Projected Cash Flow

Cash flow will have to be carefully monitored, as in any business, but The Daily Perc is also the beneficiary of operating a cash business. After the initial investment and start-up costs are covered, the business will become relatively self-sustaining, with the exception of seasonal dips, which TDP has attempted to account for through changes in the menu items.

Assuming an initial investment and financing of $515,000, which would include $25,500 of operating capital, The Daily Perc anticipates no cash flow shortfalls for the first year or beyond. March and May are the greatest cash drains, since TDP will be experiencing the cost of a second Drive-thru and mobile unit start-up. Again, TDP sees heavier than normal drains of cash in December and January, as there will be certain accounts payable coming due. A detailed pro forma cash flow for the first year of operations is included in Appendix 1-E.

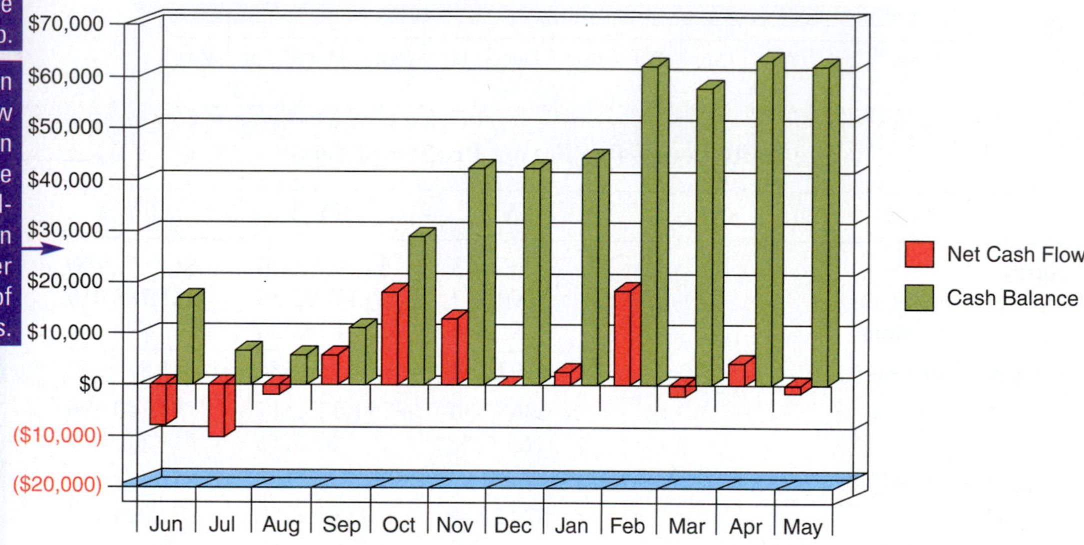

BUSINESS PLAN

The Daily Perc—Pro Forma Cash Flow

	FY 1	FY 2	FY 3
Cash Received			
Cash from Operations			
Cash Sales	$558,043	$2,348,900	$6,022,950
Subtotal Cash from Operations	$558,043	$2,348,900	$6,022,950
Additional Cash Received			
Sales Tax, VAT, HST/GST Received	$0	$0	$0
New Current Borrowing	$0	$0	$0
New Other Liabilities (Interest-free)	$0	$0	$0
New Long-term Liabilities	$181,463	$253,970	$729,992
Sales of Other Current Assets	$0	$0	$0
Sales of Long-term Assets	$0	$0	$0
New Investment Received	$0	$0	$0
Subtotal Cash Received	$739,506	$2,602,870	$6,752,942

	FY 1	FY 2	FY 3
Expenditures			
Expenditures from Operations			
Cash Spending	$242,374	$846,050	$2,024,250
Bill Payments	$240,175	$1,091,066	$2,573,382
Subtotal Spent on Operations	$482,549	$1,937,116	$4,597,632
Additional Cash Spent			
Sales Tax, VAT, HST/GST Paid Out	$0	$0	$0
Principal Repayment of Current Borrowing	$1,500	$0	$0
Other Liabilities Principal Repayment	$0	$0	$0
Long-term Liabilities Principal Repayment	$26,469	$0	$0
Purchase Other Current Assets	$0	$0	$0
Purchase Long-term Assets	$191,850	$429,700	$1,356,993
Dividends	$0	$0	$0
Subtotal Cash Spent	$702,368	$2,366,816	$5,954,625
Net Cash Flow	$37,139	$236,054	$798,317
Cash Balance	$62,639	$298,693	$1,097,010

7.5. Projected Balance Sheet

The Daily Perc's projected balance sheet shows an increase in net worth to just over $1 million in FY 3, at which point it also expects to be making 21.5% after-tax profit on sales of $6.02 million. With the present financial projections, TDP expects to build a company with strong profit potential, and a solid balance sheet that will be asset heavy and flush with cash at the end of the third year. The Daily Perc has no intention of paying out dividends before the end of the third year, using the excess cash for continued growth. The first year projected balance sheet for TDP appears in Appendix 1-F.

The Daily Perc Business Plan provided by Business Plan Pro® and used by permission of Palo Alto Software.

Cash from operations and cash sales are the same for this particular business.

TDP is anticipating that no taxes are collected on food or other sales. Some states and certain businesses will have to collect these taxes and reflect them in the cash flow.

Expansion plans include no short-term borrowing.

Borrowing for expansion.

Assuming all investment occurs before the operations begin.

Since no taxes are collected, none are paid out.

Indicates the repayment of principal on current debt. Typically, there will be some each year if there is new debt.

No principal repayment reflected in this cash flow. Normally, a portion of the long-term debt is repaid annually, so that there would be a value in each year.

This number is higher than the new long-term debt and investment total, indicating that a significant portion of the expansion will be paid through operations.

Shows a strong positive cash balance, such that TDP might even be able to reduce debt significantly if desired.

Clear statement of goal.

Investors know not to expect any dividends during this period, because TDP makes it explicit.

Shows a snapshot of the assets and liabilities at the end of each year.

Matches cash flow statement.

If TDP extended credit to its customers so that there were Accounts Receivable, it would be reflected here.

Assets at their initial value.

Depreciation accumulated over the life of the assets.

Typically, a business has a chart to record depreciation for each long-term asset.

Net value of assets after depreciation is subtracted.

Reflects trade credit that TDP receives from its suppliers.

Total long-term portion of debt remaining. Remember, each year the part of long-term debt that is due within 12 months becomes current debt.

Equity from investors.

Initial profit or loss (likely a loss due to start-up costs) plus each year's earnings.

Equals Paid-in Capital plus Retained Earnings plus Earnings (Net Profit).

Ratios match up with the path set out in the business plan.

Comparing TDP to an industry profile. Indicate which SIC or NAICS code you are comparing it to, [?] with the source of the industry data.

The Daily Perc—Pro Forma Balance Sheet

	FY 1	FY 2	FY 3
Assets			
Current Assets			
Cash	$62,639	$298,693	$1,097,010
Inventory	$35,159	$134,826	$328,252
Other Current Assets	$0	$0	$0
Total Current Assets	$97,798	$433,519	$1,425,263
Long-term Assets			
Long-term Assets	$323,250	$752,950	$2,109,943
Accumulated Depreciation	$21,785	$114,695	$310,790
Total Long-term Assets	$301,465	$638,255	$1,799,153
Total Assets	$399,263	$1,071,774	$3,224,416

	FY 1	FY 2	FY 3
Liabilities and Capital			
Current Liabilities			
Accounts Payable	$43,909	$93,775	$222,054
Current Borrowing	$7,500	$7,500	$7,500
Other Current Liabilities	$0	$0	$0
Subtotal Current Liabilities	$51,409	$101,275	$229,554
Long-term Liabilities	$286,394	$540,364	$1,270,356
Total Liabilities	$337,803	$641,639	$1,499,910
Paid-in Capital	$225,270	$225,270	$225,270
Retained Earnings	($173,770)	($163,810)	$204,865
Earnings	$9,960	$368,675	$1,294,371
Total Capital	$61,460	$430,135	$1,724,505
Total Liabilities and Capital	$399,263	$1,071,774	$3,224,416
Net Worth	$61,460	$430,135	$1,724,505

7.6. Business Ratios

Standard business ratios are included in the following table. The ratios show a plan for balanced, healthy growth. The Daily Perc's position within the industry is typical for a heavy-growth start-up company. Industry profile ratios based on the Standard Industrial Classification (SIC) code 5812, Eating Places, are shown for comparison.

Comparing the ratios in the third year with the industry, this pro forma plan appears to be within an acceptable difference margin.

TDP's return on net worth and net worth number differ from the Industry Profile due to the lack of overhead when compared to a typical walk-in café. The Drive-thru and Mobile business model is lean, thus allowing for an increased return ratio and providing a lower Net Worth.

The Daily Perc—Ratio Analysis

	FY 1	FY 2	FY 3	Industry Profile
Sales Growth	0.00%	320.92%	156.42%	7.60%
Percent of Total Assets				
Inventory	8.81%	12.58%	10.18%	3.60%
Other Current Assets	0.00%	0.00%	0.00%	35.60%
Total Current Assets	24.49%	40.45%	44.20%	43.70%
Long-term Assets	75.51%	59.55%	55.80%	56.30%
Total Assets	100.00%	100.00%	100.00%	100.00%
Current Liabilities	12.88%	9.45%	7.12%	32.70%
Long-term Liabilities	71.73%	50.42%	39.40%	28.50%
Total Liabilities	84.61%	59.87%	46.52%	61.20%
Net Worth	15.39%	40.13%	53.48%	38.80%
Percent of Sales				
Sales	100.00%	100.00%	100.00%	100.00%
Gross Margin	65.52%	67.32%	68.90%	60.50%
Selling, General & Administrative Expenses	44.74%	30.63%	29.15%	39.80%
Advertising Expenses	3.23%	1.53%	1.20%	3.20%
Profit before Interest and Taxes	4.68%	17.31%	22.86%	0.70%
Main Ratios				
Current	1.90	4.28	6.21	0.98
Quick	1.22	2.95	4.78	0.65
Total Debt to Total Assets	84.61%	59.87%	46.52%	61.20%
Pre-tax Return on Net Worth	16.21%	85.71%	75.06%	1.70%
Pre-tax Return on Assets	2.49%	34.40%	40.14%	4.30%

	FY 1	FY 2	FY 3	
Additional Ratios				
Net Profit Margin	1.78%	15.70%	21.49%	n.a
Return on Equity	16.21%	85.71%	75.06%	n.a
Activity Ratios				
Inventory Turnover	7.02	8.62	7.70	n.a
Accounts Payable Turnover	6.47	12.17	12.17	n.a
Payment Days	27	22	21	n.a
Total Asset Turnover	1.40	2.19	1.87	n.a
Debt Ratios				
Debt to Net Worth	5.50	1.49	0.87	n.a
Current Liabilities to Liabilities	0.15	0.16	0.15	n.a
Liquidity Ratios				
Net Working Capital	$46,389	$332,244	$1,195,708	n.a
Interest Coverage	1.62	10.71	16.74	n.a
Additional Ratios				
Assets to Sales	0.72	0.46	0.54	n.a
Current Debt/Total Assets	13%	9%	7%	n.a
Acid Test	1.22	2.95	4.78	n.a
Sales/Net Worth	9.08	5.46	3.49	n.a
Dividend Payout	0.00	0.00	0.00	n.a

The Daily Perc Business Plan provided by Business Plan Pro® and used by permission of Palo Alto Software.

Explanation of TDP's variance industry data.

High growth. TDP is starting at a low base and adding locations.

Higher than industry norms, probably because the low base requires further discussion.

This significant variance should be described in the text.

TDP is carrying a lower trade debt and current portion of long-term debt.

Described in the business plan text.

Matches the income statement.

Not detailed in the income statement.

Radical difference from the industry warrants an explanation.

Quick ratio is also radically different.

Explained in the text.

Explained in the text.

BUSINESS PLAN

Description of the total need.

Uses the precise wording of previous sections. Reiterates the structure of the equity offering. Does not tell the sources of these in significant detail nor is there information regarding the intended or secured sources of debt financing.

TDP offering multiple exit strategies.

Exit options that make investment more attractive. This should strengthen the business plan.

Franchising strategy as a form of replication.

Expansion strategy fueled by an IPO or private offering.

Three years is relatively quick for such a scenario.

Exit through buyout by a competitor.

This falls within the $4 million to $9 million estimate provided earlier.

Calculation of the purchase price per unit permits the calculation of return on investment.

ROI calculation.

Why a cash/stock combination is preferable.

8. Funding Request and Exit Strategy

8.1. Funding Request

The Daily Perc, LLC requires initial financing of $515,000 for its start-up phase without any anticipated need for additional equity or debt except for as needed to complete the purchase of additional facilities and/or equipment.

The plan calls for the sale of 100 membership units in the company to family members, friends, and Angel Investors. Each membership unit in the company is priced at $4,250, with a minimum of five units per membership certificate, or a minimum investment of $21,250 per investor.

If all funds are raised, based on the pricing established in the financial section of this plan, Bart and Terri Fisher will maintain ownership of no less than 51% of the company.

8.2. Exit Strategy

There are three scenarios for the investors and management to recover their investment—two with significant returns on each dollar invested.

Scenario One:

The Daily Perc becomes extremely successful and has requests from other communities for Daily Perc operations to be opened there. This opens the door for franchising opportunity. When one looks at the wealth that has been created by the likes of McDonald's, Wendy's, Kentucky Fried Chicken, Burger King, and Taco Bell, the value of franchising a great idea cannot be dismissed. However, developing a franchise can be extremely costly, take years to develop, and be destroyed by one or two franchisees who fail to deliver the consistency or value on which the founding company had built its reputation.

Scenario Two:

The Daily Perc chooses to become the Drive-thru version of Starbucks, obtaining several million dollars through an initial public or private offering that would allow the company to open 20 to 30 facilities per year in the region of the country between the mountain ranges, in both major and small metropolitan communities. This is the preferred Exit Strategy of the Management Team. The danger in this is that competitors would rise up and establish a foothold on a community before—or in the midst of—the arrival of The Daily Perc, causing a potential for a drain on revenues and a dramatic increase in advertising expenditures to maintain market share. Knowing these risks—and planning for them—gives TDP the edge needed to make this scenario work.

Scenario Three:

By the third year, the growth and community support for The Daily Perc will have made the news in more than just the metropolitan area. It can be assumed that competitors, such as Starbucks or Quikava, will have seen the press and realized the value proposition in The Daily Perc's business plan. This will make TDP an attractive target for buyout. The company could be purchased by a much larger competitive concern by the end of the third year.

Taking a conservative approach to valuation and estimating that The Daily Perc would be valued at $7.5 million, and assuming that all 250 units of ownership in TDP are distributed to investors, a cash purchase of TDP would net each unit $30,000. With each unit selling at $4,250, that constitutes a Return on Investment of 705% over the three years. However, any buyout will most likely involve a cash/stock combination. A cash/stock buyout would be favorable, since the buying company would pay a higher price and the transaction would not have such severe tax consequences to the sellers.

Conclusion:

Of the three scenarios, the management team prefers Scenario #2. The same numbers would relate to a public or private offering as are used in Scenario #3, but to make an

The Daily Perc Business Plan provided by Business Plan Pro® and used by permission of Palo Alto Software.

offering available, there would be a dilution of shares that would provide additional shares for sale to the new investors.

Assuming the capital acquisition described in this plan is completed, there will be 250 units of the company in the hands of investors, constituting 100% of the authorized and issued units. For purposes of future fund-raising, it will be necessary to authorize a stock split of perhaps 5,000 to one, turning the current 250 units into 1,250,000 units.

Using the balance sheet for the third year, which estimates a Net Worth of just over $1.7 million, cash balances of $1.1 million, and earnings of $1.3 million, based on thirteen Drive-thrus and four Mobile Cafés, it is not unrealistic to put a market value of $15 million to $25 million on the company. At present, such companies are trading in multiples of 20 to 30 times earnings, and it is simple mathematics to multiply the success of TDP by the number of commuter-heavy metropolitan areas in the United States.

With a corporate valuation of $7,500,000, each of the new units would have a market value of $6/unit. By authorizing an additional 750,000 units, there would be a total of 2,000,000 units with a market value of $3.75 per share. By offering the 750,000 shares at the price of $3.75 per unit, TDP would raise an additional $2,812,500 in expansion capital, which would be sufficient to open locations in an additional three to five cities.

Returned to the $7.5 million valuation from above.

Specific number of additional shares. The value ($7.5 million) divided by the total number of shares (2 million) yield the market value of $3.75 per share.

By multiplying the number of new shares (750,000) by the price per share ($3.75), TDP calculates the infusion of capital.

Using milestones to ensure measurement.

8.3. Milestones

The Milestone table reflects critical dates for occupying headquarters, launching the first Drive-thru and subsequent Drive-thrus, as well as deployment of the mobile units. The Daily Perc also defines our break-even month, our Web site launch and subsequent visitor interaction function, and other key markers that will help us measure our success in time and accomplishment.

The Daily Perc—Milestones

Milestone	Start Date	End Date	Budget	Manager	Department
Light Web Site	6/1/YR1	8/15/YR1	$5,600	COO	Mktg.
Open First Drive-thru	7/15/YR1	8/31/YR1	$105,400	COO	Admin.
First Break-even Month	12/1/YR1	12/31/YR1	$0	COO	Finance
Open Second Drive-thru	12/15/YR1	2/1/YR1	$105,400	COO	Admin.
Receive First Mobile Unit	3/1/YR1	3/30/YR1	$86,450	COO	Admin.
Launch Web Site Voting	5/1/YR1	6/1/YR1	$12,500	COO	Mktg.
Open Third Drive-thru	4/15/YR1	6/1/YR1	$105,400	COO	Admin.
Receive Second and Third Mobile Units	7/15/YR2	9/1/YR2	$172,900	COO	Admin.
Open Fourth Drive-thru	12/15/YR2	2/1/YR2	$105,400	COO	Admin.
Install Point-of-Sale System	12/1/YR2	2/1/YR2	$21,000	CIO	MIS
Occupy Headquarters	4/1/YR2	5/15/YR2	$45,000	COO	Admin.
Open Fifth Drive-thru	4/15/YR2	6/1/YR3	$105,400	COO	Admin.
Receive Fourth Mobile Unit	4/15/YR2	6/1/YR3	$86,450	Equip.	Admin.
Open Drive-thrus 6 and 7	7/15/YR3	9/15/YR3	$210,800	COO/Dir.	Mgmt.
Open Drive-thrus 8, 9, and 10	10/15/YR3	12/15/YR3	$316,200	COO/Dir.	Mgmt.
Open Drive-thrus 11, 12, and 13	1/15/YR3	3/1/YR3	$316,200	COO	Admin.
Expand to Kansas City	1/15/YR3	6/1/YR3	$176,943	COO	Mgmt.
Open First Franchise	10/31/YR3	9/1/YR4	$45,000	CFO	Finance
Initiate Exit Strategy	10/1/YR4	1/1/YR4	$100,000	CFO	Mgmt.

Appendices

The appendices for The Daily Perc business plan appear in Appendix 1.

Appendix 3

Sample Student Business Plan

University Parent, Inc.

Fesehaye Abrhaley
Michelle Dorenkamp
Kara Grinnell
Ryan Roth
Sarah Schupp

University Parent, Inc.

Table of Contents

Appendix

2890 Shadow Creek - Boulder, Colorado - 303.579.9871 - info@upi.com

University Parent, Inc.

Executive Summary

University Parent, Inc.
University Parent (UPI) produces institution-specific guides and comprehensive websites for parents of college students. Revenues are generated through the sale of advertising in the local guides and on the websites.

Today, there are 32 million parents of college students
According to surveys and interviews conducted by UPI, parents do not receive the information they need from colleges. They want to know where to have a nice dinner in their student's college town, where to stay, and fun activities to do while visiting. They also want to know how to parent their college student and need to understand the issues their child is facing such as managing money, avoiding credit card debt, and balancing school, a part-time job, and extra-curricular activities.

UPI can help
UPI will produce three free guides per year for each college that will be distributed during summer orientation and August move-in, Fall Parent's Weekend, and in the Spring to prospective parents through the Admissions Office and Campus Tour Office. At the University of Colorado, over 25,000 prospective parents tour the campus. The magazines will be distributed through the university, hotels, and restaurants. The magazine content will include: restaurant reviews, a lodging directory, a shopping guide, calendar of events, graduation requirement Information, map of the city, and a Q&A section.

Proven track record
The first issue of the *Parent's Guide to Boulder* was published in October 2003 and immediately profited from advertising sales. The second edition will be published June 2004, and due to advance advertising sales, will also be profitable. Demand for these first guides have proved that advertisers are committed to purchasing space in the guide and that parents are interested in reading the guide.

Experienced, enthusiastic management team
Sarah Schupp is the founder, CEO, and Chairman of the UPI Board of Directors. She published the initial *Parent's Guide to Boulder* in 2003. A graduate of the University of Colorado with degrees in Business Administration and English Literature, Sarah is capable of expanding the vision of UPI to Colorado and Texas. In Year 3, UPI plans to hire a CEO with national rollout experience.

Other UPI employees include VP Marketing Michelle Dorenkamp, CFO Kara Grinnell, and CTO Ryan Roth. In addition to an excellent management team,

UPI is in the process of developing a board of twelve directors that bring experience in advertising, magazine writing, start-ups, and venture capital.

Plan for expansion

Because of the initial success of the *Parent's Guide to Boulder*, UPI is currently expanding its marketing base to Colorado State University and the University of Denver. A regional office in Boulder will handle advertising sales for the three guides. UPI plans to broaden its base beginning in Year 2, with a goal of being in 44 schools by Year 5.

The offering

UPI is offering 35% of the company for $500,000. This will provide investors with a 60% rate of return, translating to $4.3 million in Year 5 when UPI plans to sell to Hearst Publishing or Conde Nast Publishing. UPI breaks-even in Year 2, generating revenues of $1.8 million. In Year 5, UPI will have revenues of $12 million and a net profit of $4.1 million.

Company Overview

With two successful publications for the University of Colorado and established relationships with over 35 advertisers, UPI is positioned for nation-wide expansion. In October of 2004, UPI plans to produce a total of 9 publications and 3 websites for the University of Colorado, the University of Denver, and Colorado State University. We project UPI will produce 132 publications and high-traffic websites for 44 colleges and universities by Year 5. This will result in net revenues of $12.3 million, net profits of $4.1 million, and a valuation of $70 million. Also in Year 5, UPI plans to market the company to suitable buyers such as Hearst Publishing or Conde Nast Publishing.

University Parent, Inc.

Product/Service Description

Introduction

You arrive on campus to drop off your freshman student. This is always one of the hardest times of the year for you. Leaving your child miles from home, millions of questions are running through your head. How do they register for classes? How many credits will they need to graduate? What issues will they face being away from home? As you are signing in for orientation, you receive a magazine that specifically answers these questions. Not only does it answer campus life questions, it also offers restaurant reviews, lodging suggestions, and a detailed map of the city. The magazine directs you to a website where you can talk to other parents who have your same concerns. Suddenly you have a sense of relief. Now you have a source of information at your fingertips.

As a Boulder business, you have always wondered how you can directly advertise to CU parents who visit often and spend thousands of dollars while visiting. One day a packet arrives at your business with the first *Parent's Guide to Boulder* from the 2003 Parent's Weekend and a rate card. You are excited that there is now a reasonably priced and direct way to contact CU parents and inform them of your business. You know that purchasing advertising will be well worth every dollar. (Boulder, Colorado served as UPI's test market.)

Description

University Parent produces a comprehensive local guide as well as a website for parents of college students. Through its compilation of articles, pictures, maps, current events, and advertisements, it provides a convenient, thorough source of information for CU parents.

Parent

Guide Feature	Benefit
Distribution through the university, hotels, and restaurants	Convenience
Provides useful information about their student's environment and community	Comfort, Sense of Security
Makes navigating Boulder easier and allows for advance planning	Saves Time
Free! Gives information and coupons for good values in: lodging, eating, shopping, and having a good time	Saves Money

2890 Shadow Creek – Boulder, Colorado – 303.579.9871 – info@upi.com

University Parent, Inc.

Advertiser

Guide Feature	Benefit
Targets specific niche	Targeted ROI
Mid-ranged priced advertising	Saves Money
Effective distribution channels	Reaches Target Market, Generates Revenue

Market Comparison
Unlike other publications in college towns, UPI offers its readers focused, relevant information that is unavailable through local newspapers and magazines. It also offers advertisers a targeted, identifiable market.

Stage of Development
UPI produced its first guide in Boulder for Parent's Weekend '03. The profitability of the first guide demonstrated UPI's ability to sell advertising and to produce a useful product. UPI is currently marketing and creating articles for its Summer '04 publication. Our CTO, Ryan Roth, launched the Guide to Boulder's website in April of '04, http://www.guidetoboulder.com. Advertising sales for the website are scheduled to begin in May '04.

Client Base
UPI currently has over 35 clients for the *Parent's Guide to Boulder.* These advertisers include: Wells Fargo, Walnut Realty, McGuckin Hardware, the CU Book Store, the CU Foundation, Greenbriar Inn, Boulder Broker Inn, Boulder Outlook Hotel & Suites, Boulder Express Shuttle, and many more. Of the initial advertisers in the Fall '03 guide, 100% of advertisers solicited purchased advertising for the Summer '04 guide.

Potential Readership Base

Demographic

32 million U.S. parents of college students, growing at an annual rate of 6%

We expect 20% of each college's parent population to read our magazines

Family Income

Most families sending children to college have a combined household income ranging from $80,000 to $150,000

Cost of Education

A college education is likely the biggest investment they will make in their student

A college education costs anywhere from $30,000 to $200,000

Parents typically provide for their children while in college, paying for expenses such as transportation (car, bike), car insurance, textbooks, clothing, computers and software, food, rent, etc.

2890 Shadow Creek - Boulder, Colorado - 303.579.9871 - info@upi.com

These expenses average between $800–$1,500 per month.

Potential Advertisers

Independent marketing firms that handle national accounts
Local business owners and/or Marketing Managers representing hotels, restaurants, retail stores, travel agencies that must make buying decisions based on distribution and cost.

Industry and Marketplace Analysis

The publication industry has over 17,000 magazines that gross $24 billion in revenue each year. Historically, this industry has grown at a rate of 7 percent, and is expected to grow 6 percent in the future. There is little demand for new titles with the exception of demand for specialty, niche magazines that enable advertisers to reach a well-defined market. Our primary, unexplored niche consists of parents of college students. According to surveys, virtually all CU parents (95%) are uninformed about campus activities, news, and pertinent issues. Currently no other publications are addressing these needs and concerns of CU parents.

In recent years, there has been an increase in online magazines and online versions of print magazines. Major threats in the periodical industry include other advertising mediums such as television, radio, and print. The most competition for publications is in print advertising, which ranges from daily newspapers to monthly magazines. Another threat to the publication industry is the rising cost of paper, which is driving down profits. Some of the internal market changes revolve around a concern over rising paper costs because of deforestation.

Leading advertisers in the magazine industry include: automobile manufacturers, consumer goods companies, entertainment conglomerates, and tobacco firms. Some of the internal market changes revolve around a concern over rising paper costs because of deforestation.

Leading advertisers in the magazine industry include: automobile manufacturers, consumer goods companies, entertainment conglomerates, and tobacco firms. The publication industry is affected by changes in economic conditions since revenue is advertising-dependant.

University Parent, Inc.

Marketing Strategy

Introduction
UPI's target readership market will include students, parents of present and future students, university faculty and staff, and high school counselors. Aggressive distribution will insure that all sectors of our target market will receive our free guide as well as website information. Our target market for advertising is businesses that want to make parents of college students aware of their products and/or services. We provide these businesses an opportunity to reach a specific, identifiable market at a reasonable cost.

Target Market Advertising Strategy
We will position ourselves as the only publication offering information specifically for parents of CU students and as the only publication offering businesses the opportunity to advertise to these parents.

In Boulder, the primary advertising media are the *Colorado Daily*, *Daily Camera*, *The Onion*, and *Boulder Magazine*. UPI's targeted, niche market strategy offers businesses a superior, more cost-effective media product at a lower cost than these publications. UPI will produce a quarterly mailing to businesses in Boulder that offer a product/service that CU parents may be interested in purchasing. The mailing will be directed to the "businesses' owners" and will include a previous *Parent's Guide to Boulder*, a cover letter specifying why advertising with UPI is effective, testimonials from current advertisers, and a rate card.

As UPI moves into additional markets, this strategy will be replicated and customized as needed.

Pricing Strategy
University Parent will generate revenue from two sources: print advertising in our guides and online advertising on our website.

Print advertising prices (per guide):

Size	Full Color
Eighth Page	$250
Quarter Page	$400
Half Page	$600
Full Page	$800
Back Cover, Inside Cover, Back Inside	$1000

2890 Shadow Creek - Boulder, Colorado - 303.579.9871 - info@upi.com

University Parent, Inc.

Website advertising prices (per month):

Size	Full Color
2" x 1"	$400
2" x 2"	$500
Banner, 1" x 7"	$700
Pop Up	$1000
Ad in email newsletter	$500

Businesses can purchase yearlong magazine and website advertising at a10% discount. The website advertising prices are likely to change based on our website's traffic. The higher the traffic, the higher the price we can charge.

Distribution Strategy

UPI will distribute guides to parents through the university admissions office, parent relations office, and campus tour office. The guide will also be distributed in hotels, restaurants, businesses, and through the Chamber of Commerce. There will be an option on the website to download the guide or have it mailed for a small fee (postage).

Advertising, Sales & Promotion Strategy

UPI will be promoted to advertisers through local networking at Boulder Chamber of Commerce events, press releases in local papers, direct mailings, and referral incentives for current clients. In addition, the website will serve as an effective tool to inform both businesses and parents of our services.

Marketing & Sales Forecasts

UPI's revenue is generated through print and website advertising sales. We project revenues from print advertising at 54% and website advertising sales at 46% of total revenues.

Advertising revenues are calculated by using the print advertising rates multiplied by expected sales for three guides. UPI projects sales of 25 print advertisements per issue at an average cost of $1,000 and 72 website sales per year per institution at an average cost of $750.

Revenue (In thousands $)

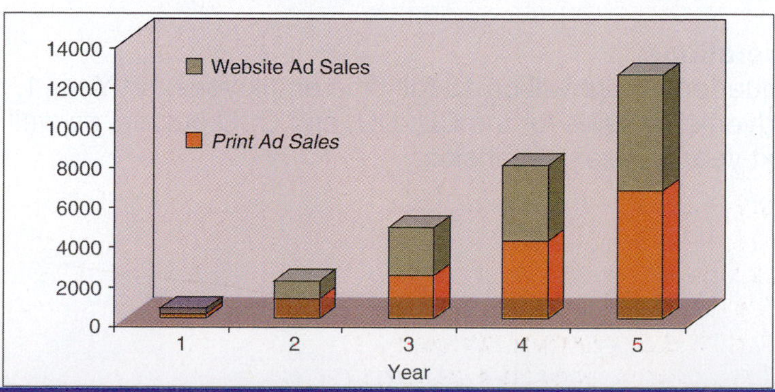

2890 Shadow Creek - Boulder, Colorado - 303.579.9871 - info@upi.com

Revenue Projections

	Year 1	Year 2	Year 3	Year 4	Year 5
Product A—Magazine					
Number of Schools	3	9	22	32	44
Total Issues/Year	9	36	66	96	132
Magazines Printed/Year	90,000	360,000	660,000	960,000	1,320,000
Printing Cost/Per Magazine	0.25	0.23	0.21	0.19	0.17
Number of Units/Ad	225	900	1,800	2,925	4,425
Avg. Price/Ad Page	$1,000	$1,100	$1,210	$1,331	$1,464
Print Adv Total	$225,000	$990,000	$2,178,000	$3,893,175	$6,478,643
Product B—Website					
Advertisements Sold/Yr	360	1,080	2,640	3,840	5,280
Price per unit	$750	$825	$908	$998	$1,098
Web Adv Total	$270,000	$891,000	$2,395,800	$3,833,280	$5,797,836
Net Revenue	$495,000	$1,881,000	$4,573,800	$7,726,455	$12,276,479

Operations Plan

Operations Strategy

Our strategy is to establish a reputation with readers and advertisers that UPI consistently delivers well-received, well-designed, informative magazines and websites. We will develop this reputation by providing products that are professionally designed, error-free, and exceed the expectations of both our readers and our advertisers. We will measure our success through in-person as well as online surveys of our customers.

Our goal is to have highly satisfied customers—our parent readers and our advertisers. To that end, UPI will provide training for all employees that stresses the necessity of exceeding the expectations of our customers in ways such as delivering advertising proofs early or following up with a parent's question promptly and thoroughly.

Scope of Operations

At UPI headquarters, there will be 15 full-time employees. In Year 1, this office will handle advertising sales for the CU, DU, and CSU guides, as well as negotiate next year's Texas expansion.

University Parent, Inc.

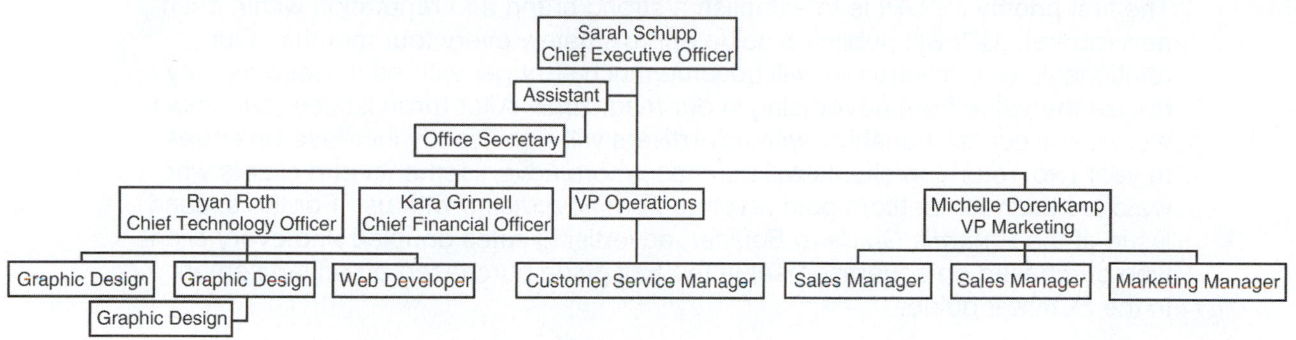

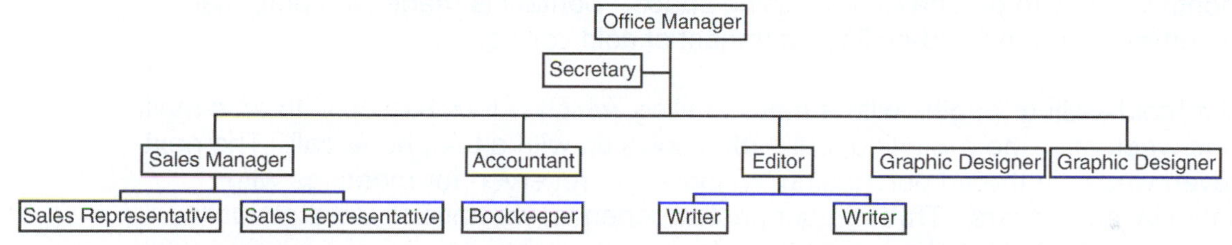

Ongoing Operations

UPI headquarters will coordinate with the regional offices to produce a website and three magazines annually for each college. Issues will be published every summer, fall, and spring. The website will be updated as needed, daily if necessary. Advertising sales as well as contact with parents and university faculty and staff will be continuous throughout the year

Operating Expenses

	Year 1	Year 2	Year 3	Year 4	Year 5
Total Operating Expenses	$854,967	$1,547,676	$2,588,328	$3,611,938	$5,083,166
% of Revenue	172.7%	82.3%	56.6%	46.7%	41.4%

2890 Shadow Creek – Boulder, Colorado – 303.579.9871 – info@upi.com

University Parent, Inc.

Development Plan

Development Strategy

The first priority for UPI is to establish a strong brand and reputation within each new market. UPI will publish a guide approximately every four months. Our relationship with advertisers will become much stronger with each issue as they realize the value from advertising in our magazine. After three issues (one year), we believe our relationships with advertisers will significantly increase revenues. In year two, returning clients will purchase more advertisements and clients who watched their competitors gain revenue from advertising with us. For the second issue of the *Parent's Guide to Boulder,* advertising sales doubled and every client who purchased an advertisement in the Fall guide purchased an advertisement in the Summer guide.

During the publication cycle for each issue, the first order of business is to brainstorm new ideas and themes. Once the themes are decided, we make those themes available to the advertisers. We then give advertisers a three-month window to purchase advertising space. Contact is made with potential advertiser through "cold-selling," a variant of cold calling.

The "cold-selling" begins with a mass mailing, which is followed up with an e-mail. One week after the e-mailing, our staff follows up with a telephone call. The next seven weeks in the ad purchasing "window" are reserved for meetings with potential advertisers. Through our past experience, we have found that such meetings are vital for closing most deals.

The artwork acceptance window is open from the moment an advertising contract is signed until the artwork acceptance deadline, one week after the close of advertising sales. The first payment for the advertisement is due on the last day of advertisement sales. The second payment is due one week before we send the magazine to the printer.

While ad sales are in full swing, the design of the magazine is developed. Concurrently, article research and story writing for the magazine are performed. Immediately after the design and story writing are finalized, we finalize the layout and update the website; both of these occur over a two-week period.

As soon as the layout is finished, the final copy is sent to the printer. Within 5 days, the printer overnights a digital proof for UPI's approval. Once approved, printing takes approximately one week. Once the copies are received, the magazine is ready for distribution. Distribution takes place over a two-week period. Most magazines are mailed directly from the printer to the distribution point. These distribution points include: the university, hotels, restaurants, and other local businesses.

University Parent, Inc.

Roll-Out Plan

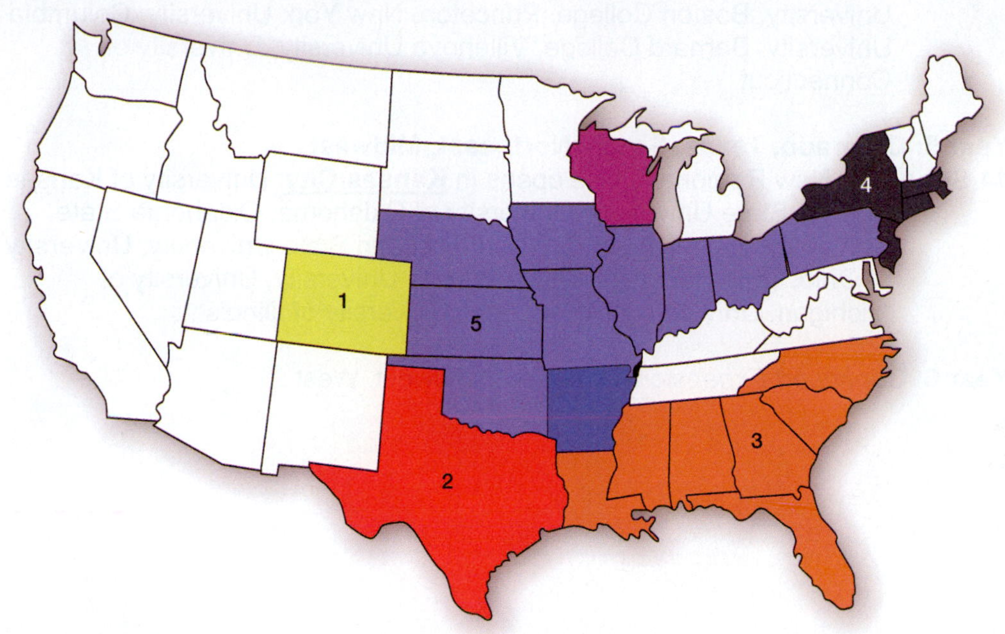

Year 1: Colorado
3 Schools: CU, University of Denver, and Colorado State University

Year 2: Colorado and Texas
9 Schools: *New Regional Office opens in **Dallas**: Southern Methodist University, University of Texas at Austin, A&M, Trinity University, Baylor University, Rice University

Year 3: Colorado, Texas, South
22 Schools: *New Regional Office opens in **Atlanta**: University of Georgia, University of the South, University of North Carolina, University of South Carolina, Duke University, University of Florida, Rollins College, University of Virginia, University of Richmond, University of Louisiana, Louisiana State University

2890 Shadow Creek - Boulder, Colorado - 303.579.9871 - info@upi.com

Year 4: Colorado, Texas, South, Northeast
32 Schools: *New Regional Office opens in **Boston**: Harvard, MIT, Tufts, Boston University, Boston College, Princeton, New York University, Columbia University, Barnard College, Villanova University, University of Connecticut

Year 5: Colorado, Texas, South, Northeast, Midwest
44 Schools: *New Regional Office opens in **Kansas City**: University of Kansas, Kansas State University, University of Oklahoma, Oklahoma State University, University of Missouri, Missouri State University, University of Ohio, Ohio State University, Purdue University, University of Michigan, University of Wisconsin, University of Illinois

Year 6: *Continued Expansion*: Northeast, Midwest, West

University Parent, Inc.

Management

Sarah Schupp, Chief Executive Officer
Sarah founded *The Parent's Guide to Boulder* in June of 2003. A graduate of the University of Colorado with degrees in Business Administration and English Literature, Sarah is capable of expanding the vision of UPI across the U.S. In addition, she has developed relationships with the University of Colorado through her 2004 position as the Senior Class President and member of the President's Leadership Class.

Ryan Roth, Chief Technology Officer
Ryan comes to UPI with an extensive background in high-level web technology and information system deployment strategies. As team leader of numerous successful system development projects, Ryan is a valuable addition to UPI as Chief Technology Officer. He joined our team in early 2004 to provide in-depth, focused research on technology issues and solutions to provide University Parent with customized solutions unmatched by any other magazine publisher today. Ryan graduated from the Leeds School of Business at the University of Colorado with a B.S. in Business Administration and an emphasis in Information Systems.

Kara Grinnell, Chief Financial Officer
Kara is equipped with the financial knowledge needed to accomplish all the tasks included in the job of Chief Financial Officer. With a degree in Finance from the University of Colorado, Kara has the appropriate background to help UPI meet its financial goals. Kara has firsthand field experience with financial measurements and is prepared to help UPI become a $100 million venture.

Michelle Dorenkamp, VP Marketing
Michelle will graduate with a Bachelor of Science Degree in Business from the University of Colorado in May 2004. For the past three summers, she has worked in marketing and advertising for a real estate company. She has successfully worked with companies doing a direct mail campaign similar to the one that will be used to attract advertisers for the local guides.

University Parent, Inc.

Business Risks

Another company will copy our idea.
Because of a magazine's low start-up costs, it is likely that people will copy our concept. However, we can mitigate this risk by negotiating with national advertisers for annual contracts and with universities for distribution rights. Another way we can mitigate this risk is through strategic growth. By identifying the best regions for expansion, we will capture a new region each year. We are targeting geographically central locations with a high concentration of colleges and universities.

Universities will not cooperate to help us distribute the guide.
When selling advertisements to businesses, our greatest strength is that universities allow us to distribute the guide on campus. This distribution point makes advertisers believe their ROI will be greater because parents pay close attention to materials given to them by the university. However, our guide is an effective public relations tool for universities to give to parents and by maintaining appropriate content, we eliminate this obstacle.

Businesses will not buy advertising.
Our revenue projections are based on selling 25 or more print advertisements per issue and 10 Web ads per month per location. If businesses do not believe that our magazine will serve as an effective marketing tool, they will not purchase advertising. We must prove to advertisers that parents do and will read our magazine and will make buying decisions based on our information.

Each university has a different environment with different demographics.
Because we are producing guides with location-specific information, we must insure that the information we publish is accurate and appropriate for the area. If we miss the target demographic or culture of the area, parents will not read the guide and advertisers will not purchase advertising. To make sure we understand the area, representatives from our regional office will be familiar with every location in their region and will have student interns at each school that will help UPI understand the area and its parent population. In addition, we will use our website to collect marketing data. Weblogs, an online parent chat room, will allow us to track parents' comments and their geographic location, which will enable us to understand the issues at each university.

University Parent, Inc.

Financial Plan

Financial Summary

Revenue for UPI is derived from magazine and website advertising sales. UPI plans to sell advertising to both national and local advertisers. As more people read our magazine and visit our website, the prices we can charge advertisers will increase.

The following table summarizes five years of pro forma financial statements. Assumptions for the financial statements are located in Section G of the Appendix.

	Year 1	Year 2	Year 3	Year 4	Year 5
Operating Revenue	**$495,000**	**$1,881,000**	**$4,573,800**	**$7,726,455**	**$12,276,479**
Operating Expenses					
Salaries, Wages, & Benefits	$323,000	$692,230	$1,152,524	$1,526,238	$1,907,539
Depreciation	$6,667	$20,000	$40,000	$60,000	$80,000
Rent & Utilities	$40,000	$85,600	$131,592	$180,803	$233,460
Total Operating Expenses	**$854,967**	**$1,547,676**	**$2,588,328**	**$3,611,938**	**$5,083,166**
Income Taxes	$0	$0	-$550,989	-$1,542,198	-$2,749,048
Net Income (Loss)	**($401,329)**	**$197,583**	**$1,227,012**	**$2,313,297**	**$4,123,572**

2890 Shadow Creek - Boulder, Colorado - 303.579.9871 - info@upi.com

University Parent, Inc.

Balance Sheet
Years 0–5 ($)

	Begin	Year 1	Year 2	Year 3	Year 4	Year 5
ASSETS						
CURRENT ASSETS						
Cash	530,000	117,763	281,640	1,616,578	4,006,443	8,252,410
Accounts Receivable		0	0	0	0	0
Inventories		0	0	0	0	0
Other Current Assets		113	3,947	50,228	63,484	75,729
Total Current Assets	530,000	117,875	285,588	1,666,806	4,069,927	8,328,139
PROPERTY & EQUIPMENT	0	16,533	50,133	81,733	109,333	136,133
TOTAL ASSETS	530,000	134,409	335,721	1,748,539	4,179,261	8,464,272
LIABILITIES & SHAREHOLDERS' EQUITY						
CURRENT LIABILITIES						
Short-Term Debt	0	0	0	0	0	0
Accounts Payable & Accrued Expen		5,625	9,281	191,445	306,567	464,840
Other Current Liabilities		113	186	3,829	6,131	9,297
Current Portion of Long-term Debt	0	0	0	0	0	0
Total Current Liabilities	0	5,738	9,467	195,274	312,698	474,137
LONG-TERM DEBT (less current portion)	0	0	0	0	0	0
STOCKHOLDERS' EQUITY						
Common Stock	30,000	30,000	30,000	30,000	30,000	30,000
Preferred Stock	500,000	500,000	500,000	500,000	500,000	500,000
Retained Earnings		(401,329)	(203,746)	1,023,266	3,336,563	7,460,135
Total Equity	530,000	128,671	326,254	1,553,266	3,866,563	7,990,135
TOTAL LIABILITIES & EQUITY	530,000	134,409	335,721	1,748,539	4,179,261	8,464,272

2890 Shadow Creek – Boulder, Colorado – 303.579.9871 – info@upi.com

University Parent, Inc.

Offering

Investment Requirements
UPI initially requires $500,000 in seed funding for the first year of operations. This amount will fund the expansion to the University of Denver and Colorado State University as well as funding new employee salaries and the opening of a Colorado regional office in Boulder. Investors will own 35% of the venture.

Valuation
Using the venture capital method, in Year 5, assuming net earnings of $4.1 million, and an industry P/E ratio of 17.3, UPI will have a market value of $70 million.

Financing
UPI seeks $500,000 in seed funding in Year 0. This round will provide the investor with a 35% stake in the venture at a 60% annual rate of return.

Exit Strategy
In Year 5, UPI we be marketed to Hearst Publishing and Condé Nast Publishing. These are logical acquirers because both companies own over 30 niche magazines.

University Parent, Inc.

Appendices

2890 Shadow Creek – Boulder, Colorado – 303.579.9871 – info@upi.com

University Parent, Inc.

Appendix A, Income Statement, Years 1–5 ($)

	Year 1	Year 2	Year 3	Year 4	Year 5
NET REVENUES	495,000	1,881,000	4,573,800	7,726,455	12,276,479
COST OF REVENUE	26,362	90,741	152,471	204,023	255,692
% of Revenues	5.3%	4.8%	3.3%	2.6%	2.1%
GROSS PROFIT	468,638	1,790,259	4,421,329	7,522,432	12,020,787
% of Revenues	94.7%	95.2%	96.7%	97.4%	97.9%
OPERATING EXPENSES					
Sales & Marketing	240,750	364,610	674,953	1,023,764	1,734,098
Research & Development	219,800	291,186	360,569	434,809	514,245
General and Administration	394,417	891,880	1,552,806	2,153,364	2,834,823
Total Operating Expenses	854,967	1,547,676	2,588,328	3,611,938	5,083,166
% of Revenues	173%	82%	57%	47%	41%
EARNINGS FROM OPERATIONS	(386,329)	242,583	1,833,001	3,910,495	6,937,620
EXTRAORDINARY INCOME/(EXPENSE)	(15,000)	(45,000)	(55,000)	(55,000)	(65,000)
EARNINGS BEFORE INTEREST & TAXES	(401,329)	197,583	1,778,001	3,855,495	6,872,620
INTEREST INCOME/(EXPENSE)	0	0	0	0	0
NET EARNINGS BEFORE TAXES	(401,329)	197,583	1,778,001	3,855,495	6,872,620
TAXES	0	0	(550,989)	(1,542,198)	(2,749,048)
NET EARNINGS	(401,329)	197,583	1,227,012	2,313,297	4,123,572
% of Revenues	-81.1%	10.5%	26.8%	29.9%	33.6%

2890 Shadow Creek - Boulder, Colorado - 303.579.9871 - info@upi.com

University Parent, Inc.

Appendix B, Balance Sheet, Years 0–5 ($)

	Begin	Year 1	Year 2	Year 3	Year 4	Year 5
ASSETS						
CURRENT ASSETS						
Cash	530,000	117,763	281,640	1,616,578	4,006,443	8,252,410
Accounts Receivable		0	0	0	0	0
Inventories		0	0	0	0	0
Other Current Assets		113	3,947	50,228	63,484	75,729
Total Current Assets	530,000	117,875	285,588	1,666,806	4,069,927	8,328,139
PROPERTY & EQUIPMENT	0	16,533	50,133	81,733	109,333	136,133
TOTAL ASSETS	530,000	134,409	335,721	1,748,539	4,179,261	8,464,272
LIABILITIES & SHAREHOLDERS' EQUITY						
CURRENT LIABILITIES						
Short-Term Debt	0	0	0	0	0	0
Accounts Payable & Accrued Expen		5,625	9,281	191,445	306,567	464,840
Other Current Liabilities		113	186	3,829	6,131	9,297
Current Portion of Long-Term Debt	0	0	0	0	0	0
Total Current Liabilities	0	5,738	9,467	195,274	312,698	474,137
LONG-TERM DEBT (less current portion)	0	0	0	0	0	0
STOCKHOLDERS' EQUITY						
Common Stock	30,000	30,000	30,000	30,000	30,000	30,000
Preferred Stock	500,000	500,000	500,000	500,000	500,000	500,000
Retained Earnings		(401,329)	(203,746)	1,023,266	3,336,563	7,460,135
Total Equity	530,000	128,671	326,254	1,553,266	3,866,563	7,990,135
TOTAL LIABILITIES & EQUITY	530,000	134,409	335,721	1,748,539	4,179,261	8,464,272

University Parent, Inc.

Appendix C, Cash Flow Statement, Years 1–5 ($)

		Year 1	Year 2	Year 3	Year 4	Year 5
OPERATING ACTIVITIES						
Net Earnings		(401,329)	197,583	1,227,012	2,313,297	4,123,572
Depreciation		7,467	24,400	48,400	72,400	97,200
Working Capital Changes						
(Inc.)/Dec. Accts. Rec.		0	0	0	0	0
(Inc.)/Dec. Inventories		0	0	0	0	0
(Inc.)/Dec. Other CA		(113)	(3,835)	(46,281)	(13,256)	(12,245)
(Inc.)/Dec. Accts Pay Expenses		5,625	3,656	182,163	115,122	158,274
(Inc.)/Dec. Other CL		113	73	3,643	2,302	3,165
Net Cash Provided/(Used) Operating Activities		(388,237)	221,878	1,414,937	2,489,865	4,369,967
INVESTING ACTIVITIES						
Property & Equipment		(24,000)	(58,000)	(80,000)	(100,000)	(124,000)
Other						
Net Cash Used in Investing		(24,000)	(58,000)	(80,000)	(100,000)	(124,000)
FINANCING ACTIVITIES						
(Inc.)/Dec. Short-Term Debt		0	0	0	0	0
(Inc.)/Dec. Curr. Portion LTD		0	0	0	0	0
(Inc.)/Dec. Long-Term Debt		0	0	0	0	0
(Inc.)/Dec. Common Stock		0	0	0	0	0
(Inc.)/Dec. Preferred Stock		0	0	0	0	0
Dividends Declared		0	0	0	0	0
Net Cash Provided/(Used) by Financing		0	0	0	0	0
INCREASE/(DECREASE) IN CASH		(412,237)	163,878	1,334,937	2,389,865	4,245,967
CASH AT BEGINNING OF YEAR		530,000	117,763	281,640	1,616,578	4,006,443
CASH AT END OF YEAR	530,000	117,763	281,640	1,616,578	4,006,443	8,252,410

2890 Shadow Creek – Boulder, Colorado – 303.579.9871 – info@upi.com

University Parent, Inc.

Appendix D, Monthly and Quarterly Cash Flow Statements, Years 1–5 ($)

		Year 1	Year 2	Year 3	Year 4	Year 5
OPERATING ACTIVITIES						
Net Earnings		(401,329)	197,583	1,227,012	2,313,297	4,123,572
Depreciation		7,467	24,400	48,400	72,400	97,200
Working Capital Changes						
(Inc.)/Dec. Accts. Rec.		0	0	0	0	0
(Inc.)/Dec. Inventories		0	0	0	0	0
(Inc.)/Dec. Other CA		(113)	(3,835)	(46,281)	(13,256)	(12,245)
(Inc.)/Dec. Accts Pay Expenses		5,625	3,656	182,163	115,122	158,274
(Inc.)/Dec. Other CL		113	73	3,643	2,302	3,165
Net Cash Provided/(Used) Operating Activities		(388,237)	221,878	1,414,937	2,489,865	4,369,967
INVESTING ACTIVITIES						
Property & Equipment		(24,000)	(58,000)	(80,000)	(100,000)	(124,000)
Other						
Net Cash Used in Investing		(24,000)	(58,000)	(80,000)	(100,000)	(124,000)
FINANCING ACTIVITIES						
(Inc.)/Dec. Short-Term Debt		0	0	0	0	0
(Inc.)/Dec. Curr. Portion LTD		0	0	0	0	0
(Inc.)/Dec. Long-Term Debt		0	0	0	0	0
(Inc.)/Dec. Common Stock		0	0	0	0	0
(Inc.)/Dec. Preferred Stock		0	0	0	0	0
Dividends Declared		0	0	0	0	0
Net Cash Provided/(Used) by Financing		0	0	0	0	0
INCREASE/(DECREASE) IN CASH		(412,237)	163,878	1,334,937	2,389,865	4,245,967
CASH AT BEGINNING OF YEAR		530,000	117,763	281,640	1,616,578	4,006,443
CASH AT END OF YEAR	530,000	117,763	281,640	1,616,578	4,006,443	8,252,410

2890 Shadow Creek - Boulder, Colorado - 303.579.9871 - info@upi.com

University Parent, Inc.

Appendix E, Break-Even Analysis, Years 1–5 ($)

	Year 1	Year 2	Year 3	Year 4	Year 5
Revenue	495,000	1,881,000	4,573,800	7,726,455	12,276,479
Cost of Revenue					
Variable	24,562	85,341	141,671	186,023	228,692
Fixed	1,800	5,400	10,800	18,000	27,000
Total	26,362	90,741	152,471	204,023	255,692
Operating Expenses					
Variable	49,500	188,100	457,380	772,646	1,227,648
Fixed	805,467	1,359,576	2,130,948	2,839,292	3,855,519
Total	854,967	1,547,676	2,588,328	3,611,938	5,083,166
Total Costs & Expenses					
Variable	74,062	273,441	599,051	958,668	1,456,340
Fixed	807,267	1,364,976	2,141,748	2,857,292	3,882,519
Total	881,329	1,638,417	2,740,799	3,815,960	5,338,858
Variable Costs/Revenue Ratio	0.15	0.15	0.13	0.12	0.12
Break-Even Point Revenues	949,301	1,597,154	2,464,540	3,262,032	4,405,087

Appendix F, Capital Expenditure Detail

	Year 1	Year 2	Year 3	Year 4	Year 5
Net Revenues	495,000	1,881,000	4,573,800	7,726,455	12,276,479
Capital Expenditures					
Computers, Software, & Office Equipment	20,000	40,000	60,000	80,000	100,000
Plant & Equipment	0	0	0	0	0
Other	4,000	18,000	20,000	20,000	24,000
Total Capital Expenditures	24,000	58,000	80,000	100,000	124,000

2890 Shadow Creek – Boulder, Colorado – 303.579.9871 – info@upi.com

University Parent, Inc.

Appendix G, Financial Assumptions

General Assumptions

First Month of Operations	June 2004
Estimated Inflation	2.5%
Corporate Tax Rate	38%

Annual Projections

	Year 1	Year 2	Year 3	Year 4	Year 5
Product A—Magazine					
Number of Schools	3	9	22	32	44
Total Issues/Year	9	36	66	96	132
Number of Units/Ad	225	900	1,800	2,925	4,425
Avg. Price/Ad Page	$1,000	$1,100	$1,210	$1,331	$1,464
Print Advertising Sales	$225,000	$990,000	$2,178,000	$3,893,175	$6,478,643
Product B—Website					
Advertisements Sold/Year	360	1,080	2,640	3,840	5,280
Price per Unit	$750	$825	$908	$998	$1,098
Web Advertising Sales	$270,000	$891,000	$2,395,800	$3,833,280	$5,797,836

Printing Costs

	Year 1	Year 2	Year 3	Year 4	Year 5
Magazines Printed/Year	90,000	360,000	660,000	960,000	1,320,000
Printing Cost/Magazine	0.25	0.23	0.21	0.19	0.17
Total Costs	22,500	82,800	138,600	182,400	224,400

Funding

Total Shares Outstanding	2,000,000
Preferred Shares (Investors)	700,000 (35%)
Common Shares (Founders/Employees)	130,000 (65%)
Expected Investor IRR	60%
Total Funding Required	$500,000
Founders' Contribution	$30,000

2890 Shadow Creek - Boulder, Colorado - 303.579.9871 - info@upi.com

University Parent, Inc.

Appendix H, Development Timeline, Year 1

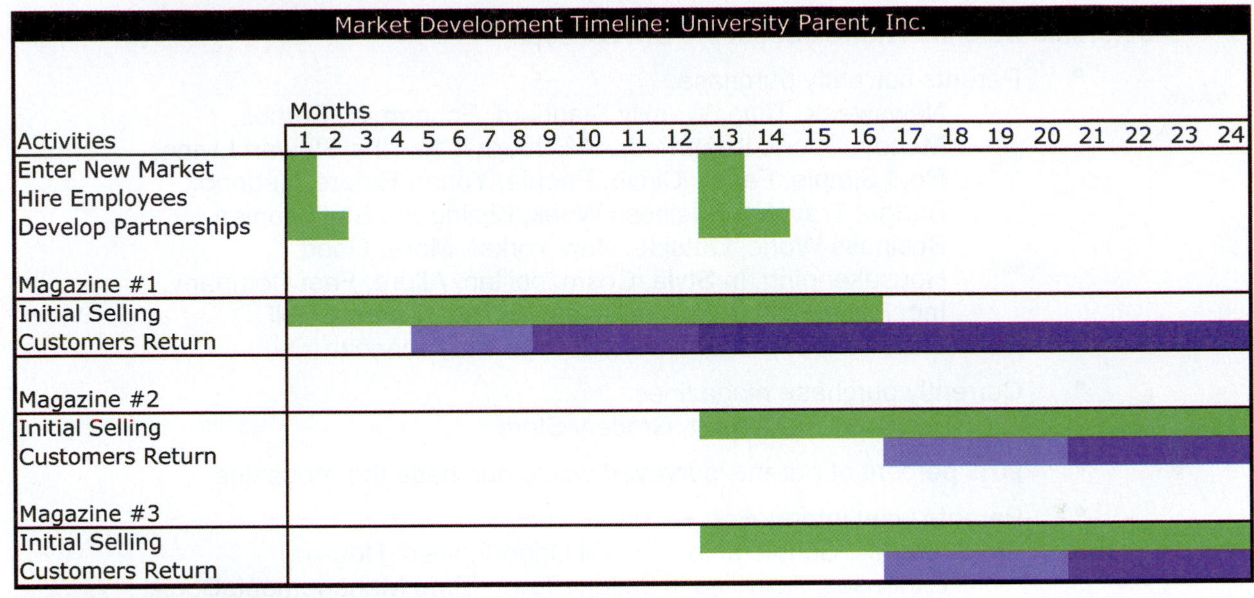

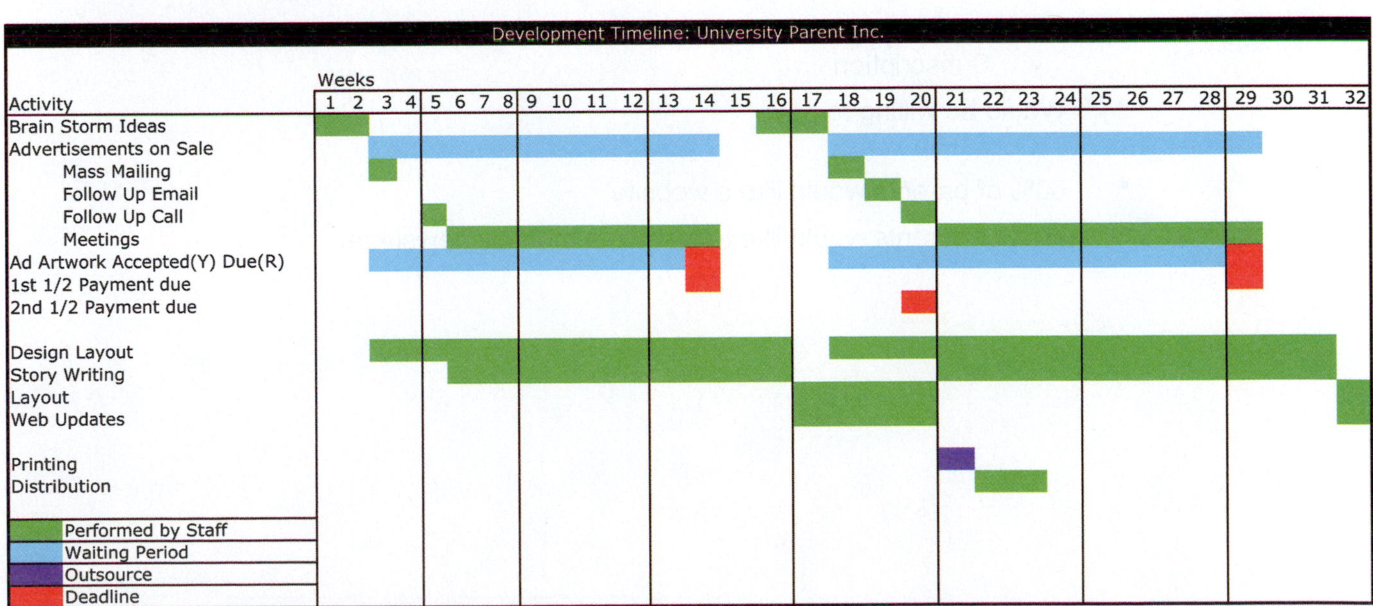

2890 Shadow Creek – Boulder, Colorado – 303.579.9871 – info@upi.com

Appendix I, Customer Survey Results

40 Parents were interviewed about the UPI concept.

- Parents currently purchase:
  - ✓ Newsweek, Time, Weekly Standard, Economist, Forbes, Money, Sports Illustrated, AAE Journal, Martha Stewart Living, Real Simple, Family Circle, People, Young Riders, Redbook, Budget Traveler, Business Week, Kiplingers, Smithsonian, Business World, Outside, New Yorker, More, Good Housekeeping, In Style, Cosmopolitan, Allure, Fast Company, Inc, Prevention, Readers Digest, Sunset, Tennis, Golf, Consumer Reports, Veranda, Scientific American
- Currently purchase magazines:
  - ✓ Subscription, Airport, Grocery Store
- 90% percent of parents surveyed would purchase the magazine
- Parents want information about:
  - ✓ Grades, Scholarships, Travel Opportunities, Housing Expenses, Activities in College Town, Time Management, Social Life, Programs, Internships, Job Placements, Curriculum, Student Safety, Speakers, Career Guidance, Graduation Requirements, Student Groups, Transportation
- Currently receive information:
  - ✓ From the student, from the college, media
- Would like to purchase UP:
  - ✓ Subscription
- Would be willing to pay:
  - ✓ $1–$5
- 60% of parents would like a website
- 70% of parents would like to receive a monthly newsletter

Appendix 4

BizBuilder Business Plan

Congratulations! If you've made it this far, you have given yourself a comprehensive, basic education in entrepreneurship and you will have made progress toward writing a business plan that will work for your operations and impress potential investors and lenders.

At this point, you will probably want to expand and enhance your business plan to reflect all that you have learned. Worksheets to complete for the following questions are on the BizBuilder section of the Web site. Use them to create a more professional-looking business plan. Follow the guidelines in Chapter 2 to ensure the quality of the business plan. These features will make your plan a better road map for running your organization and will make it more attractive to investors.

The BizBuilder section also includes a PowerPoint template you can use to create a Business Plan Presentation. With a PowerPoint Business Plan Presentation, you can quickly show potential employees, partners, and investors the highlights of your plan.

The BizBuilder Business Plan includes an additional section for students wishing to start a not-for-profit organization. If you are starting a nonprofit, please fill out this section and adjust your business plan accordingly.

Business Plan Pro software is also included with this book to give you another option for preparing your plan. Explore Business Plan Pro to see if it's a better fit for your business plan. Both the BizBuilder section of the Web site and the Business Plan Pro CD can help you write a professional business plan.

BizBuilder Business Plan Worksheet Questions/Notes

Cover Page

A. What is the full name of your organization?

B. Provide contact information for the organization including the names of majority owners.

C. What confidentiality/nondisclosure language will you include?

D. Provide the date of the plan.

Table of Contents (Can Be Placed Before or After the Executive Summary)

A. List the key sections of the plan and the page numbers.

1.0 Executive Summary

A. What is the name of your organization?

B. Describe your business idea and the nature of the target market.

C. What type of organization are you starting?

D. What products and/or services will you offer?
E. What is your marketing and sales strategy? Explain how your business idea will satisfy a customer need.
F. Describe the key success factors for the organization.
G. Calculate the "economics of one unit" for your organization.
H. What are your short-term business goals (less than one year)?
I. What are your long-term business goals (from one to five years)?
J. What resources and skills do you (and the other owners and managers) have that will help make your organization successful? What other skills are needed and how will they be obtained?
K. If there is more than one owner, describe how the ownership will be shared.
L. What are the sources and uses of funds?
M. Include a summary of the financial projections.
N. What is the growth and exit strategy?

2.0 Mission, Vision, and Culture

A. Write a mission statement for your organization in 21 words or fewer that clearly states your competitive advantage, strategy, and tactics.
B. Create a vision statement for your organization.
C. Describe the core beliefs you will use to run your organization and how they will be reflected in its culture.
D. Identify the ways you plan to run a socially responsible organization.

3.0 Company Description

A. What industry are you in?
B. What type of organization is it (manufacturing, wholesale, service)?
C. What needs will this business satisfy?
D. What is your strategic advantage?
E. What is your organization's legal structure (sole proprietorship, partnership, LLC, C corporation, etc.)?
F. Why did you choose this legal structure?
G. In what state are you registered or do you intend to register?
H. Where will you physically operate the organization?
I. What is the geographic reach of the organization?
J. Who will be the owner(s), partners, or stockholders for your company?
K. If your business is incorporated, describe what percentage of the company is owned by each shareholder.

4.0 Opportunity Analysis and Research

A. Describe your research methods (surveys, focus groups, general research, and statistical research).
B. Describe your target customer along as many dimensions as you have defined (demographic, geographic, needs, trends, and decision-making process).

4.1 Industry Analysis

A. What is the industry or set of industries in which your organization operates (include the NAICS codes)?
B. What factors influence the demand for your product or service?
C. What factors influence the supply for your product or service?
D. How large is your industry (historic, current, projected size)?
E. What are the current and anticipated characteristics and trends in the industry?
F. What are the major customer groups for the industry (consumers, governments, businesses)?
G. How large is your target market (number of customers, size of purchases, frequency of purchases, trends)?

4.2 Environmental Analysis

A. Perform a SWOT analysis of your organization.
B. What external/environmental factors are likely to impact your business?
C. Are there customers for your business in other countries? How do you plan to reach them?

4.3 Competitive Analysis

A. How do you define/describe your competition, both direct and indirect?
B. Describe your competitive advantage.
C. Find three competitors and describe them.
D. Describe any international competitors you have found who may be able to access your customers. How do you intend to compete?
E. Describe your strategy for outperforming the competition.
F. What tactics will you use to carry out this strategy?
G. What barriers to entry can you create to block out competitors?

5.0 Marketing Strategy and Plan

A. Explain how your marketing plan targets your market segment.
B. What percentage of the market do you feel you need to capture for your business to be profitable?
C. Write a positioning statement for your business.
D. How do you plan to grow the organization (self-generated, franchising, acquisition)?

5.1 Products/Services

A. What products/services do you intend to sell?
B. Explain how your product will meet a customer need.
C. Where is your product/service in the product life cycle?
D. Describe the features and benefits of the product/service your business will focus on selling.
E. What existing copyrights or patents do you own or expect to own?

F. How will your organization help others? List all the organizations to which you plan to contribute. (Your contribution may be time, money, your product, or something else.)

G. Do you intend to publicize your philanthropy? Why, or why not? If you do, explain how you will work your philanthropy into your marketing.

5.2 Pricing

A. Describe your pricing strategy and structure, and the gross margins you expect to generate.

B. What will your discount structure, if any, be?

C. Will you accept personal checks from customers? Credit cards? Will you offer charge accounts or customer credit?

5.3 Promotion

A. Identify the ways you plan to promote your product or service, including the message, the media, and the distribution channels. Describe why you have chosen these methods and why you think they will work.

B. Show examples of marketing materials you intend to use to sell.

C. What is your business slogan?

D. Do you have a logo for your business? How do you intend to protect it?

E. Where do you intend to advertise (be specific, including identifying reach and frequency)?

F. How do you plan to get publicity for your organization?

G. List ways you intend to provide superior customer service.

H. Write a one-minute sales pitch for your product/service and describe five sales prospects you intend to pitch.

I. How will you keep your customer database? What essential questions will you ask every customer for your database?

5.4 Place

A. Where do you intend to sell your product? Describe the advantages and disadvantages of your location(s).

B. What are the surrounding businesses? Access routes?

C. If vehicular traffic is important to your organization, what is the traffic count for this location?

D. What is the workforce availability in the area as it pertains to your needs?

6.0 Management and Operations

6.1 Management Team

A. Create an organizational chart for your business.

B. Will you be hiring employees? If so, describe what their qualifications should be, what you intend to pay them, and how they will help your business.

C. Do you intend to pay yourself a salary, wage, dividend, or commission? Explain.

D. What will your policies toward employees be? How will you make your organization a positive and rewarding place to work?
E. Describe the corporate governance plan for your organization. It should include five policies (rules) that will be the backbone of your organization's ethics.
F. Provide information for each of your mentors or advisors. If there is a board of advisors, list each member and describe his/her commitment to the board.
G. Provide contact information for your accountant, attorney, banker, and insurance agent.

6.2 Research and Development

A. What type of research are you doing? What do you intend to do?
B. What are others in the industry doing?
C. How will you protect your intellectual property?

6.3 Physical Location

A. Describe the actual physical place in greater detail than above.
B. What are the zoning laws in your area? Does your business comply?

6.4 Facilities

A. What type of building and equipment will you have?
B. Identify which technological tools you plan to use for your organization, and explain why.
C. How do you plan to get access to the technology you need?

6.5 Inventory, Production, and Quality Assurance

A. Where are you purchasing the products you plan to sell, or the parts you will use to manufacture those products? Illustrate your supply chain.
B. Do you intend to manufacture your product? If so, describe the manufacturing processes you will use. If not, describe how your product is manufactured.
C. Are there any economies of scale to be attained for your business? At what point do you anticipate attaining them?
D. Have you developed and/or adopted any innovations in production, inventory management, or distribution that are significant? What are they and why are they meaningful?
E. How do you plan to distribute your product to your target market?
F. Show the production-distribution channel for your business, and the markups along the chain.
G. What is the estimated delivery time between when you place an order with your supplier and when you will have the product available for your customers?
H. What method(s) will you use to define and ensure the quality of your products/services?
I. What types of insurance will your business need, and why?
J. What methods will you use to ensure that you comply with federal, state, and local tax laws?

K. What laws—such as minimum wage and age requirements, health and safety regulations, or antidiscrimation laws—will affect your business?

7.0 Financial Analysis and Projections

A. Describe your recordkeeping system.
B. List the types of bank accounts you will open for your organization.

7.1 Sources and Uses of Capital

A. How much capital do you need? When? What type and on what terms?
B. How will you use the money that you raise? Be specific.
C. List the items you will need to buy to start your business and add up the items to get your total start-up capital. Then, add a cash reserve of one-half your total start-up capital.
D. List the sources of financing for your start-up capital. Identify each source as equity, debt, or gift. Indicate the amount and type for each source.
E. What is your payback period? In other words, how long will it take you to earn enough profit to cover start-up capital?
F. Describe financing sources that might be willing to invest in your business in exchange for equity.
G. Describe any debt financing you intend to pursue. What is your debt ratio? What is your debt-to-equity ratio? Add a cash reserve of one-half your total start-up capital.
H. Do you plan to use bootstrap financing? Explain.
I. Do you plan to pursue venture capital? Why, or why not? List potential sources of venture capital.

7.2 Cash Flow Projections

A. List and describe your monthly fixed costs and add a cash reserve that covers three months of fixed costs.
B. Create a projected cash flow statement for your business for the first four quarters and the second and third years of operation.
C. Calculate the burn rate for your business.

7.3 Balance Sheet Projections

A. Create a projected balance sheet for your business for the first four quarters and the second and third years of operation.
B. Create a pie chart showing your current assets, long-term assets, current liabilities, and long-term liabilities.

7.4 Income Statement Projections

A. Create a projected income statement for your business for the first four quarters and the second and third years of operation.
B. Create a bar chart showing your gross revenues, gross profit, and net income.

7.5 Breakeven Analysis

A. Use Excel or another spreadsheet program to create a spreadsheet projecting the expenses for your business. Use this data to perform a breakeven analysis.

7.6 Ratio Analysis

A. Use your projected financial statements to calculate all of your key ratios.

B. Compare these ratios to your industry using publicly available data.

7.7 Risks and Assumptions

A. List the risks and assumptions that underlie your financial projections.

B. Identify any external factors that you feel should be disclosed as substantial risks.

8.0 Funding Request and Exit Strategy

8.1 Amount and Type of Funds Requested

A. Clearly state how much money you are requesting in this plan and the terms under which you anticipate obtaining the funds.

B. Do you intend to use debt to finance your business? Explain.

C. Do you plan to issue bonds to finance your business at some point in the future?

8.2 Exit Plan

A. How will investors get paid back/out? Public offering? Employee buyout? Merger or acquisition? Liquidation? Stock buyback?

B. When will this happen?

C. Do you plan to franchise your business, or license any of your products? Explain.

8.3 Milestones

A. Create a PERT chart for your organization to make your plans clear to potential investors.

Appendices

Resumes and Position Descriptions

A. Include a resume for each key team member.

B. Add position descriptions for any vital start-up positions that are not yet filled.

Sample Promotional Materials

A. Include any sample logos, letterhead, advertisements, brochures, or other items that can be inserted into the plan.

B. Add photos of any promotional items, signage, or larger materials to provide examples.

Product Illustrations/Diagrams

A. If you have nonproprietary drawings or properly authorized proprietary drawings, illustrations, or diagrams of your product or service concept, insert them here.

B. Any floor plans, assembly layouts, or the like should be included.

Detailed Financial Projections

A. Monthly financials and other financial projections that are in too great of detail for inclusion in the main document go here.

B. Include detailed assumptions and notes underlying the projections.

C. Significant contracts.

If You Are Starting a Not-for-Profit Organization, Also Consider

1. What is the name of your nonprofit?
2. What problem(s) are you trying to reduce or eliminate?
3. Describe the mission of your organization.
4. Describe the programs and services you plan to create.
5. How will your organization achieve the changes you intend to bring about?
6. What is the unit of change (per person, animal, house, etc.)?
7. How will you measure these changes?
8. Who are your competitors?
9. How much will it cost you to deliver a unit of service?
10. What are your sources of funding?

Appendix 5

Resources for Entrepreneurs[1]

Books

On Starting a Business—and Succeeding

101 Successful Businesses You Can Start on the Internet, by Daniel S. Janal (International Thompson Publishing, Inc., 1997).

The Art of the Start: The Time-Tested, Battle-Hardened Guide for Anyone Starting Anything, by Guy Kawasaki (Portfolio, 2004).

Good to Great: Why Some Companies Make the Leap...and Others Do Not, by Jim Collins (HarperBusiness, 2001).

How to Make 1000 Mistakes in Business and Still Succeed: The Guide to Crucial Decisions in the Small Business, Home-Based Business and Professional Practice, by Harold L. Wright (Wright Track, 1995).

In Search of Excellence: Lessons from America's Best-Run Companies, by Thomas J. Peters and Robert H. Waterman (Harper, 2004).

The Innovator's Dilemma: When New Technologies Cause Great Firms to Fail, by Clayton M. Christensen (Harvard Business School Press, 1997).

The Innovator's Solution: Creating and Sustaining Successful Growth, by Clayton M. Christensen and Michael E. Raynor (Harvard Business School Press, 2003).

Mancuso's Small Business Resource Guide, by Joseph Mancuso (Sourcebooks Inc., 1996).

Online Success Tactics: 101 Ways to Build Your Small Business, by Jeanette S. Cates (Twin Towers Press, 2002).

Start Your Own Business, 4th ed., by Rieva Lesonsky (Entrepreneur Press, 2007).

What No One Ever Tells You About Starting Your Own Business: Real-Life Start-Up Advice from 101 Successful Entrepreneurs, 2nd ed., by Jan Norman (Kaplan Business, 2004).

The Young Entrepreneur's Guide to Starting and Running a Business, compl. rev. edition, by Steve Mariotti (Three Rivers Press, 2000).

On Thinking Like an Entrepreneur

The 7 Habits of Highly Effective People, rev. edition, by Stephen Covey (Free Press, 2004).

The 48 Laws of Power, by Robert Greene (Penguin, 2000).

Awakening the Entrepreneur Within: How Ordinary People Can Create Extraordinary Companies, by Michael Gerber (Harper, 2009).

The Entrepreneurial Mindset: Strategies for Continuously Creating Opportunity in an Age of Uncertainty, by Rita Gunther McGrath and Ian MacMillan (Harvard Business School Press, 2000).

Focus: The Future of Your Company Depends on It, by Al Ries (Harper, 2005).

Oh, the Places You'll Go!, by Dr. Seuss (Random House, 1990).

Secrets of the Young & Successful: How to Get Everything You Want Without Waiting a Lifetime, 2nd ed., by Jennifer Kushell and Scott M. Kaufman (Ys Media Corp., 2006).

[1] Please note that the publisher cannot guarantee that listed URLs will remain active, and is not responsible for future changes to the content of the Web sites.

The Student Success Manifesto: How to Create a Life of Passion, Purpose, and Prosperity, by Michael Simmons (Extreme Entrepreneurship Education Co., 2003).

Success Through a Positive Mental Attitude, by Napoleon Hill and W. Clement Stone (Thorsons, 1997).

Think and Grow Rich: A Black Choice, by Dennis Paul Kimbro and Napoleon Hill (Fawcett, 1992).

Think and Grow Rich: The Secret to Wealth Updated for the 21st Century, by Napoleon Hill (CreateSpace, 2010).

Traction: Get a Grip on Your Business, by Gino Wickman (eos, 2007).

A Whack on the Side of the Head: How You Can Be More Creative, 25th anniv. rev. edition, by Roger Von Oech (Business Plus, 2008).

On How Other Entrepreneurs Succeeded

The Accidental Entrepreneur: The 50 Things I Wish Someone Had Told Me About Starting a Business, by Susan Urquhart-Brown (AMACOM, 2008).

Ben & Jerry's: The Inside Scoop: How Two Real Guys Built a Business with a Social Conscience and a Sense of Humor, by Fred Lager (Three Rivers Press, 1995).

Entrepreneurs in Profile: How 20 of the World's Greatest Entrepreneurs Built Their Business Empires...and How You Can Too, by Steve Mariotti and Michael Caslin with Debra DeSalvo (The Career Press, Inc., 2002).

Founders at Work: Stories of Startups' Early Days, by Jessica Livingston (Apress, 2007).

Kitchen Table Entrepreneurs: How Eleven Women Escaped Poverty and Became Their Own Bosses, by Martha Shirk, Anna Wadia, Marie Wilson, and Sara Gould (Westview Press, 2004).

Life and Def: Sex, Drugs, Money, + God, by Russell Simmons (Three Rivers Press, 2002).

Losing My Virginity: How I've Survived, Had Fun, and Made a Fortune Doing Business My Way, by Richard Branson (Three Rivers Press, 1999).

The Men Behind Def Jam: The Radical Rise of Russell Simmons and Rick Rubin, by Alex Ogg (Omnibus Press, 2002).

The Republic of Tea: How an Idea Becomes a Business, by Mel Ziegler, Patricia Ziegler, and Bill Rosensweig (Doubleday, 1992).

The Republic of Tea: The Story of the Creation of a Business, as Told Through the Personal Letters of Its Founders, by Mel and Patricia Ziegler (Doubleday Business, 1994).

Steve Jobs: Wizard of Apple Computer, by Suzan Wilson (Enslow Publishers, 2001).

Student Entrepreneurs: 14 Undergraduate All-Stars Tell Their Stories, by Michael McMyne and Nicole Amare (Premium Press America, 2003).

Trump: The Way to the Top: The Best Business Advice I Ever Received, by Donald Trump (Crown Business, 2004).

You Need to Be a Little Bit Crazy: The Truth About Starting and Growing Your Business, by Barry J. Moltz (Authorhouse, 2008).

On Negotiating

The Art of Woo: Using Strategic Persuasion to Sell Your Idea, by G. Richard Shell and Mario Moussa (Penguin Group, 2007).

Bargaining for Advantage: Negotiation Strategies for Reasonable People, by G. Richard Shell (Penguin Group, 2006).

Difficult Conversations: How to Discuss What Matters Most, 1st ed., by Douglas Stone, Bruce Patton, Sheila Heen, and Roger Fisher (Penguin, 2000).

Winning, by Jack Welch (HarperCollins, 2005).

On Accounting

The Accounting Game, 2nd ed., *Basic Accounting Fresh from the Lemonade Stand,* by Judith Orloff and Darrell Millis (Sourcebooks, Inc., updated rev. edition, 2008).

Barron's Accounting Handbook, 5th ed., by Joel G. Siegel and Jae K. Shim (Barron's Educational Series, 2010).

E-Z Accounting, 5th ed., by Peter J. Eisen (Barron's Educational Series, 2009).

On Investing, Money Management, and Personal Finance

The Entrepreneur's Guide to Finance and Business: Wealth Creation Techniques for Growing a Business, by Steven Rogers (McGraw-Hill, 2002).

Irrational Exuberance, 2nd ed., by Robert J. Shiller (Broadway Business, 2006).

The Laws of Money, The Lessons of Life: Keep What You Have and Create What You Deserve, by Suze Orman (The Free Press, 2003).

The Millionaire Next Door, by Thomas J. Stanley and William D. Danko (Pocket, 1998).

The Motley Fool Investment Guide for Teens: 8 Steps to Having More Money Than Your Parents Ever Dreamed Of, by David Gardner, Tom Gardner, and Selena Maranjian (Fireside, 2002).

Rich Dad, Poor Dad: What the Rich Teach Their Kids About Money—That the Poor and Middle Class Do Not!, by Robert T. Kiyosaki and Sharon L. Lechter (BusinessPlus, 2010).

Understanding Wall Street, 5th ed., by Jeffrey B. Little (McGraw-Hill, 2009).

On Marketing

The 22 Immutable Laws of Branding: How to Build a Product or Service into a World-Class Brand, 1st ed., by Al Ries and Laura Ries (Harper Paperbacks, 2002).

Blue Ocean Strategy: How to Create Uncontested Market Space and Make Competition Irrelevant, by W. Chan Kim and Renée Mauborgne (Harvard Business School Press, 2005).

Conversation on Networking: Finding, Developing, and Maintaining Relationships for Business and Life, by Steven Smolinsky and Kay Keenan (Forever Talking Press, 2006).

Made to Stick: Why Some Ideas Survive and Others Die, by Chip Heath and Dan Heath (Random House, 2007).

Purple Cow: Transform Your Business by Being Remarkable, by Seth Godin (Portfolio, 2003).

The Sales Bible: The Ultimate Sales Resource, New Edition, by Jeffrey Gitomer (HarperCollins, 2008).

Social Marketing: Improving the Quality of Life, 2nd ed., by Philip Kotler, Ned Roberto, and Nancy Lee (Sage Publications, Inc., 2002).

The Tipping Point: How Little Things Can Make a Big Difference, by Malcolm Gladwell (Back Bay Books, 2002).

Magazines

Black Enterprise	*http://www.blackenterprise.com*
Brass	*http://www.brassmagazine.com*
BusinessWeek	*http://www.businessweek.com*
Entrepreneur	*http://www.entrepreneur.com*

Fast Company	*http://www.fastcompany.com*
Forbes	*http://www.forbes.com*
Fortune	*http://money.cnn.com/magazines/fortune/*
Harvard Business Review	*http://hbr.org/*
Hispanic Business	*http://www.hispanicbusiness.com*
Inc. Magazine	*http://www.inc.com*
Kiplinger's	*http://www.kiplinger.com/magazine/*
Money	*http://money.cnn.com/magazines/moneymag/*
Smart Money	*http://www.smartmoney.com*
Young Money	*http://www.youngmoney.com*

Web Sites

Association Directory, http://info.asaenet.org, from the American Society of Association Executives.

BizBuySell at *http://www.bizbuysell.com* sends registered users who might want to buy your business e-mails, alerting them that you want to sell.

Business Owners Idea Café at *http://www.businessownersideacafe.com* provides a tool for figuring out how much capital you will need to get your business off the ground.

Census data is available at *http://www.census.gov.*

Copyright Office: http://www.copyright.gov.

Currency Converter: http://finance.yahoo.com/currency?u.

Download.com at *www.download.com* has free software. Be sure to run any software through your virus-detection program before installing it on your hard drive.

E-Commerce Guide: http://www.ecommerce-guide.com.

Internal Revenue Service: *http://www.irs.gov.* You can download any tax form you need from the IRS Web site.

Internet Public Library at *http://www.ipl.org* is a good source for industry and market statistics.

InterNIC, http://www.internic.net, is where you can register the name of your Web site.

Practical Money Skills: http://www.practicalmoneyskills.com.

Standards of Corporate Responsibility at *http://www.svn.org/initiatives/standards.html* provides ideas on how to make your business socially responsible.

Surveys can be created using *http://www.surveymonkey.com.*

Buying Wholesale

The following is a list of Web sites where you can purchase products wholesale:

American Science and Surplus, http://www.sciplus.com; science, chemistry, and lab-related toys and equipment.

Craft Catalog, http://www.craftcatalog.com; provides crafts and art supplies, including brushes, paints, and sewing materials.

CR's Crafts, http://www.crscraft.com; doll and bear supplies.

Golf Discount, http://www.golfdiscount.com; golf clubs, balls, spikes, and shoes.

Harold Import Company, http://www.haroldimport.com; gifts, tabletop items, kitchenware, housewares.

Johnny's Selected Seeds, http://www.johnnyseeds.com; supplier of plant, flower, and herb seeds, along with garden accessories.

Off Price Clothing, http://www.offpricemarket.com/; returned and recycled clothing at low prices.

Oriental Trader, http://www.orientaltrading.com; large provider of wholesale gift items.

Party Pro, http://www.partypro.com; party and paper supplies.

Sav-On Closeouts, http://www.sav-on-closeouts.com; wholesale novelties and closeouts.

St. Louis Wholesaler, http://stlouiswholesale.com; sunglasses, jewelry, and toys.

VendMart, Inc., http://www.vendmart.com; snack, laundry supplies, and other vending machine items.

WholesaleCentral.com, http://www.wholesalecentral.com; a large collection of categories and subcategories, along with a great search feature. Business-to-business only.

Additional Resources

The **Small Business Administration (SBA)** is a federal agency created to support and promote entrepreneurs. The SBA offers free and inexpensive pamphlets on a variety of business subjects. Some local offices offer counseling to small business owners.

Contact the SBA at: Small Business Administration, 409 Third Street SW, Washington, DC 20416, (800) 827–5722, or visit *http://www.sba.gov*.

The **Minority Business Development Agency (MBDA)** is a federal agency created to foster the establishment and growth of minority-owned businesses. MBDA provides funding for a network of Minority Business Development Centers (MBDCs), Native American Business Development Centers (NABDCs), and Business Resource Centers (BRCs). The centers provide minority entrepreneurs with one-on-one assistance in writing business plans, marketing, management and technical assistance, and financial planning to assure adequate financing for business ventures.

To find a Minority Business Development Center in your area, visit *http://www.mbda.gov*.

The **Service Corps of Retired Executives (SCORE)** is a group of retired businesspeople who volunteer as counselors and mentors to entrepreneurs.

To locate an office near you, contact SCORE Association, 409 3rd Street SW, 6th Floor, Washington, DC 20024, (800) 634-0245, *http://www.score.org*.

The **National Association of Women Business Owners** helps female entrepreneurs network. You can join a local chapter of female entrepreneurs in your area.

National Association of Women Business Owners, 601 Pennsylvania Avenue, NW, South Building, Suite 900, Washington, DC 20004, (800) 55-NAWBO, *http://www.nawbo.org*.

The **United States Department of Agriculture (USDA)** is a federal agency that provides financial and business support in rural communities through its Business and Community Development Programs. It also offers Cooperative Services Programs to promote the use of cooperatives to distribute and market agricultural products. Much like SBA-supported Small Business Development Centers, there are Rural Business Entrepreneurship Centers nationwide.

USDA, 1400 Independence Avenue, SW, Washington, DC 20250, (202) 720-2791, *http://www.usda.gov*.

Awards for Entrepreneurs

If you are an entrepreneur under 25, you may qualify for awards that promote youth entrepreneurship and education.

Ernst & Young Entrepreneur of the Year Award

http://www.ey.com/US/en/About-us/Entrepreneur-Of-The-Year/

To qualify for the Ernst & Young award, you must be an owner/manager primarily responsible for the recent performance of a privately held or public company that is at least two years old.

Guardian Life Insurance "Girls Going Places" Scholarship Award

http://www.guardianlife.com/womens_channel/girls_going_places/

For girls ages 12 to 18 to further entrepreneurial pursuits, or for college.

National Association for the Self-Employed Future Entrepreneur of the Year Award

http://benefits.nase.org/show_benefit.asp?Benefit=Scholarship

This scholarship is given to a young man or woman who is a micro-business owner and demonstrates leadership and academic excellence, ingenuity, and entrepreneurial spirit.

NFIB Young Entrepreneur Award

http://www.nfib.com/page/nfibYoungEntrepreneurAward.html

The NFIB Young Entrepreneur Foundation grants NFIB Young Entrepreneur Awards to high school seniors nationwide.

NFTE Global Young Entrepreneur of the Year

http://www.nfte.com

NFTE graduates can win an all-expenses-paid trip to New York City for NFTE's annual "Dare to Dream" Awards Dinner and a grant to be applied toward the awardee's business, or college education.

SBA Young Entrepreneur of the Year Award

http://www.sba.gov

At National Small Business Week, one outstanding entrepreneur is named to represent each state, the District of Columbia, Puerto Rico, and Guam as the state Small Business Person of the Year. From this group, the National Small Business Person of the Year is chosen.

Staples Youth Social Entrepreneurship Competition

http://www.genv.net/en-us/staples-yse

For young people between the ages of 12 and 24 who are operating a youth-led social venture, and are able to demonstrate impact. Hosted by Ashoka and Staples, Inc.

Appendix 6

Useful Formulas and Equations

Liquidity Ratios

$$\text{Current Ratio} = \frac{\text{Current Assets}}{\text{Current Liabilities}}$$

$$\text{Quick Ratio} = \frac{\text{Current Assets} - (\text{Inventory} + \text{Prepayments})}{\text{Current Liabilities}}$$

Activity Ratios (Efficiency Ratios)

$$\text{Accounts Receivable Turnover} = \frac{\text{Annual Net Credit Sales}}{\text{Average Accounts Receivable}}$$

$$\text{Average Collection Period} = \frac{\text{Accounts Receivable}}{\text{Average Daily Credit Sales}}$$

$$\text{Inventory Turnover} = \frac{\text{Cost of Goods Sold}}{\text{Average Inventory}}$$

$$\text{Days' Sales in Inventory} = \frac{\text{Ending Inventory}}{\text{Daily Cost of Goods Sold}}$$

Profitability Ratios

$$\text{Gross Profit Margin} = \frac{\text{Gross Profit}}{\text{Net Sales}}$$

$$\text{Return on Sales} = \frac{\text{Net Income}}{\text{Sales}}$$

$$\text{Return on Assets (ROA)} = \frac{\text{Net Income} + \text{Interest} + \text{Income Taxes}}{\text{Average Total Assets}}$$

$$\text{Return on Common Equity (ROE)} = \frac{\text{Net Income} - \text{Preferred Stock Dividends}}{\text{Average Common Stockholders Equity}}$$

Market Ratios

$$\text{Earnings per Share (EPS)} = \frac{\text{Net Income} - \text{Preferred Stock Dividends}}{\text{Common Shares Outstanding}}$$

$$\text{Return on Investment (ROI)} = \frac{\text{Net Income}}{\text{Average Owners' Equity}}$$

Debt Ratios (Leverage Ratios)

$$\text{Debt Ratio} = \frac{\text{Total Liabilities}}{\text{Total Assets}}$$

$$\text{Debt-to-Equity Ratio} = \frac{\text{Total Debt} + \text{Value of Leases}}{\text{Total Equity}}$$

$$\text{Times Interest Earned or Interest Coverage} = \frac{\text{EBIT}}{\text{Interest Expense}}$$

Appendix 7

Accounting Journal Distribution Guide

The following table is a general guide to help you make the best choice when distributing income and expenses in an accounting journal. In some cases there is more than one correct choice. If so, make the best choice for your situation, and then stick with that method. Then apply that decision consistently.

Always use the accounting format ( ) to designate a negative value entry. For example, negative $150.00 is written as (150.00).

Purchases—$ Out

Category	Type of Transaction	Explanation
FC	Accounting/bookkeeping service	
FC	Advertising (all types)	Not driven by sales.
FC	Bank fees	
FC	Brochures	
FC	Bus tickets	
FC	Business cards	
(CAPITAL INV.)	Cash taken out by owner (Draw)	Negative because you're taking money out of the business; use ( ).
FC	Catalog designed	
FC	Catalog printed	
FC	Cleaning service	
INV. COSTS	Contracted direct labor	Labor paid "per piece" for work directly producing the product or service.
FC	Computer, business only	
FC	Computer supplies, business only	
FC	Consulting fees	
INV. COST	Costs listed in your EOU model	
FC	Development of Web site	
(CAPITAL INV.)	Draw of cash by owner	Negative because you're taking money out of the business; use ( ).
FC	Electric bill	
FC	Entertainment, business only	Keep good documentation; frequently questioned by auditors.
Same category used for the wages	Employers share of Social Security tax, unemployment insurance and other payments made for employees	It is a cost of hiring labor, whether it goes directly to the employee or not. These taxes add approximately 10 percent to the cost of hiring.
FC or CAP. EQUIP'T	Equipment or machinery	Depends on whether it will last more than 1 year or not.
FC	Equipment; lasting less than 1 year	
CAP. EQUIP'T	Equipment; lasting more than 1 year	
FC or INV. COST	Fees for use of equipment	

Category	Type of Transaction	Explanation
FC	Flyers	
FC	Furniture, for your own use	
FC	Gas bill, natural or LP	
FC	Gas for vehicle	
FC	Insurance	
FC	Internet service, ISP	
VC or INV. COST	Labor, direct work on product, incl. paid on a "per unit" basis	Depends on whether it is in your SUS model; either way will work.
FC	Labor, not on product, and paid by the hour	
FC	Legal fees	
Other Costs	Loan payments (any kind)	
FC	Machinery, lasting less than 1 year	
CAP. EQUIP'T	Machinery, lasting more than 1 year	
FC	Market research	
FC	Marketing costs	
FC	Marketing materials	
INV. COST	Materials used up in product or service	Services purchased
FC	Mechanical pencils; other bookkeeping	Supplies
FC	Office supplies	
FC	Other car expense, cost per mile	You normally pay for the use of a nonbusiness vehicle by the mile, including gas; 55 cents/mile is acceptable, but the amount is increased periodically.
VC, INV. COSTS, or Other Costs	Packing materials, ship end product to customer	Depends on whether it is included in your product price.
INV. COSTS	Packing materials, ship product to subcontractor	Part of your process to create the product or service.
FC	Parking fees	
Other Costs	Payments on loan (any kind)	
FC	Payroll, general	Not linked to production of product or service.
VC or INV. COST	Payroll for direct labor on product or service	Linked to production of product or service in your EOU model.
FC	Phone bill	
FC	Postage	
FC	Posters	
INV. COST	Product or service to be resold	
FC or Other Costs	Property tax	
INV. COST	Raw materials	
(REVENUES)	Rebates to customers	Is a planned part of the sale and should be averaged in with your sale price; enter as negative value with ( ).
FC	Receipt booklet	
FC	Recycling costs	
(REVENUES)	Refunds on sales	Represents a sale not made, even though not preplanned.
FC	Registration fees	
Use category that reflects what is being paid for	Reimbursements for business expenses (Be sure they are legitimate.)	Include a note about the purpose of the reimbursement and keep thorough documentation; frequently challenged by auditors who suspect that people are draining cash out of the business.
FC	Rent	
FC	Repairs, minor	
VC	Royalties owed on sales	Do not count as INV. COSTS because you do not pay unless the product is sold.
FC	Salaries of employees, not direct labor	
INV. COSTS	Salaries of employees, direct labor	Only if 100 percent working on product or service.

Category	Type of Transaction	Explanation
FC	Salary of owner	
VC	Sales commissions	
Other Costs	Sales tax collected and then paid to government	Collect sales tax as revenue. Pay out as Other Costs.
FC	Services, any type	
INV. COST	Shipping, inbound for product	
FC	Shipping not for product, inbound and outbound	
INV. COST	Shipping of product to and from subcontractor	
VC	Shipping, outbound to customer	
FC	Shop supplies (not direct product)	If used in making the product or service, use INV. COSTS.
FC	Software, business only	
VC	Special packaging not included in the product price	If it is in your EOU model, it is your product price; then use INV. COST.
INV. COST	Supplies used on product or service	
FC	Supplies, general	
Other Costs	Taxes, business profit	
FC	Tools, lasting less than 1 year	
CAP. EQUIP'T	Tools, lasting more than 1 year	
FC	Transportation, misc.	
VC	Transportation to deliver products to customer	If it happens after the sale is made, it cannot be INV. COSTS.
INV. COST	Transportation to get products	The same as inbound shipping, only you pay with your time and cash spent.
FC	Trash removal	
Same category used for the wages	Unemployment tax	It is a cost of hiring labor, whether it goes directly to the employee or not.
FC	Vehicle maintenance	
CAP. EQUIP'T	Vehicle purchase	
Other Costs	Warrantees paid	Not part of the original, planned sale; warrantee costs should be watched carefully to see if you have a bad product.
FC	Web site development	
FC	Web site hosting	

Receipts of Money—$ In

Category	Type of Transaction	Explanation
CAPITAL INV.	Additional investment by owner	
CAPITAL INV.	Additional investment from new partner(s)	
REVENUE	Extra charges to customers that are not part of the planned sale	They are still part of the sale.
(Other Costs)*	Gain from sale of equipment	Negative because you're bringing in money.
(Other Costs)*	Insurance settlement	Negative because you're bringing in money. It is not revenue because it is not a normal part of your business.
(Other Costs)*	Receive cash from line of credit; a type of short-term loan	A line of credit (LOC) is an ST loan; include it on the balance sheet under ST liabilities.
(Other Costs)*	Receive cash from loan, less than 1 year; short term	Include in ST liabilities on balance sheet.
(Other Costs)*	Receive cash from loan, more than 1 year; long term	Include in LT liabilities on balance sheet.
Other Costs*	Loss from sale of assets	Enter as a positive value, because it costs you to lose value on an asset. You will make this entry when you receive cash from the sale of the asset.
CAPITAL INV.*	Original investment by owners	
REVENUE	Revenue	
(Other Costs)	Sale of other assets, such as intellectual property	Enter as a negative because you're bringing in money, not spending it. Use ( ) to show neg.
CAPITAL INV.	Sale of percentage of the business, taking in partner(s)	
CAPITAL INV.*	Sale of stock to investors	
(Other Costs)	Sale of capital equipment	Enter as a negative because you're bringing in money, not spending it. Use ( ) to show neg.
REVENUE	Sales of your product/service	
REVENUE	Shipping and handling fees charged to customers	
CAPITAL INV.	Start-up capital; original investment	

**Note: Any example of negative value in Other Costs, signified by (Other Costs) is money received that does not fit the existing categories. Such receipts of income could be distributed into an Other Income column for nonrevenue, noninvestment income.*

Appendix 8

Using Business Plan Pro®

Access to Business Plan Pro is available from within the MyBizSkillsKit for Entrepreneurship or on a CD that can be packaged with the textbook. Business Plan Pro planning software is commercial software that you can use to create a professional-looking business plan. We recommend that you build your business plan using the BizBuilder Business Plan Template located on the Companion Web site or within MyBizSkillsKit, because it mirrors the planning process presented in the textbook and contains more detailed questions in some areas than Business Plan Pro that will be helpful to you in the preparation of your plan.

Once you have created your plan using the BizBuilder Template, it is easy to cut and paste material from your planning document into Business Plan Pro. You may want to do this to get a more professional-looking product and make use of the spreadsheet and wizards for charts and graphs. Business Plan Pro also contains several sample plans that you can review for ideas and alternate formats.

Business PlanPro includes:

- 68 sample business plans for you to study and compare to your business plan. Use the Sample Plan Browser to search the extensive sample plan library.
- Easy Plan Wizard that guides you through writing your plan.
- Spreadsheet tables with columns, rows, and formulas to automatically calculate totals as you enter your numbers.
- Financial statements that you can customize to meet your business's needs.
- Plan Review Wizard that reviews your plan for completeness, compares your financial statements to standard accounting practices, and checks for errors.
- Pie and bar charts that can be automatically created from your spreadsheets.
- A professional-looking printout of your business plan.
- Links to useful Internet resources.

If you would like to create a plan using Business Plan Pro, you will need to have the following installed on your computer: Microsoft Internet Explorer (6.0 or higher) and Adobe Acrobat Reader (8.0 or higher). You can find both programs online; just be sure to install Internet Explorer before you attempt to install Adobe Acrobat Reader.

If you are accessing Business Plan Pro through the MyBizSkillsKit, simply click on the link, register, and you are good to go. If you are accessing the program from a CD, the serial number you will need in order to install Business Plan Pro on your computer is on the back of the CD-ROM that came with your book. There is a quick-start tutorial on the CD and more tutorials online at http://www.paloalto.com/su/bp/tutorials.

Appendix 9

Glossary

accrual method accounting method wherein transactions are recorded at the time of occurrence, regardless of the transfer of cash.
acquisition a business purchase.
active listening focusing solely on what the other person is saying in a conversation and then validating understanding of the content and meaning.
advertising paid promotion through media outlets.
advisory board or council a group that provides advice and counsel, but is not a board of directors.
angel investor a wealthy individual who invests in businesses.
arbitration a method of dispute resolution using an arbitrator to act as the decision maker rather than through the courts.
area franchise or multiple-unit franchise a type of franchise that gives the exclusive rights to open franchisee-operated units within specified areas.
asset any item of value.
asset valuation a method that analyzes the underlying value of a firm's assets as a basis for negotiating the price.
audit a review of financial and business records to ascertain integrity and compliance with standards and laws, particularly by the U.S. Internal Revenue Service.

balance sheet a financial statement summarizing the assets, liabilities, and net worth of a business.
bankruptcy the legal process in which an individual or business declares the inability or impaired ability to pay debts as they come due.
barriers to entry the factors that contribute to the ease or difficulty of a new competitor joining an established market.
behavioral interview an interview designed to determine the fit of a prospective employee with the requirements of the position, using prior-experience examples.
benchmarking the comparison of a company's performance against that of companies in the same industry or against best practices, standards, or certification criteria.
blog (short for Web log) a journal that appears on the Internet periodically (perhaps daily) and is intended for the public.
blogosphere the term used for all the blogs on the Internet.
boilerplate language a standard format for specific types of legal agreements.
book value valuation of a company as assets minus liabilities.
bootstrap financing financing a business by creatively stretching existing capital as far as possible, including extensive use of the entrepreneur's time.
brand spiraling integrating a company's conventional offline branding strategy with its Internet strategy by using conventional approaches to direct traffic to its online sites.

breach of contract the failure of a signatory to perform as agreed.
breakeven point when the volume of sales exactly covers the fixed costs.
burn rate the pace at which a company spends capital before generating positive cash flow.
business broker a company or individual that buys and sells businesses for a fee.
business plan a document that thoroughly explains a business idea and how it will be carried out.
business-format franchising a form of franchising in which the franchisee secures the product and trade-name benefits and also the operating, quality assurance, accounting, and marketing methods, and the support of the franchisor.
buzz marketing another name for word-of-mouth marketing.

capital money or property owned or used in business.
capitalism the free-market system; characterized by individuals and companies competing for economic gains, private property ownership and wealth; free-market forces determine prices.
cash accounting method the method wherein transactions are recorded as cash is paid out or received.
cash flow statement a financial statement showing cash receipts less cash disbursements for a business over a period of time.
cash flow valuation a method of calculating the worth of a business by using projected future cash flows and the time value of money.
cash reserve emergency funds and a pool of cash resources.
cause-related marketing marketing inspired by a commitment to a social, environmental, or political cause.
center-of-gravity method location-decision approach that calculates the best cost location for a distribution center serving multiple sites.
certificate an official document that verifies something.
chain-of-command hierarchy of reporting and communications.
charge account credit extended by a company allowing qualified customers to make purchases up to a specified limit, without paying cash at the time of purchase.
clustering locating near direct competitors as a strategy.
code of conduct a set of official standards of employee behavior for a company.
code of ethics a statement of the values of a company.
code of ethics and business conduct a combination of a written statement of values with a set of official standards of employee behavior.
commission a percentage of a sale paid to a salesperson or other employee.
competitive analysis research that compares an organization with several direct and indirect competitors by name in a manner that is meaningful to targeted customers.
competitive strategy the combination of the business definition with its competitive advantage.
compound interest used with interest or rate of return and applied when earnings also accumulate interest or other returns, in addition to earnings on principal.
conflict of interest a circumstance in which personal benefits and professional obligations interfere with one another.
contingency a condition that must be met in order for something else to occur.
continuous improvement always identifying and implementing changes throughout an organization to focus on the requirements of internal and external customers.

contract an agreement between two or more parties that is enforceable by law.
contribution margin gross profit per unit—the selling price minus total variable costs plus other variable costs.
conversion franchising a type of franchising defined by existing or stand-alone businesses or local chains becoming part of a franchise operation.
cooperative advertising fee a fee paid by franchisees to contribute to a shared advertising fund that is separate from royalty fees.
core values the fundamental ethical and moral philosophy and beliefs that form the foundation of the organization, and provide broad guidance for all decision making.
corporate governance rules and safeguards to ensure that executives behave legally and ethically.
corporate social responsibility the ethical obligation of a company to its community.
corporation a legal entity composed of stockholders under a common name.
cost of goods sold (COGS) the cost of selling "one additional unit" of a tangible item.
cost of services sold (COSS) the cost of selling "one additional unit" of a service.
cost per rating point (CPRP) a measure of the efficiency of a media vehicle to a company's target market, calculated by dividing the cost of the media buy by the vehicle's rating.
cost per thousand (CPM) the cost of reaching 1000 members of the media vehicle's audience.
cost/benefit analysis a decision-making process in which the costs of taking an action are compared to the benefits.
cost-plus pricing takes the organization's product cost and adds the desired markup.
credit the ability to borrow money.
credit history a record of credit extended and the repayment thereof.
credit reporting agency (CRA) an organization that collects and analyzes information supplied by financial institutions, and others who extend credit, and then resells it.
creditor person or organization that is owed money.
culture the beliefs, values, and behavioral norms of an organization.
currency money that can be exchanged internationally.
current assets cash or items that can be quickly converted to cash or will be used within one year.
current liabilities debts that are scheduled for payment within one year.
current ratio liquidity ratio consisting of the total sum of cash plus marketable securities divided by current liabilities.
customer relationship management (CRM) company-wide policies, practices, and processes that a business uses with its customers to generate maximum customer satisfaction and optimal profitability.
customer service everything a business does to keep the customer happy.

data mining a computer program to analyze and sort data, to identify the best existing customers and model those who might become even better customers.
database a collection of information that is generally stored on a computer and organized for sorting and searching.
debt ratio measures total debt versus total assets.
debt service the amount a borrower is obligated to pay in a given period until a loan is repaid.

debt-to-equity ratio compares total debt to total equity.
deductible the amount of loss or damage a policyholder covers before the insurer pays on a claim.
default the results of a borrower failing to meet the repayment agreement on a debt.
demographics population statistics.
depreciation the percentage of value of an asset subtracted periodically to reflect its declining value.
development plan a document stating how an employee will attain specific performance.
direct marketing a method that includes telemarketing, direct mail, in-person selling, and other personalized marketing.
discount (referring to bonds) the difference between a bond's trading price and its par value when the trading price is below par.
diversification the addition of product or service offerings beyond the core product or service.
dividend each stockholder's portion of the profit-per-share paid out by a corporation.
due diligence the exercise of reasonable care in the evaluation of a business opportunity.
dumping companies pricing products below cost and selling large quantities in foreign markets.

e-active marketing the two major components of Internet marketing—e-commerce and interactive marketing—in combination.
earnings valuation a method that assesses the value of a firm based upon a stream of earnings that is multiplied either by an agreed-upon factor (the capitalization factor) or by the price/earnings ratio (for a publicly traded company).
economic order quantity (EOQ) the amount of inventory to order that will equal the minimum total ordering and holding costs.
economic risk the possibility that changes in the economy of a country where a company does business will cause financial or other harm to the business.
economics of one unit of sale (EOU) the amount of gross profit that is earned on each unit of the product or service a business sells.
edutainment combining education and entertainment to make a more lasting impression upon the audience.
elastic demand customer demand moving significantly upward or downward when the price of a product changes.
electronic rights the right to reproduce someone's work online.
electronic storefront an online site that customers can visit to view a company's catalog, price lists, and documentation.
elevator pitch a brief (15 second to 2 minute) presentation that conveys in an engaging way what a business is proposing and why the listener should be interested.
embargo the total prohibition on imports of all or specific products from one or more nations.
embezzlement the crime of stealing money from an employer.
entrepreneur a person who organizes and manages a business, assuming the risk for the sake of potential return.
environmental analysis a review that addresses the roles of the community, region, nation, or the world, as they relate to a business.
ethical dilemma a circumstance when personal values conflict and muddy decision-making.

ethical imperialism a belief that ethical standards are universal and that those of your nation are held everywhere you will do business.
ethical relativism situation where ethical standards are believed to be subject to interpretation.
ethics a system of moral conduct and judgment that helps determine right and wrong.
exporting the sale of goods or services produced domestically to foreign customers.

face value the amount of a bond, also known as par, to be repaid by a corporation or government at its maturity date.
factor-rating method location-decision approach whereby decision criteria are prioritized and weighted to eliminate subjective decisions.
fair market value the price at which a property or business is valued by the market; the price it would fetch on the open market.
family business a firm that has two or more members of the same family managing and/or working in it, and that is owned and operated for the benefit of that family's members.
feasibility analysis a study to assist in making a "go/no go" decision based upon a close examination of product/service, market, industry, and financial data in a sufficient degree of detail to ensure confidence in the results.
financing the act of providing or raising funds (capital) for a purpose.
fiscal year the financial reporting year for a company.
fixed operating costs expenses that do not vary with changes in the volume of production or sales.
fixed-position layouts used for the production of large objects where materials and teams are brought to a single location, as in manufactured housing.
float the time between a payment transaction and when the cash is actually in the payee's account.
follow-the-leader pricing a pricing strategy that is similar to a meet-or-beat-the-competition strategy but uses a particular competitor as the model for pricing.
foreign exchange (FX) rate the relative value of one currency to another.
foundation a not-for-profit organization that manages donated funds, which it distributes through grants to individuals, or to other nonprofit organizations, that help people and social causes.
franchise a business that markets a product or service developed by a franchisor, typically in the manner specified by the franchisor.
franchise agreement contract that explains the specific parameters of the relationship between the parties in a franchise.
Franchise Disclosure Document (FDD) the primary source of information for prospective franchisees regarding franchisors.
franchisee the second party to the franchise agreement, the owner of the unit or territory rights.
franchising the system of operating a franchise governed by a legal agreement between a franchisor and franchisee.
franchisor the person who develops a franchise or a company that sells franchises and specifies the terms and particulars of the franchise agreement.
free-enterprise system economic system in which businesses are privately owned and operate relatively free of government interference.
frequency how often individuals will be exposed to an advertisement during a particular time frame.
future value the amount an asset will gain over time.

gazelle a company that achieves an annual growth rate of 20 percent or greater, typically measured by the increase of sales revenue.

goodwill an intangible asset generated when a company does something positive that has value.

grapevine an informational communication channel that transmits information and rumors.

green entrepreneurship enterprise activities that avoid harm to the environment or help to protect it in some way.

gross profit total sales revenue minus total cost of goods sold.

gross ratings points (GRP) are calculated by multiplying the media vehicle's rating (reach) by the OTS, or number of insertions, to measure the intensity or impact of a media plan.

guerilla marketing original, unconventional, and inexpensive small-business strategies.

harvesting the act of selling, taking public, or merging a company to yield proceeds for the owner(s).

human resources the segment of a business that hires, trains, and develops a company's employees.

hyperlink word(s) that when clicked on transfer a computer user to a new Web page.

hypertext Web-based documents that combine text and graphics.

importing the sale of products produced in a foreign country to customers in your home country.

income statement a financial document that summarizes income and expense activity over a specified period and shows net profit or loss.

industry analysis a critical view of industry definition, industry size and growth (or decline), product and industry life cycle, and any current or anticipated legal or regulatory concerns.

inelastic demand the type of demand that does not change in a significant way when prices change.

inflation the gradual, continuous increase in the prices of products.

initial public offering (IPO) first offering of corporate stock to investors on the open (public) market.

in-kind donation a contribution of products or services that may include employee time rather than cash.

installment credit loans to be paid back in increments over time.

institutional advertising provides information about an organization, rather than a specific product, and is intended to create awareness about the firm and enhance its image.

insurance a system of protection for payment provided by insurance companies to protect individuals and organizations from having property or wealth damaged or destroyed.

international outsourcing the process of contracting with foreign companies to secure labor for a domestic company.

Internet franchise a type of franchise company that does not depend upon physical location for the delivery of its products or services; rather, it is a "virtual" business.

interview guide a document to assist in question development regarding an applicant's knowledge, skills, abilities, and interests.

inventory costs expenses associated with materials and direct labor for production until the product is sold.

investment something that a person or entity devotes resources to in hopes of future profits or satisfaction.

job offer letter a formal written invitation extended by an employer to a candidate selected for hiring that states basic employment terms—such as the position offered, the starting date, the salary, and so forth.
job profile identifies the knowledge, skills, and abilities required to perform the specific tasks of a job.
job shop a subcontractor for a manufacturer.
just-in-time manufacturing (JIT) manufacturing methodology focusing on making the smallest amount of product needed, quickly and efficiently.

leader a person who get things done through influence, by guiding or inspiring others to voluntarily participate in a cause or project.
leasehold improvements changes made to adapt a rented property for a particular business.
letter of agreement a document that puts an oral understanding in writing, in the form of a business letter.
letter of credit a financing instrument that is usually issued by a bank on behalf of a customer that promises to pay a certain sum of money once specific conditions are met.
leveraged financed by debt, as opposed to equity.
liability a business debt.
license an official document that grants the right to engage in an activity for a specified time.
licensing renting a brand or other intellectual property to increase sales of products.
lifestyle business a microenterprise that permits its owners to follow a desired pattern of living, such as supporting college costs or taking vacations.
lifetime value the profit earned from a particular customer or customer segment.
limited partnership business partnership wherein there is a general partner with unlimited liability and one or more limited partners, with no official input in daily operations and limited liability.
line extension using an established brand to promote different kinds of products.
line organization an organizational structure where each person reports to a single supervisor.
line-and-staff organization an organizational structure that includes the line organization, plus staff specialists (such as legal) who assist management.
liquidation the sale of all assets of a business concurrent with its being closed.
liquidity the ability to convert assets into cash.
location breakeven analysis a location selection method using cost-volume analysis.
logo short for logotype, a company trademark or sign.
long-term assets those that will take more than one year to use.
long-term liabilities debts that are due after one year.
lurk reading messages and getting a feel for discussions on a Web site, newsgroup, or the like, without participating in the online conversation.

manufacturing making or producing a tangible product.
market a group of people or organizations that may be interested in buying a given product or service, has the resources to purchase it, and is permitted by law and regulation to do so.
market clearing price the particular price at which the supply of products and/or services matches the demand for them.

market research is the collection and analysis of data regarding target markets, industries, and competitors.
market segment a group of consumers or businesses that have a similar response to a particular type of product or service.
marketable securities investments that can be converted into cash within 24 hours.
marketing the development and use of strategies for getting a product or service to customers and generating interest in it.
marketing mix the combination of the four factors—product, price, place, and promotion—that communicates a marketing vision.
marketing plan a statement of the marketing goals and objectives for a business and the intended strategies and tactics to attain them.
markup pricing a cost-plus pricing strategy in which you apply a predetermined percentage to a product's cost to obtain its selling price.
master franchise a specific type of franchise that allows individuals and organizations to buy the right to subfranchise within a delineated geographic territory.
maturity the date at which a loan must be repaid, including when a bond must be redeemed by the issuer.
media buyer the person who purchases time/space and negotiates pricing and scheduling details.
media planner the person that creates a media plan with a specific advertising schedule.
media schedule spells out the particular media vehicles to be used, the volume of usage, and the timing.
media strategy the identification of the media a business will use and the creative decisions involved.
merchant card services financial systems to permit acceptance of major credit cards.
merger the joining of two companies to share their respective strengths.
microenterprise a firm with five or fewer employees, initial capitalization requirements of under $35,000, and the regular operational involvement of the owner.
mission a concise communication of a business's strategy, including a business definition and explanation of competitive advantage.
mission statement a brief, written statement that informs customers and employees what an organization's goal is, and describes the strategy and tactics to meet it.
mobile social networking the updating of social-network sites via mobile handsets.

net profit the remainder of revenues minus fixed and variable costs and taxes.
net worth (owner's equity) the difference between assets and liabilities.
newsgroup an online discussion group focused on specific topics or interests.
noncash expenses adjustments to asset values not involving cash, such as depreciation.
nondisclosure agreement a legal document enumerating the type of information that is to remain confidential.
notary a person who has been authorized by the state to witness the signing of documents.
not-for-profit organization an entity formed with the intention of addressing social or other issues, with any profits going back into the organization to support its mission.

offshoring relocating company operations to foreign locations.
operating ratio an expression of a value versus sales.

operational plan the stated short-term methods for achieving tactical goals.
operations a set of actions that produce goods and services.
opportunities to see (OTS) the cumulative number of ad exposures in a given time period—usually four weeks.
opportunity cost the value of what must be given up in order to obtain something else.
owner's equity (net worth) the difference between assets and liabilities.

par the face value of a bond (typically $1000) or the stated value of a stock.
partnership a business with two or more owners that make decisions for the business together and share the profits, losses, assets, and liabilities.
patent an exclusive right, granted by the government, to produce, use, and sell an invention or process.
payback period estimated time required to earn sufficient net cash flow to cover the start-up investment.
payroll tax employers must deduct this tax from their employees' pay and forward it to the designated governmental entity.
penetration pricing a pricing strategy that uses a low price during the early stages of a product's life cycle to gain market share.
performance appraisal the formal process used to evaluate and support employees' performance.
permit an official document that gives a party the right to put on a specific event.
personal guarantee the promise to pay issued by an individual.
personalized pricing a dynamic pricing strategy in which a company charges a premium above the standard price for a product or service to certain customers who will pay the extra cost.
philanthropy a concern for human and social welfare that is expressed by giving money through charities and foundations.
piggybacking or co-branding occurs when two franchises share locations and resources.
pilferage theft of inventory.
pitch letter correspondence designed to explain the story behind a press release, and why it would be interesting and relevant to the media outlet's readers, listeners, or viewers.
pocket price the portion of the full price that remains after all pricing factors are deducted.
policy loan a loan made against an insurance policy that has cash value.
political risk the possibility of a country's political structure and policies impacting a foreign company transacting business within its geopolitical borders.
position description includes the knowledge, skills, and abilities from the job profile, as well as the reporting and working relationships and the goals and objectives.
positioning distinguishing a product or service from similar products or services being offered to the same market.
premium (regarding bonds) the amount above par for which a bond is trading in the market.
premium the cost of insurance.
present value what the future amount of an asset or other investment is worth at face value discounted back to the present.
press release an announcement sent to the media to generate publicity that states the "who, what, when, where, and why" of a story.
prestige pricing the pricing strategy in which a firm sets high prices on its products or services to send a message of uniqueness or premium quality.

statute of limitations the time period in which legal action may be taken.
stealth marketing undercover, or deceptive, marketing efforts that are intended to appear as if they happened naturally.
strategic plan typically a three to five-year overall plan to achieve long-term growth, including sales, and positioning goals.
strategy a plan for how an organization or individual intends to outdo its competitors.
supply chain management (SCM) the management of sourcing, procuring, production, and logistics to go from raw materials to end customers across multiple intermediate steps.
sustainable situation in which current needs are met while preserving resources for the future.

tactical plan the short-term (one year or less) implementation plan that has limited, specific objectives.
tactics the specific ways in which a business carries out its strategy.
target market groups that are defined by common factors such as demographics, psychographics, age, or geography that are of interest to a particular business.
tariffs taxes or duties on goods and services imported into a country.
tax abatement legal reduction in taxes.
tax credit direct reduction of taxes.
tax evasion the deliberate avoidance of an obligation to pay taxes; may lead to penalties or imprisonment.
tolerance the range of acceptable size variation.
tooling cost the expense of creating specialized equipment for a manufacturing process.
total quality management (TQM) the quality-assurance methodology of striving for strategic advantage through quality.
trade intermediary organization that serves as a contract distributor of products traded between countries.
trade mission an international trip taken by government officials and businesspeople organized to promote exports or to attract investment.
trademark any word, name, symbol, or device used by an organization to distinguish its product.
trade-off the act of giving up one thing for another.
traffic generators complementary businesses that attract customer traffic to a retailing area.

uniform resource locator (URL) a Web page address.
unique selling proposition (USP) the distinctive feature and benefit that sets a company apart from its competition.
unit of sale the basic unit of the product or service sold by the business.

value-engineer to reduce the cost in a product while maintaining quality standards.
variable costs expenses that vary directly with changes in the production or sales volume.
variable pricing strategy provides different prices for a single product or service.
venture capitalist an investor or investment company whose specialty is financing new, high-potential entrepreneurial companies, and second-stage companies.
venture philanthropy a subset or segment of social entrepreneurship wherein financial and human capital is invested in not-for-profits by individuals and for-profit enterprises, with the intention of generating social rather than financial returns on their investment.

vertical integration the process of going forward or backward on the idea-to-market continuum.
viral marketing the process of promoting a brand, product, or service though an existing social network, where a message is passed from one individual to another—much as a virus spreads.
vision a broader and more comprehensive perspective on an organization than its mission; built on the core values and belief systems of the organization.
visual control inventory-management method in which an individual assesses the stock level on hand by visual inspection and reorders when the supply is low.
voluntary exchange a transaction between two parties who agree to trade money for a product or service.

wage fixed payment per hour for work performed.
wealth the value of assets owned versus the value of liabilities owed.
whistle-blower a person that reports unethical or illegal conduct to a manager or to the public.
wholesale buying in bulk from manufacturers and selling smaller quantities to retailers.
working capital the value of current assets minus current liabilities.

Index